THE MEDIA

OF MASS

COMMUNICATION

STUDY EDITION

NINTH EDITION

John Vivian

Winona State University

Allyn & Bacon

Boston   New York   San Francisco
Mexico City   Montreal   Toronto   London   Madrid   Munich   Paris
Hong Kong   Singapore   Tokyo   Cape Town   Sydney

Editor-in-Chief: Karon Bowers
Acquisitions Editor: Jeanne Zalesky
Development Editors: Carol Alper and Hilary Jackson
Series Editorial Assistant: Megan Lentz
Marketing Manager: Suzan Czajkowski
Production Editor: Claudine Bellanton
Manufacturing Buyer: JoAnne Sweeney
Editorial Production and Electronic Composition: Elm Street Publishing Services
Interior Design: Henry Rachlin
Photo Researcher: Laurie Frankenthaler
Cover Administrator/Designer: Joel Gendron

For related titles and support materials, visit our online catalog at www.pearsonhighered.com.

Between the time website information is gathered and then published, it is not unusual for some sites to have closed. Also, the transcription of URLs can result in typographical errors. The publisher would appreciate notification where these errors occur so that they may be corrected in subsequent editions.

A previous edition was published under *The Media of Mass Communication*, Ninth Edition, copyright © 2009 by Pearson Education, Inc.

10 9 8 7 6 5 4 3 2   13 12 11 10 09

Allyn & Bacon
is an imprint of

www.pearsonhighered.com

ISBN-10: 0-205-63254-8
ISBN-13: 978-0-205-63254-1

to HAROLD VIVIAN, **my father**, who sparked my curiosity about the mass media at age 5 by asking what was black and white and read all over.

and

to ELAINE VIVIAN, **my mother,** who nurtured this curiosity by keeping the house stocked with books, magazines and reading material of every sort.

Why You Need This New Edition

D on't blink. If you do, the landscape of the media of mass communication will have morphed and warped into a new reality when you open up. The rapidity of change in the mass media and in the world in which the media function necessitated this new edition of *The Media of Mass Communication*. This edition is my effort at the most up-to-date package possible to accompany your course. The book is more than a snapshot, though. You will find *MMC* a foundation for strengthening understanding of the mass media. More firmly rooted in principles and foundations, you will find yourself in good stead for staying atop of hard-to-anticipate changes that are coming fast, even as you read this.

Another reason for this new ninth edition is from my experience as a teacher. I am always hunting for new ways to present material in my classes, to do it better. This revision includes improvements ranging from little things, like word choices, examples and illustrations, to major things like a stronger emphasis on themes, new topics and new features to help you pull everything together. Consider these changes:

▶ **Current Issues.** Mass media have had a role, not altogether exemplary, in public awareness about the global warming crisis. You will learn about it in this edition. The changing role of the Internet in our lives is a recurrent theme. So is the decline of traditional media, particularly magazines and books but also the troubled future for television and radio as we know them. You will find discussions on gaming as an emerging media vehicle for advertising. There also is new discussion on dilemmas posed by the phenomenal rise of blogging and online activities like Facebook and YouTube. And what does media titan Rupert Murdoch know that nobody else does? Why would he bail out of his ownership control of the DirecTV satellite service and buy the *Wall Street Journal?* This edition is as current as I could make it.

▶ **Global Emphasis.** Flip through the pages, and you will see photos that illustrate a new global thrust in this edition. Chadors and kaffiyehs underscore the edition's expanded attention to media in Arab regions. You will find significantly increased attention to the mass media of China, which is essential to an understanding of evolving relationships in political realities and the global marketplace.

▶ **Streamlined Organization.** To make it easier to cover the material in a semester's time, we've reduced the number of chapters from 21 to 20. All of the chapters are now included in the main text. Key online content from previous editions has been integrated throughout.

▶ **New Pedagogical Features.** I think of this as a pedagogy-enhanced edition. In addition to the features that previous users have enjoyed, I've added some new ones. Read about the details of these new learning tools in the "Using This Book" section of the preface.

   ▶ Learning Check
   ▶ Case Studies, enhanced with questions and activities
   ▶ Illustrated Timelines
   ▶ Enhanced Chapter Wrap-Ups
   ▶ Thematic Chapter Summaries

▶ **Updated MyCommunicationLab for Mass Communication.** (www.mycommunicationlab.com) New features in this interactive and instructive online solution help foster student understanding of media literacy and make learning fun! See details under "Supplements" in the preface.

Contents

PUBLIC RELATIONS: A Thematic Chapter Summary   **314**

13 Advertising   317

ADVERTISING: A Thematic Chapter Summary   **342**

18 Mass Media and Governance   461

19 Mass-Media Law   479

20 Ethics

Preface

Since the first edition of the *Media of Mass Communication* in 1991, more than a million students have found this book to be their first academic look at the media environment that so much shapes not only their daily routines, but their lives and their understanding of our whole culture. For a teacher this is gratifying. Through *MMC* and a growing network of colleagues who have adopted the book, my reach as a teacher has been extended far, far beyond the confines of my own classrooms. I am indebted deeply to adopters and their students, who pepper me almost daily with their reactions to the book and with news and tidbits to keep the next edition current.

The reach of *MMC* is wider than ever. There are editions in China in both English and Chinese, in India and in Indonesia. A Canadian adaptation is in its fourth edition. In all, *MMC* has been published in 21 variations over the years, each updated to keep students up-to-speed with our ever-changing and fast-changing media of mass communication.

Most gratifying to me is the community that has grown up around *MMC*. These are people, many of whom have become valued friends, whose thoughts have made the book an evolving and interactive project. In countless messages, adopters have shared what works in their classes and how it might work elsewhere. Students write the most, sometimes puzzled over something that deserves more clarity, sometimes with examples to illustrate a point. All of the comments, questions and suggestions go into a mix to add currency and effectiveness with every updated edition.

How This Book Is Organized

This book has three sections, each intended to examine a different aspect of the mass media.

The Mass Media   Chapter 1, "Mass-Media Literacy," provides a foundation for understanding the mass media and the dynamics that affect the messages they transmit. Chapter 2 focuses on media technology, including the historical development of media beginning with Gutenberg's press and continuing to today's digital media. This chapter also introduces models of the mass communication process. The next eight chapters deal with each of the major mass media—books, newspapers, magazines, sound recordings, movies, radio, television and the Internet.

Mass Messages   Then come chapters on the major content forms disseminated by the media to mass audiences. These include news, public relations, advertising and entertainment. Also included is a chapter on media research, with special attention to measuring the audience for mass messages.

Mass-Media Issues   The rest of the book focuses on specific issues, including media effects, global mass media, media and governance, media law and media ethics.

Using This Book

This edition retains many of the popular features that have helped your predecessors master the subject. This edition also introduces some new features.

❱ ***Introductory Vignettes.*** Chapters open with evocative stories that illustrate important issues about the mass media and also colorful descriptions about people who contributed significantly to the mass media.

Learning Ahead Lists. Each chapter begins with learning goals to help you guide your thoughts as you read through the chapter.

Study Previews. To help you prepare for the material ahead, each major section begins with a preview of the concepts to be covered there.

Learning Checks. Questions peppered through chapters help you be sure you've grasped the main points. These questions are intended also to help you relate what you've learned to your own experience that you have brought to the course.

Running Glossaries. You will also find glossary definitions in the margins, on the same page that the name of concept is introduced in the text.

Media People Boxes. This feature introduces personalities who have had a major impact on the media or whose story illustrates a major point of media history.

Case Studies. Case studies, one per chapter, lay out issues and problems that encourage you to put together the knowledge, experience and values you brought to the course with new information and ideas from the book. Most case studies deal with perennial issues that will recur in new forms as the years go on. Each case study includes a three-step series of questions and activities to guide you through your own assessment of the issue and a conclusion.

Media Timelines. These full-page features cast key developments in the mass media in a graphic chronology. Important too is that the timelines put these media developments in the larger context of what was happening intellectually, politically and socially in the larger society. You will find the timelines useful in connecting the dots between what you are learning about the mass media to what you already know and what you are learning in other courses in other fields.

Chapter Wrap-Ups. The end-of-chapter wrap-ups are expanded in this edition to include a summary paragraph on every section in the chapter. These are a handy review.

Review Questions. These questions are keyed to the major topics and themes in the chapter. Use them for a quick assessment of whether you have caught the major points.

Concepts, People and **Terms.** The most important concepts, terms and people introduced in the chapter are listed with their page numbers.

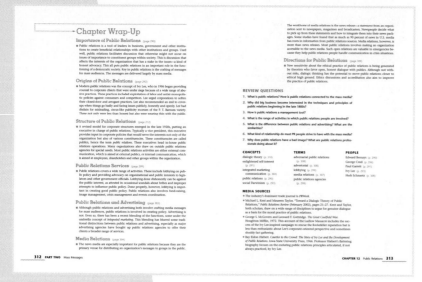

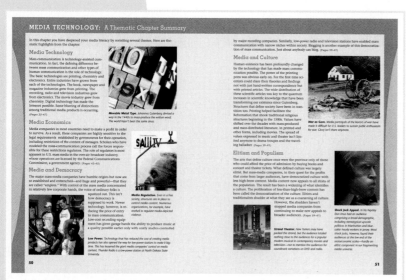

Media Sources. You also will find a brief list of suggested reading for further learning, some of it the latest thinking on the subject, some the classic works in the field.

Thematic Chapter Summaries. At the end of every chapter you will find a two-page spread that ties the chapter's content to the book's major themes. These changes are in nutshell paragraphs, photos and captions. These thematic summaries are an additional framework for understanding the mass media. They offer a unifying perspective—a kind of cross-referencing of material in every chapter to material in every other chapter.

Instructor Supplements

A complete and integrated package of resources augments lessons from the book in the classroom.

PRINT RESOURCES

Instructor's Resource Manual. The manual, by Yvonne Bland of Robert Morris University, is designed to ease time-consuming demands of instructional preparation, to enhance lectures, and to provide helpful suggestions to organize the course. The manual consists of helpful teaching resources and lecture enrichment including outlines, synopses, glossaries, activities, and at-a-glance guides to the wealth of available resources.

Test Bank The test bank, by Judy Oskam of Texas State University, includes more than 2,500 multiple choice, true/false, matching, fill-in-the-blank, short answer and essay questions.

ELECTRONIC RESOURCES

Computerized Test Bank. The Computerized Test Bank provides test questions electronically. The user-friendly interface enables instructors to view, edit and add questions as well as transfer questions to tests and print tests in a variety of fonts. Search and sort features allow instructors to locate questions quickly and arrange them in a preferred order. The Computerized Test Bank is available on the Web through the Instructor's Resource Center at www.pearsonhighered.com/irc.

PowerPoint™ Package. This collection of lecture outlines and graphic images by Yvonne Bland of Robert Morris University, is keyed to every chapter and is available on the Web at the Instructor's Resource Center (www.pearsonhighered.com/irc.).

Updated MyCommunicationLab for Mass Communication (Access Code Required). Available at www.mycommunicationlab.com, this interactive and instructive online solution helps foster student understanding of media literacy. Flexibly designed to supplement a traditional lecture course or completely administer an online course, MyCommunicationLab combines assignable multimedia, video, activities, research support, tests, and quizzes to make teaching and learning fun!

▶ *A Day in the Life.* These mini-documentaries that allow students to experience what it is really like to work in mass communication by viewing "a day in the life of" professionals, including producers at a hit record label, a video game developer, and a public relations startup company.

▶ *MyMediaFeed.* This feature encourages media literacy by asking students to compare live media feeds from various news sources, and to critically evaluate the content, ownership and style of these media feeds, while interacting with multimedia news formats. Each media feed activity is followed by assignable critical thinking questions, further encouraging students to critically consider the media that influence their daily lives.

Mass Communication Interactive Video. Specially selected news segments from ABC news programs include on-screen critical-thinking questions and deal with a variety of media issues and problems to help bring media issues to life in the classroom. The program includes an accompanying video user's guide.

VideoWorkshop for Introduction to Mass Communication: Instructor Teaching Guide with CD-ROM. The VideoWorkshop program, by Elsa Peterson, includes quality video footage on an easy-to-use CD-ROM, plus a Student Learning Guide and an Instructor's Teaching Guide. The result? A program that brings textbook concepts to life with ease and that helps students understand, analyze and apply the objectives of the course.

Mass Communication Video Library. This library of videos, produced by Insight Media and Films for the Humanities and Sciences, includes full-length videos such as *Functions of Mass Communication, Making of a Newspaper, Illusions of News* and *The Truth About Lies.* Some restrictions apply.

Digital Media Archive for Communication 3.0. The Digital Media Archive CD-ROM contains electronic images of charts, graphs, maps, tables and figures, along with media elements such as video, audio clips, and related Web links. These media assets are fully customizable to use with the pre-formatted PowerPoint™ outlines or to import into the instructor's own lectures. (Windows and Mac).

iClicker Classroom Response System. iClicker, an easy-to-use classroom response system, enables instructors to pose questions, record results, and display those results instantly in the classroom.

Designed to encourage active learning, iClicker is easy to integrate into lectures:

▶ Students use a personal remote that they bring to class.

▶ The instructor asks multiple-choice questions during class. Students simply click their answer into their remote.

▶ A classroom receiver connected to the instructor's computer tabulates all answers and displays them graphically in class.

▶ Results can be recorded for grading, attendance, or simply used as a discussion point.

Student Supplements

Students can take advantage of a selection of study and enrichment materials.

PRINT RESOURCES

Study Card for Introduction to Mass Communication.   Colorful, affordable, and packed with useful information, Allyn & Bacon's Study Cards make studying easier, more efficient and more enjoyable. Course information is distilled down to the basics, helping students quickly master the fundamentals, review a subject for understanding or prepare for an exam. Because they're laminated for durability, students can keep these Study Cards for years to come and pull them out any time for a quick review.

Research Navigator™ Guide. This updated booklet by Ronald Roat of Southern Indiana University and Linda Barr, includes tips, resources, and URLs to help students conduct research on Pearson Education's research Web site, www.researchnavigator.com. The guide contains a student access code for the Research Navigator database, offering you unlimited access to a collection of more than 25,000 discipline-specific articles from top-tier academic publications and peer-reviewed journals, as well as the New York *Times* and popular news publications. The guide introduces you to the basics of the Internet and the World Wide Web. It includes tips for searching for articles on the site and a list of journals useful for research in mass communication. Also included are hundreds of Web resources for mass communication, as well as information on how to correctly cite research.

Careers in Media.   This supplement, by Frank Barnas and Mike Savoie of Valdosta State University, profiles employment opportunities in media and points out often overlooked options for seeking a job in the highly selective and competitive media world. Included is a discussion of portfolio development and valuable appendices with state and job Web sites.

ELECTRONIC RESOURCES

Updated MyCommunicationLab for Mass Communication (Access Code Required).   Available at www.mycommunicationlab.com, this interactive and instructive online solution helps students foster understanding of media literacy. MyCommunicationLab combines multimedia, video, activities, research support, tests and quizzes to make learning fun!

> *A Day in the Life* is a selection of mini-documentaries that allow you to experience what it is really like to work in the mass communication field by viewing "a day in the life of" professionals, including producers at a hit record label, a video game developer and a public relations startup company.

> *MyMediaFeed* encourages media literacy by teaching students to compare live media feeds from various news sources, and to critically evaluate the content, ownership, and style of these media feeds, while interacting with multimedia news formats. Each media feed activity is followed by critical-thinking questions, further encouraging students to critically consider the media that influence their daily lives.

Introduction to Mass Communication Study Site.   Available at www.pearsonmasscommunication.com, this Web site features study materials for the introductory mass communication course, including flashcards and a complete set of practice tests for all major topics. Web links to valuable sites where students can further explore important topics in the field are also included.

News Resources for Mass Communication (Access Code Required).   News Resources for Mass Communication with Research Navigator is one-stop access to keep students abreast of the latest news events and for all of their research needs. Highlighted by an hourly feed of the latest news in the discipline from the New York *Times,* you will stay on the forefront of currency throughout the semester. In addition, Pearson's Research Navigator™ is the easiest way for you start a research assignment or research paper. Complete with extensive help on the research process and four exclusive databases of credible and reliable source material including the EBSCO Academic Journal and Abstract Database, New York *Times* Search by Subject Archive and *Financial Times* Article Archive and Company Financials, Research Navigator helps students quickly and efficiently make the most of their research time.

VideoWorkshop for Introduction to Mass Communication: Student Learning Guide with CD-ROM. The VideoWorkshop program, by Elsa Peterson, includes quality video footage on an easy-to-use CD-ROM, plus a Student Learning Guide. The result? A program that brings textbook concepts to life with ease and that helps you understand, analyze and apply the objectives of the course.

Acknowledgments

The greatest ongoing contribution to making *The Media of Mass Communication* the most adopted survey textbook in the history of the subject has been made by Carol Alper, senior development editor at Allyn & Bacon. She has not only applied her lively imagination and good sense to the book's contents, but has also coordinated the complexities of moving the manuscript through production. Infusing new energy and innovation at conceptual stages, experienced mass communication development editor Hilary Jackson shepherded the project at critical early steps. This all has been done with the energetic support of Allyn & Bacon's mass communication editor, Jeanne Zalesky, who picked up the momentum from her predecessor, Karon Bowers, to make this the most significant revision in the history of *MMC.* It has been a team effort. Case studies, for example, came from Jenny Lupica, Brian Mickelson, Kay Turnbaugh, Emiley Zalesky and Jeanne Zalesky. Kudos go to production administrator Claudine Bellanton and project manager Eric Arima. Photo researcher Laurie Frankenthaler's tireless pursuit of photographs and permissions to tell the story of the media of mass communication makes this edition dazzle.

Besides my students and colleagues at my academic home, Winona State University, who made contributions in ways beyond what they realize, I am indebted to many students elsewhere who have written thoughtful suggestions that have shaped this edition. They include Niele Anderson, Grambling State University; Krislynn Barnhart, Green River Community College; Mamie Bush, Winthrop University; Lashaunda Carruth, Forest Park Community College; Mike Costache, Pepperdine University; Scott DeWitt, University of Montana; John Dvoroak, Bethany Lutheran College; Denise Fredrickson, Mesabi Range Community and Technical College; Judy Gaines, Austin Community College; James Grades, Michigan State University; Dion Hillman, Grambling State University; Rebecca Iserman, Saint Olaf University; Scott Wayne Joyner, Michigan State University; Chad Larimer, Winona State University; Amy Lipko, Green River Community College; Nicholas Nabokov, University of Montana; Andrew Madsen, University of Central Florida; Scott Phipps, Green River Community College; Colleen Pierce, Green River Community College; June Siple, University of Montana; and Candace Webb, Oxnard College.

I also appreciate the suggestions of other colleagues whose reviews over the years have contributed to *MMC's* success:

Edward Adams, Brigham Young University
Ralph D. Barney, Brigham Young University
Thomas Beell, Iowa State University
Ralph Beliveau, University of Oklahoma

Robert Bellamy, Duquesne University
ElDean Bennett, Arizona State University
Lori Bergen, Wichita State University
Michelle Blackstone, Eckerd College
Bob Bode, Western Washington University

Timothy Boudreau, Central Michigan University

Bryan Brown, Missouri State University

Patricia Cambridge, Ohio University

Jane Campbell, Columbia State Community College

Dom Caristi, Ball State University

Meta Carstarphen, University of North Texas

Michael L. Carlebach, University of Miami

Michael Cavanagh, State University of New York at Brockport

Danae Clark, University of Pittsburgh

Jeremy Cohen, Stanford University

Michael Colgan, University of South Carolina

Ross F. Collins, North Dakota State University

Stephen Corman, Grossmont College

James A. Danowski, University of Illinois, Chicago

David Donnelly, University of Houston

Thomas R. Donohue, Virginia Commonwealth University

Michele Rees Edwards, Robert Morris University

Kathleen A. Endres, University of Akron

Glen Feighery, University of Utah

Celestino Fernández, University of Arizona

Donald Fishman, Boston College

Carl Fletcher, Olivet Nazarene University

Laurie H. Fluker, Southwest Texas State University

Kathy Flynn, Essex County College in Newark, New Jersey

Robert Fordan, Central Washington University

Ralph Frasca, University of Toledo

Mary Lou Galician, Arizona State University

Andy Gallagher, West Virginia State College

Ronald Garay, Louisiana State University

Donald Godfrey, Arizona State University

Neil Gustafson, Eastern Oregon University

Donna Halper, Emerson College

Larry David Hansen, Madison Area Technical College

Bill Holden, University of North Dakota

Peggy Holecek, Northern Illinois University

Anita Howard, Austin Community College

Elza Ibroscheva, Southern Illinois University, Edwardsville

Carl Isaacson, Sterling College

Nancy-Jo Johnson, Henderson State University

Carl Kell, Western Kentucky University

Mark A. Kelley, The University of Maine

Wayne F. Kelly, California State University, Long Beach

Donnell King, Pellissippi State Technical Community College

William L. Knowles, University of Montana

John Knowlton, Green River Community College

Sarah Kohnle, Lincoln Land Community College in Illinois

Charles Lewis, Minnesota State University, Mankato

Lila Lieberman, Rutgers University

Amy Lignitz, Johnson County Community College in Kansas

Larry Lorenz, Loyola University

Linda Lumsden, Western Kentucky University

John N. Malala, Cookman College

Reed Markham, Salt Lake Community College

Maclyn McClary, Humbolt State University

Daniel G. McDonald, Ohio State University

Denis Mercier, Rowan College of New Jersey

Timothy P. Meyer, University of Wisconsin, Green Bay

Jonathan Millen, Rider University

Joy Morrison, University of Alaska at Fairbanks

Gene Murray, Grambling State University

Richard Alan Nelson, Kansas State University

Thomas Notton, University of Wisconsin–Superior

Judy Oskam, Texas State University

David J. Paterno, Delaware County Community College

Terri Toles Patkin, Eastern Connecticut State University

Sharri Ann Pentangelo, Purdue University

Deborah Petersen–Perlman, University of Minnesota–Duluth

Tina Pieraccini, State University of New York at Oswego

Leigh Pomeroy, Minnesota State University, Mankato

Mary-Jo Popovici, Monroe Community College

Thom Prentice, Southwest Texas State University

Hoyt Purvis, University of Arkansas

Jack Rang, University of Dayton

Benjamin H. Resnick, Glassboro State College

Rich Riski, Penninsula College

Ronald Roat, University of Southern Indiana

Patrick Ropple, Nearside Communications

Marshel Rossow, Minnesota State University, Mankato

Julia Ruengert, Pensacola Junior College

Cara L. Schollenberger, Bucks County Community College

Quentin Schultz, Calvin College

Jim Seguin, Robert Morris College

Todd Simon, Michigan State University

Ray Sinclair, University of Alaska at Fairbanks

J. Steven Smethers, Kansas State University

Karen A. Smith, College of Saint Rose

Mark Smith, Stephens College

Howard L. Snider, Ball State University

Brian Southwell, University of Minnesota

Alan G. Stavitsky, University of Oregon

Penelope Summers, Northern Kentucky University

Larry Timbs, Winthrop University

John Tisdale, Baylor University

Edgar D. Trotter, California State University, Fullerton

Helen Varner, Hawaii Pacific University

Rafael Vela, Southwest Texas State University

Stephen Venneman, University of Oregon

Kimberly Vos, Southern Illinois University

Michael Warden, Southern Methodist University

Hazel G. Warlaumont, California State University, Fullerton

Ron Weekes, Ricks College

John Weis, Winona State University

Bill Withers, Wartburg College

Donald K. Wright, University of South Alabama

Alan Zaremba, Northeastern University

Eugenia Zerbinos, University of Maryland

Keeping Current

To you, the student, I want to emphasize that this book is a tool to help you become more intelligent and discerning as a media consumer. If you plan on a media career, the book is intended to orient you to the courses that will follow in your curriculum. This book, though, is only one of many tools for staying on top of the subject for many years to come.

Stay in Touch

Please feel free to contact me with questions and also ideas for improving the next edition. My e-mail: jvivian@winona.edu

May your experience with *The Media of Mass Communication* be a good one.

—John Vivian
Winona State University

1

Mass-Media Literacy

Great Moral Issues

Great moral issues define a society. Slavery, right or wrong? Abortion on demand? Stem cell research? Citizenship for illegal aliens? These are issues on which mass media comprise the primary forum for the debate as society struggles toward consensus.

On slavery, Quakers in the 1700s drew on their theology for an unequivocal position: Evil. Later when the Constitution created the new American republic, slavery was debated as a constitutional issue. But not until the 1800s, with the proliferation of printing presses, did the Quaker-inspired position for abolition bore into public consciousness as a defining moral issue for a new generation. Quaker-inspired newspapers, first published by white abolitionists, then also by blacks who had been freed from slavery, fanned the moral and intellectual struggle until it boiled over into politics. One by one the movement picked up followers. These included people who earlier hadn't had strong feelings on the issue. Also, there were converts.

The abolitionist movement spread from fringe publications to the mainstream. By the time of the Civil War in the 1860s, slavery was a leading subject in daily newspapers. Historians see a book, the novel *Uncle Tom's Cabin* by Harriet Beecher Stowe, as pivotal.

The struggle was horribly painful and not entirely settled by the war. But over the next century, amid continuing media attention to social justice, consensus emerged. Nobody today would advocate slavery. Or even backtracking.

No less defining for society and its moral values is today's issue of stem cell research, with almost the entire debate going on in the mass media.

LEARNING AHEAD

- More than most people realize, we are awash in a mass-media environment.
- Media literacy begins with an awareness of our media environment.
- Communication through mass media has profoundly affected human existence.
- The media's role in binding people together is changing with more media choices.
- Profit potential drives mass-media behavior in a capitalistic environment.

Michael J. Fox. *Actor Michael J. Fox, who suffers from debilitating Parkinson's disease, chose to become a poster child for expanded stem cell research in 2006 political campaigns. His media presence was a powerful factor, perhaps a turning point, in the development of society-wide consensus on the morality of medical research using embryonic stem cells.*

1

His body spasmodic because he'd chosen to forgo his medication that day, actor Michael J. Fox made a powerful case on television during the 2006 midterm elections for expanded stem cell research. Fox was hardly the first person to argue that the scientific tools are at hand to ease if not end the human misery wrought by chronic diseases like his own Parkinson's disease. Fox's involuntary convulsing gave potency to his argument. The television spots also provided the opposition with a springboard to argue the case that the medical use of embryonic stem cells is murder of human beings.

Some day the stem cell debate will be behind us, no matter its final outcome. A century from now historians will be pondering what the turning points were in the debate. The historians will focus on the role of the messages that the principals in the debate, all mass communicators, put into society-wide dialogue through the mass media. For now we'll leave it to commentators in the mass media to sort through whether Michael J. Fox's pleas will make a difference.

In the meantime, think about former cutting-edge issues that through debate in the mass media either have been resolved or are in the process of being resolved:

- Should women be allowed to vote?
- Are Darwin's provocative thoughts on the evolution of species the work of the devil?
- Are American Indians due restitution because of the U.S. government's history of genocidal policies?
- Is rap music the ruination of a generation?
- Do portrayals of violence in books beget real-life violence? How about portrayals on television? In the movies?
- Is the creation of jobs more important than the resulting environmental damage from industrial pollution?
- Do individuals have the right to choose to die?

That's a lot of weighty stuff to consider. As with all the profound issues with which educated people deal, mass communication's role is so key that it cannot be ignored.

This chapter is your start on a keener understanding of the media of mass communication and their significance in our lives, both individually and collectively. This understanding is called media literacy. The more sophisticated your media literacy, the better equipped you are to deal with the overwhelming deluge of messages from the mass media. You'll also be better able to participate intelligently in the dialogue.

Media Ubiquity

STUDY PREVIEW

We swim in an ocean of mass communication, exposed 68.8 percent of our waking hours to media messages. So immersed are we in these messages that we often are unmindful of their existence, let alone their influences.

MEDIA EXPOSURE

● **mass media**
Strictly speaking, mass media are the vehicles through which messages are disseminated to mass audiences.

The term also is used for industries built on mass media: *the television and book media.*

The term is also used for companies in the business of delivering mass messages with mass media: *Viacom is a media company.*

So awash are we in **mass-media** messages that most of the time we don't even think about them. Scholars at Ball State University found that people are intentionally involved in a media activity, like watching television or browsing the Internet, 30 percent of their waking hours—almost five hours a day. Additional media exposure is passive, like audio wallpaper. In the 21st century, mass media are essential in most of our daily lives, sometimes in our faces, like air, ubiquitous but invisible. Or at least unnoticed, taken for granted.

CONCURRENT MEDIA USAGE

Incredible as it may seem, the Ball State study found that besides five hours of media involvement a day, people average more than an additional six hours with the media while doing something else. That's an additional 39 percent of our waking hours. This includes half-watching television while cooking dinner or catching a billboard while commuting. All tallied, the media are part of our lives about two-thirds of the time we're not sleeping—68.8 percent to be precise. Perhaps we need the rest.

● **media multi-tasking**
Simultaneous exposure to messages from different media

Mass media have become so integrated into people's lives that **media multi-tasking** is no chore. The Ball State researchers found that roughly one-third of the time people spend with mass media involves simultaneous contact with two or more other media. This includes reading a newspaper with one ear tuned to a television program, listening to the radio with the other ear, and simultaneously surfing the Net.

As startling as the Ball State study may seem, the findings are hard to dispute. Researchers tracked 294 Midwesterners for 12 hours a day, 5,000 hours in all, recording their media use every 15 seconds on a handheld device. That's a sample size and methodology that commands respect.

● **mass communication**
Technology-assisted process by which messages are sent to large, faraway audiences

Strictly speaking, the media exposure tracked in the Ball State study was not all mass communication. By definition, **mass communication** is the technology-assisted transmission of messages to mass audiences. The Ball State study included technology-assisted one-on-one communication such as instant messaging and e-mail, which primarily are forms of interpersonal communication. The fact, however, is that distinctions between mass communication and some interpersonal communication are blurring. Video gaming, for example, can be a solo activity. Video gaming can also be interpersonal with two people together or apart.

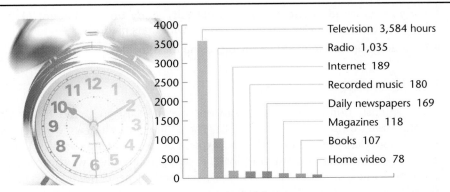

Television 3,584 hours
Radio 1,035
Internet 189
Recorded music 180
Daily newspapers 169
Magazines 118
Books 107
Home video 78

Media Usage

The research firm Veronis Suhler Stevenson found that the reported amount of television viewing easily led other media in the average hours of consumer use per person in 2004. Veronis projected even more television viewing by 2008.

Time Spent with Media

Mass media are everywhere all the time. An extensive Ball State University study found that we spend 68.8 percent of our waking hours with the media, much of it while doing something else. Also, we sometimes expose ourselves to additional media messages at the same time.

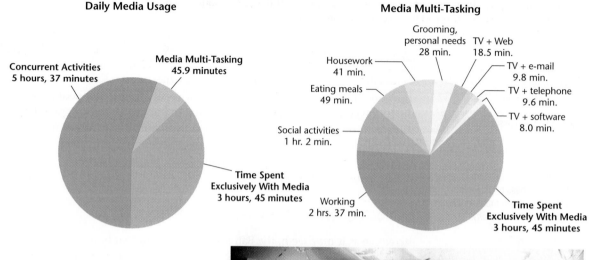

Daily Media Usage

Concurrent Activities
5 hours, 37 minutes

Media Multi-Tasking
45.9 minutes

Time Spent
Exclusively With Media
3 hours, 45 minutes

Media Multi-Tasking

Grooming, personal needs
28 min.

TV + Web
18.5 min.

Housework
41 min.

TV + e-mail
9.8 min.

Eating meals
49 min.

TV + telephone
9.6 min.

Social activities
1 hr. 2 min.

TV + software
8.0 min.

Working
2 hrs. 37 min.

Time Spent
Exclusively With Media
3 hours, 45 minutes

Inventory of Devices. *Media devices abound as part of our personal landscapes. How does your own inventory compare with this well-stocked college dorm room?*

Also, video gaming can be a mass activity with dozens, theoretically thousands, clearly making it a form of mass communication. By lumping technology-assisted communication and mass-media communication together, the Ball State data merely reflect the emerging reality that we are living a media-saturated existence.

LEARNING CHECK ◄

▶ Are you surprised at the Ball State University study on the amount of time people spend consciously and unconsciously with mass media?

▶ What are your own patterns and habits using mass media?

INESCAPABLE SYMBIOSIS

As a demonstration of willpower, someone occasionally goes cold turkey and abstains from exposure to the mass media. The oddity makes it news, whether it's a grade school class exercise or a scientific experiment with careful controls. Usually media-free demonstrations are short-lived. Except perhaps when we backpack into the remote wilds, most of us have a happily symbiotic dependence on mass media. We depend on media. And media industries, of course, are dependent on having an

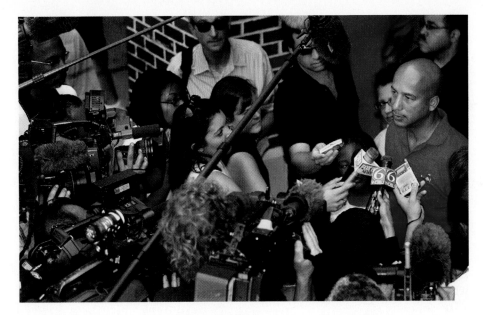

If Not from Reporters, from Whom? *It's through the mass media that people learn what's going on beyond the horizon. The media also are the vehicle through which leaders communicate with the public. Here, New Orleans Mayor Ray Nagin speaks with reporters about the Hurricane Katrina recovery. The reporters then packaged his account for their audiences.*

audience. What would be the purpose of a radio station, for example, if nobody listened?

■ **Personal Dependence.** Most days the most-listened-for item in morning newscasts is the weather forecast. People want to know how to prepare for the day. Not knowing that rain is expected can mean getting wet on the way home or not allowing extra time if the roads are slick. For most us, modern life simply wouldn't be possible without media. We need media for news and information; for entertainment, amusement and diversion, and for the exchange of ideas.

■ **Information.** Mass-media-delivered information comes in many forms. Students heading for college, especially if they plan to live in a dorm, receive a brochure about the dread disease meningitis. It's a life-or-death message about reducing the contagion in cramped living quarters. The message "Inoculate now" is from a mass medium—a printed brochure or a mass-mailed letter from the campus health director.

The most visible mass-media-delivered information is news. People look to newscasts and newspapers, even David Letterman and Argus Hamilton, to know what's going on beyond the horizon. If not for the mass media, people would have to rely on word of mouth from travelers to know what's happening in Iraq, Hollywood, or the state Capitol.

Information takes many forms. For example, advertising offers information to help consumers make intelligent decisions.

■ **Entertainment.** Before mass media came into existence in the mid-1400s, people created their own diversion, entertainment and amusement. Villagers got together to sing and swap stories. Traveling jugglers, magicians and performers dropped by. What a difference mass media have made since then. In 2006 the Ron Howard movie *The Da Vinci Code*, in its first weekend, opened to 80 million people in the United States and 120 million abroad. Do you know anyone who hasn't had television or radio on for entertainment in the past week? The past 24 hours?

● **marketplace of ideas**
The concept that a robust exchange of ideas, with none barred, yields better consensus

■ **Persuasion.** People come to conclusions on pressing issues by exposing themselves to competing ideas in what's called the **marketplace of ideas.** In 1644 the thinker-novelist John Milton eloquently stated the concept of the value of competing ideas: "Let truth and falsehood grapple; whoever knew truth put to the worse in a free and open encounter." Today more than ever, people look for

Marketplace of Ideas. *In his tract* Areopagitca *in the 1600s, English thinker John Milton made an eloquent case for free expression. Milton's idea was that individuals can use their power of reasoning to improve their situation and come to know great truths by exchanging ideas freely. The mass media are the primary vehicle for persuasive discourse.*

truth by exposing their views and values to those of others in a mass-media marketplace. Milton's mind would be boggled by the volume. Consider the diversity: Talk radio, newspaper editorial pages, blogs, anti-war lyrics from iTunes.

The role of persuasion is especially important in a democratic society, where public policy bubbles up from the citizenry over time. Consider the debate for decades on limiting young people's access to alcohol. Should the legal drinking age be 18? 21? None at all? Or should booze be banned entirely? As the debate has worn on, with both sides making their cases, public policy representing a grassroots majority has evolved. The media have been essential in this process.

The most obvious persuasion that the mass media carry is advertising. People look to ads to decide among competing products and services. What would you know about Nikes or iPods if it weren't for advertising to which you exposed yourself or heard about from a friend who saw or heard an ad?

■ **Media Dependence.** Not only do people in their contemporary lifestyles need mass media, but the industries that have built up around the media need an audience. This is the interdependence—the symbiosis. To survive financially, a publishing house needs readers who will pay for a book. A Hollywood movie studio needs people at the box office or video store. Media companies with television, radio, newspaper and magazine products cannot survive financially unless they can deliver to an audience that advertisers want to reach. Advertisers will buy time and space from media companies only if potential customers can be delivered.

We live in an environment that interconnects with mass media. The interdependence is a generally satisfying although not problem-free fact of modern life.

LEARNING CHECK ◄ ···

▶ **Why do people need mass media today? And why do mass media need people?**

▶ **What is the role of persuasion in a democratic society?**

Media Literacy

···

STUDY PREVIEW

Understanding mass media begins with a factual foundation. Added layers of sophistication of understanding come from knowing the dynamics that shape media content and their effects. In the process of improving media literacy, we enable ourselves to assess media issues intelligently.

HIERARCHY OF MEDIA LITERACY

● **media literacy**
Competence or knowledge about the mass media

By literacy, people usually mean the ability to read and write. Literacy also can mean command of a specific discipline such as history or physics. **Media literacy** is possessing the knowledge to be competent in assessing messages carried by mass media. Media literacy is essential in this Age of Mass Communication that envelops our lives dawn to dusk, cradle to grave. Think about not having modern media literacy. Thomas Jefferson, although brilliant and learned in his time, would be in absolute wonderment at hearing a radio for the first time. As foolish as he would seem to you and me today, a resurrected Jefferson might ask how so many little people could fit inside so tiny a box and make so much noise. Jefferson would be laughable for his lack of media literacy.

Cultivating Readers

Newspapers are worried that young people don't read them. Long before television, Yahoo, iPods, MySpace and blogs, newspapers were the dominant media. They were the one source everyone turned to for information about the world. Not so anymore.

Newspaper circulation, after slipping for several years, dipped precipitously in 2005. Research firm Veronis Suhler Stevenson reported that the number of hours spent annually with a daily newspaper was down to 169 per U.S. adult and would fall almost another 1 percent in 2008. The greatest loss was projected for young adults, an audience that many advertisers covet.

Anxious to change those statistics, newspapers stepped up their industry's long-standing Newspapers in Education program aimed at elementary school readers. The goal is to excite a new generation about current affairs, which the industry hopes will stem circulation losses. For years, many papers have carried the boilerplate NIE features that incorporate newspapers into the classroom. In the 1990s, NIE's Barbara Goldman created It's News to Me, a board game available in many toy stores. Now she's devised flash cards that newspapers can buy emblazoned with their brand names and sell to schools. The cards have questions that can be answered by reading the local paper.

But what about teens and young adults? Why don't they read newspapers?

One theory is that mass audiences are hardly static. Today's youth are a fickle bunch. A prime-time television hit one year can flicker out the next. YouTube grew from idea to billion-dollar reality in less than two years.

Another theory is that "old media" don't employ enough young people.

The Associated Press, the giant news agency that reaches over 1 billion people daily and is known for its to-the-point reporting, created Asap, a special service aimed at young people 25 to 34 years old. Asap boasts "bold and innovative coverage" that embraces diverse interactive media elements, including video, blogs, diaries and photos. A team of writers, mostly in their 20s and 30s, draws from the work of 2,000 AP reporters worldwide with a fresh, if not sometimes flip, tone. About 200 U.S. newspapers have subscribed, posting Asap content on Web sites or in their papers.

Youth Outlook, a project of the nonprofit alternative Pacific News, employs only young writers and does not count on sources from "old media," like the AP. Pacific says that the writers and editorial staff of its youth media are all in their 20s or younger. "Young people can tell if the stories are coming from peers or just being reported by other," says Kevin Weston, 37, the director of Youth Outlook.

Will these innovations bring back young readers? Have today's newspapers figured out why young people don't need newspapers as much as newspapers need them?

It's News to Me! The newspaper industry's Newspapers in Education project is trying to excite a new generation of readers about current affairs. One initiative was Barbara Goldman's It's News to Me, a board game. Now her flash cards pose questions that can be answered by checking the local paper.

DEEPENING YOUR MEDIA LITERACY

Where are newspaper readers going? Can a mass medium that's in its maturity, like newspapers, stall the shift of its audience to newer medium forms?

EXPLORE THE ISSUE

What is your dominant local newspaper? Choose a metropolitan daily in a different major city.

DIG DEEPER

Check into the circulation patterns of both newspapers going back to 1990. You can do this with data provided quarterly by each newspaper to the Audit Bureau of Circulations. If you have difficulty finding ABC data at your library or online, the circulation director at the newspapers will be pleased to provide it.

Check also on the 1990 and 2000 census data for these two newspapers' home cities.

WHAT DO YOU THINK?

Does the circulation of the two newspapers reflect population changes? What is your theory on why this is so or why it is not? Is there a reason for concluding that the national slippage in young readers applies to these newspapers? If one or both is an exception, why?

When the New York cable television system owned by Time Warner had to decide whether to go with CNN or Fox News, guess what? CNN, owned by Time Warner, got the nod for the lone available channel. Rupert Murdoch was furious. At the time he was trying to establish footholds everywhere he could for his new Fox News channel. He ordered his New York newspaper, the *Post*, to stop running the Time Warner cable schedule.

Not even Murdoch could argue that his power play was in the interest of *Post* readers. It was a demonstration, though, of the power that Murdoch wields over his media empire, which includes 20th Century-Fox, HarperCollins, the *Wall Street Journal* and other newspapers, and **satcast** companies on several continents.

Murdoch is frank about being driven by the bottom line. To critics who claim that his Fox News is biased to the conservative right politically, he responds with a suggestion that he himself is apolitical. "Conservative talk is more popular," he explained.

Who is Rupert Murdoch? From his father he inherited a chain of Australian newspapers. Then he acquired some British newspapers. After several forays into U.S. media, he took a major plunge and bought 20th Century-Fox and announced a daring plan to up-end the U.S. television industry by launching a fourth network. The Murdoch empire, which operates under the News Corp. name, has become a global system for content creation and delivery under a single corporate umbrella.

Murdoch, now in his 70s, has steered through perils and challenges galore. He's hardly risk-averse. The common denominator in his career is to let nothing interfere with News

Media Baron. *Born with the silver spoon of an Australian newspaper empire in his mouth, Murdoch turned the spoon platinum. He built one of the planet's largest media empires through his News Corporation. He even went for U.S. citizenship because his alien status threatened to impede expanding his Fox television and movie holdings in the United States. His ventures include HarperCollins books, the* Wall Street Journal, *numerous metro newspapers in several countries and satcast services abroad.*

Corp. growth and profits. In the 1980s, for example, when his Australian citizenship became an obstacle to building his network of Fox television stations, he applied for U.S. citizenship and took the exam. Problem solved. For Murdoch, citizenship is a means to an end.

When he needed friends in Congress on a broadcast regulation issue, Murdoch's book subsidiary, HarperCollins, offered House Speaker Newt Gingrich an extraordinarily sweet $4.5 million advance for an autobiography. Gingrich hadn't even started the book. When word about the deal leaked out, the book industry was aghast. There was no way a Gingrich book could ever earn back such an advance. The deal exposed, Murdoch denied he was trying to buy influence. His problems on the Hill and the book deal, he said, were an unfortunate coincidence.

Murdoch has no problem backpedaling. In one speech, waxing on the future of democracy, Murdoch predicted that advanced communication

technology would spell the end of totalitarian regimes. He hadn't reckoned that the totalitarian leadership in China might hear the speech. They did. When the Chinese threatened to deny permission for Murdoch's StarTV satellite to transmit into China, he moved quickly to placate the Chinese totalitarians. He signed a deal for HarperCollins to publish a book by the daughter of head of state Deng Xiaoping. Also, he canceled another book that probably would have provoked the Chinese. Knowing that the Chinese were wary of the BBC World Service independent news broadcasts, he discontinued BBC from his StarTV satcast service.

Murdoch has become synonymous with media power. Former CBS executive Howard Stringer once called him "the leader of a new Napoleonic era of communications." Critics claim that his emphasis on corporate profits has undermined the notion that the mass media have a primary responsibility to serve the public.

WHAT DO YOU THINK?

▶ In *Fourth Estate*, a slightly veiled novel based on Murdoch, British author Jeffrey Archer portrays a ruthless, financially successful media mogul. Based on what you know about Murdoch, is Archer being fair?

▶ Can a media company both maximize profits and provide excellent content to the audience?

● **satcast**
Broadcasting directly to consumers via satellite

■ **Factual Foundation.** Nobody today is as out of touch with the media as our hypothetical Thomas Jefferson. Not uncommon are preschoolers who fiddle with computer keyboards. Certainly no teenager believes that a shrunken Alicia Keys really exists inside a television flat screen. Everyone today has a running start on media literacy.

A sophisticated understanding of a subject, whether carpentry or rocket science, begins with factual knowledge and vocabulary. So does media literacy. Thomas Jefferson would need to learn the word *radio*, something not yet invented in the late 1700s. He would need to learn the switches, buttons and knobs for on/off, for volume, and for channel selection—just as you did at some point. The foundation for media literacy is a factual foundation.

■ **Media Dynamics.** Media literacy has various levels. Understanding the dynamics that shape media content is one of these levels. Economics, as an example, explains a lot about media behavior. To survive, a media company needs to build an audience either for direct sale, as with a book, or to attract advertisers, as with television.

Besides economics, personalities can be a dynamic that shapes media content. Jon Stewart decides who makes it on the *Daily Show* and who doesn't. At book publisher HarperCollins, the top boss at the parent company sometimes decides himself what book to push and what book to cancel. Yes, for that reason alone we need to know what makes Rupert Murdoch tick. Murdoch, as the media baron who controls HarperCollins' parent company, sometimes micromanages the call on what gets published. Government regulations and law are another dynamic.

In our media-saturated environment, the more we know about media dynamics, the better equipped we are to make sense of our world. Why did a country music radio station stop playing the Dixie Chicks? Why have rock radio stations become an endangered species? How do Dodge television commercials get by with those risqué double entendres? Is the Democratic or the Republican National Committee behind the latest attack ads?

■ **Media Effects.** With the mass media so omnipresent in our lives, we must bear some imprint from so much exposure. How much? Everybody, it seems, has an opinion. Undoubtedly you've heard people talk about the latest violent crime and blame television or the movies or video games. Morals gone lax? The media are handy whipping boys. The fact, however, is that we know far less about media effects than we need to. Scholarship on effects is less conclusive than the conventional wisdom of uninformed conversational banter would have it.

Despite all the unanswered questions, we can ignore media effects only at our own peril. The greater our media literacy as individuals, the better we are equipped to separate alarmist claptrap from what merits truly significant concerns. Exactly how alarmed should we be at Janet Jackson's momentarily exposed mammary in that Super Bowl wardrobe malfunction? Or a gruesome onscreen battle at the multiplex? Or bald lies in political ads?

Only through media literacy can we proceed together to weed out truly dangerous media effects from those that are disturbing perhaps but inconsequential. There is no shortcut to media literacy if we are to come up with intelligent public policies on the mass media. Nor is there an alternative to media literacy for us as individuals to make well-informed media choices.

■ **Media Issues.** Public dialogue on today's great social, political, economic and cultural issues by which we will define our future as a society requires keen levels of media literacy. Unless we can connect the dots in both related and disparate fields, we are impossibly handicapped in sorting through complex media issues.

Peter King

Bill Keller

Journalistic Treason? *Was it overblown political rhetoric for Peter King, a Republican member of Congress from New York, to accuse the New York* Times *of treason for revealing the breadth of Bush administration wiretapping? President Bush himself was irate at the revelations although he stopped short of using the T word. The executive editor of the* Times, *Bill Keller, admitted that the decision to publish did not come easily but that, in the end, the government's argument for secrecy was less compelling than the people's right to know. For citizens to sort through such issues requires that they have a competent level of media literacy.*

Think about the media bashing against early U.S. news reports, including the specter of treason, that the Iraq War policy was not going well. What does the U.S. Constitution say? What do the political theorists say? Consider those ads for sugar-laden breakfast cereals aimed at kids. What do developmental psychologists say? How about ethicists on the morality of advertising as a driving force in what media companies produce? Put another way, if the media industries are capable of reshaping society, do they therefore have a responsibility for quality in content? It's the perennial *National Enquirer* vs. New York *Times* dichotomy.

Of course, just as no one knows every word in the language, nobody can be a complete media expert. That the task is daunting, however, is no excuse to opt out—any more than would be refusing to learn to read because total mastery of the vocabulary is beyond human grasp. The challenge is to build media literacy, first with a foundation in facts, and then, with increasing sophistication, an understanding of the dynamics, effects and issues.

LEARNING CHECK ◄ ·······································

▶ **What is media literacy? Why is it important?**

▶ **Give examples of elements in the hierarchy of media literacy.**

MEDIA AWARENESS

Most of our media exposure is invisible or at least unnoticed at a conscious level—the background music at a mall store, the advertising blurb on a pen, the overblown entrée description on a menu with the stacked-higher-than-life photo of a burger. Many media messages blur into our landscape as part of the environment that we take for granted. One measure of media literacy is awareness of the presence of media messages.

Some awareness requires higher media literacy than others.

■ **Message Form.** Fundamental media literacy is the ability to see the difference between a one-on-one message and a mass message. This is not always easy. Consider a mass mailing with a personal salutation: "Hi, Karla." It's naïve—media illiteracy, we could call it—for Karla to infer from the salutation that she's getting a personal letter.

■ **Message vs. Messenger.** Once there was a monarch, as the story goes, who would behead the bearer of bad news. The modern-day media equivalent is faulting a news reporter for telling about a horrible event, or criticizing a movie director for rubbing your face in an unpleasant reality. Media literacy requires distinguishing between messages and the messenger. A writer who deals with the drug culture is not necessarily an advocate. Nor necessarily is a rapper who conjures up clever rhymes for meth.

■ **Motivation Awareness.** Intelligent use of the mass media requires assessing the motivation for a message. Is a message intended to convey information? To convince me to change brands? To sour me on a candidate? The answer usually requires thinking beyond the message and identifying the source. Is the message from a news reporter who is trying to be detached and neutral about the subject? Or is the message from the Democratic National Committee? It makes a difference.

■ **Media Limitations.** The different technologies on which media are shaped affect messages. CDs, for example, can deliver music superbly but books cannot. Both CDs and books are mass media, but they have vastly different potentials.

Someone who criticizes a movie for departing from the particulars of the book on which it's based may well lack sufficient media literacy to recognize that a 100-minute movie cannot possibly be literally true to a 90,000-word novel. Conversely, Ang Lee's 2005 movie *Brokeback Mountain* did things visually and audiologically that Annie Proulx could not do in her *New Yorker* short story on which the movie was based. It's as pointless to criticize a movie for not being a book as it is to criticize a tuna fish for not tasting like celery.

■ **Traditions.** The past informs our understanding of the present. A long-standing strain in U.S. journalism, for example, was born in the Constitution's implication that the news media should serve as a watchdog on behalf of the people against government folly and misdeeds. Another tradition is for artistic expression that is free from government restraint. Media literacy is impossible without an appreciation of the traditions that have profoundly shaped the parameters of media performance and reasonable expectations.

Too, media literacy requires an understanding of other traditions. The role of mass media in China, for example, flows from circumstances and traditions radically different from those in Western democracies. Even among democracies, media performance varies. News reporting about criminal prosecutions in Britain, as an example, is much more restrained than that in the United States.

■ **Media Myth.** Video games are the latest whipping boys for violent crime. The fact is that the oft-heard conventional wisdom that media violence begets real-life violence has never been proved, despite hundreds of serious studies by social scientists. In fact, no matter how cleverly criminal defense attorneys have tried to scapegoat violent behavior on video gaming, television or movies, the courts always have rejected the argument. This is not to say that there is no link between violence in the media and violence in real life. Rather, it's to say that a simple, direct lineage has yet to be confirmed.

Media myths galore are afloat, polluting intelligent dialogue and understanding of important issues, including media violence. To separate real phenomena from conjecture and nonsense requires media literacy.

LEARNING CHECK ◄••

▶ **Give examples of media awareness as indicators of media literacy.**

▶ **How do media myths impede attaining a high level of media literacy?**

Human Communication

STUDY PREVIEW

Mass communication is a process that targets technologically amplified messages to massive audiences. Other forms of communication pale in comparison in their ability to reach great numbers of people.

ANCIENT COMMUNICATION

- **interpersonal communication**
Between two individuals, although sometimes a small group, usually face-to-face

- **group communication**
An audience of more than one, all within earshot

Human communication has many forms. Cave dwellers talked to each other. When Tor grunted at Oop, it was **interpersonal communication**—one on one. Around the campfire, when Tor recounted tales from the hunt for the rest of the tribe, he was engaging in **group communication.** Traditionally, both interpersonal and group communication are face-to-face. Technology has expanded the prehistoric roots of human communication. When lovers purr sweet nothings by telephone, it's still interpersonal communication. A rabble-rouser with a megaphone is engaging in group communication.

MASS COMMUNICATION

Fundamental to media literacy is recognizing the different forms of communication for what they are. Confusing interpersonal communication and mass communication, for example, only muddles an attempt to sort through important complex issues.

- **mass communication**
Technology-assisted process by which messages are sent to large, faraway audiences

    Mass communication is the sending of a message to a great number of people at widely separated points. Mass communication is possible only through technology, whether it be a printing press, a broadcast transmitter or an Internet server.

    The massiveness of the audience is a defining characteristic of mass communication:

■ **Distance.** The mass audience is beyond the communicator's horizon, sometimes thousands of miles away. This is not the case with either interpersonal or group communication. Even technology-assisted group meetings via satellite or videoconferencing, although connecting faraway points, are not mass communication but a form of group communication.

■ **Audience.** The mass audience is eclectic and heterogeneous. With sitcoms, for example, the television networks seek mega-audiences of disparate groups—male and female, young and old, liberal and right-wing, devout and nonreligious. Some media products narrow their focus, like a bridal magazine. But a bridal magazine's intended audience, although primarily young and female, is still diverse in terms of ethnicity, income, education and other kinds of other measures. It still is a mass audience.

- **feedback**
Response to a message

■ **Feedback.** The mass audience generally lacks the opportunity for immediate **feedback.** In interpersonal communication, a chuckle or a punch in the nose right then and there is immediate feedback. With most mass communication, response is delayed—a letter to the editor, a canceled subscription. Even an 800-call to a television news quiz is delayed a bit and is certainly less potent than that punch in the nose. Also, the recipient of an e-mailed message doesn't necessarily read it right away.

LEARNING CHECK ◄

▶ Can you give examples of personal, group and mass communication besides those cited here?

▶ Is a football cheerleader with a megaphone a mass communicator? How about someone in a videoconference meeting?

Media and Society

STUDY PREVIEW

With the advent of network radio, people across the geographically huge and diverse United States found themselves bound culturally as never before. Later, television networks added to the cultural cohesion. That mass audience of yore, however, is fragmenting. Media companies cater increasingly to niches, not the whole.

UNIFICATION

Media literacy can provide an overview of mass media's effects on society and culture. The most sweeping effect of mass media has been as a cultural unifier.

■ **Newspapers, Books.** The mass media bind communities with messages that become a shared experience. History is peppered with examples. When Horace Greeley created a national weekly edition of his New York *Tribune* in the 1840s, readers throughout the country, even on the remote frontier, had something in common. Meanwhile, the first distinctly American novels, appearing in the early 1800s, helped give the young nation a cultural identity. The mass media of the time, mostly books and newspapers, created an awareness of something distinctly American. Shared knowledge, experience and the values flowing therefrom are, after all, what a culture is.

■ **Radio.** The national radio networks beginning in the 1920s, seeking the largest possible audiences, contributed intensely to cultural cohesion. Americans everywhere laughed together, simultaneously even, with the on-air antics of Eddie Cantor, Jack Benny, and Fibber McGee and Molly. Pop music became a coast-to-coast phenomenon. Even the networks' names suggested their role in making a national identity—the *National* Broadcasting Company and the *Columbia* Broadcasting System and later the *American* Broadcasting Company. It was radio that gave President Franklin Roosevelt a national audience in the Depression from which to rally massive majorities behind daring economic and social reforms. Hollywood shifted to patriotic war themes in feature movies, which along with outright propaganda, like Frank Capra's *Why We Fight* series, were a powerful part of the media mix that made it easy for Roosevelt to unify the nation for war in the 1940s, despite the country's ethnic, religious and social diversity.

■ **Television.** Later the television networks became major factors in the national identity. Audiences of unprecedented magnitude converged on the networks, all promulgating the same cultural fare. Even network newscasts, when they were introduced, all had a redundancy.

Through most of the 20th century, the most successful mass media companies competed to amass the largest possible audiences. The companies sought to bring everybody into their tents. True, there were racist hate-mongers with radio programs. Also, political dissidents had their outlets. But the media, especially those dependent on advertising revenue, had a largely homogeneous thrust that simultaneously created, fed and sustained a dominant monoculture.

The role of mass media as a binding influence is most clear in news coverage of riveting events. Think 9/11. Think Hurricane Katrina. Even the Super Bowl. On-screen news graphics are a regular binding influence: *America in Crisis, America's Most Wanted, Our Porous Borders.* Lou Dobbs on CNN has found broad appeal with his "War on the Middle Class" theme. Almost everybody's self-perception is as middle class or aspiring to be.

MORAL CONSENSUS

The mass media contribute to the evolution of what society regards as acceptable or as inexcusable. News coverage of the impeachment of President Clinton did this. On a lesser scale, so did revelations about the drug addiction of talk-show host Rush Limbaugh, who for years stridently called for harsh crackdowns on sellers and users of illegal drugs. The lists of people convicted of underage alcohol consumption, a staple in many small-city newspapers, keep the question before the public about whether the legal age should be 21 or 18, or whether there should be any restriction at all or, at the other extreme, a return to prohibition. At many levels, the mass media are essential to the ongoing process of society identifying its values.

You might ask whether the media, in covering controversy, are divisive. The short answer: No. Seldom do the media create controversy. For the most part, media merely cover it. Thorough coverage, over time, helps to bring about societal consensus—sometimes for change, sometimes not. For example, most Americans once opposed legalizing abortion. Today, after exhaustive media attention, a majority belief has emerged that abortion should be available legally in a widening array of circumstances. Racial integration was settled upon as public policy in the latter 20th century. The debate, conducted almost entirely through mass media, is well along in many fundamental issues, such as gun control, gay marriage and, never ending, government budget priorities.

FRAGMENTATION

The giant Gannett newspaper chain launched a national daily, *USA Today*, in 1982, with editing techniques that pandered explicitly to an American identity. The paper had a first-person "our" tone throughout in referring to national issues. *USA Today* rose to become the largest daily in the nation, reflecting and also fueling a homogeneity in American culture. At the same time, however, a phenomenon was at work elsewhere in the mass media to turn the conventional wisdom of the time about mass audiences on its head. In a process called **demassification,** media companies shifted many of their products from seeking the largest possible audience to focusing on audience segments.

● **demassification**
Media's focus on narrower audience segments

Demassification began on a large scale with radio. In the 1950s the major radio networks, NBC, CBS and ABC, pirated their most popular radio programming and put it on their new television networks. There was an exodus of audience and advertisers from radio. Suddenly, the radio industry was an endangered species. Stations recognized that they couldn't compete with network television for the mass audiences anymore and began seeking audience segments with specialized music. Radio became a demassified medium with a growing number of musical genres. Stations each sought only a local slice of the mass media—**sub-mass audiences** they could be called. Or niche audiences. The new radio programming was designed not for universal appeal but for audience niches. These were audience segments that television networks didn't bother to seek in their quest to build audiences that left no one out.

● **sub-mass audience**
A section of the largest mass audience, with niche interests

Like radio, magazines geared for universal audiences lost national advertising to early network television. They survived only by reinventing themselves and focusing on audience segments.

ACCELERATING DEMASSIFICATION

Media demassification accelerated in the 1980s with technology that gave the cable television industry the ability to deliver dozens of channels. Most of these channels, while national, were taking the demassified course of magazines and gearing programs to audience niches—sports fans, food aficionados, speed freaks. The term

● narrowcasting
Seeking niche audiences, as opposed to broadcasting's traditional audience-building concept

narrowcasting, as opposed to broadcasting, entered the vocabulary for media literacy. Then a wholly new technology, the Internet, offered people more alternatives that were even narrower.

What has demassification done to the media's role as a contributor to social cohesion? Some observers are quick to link media fragmentation with the political polarization of the country, epitomized by Blue State and Red State divisions. Clearly there are cultural divides that have been nurtured if not created by media fragmentation. Music, as an example, is defined today by generational, racial, ethnic and socioeconomic categories, contrary to the homogenizing of tastes that radio fostered at the national level in its heyday in the 1930s and 1940s. At the same time, there remain media units that amass huge audiences in the traditional sense. Even in the slow summer months, CBS easily draws 9 million viewers to *CSI*. And *USA Today*, with a 2.3 million circulation, is by far the largest daily newspaper in the country.

A great drama of our times is the jockeying of the mass media for audience in an unpredictable and fast-changing media landscape. In pursuit of audience, whether mass or niche, media companies are experimenting with alternative platforms to deliver content that will find a following—or keep a following. Movies aren't only at the multiplex anymore and soon may be on iPods. ABC's *Lost* isn't only on prime time but is also downloadable. *USA Today* is online. CNN has multiple online platforms.

LEARNING CHECK ◄ ⋯⋯⋯⋯⋯⋯⋯⋯⋯⋯⋯⋯⋯⋯⋯⋯⋯⋯⋯

▶ **Historically, what was the effect of mass media's seeking the largest possible audiences?**

▶ **What triggered media demassification? So what?**

▶ **Are mass media today a factor of unification or division in society?**

Media Economics

STUDY PREVIEW

Most media behavior can be explained by economics. Who pays the bills? Advertising generates most of the revenue for newspapers, magazines, radio and television. Books, movies and music rely largely on direct sales to consumers. A great issue with advertising-funded media is whether he who pays the piper calls the tune.

REVENUE STREAMS

Media literacy requires an understanding of the dynamics that shape media content. In a capitalistic environment, economics is the primary driver of the behavior of media companies. With rare exceptions, media companies are businesses whose success is measured by their owners in profits. In short, capitalism rewards enterprises that generate profits. This means producing products that people are willing to buy in enough quantity and at a sufficient price to meet and, if successful, exceed expenses.

● revenue stream
Source of income

Most media have numerous sources of income, called **revenue streams.** Advertising is a major revenue source.

■ **Advertising.** Major segments of the media industry use their audiences to attract advertising. Newspapers and magazines sell space to advertisers to reach potential customers. Television and radio sell airtime.

The purchase of media space and time is a major corporate activity. It's through advertising that corporations reach potential customers. In the United States, General Motors puts $4 billion a year into advertising, That's somewhere near $14 per capita. Procter & Gamble, the second-largest U.S. advertiser, pitches in almost $3.9 billion, another $14 per capita. In the process of buying access to potential customers, advertisers also are subsidizing consumer media habits.

If not for advertising, *Time* magazine as we know it wouldn't exist. Nor would CNN or the New York *Times*. Almost all newspaper, magazine, radio and television outlets have advertising as their main revenue stream.

The importance of advertising in the financial structure of mass media is hard to overstate. Some years ago it was estimated that a copy of *Time* would run $16 at the newsstand if it weren't for advertising. Today the cover price undoubtedly would be even more. In effect, advertising subsidizes consumers who, for example, buy *Time* for only $5 for a single copy off a newsrack or subscribe for as little as 50 cents a copy.

What do advertisers get for their money? In their purchased time and space, advertisers generally are free to say whatever they want. It's their space. They paid for it.

● **editorial content**
Mass media content other than advertising

Stories occasionally surface about advertisers that assume they also are buying control of what's called **editorial content**—the nonadvertising part of a media product's content. In a classic case study, General Motors went into a tiff and withdrew its advertising from the *Wall Street Journal* because of a negative news story. To its credit, the *Journal* stuck to the classic model of editorial independence in media-advertiser relations and refused to bend. GM eventually came back because it needed the *Journal* to reach potential customers. Not all media, however, have the financial wherewithal to stand up to advertiser pressure or bullying. In some communities, a major local advertiser, like a grocery chain, can wield tremendous power over editorial content.

■ **Subscriptions.** The role of subscription revenue varies. At most newspapers, newsrack coins and subscription orders are secondary revenue streams that, at best, cover delivery costs. The cost of producing the product is borne mostly by advertising. For most magazines also, subscriptions are a minor revenue stream.

Commercial radio and television in the United States have no mechanisms for subscriptions. For all practical purposes, selling time to advertisers is the sole source of revenue. There are notable exceptions, however. Cable networks charge local cable companies a monthly fee that is passed on to the cable customers. The Sirius and XM satellite radio services rely mostly on subscriptions.

A variation is the volunteer subscriptions that ad-free public television and radio stations encourage listeners to pay—a donation.

■ **Direct Sales.** The economics of the book, recorded music and movie industries are built on individual unit sales to consumers. Books are sold mostly one at a time. People buy music one song or album at a time. At the movies it's one ticket at a time.

In one sense, direct sales are the purest relationship between a media product and its audience. A book, for example, succeeds or fails on direct sales—not whether a widget manufacturer sees a book as a way to peddle widgets. There is minimal possibility for a book's content to be tainted by an advertiser. Generally there is no third party in the relationship between a book and its reader. It's the same for recorded music. Historically, movies have relied on direct sales, although the growing number of paid product plugs in scripts is eroding the pristine movie-audience relationship.

■ **Other Revenue.** A diverse range of other revenue supports various mass media to differing degrees. Corporations and charitable foundations are major donors to noncommercial television and radio. So-called public broadcasting, like PBS and National Public Radio, leans on government funding. Merchandise tie-ins, like Batman toys, are significant for Hollywood, not to mention DC Comics.

LEARNING CHECK ◄ •••

▸ **What are mass media's most significant revenue streams?**

▸ **Which media are least vulnerable to advertiser pressure to shape content?**

CORPORATE STRUCTURES

Another dynamic for media literacy is the corporate structure within which media products exist. Knowing the entities comprising News Corporation, for example, explains a lot of the content output of corporate stablemates Fox television and HarperCollins books.

● **Frank Gannett**
Founder of the Gannett newspaper chain

▪ **Media Chains.** We are in an era of Big Media, with more cross-ownerships than most people realize. The Gannett media chain is one example. Like most media chains, Gannett started small, with **Frank Gannett** and a few associates pooling enough money in 1906 to buy a half interest in the Elmira, New York, *Gazette*. They added a few small-town papers and eventually created the Empire State group of dailies and moved the headquarters to Rochester. Gradually more papers were added. Today Gannett owns 99 daily newspapers coast-to-coast, including *USA Today*. The company also owns 17 dailies in Britain. The company's holdings also include television stations. Along the way, Gannett has been in and out of radio, billboards, magazines, polling, and other enterprises.

To gather capital for further expansion and to build its business, Gannett periodically sells ownership shares to investors. These investors have a growing role in choosing managers of the company's properties and adopting policies to increase profits as a return on their investments.

Today most media operations with names that consumers recognize are parts of giant conglomerates whose policies are decided by the shareholders who own the most stock. These are giant enterprises. Time Warner generates revenue of $37 billion a year from movies, books, television, magazines, online sites and other media operations. What all controlling shareholders have in common is their goal of improving the return on their investments.

These are the largest U.S. media companies ranked by domestic revenue:

Time Warner	$37.0 billion	News Corp.	11.4 billion
Viacom	21.5 billion	DirecTV	9.8 billion
Comcast	20.1 billion	Cox	8.6 billion
Disney	17.4 billion	Echo Star	6.7 billion
NBC Universal	12.5 billion	Clear Channel	6.5 billion

Each company's board of directors chooses executives to achieve these goals, and those executives appoint subordinates to do the job. In a hierarchical business structure, decisions by the board determine the shape of the media we deal with day-in and day-out—to buy or sell AOL, to reintroduce *Life*, to put more resources into *People* to strengthen its market dominance, to back off animated movies, or to further saturate the market with more animations. These decisions, made in boardrooms, are off the radar of all but the most savvy and media-literate.

▪ **Capitalist Environment.** The structure of U.S. mass media is a money-driven system. Executives who don't deliver profits are replaced. If profits lag, investors

A Profile of News Corporation with a Sample of Subsidiary Units, Whose Global Revenues Exceed $23 Billion a Year

	Subsidiary Unit	Yearly Revenue		Subsidiary Unit	Yearly Revenue
Newspapers	Wall Street Journal New York Post London Times News of the World Australian newspapers	$6.5 billion	**Satcast**	StarTV Sky Italia Latin America services	$2.3 billion
			Books	HarperCollins	1.3 billion
Movies	20th Century-Fox Fox Searchlight 20th Century-Fox Television	5.9 billion	**Magazines**	TV Guide Weekly Standard Inside Out	1.1 billion
			Internet	MySpace.com Broadsystem Ventures	1.0 billion
Television	Fox network 35 U.S. stations Latin American stations Asian stations	5.3 billion	**Radio**	Sky Radio	200 million
Cable	Fox News Channel Fox Movie Channel Fox Business Channel Fox regional sports networks	2.7 billion			

pull out their money, reducing the capital available for operations and growth. Investors as a group couldn't care less whether their money is in the stock of a mass media company or a widget manufacturer. The investment with the greatest profit potential is a magnet.

Profit generation is complex. Different operations have a different mix of advertising and other revenue streams. A high-yield operation, as AOL once was for Time Warner, can fade and need to be either sold or somehow reinvented. Competition can change everything, whether from a direct competitor or some new enterprise that sucks away audience—as the online news has done for traditional news media. An enterprise that generates strong profits at the moment may not have strong prospects down the road. What to do? Cut expenses and ride the road to lesser revenue? Sell? Shut down? And what effect do these questions have on you as a media consumer?

LEARNING CHECK ◄ •••

▶ Why have media chains and conglomerates come into being?

▶ Who owns your daily newspaper? Your favorite local radio station? The dominant local television station?

The pre-Oprah reigning ringmaster of daytime television, Phil Donahue, is sounding the perils of corporate conglomeration of the media. In a fund-raising letter distributed by the pressure group Free Press, Donahue talks about "deadly serious damage" being inflicted by giant corporate media. Donahue sees giant media corporations in collusion with government, spewing propaganda for partisan political causes in exchange for government regulations that will enhance the media corporations' profits. At stake, Donahue says, is free speech. Using radio as an example, Donahue minces no words:

"Does your local radio station carry high school football games on Friday night? How about births and deaths in the community that day? No? That's because your radio station is probably a computer where no live person works. The music you hear is sliced and diced at a distant location and fed to the hundreds of human-free stations along the loop owned by one company. News? Are you serious? News means people, expenses, lower profits. Cue the canned music.

"The massive media monopolies that control content are the biggest

Evils of Media Conglomeration. *Talk-show veteran Phil Donahue, who's seen the media industry from the inside, decries the effect of Big Media ownership on media content. Cost-cutting, he says, has undermined serving the audience.*

enemies to free speech. They dine with and cater to the public servants who protect them in Congress."

Donahue says he can't tolerate the carpet-bombing of children by television advertisers, the two-minute hit-and-run newscasts, or the absence of diverse opinions on the political shout shows.

The Free Press organization that Donahue supports has had successes:

• Free Press helped rally people to send more than 1 million messages to Congress to reinstate full funding

for the PBS and NPR non-commercial broadcast systems. Commercial station owners had long loathed PBS and NPR for siphoning audience away from their stations.

• Free Press mobilized 60,000 messages against the Sinclair television chain for planning to air a film smearing Democratic candidate John Kerry in prime time on all of its 62 stations a few days before the 2004 presidential election. Sinclair executives had been big financial backers of Republican candidate George Bush. Under pressure, Sinclair canceled the show.

• Free Press claimed at least partial credit for pressing Congress to cut funding for government agencies to issue "video news releases" that promote partisan projects in the guise of news stories.

WHAT DO YOU THINK?

▶ The major factors in determining media content are audience size, advertising appeal and doing social good? Which do you see as the most influential?

▶ Is Phil Donahue overstating his point when he calls big media companies the enemies of free speech. Or is he right on?

Chapter Wrap-Up

Media Ubiquity (Page 3)

■ Two-thirds of our waking hours are spent consciously or subconsciously with the mass media. The media are a major component of our ecosystem. We can be oblivious to their effects unless we cultivate an understanding of how the media work and why. This understanding is called media literacy.

Media Literacy (Page 6)

■ Media literacy begins with a factual foundation and becomes keener with an understanding of the dynamics that influence media messages. There are degrees of awareness, including abilities to understand and explain media behavior and effects and to identify significant media issues.

Human Communication (Page 12)

■ Mass media operate through a process called mass communication. The process technologically amplifies messages, sending them potentially to massive audiences. Other forms of communication, such as interpersonal, can't approach the great numbers of people that mass media reach through mass communication.

Media and Society (Page 13)

■ The effect of mass media on culture is changing. At one time the media bound people culturally, especially early radio networks, then television, and people across the geographically huge and diverse United States heard the same comedy, drama and music. The result: A strong cultural cohesion. That mass audience of yore, however, is fragmenting. Media companies pander increasingly to niches, not the whole. The result: Fragmentation in the culture, which is sometimes polarizing, at other times simply diverging. Either way, there has been a loosening of cultural cohesion.

Media Economics (Page 15)

■ Most media behavior, including demassification, can be explained by economics. Advertising, a significant driver of media behavior, has gravitated to media products that deliver audiences of the advertisers' most likely customers—not blanket mass audiences but sub-mass audiences. A great issue with advertising-funded media is whether he who pays the piper calls the tune. The problem is that the economic structure of many media companies creates a conflict between serving the interests of their advertisers and serving the interests of their audiences. Having two masters is problematic.

REVIEW QUESTIONS

1. Do your own media habits differ from what the Ball State University study suggests, which is that media exposure is a dominant ingredient in the daily lives of most people?

2. What were your strengths in media literacy at the start of your current course? Any voids?

3. How are interpersonal, group and mass communication different? Give examples of each.

4. Mass media have had tremendous effects on shaping society and culture in the United States. Describe how these dynamics have worked throughout history.

5. For better or worse, how do economics shape mass media content?

CONCEPTS	TERMS	PEOPLE
media multi-tasking (Page 3)	satcast (Page 12)	Rupert Murdoch (Page 8)
marketplace of ideas (Page 5)	feedback (Page 12)	John Milton (Page 6)
media literacy (Page 6)	mass media (Page 3)	Frank Gannett (Page 17)
mass communication (Page 3)	narrowcasting (Page 15)	Phil Donahue (Page 19)
demassification (Page 14)	editorial content (Page 16)	

MEDIA SOURCES

- Newsmagazines, including *Time* and *Newsweek*, cover mass-media issues more or less regularly. So do the New York *Times, Wall Street Journal* and other leading newspapers. Periodicals that track mass media as businesses include *BusinessWeek, Forbes* and *Fortune*.

- Kara Swisher. *There Must Be a Pony in Here Somewhere*. Crown, 2003. Swisher, a *Wall Street Journal* reporter, chronicles the giddy incorporation of AOL into Time Warner through the disenchantment that led to purging AOL from the corporate name in 2003.

- Benjamin M. Compaine and Douglas Gomery. *Who Owns the Media? Competition and Concentration in the Mass Media Industry*, third edition. Erlbaum, 2000. The authors update the 1979 and 1992 editions with details on further concentration, more attention to the cable and home video business and discussion of the effect of technological convergence.

- Sumner Redstone with Peter Knobler. *A Passion to Win*. Simon & Schuster, 2001. This is the autobiography of Viacom's architect, published by his Simon & Schuster subsidiary and marketed heavily through his Blockbuster video rental chain.

- Ben Bagdikian. *The Media Monopoly*, fifth edition. Beacon, 1997. Bagdikian, perhaps the best-known critic of media conglomeration, includes data on the digital revolution in this update of his classic work.

Media Trends

In this chapter you have deepened your media literacy by visiting several themes. Here are highlights from this chapter that suggest where media are heading.

Media and Democracy

The mass media are at the core of democracy. If people at the grassroots are to participate in shaping their common course, they need information. This will be even more true in the future The mass media are information purveyors. People also need a forum for exchanging their reactions to information and their ideas. The mass media are that forum. **(Pages 4–6)**

Bringing the Country Together. *President Franklin Roosevelt used the new medium of radio in the 1930s to rally national support for fundamental social and economic reforms to deal with the Great Depression.*

Media and Culture

We live in a culture that's increasingly media-saturated. So ubiquitous are mass media that their presence largely is invisible. Occasionally we're jarred by in-your-face content, but mostly the mass media are taken for granted—like air. Just as air affects us, and deserves scientific examination and monitoring, so do media. **(Pages 3–6)**

Consensus Builder. *Media attention to divisive issues can help wring societal consensus. The Michael J. Fox pleas for stem-cell research funding in the 2006 political campaign stirred pro and con dialogues a step toward consensus.*

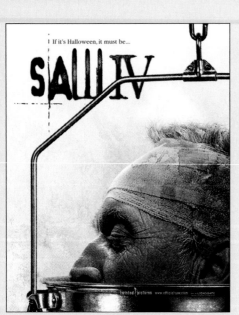

Media Effects

Media messages influence our daily decision making in ways we often don't recognize. What influences you, for example, toward one brand of toothpaste or line of gym shoes? Media effects are a two-way street. Media affect us, but also, because media are economically dependent on audience, we as media consumers influence the media and do so in ways we often don't recognize. **(Pages 3–6)**

Violence Progenitor? *Slasher movies have reignited media criticism about negative effects on individuals and society. Research, however, is inconclusive as to whether media violence begets real-life violence. We need to know more about media effects.*

Audience Fragmentation

Mass media build social cohesion by giving far-flung audiences something in common. A sense of nationhood was nurtured, for example, by books on the American experience in the early 1800s. A century later, radio networks gave Americans everywhere the same comedies, drama and newscasts. Although media continue to be a unifier, new technologies have created economics for gearing messages to sub-mass audiences, which is figuring into the fragmentation of society. (Pages 13–15)

Media Melding. *Distinction between and among media are blurring with delivery devices that combine text, audio and visuals, including moving images.*

Media Economics

Most media behavior, including content decisions, can be explained by the profit motivation of media owners. Companies operate in their economic self-interest. This has led to waves of consolidation into fewer and fewer companies, all of them giants, with occasional spin-offs when it serves profit goals. Media companies today are scrambling to find ways to ensure their continued profitability in a rapidly changing media landscape. (Pages 15–18)

Media Technology

Citizens as News Reporters

When a gunman started shooting in Norris Hall at Virginia Tech there were no traditional news journalists with their video cameras on the scene. But within minutes CNN broadcast video footage showing the chaos. As police moved in, viewers not only saw but heard the gunfire and ensuing panic. A student, Jamal Albarghouti, who had been carrying his video-capable cell phone in his pocket as he walked on campus quickly moved toward the scene with his camera-phone running. Albarghouti notified CNN. His images were viewed on CNN by millions throughout the day as the story of the tragedy unfolded. CNN anchors referred to Albarghouti as their I-Reporter on the scene.

The on-the-spot video was just one example of the way that new technology had an impact on how we learned about the Virginia Tech tragedy. Tech-savvy Virginia Tech's students, like college students everywhere, routinely use social networking sites, such as Facebook or MySpace, to stay connected with their friends and family. It should come as no surprise that they turned to these sites to instantly let people know that they were not among the victims, to share details of what was happening on campus, to let people everywhere know about campus vigils or other events, to post memorials commemorating the victims, or even just to stay connected to loved ones far away.

Other virtual communities, such as the temporary Web site vttragedy.com, were quickly set up as another forum for people to share information and connect with others around the world who wanted to share their sympathies with the grieving

LEARNING AHEAD

- Mass communication is a technology-based process.
- Mass production of the written word became possible with movable metal type.
- Chemistry is the technological basis of movies.
- Mastery of the electromagnetic spectrum led to radio and television.
- Orbiting satellites and fiber optics have improved media efficiency.
- Traditional media products and new products are emerging from digital technology.
- Models help explain the technology-driven process of mass communication.

Cell Phone in Hand. *Mourning Virginia Tech students clutch each other after a campus massacre that claimed 33 lives, including the shooter's. It was a tragedy in which hundreds of students with video-capable cell phones became citizen journalists.*

campus community. The Virginia Tech campus newspaper immediately began to post news on their online site, collegiatetimes.com, and scooped even the New York *Times*, which acknowledged the Virginia Tech Web site by posting a link to it.

Traditional reporters, hungry for sources of news about the tragedy, logged on to the various blogs and were able to use them as sources to quickly find eyewitnesses to interview themselves. Martin Clancy, producer for ABC News Digital, says, "This is a really much more efficient way to gather information and to get input and to discover perspectives you didn't even know existed." Even President Bush referred to the blog coverage of the events of the day when he addressed the campus later that evening to express his sympathies and offer support.

Media Technology

STUDY PREVIEW

Technology is basic in mass communication. If not for the technology of printing presses, books as we know them wouldn't exist. If not for electronic technology, television and radio wouldn't be.

TECHNOLOGY DEPENDENCE

● **interpersonal communication**
Usually two people face to face

One defining characteristic of mass communication is its reliance on technology. People can communicate face-to-face, which is called **interpersonal communication,** without technological assistance. For centuries people communicated in large groups, as in town-hall meetings and concert halls, without microphones—just the human voice, albeit sometimes elevated to extraordinary volume. For mass communication, however, with audiences much more far-flung than those in the largest auditorium, machinery is necessary.

EVOLVING MEDIA LANDSCAPE

Media technology, the product of human invention, exists in several forms, each one distinctive. Around each of these technologies, industries have been built that are closely allied with each specific technology.

■ **Printing Technology.** The printing press, dating to the 1440s, spawned the book, newspaper and magazine industries. After centuries, each still exists in a largely cubbyholed niche in the media landscape.

■ **Chemical Technology.** Photography and movies have relied on chemical technology throughout most of their history.

■ **Electronic Technology.** The first of the electronic media, sound recording, actually preceded the widespread use of electricity but quickly became an electrically powered medium. Radio was electrical early on. Television was electronic from the get-go.

■ **Digital Technology.** Traditional mass media all adapted to digital technology, to varying degrees, beginning in the first decade of the 21st century, but the industries built on the original printing, chemicals and electronic forms remain largely distinctive. Book companies like HarperCollins still produce books. CBS is still primarily in the television business. The distinctive newest medium built on digital technology is the Internet. Even as companies built on older technologies have swirled in a frenzy to find ways to capitalize on the new medium, the Internet itself has created entirely new categories of media companies. Think Wikipedia. Think Facebook.com. Think Google.

Meanwhile, printed and bound books are still with us, as are Channel 2 on television, Paramount Pictures and commute-time radio.

LEARNING CHECK ◄ ••
▶ **What are the four primary technologies on which mass media are built?**
▶ **What industries have built around the different media technologies?**

Printing

STUDY PREVIEW

With the invention of movable metal type in the mid-1440s, suddenly the written word could be mass-produced. The effect on human existence was profound. Incorporating photographic technology with printing in the late 1800s added new impact to printed products.

MOVABLE METAL TYPE

● **movable metal type**
Innovation that made the printing press an agent for mass communication

● **Johannes Gutenberg**
Metallurgist who invented movable metal type in mid-1440s

Although printing can be traced back a couple thousand years to eastern Asia, an invention in the mid-1440s made mass production of the written word possible for the first time. The innovation: **movable metal type.** A tinkerer in what is now the German city of Mainz, **Johannes Gutenberg,** was obsessed with melting and mixing metals to create new alloys. He came up with the idea to cast the individual letters of the alphabet in metal, and then assemble them one at a time into a page for reproduction by pressing paper onto the raised, inked characters. The metal characters were sturdy enough to survive the repeated pressure of transferring the inked letters to paper—something not possible with the carved wood letters that had been used in earlier printing.

In time, industries grew up around the technology, each producing print media products that are still with us today—books, magazines and newspapers. But historically, the impact of Gutenberg's invention was apparent much earlier. Printing with Gutenberg's new technology took off quickly. By 1500 printing presses were in place throughout Europe. Suddenly civilization had the mass-produced written word.

Movable Metal Type. Johannes Gutenberg melted metals into alloys that he cast as individual letters, then arranged in a frame the size of a page to form words, sentences and whole passages. Once a page was full, the raised letters would be inked and a sheet of paper pressed onto them to transfer the impression. Dozens, even hundreds of impressions could be made, one page at a time. Then the type would be removed and reassembled for another page. Tedious? Yes, but it sure beat the tedium of scribists producing handwritten manuscripts letter by letter.

Johannes Gutenberg was eccentric—a secretive tinkerer with a passion for beauty, detail and craftsmanship. By trade he was a metallurgist, but he never made much money at it. Like most of his fellow 15th-century Rhinelanders in present-day Germany, he pressed his own grapes for wine. As a businessman, he was not very successful, and he died penniless. Despite his unpromising combination of traits, quirks and habits—perhaps because of them—Johannes Gutenberg wrought the most significant change in history: The mass-produced written word. He invented movable metal type.

Despite the significance of his invention, there is much we do not know about Gutenberg. Even to friends he seldom mentioned his experiments, and when he did, he referred to them mysteriously as his "secret art." When he ran out of money, Gutenberg quietly sought investors, luring them partly with the mystique he attached to his work. What we know about Gutenberg's "secret art" was recorded only because Gutenberg's main backer didn't receive the quick financial return he'd expected on his investment and sued. The litigation left a record from which historians have pieced together the origins of modern printing.

The date when Johannes Gutenberg printed his first page with movable type is unknown, but historians usually settle on 1446. Gutenberg's

● **Gutenberg Bibles**
Bibles printed by Gutenberg with movable type. Surviving Bibles are all collector items.

Johannes Gutenberg

Gutenberg Bible. *Although his technology for mass-producing the written word was primitive, Johannes Gutenberg's work was masterly. He mixed up excellent inks from scratch. His blacks the blackest blacks and his colors vibrant. Gutenberg was never rushed. He produced only 200 Bibles with his movable type. The survivors are now all museum pieces.*

printing process was widely copied—and quickly. By 1500, presses all over Western Europe had published almost 40,000 books.

Today, Gutenberg is remembered for the Bibles he printed with movable type. Two hundred **Gutenberg Bibles,** each a printing masterpiece, were produced over several years. Gutenberg used the best paper. He concocted an especially black ink. The quality amazed everybody, and the Bibles sold quickly. Gutenberg could have printed hundreds more, perhaps

thousands. With a couple of husky helpers he and his modified wine press could have produced 50 to 60 pages an hour. However, Johannes Gutenberg, who never had much business savvy, concentrated instead on quality. Forty-seven Gutenberg Bibles remain today, all collector's items. One sold in 1978 for $2.4 million.

WHAT DO YOU THINK?

▶ Would you rank Johannes Gutenberg among the 10 most influential persons in human history?

GUTENBERG'S IMPACT

The impact was transformational. Scientists who earlier had carried on time-consuming hand-written correspondence with colleagues now could print their theories and experiments for wide dissemination.

Modern science thus took form. Religious tracts could also be mass-produced, as could materials with serious challenges to religion. The growing quantity of printed materials fueled literacy and, slowly, a standardization in written languages. What Gutenberg begat can be called the Age of Mass Communication,

Halftone. *The halftone process, invented by Frederick Ives, uses variously sized dots to transfer ink to paper. The dots are invisible except under close examination. At a reading distance, however, the bigger dots leave darker impressions, the smaller dots a lighter impression. The effect looks like the varying tones in a photograph.*

Frederick Ives

but his innovation also spurred Western civilization into the ongoing Age of Science and Age of Reason. Civilization hasn't been the same since.

LEARNING CHECK ◄

▶ **What was the link between Gutenberg and the scientific revolution of the 1600s and 1700s?**

▶ **What breakthrough in technology made mass production of photographs possible in newspapers and other print media?**

PRINT-VISUAL INTEGRATION

Although visuals are not a mass medium, photography increased the communicative power of the printed word in the late 1800s. Experiments at Cornell University in the 1870s led to technology that could mass-produce images in books, newspapers and magazines. This new technology, pioneered by **Frederick Ives,** was the **halftone.** Ives divided a photograph into a microscopic grid, each tiny square having a raised dot that registered a separate tonal gray from a photograph—the bigger the dot, the more ink it would transfer to the paper and the darker the gray. At the typical reading distance of 14 inches, the human eye can't make out the grid, but the eye can see the image created by the varying grays. Although crude, this was the first halftone.

At the New York *Daily Graphic*, **Steve Horgan** adapted Ives' process to high-speed printing. In 1880, the *Graphic* published a halftone image of Shantytown—a break from the line drawings that were the *Graphic's* original claim to distinction. Ives later improved on Horgan's process, and visual communication joined the Age of Mass Communication.

● **Frederick Ives**
Invented halftone in 1876

● **halftone**
Reproduction of an image in which the various tones of gray or color are produced by variously sized dots of ink

● **Steve Horgan**
Adapted halftone technology for high-speed newspaper presses

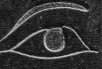

TECHNOLOGY MILESTONES	PIVOTAL EVENTS

1400s/1500s

Movable Type
Mass communication began with the Gutenberg printing process (1440 on).

- Columbus discovered Americas (1492)
- Luther sparked Protestant Reformation (1517)

1600s

Books
Cambridge Press issued first book in British North American colonies (1640). Cambridge Press also issued religious pamphlets, materials.

Newspapers
Ben Harris printed *Publick Occurrences,* first newspaper in the English colonies (1690).

- Pilgrims established colony (1620)
- French and Indian wars (1689–1763)

Gutenberg

Publick Occurrences

1700s

Magazines
Andrew Bradford and Benjamin Franklin introduced competing magazines in British colonies (1741). Meanwhile, weekly newspapers existed in larger colonial cities, reprinting items from Europe and each other.

- Industrial Revolution began (1760s)
- Revolutionary War (1776–1781)

1800s

Recording
Thomas Edison introduced Phonograph, which could record and play back sound (1877). Meanwhile, the book, newspaper, magazine industries flourished.

Movies
William Dickson devised motion picture camera (1888). Meanwhile, newspapers were in their heyday as dominant medium.

- Size of United States doubled with Louisiana Purchase (1803)
- Morse invented telegraph (1844)
- U.S. Civil War (1861–1864)
- U.S. coasts linked by rail (1869)

Bradford's magazine

1900s

Radio
Guglielmo Marconi transmitted first message by radio waves (1895). Meanwhile, sensationalism and muckraking attracted growing newspaper and magazine audiences.

Television
Philo Farnsworth discovered how to pick up moving images electronically for live transmission (1927). Meanwhile, radio networks created national audiences unprecedented in their reach.

Internet
U.S. military established computer network that became the Internet (1969). Television firmly dominated as an entertainment medium and was maturing as a news medium.

- Right to vote extended to women (1920)
- Great Depression (1930s)
- World War II (1941–1945)
- Russian–Western rivalry triggered Cold War (1945)
- Humans reached moon (1969)
- Soviet empire imploded (1989)

Edison Invention

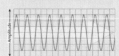
Mastering the Airwaves

2000s

Convergence
Delivery of mass messages fragmented into a growing number of digital mechanisms. By and large, the historic media industries remained in place producing content.

- 9/11 terrorist attacks (2001)
- Iraq War (2003–)
- Hurricane Katrina (2005)

Digital Era

Magazines, notably the early ***National Geographic,*** experimented with halftones too. When *Time* founder **Henry Luce** launched *Life* in 1934, photography moved the magazine industry into new visual ground. The oversize pages with slick, super-white paper gave *Life* photographs an intensity not possible with newsprint. *Life* captured the spirit of the times photographically and demonstrated that a wide range of human experiences could be recorded visually. Both real life and *Life* could be shocking. In 1938 a *Life* spread on human birth was so shocking for the time that censors succeeded in banning the issue in 33 cities.

LEARNING CHECK ◄ ....

▶ Using a newspaper picture, show how halftones give the illusion of a photograph.

▶ Without halftones, what pre-Gutenberg methods could print media use for illustrations?

Chessmistry

....

STUDY PREVIEW

Historically, photography is rooted in chemistry. The distinct technology had come of age by the time of the U.S. Civil War, creating a new kind of archival record. When techniques were devised to integrate photography into Gutenberg-legacy printing, the mass media suddenly were in a new visual era. Movies also drew on chemical technology but evolved along a separate path.

PHOTOGRAPHY

The 1727 discovery that light causes silver nitrate to darken was a breakthrough in mass communication. Scientists dabbled with the chemical for the next century. Then in 1826 **Joseph Níepce** found a way to capture and preserve an image on light-sensitive material. Photography was born—a chemical process for creating and recording a visual message. The technology was sufficiently established by the 1860s to create a new type of historical archive. Teams of photographers organized by **Mathew Brady** created an incredible visual record, much of it horrific, of the U.S. Civil War.

Over the next half century, technology developed for reproducing photographs on printing presses. Brady's legacy was issued in book form. Emotional advertisements stirred sales, promising lifelike images of "soldiers dashing and flags flying and horses leaping all over." The time was right, and hundreds of thousands of copies were sold to a generation of Civil War veterans and their families. By the time World War I began, however, the market was saturated. Also, people had new gruesome photographs from the European front. New grisliness replaced the old.

Also, a new application of photographic chemistry—the motion picture—was maturing.

LEARNING CHECK ◄ ....

▶ Explain this assertion: Photography and words are not mass media but are essential for the media to exploit their potential.

▶ How did Mathew Brady build public enthusiasm for photography in mass communication?

MOVIES

The motion picture, a late-1800s development, was rooted in chemistry too. The new media linked the lessons of photography to the recognition of a phenomenon called **persistence of vision.** It had come to be recognized in the late 1800s that

Visual Impact. With new technology in the late 1800s that could produce photographs on printing presses, newspapers and magazines suddenly had new potency in telling stories. The potential of photography to send printed media in a new direction was illustrated with painfully gory battlefield scenes from the Civil War. This visual perspective on war was mostly the work of teams of photographers organized by entrepreneur Mathew Brady.

Mathew Brady

the human eye retains an image for a fraction of a second. If a series of photographs captures motion at split-second intervals, those images, if flipped quickly, will trick the eye into perceiving continuous motion. For most people the illusion of motion begins with 14 photos per second.

● **William Dickson**
Developed the first movie camera

● **George Eastman**
Developed celluloid film

● **Lumière brothers**
Opened first motion picture exhibition hall

■ **Cameras.** At the research labs of prolific inventor and entrepreneur Thomas Edison, **William Dickson** developed a camera that captured 16 images per second. It was the first workable motion picture camera. Dickson used celluloid film perfected by **George Eastman,** who had popularized amateur photography with his Kodak camera. By 1891 Edison had begun producing movies.

■ **Projectors.** Edison's movies were viewed by looking into a box. In France the **Lumière brothers** Auguste and Louis brought projectors to motion pictures. By running the film in front of a specially aimed, powerful lightbulb, the Lumières projected movie images onto a wall. In 1895 they opened an exhibition hall in Paris—the first movie house. Edison recognized the commercial advantage in projection and himself patented a projector that he put on the market the next year.

LEARNING CHECK ◄

▶ **How are photography and motion pictures similar? How are they different?**

▶ **How does persistence of vision work?**

Electronics

STUDY PREVIEW

Electricity transformed people's lives beginning in the late 1800s with dazzling applications to all kinds of activities. The modern music industry sprang around these new systems for recording and playing back sound. Radio and television, both rooted in electricity, were among the technologies around which new industries were created.

ELECTRICITY AS TRANSFORMATIONAL

The harnessing of electricity had a profound impact on American life beginning in the late 1800s. The infrastructure for an electricity-based lifestyle was wholly in place half a century later when, in the 1930s, the government launched a massive project to extend electricity-distribution networks to every end-of-the road farmhouse. During this period, inventors and tinkerers came up with entirely new media of mass communication.

For two centuries mass media had comprised only the print media, primarily books, newspapers and magazines. In the span of a generation, people found themselves marveling at a dizzying parade of inventions ranging from the lightbulb to streetcars. Among the new delights were phonographs, radio and then television.

Consider how much these new media transformed lifestyles. A person who as a child had read into the night by kerosene lantern could in adulthood be watching television.

RECORDINGS

● **phonograph**
First sound recording and playback machine

Sound recording did not begin as an electronic medium. The first recording machine, the **phonograph** invented by Thomas Edison in 1877, was a cylinder wrapped in tinfoil that was rotated as a singer shouted into a large metal funnel. The funnel channeled the vibrations against a diaphragm, which fluttered and thus cut grooves into the rotating tin. When the cylinder was rotated in a playback machine, a stylus picked up sound from the varying depths of the groove. To hear the sound, a person placed his or her ear next to a megaphone-like horn and rotated the cylinder.

● **Emile Berliner**
Invented machine to mass produce sound recording

Inherent in Edison's system, however, was a major impediment for commercial success: A recording could not be duplicated, let alone mass-produced. In 1887 **Emile Berliner** introduced a sturdy metal disk to replace Edison's foil-wrapped cylinder. From the metal disk Berliner made a model and then poured thermoplastic material into the mold. When the material hardened, Berliner had a near-perfect copy of the original disk—and he could make hundreds of them. The process was primitive by today's standards—entirely mechanical, nothing electronic about it. But it was a marvel at the time.

● **Joseph Maxwell**
Introduced electrical sound recording in 1920s

Those early machines eventually incorporated electrical microphones and electrical amplification for reproducing sound. These innovations, mostly by **Joseph Maxwell** of Bell Laboratories in the 1920s, had superior sensitivity. To listen, it was no longer a matter of putting an ear to a mechanical amplifying horn that had only narrow frequency responses. Instead, loudspeakers amplified the sound electromagnetically.

LEARNING CHECK ◄ •

▶ **Why would be it be a mistake to call Thomas Edison's first sound recording and playback machine an instrument of mass communication?**

▶ **How would you rank the importance of these inventors in the history of sound recording? Thomas Edison, Emile Berliner and Joseph Maxwell? Why?**

ELECTROMAGNETIC SPECTRUM

● **telegraph**
Electricity-enabled long-distance communication, used mostly from Point A to Point B

● **Samuel Morse**
Inventor of telegraph in 1844

The introduction of electricity into mass communication occurred with the **telegraph.** After experimenting with sending electrical impulses by wire for more than a decade, **Samuel Morse** talked Congress into spending $30,000 to string electricity-conducting wires 41 miles from Washington to Baltimore. In 1844, using his code of dots and dashes, Morse sent the famous message "What hath God wrought." The demonstration's high visibility showed that real-time communication was possible over great distances. Morse's instantaneous-communication gizmo overcame an impediment of the printed word—the inherent delay of producing and delivering a physical product.

Granville Woods. *New possibilities for communication were suggested in his invention of railway telegraphy in 1887. The invention allowed train conductors to communicate with each other in transit and with dispatchers.*

● **Heinrich Hertz**
Demonstrated existence of radio waves in 1887

● **Guglielmo Marconi**
Transmitted first wireless message in 1895

The possibilities of the Morse invention electrified people—and investors. Within only four years, by 1848, promoters had rounded up the money to construct a system that linked the most populous parts of the United States, up and down the eastern seaboard and inland as far as Chicago and Milwaukee. By 1866 a cable had been laid on the floor of the Atlantic Ocean to connect North America with Europe for telegraphic communication.

Although telegraph messages basically were Point A to Point B communication, the way was opened for applying electricity to explicitly mass communication—perhaps even without wires.

■ **Wireless.** The suggestion of wireless communication was inherent in a discovery by **Granville Woods** in 1887 of a way to send messages to and from moving trains. Railway telegraphy, as it was called, reduced collisions. Although the invention was intended for electric trains, which drew their power from overhead lines and on-ground rails, Woods' work also posed the question: Could communication be untethered?

For hundreds of years scientists had had a sense that lightning emitted invisible but powerful electrical waves. The word *radi*, from the Latin *radius*, was used because these waves rippled out from the electrical source. A German scientist, **Heinrich Hertz,** confirmed the existence of these waves in 1887 by constructing two separate coils of wire several feet apart. When electricity was applied to one coil, it electrified the other. Thus electricity indeed could be sent through the air on what soon were called Hertzian waves.

The scientific journals, full of theories about Hertzian waves, intrigued the young Italian nobleman **Guglielmo Marconi.** Whether he realized it or not, Marconi was self-educating himself as an engineer. Obsessed, refusing to take time even for food, he locked himself in an upstairs room at his father's estate near Bologna and contemplated and fiddled. By grounding Hertz's coils to the earth, Marconi discovered in 1895 that he could send messages farther and farther. Soon he was ringing a bell across the room by remote control, then downstairs, then 300 feet away—the first wireless message.

Marconi suddenly was hopeful that he was disproving the notion among scientists at the time that Hertzian waves could not penetrate solid objects, let alone Earth. He devised an antenna, which further extended transmission range. Also, he hooked up a Morse telegraph key, which already was widely used to tap out dots and dashes for transmission on telegraph lines. Marconi had his brother go three miles away over a hill with instructions to fire a rifle if the Morse letter *s*, dot-dot-dot, came through a receiver. Metaphorically, it was a shot heard around the world.

Although Marconi didn't realize it at the time, the earth in fact impedes radio waves, but those waves that emanate upward then ricochet off the ionosphere back

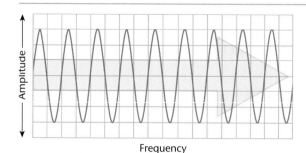

Radio Waves

If you could see electromagnetic waves, they would look like the cross section of a ripple moving across a pond except they would be steady and unending. In 1895, Guglielmo Marconi figured out how to hitch a ride on these waves to send messages.

Guglielmo Marconi

to Earth. Transmissions go far, far beyond the horizon. Marconi saw immediate business potential for establishing communication with ships at sea—something hitherto limited to semaphore flags and mirrors, which, of course, meant that ships were incommunicado with anything over the horizon. Marconi made a fortune.

LEARNING CHECK ◄

▶ How was the telegraph a precursor of radio?

▶ Marconi's wireless was based on what scientific and technical breakthroughs?

▶ Marconi saw radio as a point-to-point medium rather than as a mass medium. What's the difference?

■ **Television.** For most of its history, dating to experimental stations in the 1930s, television used the airwaves somewhat like radio does. But the technology of television, to capture movement visually for transmission, involved drastically different concepts. Physicists at major universities and engineers at major research labs had been toying for years to create "radio with pictures," as early television was called.

● **Philo Farnsworth**
Inventor of television

But it was a south Idaho farmboy, **Philo Farnsworth,** who, at age 13 while out plowing the field, came up with a concept that led to his invention of television.

Plowing the fields, back and forth in rows, the young Farnsworth had an epiphany. Applying what he knew about electricity from science magazines and tinkering, he envisioned a camera-like device that would pick up light reflected off a scene, with the image being sent radio-like to a receiver that would convert the varying degrees of light in the image and zap them one at a time across stacked horizontal lines on a screen, back and forth so rapidly that the image on the screen would appear to the human eye as real as a photograph. And then another electron would be zapped on to the same across the screen so to speak, "furrows," to replace the first image—with images coming so quickly that the eye would perceive them as motion. Farnsworth called his device an **image dissector,** which literally was what it did.

● **image dissector**
First device in early television technology

Like motion picture technology invented 40 years earlier, television froze movement at fraction-of-a-second intervals and played them in fast sequence to create an illusion that, like movies, capitalized on the persistence of vision phenomenon. Unlike movies, Farnsworth did not do this with photographic technology. Television uses electronics, not chemicals, and images recorded by the camera are transmitted instantly to a receiving device, called a *picture tube*, or to a recording device for later transmission.

Although Farnsworth had sent the first television picture, from one room in his San Francisco apartment to another, in 1927, the complexities of television technology delayed its immediate development. So did national survival while Americans focused on winning World War II. By the 1950s, however, a radio-like delivery infrastructure for television was in place.

LEARNING CHECK ◄

▶ Philo Farnsworth called his invention an image dissector. How were images dissected?

▶ What is the role of persistence of vision in television technology?

▶ How is persistence of vision employed differently in television and movies?

New Technologies

STUDY PREVIEW

Satellite and fiber-optic technologies in the late 1900s improved the speed and reliability of delivering mass messages. These were backshop developments that were largely invisible to media consumers. Plainly visible, though, was the related advent of the Internet as a new mass medium.

ORBITING SATELLITES

More than 50 years ago the Russians orbited Sputnik, the first human-made satellite. The accomplishment ignited a rush to explore space near Earth. Technology surged. Weather forecasting became less intuitive, more scientific and many times more accurate. With geopositioning signals from satellites, maps had new, everyday applications that only Spock could have imagined. Communication was transformed too, with signals being bounced off satellites for a straight-line range that far exceeded anything possible with the existing network of ground-based relay towers located every 10 or so miles apart.

For communication, the key to utilizing satellites was the **geosynchronous orbit.** It was a concept of sci-fi author **Arthur C. Clarke,** who also was a serious scientist. Clarke figured out in 1945 that a satellite 22,300 miles above the equator would be orbiting at the same speed as Earth's rotation, thus always being above the same point below on Earth—an ideal platform for continuous service to pick up signals from Earth stations and retransmit them to other Earth stations. It was like a 22,300-mile-high relay tower. With only one relay, not hundreds, signals would move faster and with more reliability. The **Telstar** communication satellite, launched in 1960, took the first telephone signals from **uplink** stations on Earth, amplified them, and returned them to **downlink** stations. Television networks also used Telstar.

Satellite technology, however, did not change the fundamental structures of the industries that had built up around print, chemical and electronic technology. Rather, satellites were an efficient alternative for delivering traditional media products. Prime-time network programming still came from the networks. Although *USA Today* was sending pages by satellite to several dozen printing plants around the country, readers still picked up the paper every morning from newsracks. In short, satellite technology was important for enabling media companies to improve delivery of their products but was largely invisible to consumers.

LEARNING CHECK ◄

▸ **What was the genius of Arthur C. Clarke as a mass communication futurologist?**

▸ **How does a geosynchronous orbit work?**

BACK TO WIRES

Even as possibilities with satellites were dazzling scientists, the old reliable of mass communication—the wire, sometimes called a **landline**—was in revival. A radio repair-shop owner in Astoria, Oregon, wired the town in 1949 to receive television signals from Seattle, which was too far away for signals to be received unless they were intercepted by a high antenna. In mountainous West Virginia, entrepreneurs also were stringing up local cable systems to distribute television signals that were blocked by terrain. **Cable television,** as it was called, was a small-town success. On the television industry's radar, however, cable was merely a blip. Local cable operators only passed on signals from elsewhere; they didn't add any content.

The role of the cable industry changed in 1975 when the Time Inc. media empire put HBO on satellite as a programming service for local cable companies. With exclusive programming available to subscribers, cable suddenly was hot. More cable programming services, all delivered by satellite, came online. Wall Street investors poured billions of dollars into wiring major cities, where huge population masses were eager for HBO, CNN and other new programming available only through cable operators.

In the 1960s, meanwhile, Corning Glass had developed a cable that was capable of carrying light at incredible speeds—theoretically, 186,000 miles per second. The potential of these new **fiber-optic cables,** each strand carrying 60,000 messages simultaneously, was not lost on the telephone industry. So fast was the fiber-optic network that the entire *Oxford English Dictionary* could be sent in just seconds. Soon hundreds of crews with backhoes were replacing copper wires, which had constituted the backbone of telephone communication, with fiber-optic cables. Coupled

● geosynchronous orbit
Orbit in which a satellite's period of rotation coincides perfectly with Earth's rotation

● Arthur C. Clarke
Devised the concept of satellites in geosynchronous orbits for communication

● Telstar
First communication satellite

● uplink
A ground station that beams a signal to an orbiting communication satellite

● downlink
A ground station that receives a signal relayed from a communication satellite

● landline
Conventional telecommunication connection using cable laid across land, typically buried or on poles

● cable television
Television transmission system that uses cable rather than an over-air broadcast signal

● fiber-optic cables
Thin, flexible fibers of glass capable of transmitting light signals

Philo Farnsworth was 11 when his family loaded three covered wagons and moved to a farm near Rigby in eastern Idaho. Cresting a ridge, young Farnsworth, at the reins of one wagon, surveyed the homestead below and saw wires linking the buildings. "This place has electricity!" he exclaimed. Philo obsessed about the electricity, and soon he was an expert at fixing anything electrical that went wrong.

The day when the Farnsworths settled near Rigby in 1919 was a pivotal moment in young Farnsworth's life that led to technology on which television is based.

The next pivotal moment came two years later when Philo Farnsworth was 13. He found an article saying that scientists were working on ways to add pictures to radio but they couldn't figure out how. He then went out to hitch the horses to a harvesting machine to bring in the potatoes. As he guided the horses back and forth across the field, up one row, down the next, he visualized how moving pictures could be captured live and transmitted to a faraway place. If the light that enables people to see could be converted to electrons and then transmitted one at a time, but very quickly as a beam, back and forth on a surface, then, perhaps, television could work.

The ideas simmered a few months and then, when he was 14, Farnsworth chalked a complicated diagram for "electronic television" on his chemistry teacher's blackboard. The teacher, Justin Tolman, was impressed. In fact, 15 years later Tolman would reconstruct those blackboard schematics so

Television Inventor. *Thirteen-year-old Philo Farnsworth came up with the concept of live transmission of moving images by zipping electrons back and forth on a screen— just as he was doing, back and forth, in harvesting a potato field. Barely in his 20s, Farnsworth moved from theory to practice with what he called an image dissector.*

convincingly that Farnsworth would win a patent war with RCA and force RCA to abandon its claim that its Vladimir Zworykin invented television.

Farnsworth's native intelligence, earnestness and charm helped to win over the people around him. When he was 19, working in Salt Lake City, Farnsworth found a man with connections to San Francisco investors. With their backing, the third pivotal moment in Farnsworth's work, he set up a lab in Los Angeles, and later in San Francisco, and put his drawings and theories to work. In 1927, with handblown tubes and hand-soldered con-

nections, Farnsworth had a gizmo he called the image dissector. It picked up the image of a glass slide and transmitted it. The Idaho farmboy had invented television.

WHAT DO YOU THINK?

▶ Describe how Philo Farnsworth's image dissector worked.

▶ Farnsworth's horizontal electrons zaps have been replaced by pixels, but the fundamental insight that led to his invention of television remains on video screens today. What is this enduring legacy?

with other new technologies, notably digitization of data, the new satellite-based and fiber-optic landline communication systems enabled the introduction of a new medium—the Internet.

LEARNING CHECK ◀ ••

▶ **What has been the effect of geosynchronously orbiting satellites on the television industry?**

▶ **What technologies transformed the sleepy small-town cable television industry beginning in the 1970s?**

Digital Integration

STUDY PREVIEW

Digital technology has brought efficiency to almost every aspect of humans'
lifestyles, including products from traditional mass-media companies. A wholly
new medium, the Internet, is built entirely on binary digital signals. This newest
media technology is melding the once-distinctive delivery systems of many
products from old-line media companies.

SEMICONDUCTOR

● **semiconductor**
Silicon chip that is used
in digitization

Researchers at AT&T's Bell Labs knew they were on to something important for telephone communication in 1947. Engineers Jack Bardeen, Walter Brattain and William
Shockley had devised glasslike silicon chips—pieces of sand, really—that could be used
to respond to a negative or a positive electrical charge. The tiny chips, called
semiconductors, functioned very rapidly as on/off switches. With chips, the human
voice could be reduced to a stream of digits—1 for on, 0 for off—and then transmitted
as rapid-fire pulses and reconstructed so quickly at the other end of the line that the
sound was like the real thing. Bardeen, Brittain and Shockley won a Nobel Prize.

Little did they realize that they had laid the groundwork for revolutionizing
not just telephonic communication but all human communication.

Bell Labs then took digital on/off binary signals to a new level. By breaking
messages into pieces and transmitting them in spurts, Bell suddenly, in 1965, could
send multiple messages simultaneously. People marveled that 51 calls could be carried at the same time on a single line. The capacity of telephone systems was dramatically increased without a single new mile of wire being laid.

The potential of the evolving technology was no less than revolutionary. Not
only could the human voice be reduced to binary digits for transmission but so

Jack Bardeen, Walter Brattain and William Shockley

Nobel Winners. *The 1956 Nobel Prize went to the inventors of the semiconductor. They had devised tiny, low-cost crystals
that could be used as switches to transmit data that had been converted to binary codes of 0s and 1s. Digital communication
followed, with innovations that led to today's global communication networks.*

could text and even images. Futurologists asked: "Who needs paper?" Might digitization even replace the still-new-fangled technology of television that had flowed from Philo Farnsworth's pioneering work?

Digitization, alas, did not replace Gutenberg-based print media, and the core media industries are still pigeonholed easily into their traditional categories—books, newspapers, magazines, movies, sound recordings, radio and television. The technology did, however, spawn new media industries built around the new technologies. America Online was in the first generation. Now Google, MySpace and YouTube are leaders. Tomorrow? Stay tuned.

LEARNING CHECK ◄ ···

▶ What has proved to be the significance of binary digital signaling?

▶ How have traditional media industries been affected by binary digital signaling?

INTERNET ORIGINS

The U.S. military saw potential in digitized communication for a noncentralized network. Without a central hub, the military figured that the system could sustain itself in a nuclear attack. The system, called ARPAnet, short for Advanced Research Projects Agency Network, was up and running in 1969. At first, the network linked contractors and universities so that military researchers could exchange information. In 1983 the National Science Foundation, whose mandate is to promote science, took over and involved more universities, which tied their own internal computer-based communication systems into the larger network. As a backbone system that interconnected networks, the term *internet* fit.

MEDIA CONVERGENCE

The construction of a high-capacity network in the 1990s, which we call the **Internet,** is emerging as the delivery vehicle of choice for any and all media products. The technological basis, called **digital,** is distinctive. Messages, whether text, audio, image or a combination, are broken into millions of bits of data. The bits are transmitted one at a time over the Internet, which has incredibly high capacity and speed, then reassembled for reception at the other end. The process is almost instantaneous for text, whose digital bits of data are small and easily accommodated. Audio and visual messages can take longer because far more data bits are required to reconstruct a message at the reception point.

A digitization revolution, called **media convergence,** is in progress.

■ **Distribution.** The Internet has an unmatchable efficiency in delivering messages. In contrast, a newspaper company needs a fleet of trucks and drivers for predawn runs from the production point to intermediate distribution points. There, individual carriers pick up papers for delivery to individual customers. Magazine companies rely on the postal system, which takes at least a day and countless gallons of fuel to deliver magazines. Book publishers have massive inventories, which require expensive warehousing, and then high shipping costs. Although books, newspapers and magazines have not vanished from the media landscape, these companies are shifting to delivering at least some of their content by the Internet.

■ **Devices.** With a single device, consumers can pick up media content whatever its origin. The device can be a desktop or laptop computer or something handheld. What the devices have in common is an Internet connection.

■ **Distinctions.** Digitization is breaking down old distinctions. Newspaper people increasingly talk about being in the news business, not the newspaper business. Radio people do likewise, talking about being in the music business, not the radio business. The new emphasis is on content. Consumers acknowledge this underlying shift. Instead of reading a newspaper, for example, more people

● **Internet**
A high-capacity global telephone network that links computers

● **digital**
Technology through which media messages are coded into 1s and 0s for delivery transmission and then decoded into their original appearance

● **media convergence**
Melding of print, electronic and photographic media into digitized form

Crossroads of Real and Virtual Life

Late on a February night in 2007 a small group of Republicans wearing Bush '08 tags vandalized the John Edwards presidential campaign head-quarters. They defaced the area with obscenities, Marxist posters and slo-gans, and Photoshopped images of Edwards in blackface. Only a month later, the French presidential candidate Jean-Marie Le Pen's headquarters was attacked. Violence and bloodshed followed between security guards and the armed protestors.

Fortunately for Edwards and Le Pen, their campaign headquarters could be repaired with a few clicks of a computer mouse. These were cy-ber-attacks. Safe in the virtual world of Second Life, the vandals have yet to receive any physical punishment.

Launched in 2003 Second Life is a virtual world of more than 8 1/2 mil-lion members worldwide. They call themselves residents. Second Life is just one of the many virtual worlds inspired by Neal Stephenson's novel *Snow Crash* and other books associated with the cyberpunk literary movement.

Make Believe. So immersed are avatars in Second Life that it's becoming the ad-vertising platform du jour? Everybody, it seems, wants to be there. CNN and Reuters have established Second Life news bureaus. The Minnesota state college system has bought space to tout its online courses.

Second Life facilitates all kinds of real-world activities for residents. Opportunities include actual monetary gain, fundraising, political activism, social networking, dancing, job searching, gambling and worship. By creating an individual "avatar," residents navi-gate their virtual existence in the look and body of their own making. They develop on-line skills to create virtual buildings, vehicles and machines that can be traded or sold to support the Second Life economy. These skills can also be carried over to their real-world existence.

The virtual audience of Second Life presents a multitude of opportunities for real-world mass communication. Successful media companies, such as Dell and Warner Brothers, have issued news releases in Second Life. Reuters employs an "in-world" corre-spondent to cover daily events in the metaverse. The online newsletter Second Opinion keeps residents informed of the latest news and virtual economy while AvaStar provides members with a lively tabloid. Real-world politicians have been taking advantage of this new media outlet by hosting campaign headquarters, taking political polls and holding press conferences in Second Life.

The virtual media platform created by Second Life residents has captured the atten-tion of many organizations traditionally reliant on social media for their marketing, public relations and advertising. Only time will tell if this new virtual audience is worth their investment.

DEEPENING YOUR MEDIA LITERACY

EXPLORE THE ISSUE

Go to www.secondopinion.com to read the latest news in Second Life.

DIG DEEPER

How is the news within the virtual world of Second Life different from your local com-munity news? Is the virtual audience any different from a physical audience?

WHAT DO YOU THINK?

How do issues or events taking place in Second Life have an impact on the real world? How do you think Second Life will affect mass-media in the future?

talk about reading news. Instead of watching television, people watch a sitcom. This makes sense as digital devices supplant Gutenberg print technology and combine radio, television, movie and recording reception appliances into single devices.

■ **Production.** For almost a century, print media publishers have recognized their inherent disadvantage in production costs. Presses for a big-city daily require millions of dollars in investment. In contrast, as publishers have seen it, albeit simplistically, their broadcast counterparts merely flick a switch. But with digitized delivery, the broadcast equivalent of a printing press, even transmitter and tower maintenance seem hopelessly expensive. Production costs for newspaper content also can be cut drastically with Internet delivery.

■ **Democratization.** The relatively low cost of Internet production and delivery may have its greatest impact in broadening the sources of media content. Almost anybody can afford to create messages for Internet delivery and, theoretically anyway, reach everyone on the planet who has a reception device. In contrast to a generation ago, the price of entry into the mass media no longer requires millions of dollars for production facilities and millions more for start-up costs, including costs for personnel. Ask any blogger or garage band. Media moguls are struggling to identify ways to maintain their dominance. We are in a turbulent environment of change that's still playing out but that has been described, perhaps with prescience, perhaps prematurely, as the democratization of mass communication.

LEARNING CHECK ◄

▶ **What are the primary print media? What are the primary electronic media?**

▶ **Has electronic media replaced print media?**

▶ **What is the future for major mass media?**

Technology and Mass Communication

STUDY PREVIEW

Theorists have devised models to help understand and explain the complex and mysterious technology-dependent process of mass communication. But many models, now more than 50 years old, have been outdated by rapid changes in technology. These changes have added more complexity and mystery to how mass communication works.

LASSWELL MODEL

● **Harold Lasswell**
Devised the narrative communication model

● **channel**
The medium through which a message is sent to a mass audience

● **effect**
The consequence of a message

Scholars got serious about trying to understand how mass communication works in the 20th century. Theories came and went. One of the most useful explanations, elegant in its simplicity as an overview, was articulated in the 1950s by Yale professor **Harold Lasswell.** It is a narrative model that poses four questions: Who says what? In which **channel?** To whom? With what **effect?**

With his reference to *channel*, Lasswell clearly differentiated his model as not just another model for human communication. His channel component clearly made his model one of mass communication technology. Lasswell's channel was a technology-defined mass medium—a book, a movie, a television program.

The Lasswell model is easy to apply. Pick any media message, say, former Vice President Al Gore's documentary *An Inconvenient Truth:*

- **Who says what?** Gore told a story based on expert testimony and recorded evidence about global warming. His message was that global warming is a human-accelerated phenomenon that threatens Earth as a habitat for life as we know it.

- **In which channel?** The documentary itself was a movie. Also, it was distributed widely in video form for home and group audiences. There also was a book bearing the same title.
- **To whom?** Although unfriendly critics tried to dismiss the work as intended for penguins, the movie's video and book quickly became best sellers.
- **With what effect?** Public attention quickly embraced the notion that it was possible for human beings, acting quickly, to counter the deterioration of Earth as a habitable planet. Under Governor Arnold Schwarzenegger, California shifted into high gear with new public policies to reduce greenhouse emissions. The U.S. Supreme Court upheld tougher emission standards that big industries had resisted.

LEARNING CHECK ◀

▶ How does the Lasswell model of mass communication differ from models for interpersonal communication, such as between friends conversing face-to-face?

▶ Find a bylined newspaper article that discusses a breakthrough on a recent controversial issue. Then apply the four steps in the Lasswell communication process to the article.

VALUES AND LIMITATIONS OF MODELS

For all their usefulness, models of mass communication fall short, way short, of capturing the complexities occurring in our media systems. The volume of messages is incalculable. The word *zillions* comes to mind. What we do know about the volume is that it's increasing rapidly. Nobody has come up with a model to portray the overlays and interplay of all the content moving through the mass media.

All models, whether of ships, planes, automobiles, have the same deficiency. By definition, a model is a facsimile that helps us see and understand the real thing. But no model shows everything. An aircraft engineer, for example, can create a model of an airplane's propulsion system. Although essential to illustrating how the plane will be powered, a model of its propulsion system doesn't illustrate the plane's aesthetic features, nor its ventilation system, nor its electrical system, nor any of hundreds of other important features. Engineers are able to overlay various models to show connections and interrelations—which itself is a major challenge—but far short of what it would take to illustrate all that is going on. It's the same with communication: Too much is occurring at any given nanosecond. So, like all models, mass communication models are useful illustrations but limited because there is far, far more to what's happening than can be reduced to a schematic.

Different models illustrate different aspects of the process. That the process is too complex for a single model to convey it all is clear from the Lasswell model. Sweeping as it is, the Lasswell model is far less than a detailed framework for understanding how mass communication works; but it is a starting point.

LEARNING CHECK ◀

▶ What are the advantages and disadvantages of any model?

▶ Can complex phenomena like mass communication be reduced to a model?

CONCENTRIC CIRCLE MODEL

One of the most useful models from the late 20th century was conceived by Ray Hiebert, Donald Ungurait and Thomas Bohn. It is a series of concentric rings with the source of the message at the center. The source encodes information or an idea, which then ripples outward to the outermost ring, which is the receiving audience. In between are several elements unique to the mass communication—including gatekeepers, a technologically based medium, regulators and amplification. The model creates a framework for tracking the difficult course of a message through the mass communication process. In effect, the model portrays mass communication as an obstacle course.

Steve Jobs. *The ongoing technical and corporate convergence of the mass media is epitomized in Jobs' linking computers and the Internet through his position at Apple with his role in movies through Disney and Pixar and with the revolution he stirred in the music industry with the iPod and iTunes store.*

Working in a garage, Steve Jobs and a buddy built an over-the-top desktop computer, which became the foundation for Apple Computer. No wonder, when people think of Jobs, they think of computers. Think again. Jobs, now a multibillionaire in his 50s, has positioned Apple at the convergence point of computers and television and a whole lot of other media channels.

Jobs' latest breakthrough, in 2002, was the iPod portable music device, which triggered a transformation of music retailing and the music industry. The device morphed into the video iPod in 2005, whose first version could take 150 hours of video downloads from the Internet.

Meanwhile, Jobs, who ran both Apple and Pixar Animation Studios, known for the blockbuster movies *Toy Story* and *Finding Nemo,* sold Pixar to Disney ABC for an incredible $7.4 billion. The deal made Jobs the largest Disney shareholder and put Jobs on the Disney board of directors.

During preliminaries, with Disney and Pixar still in a dance about merging, Jobs pushed for ABC content to be made available for the video iPod. Negotiations took only three days, unbelievably fast by usual business standards. Mickey Mouse and Goofy features from Disney archives immediately were available on video iPods at $1.99. So were episodes of ABC's *Desperate Housewives* and *Lost.* Executives at competing television networks saw no choice but to sign on, despite worries about eroding their historic monopoly on distributing programs through their local affiliates.

The Apple innovations under Jobs may not end with handheld devices. Insiders are talking about the living room of 2010 having a single box, an Apple TV that replaces a CD player, a DVD player, a set-top cable box, and a stereo. An Apple TV, with digital signals from the Internet or wireless relays, could do even more. The one-hour shows now available from Apple's iTunes may soon carry movie-length features. Disney is also trying to move dramatically more content to the Internet. To the consternation of the movie-house industry, this includes re-leasing movies on the Internet the same day they are released in theaters.

Incredible new technologies are forcing basic changes. The familiar territory of industry infrastructures that have been in place since the mid-1900s is in profound transition. What's ahead? A shake-up like nothing before.

WHAT DO YOU THINK?

▶ In what ways will the new technology affect the basic function of mass communication?

▶ What changes would you make to Lasswell's basic model to account for changes in technology?

● **amplification**
Giving a message to a larger audience

■ **Medium.** Hiebert, Ungurait and Bohn, aware that media affect messages, put the label *mass media* on one of their rings. Media make a difference. A message that lends itself to visual portrayal, like a comedian's sight gag, will fall flat on radio. The medium is indeed critical in ensuring that an outward-rippling message makes its way to the goal—an effect, which Hiebert, Ungurait and Bohn place at the outermost ring.

■ **Amplification.** Important in understanding mass communication is knowing how a mass medium boosts a message's chance of reaching an audience and having an effect. Radio exponentially increases a commentator's audience. A printing press amplifies a message the same way. Indeed, it's the **amplification** made possible

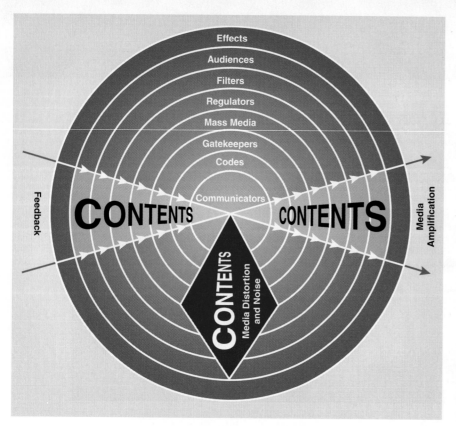

Concentric Circle Model
The concentric circle model illustrates a great number of obstacles for a mass-communicated message to reach an audience. These include obstacles in the technology, including coding for transmission. It's a detailed model that acknowledges that the media amplify messages, which can compound their effects. Feedback is shown, too. In mass communication, feedback usually is muted and almost always is delayed.

by media technology that sets *mass* communication apart from chatting with a neighbor or making a class presentation.

■ **Message Controls.** Most mass communication involves a team, usually dozens of people, sometimes hundreds. Consider video of a terrorist attack shot by an AP photographer in Iraq. The video passes through a complex gatekeeping process, with editors, packagers, producers and others making decisions on how much of the rough footage ends up in distribution to television stations—or whether the images will make the cut at all. **Gatekeepers** are media people who make judgments on what most merits inclusion in what is sent to networks, stations and Web site operators.

Gatekeeping is an unavoidable function in mass communication because there is neither time nor space for all the messages that might be passed through the process. Gatekeepers are editors who decide what makes it through their gates and in what form.

Like gatekeepers, **regulators** can affect a communicator's messages substantially, but regulators are not media people. A military censor who stops a combat story is a regulator. Some regulators function more subtly than a censor but nonetheless powerfully affect messages. The Federal Communications Commission, which regulates U.S. broadcasting, is a mighty force in its authority to grant and deny licenses to over-air stations. In 2006 FCC fines for vaguely defined indecency prompted broadcasters to rein in scriptwriters and producers who had been pushing the envelope. The regulation process can be heavy-handed. China, for example, has insisted that U.S. and other countries' media companies comply with vaguely defined but stridently enforced bans on subjects the government sees as challenges to its authority. Censorship, yes, but Google, Yahoo, StarTV and other transnational media companies eager to profit from access to potentially huge Chinese audiences have chosen to comply.

● **gatekeepers**
Media people who influence messages en route

● **regulators**
Nonmedia people who influence messages

Gatekeepers. *At the Baltimore, Maryland,* Afro American, *as at news organizations worldwide, editors sit down daily to decide what to include in their next edition or newscast. Not everything that could be reported will fit. This decision-making process is called gatekeeping. Some stories will make it, some will be trimmed, some will be spiked.*

● **noise**
Impediment to communication before a message reaches a receiver

● **semantic noise**
Sloppy message crafting

● **channel noise**
Interference during transmission

● **environmental noise**
Interference at reception site

● **filter**
Receiver factor that impedes communication

● **informational filter**
Receiver's knowledge limits that impede deciphering symbols

● **physical filter**
Receiver's alertness impeding deciphering

● **psychological filter**
Receiver's state of mind impeding deciphering

■ **In-Process Impediments.** If speakers slur their words, the effectiveness of their messages is jeopardized. Slurring and other impediments to the communication process before a message reaches the audience are called **noise.** In mass communication, based as it is on complex mechanical and electronic equipment, the opportunities for noise interference are countless because so many things can go wrong.

Mass communicators themselves can interfere with the success of their own messages by being sloppy. This is called **semantic noise.** Sloppy wording is an example. So is slurring. **Channel noise** is something that interferes with message transmission, such as static on the radio. Or smudged ink on a magazine page. Or a faulty microphone on a television anchor's lapel. An intrusion that occurs at the reception site is **environmental noise.** This includes a doorbell interrupting someone reading an article, which distracts from decoding. So would shouting kids who distract a television viewer.

■ **Deciphering Impediments.** Unwittingly, people who tune in to mass messages may themselves interfere with the success of the mass communication process. Such interference is known as a **filter.**

If someone doesn't understand the language or symbols that a communicator uses, the communication process becomes flawed. It is a matter of an individual lacking enough information to decipher a message. This deficiency is called an **informational filter.** This filter can be partly the responsibility of the communicator, whose vocabulary may not be in tune with the audience. More often, though, filters are a deficiency in the audience.

There also are physical filters. When a receiver's mind is dimmed with fatigue, a **physical filter** may interfere with the communication process. A drunk whose focus fades in and out suffers from a physical filter. Mass communicators have little control over physical filters.

Psychological filters also interfere with communication. Conservative evangelist James Dobson and Parkinson's sufferer Michael J. Fox, for example, likely would decode a message on stem cell research far differently.

The Hiebert, Ungurait and Bohn model was incredibly useful in diagramming the process of mass communication—until new technologies ushered in the Internet and transformed a lot of mass communication. Twentieth-century models quickly became, well, so old.

LEARNING CHECK ◄ ••

▶ What are the similarities in the processes of interpersonal and mass communication? And the differences?

▶ What mechanisms, short of censorship, does government use to influence media messages?

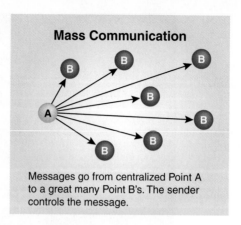

Linear Communication

Point A → Point B

The telegraph moves messages from Point A to Point B. The sender controls the message.

Mass Communication

Messages go from centralized Point A to a great many Point B's. The sender controls the message.

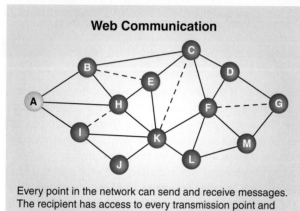

Web Communication

Every point in the network can send and receive messages. The recipient has access to every transmission point and controls what is received.

Points Model

Web communication shifts much of the control of the communication through the mass media to the recipient, turning the traditional process of mass communication on its head. Receivers are no longer hobbled to sequential presentation of messages, as on a network television newscast. Receivers can switch almost instantly to dozens, hundreds even, of alternatives through a weblike network that, at least theoretically, can interconnect every recipient and sender on the planet.

21st-CENTURY MODELS

Scholars again are at work on devising models to help explain the new mass communication. Clearly, the coding of Internet messages has become largely automated. There are no typesetters or press operators. Nor are there broadcast control room engineers. Gatekeeping is minimal. Bloggers blog unfettered. The closest that Facebook comes to editing are anonymous campus monitors whose controls are so light-fingered as to be almost nonexistent. Regulators? Governments have scratched the surface on transnational copyright issues, but largely the governments of Western countries have dallied in trying to apply old regulation models to the Internet.

In part the problem is that the heart of the technology for the Internet is decentralized. There are no central sources that can be regulated—no newsroom, no production centers, no presses. In some ways it's a free-for-all. One useful way to envision the Internet is to think of old telegraph communication in the 1800s, in which messages went from Point A to Point B. In the 1900s, technology ushered in an explosion of mass communication. Radio, for example, picked up on the mass communication model of print media. Messages went from a single Point A to many, many recipients—magazine readers by the millions, radio listeners by the millions and television viewers by the millions. That was the process that Hiebert, Ungurait and Bohn's concentric circle model captured so well.

In the 21st century with the Internet, every Point A is theoretically reached by every Point B and C and also Points X, Y, and Z. It's not a linear Point A to Point B. Nor is it a message emanating from Point A to multiple points. It's a web of interactive messages reaching an incalculable number of points, which in part is why the term *World Wide Web* came to be.

LEARNING CHECK ◀

▸ How has the technology underlying the Internet rendered early mass communication models obsolete?

▸ Compare models for the communication technology of the telegraph in the 1800s, the communication technology of radio and television in the 1900s and the communication technology of the Internet in the 21st century.

Chapter Wrap-Up

Media Technology (Page 26)

■ Mass communication is unique among various forms of human communication because it cannot occur without technology. These technologies include modern printing. Books, newspapers and magazines are rooted in printing technology. Motion pictures are rooted in chemical technology. Sound recording, radio and television are called electronic media for a reason. The latest media technology is binary digital signals.

Printing (Page 27)

■ The importance of Johannes Gutenberg to human civilization cannot be overstated. In the 1440s Gutenberg invented movable metal type, which permitted mass production of the written word. Previously difficult communication among faraway people became possible. Human communication multiplied exponentially. Especially important were exchanges among scientists and other scholars who were expanding the bounds of human knowledge. Pivotal movements in human history began, including the Age of Reason and the Age of Science and quantum leaps in literacy. These all could be called part of the Age of Mass Communication, now about 500 years old.

Chemistry (Page 31)

■ Photography was discovered through chemistry. The significance of photography technology is that it became largely subsumed by printed media, notably newspapers and magazines. This dramatically increased the powerful effects of printed media messages. Movies also drew on chemical technology but evolved along a separate path.

Electronics (Page 32)

■ Electricity and the mastery of electromagnetic waves brought us entirely new delivery mechanisms for mass messages. Most notable were radio, which established itself in the early 1900s, and later television. The electronic media transmitted messages invisibly through the air by shaping and warping electromagnetic waves that are omnipresent in the physical universe. Latter-day variations include cable delivery, but even the cable industry is dependent on over-air signals from program suppliers. Electronic media of a different sort include sound recording, which, although not electronic to begin with, has become so.

New Technologies (Page 35)

■ Speed and reliability in delivering mass messages increased dramatically with satellite and fiber-optic technologies in the late 1900s. The improvements were mostly invisible to media consumers, except that everyone recognized that the inventory of media products was increasing and creating more choices. People who once could receive only a handful of television signals could suddenly, with new satellite and cable services, receive dozens of channels, even hundreds. The volume of media content, including news coverage, grew exponentially. So did entertainment choices. For movies it was no longer what the neighborhood movie house was showing but what was stocked at a local video rental shop.

Digital Integration (Page 38)

■ In merely 40 years the Internet has grown from a concept to a major mass medium. Built entirely on binary digital signals, the Internet is melding the once-distinctive delivery systems of many products from old-line media companies. In addition, entirely new media products and content forms have been invented. Ten years ago nobody would have had any idea what blogging means or how to perform a Google.

Technology and Mass Communication (Page 41)

■ The mass communication process is complex and mysterious. In attempts to understand the process, scholars have devised a broad range of models and schematics and invented terminology to explain some of the phenomena they observe when they dissect the process. Although useful in some ways, modeling the mass communication process leaves many questions and issues open to further inquiry. If we had all the answers to how the process works, every advertising campaign would be a success, every book a best seller, and every television pilot the next *American Idol*.

REVIEW QUESTIONS

1. What is the technology basis of books? newspapers? magazines? sound recordings? movies? radio? television? the Internet?

2. What were the early effects of Gutenberg's movable type on civilization? Can you speculate on what our culture would be like without Gutenberg's invention?

3. Photography and movies are both rooted in chemical technology, but one is a mass medium and the other is not. Explain this distinction using this paradigm: A photograph is to a book what a script is to a movie.

4. How were systems for delivering mass messages widened with electricity and electronic technology?

5. Describe the components that led to the creation and refinement of our latest mass medium, the Internet.

6. The digital technology underlying the Internet is changing the industries that were built around older mass media. What are these changes? Will traditional media companies as we know them survive?

7. What are the strengths of the Lasswell mass communication model? The concentric circle model? What are their inadequacies?

CONCEPTS

channel (Page 41)

gatekeepers (Page 44)

interpersonal communication (Page 26)

media convergence (Page 39)

persistence of vision (Page 31)

TERMS

filters (Page 45)

halftone (Page 29)

movable metal type (Page 27)

noise (Page 45)

regulators (Page 44)

PEOPLE

Mathew Brady (Page 31)

Arthur C. Clarke (Page 36)

Philo Farnsworth (Page 35)

Johannes Gutenberg (Page 27)

Harold Lasswell (Page 41)

MEDIA SOURCES

- Linda Simon. *Dark Light: Electricity and Anxiety from the Telegraph to the X-Ray.* Harcourt, 2004. Simon, a literary scholar, finds both excitement and fear in 19th-century novels and short stories about the transforming effect of electricity on life and values.

- Stephen W. Littlejohn. *Theories of Human Communication,* eighth edition. Wadsworth, 2004. In this classic treatment, Professor Littlejohn traces developments in communication theory and synthesizes the research. One chapter focuses on mass communication.

- Denis McQuail and Sven Windahl. *Communication Models for the Study of Mass Communication,* second edition. Longman, 1993. McQuail and Windahl include dozens of models from the first 30 years of mass communication research with explanatory comments. Included in the discussion are Shannon-Weaver and helix models.

In this chapter you have deepened your media literacy by revisiting several themes. Here are thematic highlights from the chapter:

Media Technology

Mass communication is technology-assisted communication. In fact, the defining difference between mass communication and other types of human communication is the role of technology. The basic technologies are printing, chemistry and electronics. Entire industries have grown from each of the technologies. The book, newspaper and magazine industries grew from printing. The recording, radio and television industries grew from electronics. The movie industry grew from chemistry. Digital technology has made the Internet possible. Some blurring of distinctions among traditional media products is occurring. **(Pages 25–47)**

Movable Metal Type. *Johannes Gutenberg devised a way in the 1440s to mass-produce the written word. The world hasn't been the same since.*

Media Economics

Media companies in most countries need to make a profit in order to survive. As a result, these companies are highly sensitive to the legal requirements established by governments for their operation, including restrictions of the content of messages. Scholars who have modeled the mass-communication process call the forces responsible for these restrictions regulators. The role of regulators is most apparent in U.S. mass media in the over-air broadcast industry, whose operations are licensed by the Federal Communications Commission, a government agency. **(Pages 42–45)**

Media and Democracy

The major mass-media companies have humble origins but now are so established and entrenched—and huge and powerful—that they are called "empires." With control of the mass media concentrated in relatively few corporate hands, the voice of ordinary folks is squeezed out. This isn't how democracy is supposed to work. Newer technology, however, is reducing the price of entry to mass communication. Low-cost recording equipment has given garage bands the ability to produce music at a quality possible earlier only with costly studios controlled

Media Regulation. *Even in a free society, structures are in place to control media content. Numerous organizations, for example, have worked to regulate media-depicted violence.*

Low Power. *Technology that has reduced the cost of creating media products has also opened the way for low-power stations to make it big time. This has loosened the giant media companies' control on media content. Thunder Radio is a low-power station at North Dakota State University.*

by major recording companies. Similarly, low-power radio and television stations have enabled mass communication with narrow niches within society. Blogging is another example of this democratization of mass communication. Just about anybody can blog. **(Pages 39–41)**

Media and Culture

Human existence has been profoundly changed by the technology that has made mass communication possible. The power of the printing press was obvious early on. For the first time scientists could share their theories and findings not with just hand-written correspondence but with printed articles. The wide distribution of these scientific articles was key to the quantum increases in scientific knowledge that have been transforming our existence since Gutenberg. Structures that define society have been in transition too. Printing helped facilitate the Reformation that shook traditional religious structures beginning in the 1500s. Values have shifted over the decades with mass-produced and mass-distributed literature, in printed and other forms, including movies. The spread of values expressed in music and theater isn't limited anymore to drama troupes and the traveling balladeer. **(Pages 39–41)**

War as Gore. *Media portrayals of the horrors of war have made it difficult for U.S. leaders to sustain public enthusiasm for war. Glory isn't there anymore.*

Elitism and Populism

The arts that define culture once were the province only of those who could afford the price of admission by buying books and concert and theater tickets. What defined culture was largely elitist. But mass-media companies, in their quest for the profits that come from larger audiences, have democratized culture with less high-brow content. Media content now appeals to all strata of the population. The result has been a widening of what identifies a culture. The proliferation of less-than-high-brow content has been called the democratization of the culture. Elitists and traditionalists shudder at what they see as a coarsening of culture. However, the shudders haven't stopped media companies from continuing to make new appeals to broader audiences. **(Pages 39–41)**

Shock Jock Appeal. *In his heyday Don Imus had an audience comprising a broad demographic, including stereotypical upscale politicos in Manhattan and blue-collar hourly workers in Jersey. Most shock jocks, however, found their audiences at the low end of the socioeconomic scales—hardly an elitist component in our fragmenting media universe.*

Strand Theater. *New Yorkers may have packed the Strand, but the audience totaled nothing close to the audiences for a popular modern musical in contemporary movies and television—not to mention the audiences for soundtrack variations on DVD and radio.*

51

3

Books

The Wikipedia Breakthrough

Sometime in the 1960s Jimmy Wales's folks bought a *World Book* encyclopedia set from a door-to-door salesman. Jimmy became hooked on information. In college he became committed to the notion that people can best acquire wisdom by pooling what they know. He calls himself "an Enlightenment kind of guy."

Wales put his idea on the Web in 2000 with an ambitious project for an online reference book. Nupedia, he called it. Like dozens of other encyclopedias before, all in printed form, Nupedia solicited experts to write articles, ran the articles by a review panel and then posted them. Things went slowly. A year later, Nupedia had only 21 entries.

Then, secondhand from an assistant, **Jimmy Wales** heard about a simple software tool called *wiki*. The software enabled several people to collaborate on writing and editing. Why not thousands? Millions? By 2001 Wales had modified Nupedia to accept online contributions directly from, well, anyone—with anyone able to edit entries online and do so instantly. It was a process called open editing. An e-notice went out to 2,000 people on Nupedia's mailing list: "Wikipedia is up! Humor me. Go there and add a little article. It will take all of five or 10 minutes."

Five years later **Wikipedia,** as the project was renamed, carried 1 million articles, compared to 120,000 in *Encyclopedia Britannica*, the printed encyclopedia against which all others are judged. Being on the Web, Wikipedia has no physical limit on its size. The site has become the 17th-most visited on the Internet. There are 14,000 hits per second.

LEARNING AHEAD

- We learn the lessons of past generations mostly from books.
- A few large, growing companies dominate the book industry worldwide.
- The book industry has been laggard in exploiting new technology.
- Books fall into broad categories: trade books and textbooks.
- Technology and aliteracy are challenges for the book industry.

● **Jimmy Wales**
The founder of Wikipedia

● **Wikipedia**
A massive online encyclopedia written and edited by users

Wikipedia Founder. Only five employees led by Jimmy Wales keep Wikipedia humming. The entries, all from volunteers, are growing to many multiples of those in traditional encyclopedias.

53

In many ways, Wikipedia represents much of the free-for-all that is the Web. Among Wikipedia's few rules are these: First, articles must be from a neutral point of view. Second, content must be verifiable and previously published. Contributors must be anonymous.

Despite these rules, nonsense does get posted. Too, there are vandals who take perverse joy in messing up entries. Wales has robots that roam entries for disruptive submissions. When accuracy is an issue, volunteer administrators make judgment calls. When contributors differ on facts, Wales runs the facts by a mediation committee and an arbitration committee.

How accurate is Wikipedia? Stories are legion about members of Congress cleaning up entries posted about them. Voting records have been tampered with in self-serving ways. Some members of Congress modified entries about themselves in 2006 to distance themselves from President Bush when his popularity plummeted. Wikipedia, which tracks all changes, restored the balanced accounts, although that took time. On several occasions every member of Congress has been barred from posting changes while Wikipedia administrators sorted out the facts and the truth.

A survey by the journal *Nature* in 2005 tested 43 entries in Wikipedia and in the *Encyclopedia Britannica* and found both amazingly accurate. Wikipedia did, however, have four errors for every three in *Britannica*, but errors were rare both places.

Whatever the pros and cons of Wikipedia, it represents the techno-driven directions we can expect books to take.

Influence of Books

....

STUDY PREVIEW

Mass-produced books, first introduced in the mid-1400s, changed human history by accelerating the exchange of ideas and information among more people. Books have endured as a repository of culture. They are the primary vehicle by which new generations are educated in their society's values and by which they learn the lessons of the past.

REDEFINING THE BOOK

Once, everyone pretty much knew what a book was. Books were bound, which made them distinct from newspapers. They had stiffer covers than magazines, usually cardboard, sometimes laminated with plastic or cloth or even leather, which made them more durable. Get ready to rethink what a book is. Old definitions, going back to Gutenberg Bibles in the mid-1400s, don't fit any of the directions that innovations as diverse as Wikipedia and e-books suggest.

Does this mean that the book is dead? Hardly. Long-form literature such as novels, and long-form nonfiction such as biographies, will not disappear. For the future, the most useful definition for books is long-form, word-driven media content. Books will endure, albeit less so in the physical Gutenberg-era format that goes back almost five centuries.

So what format will replace the bound and printed book? That question has industry leaders scratching their heads as they experiment tepidly with alternatives. Perhaps significantly, the greatest innovations have not come from within the book industry, which seems mired in traditional ways of doing business. Rather, it's upstarts like Wikipedia that are leading the change. The market is vanishing for $2,100 32-volume home sets of the *Encyclopedia Britannica* that takes up 5 1/2 feet of shelf space. Are e-books the answer, with content that's downloadable and readable on digital devices? The jury is still out after disappointing early receptions in the marketplace. Even so, e-books are appearing in a lot of crystal balls these days.

LEARNING CHECK ◄···

▶ What is a more useful definition of books than the physical description of printed pages bound between covers?

▶ Do we have reason to be concerned whether books will survive?

TRANSFORMING HUMAN EXISTENCE

Bound volumes of manuscript date to ancient times, but it was Johannes Gutenberg's movable type innovation of the 1440s that jump-started mass production of the written word. By 1490 every major city in Europe had at least one printer using Gutenberg technology. Books were being pumped into circulation at unprecedented rates and transforming human existence.

■ **Scientific Progress.** The impact of the printing press on scientific inquiry was explosive. Scientists had been stymied by delays in learning what their colleagues were thinking and learning. With mass-produced reports on their work, scientists could build on each other's discoveries. This ushered in the Scientific Revolution, which took off in the 1600s and has been transforming our existence ever since.

■ **Social Reform.** The cost of producing books dropped dramatically with mass production, making the printed word available beyond the socially elite. Exposed to new ideas, people honed their focus on the human condition and social structures and governance in new ways. Revolutionary ideas took root. Martin Luther advanced his Protestantism with printed materials. Tracts and treatises promoting free inquiry came into circulation. It can be asked whether the Renaissance, a period of intellectual, artistic and cultural awakening in the 1500s and 1600s, could have come to fruition without the printing press.

■ **Literacy.** Although the first works using Gutenberg technology were in Latin, soon books and other materials were being printed in native languages. Geoffrey Chaucer's classic *Canterbury Tales*, although written in 1387, was read by relatively few people until the Gutenberg printing press arrived in England. Chaucer's book, in fact, became the first book printed in the English language.

LEARNING CHECK ◄···

▶ How have books been pivotal in the drastic changes in the ways humankind has come to view the world and itself since Gutenberg?

Books and American Culture

··

STUDY PREVIEW

Books have reflected and shaped American culture, from the time the early colonists saw geography and the environment as obstacles to overcome. Books remain a primary vehicle for redefining values, like the more recent notion that humans need to find ways to co-exist with forces of nature. Through books, our leading thinkers tackle great issues like the nature of humankind, including our origins, and how we can best go about organizing ourselves socially and politically.

BOOKS IN NATIONAL DEVELOPMENT

Books were transformational in the early American experience.

■ **Thomas Paine.** Up and down the eastern seaboard, British colonists were shocked that fellow colonists had been killed in combat against British troops in Massachusetts in 1775. That was on the eve of the Revolutionary War. In a 50-page polemic, *Common Sense*, colonial writer Thomas Paine captured the colonists' frustration and anger. Paine attacked King George III as "a wretch who was able to sleep with the blood of Bunker Hill upon his soul." The word *independence* resonated throughout the pamphlet. In three months, *Common Sense* sold 125,000 copies—some historians say it was closer to 250,000—one for every 10 colonists.

Paine was no mere armchair commentator. In 1776 he joined George Washington's army. When the British forced Washington's army to retreat into New Jersey, Paine wrote an essay, the opening lines of which have endured: "These are the times that try men's souls. The Summer soldier and the sunshine patriot will, in this crisis, shrink from the service of their country; but he that stands it now, deserves the love and thanks of man and woman." Washington saw the value of the essay to encourage his dejected soldiers. He ordered every corporal to read Paine's essay to his squad. Inspired by Paine, Washington's soldiers retook Trenton.

Paine's subsequent rousing essays, reprinted by newspapers throughout the newly declared nation, fueled more sales of *Common Sense*. Paine's words, in book form, were part of the soul of the creation of the American republic.

■ **James Fenimore Cooper.** In colonial America, people mostly read British literature. Not until the 1820s, half a century after the founding of the new republic, did works reflecting the American experience begin to appear. In 1821 James Fenimore Cooper began acquiring an international reputation with his novel *The Spy*. Then came his Leatherstocking series. The books drew on the distinctive frontier society that had evolved over two centuries. Cooper gave Americans an insight that they had an identifiable culture with values flowing from their unique experience as a people.

■ **Harriet Beecher Stowe.** In 1862 with the Civil War in progress, Harriet Beecher Stowe, who had written *Uncle Tom's Cabin* in 1852, found herself invited to a White House reception. President Abraham Lincoln rose to greet her: "Why, Mrs. Stowe, right glad to meet you. So you're the little woman who wrote the book that made this great war. Sit down, please." Lincoln wasn't merely being gracious. Stowe's tale of slave life had stirred abolitionist fervor exponentially beyond thousands of earlier tracts, editorials and polemics. Within months of its release, *Uncle Tom's Cabin* had sold 200,000 copies—the first blockbuster. The book was historically pivotal, propelling the anti-slavery movement to center stage.

■ **John Howard Griffin.** A century after Stowe, segregation remained a reality in the United States, albeit muted. John Howard Griffin, a white man, dyed his skin dark and traversed southern states to experience racism from the inside out. His book, *Black Like Me*, published in 1959, offered unmatched insights into social injustice and travesties that white readers could not otherwise have known. Griffin helped set the stage for a renewed civil rights movement and major reforms that became law. His was another example of the power of long-form journalism—the book.

■ **Rachel Carson.** The patron saint of environmentalism is Rachel Carson, whose book *Silent Spring* in 1962 alerted everyone to the dangers posed by pesticides and a wide range of other environmentally unfriendly human activity. Carson's work began a shift away from the traditional American idea that nature was an enemy to be overcome. American thinking began turning away from the virtues of clearing the forest, overcoming the mountains, damming the rivers, and subduing nature toward finding ways for the human species to co-exist with nature.

James Fenimore Cooper

A New American Identity. *Books became a major contributor to a distinctive American identity in the early days of nationhood. James Fenimore Cooper, among others, created stories that flowed from the American experience and gave Americans a perception of themselves as a people with their own traditions. Indeed, can there be a society or a culture without its own literature? Cooper's stories, including* The Last of the Mohicans, *were products of the frontier, which was a unique American subject.*

◼ **Ralph Nader.** The modern consumer movement received a major boost when Ralph Nader tackled General Motors in *Unsafe at Any Speed* in 1963. Nader's target, the unstable rear-engine Chevrolet Corvair, was soon withdrawn from the market. Although criticized as an alarmist, Nader persisted writing book after book, hoping to empower consumers to stand up against corporate power.

LEARNING CHECK ◂ ⋯⋯⋯⋯⋯⋯⋯⋯⋯⋯⋯⋯⋯⋯⋯⋯⋯⋯⋯⋯⋯

▸ **Would the upstart United States have come into nationhood and defeated the British without Thomas Paine?**

▸ **List authors whose books have helped define and redefine the values that make the United States a distinctive society with identifiable and unique values. Try to go beyond the authors listed here.**

BOOKS AND DEFINING ISSUES

The power of the book is no better illustrated than in Charles Darwin's *Origin of Species* in 1859. The British naturalist argued that all species have evolved over time from common ancestors through the process he called natural selection. Darwin's ideas, addressing so many perplexing questions about human existence, caught on quickly. Human beings suddenly saw themselves in a different, less mystical light. To be sure, resistance from traditionalists was strident—indeed the debate still continues—but the scientific community had embraced Darwinism nearly unanimously as the most plausible explanation of how species originated. To be sure, it was Darwin's ideas that brought about the sea change in human self-perception, but the vehicle for his idea was the book and a torrent of subsequent works that savagely debated the issue until, gradually, consensus had reached almost all corners.

Books have gravitas. Anyone serious about seeking the U.S. presidency needs to have written at least one book, usually a biography, before announcing his or her

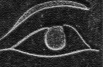

media timeline

BOOK MILESTONES	PIVOTAL EVENTS

1400s

Movable Type
Johannes Gutenberg printed Bibles using movable type (1400s)

University Press
Oxford University established first university press (1478)

Gutenberg's print shop

- Printing presses sprouted in major European cities (1460s–)

1500s

- Martin Luther launched Reformation (1517)
- Postal systems facilitated spread of printed materials (1500s)

1600s

Massachusetts Bay Colony
Puritans established Cambridge Press (1638)

James Fenimore Cooper

- Harvard University founded (1636)
- Age of Science, Age of Reason began (1600s–)
- Colonization of eastern seaboard (1620s–)
- Isaac Newton discovered natural laws (1687)

1700s

Tract for Independence
Thomas Paine stirred patriot fervor with *Common Sense* (1776)

- Industrial Revolution (1760s–)
- Revolutionary War (1776–1781)

1800s

American Literature
James Fenimore Cooper emerged as first U.S. writer with an international reputation (1821)

McGuffey Reader
William Holmes McGuffey wrote first textbook (1836)

Cheap Reading
Beedle brothers introduced dime novels (1860)

GPO
Congress established Government Printing Office (1895)

McGuffey Readers

- Public education took root as a social value (1820s)
- Morse invented telegraph (1844)
- U.S. Civil War (1861–1864)
- Railroad linked Atlantic and Pacific coasts (1869)

1900s

Paperback
Robert de Graff introduced modern paperback (1939)

Amazon.com
Pioneer online bookseller (1995)

Personal Digital Readers
E-book introduced (1998)

- Right to vote extended to women (1920)
- Great Depression (1930s)
- World War II (1941–1945)
- Humans reached moon (1969)
- Military founded predecessor to Internet (1969)

2000s

Nupedia
Jimmy Wales launched Wikipedia predecessor (2000)

Google Print Library
Google began digitizing all books ever published (2005)

Espresso
Print-on-demand machines introduced in bookstores (2005)

Jimmy Wales rewrote the concept of an encyclopedia

- 9/11 terrorist attacks (2001)
- Iraq War (2003–)
- Hurricane Katrina (2005)

candidacy. By 2008 Barack Obama had two—a biography and a second book on his views. His nemesis for the Democratic nomination, Hillary Clinton, had multiple titles too. These campaign books, most of them ghostwritten, generally are little remembered after a campaign. Exceptions include John Kennedy's *Profiles of Courage* and Hillary Clinton's *It Takes a Village*. Without a book a candidate seems less worthy.

Perhaps religion is where books have been their most influential. The holy books the Bible and the Koran are all-time leaders. The great religious revival periods in U.S. history were marked by evangelical work that attracted great followings. One religious book, *In His Steps* by Charles Sheldon in 1896, is among the most best-selling books of all time, translated into 51 languages. L. Ron Hubbard's long run with Scientology titles includes translations into 71 languages.

Today, with faithful diehards of Christianity and Islam re-engaging in a Crusades-like confrontation from the Middle Ages, both absolute in their beliefs but unable to cite supporting evidence on basic issues, a literature of virulent atheism, rooted in rational discourse, has taken form. This may be the telling intellectual battleground of the 21st century, with thinkers like Christopher Hitchens, Richard Dawkins and Sam Harris wielding new influence—and popularizers like humorist Bill Maher and magicians Penn and Teller taking their points beyond the books to even broader audiences.

This is not say that everything published between two covers contributes mightily to society's sorting through its fundamental values. That would be an unreasonable expectation for an industry that produces 195,000 titles a year, and whose range includes textbooks, Harlequin romances, and pop-sellers. True, Stephen King and Danielle Steel may be saying something about the culture in their best sellers, but hardly are their works agents of change. But who knows? King may endure as the next Edgar Allan Poe. Perhaps Steel's next work will be a new generation's *Gone with the Wind*. And just how timeless will J. K. Rowling's *Harry Potter* series prove to be?

LEARNING CHECK ◄ ·

▶ **The human perception of the world hasn't been the same since Charles Darwin. How would you be viewing yourself and your role in the world if Darwin hadn't written** *The Origin of Species*?

▶ **What advice would you offer a rising political figure who wants to write a book for the gravitas it would lend to a candidacy for the White House?**

Book Industry

· ·

STUDY PREVIEW

Mergers and acquisitions have reduced the book industry to fewer and fewer companies, all with global interests. Even so, small publishing houses continue, many profitably, in niches.

SCOPE OF THE BOOK INDUSTRY

The number of new books is skyrocketing. New titles total 195,000 a year in the United States alone. Sales at 710 million copies were up 9.3 percent in 2004. Projections peg growth at 3.5 percent a year, despite a documented phenomenon that young people are reading less than preceding generations.

MAJOR HOUSES

Publishing houses think of themselves as widely recognized brand names: Simon & Schuster, Doubleday, HarperCollins, Penguin. To most people, though, a book is a book is a book, no matter the publisher—although there are exceptions, such as

Harlequin, which is almost a household word for pulp romances. Scholars are exceptions. Their vocabularies are peppered with publishers' names, perhaps because of all the footnotes and bibliographies they have to wade through.

Major publishing houses once had distinctive personalities that flowed from the literary bent of the people in charge. Scribner's, for example, was the nurturing home of Tom Wolfe, Ernest Hemingway and F. Scott Fitzgerald from the 1920s into the 1950s and very much bore the stamp of Charles Scribner and his famous editor Maxwell Perkins. Typical of the era, it was a male-dominated business, everybody wearing tweed coats and smoking pipes. Today the distinctive cultures have blurred as corporate pride has shifted more to the bottom line.

BOOK INDUSTRY CONSOLIDATION

As with other mass-media industries, book publishing has undergone consolidation, with companies merging with each other, acquiring one another, and buying lists from one another. Some imprints that you still see are no longer stand-alone companies but part of international media conglomerates. Random House, a proud name in U.S. book publishing, is now part of the German company Bertelsmann. The company also owns the Bantam, Dell and Doubleday imprints, among other media subsidiaries, including numerous magazines.

Harcourt was sold to Reed Elsevier of Europe and Thomson of Canada in 2001. Half of Simon & Schuster, once the world's largest book publisher, was sold to Pearson, a British conglomerate, in 1999. St. Martin's Press is now part of Holtzbrinck of Germany. HarperCollins is in the hands of Rupert Murdoch, whose flagship News Corp. has its headquarters in Australia. Warner Books became part of French publishing giant Lagardere in 2006. In short, fewer and fewer companies are dominating more and more of the world's book output. And many once-U.S. companies now have their headquarters abroad.

LEARNING CHECK ◄ ••

▶ **Do you think the consolidation of the book industry into major publishing houses has reduced the diversity of new fiction in our society? Of nonfiction?**

NICHE PUBLISHING

Although major houses dominate publishing, about 12,000 other companies in the United States issue books. The catalogs of most contain only a few titles, but altogether these companies comprise a significant portion of the nation's book inventory. Some specialize in regional titles, others in poetry and other niches for limited audiences.

As part of their mission to advance and disseminate knowledge, universities have been in the publishing business since 1478. That's when Oxford University Press was founded. Today 99 U.S. universities own imprints that publish works, mostly scholarly, that commercial publishers wouldn't find economically feasible. University press contributions have been notable. Harvard, for example, brought out *The Double Helix* by James Watson, a landmark in the biosciences. Harvard also published the poetry of Ezra Pound.

As higher-education budgets have tightened in recent years, some **university presses** have disappeared. Others are under financial pressure to seek profitable titles to offset other losses and even turn a profit. Some have found niches in regional histories, travelogues and, egads, even cookbooks.

● **university presses**
University-sponsored book publishing operations, traditional focus on scholarly work

LEARNING CHECK ◄ ••

▶ **Is the profit model that's at the heart of the book industry a good fit for university presses? Why or why not?**

New Technology and Books

The book industry is vulnerable to criticism as dowdy and stuck in a centuries-old business model. Innovations have been imposed mostly by outsiders. Today it's Google and Wikipedia that are redefining the industry.

TRADITION-BOUND INDUSTRY

No surprise, as the oldest of mass-media businesses, the book industry is bound up in traditional ways of doing things. Modest innovations, like the modern paperback in the 1930s, threw the industry into a loop. The online retail model of Amazon.com in the 1990s did the same. The industry is defensive about being called tradition-bound, but the record clearly shows that the great innovations have come from out-of-the-box thinking from outside the industry.

Wikipedia wasn't conceived by editors at the *Encyclopedia Britannica*, whose embrace of digital technology had been limited to truncated CD editions. Barnes & Noble may have fine-tuned traditional book retailing with its flashy superstores, but it was an upstart entrepreneur in Seattle, **Jeff Bezos,** who came up with Amazon.com. The idea to digitize every book ever published for a single searchable database didn't come from a publishing house boardroom in New York or Boston but from the Google crew in California's techno-obsessed Silicon Valley.

● **Jeff Bezos (pronounced BAY-zos)** Founder of online book retailer Amazon.com

LEARNING CHECK ◄

▸ **How much validity do you attach to the charge that the book industry is resistant to change?**

▸ **What do you see as the shape of the book industry a quarter century from now?**

PROTECTING THE FRANCHISE

It is a pattern among media, once established, to protect their franchise. The television industry opposed newcomer cable. Radio opposed Sirius and XM. The book industry, perhaps because its roots are so deep in history, has been especially resistant to innovation. The Association of American Publishers, for example, went to court in 2005

E-Commerce Pioneer. As Jeff Bezos saw it back in 1994, the Web had great potential for e-commerce. But what to sell? Figuring that products that lent themselves to direct mail would also work well on the Web, Bezos settled on books. He founded Amazon.com in the garage of his Seattle home, pioneering book retailing on the Web. By 2000 sales topped $1 billion.

to stop a Google project from digitizing every book ever printed in English, as well as other languages.

Book industry executives don't cotton at all to being likened to techno-Neanderthals. The fact, though, is that the industry's embrace of technology has been at the periphery, like audiobook variations of the core print product and Web site add-ons for core-product textbooks. Forays into new models for distributing their products have been similarly modest. On-site bookstore custom publishing, for example, merely changes delivery of the traditional product. There have been tepid experiments to deliver books to handheld devices—**e-books**—but they fizzled because of what some critics say was a half-hearted investment in the new product and lackluster promotion. A few textbook publishers have tested direct-to-student sales but backed off rather than offend booksellers, the publishing industry's partners for 500 years.

Is the book industry doomed by old thinking? Actually, some industry leaders acknowledge the problem. Richard Sarnoff, president of corporate development at Random House, is working on selling online access directly to readers. It's a pay-per-view plan at 4 cents a page. At HarperCollins, chief executive Jane Friedman sees an end to the blockbuster mentality that has major publishers channeling resources into authors and titles in hopes of superprofits but at high risk if a book flounders. Friedman says that the book industry needs to reinvent itself: "Chasing best-sellers is a fool's game."

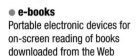

● **e-books**
Portable electronic devices for on-screen reading of books downloaded from the Web

E-Books. *When 400,000 Stephen King fans down-loaded his* Riding the Bullet *in 2000, e-books seemed to be the future. Alas,* Bullet *turned out to be a one-time wonder. Early dedicated-purpose computer tablets for storing a downloaded library failed in the marketplace. Retailer Barnes & Noble, which had high hopes for the product, shut down its eBooks store in 2003. Hardware makers keep designers busy on new versions of the e-book gizmos, but the book industry is wary.*

Stephen King

Jane Friedman, chief executive at HarperCollins, is unlearning fundamental lessons from her career climb over 30 years. The book industry's future, as Friedman sees it, is not in blockbusters. Big-name authors are risky, she says. Guaranteed advances in the upper six figures, sometimes higher, don't ensure that a book won't flop and leave a publisher bleeding red ink.

Friedman sees a new model for publishers that emphasizes long-term profits from what she calls "small books."

Her doubts about blockbusters are understandable. A rule of thumb is that 4 percent of new titles earn a good profit, but only a few of those make spectacular money. In 2005, for example, only 200 books accounted for 10 percent of U.S. book industry sales. One book, *Harry Potter and the Half-Blood Prince*, with 7 million copies, accounted for 1 percent of the year's total sales.

So what is Friedman's vision?

She sees new life for books that now, after their introduction, languish in warehouses until they're shredded to make room for newer titles. With digital storage, these backlist books can remain available indefinitely. With print-on-demand technology, one copy at a time can be printed. Over the long term, Friedman says, many backlist books can generate continuing sales and profits.

Also, she says, small books could sell significantly better if marketed to people with specific interests and who otherwise have no idea the books are available.

Book Industry Contrarian. *The heavy investment to create a best seller is risky. A book can flop despite aggressive marketing. And sales, even when spectacular, are short-lived. At HarperCollins, Jane Friedman sees a less rocky future with niche books that have more modest initial sales but long lives and steady revenue.*

Friedman's ideas on targeted marketing are clearly contrarian in an industry where intiuitive assessments of manuscripts has been the tradition. She's blunt: "Publishers have never looked at who the consumer is."

The book industry needs to reinvent itself, she says: "Chasing bestsellers is a fool's game."

WHAT DO YOU THINK?

▶ Is Jane Friedman right about the blockbuster having reached its zenith as a 150-year obsession among major publishing houses?

▶ What do you think of Friedman's prediction for the future of "small books"?

Whether the book industry as we know it will adapt to new models is an unanswered question. This is not to suggest that the novel and word-driven long-form journalism are at risk. The question is whether it will be a Random House or a Google that shapes the future of the book.

LEARNING CHECK ◀ •••••••••••••••••••••••••••••••••••

▶ **Why did the early e-books fizzle?**

▶ **Can books in a format downloadable to a designated-purpose reading tablet catch on? Explain your answer.**

Book Products

STUDY PREVIEW

When most people think about books, fiction and nonfiction aimed at general readers come to mind. These are called trade books, which are a major segment of the book industry. Also important are textbooks, which include not only schoolbooks but also reference books and even cookbooks. There are countless ways to further dissect book products, but textbooks and trade books are the major categories.

TRADE BOOKS

● **trade books**
General-interest titles, including fiction and nonfiction

The most visible part of the $28.8 billion a year that the U.S. book publishing industry produces is **trade books.** These are general-interest titles, including fiction and nonfiction, that people usually think of when they think about books. Trade books can be incredible best sellers. Since it was introduced in 1937, J. R. R. Tolkien's *The Hobbit* has sold almost 40 million copies. Margaret Mitchell's 1936 *Gone with the Wind* has passed 29 million. Most trade books, however, have shorter lives. To stay atop best-seller lists, Stephen King, J. K. Rowling, Danielle Steel and other authors have to keep writing. Steel, known for her discipline at the keyboard, produces a new novel about every six months.

Although publishing trade books can be extremely profitable when a book takes off, trade books have always been a high-risk proposition. One estimate is that 60 percent of them lose money, 36 percent break even, and 4 percent turn a good profit. Only a few become best sellers and make spectacular money.

TEXTS AND REFERENCES

● **textbooks**
Educational, professional, reference titles

Although the typical successful trade book best seller can be a spectacular money-maker for a few months, a successful **textbook** has a longer life that provides steady income. For example, Curtis MacDougall wrote a breakthrough textbook on journalism in 1932 that went through eight editions before he died in 1985. Then the publisher brought out a ninth edition, with Robert Reid bringing it up to date. This gave MacDougall's *Interpretative Reporting* a life span of more than 60 years. Although

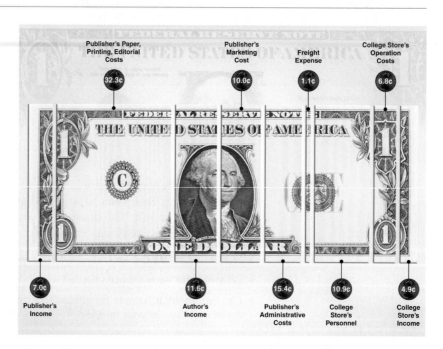

Textbook Dollar

Students grumble about textbook costs, which fuel suspicions about profiteering. By most business and retail standards, however, profits are slim. The National Association of College Stores says pre-tax profits on new text books average 7.0 percent for publishers and 4.9 percent for retailers. Author royalties average 11.6 percent. For used books, however, the breakdown is drastically different. College stores often have twice the markup. On used books, there are no expenses for manufacturing, publishing house overhead, author royalties or marketing.

McGuffey Readers. *For a century McGuffey's readers taught children to read, contributing to quantum increases in literacy. The first book in the McGuffey series appeared in 1836.*

Just out of college, William Holmes McGuffey arrived at Miami University in Ohio on horseback in 1826. In his saddle bags were a few books on moral philosophy and languages. At the university he tested his theories about education on neighborhood kids who gathered on his porch next to the campus. McGuffey confirmed that children learn better when sentences are accompanied by a picture. He also noted that reading out loud helps and that spelling is not very important in learning to read. McGuffey took notes on his observations and tested his ideas on other age groups. He also collected a mass of stories from a great variety of places.

In 1833 the Truman & Smith publishing company was scouting for someone to write a series of readers and found McGuffey. He culled his favorite stories for the new reader. Many were from the Bible, and most made a moral point. In 1836 the first of McGuffey's *Eclectic Readers* appeared. McGuffey still had lots of material that he had used with the children on his porch, and a second, third and fourth reader followed. Truman & Smith marketed the books vigorously, and they soon had a national following.

WHAT DO YOU THINK?

▶ To engage his pupils, William Holmes McGuffey used ancient tales full of morality lessons. Do you find your textbooks at all preachy?

▶ Do you see a correlation between the success of McGuffey's readers and the rise of literacy and the growing value placed on public education from the 1820s on? Explain your answer.

---

textbook publishers don't routinely announce profits by title, *Interpretative Reporting* undoubtedly has generated more income than many trade book best sellers.

Textbooks, the biggest segment of the book market, include reference and professional books, college textbooks, and elementary and high school textbooks and learning materials.

■ **Professional and Reference Books.** Dictionaries, atlases and other reference works represent about 10 percent of textbook sales. Over the years the Christian Bible and Noah Webster's dictionary have led reference book sales. Others also have had exceptional, long-term success that rivals trade books. Even after Benjamin Spock died in 1998, his *Baby and Child Care*, introduced in 1946, kept on selling. Total sales are past 50 million. Next on the list: *The Better Homes and Gardens Cookbook*.

■ **Textbooks.** College textbooks sell in great numbers, mostly through the coercion of the syllabus. Although textbooks are written for students, publishers pitch them to professors, who then order them for their students. Books for elementary and high school students comprise the **el-hi** market.

● **el-hi**
The elementary and high school book market

LEARNING CHECK ◄ •

▶ The book publishing industry is largely divided into two components—text and trade. Can you identify any books that could fit into both categories? How about books that don't fit easily into either category?

Book Trends

The blockbuster long has been the golden grail at major book publishing houses. Digitization, however, has created a large and growing market segment for niche and short-run titles.

BLOCKBUSTERS

Ever since *Uncle Tom's Cabin*, major publishing houses have been obsessed with finding the next blockbuster. How big can a best seller be? No one knows. Every new top-seller sets a new goal to surpass. Two of the top-selling novels in history have appeared since 2000—J. K. Rowling's latest *Harry Potter* book, which averages 60 million copies worldwide, and Dan Brown's *Da Vinci Code,* at 60.5 million and still counting.

Critics fault publishing houses for their frenzied blockbuster emphasis. In an important book, *The Death of Literature*, Alvin Kernan makes the case that publishers look for what's marketable rather than what has literary quality. The blockbuster obsession, Kernan says, stunts good literature. A premium is put on works that are written, edited and marketed to a lesser literary level, which Kernan says undermines cultural standards. Mediocre stuff, even bad stuff, displaces good stuff in the marketplace.

A classic case study to which critics point is Warner Books, which, half a century after the success of *Gone with the Wind*, sensed a market opportunity for a sequel. Warner went looking for an author to come up with a manuscript that could be marketed into best-seller status. Romance writer Alexandra Ripley was given a $600,000 advance to do the job. Perhaps it was an impossible task to produce a sequel on par with Margaret Mitchell's original. In any event, the sequel *Scarlett* took a drubbing from critics. Despite the book's dubious literary merit, Warner promoted *Scarlett* into a 1991 best seller.

Did the world need another bodice-busting romance, this time gussied up in hard cover? No, say the critics. But Warner Books did.

Warner profited tremendously from the *Scarlett* project, but despite clever marketing, not all big-budget plans for the next best seller materialize. Some flop, draining a publishing house of capital that could have gone to worthier if less flashy works. Critics say the fetish of major houses for best sellers hurts talented **mid-list** authors, who write for modest advances and whose work languishes for

● **mid-list**
Books for which publishing houses expect modest sales and promote modestly

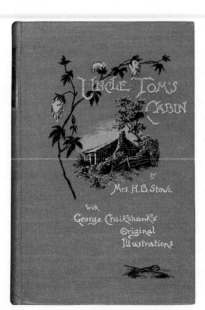

Harriet Beecher Stowe

First Blockbuster. *Publishers first tasted the immense potential of best sellers before the Civil War, when* Uncle Tom's Cabin *by Harriet Beecher Stowe sold 200,000 copies within three weeks. The major focus at major publishing houses became finding potential mega-sellers and promoting them energetically. Sometimes, say critics, the promotion more than the literary quality creates the sales success. Put another way, the tail wags the dog.*

O. J. Simpson's How-To

HarperCollins was poised to make a bundle.

ReganBooks, an imprint headed by the U.S. book industry's *enfant terrible* of the moment, Judith Regan, had signed ex-football star O. J. Simpson to write a book on how he would have murdered his wife, Nicole, and friend Ron Goldman in 1995—had he done it. Regan, known for her fine-tune twists in promoting books, wanted to use the title *I Did It*. That went too far, Simpson's attorneys insisted. The title became *If I Did It*.

Regan was a star at HarperCollins. The Vassar grad had worked at the *National Enquirer*. Later she developed best-selling tell-all books at Simon & Schuster. In 1994 Rupert Murdoch, who owns HarperCollins, offered Regan her own imprint and a television show on his Fox News. One estimate is that Regan's magic at ReganBooks generated $120 million a year.

Then came the Simpson book. Although acquitted in a lengthy criminal trial that millions of people followed daily, Simpson eventually was ordered to pay the victims' families $35 million in a civil trial. He didn't pay it, but the advance and royalties from ReganBooks, $3.5 million according to one source, reportedly were to go to Simpson's children.

If I Did It was due to hit the bookstores just in time for the 2006 holiday rush. Expecting a typical Regan best-seller, HarperCollins printed 400,000 copies. To promote the book, Regan taped a no-holds-barred interview with Simpson to air on the Fox network.

When word of the pending book became news, there was outrage. Many people were sure he had committed the murders and been spared jail by clever, top-dollar attorneys. The possibility that Simpson stood to benefit somehow was abhorrent to many people in ways that Regan had not anticipated. It was no less abhorrent to many people that HarperCollins wanted to cash in. Relatives of the victims, women's groups and victims' rights organizations went into high-gear criticism. Many independent bookstores said they would either not sell *If I Did It* or give away the proceeds. Within days, almost a dozen Fox affiliates refused to carry the Regan–Simpson interview.

Ten days before the book's scheduled release, Murdoch, whose media empire is rarely afraid to push the limits of taste, pulled the plug on the book and the show. The books were recalled and destroyed. Murdoch apologized to the victims' families: "This was an ill-considered project."

Regan said she didn't understand. She likened herself to those who keep Hitler's *Mein Kampf* in print. She compared her interview with Simpson to Barbara Walters' interviews with murders, dictators and criminals. She ignored the obvious difference that Regan Books had invested millions for the rights to Simpson's story.

A month later, Judith Regan was fired. HarperCollins' explanation was that Regan, known for a sharp tongue, had made anti-Semitic remarks to a company attorney.

Whatever the truth of the firing, Ron Goldman's father sued to obtain the rights to the book—and won.

HarperCollins, instead of making a bundle, lost millions.

Judith Regan. To promote O. J. Simpson's book If I Did It, *about the murder of his wife and her friend, publisher Judith Regan launched a promotional blitz on radio shows and other media. Then Regan's parent company ordered the book shredded in response to public outrage at commercializing the murders. The decision to shred was made by media titan Rupert Murdoch, owner of HaperCollins, whose imprints include Regan's Reganbooks.*

DEEPENING YOUR MEDIA LITERACY

EXPLORE THE ISSUE

Ask 10 people if they bought the O. J. Simpson book and why or why not. If you can, combine your data with several other students.

DIG DEEPER

Categorize your data as either populist or elitist. Figure the percentage that would have bought the book and whether more people would have bought it for populist or elitist reasons. What other trends do you see in your data?

WHAT DO YOU THINK?

Should a book with objectionable material be withdrawn from publication? Who should decide? Should the prospect of profits factor into the decision to publish a book? What does the *If I Did It* fiasco say about publishing?

want of a marketing budget. And, add the critics, society is culturally the poorer for the misguided emphasis on blockbusters.

Publishing executives acknowledge that pursuing best sellers is costly and risky, but the financial rewards for success can be substantial. Producing books with limited popular appeal, the publishers say, would put them out of business. Their argument: Without seeking the huge profits that a best seller can generate, the industry would constrict—and where, they ask rhetorically, would cultural enhancement be then?

LEARNING CHECK ◀ ···

▶ **By definition, blockbuster books make a lot of money. So what explains a growing skepticism about the value of publishers pursuing blockbuster successes?**

MARKETING PLOYS

Generating buzz has become a pre-emptive tactic in pushing a trade book to be a success in the first months of release. The period for a book to show marketplace success, however, has been compacted because major retailers now display a new title at the front of the store only a couple of weeks. To build prerelease demand, publishers begin hyping a book months ahead of its release. Critics object that the new marketing lets hype trump legitimate marketplace dynamics in creating strong sellers. As critics see it, whichever publisher has the biggest bag of tricks wins.

For its 2006 title *The Numbers*, about retirement planning, publisher Free Press applied a full-range of proven and also new tactics to goose those essential make-it or break-it early sales.

- Lined up a media-wise former editor of *Esquire* who interviews well, Lee Eisenberg, as author.
- Decided on a January release, optimum for self-improvement titles because people are still into New Year's resolutions.
- Mailed bound manuscripts, an unusual tactic, to opinion leaders the preceding June to generate early word-of-mouth enthusiasm.

Bret Easton Ellis

TwoBrets.com. *To promote* Lunar Park *by bad-boy author Bret Easton Ellis, the old-line publishing house Knopf created a Web site three months before the book was released. The goal was to stir up debate about how much of Ellis' book was autobiographical. Although impossible to measure how many visits to TwoBrets.com translated into sales, the first printing sold out quickly and the book went into a second printing.*

- Mailed uncorrected page proofs to reviewers the preceding August.
- Printed 3,500 preview copies in hardcover, not the usual paper covers, to bookstore executives and buyers.
- Created a Web site with Eisenberg and then in waves alerted 300 bloggers on financial issues, hoping for links to the author site over several weeks.
- Hired BzzAgent, a Boston marketing company that specializes in word-of-mouth promotion, to send preview copies in December to 300 Bzz agents between 35 and 60 with incomes of $45,000, offering incentives to talk up the book among friends and acquaintances.

The first printing was 125,000 copies.

LEARNING CHECK ◄ •

▶ **Cast the debate over blockbusters on the elitist-populist continuum.**

▶ **Has the era of the blockbuster been eclipsed by digital technology?**

NICHE PROLIFERATION

Evidence is growing that the pedestal on which major publishing houses have placed blockbusters may come to be shared with nonblockbusters. Nielsen Bookscan, which tracks book sales, found that three-quarters of the titles sold in 2004 were of fewer than 99 copies. The significance of the Nielsen data was that these extremely low-volume sales were of 950,000 titles. Looking at the data, Chris Anderson, editor of tech-savvy *Wired* magazine, said that "all these onesies and twosies" add up. There is other evidence that the time has come for niche books. At online retailer Amazon.com, about a quarter of book sales are outside the top 100,000 sellers.

Hyperefficient digital economics explains what's happening. Consumers have easy access to online reviews and catalog-type information. Too, search engines can steer consumers to sellers that have obscure titles available.

Niche books will become an even more important segment of the book industry as publishers and retailers embrace emerging technology.

■ **Digital Storage.** Publishers are acquiring the ability to store books digitally, eliminating the expensive warehousing of paper products. Formerly, titles went **out of print** when the last copy was sold and a publisher couldn't justify the cost of a new pressrun of several hundred copies and warehousing them for perhaps years to meet trickling demand.

● **out of print**
A book unavailable because slow sales don't warrant the cost of printing and warehousing a new batch

■ **Digital Distribution.** Printing now can be short runs, as little as a single copy, with new printing and binding equipment. **Print-on-demand** machines, called POD, already are tapping digitally stored books for one-at-a-time production even as a customer waits in a store. The machines tap into a publisher's computers for on-site downloads.

● **print-on-demand (POD)**
Equipment that prints and binds books in low volumes, even a single copy

The general view is that high-volume books, including short-lived blockbusters, will continue to be important in the book industry but that a new and more dependable revenue stream from niche sales is emerging. Niche books are not only titles that are past their prime but also books intended at the start only for niche audiences.

LEARNING CHECK ◄ •

▶ **How is digital technology enabling the niche-publishing phenomenon?**

▶ **What changes will print-on-demand technology bring to the book industry? To book retailers? To readers?**

Book Challenges and Issues

STUDY PREVIEW

The search-engine company Google and publishers are in a kerfuffle over a project to digitize all the books in the English language. That, however, is not the book industry's greatest problem. A haunting albeit unanswered question: Are young people, the industry's next generation of customers, reading books anymore?

GOOGLE PRINT LIBRARY

● **Google Print Library**
Project to digitize all books in the English language

The greatest innovation in the book industry is coming not from publishers but from Google, the search engine company. Google set out on a massive project in 2005 to digitize the entire collection at the libraries of Harvard, Oxford, Stanford, the University of Michigan and the New York Public Library. The massive project, called the **Google Print Library,** would put virtually all the books in the English language, 15 million titles, on a searchable database. The project, predicted to take years, was designed to offer free access to complete books in the public domain and no longer covered by copyright. For works still covered by copyright, Google would provide only snippets generated by a search term. There then would be sponsored links to publishers, booksellers and libraries for the full work.

Book publishers were envious of Google's innovation and the profits the company stood to make by placing paid advertisements geared to search results. Publishers wanted a share and even went to court to stop Google.

Google's supporters, however, saw the book industry as short-sighted. Imagine that you want to find out everything written about early U.S. book publisher Isaiah Thomas. If he is mentioned in an older book not covered by copyright, you could have instant access to the entire book. If he is mentioned in a book that is covered by copyright, Google would provide a snippet that includes the reference to Thomas, perhaps a sentence or a paragraph, accompanied by links to sources where you could locate the full book. As Google saw it, publishers would benefit because people would buy books they otherwise might never have known existed.

Google Guys. *With the fortune they amassed from Google, Sergey Brin and Larry Page have cast their net widely for new projects. The in-process Google Print Library aims to digitize the entire inventory of books ever published into a giant reference source. Google would sell on-screen advertising, as it does for its other search engine products.*

Publishers were not alone in resisting innovations from cybercompanies that could create profits. The music recording industry was pressing for a bigger cut from iTunes and other online music vendors. Hollywood was doing the same.

LEARNING CHECK ◄···

▶ **Should book publishers share in the profit that Google expects to make from advertising on its Library Project pages?**

YOUNG READERS

Despite the era's conventional wisdom that young people are dazzled by graphics and don't read much, there is evidence to the contrary. In the early part of the 21st century, bookstores reported increases of 20 to 75 percent in young buyers. Some called it the Harry Potter effect, which indeed prompted a swelling of new titles for 10- to 14-year-olds. Established authors including Isabel Allende, Clive Barker, Michael Crichton and Carl Hiaasen all wrote books for the juvenile market. Some observers noted that teenagers, spurred earlier than ever to do well on college admissions tests, worked harder at getting a sense of a larger world. Too, the book industry became increasingly clever with marketing lures, including Hollywood and celebrity tie-ins and book readings at teen clubs.

Even so, concern is growing that young people are drifting away from books. A landmark study by the National Endowment for the Arts, called *Reading at Risk*, found that fewer than half of American adults read literature, loosely defined as fiction or poetry. That was a 10 percent decline over 20 years. For young adults, the drop was 28 percentage points. It's not that people can't read, which would be illiteracy. Instead, people are increasingly **aliterate,** which means they can read but don't.

● **aliterate**
Choosing not to read although able to do so

The findings of the National Endowment study, although alarming, may be overstated. The fact is that adult fiction titles grew 43.1 percent in 2004 to more than 25,000 titles, which perhaps means that fewer people are reading more books. Too, as book industry spokesperson Patricia Schroeder has noted, people in serious eras spend less time with fiction and more time with biography, history, current events and other nonfiction. Clearly, more time is spent on alternatives to books, like on-screen news and blogs.

LEARNING CHECK ◄···

▶ **How would you respond to someone who sees books and other print media as past their heyday as major mass media?**

▶ **What can book publishers do to bring young people back to reading books, as did earlier generations?**

▶ **Do the findings of *Reading at Risk* coincide with your own observations and experiences?**

Chapter Wrap-Up

Influence of Books (Page 54)

■ As long-form literature and journalism, books have a history of a transformational impact on cultural and social values. This legacy goes back to Johannes Gutenberg in the 1440s. Books have been the major forum for the exchange of scientific thought. Thinkers in many fields have fueled social and other reforms through books. Thanks in large part to books, few assumptions and values from the 15th century have survived. Literacy has made quantum leaps.

Books and American Culture (Page 55)

- Books have reflected and shaped American culture, from the early mindset of seeing geography and the environment as obstacles to be overcome through human genius and industry. Books remain a primary vehicle for redefining values. Books have been important, for example, in the revisionist notion that humankind needs to find ways to co-exist with forces of nature. Through books our leading thinkers tackle great issues like the nature of humankind, including our origins, and how we can best go about organizing ourselves socially and politically.

Book Industry (Page 59)

- The book industry is large. In the United States alone, more than 700 million books a year are sold. About 195,000 new titles come out every year. Major publishing houses have undergone consolidation into a handful of big players, most under foreign ownership. Despite this conglomeration, about 12,000 small players, most with modest niche catalogs, are altogether a major segment of the industry. Significant among smaller publishers are university-operated presses that issue works that might not make it commercially but are important in the intellectual circles where seminal thinking on critical issues is occurring.

New Technology and Books (Page 61)

- The book industry, going back 500 years, is tradition-bound and resistant to change. The industry has been slow, for example, to embrace technology, which could upend familiar ways of going about its business. Even so, change is being forced on the industry by outside forces that are capitalizing on new technology. The reference book component of the publishing industry faces major shrinkage with the rapid growth of the innovative and free Wikipedia. The search engine company Google is digitizing the contents of all the world's libraries for full-text online access to works in the public domain and searchable access to the contents of copyright-protected works. Although the book industry is suing to stop Google, the history of technology shows that technology isn't easily stopped.

Book Products (Page 64)

- Books fall into two broad categories—trade books, which include most of what you find at bookstores, and textbooks, which include professional and reference works. There are countless subcategories and other ways to dissect the industry's products—paperback and hardcover, fiction and nonfiction, comic books and graphic novels, as well as subspecies like audiobooks and on-again, off-again efforts to find marketplace acceptance of e-books.

Book Trends (Page 66)

- The blockbuster long has been the golden grail at major book publishing houses. Digitization, however, has created a large and growing market segment for niche and short-run titles. Although book sales are projected to grow, there is concern in the book industry about an emerging aliterate generation. These include young people, many of them college students, who can read but don't. The book may be diminishing as a vehicle for entertainment, amusement and escape in an age with easy access to alternative media.

REVIEW QUESTIONS

1. List as many changes as you can in how people perceive themselves and their role in the world compared to pre-Gutenberg times. Then relate these changes to the work of particular thinkers and reformers over the past 500 years. Did any of the changes you identified occur without books playing some kind of role?

2. How did books contribute to the development of nationhood in the young United States? To the creation of a distinctive American identity?

3. The book industry is dominated by a few major publishing houses, but it would be wrong to overlook the role of small publishers. What role do these small publishing houses play in the book industry?

4. The book industry is often criticized as reluctant to embrace technological change. It's a charge that makes industry leaders bristle. Evaluate the examples they cite of self-generated changes the industry has undergone.

5. What are the two major categories of products from the book industry? Make a case for each category as having the more enduring impact on cultural values and society.

6. Do you see the era of the blockbuster book ending? Why or why not? What role will aliteracy play in the future of the book industry?

CONCEPTS

aliterate (Page 71)

university presses (Page 60)

mid-list (Page 66)

out of print (Page 69)

print-on-demand (POD) (Page 69)

TERMS

e-books (Page 62)

el-hi (Page 65)

Google Print Library (Page 70)

trade books (Page 64)

Wikipedia (Page 53)

PEOPLE

Jeff Bezos (Page 61)

James Fenimore Cooper (Page 56)

Charles Darwin (Page 57)

Johannes Gutenberg (Page 55)

Jimmy Wales (Page 53)

MEDIA SOURCES

- Chris Anderson. *The Long Tail: Why the Future of Business Is Selling Less of More.* Hyperion, 2006. Anderson, editor of *Wired*, says blockbusters are becoming less important with the advent of technology that has expanded the marketplace into microniches.

- Jason Epstein. *Book Business: Publishing Past, Present and Future.* Norton, 2001. Epstein, former editorial director at Random House, offers a history of book publishing.

- Michael Korda. *Making the List: A Cultural History of the American Bestseller 1900–1999.* Barnes and Noble, 2001. Korda, longtime editor at Simon & Schuster, argues that best-seller lists are telling indicators of changing social values. Korda is informed, witty, and provocative.

In this chapter you have deepened your media literacy by revisiting several themes. Here are thematic highlights from the chapter:

A Google Library. *Sergey Brin and Larry Page see a massive online library in Google's future.*

Media Technology

The book industry has used digital technology for new efficiencies in production and promotion, but its core product remains ink on paper in bound volumes. That the industry is wedded to its traditions may be no surprise. The book manufacturing and distribution infrastructure has been in place 500 years. Technological innovation is afoot, however—from the outside. Wikipedia, with no roots in the book industry, captured the public's imagination in 2005. Almost overnight, traditional encyclopedias joined the horse and buggy. By 2010 the search engine company Google expects to have digitized every public domain book in English into a searchable database for downloading. Although the book industry is fighting it, Google also plans to add current works into its searchable database. **(Pages 53–54 and Pages 70–71)**

Media Economics

Ever since the huge commercial success of Harriet Beecher Stowe's *Uncle Tom's Cabin* that preceded the Civil War, major publishing houses have been trying to outdo every best seller. It's the profits of scale. The larger the mass production, the less the unit cost and the more the profit. The quest for blockbusters, however, is risky. Huge investments are required. When a book flops, losses can be catastrophic. Also, most blockbusters flare out quickly. A year later, the market for most blockbusters has been saturated. Some industry leaders, including Jane Friedman of HarperCollins, are talking about a new era of "smaller books." Friedman doesn't mean shorter manuscripts but rather more modest sales offset by a longer life in the marketplace. **(Pages 66–68)**

Death of the Blockbuster. *HarperCollins' Jane Friedman may not go that far, but she sees a bright future for "smaller books."*

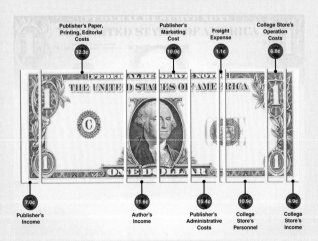

Unseen Costs. *Most consumers, including textbook purchasers, miss seeing the expenses that manufacturers, wholesalers and retailers incur to deliver the product.*

Publisher's Paper, Printing, Editorial Costs — 32.3¢
Publisher's Marketing Cost — 10.0¢
Freight Expense — 1.1¢
College Store's Operation Costs — 6.8¢
Publisher's Income — 7.0¢
Author's Income — 11.6¢
Publisher's Administrative Costs — 15.4¢
College Store's Personnel — 10.9¢
College Store's Income — 4.9¢

Audience Fragmentation

If indeed the obsession with finding the new blockbuster is easing, as some predict, major publishing houses may have more resources available to better serve smaller audiences with stronger mid-list catalogs. Literati would welcome the shift. Critics say that mid-list authors have had their works slighted in promotion budgets as publishers divert resources to big projects. Some works, many of good quality, never make it through the manuscript acceptance process for the same reason. By gearing products more to audience fragments, publishing houses could enrich the diversity of our literature. **(Pages 66–69)**

Media and Democracy

Literary grace is hardly a prerequisite for U.S. presidents, but every recent president has been an author—of sorts. A book is *de rigueur* for a presidential candidate. What gravitas would a candidate have without articulating positions between hard covers? The role of books in political dialogue dates to Thomas Paine, whose 1775 polemic *Common Sense* helped inspire colonists to fight their war against England. The great political thinkers all have expressed their positions in books, which historically have been a primary forum for debate on the great issues. As for recent presidential candidates, some have kept ghostwriting a growing occupation. **(Pages 56–57)**

New York Times. *Booksellers keep abreast of new titles in a broad range of trade book genres through the* Times.

Media and Culture

Agree with them or not, the new strident generation of atheists is challenging traditional religions through the book. This is to be expected. Historically the book has been the vehicle for examining the great, enduring and elusive questions about the religious, cultural and social values we have inherited and that we create. Every religious movement has its literature. Some is heavy-duty, some mere pop psychology in the self-help spirit. Altogether, the vast output of books on cultural issues constitutes a major influence on the values on which we individually and collectively base our lives. **(Pages 54–55)**

Foundations. *McGuffey started his* Eclectic Readers *in 1836.*

Elitism and Populism

A book industry commentator, Alvin Kernan, makes a case that our culture has paid a heavy price for publishers' obsession with blockbusters. Kernan argues that major publishing houses, in their quest of profits, are using resources for big projects with mass appeal rather than for books that could contribute to moving the culture forward. He is making an elitist argument. By pandering to mass tastes, he says, the book industry is abdicating its responsibility to wield its resources to do truly good things. **(Pages 66–68)**

Need Bookshelves. *With digital delivery growing for all media products, tomorrow's college students will have shelf space for things other than books.*

Media Future

That young people have glommed onto digital media whose content is not word-driven is giving pause to the book industry. If coming generations are less imbued with reading as a leisure activity, does long-form literature and journalism have a future? Maybe the pendulum will swing away from graphics-laden and audio-based media. Maybe there will be a resurgence of the book. Despite the industry's concern that its role as a mass medium may have peaked, sales continue to grow 3 to 5 percent annually. Go figure. **(Page 71)**

4

Newspapers

Emphasis on Local News

Don't tell Mary Junck that newspapers are past their prime as a mass medium. Since 1999, when she took over the Lee Enterprises newspaper chain, she has kept pre-tax earnings pushing 30 percent. Circulation declines have been turned around at some Lee newspapers, stemmed at others. At most of the company's 58 dailies, circulation is growing. Through acquisitions, the daily newspaper circulation at Lee papers leaped 75 percent in one recent year. The most recent acquisition was Pulitzer, Inc., with 14 dailies and 100 weeklies. Pulitzer became a key part of Lee's future in 2005 when a $1.5 billion merger was completed.

Lee, headquartered in Davenport, Iowa, is committed to newspapers. In 1999 it sold all its television stations to concentrate on newspapers. It bought up weeklies and specialty periodicals by the score, bringing the total to 175. Then, after shopping carefully for more dailies, Lee bought the 16-daily Howard chain, including the 92,000-circulation Escondido, California, *North County Times*, which became Lee's largest newspaper. Not far behind are the Lee dailies in Munster, Indiana, and Lincoln, Nebraska. In 2004 came the Pulitzer acquisition, which included the St. Louis *Post-Dispatch*.

Junck, reared an Iowa farmgirl, says the secret to success for 21st century newspapers includes a strong emphasis on local news. Her academic background is journalism. She edited the yearbook at Valparaiso University in Indiana and then earned a master's in journalism at the University of North Carolina. Then she rose into newspaper management in advertising. At Lee she created the position of vice president for news to help local editors strengthen their coverage. This was at a time when many

LEARNING AHEAD

- Newspapers are the major source of news for most Americans.

- Most U.S. newspapers are owned by chains, although chain ownership is in flux.

- Newspapers have gone online, but few have embraced online potential fully.

- Most U.S. newspapers are local, the nation having only three national dailies.

- The most highly regarded U.S. newspaper is the New York *Times*.

- Most leading U.S. newspapers are metropolitan dailies, although their number has dwindled.

- Gannett has committed its 85 dailies to online sites as readers' first stop for news.

Mary Junck. *She returned to her Iowa roots but not for life on a farm. Junck heads the Lee newspaper chain.*

U.S. newspapers, facing declining advertising revenue in a sour economy, were cutting back on newsroom budgets.

If anyone asks Junck about Lee's priorities, she whips out a business card with a five-point mission statement. There, prominently, is, "Emphasize strong local news." Other Junck priorities: "Grow revenue creatively and rapidly. Improve readership and circulation. Build our online future. Exercise careful cost controls."

To those who see only gloom and doom for newspapers, Mary Junck's message might seem Pollyanna-like, but don't tell that to the shareholders in Lee Enterprises. The company's doing well, thank you. Note, too, that Junck sees Lee's products as more than ink on paper. After all, one of her business card admonitions is "Build our online future."

Newspaper Industry

STUDY PREVIEW

The newspaper industry is in crisis even though still large, profitable and dominant in local coverage. Readers younger than 40 are increasingly hard to find. Attempts to reach younger readers have included flashy big-city tabloids designed as quick reads.

NEWSPAPER INDUSTRY DIMENSIONS

The newspaper industry dwarfs other news media by almost every measure. More than one out of three people in the United States reads a newspaper every day, far more than tune in the network news on television in the evening. The data are staggering:

- About 1,570 daily newspapers put out 52.4 million copies a day, more on Sundays. Because each copy is passed along to an average of 2.2 people, daily newspapers reach 116 million people a day.
- Weekly newspapers put out 50 million copies. With their estimated pass-along circulation of four people a copy, these newspapers reach somewhere around 200 million people a week.

Perhaps because television has stolen the glitz and romance that newspapers once had, the significance of newspapers is easy to miss. But the newspaper industry is large by every measure. In an article marveling at an issue of a newspaper as "the daily creation," the Washington *Post's* Richard Harwood, writing about his own newspaper, said: "Roughly 11,000 people are involved in the production and distribution each day, enough bodies to fill all the billets of an Army light infantry division." Although Harwood stretched to include even the delivery boys and girls in his startling number, his point is valid: In Washington and everywhere else, newspapers far outdistance other news media in the number of people who gather, edit and disseminate news.

Although newspaper revenue is slipping, newspapers are a medium of choice for advertising. Daily newspapers attracted $44.9 billion in advertising in 2004. Over-air television stations were second at $42.5 billion.

Except for brief downturns in the overall economy and an occasional exceptional situation, daily newspapers were consistently profitable enterprises through the 20th century. Less than double-digit returns on investment were uncommon. Although facing difficult times, the newspaper is not to be underrated.

LEARNING CHECK ◀

▶ Newspapers face challenges with readership declines but remain important. How so?

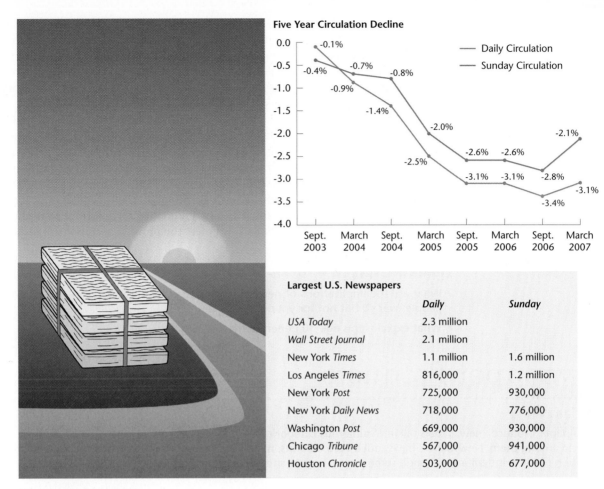

Five Year Circulation Decline

	Daily Circulation	Sunday Circulation

Data points (Daily Circulation): -0.1%, -0.7%, -0.8%, -2.0%, -2.6%, -2.6%, -2.8%, -2.1%

Data points (Sunday Circulation): -0.4%, -0.9%, -1.4%, -2.5%, -3.1%, -3.1%, -3.4%, -3.1%

Time axis: Sept. 2003, March 2004, Sept. 2004, March 2005, Sept. 2005, March 2006, Sept. 2006, March 2007

Largest U.S. Newspapers

	Daily	*Sunday*
USA Today	2.3 million	
Wall Street Journal	2.1 million	
New York *Times*	1.1 million	1.6 million
Los Angeles *Times*	816,000	1.2 million
New York *Post*	725,000	930,000
New York *Daily News*	718,000	776,000
Washington *Post*	669,000	930,000
Chicago *Tribune*	567,000	941,000
Houston *Chronicle*	503,000	677,000

Newspaper Circulation

No matter how you slice the numbers, daily newspaper circulation is in trouble in the United States. Using 2003 as a base, the Audit Bureau of Circulations has found consistent drops in its six-month tabulations, albeit an uptick in the period ending in March 2007. Even so, daily circulation had dropped more than 2 percent over five years and Sunday circulation had dropped more than 3 percent.

CONTENT: DIVERSITY AND DEPTH

In most communities, newspapers cover more news at greater depth than competing media. A metropolitan daily such as the Washington *Post* typically may carry 300 items and many more on Sundays—more than any Washington television or radio station and at greater length. City magazines in Washington, for example, offer more depth on selected stories, but the magazines are published relatively infrequently and run relatively few articles. Nationally, no broadcast organization comes close to the number of stories or the depth of the two major national newspapers: the *Wall Street Journal* and *USA Today*.

Newspapers have a rich mix of content—news, advice, comics, opinion, puzzles and data. It's all there to tap into at will. Some people go right for the stock market tables, others to sports or a favorite columnist. Unlike radio and television, you don't have to wait for what you want.

People like newspapers. Some talk affectionately of curling up in bed on a leisurely Sunday morning with their paper. The news and features give people something in common to talk about. Newspapers are important in people's lives, and as a medium they adapt to changing lifestyles. The number of Sunday newspapers, for example, grew from 600 in the 1970s to almost 900 today, reflecting an increase, at least for a few years, in people's weekend leisure time for reading and shopping. Ads in weekend papers are their guide for shopping excursions.

All this does not mean that the newspaper industry is not facing problems from competing media, new technology and ongoing lifestyle shifts. Until recently newspapers have reacted to change with surprising effectiveness. To offset television's inroads, newspapers have put new emphasis on being a visual medium and have shed their drab graphics for color and aesthetics. To accommodate the work schedule transition of Americans over recent decades from factory jobs starting at 7 a.m. to service jobs starting at 9 a.m., newspapers have emphasized morning editions, now that more people have a little extra time in the morning, and phased out afternoon editions, because more people are at work later in the day. Knowing that the days of ink-on-paper technology are limited, the newspaper industry has begun a transition to Web delivery.

Some problems are truly daunting, such as the aversion of many young people to newspapers. Also, chain ownership has raised fundamental questions about how well newspapers can do their work and still meet the profit expectations of distant shareholders.

LEARNING CHECK ◄

▶ **What are the implications of newspapers as essential lifestyle products for most people over 40 but not for younger people?**

▶ **What explains this age-40 generational dividing line?**

Newspaper Products

STUDY PREVIEW

As ink-on-paper products, newspapers fall into numerous categories—broadsheet and tabloid among them. Newspapers have added Web editions, mostly an online presentation of the print edition although some papers update sites during the day.

PRINT PRODUCTS

● **Benjamin Day**
Published the New York *Sun*

● **New York *Sun***
The first penny newspaper, 1833

● **broadsheet**
A newspaper format with full-size pages, typically six columns wide and 22 or 24 inches long

● **tabloid**
A newspaper format with pages half the size of a broadsheet; typically five columns wide and 14 to 18 inches long; *tab* for short; not necessarily sensationalistic despite a connotation the term has acquired

● **New York *Daily News***
Defined *tabloid* in public thinking as a word for sensationalism; founded 1919

The first modern newspapers in the Penny Press period were pint-size. **Ben Day's** pioneering **New York *Sun*** of 1833 was the size of a handbill. As large, steam-powered presses were introduced and as paper supplies became plentiful, page sizes grew into what came to be called **broadsheets.** Some were so wide that pages had nine two-inch columns per page, although 50-inch paper, folded into 25-inch-wide pages, became standard until the 1980s. Today, pages are more compact, most at five columns on a page. The size reduction has saved newsprint, a costly raw ingredient. A downside: Less room for news.

The word **tabloid** got its tawdry, second-rate connotation from papers featuring eye-catching but sensationalizing headlines; but newspaper people use the word in a professional sense for a half-size newspaper that is convenient to hold. Ironically, considering the association of the words *tabloid* and *sensationalism,* none of the papers in the sensationalistic Yellow Press period were tabloids—with the exception of a one-day experiment by New York publisher Joseph Pulitzer on the first day of the 20th century to illustrate the newspaper of the future.

Inspired by sensationalistic sheets that were the rage in London, two scions of the Chicago *Tribune* fortune, Joseph McCormick and Joseph Patterson, created the **New York *Daily News*** in 1919 as a photo-strong tabloid. Its wacky news selection and emphasis on crime, sex and disaster made it a quick success. Although shunned by the newspaper establishment, the *Daily News* quickly found a following. Soon it had the largest circulation in the country and redefined the term *tabloid* in the popular lexicon. There were a few imitators, mostly in cities with commuters, who preferred the handy size to read in their cramped bus and train seats on the way to work.

In recent years, with continuing readership declines, especially among young adults, newspaper executives have discovered through surveys that people prefer compact newspapers.

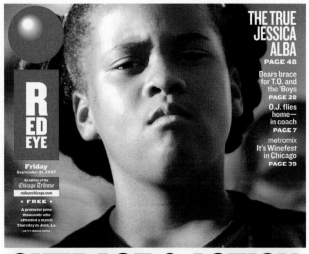

Downsizing. *Broadsheet newspapers, usually with six columns to a page, are dabbling with handier tabloid editions like the Chicago Tribune's Red Eye. A single standard for tabloid page sizes is expected to be adopted by newspaper publishers to make it easier for advertisers. Right now there are four sizes, the most popular being the roughly 8 1/2 by 11 inches and the 17-inch deep Berliner.*

Laura Gordon, in charge of a Dallas *Morning News* tabloid variation called *Quick*, makes the point that tabloids are portable in ways that broadsheets aren't: "We call it the Taco Test, the idea that you can have a newspaper open and have a taco at Taco Bell without going into other people's space."

Some dailies, including the San Francisco *Examiner*, have taken a sudden plunge. Others are testing the water. The broadsheet Chicago *Tribune* has a *RedEye* tabloid edition geared to commuters. Not to be outdone, the Chicago *Sun-Times*, historically a tabloid, rolled out a *Red Streak* edition that's snappier and more tightly edited. In London the *Times* has twin versions: one broadsheet, one tabloid. The *Independent* switched completely. Other papers have converted inside sections to tabloid to get a feel for what a fuller transition would be like.

Still, the word *tabloid* carries a stigma. Newspaper designer Mario Garcia tells about one client who, when commissioning a redesign into a tabloid format, couldn't bring himself to use the word. Alternatives include *compact newspaper* and *laptop newspaper*.

LEARNING CHECK ◄••

▸ **Is the trend in the newspaper industry toward broadsheets or tabloids?**

▸ **How did the word *tabloid* become corrupted to mean tawdry sensationalism?**

WEB EDITIONS

● **shovelware**
Posting newspaper stories on the Web after they've been published in a print edition, thereby "shoveling" them online

The Albuquerque, New Mexico, *Tribune* created the first newspaper Web site in 1992. It was **shovelware,** taking items from the print edition for reading on the Web without much adaptation. But it was a start. Other newspapers picked up on the idea, testing whether online readership would attract additional advertising. Early newspaper sites were not instant moneymakers, but they gave newspapers a foothold in the new medium and didn't cost much.

When blogs became the rage in the 2004 elections, *USA Today* put columnists and reporters online to interact with readers. The newspaper, in effect, made itself a host to reader chatrooms on a wide range of subjects. Said editor Ken Paulson: "It's about responding to news." Other papers followed.

Newspaper-sponsored blogs are not without difficulties, among them the traditional U.S. journalistic premise that news needs to be presented in a detached, neutral tone. Joe Strupp, writing in the trade journal *Editor & Publisher*, put it this way: "Reporting can stray into the quicksand of opinion—leaving many writers wishing they had kept their mouths shut." At this point in the evolution of news blogging, the idea is for reporters to go beyond carefully crafting stories toward engaging in a spontaneous dialogue to add dimension, background and interpretation—more than appears in their print coverage.

Most newspaper Web sites, however, are relatively weak compared to their potential.

LEARNING CHECK ◄

▶ How do you explain newspapers' not being innovators in online news?

▶ Can reporters in online interactive conversations avoid what's been called "the quicksand of opinion"?

FREE DISTRIBUTION

Experiments with free mini-editions have been conducted in several European cities and then imitated in the United States. Designed as quick reads, the papers, issued weekdays, boil down content into snappy tidbits aimed at mass transit commuters. Lots of the content is entertainment-oriented and of a gee-whiz variety, which editors perceive to be of interest to the elusive 20-something and 30-something readers. The question, still up in the air, is whether these sheets will attract sufficient long-term advertising for them to remain viable giveaways.

LEARNING CHECK ◄

▶ What is the content of giveaway dailies?

▶ Do free-distribution papers, with their superficial, amusement-oriented thrust, insult young readers? Or is this what young adults want?

Newspaper Ownership

STUDY PREVIEW

High profits in the newspaper industry fueled the growth of chains, which consolidated the ownership of U.S. newspapers into fewer and fewer major companies. Some chains have dissolved in recent years, with ownership of some individual papers shifting to local interests. Absentee investor groups also have picked up papers.

CHAIN OWNERSHIP

● **William Randolph Hearst**
Newspaper chain owner who dictated the contents of all his newspapers

● **newspaper chain**
A single ownership of multiple newspapers

Reasoning that he could multiply profits by owning multiple newspapers, **William Randolph Hearst** put together a chain of big-city newspapers in the late 1880s. Although Hearst's chain was not the first, his empire became the model in the public's mind for much that was both good and bad about **newspaper chains.** Like other chains, Hearst expanded into magazines, radio and television. The trend toward chain ownership continues, and today 160 chains own four of every five dailies in the United States. Chain ownership is also coming to dominate weeklies, which had long been a bastion of independent ownership.

Newspapers' profitability skyrocketed in the 1970s and 1980s, which prompted chains to buy up locally owned newspapers, sometimes in bidding frenzies.

Single-newspaper cities were especially attractive because no competing media could match a local newspaper's large audience. It was possible for new owners to push ad rates up rapidly. Local retailers, with no place else to put ads, had to go along. The profit potential was enhanced because production costs were falling dramatically with fewer labor-intensive back-shop procedures, computerized typesetting and other automation. Profits were dramatic. Eight newspaper companies tracked by *Forbes* magazine from 1983 to 1988 earned the equivalent of 23.9 percent interest on a bank account. Only soft drink companies did better.

● **Gannett**
A leading U.S. newspaper chain with 90 dailies

The **Gannett** media conglomerate's growth typifies how newspapers became chains and then grew into cross-media conglomerates. In 1906 the chain consisted of six upstate-New York newspapers. By 1982 Gannett had grown to more than 80 dailies, all profitable medium-size newspapers. Swimming in money, Gannett launched *USA Today*. Gannett not only absorbed *USA Today*'s tremendous start-up costs for several years but also had enough spare cash to outbid other companies for expensive metropolitan newspapers. In 1985 and 1986 Gannett paid $1.4 billion for the Detroit *News*, Des Moines *Register* and Louisville *Courier-Journal*. Along the way, Gannett acquired Combined Communications, which owned 20 broadcasting stations. Today Gannett owns 99 daily newspapers, 39 weeklies, 16 radio stations, 21 television stations, 130 Web sites, the largest billboard company in the nation and the Louis Harris polling organization. It bought a Sunday newspaper magazine supplement, *This Week*, beefed it up and renamed it *USA Weekend*. No longer just a newspaper chain, Gannett has become a mass media conglomerate.

● **local autonomy**
Independence from chain headquarters

Is chain ownership good? The question raised in Hearst's time was whether diverse points of view were as likely to get into print if ownership were concentrated in fewer and fewer hands. Although all the Hearst newspapers were once required to run editorials written in the home office, such is an exception to most chain practices today. Newspaper chains are more oriented to profits than manipulating public dialogue on a large scale. Executives at the headquarters of most chains focus on management and leave news coverage and editorials to local editors. While **local autonomy** is consistent with U.S. journalistic values, a corporate focus on profits raises a dark new question: Are chains so myopic about profits that they forget good journalism? The answer is that the emphasis varies among chains.

■ **Journalistic Emphasis.** Some chains, such as the New York Times Company, whose properties include the flagship New York *Times* and the Boston *Globe*, are known for their journalism. The *Times* won a record seven Pulitzers, most for its coverage of the September 11, 2001, attack on the World Trade Center.

■ **Balanced Emphasis.** Most chains are known for undistinguished though profitable newspapers. This is an apt description for Gannett.

■ **Profit Emphasis.** Several chains, including Media News, have a pattern at new acquisitions of cutting costs aggressively, reducing staffs and trimming news coverage. It is not uncommon for a new chain owner to fire veteran reporters and editors, in some cases almost halving the staff. To save newsprint, some chains cut back the number of pages. They hire inexperienced reporters right out of college, pay them poorly and encourage them to move on after a few months so that they can be replaced by other eager but inexperienced, and cheap, new reporters. The result is a reporting staff that lacks the kind of local expertise that is necessary for good journalism. Only the shareholders benefit.

In general, the following realities of chain ownership work against a strong local journalistic enterprise:

● **absentee ownership**
When a company's headquarters is located in a faraway city

■ **Absentee Ownership.** Chain executives are under pressure to run profitable enterprises, which works against good, aggressive journalism that can strain a newsroom budget. Under **absentee ownership** the top chain executives do not live in the communities that are shortchanged by decisions to emphasize low-cost news.

NEWSPAPER CHAINS—PRO AND CON

Here are the largest U.S. newspaper chains, ranked by number of dailies, with a sample of their major properties:

	Daily Circulation	Number of Dailies
McClatchy Miami *Herald*, Sacramento *Bee*, St. Paul *Pioneer Press*, Charlotte *Observer*	9.5 million	43
Gannett *USA Today*, Des Moines *Register*, Detroit *News*, Louisville *Courier-Journal*	7.6 million	86
Lee Enterprises St. Louis *Post-Dispatch*, Tucson *Daily Star*, Lincoln *Journal Star*	1.7 million	58
Tribune Company Los Angeles *Times*, Chicago *Tribune*, Baltimore *Sun*, Long Island *Newsday*	2.8 million	11
New York Times New York *Times*, Boston *Globe*, Florida dailies	1.7 million	26
Newhouse Cleveland *Plain Dealer*, New Orleans *Times-Picayune*, Newark *Star Ledger*	2.9 million	26

■ **Transient Management.** The local managers of newspapers owned by chains tend to be career climbers who have no long-term stake in the community their newspaper serves. News executives generally are not promoted from within a newspaper but are appointed by corporate headquarters. Generally these executives have short-term goals to look good to their corporate bosses so that they can be promoted to better-paying jobs with more responsibility at bigger newspapers in the chain.

■ **Weak Entry-Level Salaries.** The focus of newspaper chains on keeping costs down to enhance profits has worked against strong salaries for journalists. By 2008 entry-level salaries typically were $20,000 to $25,000 at small chain-owned dailies. The result has been a brain drain. Many talented reporters and editors leave newspapers for more lucrative jobs in public relations and other fields.

■ **High Newsroom Turnover.** Cost-conscious policies at many chain newspapers encourage newsroom employees to move on after a few pay raises so that they can be replaced by rookies at entry-level salaries. This turnover can denude a newsroom of people who are knowledgeable about the community the newspaper serves, thus eroding coverage.

LEARNING CHECK ◄ ┄┄┄┄┄┄┄┄┄┄┄┄┄┄┄┄┄┄┄┄┄┄┄┄┄┄┄┄┄┄┄┄┄

▶ **How did chains come to dominate the U.S. newspaper industry?**

OWNERSHIP TRENDS

The consolidation of the newspaper industry into a few giant chains may have peaked. In recent years some chains have faltered, liquidating their assets to the highest bidders. In some cases, other chains have gobbled up the properties. In other cases, papers have moved into private hands, sometimes local.

■ **Family Dramas.** For generations the Bancroft heirs of Dow Jones, whose flagship is the *Wall Street Journal*, had maintained the family commitment to quality journalism. Outside shareholders, however, had pressed for better returns on their investments. Gradually some heirs became less interested in newspapers. When media magnate Rupert Murdoch, known mostly for Fox television, put up $5 billion to buy the company in 2007, the Bancrofts sold.

The Sulzbergers and related heirs to the New York Times Company have faced the same kind of pressure to sell. Outside investors see more profit potential in these properties than has been generated by the families, which have maintained solid profits but balanced them with the long-term value of good journalism. The Tribune Company, known for the historically significant Chicago *Tribune*, Los Angeles *Times* and Baltimore *Sun*, also has been on the sales block.

Loyalists shudder at the prospects of a bottom-line tycoon like Murdoch taking over the papers. At the *Journal*, the employees' union tried to organize a counteroffer bankrolled by a Los Angeles investor, but Murdoch had wherewithal that could not be matched.

■ **Chain Buyers.** The Knight-Ridder chain, whose papers have amassed many Pulitzers over the years, fell on bad times with high-cost operations in Miami, Philadelphia and Detroit. Employees fretted about the quality of the papers in which they had invested their careers. Readers were concerned too. There was relief when a second respected chain, McClatchy, offered to buy Knight-Ridder assets.

■ **Investment Bankers.** Not all Knight-Ridder papers remained with McClatchy, however. In Minnesota, the deal gave McClatchy the competing dailies in Minneapolis and St. Paul. To address anti-trust concerns, McClatchy sold the Minneapolis *Star Tribune* to a Boston investment banking firm. *StarTrib* people began engaging in guessing games regarding what would happen next. Investment bankers' job is to manage money for well-heeled individuals and institutions whose goal is simple, the highest return possible. These companies generally slash costs to reap revenue quickly in order to turn their acquisitions around for resale.

■ **Local Investors.** In a reversal of the phenomenon of absentee ownership through chains, some papers have returned to local hands when chains have liquidated. The Philadelphia *Inquirer* went from Knight-Ridder to a Philadelphia group of buyers. In Los Angeles, a hometown group of movie moguls looked carefully when the Tribune Company put the Los Angeles *Times* up for sale, although nothing came of it. Critics of chain ownership in general applaud a return to local ownership because theoretically the owners would be more likely to have a stake in community service, not merely extracting maximum profits.

LEARNING CHECK ◄ ••

▶ **Why is the role of chains in the U.S. newspaper industry diminishing?**

▶ **What new patterns of newspaper ownership are emerging?**

CLUSTERS

Once, newspaper chains bought available papers anywhere they could find them. No more. Today, chains try to acquire newspapers with adjoining circulations to cut costs. By the year 2000, more than 400 dailies—about a quarter of the total— were in what is called a **cluster.** Among its 26 papers the Newhouse chain, for

● **cluster**
Jointly owned, geographically nearby newspapers

example, has eight dailies across southern Michigan. The papers come off the same press, reducing the expense of having several multimillion-dollar presses at the individual newspapers. In some clusters, editors are not in the hometown but 30 or even 70 miles away. Clustering eliminates competition for advertisers that seek customers in several communities because cluster papers offer merchants a one-stop place to run all their ads.

Clusters have downsides. Critics say that out-of-town supervising editors lose touch with the communities that the papers serve. Also, editors face pressure to look for stories that can go in multiple papers, reducing news-gathering expenses—and also reducing the traditional local orientation, a historic hallmark of U.S. newspapers. Overall, fewer voices are present in the marketplace.

Proponents argue that clustering creates economies that can save newspapers that otherwise would go under.

LEARNING CHECK ◄ ··

▶ **What are the upsides and downsides of cluster ownership of newspapers?**

National Dailies

··

STUDY PREVIEW

Although a nation of mostly local newspapers, the United States has two firmly established dailies. The flashy *USA Today*, founded in 1982, overcame doubters to become the largest-circulation daily in the United States. Close behind is the *Wall Street Journal*.

USA TODAY

● ***USA Today***
A Gannett national daily founded in 1981

A strict format, snappy visuals and crisp writing give ***USA Today*** an air of confidence and the trappings of success, and the newspaper has its strengths. In less than a decade, circulation reached 1.6 million. By 2007 *USA Today* was at 2.3 million, passing the *Wall Street Journal*. Gannett executives exude certainty about long-term prospects. The optimism is underscored by the confident if not brash page-one motto: "The Nation's Newspaper."

Unlike most U.S. dailies, *USA Today* has built its circulation mostly on single-copy sales and bulk sales, not individual subscriptions. *USA Today* sells mostly to business travelers who are on the road and want a quick fix on the news. Many of *USA Today*'s sales are at airport newsracks, where many buyers are corporate executives and middle-management travelers away from home. Gannett offers deep discounts to upscale hotels to buy the papers in bulk and slip them under guests' doors as a free morning courtesy. Stories strain to be lively and upbeat to make the experience of reading the paper a positive one. Most *USA Today* stories are short, which diverts little of a reader's time from pressing business. The brevity and crispness of *USA Today*, combined with the enticing graphics and the razzle-dazzle compendium of blurbs, earned the newspaper the derisive nickname "McPaper" after being introduced in September 1982.

● **Allen Neuharth**
Creator of *USA Today*

While being true to founder **Allen Neuharth's** original concept, *USA Today* also has evolved. In the mid-1990s editor David Mazzarella introduced longer, weightier stories and depth and enterprise coverage, albeit without sacrificing the blurb-like short stories that gave readers a quick fix on the news. In 1999 a new editor, Karen Jurgensen, began fine-tuning the newspaper in a third phase. Without sacrificing the original snappy graphic personality, Jurgensen has pushed reporters to scoop competitors on major stories and to emphasize thoroughness and depth in their enterprise coverage. Although Jurgensen doesn't have the resources to match the largest news organizations, she has enough to break important stories on a regular basis: 400 reporters, 20 U.S. bureaus and four foreign bureaus.

The introduction of *USA Today* came at a time when most newspapers were trying to distinguish themselves from television news with longer, exploratory and interpretive stories. While some major newspapers such as the New York *Times* and

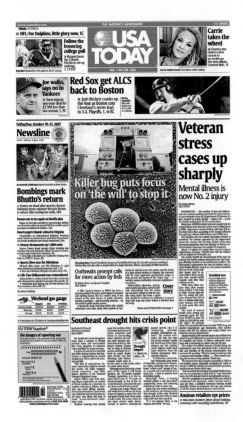

Graphics Innovator. *Since its founding in 1982, USA Today has had a profound impact on many other newspapers. The most obvious influence has been to establish newspapers as a strong visual medium with color and graphics integrated with words. The newspaper's weather coverage and high story counts also have been widely imitated.* USA Today *is designed for travelers and as a "second buy" for people who have already read their hometown daily. Subscriptions are only a small part of* USA Today's *circulation. Most sales are in distinctive TV-shaped newsracks and in airports, hotels and places where travelers pick it up for a quick fix on the news. Guaranteed in every issue are at least a few sentences about what's happening in news and sports from every state in the Union.*

Allen Neuharth

the Los Angeles *Times* were unswayed by *USA Today*'s snappy, quick-to-read format, many other newspapers moved to shorter, easily digested stories, infographics and more data lists. Color became standard. *USA Today* has influenced today's newspaper style and format.

LEARNING CHECK ◀ ••••••••••••••••••••••••••••••••••••••

▸ **What makes *USA Today* a distinctive newspaper?**

▸ **How has *USA Today* changed from the original Allen Neuharth concept? Evaluate these changes.**

WALL STREET JOURNAL

● **Wall Street Journal**
The second-largest U.S. daily newspaper

● **Charles Dow**
The cofounder of the *Wall Street Journal* in 1882

● **Edward Jones**
The cofounder of the *Wall Street Journal* in 1882

● **Barney Kilgore**
Created the modern *Wall Street Journal*

The ***Wall Street Journal,*** until recently the nation's largest newspaper, began humbly. **Charles Dow** and **Edward Jones** went into business in 1882. They roamed the New York financial district for news and scribbled notes by hand, which they sent by courier to their clients. As more information-hungry investors signed up, the service was expanded into a newsletter. In 1889 the *Wall Street Journal* was founded. Advertisers eager to reach *Journal* readers bought space in the newspaper, which provided revenue to hire correspondents in Boston, Philadelphia and Washington. By 1900 circulation had reached 10,000, and it grew to 30,000 by 1940.

The *Wall Street Journal* might have remained a relatively small albeit successful business paper had it not been for the legendary **Barney Kilgore,** who joined the newspaper's San Francisco bureau in 1929. Within two years Kilgore was the *Journal's* news editor and in a position to shift the newspaper's journalistic direction. Kilgore's formula was threefold:

- Simplify the *Journal's* business coverage into plain English without sacrificing thoroughness.
- Provide detailed coverage of government but without the jargon that plagued most Washington reporting at the time.
- Expand the definition of the *Journal's* field of coverage from "business" to "everything that somehow relates to earning a living."

Drab but Read. *The* Wall Street Journal, *the nation's largest daily, relies on its reputation for accurate and thorough reporting and good writing to attract readers. Every day the front page looks the same, with lengthy general-interest stories jumping inside. Barney Kilgore shaped the* Journal's *distinctive look and approach to coverage after taking over as editor in the 1930s. Circulation today exceeds 2 million.*

Barney Kilgore

The last part of the formula, expanded coverage, was a risk. Critics told Kilgore that the newspaper's existing readers might switch to other financial papers if they thought the *Journal* was slighting business. Kilgore's vision, however, was not to reduce business coverage but to seek business angles in other fields and cover them too. It worked. Today, with circulation at 2 million, the *Journal* is the second-largest U.S. daily.

For advertisers, the *Journal's* attraction is more than circulation totals. The median household income of *Journal* readers is $124,600. That's a lot of discretionary income and exceeds even that of the readers of the New York *Times*, which is high at $95,400.

The *Journal* puts significant resources into reporting. It is not unusual for a reporter to be given six weeks to collect research for a major story. This digging gives the *Journal* big breaks on significant stories. Although a serious newspaper, the *Journal* is neither stodgy nor prudish. Lengthy page-one pieces range from heavy-duty coverage of national politics to such diverse and unexpected stories as a black widow spider outbreak in Phoenix, archaeological research into human feces to understand lifestyles of lost civilizations, and how the admiral of landlocked Bolivia's navy keeps busy.

The *Wall Street Journal* has 500 editors and reporters, but not all are at the newspaper's Manhattan headquarters. The *Journal* has 37 foreign and 14 domestic bureaus, and its European and Asian editions have their own staffs.

The challenge for the *Journal* has been finding a balance between its original forte—covering business—and its expanding coverage of broader issues. It is a precarious balance. Numerous business publications, including *Business Week* and the Los Angeles-based *Investor's Daily*, vie for the same readers and advertisers but have more compact packages, and numerous other national publications, including the newsmagazines, offer general coverage. So far, the *Journal* has succeeded with a gradual broadening of general coverage without losing its business readers. In 2004, to broaden its appeal further, the *Journal* added a Saturday edition.

Constructive Journalism. *Since its 1908 founding, the* Christian Science Monitor *has emphasized solution-oriented journalism. The* Monitor, *based in Boston, began as an antidote to sensationalistic newspapers, emphasizing accurate and truthful coverage to help people address serious problems facing humankind.*

Mary Baker Eddy

LEARNING CHECK

▸ How did the vision of Barney Kilgore make the *Wall Street Journal* a major player in U.S. journalism?

▸ What makes the *Wall Street Journal* attractive to many advertisers?

CHRISTIAN SCIENCE MONITOR

● **Mary Baker Eddy**
Founded the *Christian Science Monitor* in 1908

● **Christian Science Monitor**
A Boston-based national U.S. newspaper

Mary Baker Eddy, the influential founder of the Christian Science faith, was aghast at turn-of-the-century Boston newspapers. The Boston dailies, like papers in other major U.S. cities, were sensationalistic, overplaying crime and gore in hyperbolic battles to steal readers from each other. Entering the fray, Eddy introduced a newspaper with a different mission. Her **Christian Science Monitor,** founded in 1908, sought to deal with issues and problems on a higher plane and to help the world come up with solutions.

Nobody, least of all Mary Baker Eddy, expected such an intellectually oriented newspaper to make money, at least not right away, so the church underwrote expenses when subscriptions, newsstand sales and advertising revenue fell short. The *Monitor* sought subscriptions nationwide and abroad, and it developed a following. Though edited in Boston, the *Monitor* was conceived as an international, not a local, newspaper, and it became the first national daily newspaper in the United States.

The *Christian Science Monitor* tries to emphasize positive news, but it also deals with crime, disaster, war and other downbeat news, and it has won Pulitzer Prizes for covering them. The thrust, though, is interpretive, unlike the sensationalistic newspapers to which Mary Baker Eddy wanted an alternative. The *Monitor* does not cover events and issues to titillate its readers. Rather, as veteran *Monitor* editor Erwin Canham explained, the newspaper's mission is "to help give humankind the tools with which to work out its salvation." The *Monitor* is not preachy. In fact, only one plainly labeled religious article appears in each issue. The *Monitor* seeks to lead and influence by example.

Vanishing Foreign Correspondent

Journalist Jill Carroll, who was kidnapped in Iraq and held for 82 days, is part of a dying breed. In 2000 U.S. newspapers employed 282 foreign correspondents. That number increased slightly after 9/11, to 304. But by 2007, it fell to 239.

One editor estimates that's about one foreign correspondent per 1.3 million people in the United States.

Only four U.S. newspapers still have regular foreign correspondents: the Los Angeles *Times*, New York *Times, Wall Street Journal*, and Washington *Post*. Pamela Constable, who has reported from more than 35 countries and is now a deputy foreign editor at the *Post*, estimates that the typical foreign bureau costs at least $250,000 a year, and that can escalate to four times as much in high-security locations like Baghdad.

As readers switch from print to other news sources such as Web sites and blogs, newspapers are replacing bureaus, which require staffs, cars and family housing. "The erstwhile bureau chief in New Delhi or Cairo, chatting with diplomats over rum punches on the veranda, is now an eager kid with a laptop and an Arabic phrase book in her backpack," says Constable.

Some broadcast networks, particularly CNN and NPR, have expanded their foreign bureaus, but overall the thrust in coverage has been new, lower-cost global news sources. These include:

Dangerous Work. After being held in Baghdad by hostile guerrilla fighters for weeks, reporter Jill Carroll of the Christian Science Monitor *found her way to freedom. It's a dangerous job. By late 2007, the Committee to Protect Journalists had tallied 123 reporter deaths for all countries, including Iraq, since 2003 when the war began. Murder accounted for 83 deaths; crossfire or other acts of war for 40. In addition, 42 support workers such as translators, had been killed.*

- McClatchy, the third largest U.S. newspaper chain, is partnering with Yahoo in a project called Trusted Voices. Traditional news stories are a blend of the "regional expertise" of correspondents and "exclusive blog reports designed to guide readers in understanding the news from these regions." It plays on the Yahoo news platform.
- Voxant's TheNewsRoom portal makes it easy for news publishers to distribute video, print, audio and still-photo content—with embedded and trackable ads—to an infinite number of Web sites and blogs through its Viral Syndication Network.
- The Associated Press is collaborating with NowPublic.com to bring citizen content into AP's news gathering.
- NewAssignment.net calls itself an "experiment in open-source reporting" and is partially funded by Reuters and involves *Wired* magazine. Actually it's a kind of outsourcing. Everyday people, working or volunteering in their spare time, create content for the news agencies. It's called crowdsourcing.

In the future the new college grad eyeing foreign reporting, armed with a laptop and a visa, may find little opportunity. Thomson Financial is planning to have about a third of the stories for its new global news service be automatically generated by computers from standardized releases.

DEEPENING YOUR MEDIA LITERACY

EXPLORE THE ISSUE

Choose a news story that originated in a foreign country.

DIG DEEPER

Can you tell whether the story originated from a foreign correspondent working for a major U.S. news organization? Or from an independent reporter? Or from a government statement or other partisan source? Does knowing the source of the story affect how you think about it?

WHAT DO YOU THINK?

What do these new sources of news mean for the American people? Do you think, as Jill Carroll believes, that "the quality of the information provided by the news media determines to a large extent the quality of the national debate and resulting policies"?

The *Monitor's* circulation peaked at 239,000 in 1971, when public interest in news was high, especially interest in the domestic turmoil over the war in Vietnam. Since then, circulation has slipped. The *Monitor* has never developed a firm advertising base, relying instead on church subsidies. But Christian Science membership has slipped too. With the church's overall income estimated at only $8.5 million a year, it's not clear how much longer the church can afford to carry out Mary Baker Eddy's goal of a strong Christian Science presence in the news media.

LEARNING CHECK ◄ ···

▶ What has set the *Christian Science Monitor* apart from other U.S. daily newspapers since its founding?

▶ What would you say to someone who assumes the *Christian Science Monitor* is a proselytizing religious newspaper?

New York *Times*

STUDY PREVIEW

The reputation of the New York *Times* rests largely on its attempt to be a newspaper of record. Outstanding reporting through its history also has contributed to its standing. Today, the newspaper seeks to be both a major regional newspaper and, through a national edition, a national newspaper.

NEWSPAPER OF RECORD

● **New York *Times***
The most respected U.S. hometown daily

Not a library anywhere would want to be without a subscription to the **New York Times,** which is one reason that the *Times* boasts at least one subscriber in every county in the country. Since its founding in 1851, the *Times* has had a reputation for fair and thorough coverage of foreign news. A large, widely respected staff covers Washington. It is a newspaper of record, printing the president's annual state of the union address and other important documents in their entirety. The *Times* is an important research source, in part because the *Times* puts out a monthly and an annual index that lists every story. More than 100 years of the *Times* pages are available online in many libraries. The editorials are among the most quoted.

In an attempt to attract younger readers, the *Times* has followed the lead of other newspapers by adding some lighter fare to the serious coverage. In 2005 a Thursday style section was launched that includes more lifestyle-oriented advertising. The *Times* even added a 10-page "Funny Pages" section at the front of the glitzy Sunday *Magazine* that includes work by graphic artists, serialized genre fiction and a venue for humor writers called "True-Life Tales." The serious book review section and one of the world's most popular crossword puzzles remain.

LEARNING CHECK ◄ ···

▶ Why is a subscription to the New York *Times* a priority for libraries?

▶ What distinguishes New York *Times* content?

NEW YORK *TIMES* HERITAGE

From its founding in 1851, the New York *Times* has been a serious newspaper, but its journalistic reputation was cemented in the 1870s when courageous reporting brought down the city government.

● **William Marcy Tweed**
Corrupt New York leader in the 1860s and 1870s who was exposed by the New York *Times*

■ **Tweed Scandal.** City Council member **William Marcy Tweed** had built a fortune with fraudulent streetcar franchises, sales of nonexistent buildings to the city and double billing. In 1868 it all got worse: Tweed and like-minded crooks and scoundrels were swept into city offices in a landslide election, and the fraud grew like a spiderweb. The *Times* launched an exposé in 1870, which prompted Tweed to call on the *Times'* largest advertisers to withdraw their advertising. Tweed also

Old Gray Lady. *True to the graphic spirit of the 19th century, when it rose in eminence, the New York* Times *is sometimes called the Old Gray Lady of American journalism. Even after color photos were added in 1997, the* Times *had a staid, somber visual personality. The coverage, writing and commentary, however, are anything but dull, and it is those things that have made the* Times' *reputation as the world's best newspaper. The paper is distinguished by international and Washington coverage, which is drawn mostly from its own staff reporters rather than the news services that most other newspapers rely on. Among Sunday features is the colorful, splashy New York* Times *Magazine, which runs lengthy examinations on serious issues. Sunday's edition also has a serious book review magazine. The New York* Times *crossword puzzle is one of the most popular in the world. The* Times *carries no comics or horoscopes, which contributes to the tone and mystique that set the newspaper apart.*

● **George Jones**
New York *Times* reporter on the Tweed Ring scandal

spread whispers that the city could reclaim the *Times* building because the ownership of the land was in doubt. Neither the management of the *Times* nor the main reporter on the story, **George Jones,** was deterred. With documents leaked from a disgruntled city employee, the *Times* reported that the Tweed Gang had robbed the city of as much as $200 million. Desperate, Tweed sent an underling to offer Jones $5 million in hush money—a bribe to back off. Jones refused and sent the underling packing: "I don't think the devil will ever make a higher bid for me than that."

Eventually, Tweed fled to Spain. When caught and returned for trial, he was quoted as saying: "If I were 20 or 30 years younger, I would kill George Jones with my own bare hands." Tweed died in jail two years later, in 1878.

● **L. B. Sullivan**
Alabama police commissioner who sued the New York *Times* for libel over a 1960 anti-racial segregation advertisement

■ **Sullivan Libel Case.** In 1960, in the heat of the U.S. racial desegregation tensions, **L. B. Sullivan,** the Montgomery, Alabama, police commissioner, was incensed at criticism in an advertisement in the New York *Times* that promoted racial integration. He sued for libel and won in Alabama courts. The *Times* could have acquiesced, paid the court-ordered settlement and put the issue behind it, but the *Times* chose an

Platform Agnosticism. *The publisher of the New York* Times *says content trumps the delivery platform.*

The mass media are in dramatic transformation. Just ask Arthur Sulzberger Jr., publisher of the New York *Times*. Despite an impressive 1.2 million copies sold weekdays and 1.7 million Sundays, growth has leveled. The *Times* might be the world's best newspaper, but as with other traditional media, its glamour is fading as the audience and advertisers shift to newer, flashier alternatives. Too, Sulzberger knows that young people, unlike their parents and grandparents, don't read newspapers much.

This might all seem depressing for a newspaper executive whose family has run the *Times* since 1896. Sulzberger himself learned the family business as a *Times* reporter for six years. But he doesn't see himself as a newspaper guy. Sulzberger calls himself a "platform agnostic." It's an insightful term. He sees the *Times* as being not so much in the newspaper business as in the news business. The content generated by the *Times*, which has 1,200 journalists in the New York newsroom alone, is the company's greatest asset. Their coverage is the key. Less relevant is the medium, or platform, that conveys the messages.

As a platform agnostic, Sulzberger is jockeying both daringly and gingerly among options for delivering news. The company has invested heavily in its NYTimes.com and Boston.com Web sites, which score 35 percent profit margins some months—all from advertising. Imagine earning that kind of interest on your checking account.

There is an audience for news. Growth for the *Times*' online ventures is projected to climb as high as 40 percent a year. NYTimes.com gets 18 million hits a day, better than 10 times the number of copies of the newspaper that are sold.

In a bid for the under-30 set, the company has bought into a giveaway tabloid, *Metro Boston*.

In television the company produces acclaimed pieces for *Frontline, Nova* and other programs. The company has put $100 million into a partnership with Discovery Communications to create the Discovery Times cable channel.

None of this is entirely new. The *Times* has long been involved in other media, including books, magazines, radio and television, adroitly testing the waters of nonnewspaper vehicles, moving in and out as lessons are learned. It was the *Times*, for example, that created the celebrity magazine *Us Weekly*. Now the company is out of the magazine business. In television it owns eight stations.

Sulzberger recognizes, of course, that all newspapers aren't about to disappear. Most of this company's revenues are from the flagship newspaper, and although flat, the revenues are a hefty $3 billion a year.

Sulzberger has created a *Times* national edition, the first U.S. metro daily to do so. The national edition is printed on 20 presses scattered across the country for home delivery to compete for readers and advertisers against *USA Today* and the *Wall Street Journal* as well as magazines and television. Abroad, the company has bought 100 percent control of the Paris-based *International Herald Tribune*, a favorite of travelers and expatriates, with 240,000 subscribers in 180 countries. The company also owns the venerable Boston *Globe* and 15 small dailies, mostly in Massachusetts and Florida.

The common denominator in Sulzberger's strategy is high-quality journalism. No company spends more on news gathering, an estimated $300 million a year. Nor does any other company have a larger news staff. The *Times* has more Pulitzer Prizes—seven in 2002 alone, six for its coverage of the 9/11 terrorism attack the year before. In the power centers of government and business, the *Times* is a must-read.

Since the *Times* was founded in 1851 the paper's tradition has been that investing in journalism will yield its own rewards. The founders 150-some years ago didn't think much beyond their medium, the newspaper, for distributing news. Sulzberger does. The future for distribution, he says, is broadband media like the Internet. In the meantime the *Times* has legs in multiple media—print, video and the Internet.

WHAT DO YOU THINK?

▸ Is Arthur Sulzberger Jr.'s "platform agnosticism" a solution for newspaper survival?

▸ Is the New York *Times* more insulated than most newspapers from devastating circulation and advertising losses? Explain your assessment.

expensive appeal to the U.S. Supreme Court to prove a First Amendment principle about free expression. The decision in *Times* **v.** *Sullivan* came in 1964, establishing new rules on libel and untethering the U.S. news media from self-imposed restraints that had discouraged important albeit controversial reporting.

■ **Pentagon Papers.** After being leaked a copy of a secret government study on U.S. policy in the Vietnam war, the *Times* conducted an exhaustive examination of the documents and decided to run a series of articles based on them. The government ordered the *Times* to halt the series, creating a showdown between the free press and the secretive Nixon administration. Not to be intimidated, the *Times* took the so-called **Pentagon Papers** case to the U.S. Supreme Court, arguing that the people in a democracy need information to make intelligent decisions on essential issues like war and peace. The Supreme Court sided with the *Times*, adding new legal obstacles to government censorship temptations and further establishing the importance of the *Times* in U.S. history.

■ **Weapons of Mass Destruction.** A black mark for the *Times* occurred during the buildup to the U.S.-led invasion of Iraq. Government sources fed veteran reporter Judith Miller information that Iraq possessed weapons of mass destruction. Miller's stories, built on this false information from her sources, fueled early public enthusiasm for the war. Neither the *Times* nor other news organizations devoted the resources needed to check into the false pro-war propaganda that the government was selectively leaking. It was not a great journalistic moment. Also, it was not the *Times* alone that was suckered.

■ **Wiretaps.** The *Times* broke the story in 2006 that the National Security Agency was tapping telephone conversations of U.S. citizens without constitutionally required court authorization. President Bush stopped just short of calling the stories treasonous, declaring the secret wiretap program essential to the government's war on terrorism. The *Times* said it had proceeded with its stories only after exhaustive consideration of security issues versus civil liberties issues. President Bush, although steamed, decided against pursuing the issue legally. Armed with the information in the *Times'* revelations, private civil liberties groups independently pursued stronger protection for citizens from government intrusions.

LEARNING CHECK ◄ ···

▶ **What has contributed the most to the New York *Times'* journalistic reputation since its founding in 1851? List additional journalistic accomplishments of the *Times*.**

Hometown Newspapers

STUDY PREVIEW

The United States has 1,570 daily newspapers, most oriented toward covering hometown news and carrying local advertising. Big-city dailies are the most visible hometown newspapers, but medium-size and small dailies have made significant strides in quality in recent decades and have eroded the metro newspapers' outlying circulation.

METROPOLITAN DAILIES

In every region of the United States is a newspaper whose name is a household word. These are metropolitan dailies with extensive regional circulation. In New England, for example, the Boston *Globe* covers Boston but also prides itself on extensive coverage of Massachusetts state government, as well as coverage of neighboring states. The *Globe* has a Washington bureau, and it sends reporters abroad on special assignments.

When experts are asked to list the nation's best newspapers, the lists inevitably are led by the New York *Times*. Other newspapers with a continuing presence include the Baltimore *Sun*, Chicago *Tribune*, Dallas *Morning News*, Houston *Chronicle*,

NEWSPAPER MILESTONES

1600s

Oxford *Gazette*
Corantos carrying news of Parliament became regularized as first newspapers (1665)

Publick *Occurrences*
In Boston Ben Harris attempted first colonial newspaper (1690)

1700s

Daily *Courant*
In London Elizabeth Mallett launched first English-language daily (1702)

1800s

North *Star*
Abolitionist paper founded by Frederick Douglass (1847)

New York *Times*
Founded by Henry Raymond, George Jones as serious alternative to penny papers (1851)

Wall *Street Journal*
Founded by financial newsletter editors Charles Dow and Edward Jones (1882)

1900s

Christian *Science Monitor*
Founded by religious leader Mary Baker Eddy as an alternative to sensationalism (1908)

Foreign-Language Papers
Their numbers peaked in United States (1914)

New York *Daily News*
Founded as photo-heavy new-style tabloid by Joseph Patterson, Robert McCormick (1919)

USA *Today*
Founded by Gannett chain's Allen Neuharth as a national daily (1982)

Online
Albuquerque, New Mexico, *Tribune* created an online edition (1992)

2000s

Chains Falter
Historic newspaper chain Knight-Ridder sold (2006)

Dow Jones
Outside buyer makes offer for Dow Jones, including flagship *Wall Street Journal* (2007)

New York *Times*
New York Times Company under shareholder pressure to sell (2007)

The Maryland Gazette, 1765

Would new owner honor Bancroft family commitment to excellent journalism?

Christian Science Monitor ought to be alternative to rampant sensationalism

Gray Lady, under pressure

Chicago's Red Eye

PIVOTAL EVENTS

- Puritans established Cambridge Press (1638)
- Plague forces Parliament to evacuate London for Oxford (1665)

- Revolutionary War (1776–1781)

- In New York, first of penny papers (1833)
- U.S. Civil War (1861–1864)
- Yellow Kid cartoon character becomes namesake for press sensationalism (1894)
- Spanish–American War (1898)

- World War I (1914–1918)
- Great Depression (1930s)
- World War II (1941–1945)
- Television emerged as commercial medium (early 1950s)
- Vietnam War (1964–1973)
- Internet emerged as commercial medium (late 1990s)

- 9/11 terrorist attacks (2001)

- Iraq War (2003–)
- Hurricane Katrina (2005)

Los Angeles *Times*, Miami *Herald*, Minneapolis *Star Tribune*, Philadelphia *Inquirer*, St. Louis *Post-Dispatch* and Washington *Post*.

LEARNING CHECK ◄ ··

▶ Which U.S. dailies would you list as having reputations for journalistic excellence?

▶ Why do most Americans never see these papers?

HOMETOWN DAILIES

While metro dailies struggle with circulation and survival, smaller newspapers have maintained a grip on their audience. A 2006 survey by the National Newspaper Association found that more than 50 percent of the people in markets of fewer than 100,000 people regard the newspaper as their primary source of local news—more than triple for television, the closest rival. It's local news, which is not provided well by television, that keeps readers—local school news, sports and last night's zoning board meeting. The NNA survey found that 78 percent of readers rank coverage as good to excellent.

On the Web, local dailies also dominate. Eighty-seven percent of respondents to the NNA survey reported visiting their local paper's Web site at least once a week.

● **hometown daily**
Edited primarily for readers in a defined region

In sheer numbers, **hometown dailies** dominate the newspaper landscape. Fifty years ago people outside metropolitan areas needed to subscribe to both their local paper and a metro for a full account of the day's events. Today, more people outside major cities rely on a mix of coverage from their hometown dailies, television and the Web to keep up with what's going on beyond the horizon. With regional and fringe circulation of metros declining, coupled with soaring trucking costs, the metros have dropped their once-profitable regionally focused editions.

LEARNING CHECK ◄ ··

▶ How do newspapers rank as a news source for most Americans?

▶ How do newspapers fit into your mix of sources for daily news?

WEEKLIES

Weekly newspapers have deep historic roots serving communities and neighborhoods. In a changing media landscape, many of these papers are positioned to continue to fill their print and Web editions with information that their readers can't find elsewhere.

■ **Community Weeklies.** Weekly newspapers are making strong circulation gains, especially in suburban communities, and some have moved into publishing twice a week. In all, almost 8,000 weekly newspapers are published in the United States, with circulation approaching 50 million. Weeklies are received in almost 60 percent of the nation's households, up almost one-third from 1970.

To the discomfort of metro dailies, many advertisers are following their customers to the suburban weeklies. Advertisers have found that they can buy space in weeklies for less and reach their likeliest customers. Ralph Ingersoll, whose weeklies give fits to the daily Long Island *Newsday* in New York, explained it this way in an interview with *Forbes*: "If you're an automobile dealer on Long Island, you can pay, say, $14,000 for a tabloid page in *Newsday*, most of which is wasted because the people that get it will never buy a car in your neck of the woods, or you can go into one of the weekender publications and pay a few hundred dollars and reach just the people likely to drive over to your shop."

Some weeklies, particularly those in upscale suburbs, offer sophisticated coverage of community issues. Others feature a homey mix of reports on social events such as who visited whom for Sunday dinner. The success of these weeklies sometimes

● **telephone book journalism**
Journalism that emphasizes listing readers' names

is called **telephone book journalism** because of the emphasis on names, the somewhat overdrawn theory being that people buy papers to see their names in print. What weeklies have in common is that they cover their communities with a detail that metro dailies have neither staff nor space to match. There is no alternative to keeping up with local news.

■ **Rural Weeklies.** Rural weeklies generally have fallen on rough times. Part of their problem is the diminishing significance of agriculture to the national economy and the continuing depopulation of rural America. In communities that remain retail centers, rural weeklies can maintain a strong advertising base. However, the Main Street of many small towns has declined as improved roads and the construction of major retail stores like Wal-Mart draw customers from 40 to 50 miles away. In earlier days those customers patronized hometown retailers, who placed significant advertising in hometown weeklies. Today many of these Main Street retailers, unable to compete with giant discount stores, are out of business.

● **shopper**
An advertising paper without news

■ **Shoppers.** Free-distribution papers that carry only advertisements have become increasingly important as vehicles for classified advertising. In recent years **shoppers** have attracted display advertising that earlier would have gone to regular newspapers. Almost all shoppers undercut daily newspapers on advertising rates. The number of shoppers has grown to about 1,500 nationwide, and they no longer are merely an ignorable competitor for daily newspapers for advertising.

By definition, shoppers are strictly advertising sheets, but beginning in the 1970s some shoppers added editorial content, usually unsolicited material, such as publicity items and occasional self-serving columns from legislators. Some shoppers have added staff members to compile calendars and provide a modicum of news coverage. Most of these papers, however, remain ad sheets with little that is journalistic. Their news-gathering efforts and expenses are minuscule compared with those of a daily newspaper.

LEARNING CHECK ◄ •

▶ **Describe the range of newspapers that are published weekly.**

▶ **How are most weeklies buffered from the competition faced by daily newspapers?**

Gannett Initiative

STUDY PREVIEW

Readership in peril, the giant Gannett chain has begun a chainwide project to reconceive news gathering and delivery. All 85 local Gannett dailies went into a 24/7 mode. Reporting for the Web was made first priority. Planning the daily print edition comes later.

INFORMATION CENTERS

For years the newspaper industry was in denial. Wishful thinking was that circulation declines somehow were an aberration that would self-correct. At the giant chain Gannett, which operates *USA Today* and 85 hometown dailies in the United States, planners saw the reality: Newspapers were losing their foothold in people's lives, especially among the under-40 set. But news was hardly out of style. The reality was that people were looking elsewhere, mostly on the Web—Craigslist, Yahoo!, YouTube and countless blogs. As Jennifer Carroll, a Gannett vice president, put it: "Amazing disruptive events" were shaking the news business and leaving newspapers out.

In 2005 Gannett quietly began to lay out a blueprint to regain relevance. In tests at papers in Iowa, Florida and South Dakota, Gannett replaced traditional

Jennifer Carroll

21st-Century News. *With a postcard theme, artist Lonnie Busch captures the essence of the Gannett newspaper chain's Information Center 24/7 project. Every local Gannett daily has shifted its emphasis to Web delivery with beefed-up local coverage. Yes, there remain daily print editions but as a second product for over-40 readers who are more comfortable with ink on paper for their news. The architect of the Gannett initiative is Jennifer Carroll, vice president of new media content.*

newspaper newsrooms with what it called **Information Centers.** Reporters begin before dawn to update breaking stories on the Web for morning readers—in contrast to stories in the print edition that had been written the day before. No mere shovelware, the Web edition is fresh. News alerts go out for mobile phones during the day as events warranted. Web readers are invited to respond to stories and each other online. In effect, stories become jumping-off points for reader interactivity. Massive databases of community information are posted—school stats, municipal budgets, crime data. It is more than could ever fit in a print edition. Reporters are issued videocams to shoot for the Web. Readers are invited to post photos and items, even bowling league and bridge club notices.

The concept is intended to regain competitiveness by building on what newspapers have always done best, local news—but also with a panopoly of expanded services possible only online.

LEARNING CHECK ◄ ···

▸ **What are the "amazing disruptive events" that Gannett executive Jennifer Carroll cites as changing the landscape of news?**

▸ **In Gannett's new-media initiative, why is shovelware out?**

MOJOS AND SCOOPS

After test runs, the concept went live. Individual Gannett papers had their own take on the concept by 2008. The switch was hardly a budget buster. The corporation put only $3 million into the project for technology upgrades. That bought a lot of videocams. Of course, individual papers bore additional expenses.

Coverage of local breaking news is stronger with **mojos.** These mobile journalists, equipped with cell phones, laptops and videocams, are on the scene quickly and can report live. A few mojos in the field can generate lots of live reporting, not Pulitzer-winning stuff but live, exciting magnets for readers. The *Arizona Republic* has 15 college journalism students out every morning early, working part time for $10 an hour, for local coverage online.

In another innovation, the *Democrat and Chronicle* in Rochester, New York, posts a database of local sex offenders, which is updated regularly. Such data, from public records, is available elsewhere, but the newspaper is establishing itself as a quick resource—no frustrating searches, no inconsistent and confusing formats from different government agencies that usually design databases for their own reference instead of public consumption or convenience. Gannett's Louisville *Courier-Journal*, as you might expect, has a database that tracks Kentucky Derby racehorses—a regular must-visit for horse people.

LEARNING CHECK ◀ ⋯⋯⋯⋯⋯⋯⋯⋯⋯⋯⋯⋯⋯⋯⋯⋯⋯⋯⋯⋯⋯⋯

▶ **Is maintaining and updating huge databases a good use of a newspaper's resources in an era of shrinking newsroom staffs?**

GANNETT LESSONS

The Gannett initiative implicitly acknowledges how lethargic newspapers had become in local coverage. Without print competition, a function partly of the growth of chains like Gannett, the incentive to be on top of news in one-paper towns gradually had diminished. Local newspapers had a monopoly on news, and broadcasters were never much of a challenge.

Except for technological bells and whistles, a lot of the Gannett concept is old, really old stuff. The New York *Daily News* pioneered the mojo concept in 1919, although nobody called it that back then. The *Daily News* had photographers roving the city in cars equipped with two-way radios to get to breaking events quickly and shoot exclusives. The idea of being on-scene and breaking news live also has roots in radio in the 1930s. Think Lakehurst, New Jersey. Think Hindenburg. Lightweight video equipment in the 1980s gave local television stations a chance to go a mojo route, but stations never committed the staffs to do it well. Also, video transmission equipment was burdensome. Some lessons that Gannett is applying have been standard practices for more than a century with news agencies like the Associated Press, which are updating stories continuously. News agency editors and reporters have always had some client somewhere on deadline every minute.

It took the shock of Internet technology, which lured readers away from newspapers in massive numbers, to shake Gannett into a new reality: How well has the Information Center concept worked? In 2007, hits on the Parsippany, New Jersey, *Daily Record* Web site were up 49 percent, to 4.9 million a month. At the Melbourne *Florida Today*, Web traffic grew 72 percent. Some Gannett editors believe Web traffic has spurred sales of the print edition. In Rochester, New York, a Sunday edition with a collection of stories on sex-offense felons outsold every other Sunday edition of the year by 4.8 percent, following several days of much of the same content appearing piecemeal in the paper's Web site.

Although Gannett is upbeat about its initiative, early data were anecdotal. In any event, Gannett was rediscovering news with a host of new technology-enabled twists and recapturing readers. The financials look positive. The rest of the newspaper industry is tracking the project closely.

To be sure, there are downsides. By realigning newsroom staffs toward breaking spot news live, fewer resources are available for in-depth and investigative reporting. Would a local Tammany Hall scandal, which put the New York *Times* on the map in 1870, miss the radar in Sioux Falls, South Dakota, where the *Argus-Leader*, typical of the Gannett papers, has stretched its staff for the petite mojo scoops of the hour?

Also, stretching staff has added stress to newsroom jobs. The Newspaper Guild, a union representing newsroom employees, has filed grievances about workload pressure brought on by staff reductions and realignments not only at Gannett but also at other papers. Too, the pressure to post news quickly online leads to errors, some merely typographical, others more serious.

LEARNING CHECK ◄••

▸ **What is new in Gannett's Information Center project? What's old?**

▸ **Is journalism from Gannett newsrooms going to be better with the shifts introduced by the Information Center concept? Discuss.**

▸ **Are mojos a good idea? Discuss the pros and cons.**

➤Chapter Wrap-Up

Newspaper Industry (Page 78)

■ Pumping out 52.4 million copies a day, the U.S. newspaper industry is a significant purveyor of news and a significant vehicle for advertising. It's also a troubled industry. Readership is down. People are finding alternatives for news, many of them online. Attempts to gain younger readers, many who have no newspaper habit whatsoever, have had mixed results.

Newspaper Products (Page 80)

■ As an ink-on-paper product, newspapers fall into numerous categories—broadsheet and tabloid among them. Newspapers have added Web editions, mostly online presentations of the print editions, although some papers update their sites during the day.

National Dailies (Page 86)

■ The United States is mostly a nation of provincial newspapers, which reflects the nation's two-tiered decentralized system of government. But three national daily newspapers, all excellent in distinctive ways, have found success: *USA Today*, the *Wall Street Journal* and the *Christian Science Monitor*. A handful of other papers have tried for national editions, but mostly they have been edited adaptations of the core hometown product.

New York *Times* (Page 91)

■ The New York *Times* cemented its journalistic reputation with exposés on massive municipal corruption in 1870, standing up to threatened boycotts and spurning huge bribery offers. In the next century the *Times* fought all the way to the U.S. Supreme Court for the right to publish government-classified documents on the Vietnam war. In this case, involving the so-called Pentagon Papers, the *Times* championed the public's right to know. The *Times* also was a key player in the Watergate scandal revelations in the Nixon era. More recently the *Times* has revealed secret government wiretapping, thereby raising nettlesome civil liberties questions. So respected is the *Times*' journalistic judgment that no other news organization is more closely tracked day-in and day-out by other news organizations for what to put on their agendas of what's most worth reporting.

Hometown Newspapers (Page 94)

■ The core of the U.S. newspaper industry is hometown dailies, most of which are published without direct local competition. Many have widely recognized names—the Chicago *Tribune*, the Washington *Post*, the Los Angeles *Times*. Less widely recognized but nonetheless household words in their communities are 1,500 other dailies nationwide. Weeklies, most in smaller communities, are important local institutions.

Gannett Initiative (Page 97)

■ With readership in peril, the giant Gannett chain has begun a chainwide project to play to the inherent strength of its 85 local dailies—local news. A corporate-wide project, dubbed Information Center, strives to make each newspaper's Web site the place to which readers go first not only for news but also for an array of information services and participatory forums. The Web is first priority in every newsroom. Planning the daily print edition comes later. Early signs indicate that the project, which entered full gear in 2007, is attracting huge increases in online traffic and perhaps even goosing print sales.

REVIEW QUESTIONS

1. Describe the role of newspapers in the lives of most Americans.

2. Explain the role of newspaper chains. Have they been good for readers?

3. Why is the United States mostly a nation of provincial newspapers?

4. Why is the New York *Times* regarded as the best U.S. newspaper?

5. Many metropolitan newspapers have lost circulation. Some have shut down. Why?

6. Is Gannett on the right path in giving priority to Web delivery?

CONCEPTS

cluster (Page 85)

absentee ownership (Page 83)

shovelware (Page 81)

tabloid (Page 80)

TERMS

Pentagon Papers (Page 94)

New York *Times* (Page 91)

shopper (Page 97)

Wall Street Journal (Page 87)

PEOPLE

Mary Baker Eddy (Page 89)

George Jones (Page 92)

Barney Kilgore (Page 87)

Allen Neuharth (Page 86)

Charles Dow, Edward Jones (Page 87)

MEDIA SOURCES

● The major newspaper industry trade journal is *Editor & Publisher*.

● Numerous histories have been written on *USA Today, Wall Street Journal, Christian Science Monitor*, and New York *Times* and other leading newspapers.

● Gene Roberts and Thomas Kunkel, editors. *Breach of Faith: A Crisis of Coverage in the Age of Corporate Newspapering*. University of Arkansas, 2003. This collection of essays notes that newspapers have become more glitzy than ever but also formulaic and bland under new pressures from giant corporate owners.

In this chapter you have deepended your media literacy by revisiting several themes. Here are thematic highlights from the chapter:

Media Technology

Joseph Pulitzer outdid himself in the run-up to the Yellow Press period with an issue of the New York *World* at a record 200 pages. High-speed presses marked a new era—in contrast to only half a century earlier when papers were mostly four tablet-size pages. Newspapers as we know them are complex products of the Industrial Revolution. Technology, however, may be the comeuppance of newspapers as a print product. The industry is shifting rapidly to Internet delivery with 24/7 Web sites. **(Pages 80–81)**

Two Hundred Pages, 2¢ a Copy. *Joseph Pulitzer showed what high-speed presses could deliver.*

Media and Democracy

More than any other U.S. institution, the New York *Times* has crusaded against government interference with a free press. This includes the 1971 battle over publishing the Pentagon Papers, which riveted public attention on a courageous public-minded press against heavy-handed government secrecy. The people sided with the press. So did the U.S. Supreme Court. The *Times* invested heavily in winning another Supreme Court battle, the 1964 *Sullivan* decision, to loosen libel laws. The decision made it harder for public officials to sue over news they don't like. The *Times'* legacy for exposing corruption dates to 1870 and the outrageous Tammany Hall scandals. **(Pages 91–93)**

NEW YORK, SUNDAY, JUNE 13, 1971
The beyond 50-mile zone from New York City, except Long Island. Higher in air delivery cities. **BQLI 50 CENTS**

Vietnam Archive: Pentagon Study Traces 3 Decades of Growing U. S. Involvement

By NEIL SHEEHAN

A massive study of how the United States went to war in Indochina, conducted by the Pentagon three years ago, demonstrates that four administrations progressively developed a sense of commitment to a non-Communist Vietnam, a readiness to fight the North to protect the South, and an ultimate frustration with this effort—to a much greater extent than their public statements acknowledged at the time.

The 3,000-page analysis, to which 4,000 pages of official documents are appended, was commissioned by Secretary of Defense Robert S. McNamara and covers the American involvement in Southeast Asia from World War II to mid-1968—the start of the peace talks in Paris after President Lyndon B. Johnson had set a limit on further military commitments and revealed his intention to retire. Most of the study and many of the appended documents have been obtained by The New York Times and will be described and presented in a series of articles beginning today.

Three pages of documentary material from the Pentagon study begin on Page 35.

Though far from a complete history, even at 2.5 million words, the study forms a great archive of government decision-making on Indochina over three decades. The study led its 30 to 40 authors and researchers to many broad conclusions and specific findings, including the following:

¶That the Truman Administration's decision to give military aid to France in her colonial war against the Communist-led Vietminh "directly involved" the United States in Vietnam and "set" the course of American policy.

¶That the Eisenhower Administration's decision to rescue a fledgling South Vietnam from a Communist takeover and attempt to undermine the new Communist regime of North Vietnam gave the Administration a "direct role in the ultimate breakdown of the Geneva settlement" for Indochina in 1954.

¶That the Kennedy Administration, though ultimately spared from major escalation decisions by the death of its leader, transformed a policy of "limited-risk gamble," which it inherited, into a "broad commitment" that left President Johnson with a choice between more war and withdrawal.

¶That the Johnson Administration, though the President was reluctant and hesitant to take the final decisions, intensified the covert warfare against North Vietnam and began planning in the spring of 1964 to wage overt war, a full year before it publicly revealed the depth of its involvement and its fear of defeat.

¶That this campaign of growing clandestine military pressure through 1964 and the expanding program of bombing North Vietnam in 1965 were begun despite the judgment of the Government's intelligence community that the measures would not cause Hanoi to cease its support of the Vietcong insurgency in the South, and that the bombing was **Continued on Page 38, Col. 1**

NIXON CRITICIZED | **Vast Review of War Took a Year**

U.S. URGES INDIANS AND PAKISTANIS TO USE RESTRAINT

Calls for 'Peaceful Political Accommodation' to End Crisis in East Pakistan

FIRST PUBLIC APPEAL

Statement Is Said to Reflect Fear of Warfare if Flow of Refugees Continues

By TAD SZULC
Special to The New York Times

WASHINGTON, June 12—The United States appealed today to India and Pakistan to exercise restraint and urged the Pakistanis to restore normal conditions in East Pakistan through "peaceful political accommodation."

It was the first public statement by the United States on the situation in the subcontinent

Continued on Page 38, Col. 1

Vietnam Study. *The New York* Times *concluded that the public's need to know transcended the government's Top Secret classification.*

Audience Fragmentation

The newspaper industry is worried that its readership is dying off. Unlike earlier generations, young people don't pick up daily papers much. The diverse coverage has less appeal than it did to mass audiences of yore. The general-interest news product is losing favor as audiences fragment toward narrowly focused information.
(Pages 79–80)

Specialty Papers. *A tradition of specialized papers continues and grows today, with many in Spanish.*

FRONTERAS *is a joint venture of Universal Press Syndicate in the United States and Danilo Black in Mexico. Used by permission. All right reserved.*

Media Economics

The newspaper industry became a linchpin in the giant market economy that shaped American life in the latter 1800s. Newspapers were the dominant medium for advertisers to reach potential customers. As the audience has fragmented, so too have the choices of advertisers for media to reach those potential customers. Today, to maintain revenue flow, newspapers are following readers to the Web and hoping advertisers stick with them. The new mantra in the newspaper business: "We're not in the newspaper business. We're in the news business." It's a content-driven definition of the industry, which some industry leaders, including publisher Arthur Sulzberger Jr. of the New York *Times*, call platform-agnostic. (Pages 79–80 and Page 94)

Medium-Agnostic. *Arthur Sulzberger Jr. of the New York* Times *says the future of newspapers is news, not necessarily ink on paper.*

Media Effects

Highbrow. *The Sunday magazine in the New York* Times *suggests not just an ordinary mass audience.*

Many people shape their lifestyles around newspapers. For some people the Sunday paper is a ritual, something to cuddle up with in bed after sleeping in late. For many people, breakfast without orange juice and the morning paper is inconceivable. Conversely, newspapers reflect lifestyles. When blue-collar jobs dominated the economy, with shifts starting at 7 a.m. and ending at mid-afternoon, most newspapers published in the afternoon. As the economy shifted to 9-to-5 white-collar jobs, with people having less discretionary time in the evening, morning papers came to dominate. Today the transition of news to the Web, with newspapers moving to catch up with the shift, suggests that a new adaptation to reader lifestyles is occurring. (Pages 79–80)

Elitism and Populism

Since the Penny Press period, newspapers have been in two broad categories of audience appeal. The earliest penny papers, followed by their Yellow Press successors, sought the largest possible audience by loading up on lowbrow fare—crime and sex stories, attention-getting stunts, and horrific tales. The instant success of the New York *Daily News*, introduced in 1919 and modeled on photo-oriented London tabloids, demonstrated how successful pandering to mass tastes could be. For years the *Daily News* was the largest-circulation daily in the nation. The legacy lives on, in some papers more than others. There also has been a sufficiently large audience for more serious content. Throughout most of its history, dating to 1851, the New York *Times* has not been the circulation leader, but it has built an unshakable following for its thorough attention to world and national affairs. (Pages 91–96)

Visual Medium. *Although newspapers have carried photos since the 1880s, Allen Neuharth underscored newspapers as a visual medium with his flashy* USA Today *in 1982.*

5

Magazines

Downscale Success

In the button-down collar offices at Time Inc. headquarters in New York, Martha Nelson has to work at keeping her chin high. Nelson is editor of *People*. Although spectacularly successful, the magazine has gone downscale into celebrity coverage. This is not the Time way. Just look at *People's* serious-minded Time stable-mates, including *Fortune, Sports Illustrated* and *Time* itself. The upside for Time executives is that *People*, under Nelson, brings in far, far more revenue than any other Time title. The weekly is a money machine.

Also, *People* has buried the competition. The closest rival, *Us*, is a distant second with less than one-third of *People's* $1.5 billion annual revenue. *Star* and *In Touch* lag even more behind in the crowded celeb-mag field.

What is the Martha Nelson magic?

People began in 1974 as a spin-off of *Time* magazine's People section. Much of the early focus was on features of ordinary people doing extraordinary things. Over time more articles focused on celebrities, sometimes with a tabloid tone. Under Nelson, who became managing editor in 2002 at age 49, celebrity content has grown to more than 50 percent.

Too, Nelson has imposed a newsy if not breathless quality to coverage. "We're responding with much more speed than we once did," she told an interviewer from the trade journal *Variety*. For Nelson, in fact, a weekly issue is not frequent enough. She takes pride in using "the *People* reporting machine," as she calls it, to break news on the magazine's Web site. Page views quadrupled in 2006 to 500 million-plus.

LEARNING AHEAD

- Early magazines helped Americans find their unique culture.

- Magazine innovations have included long-form journalism and visuals.

- The vast majority of U.S. magazine titles are unavailable on newsracks.

- A few companies, some of them multimedia conglomerates, dominate U.S. magazines.

- Most magazines today are edited for segments of the mass audience.

- Magazines face challenges today from demassified sites and television.

Martha Nelson. *She has pushed celebrity coverage to new levels and made* People *dominant.*

Nelson bristles at critics who say that *People* is too aggressive and invasive in its coverage. Although there have been instances of reporters trespassing (one reporter was arrested in Brad Pitt's backyard), Nelson says she guards against going too far. Photographers are never assigned to stake out celebrities. A photo that looks like it was taken with a long lens gets special scrutiny.

Rumors? Nelson avoids publishing them until the facts are nailed down. When rival magazines and the tabloids are speculating whether someone is pregnant or whether it'll be a boy or a girl, Nelson holds back. "We don't print rumors," she says flatly.

Avoiding gossip, says Nelson, has earned celebrity respect for *People*. Publicists for celebrities end up having to perform less damage control over *People's* coverage and reciprocate by feeding the magazine exclusives.

The Nelson formula includes going after photos aggressively. For an exclusive of Brad Pitt and Angelina Jolie's baby, *People* reportedly paid $4.1 million, although the magazine has denied it was that much. Nelson acknowledges the bidding for photos has become "crazy." She blames competitors, notably European tabloids: "If this is the situation the competition creates we are not going to be beaten for the photos that we really, really want."

Nelson came to *People* from Time's *InStyle*, of which she was the first managing editor. Nelson also was executive producer of *InStyle* television specials. Earlier she was with *Savvy, Women's Sports & Fitness* and *Ms.* In 2006 Nelson was put in charge of strategic planning for *People* and its related franchises.

Her career progression, jumping from title to title, is typical of the magazine profession. And Nelson's success is typical in the history of mass-audience magazines, finding the content qualities that satisfy audience interests at the moment.

Influence of Magazines

STUDY PREVIEW

Today, as through their whole history, major magazines constitute a mass medium through which the distinctive U.S. culture is brought to a national audience. At their best, magazines pack great literature and ideas into formats that, unlike books, almost anybody can afford. Magazines are also a national unifier because they offer manufacturers a nationwide audience for their goods.

CONTRIBUTING TO NATIONHOOD

The first successful magazines in the United States, in the 1820s, were much less expensive than books. People of ordinary means could afford them. Unlike newspapers, which were oriented to their cities of publication, early magazines created national audiences. This contributed to a sense of nationhood at a time when an American culture, distinctive from its European heritage, had not yet emerged. The American

● **Saturday Evening Post**
An early contributor to identifiable
U.S. literature

● **Postal Act of 1879**
Discounted magazine mail rates

people had their magazines in common. The **Saturday Evening Post,** founded in 1821, carried fiction by Edgar Allan Poe, Nathaniel Hawthorne and Harriet Beecher Stowe to readers who could not afford books. Their short stories and serialized novels flowed from the American experience and helped Americans establish a national identity.

With the **Postal Act of 1879,** Congress recognized the role of magazines in creating a national culture and promoting literacy—in effect, binding the nation. The law allowed a discount on mailing rates for magazines, a penny a pound. Magazines were being subsidized, which reduced distribution costs and sparked dramatic circulation growth. New magazines cropped up as a result.

LEARNING CHECK ◄ ••

▶ **How did early magazines give Americans a sense of national community?**

▶ **What motivated Congress to allow magazines to be shipped through the postal system at a penny a pound?**

NATIONAL ADVERTISING MEDIUM

Advertisers used magazines through the 1800s to build national markets for their products, which was an important factor in transforming the United States from an agricultural and cottage industry economy into a modern economy. This too contributed to a sense of nationhood.

Railroads were catalytic in these economic changes. Manufactured goods could be transported among cities by rail starting in the mid-1800s, giving rise to national brands. Products as diverse as crackers and shoes became mass-produced, displacing local production. Magazines, also distributed by the new rail connections, were an ideal vehicle for manufacturers to promote their goods widely. Rail links connected Atlantic and Pacific coasts for the first time in 1869, as the rail networks became increasingly comprehensive. Other mass media could not match the far reach of magazines. Few books carried advertisements.

LEARNING CHECK ◄ ••

▶ **How were magazines and railroads partners in transforming the U.S. economy in the mid-1800s?**

MASSIVE AUDIENCE

People have a tremendous appetite for magazines. According to magazine industry studies, almost 90 percent of U.S. adults read an average of 10 issues a month. Although magazines are affordable for most people, the household income of the typical reader is 5 percent higher than the national average. In general, the more education and higher income a person has, the greater the person's magazine consumption.

In short, magazines are a pervasive mass medium. Magazines are not only for the upper crust, however. Many magazines are edited for downscale audiences, which means that the medium's role in society is spread across almost the whole range of people. Even illiterate people can derive some pleasure and value from magazines, which by and large are visual and colorful.

The massiveness of the audience makes the magazine an exceptionally competitive medium. About 12,000 magazines vie for readers in the United States, ranging from general-interest publications such as *Reader's Digest* to such specialized publications as *Chili Pepper,* for people interested in hot foods, and *Spur,* for racehorse aficionados. In recent years 500 to 600 new magazines have been launched annually, although only one in five survives into its third year.

LEARNING CHECK ◄ ••

▶ **Almost half of Americans average 10 magazines a month. How close are your magazine habits to the average?**

▶ **What can be said about the socioeconomic and educational levels of magazine readers?**

Magazine Innovations

STUDY PREVIEW

Magazines have led other media with significant innovations in journalism, advertising and circulation. These include investigative reporting, in-depth personality profiles, and photojournalism.

LONG-FORM JOURNALISM

● **long-form journalism**
Lengthy treatments of subjects that go beyond spot news

Magazines became home to **long-form journalism** in the 1800s with fiction by major authors. The 1900s brought investigative reporting, with stories longer than newspapers typically carried.

● **muckraking**
Early 1900s term for investigative reporting

● **Theodore Roosevelt**
Coined the term *muckraking*

■ **Investigative Reporting.** Magazines honed **muckraking,** usually called "investigative reporting" today, in the early 1900s. Magazines ran lengthy explorations of abusive institutions in society. It was **Theodore Roosevelt,** the reform president, who coined the term *muckraking.* Roosevelt generally enjoyed investigative journalism, but one day in 1906, when the digging got too close to home, he likened it to the work of a character in a 17th-century novel who focused so much on raking muck that he missed the good news. The president meant the term derisively, but it came to be a badge of honor among journalists.

● **Ida Tarbell**
Exposed Standard Oil

● ***McClure's***
Pioneer muckraking magazine

● **Lincoln Steffens**
Exposed municipal corruption

● **Upton Sinclair**
Exposed the meat-packing industry

Muckraking established magazines as a powerful medium in shaping public policy. In 1902 **Ida Tarbell** wrote a 19-part series on the Standard Oil monopoly for ***McClure's.*** **Lincoln Steffens** detailed municipal corruption, and reforms followed. Other magazines picked up investigative thrusts. *Collier's* took on patent medicine frauds. *Cosmopolitan*, a leading muckraking journal of the period, tackled dishonesty in the U.S. Senate. Muckraking expanded to books with **Upton Sinclair's** *The Jungle.* Sinclair shocked the nation by detailing filth in meat-packing plants. Federal inspection laws resulted.

● **personality profile**
An in-depth, balanced biographical article

● **Harold Ross**
Pioneered the personality profile

■ **Personality Profiles.** The in-depth **personality profile** was a magazine invention. In the 1920s **Harold Ross** of the *New Yorker* began pushing writers to a thoroughness that was new in journalism. The conversational quality of Q-As, refined by Hugh Hefner at Playboy in the 1950s, added a cogent authenticity to long-form profiles. The obvious role of the interviewer in Q-As, often invisible in typical news stories, helps put what's said into context. Also, interviewees have opportunities to explain complex lines of reasoning with illuminating detail. The exhaustive nature of lengthy Q-As, such as *Playboy's*, can draw out people in ways that other journalistic forms do not. Most *Playboy* interviews are drawn from weeks, sometimes months, of face time, all recorded and then spliced into a coherent article running 7,000 words or more. Many political and religious leaders, scientists and other thinkers, celebrities too, covet the opportunity that long Q-As give them to expand and elaborate on what they have to say.

● ***Harper's Weekly***
Pioneered magazine visuals

● ***National Geographic***
Introduced photography in magazines

● **Gilbert Grosvenor**
Pioneer editor of *National Geographic*

The Q-A format has been widely imitated. It was in *Rolling Stone*, which uses Q-As regularly, that presidential candidate Wesley Clark, a retired general, said he knew from top-level Pentagon planners that the 2003 Iraq invasion was only the beginning of further U.S. military plans in the Middle East.

Not all Q-A variations are breakthrough news. *Time* magazine, for example, has introduced a "10 Questions" feature that's tightly edited, with pointed questions and answers that fit on a single page. Readable and entertaining, yes, but usually also flighty and superficial and not what Hugh Hefner had in mind.

LEARNING CHECK ◄

▶ Does the term *muckraking* capture what investigative reporting is about?

▶ What were the contributions of Harold Ross and Hugh Hefner to long-form journalism in their very different magazines?

PHOTOJOURNALISM

Magazines brought visuals to the mass media in a way books never had. **Harper's Weekly** sent artists to draw Civil War battles, leading the way to journalism that went beyond words.

The young editor of the **National Geographic**, **Gilbert Grosvenor**, drew a map proposing a route to the South Pole for an 1899 issue, putting the *Geographic* on the road to being a visually oriented magazine. For subsequent issues, Grosvenor borrowed government plates to reproduce photos, and he encouraged travelers to submit their photographs to the magazine. This was at a time when most magazines scorned photographs. However, Grosvenor was undeterred as an advocate for documentary photography, and membership in the National Geographic Society, a prerequisite for receiving the magazine, swelled. Eventually, the magazine assembled its own staff of photographers and gradually became a model for other publications that discovered they needed to play catch-up.

Aided by technological advances involving smaller, more portable cameras and faster film capable of recording images under extreme conditions, photographers working for the *Geographic* opened a whole new world of documentary coverage to their readers.

Life magazine brought U.S. photojournalism to new importance in the 1930s. The oversize pages of the magazine gave new intensity to photographs, and the magazine, a weekly, demonstrated that newsworthy events could be covered consistently by camera. *Life* captured the spirit of the times photographically and demonstrated that the whole range of human experience could be recorded visually. Both real life and *Life* could be shocking. A 1938 *Life* spread on human birth was so shocking for the time that censors succeeded in banning the issue in 33 cities.

LEARNING CHECK ◄ ·····························

▶ **Although different in mission, *National Geographic* and *Life* both established magazines firmly as a visual medium. How so?**

National Geographic. *The* Geographic *has remained in the vanguard of magazines photographically. In 1985 the magazine used a hologram, a three-dimensional photograph, of a prehistoric child's skull on its cover—the first ever in a mass-audience magazine. Three years later, for its 100th anniversary, the* Geographic *produced a three-dimensional view of Earth on the first fully holographic magazine cover. The* Geographic *is not only among the oldest U.S. magazines but also, with 6.7 million circulation, among the most read.*

Magazine Products

··

STUDY PREVIEW

The most visible category of magazines is general-interest magazines, which are available on newsracks and by subscription. Called consumer magazines, these include publications like *Reader's Digest* that try to offer something for everybody, but mostly they are magazines edited for narrow audiences. Outnumbering consumer magazines about 10 to 1, however, are sponsored magazines and trade journals.

● **Reader's Digest**
The largest-circulation newsrack magazine

● **consumer magazines**
Sold on newsracks

● **AARP The Magazine**
Has the largest circulation but is limited to AARP members

CONSUMER MAGAZINES

By most measures **Reader's Digest** is the largest-circulation U.S. **consumer magazine,** with 11 million copies sold a month, but this measure has all kinds of caveats. The Sunday newspaper magazine supplement *Parade* has 35.4 million circulation a week. At 22.4 million *USA Weekend* also is far ahead of *Reader's Digest*. Then, too, are sponsored and membership-only magazines, some with huge circulation. **AARP,** for members of the American Association of Retired Persons, is at 22.2 million. Among magazines available from newsracks, however, *Reader's Digest,*

The oversize *Life* magazine created by Henry Luce was the perfect forum for the work of Margaret Bourke-White. The giant pages, 13 1/2 inches high and opening to 21-inch spreads, gave such impact to photos that they seemed to jump off the page at readers. Bourke-White was there at the beginning, shooting the immense Fort Peck Dam in Montana for *Life's* first cover in 1936. Over her career, Bourke-White shot 284 assignments for *Life,* many of them enduring images from World War II. These included Holocaust victims in a Nazi concentration camp, great military movements and the leaders of the time in both triumph and defeat. She was among the first great photojournalists.

Bourke-White's photojournalism went beyond the news and emotions of any given day to penetrate the core of great social problems. In collaboration with writer Erskine Caldwell, whom she later married, Bourke-White created a photo documentary on the tragic lives of sharecroppers in the American South. Later, in South Africa, she went underground to photograph gold miners who were known only by numbers. Her haunting photos from the Midwest drought of the 1930s created indelible images in the minds of a generation. These were socially significant projects that moved people and changed public policy.

Fearless Photojournalist. Margaret Bourke-White not only would take her camera anywhere but also had a sense of stories that were worth telling photographically. She is remembered most for her work in Life *magazine* over 20 years beginning in the mid-1930s.

Margaret Bourke-White was fearless in her pursuit of photography. She took her camera, a weighty Speed Graphic, onto the ledges of skyscrapers to get the feel she wanted in her images. She shot the ravages of the war in Europe from airplanes. She lived her work, and was quoted once as saying, "When I die I want to die living." She died in 1971 at age 67.

WHAT DO YOU THINK?

▶ Has the impact of magazine photography been diminished by the loss of oversize magazines?

▶ Margaret Bourke-White is often quoted for saying "When I die, I want to die living." How do her photos reflect this saying?

---

a monthly compendium of articles, many condensed from elsewhere as quick reads, has been the leader for decades.

● **Henry Luce**
The founder of *Time* and later *Life*

● **Time**
The first newsmagazine

■ **Newsmagazines.** Fresh out of Yale in 1923, classmates **Henry Luce** and Briton Hadden begged and borrowed $86,000 from friends and relatives and launched a new kind of magazine: ***Time.*** The magazine provided summaries of news by categories such as national affairs, sports and business. It took four years for *Time* to turn a profit, and some people doubted that the magazine would ever make money, noting that it merely rehashed what daily newspapers had already reported. Readers, however, came to like the handy compilation and the sprightly, often irreverent writing style that set *Time* apart.

MAGAZINE MILESTONES

1700s

Colonial Magazines
In Philadelphia, Andrew Bradford printed *American Magazine*, the first in the colonies (1741)
Bradford rival Benjamin Franklin followed a couple weeks later with *General Magazine* (1741)

1800s

First Magazine Era
The *Saturday Evening Post* ushered in an era of general-interest magazines (1821)

Women's Titles
Sara Josepha Hale took reins at *Ladies' Magazine*, propelled it to success (1828)

Illustrated News
Harper's Weekly introduced visual coverage of Civil War with illustrations (1860s)

Postal Break
Congress gave discount postal rates to magazines (1879)

Magazine Photography
Gilbert Grosvenor introduced photography in *National Geographic* (1899)

1900s

Muckraking
Ida Tarbell wrote a muckraking series on Standard Oil (1902)

Compendium Magazine
DeWitt and Lila Wallace founded *Reader's Digest* (1922)

Newsmagazine
Briton Hadley and Henry Luce founded *Time*, first newsmagazine (1923)

Long-Form Journalism
Harold Ross introduced personality profiles in the *New Yorker* (1924)

Photojournalism
Henry Luce founded *Life*, coined term *photo essay* (1936)

***Life* Dies**
Network television robbed general-interest magazines of advertisers (1960s)

Q-A
Hugh Hefner introduced modern Q-A format in *Playboy* (1962)

Online
Time Warner created Pathfinder Web site (1994)

2000s

In-Store Magazines
Bella Price created *All You* for in-store Wal-Mart sales (2005)

No fashion or fluff in Sara Josepha Hale's Ladies' Magazine

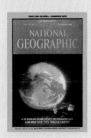

National Geographic found a quick following for visual portrayals

Life photography told stories

Every magazine is online. Some, like Slate, *exist only online*

A Wal-Mart exclusive

PIVOTAL EVENTS

- Revolutionary War (1776–1781)

- Railroad links between cities (1850s–)
- U.S. Civil War (1861–1864)
- Transcontinental rail link (1869)
- Populism widened effective political participation (1880s–)
- Samuel Gompers created powerful labor union (1881)
- Spanish-American War (1898)

- Reforms targeted corruption, monopolies, poor working conditions (1900s)
- World War I (1914–1918)
- Great Depression (1930s)
- World War II (1941–1945)
- Russian-Western Cold War (1945–1989)
- Television emerged as commercial medium (early 1950s)
- Vietnam War (1964–1973)
- Internet emerged as commercial medium (late 1990s)

- 9/11 terrorist attacks (2001)
- Iraq War (2003–)
- Hurricane Katrina (2005)

Henry Luce

Evolving Time. *Over three-quarters of a century,* Time *has expanded from a brassy summary of news into more exploratory journalism. But the magazine remains true to the concept of cofounder Henry Luce as a weekly update on broad ranges of events.*

A copycat, *Newsweek*, appeared in 1933. So did a third newsweekly, *U.S. News*, the forerunner to today's *U.S. News & World Report*. Despite the competition, *Time*, with 4.1 million copies sold weekly, has consistently led newsmagazine circulation.

While *Time, Newsweek* and *U.S. News & World Report* cover a broad range of subjects, specialized newsmagazines focus on narrower subjects. The largest category is those featuring celebrity news, including the gossipy sort. The supermarket tabloid ***National Enquirer*** focuses on the rich and famous, hyped-up medical research and sensational oddball news and is an incredible commercial success, with 2.1 million in circulation. Time Warner's *People* is at 3.6 million.

■ **Women's Magazines.** The first U.S. magazine edited to interest only a portion of the mass audience, but otherwise to be of general interest, was *Ladies' Magazine*, which later became *Godey's Lady's Book*. **Sara Josepha Hale** helped start the magazine in 1828 to uplift and glorify womanhood. Its advice on fashions, morals, taste, sewing and cooking developed a following, which peaked with a circulation of 150,000 in 1860.

The *Godey's* tradition is maintained today in the competing magazines *Better Homes & Gardens, Family Circle, Good Housekeeping, Ladies' Home Journal, Redbook, Woman's Day* and the erstwhile *Rosie* (née *McCall's*). While each sister can be distinguished from her siblings, there is a thematic connection: concern for home, family and high-quality living from a traditional woman's perspective.

These traditional women's magazines are sometimes called the **Seven Sisters.** An eighth sister is *Cosmopolitan*, although it may more aptly be called a distant

● *National Enquirer*
Magazine or newspaper?

● **Sara Josepha Hale**
Founded the first women's magazine

● **Seven Sisters**
The leading women's magazines

cousin. Under Helen Gurley Brown and later Bonnie Fuller, *Cosmopolitan* has geared itself to a subcategory of women readers: young, unmarried and working. It's the most successful in a large group of women's magazines seeking narrow groups. Among them are *Elle*, focusing on fashion, and *Essence*, for black women. The teen girl market, dominated by *Seventeen* and *YM*, has become crowded with Little Sister spin-offs *Cosmogirl*, the leading newcomer with 1.1 million circulation, *ElleGirl* and *Teen Vogue*.

■ **Men's Magazines.** Founded in 1933, *Esquire* was the first classy men's magazine. It was as famous for its pinups as for its literary content, which over the years has included articles from Ernest Hemingway, Hunter S. Thompson and P. J. O'Rourke. Fashion has also been a cornerstone in the *Esquire* content mix.

Hugh Hefner learned about magazines as an *Esquire* staff member, and he applied those lessons when he created ***Playboy*** in 1953. With its lustier tone, *Playboy* quickly overtook *Esquire* in circulation. At its peak *Playboy* sold 7 million copies a month. The magazine emphasized female nudity but also carried journalistic and literary pieces whose merit attracted many readers. Readers who were embarrassed by their carnal curiosity could claim that they bought the magazine for its articles. Critics sniped, however, that *Playboy* published the worst stuff of the best writers. Sociologists credit Hefner with both capitalizing on the post-World War II sexual revolution and fanning it. By 2004, however, *Playboy* seemed tired. Circulation was down to 3.2 million. The publisher of copycat *Penthouse* was in bankruptcy. Meanwhile, upstarts like *Maxim* at 2.5 million, *FHM* at 1.1 million and *Stuff* at 676,000 were in an ascendancy despite critics who objected to their raciness. Responding to critics, some retail outlets, notably giant retailer Wal-Mart, ceased stocking some men's titles as well as some women's magazines with provocative covers.

Not all men's magazines dwell on sex. The outdoor life is exalted in *Field & Stream*, whose circulation tops 2 million. Fix-it magazines, led by *Popular Science* and *Popular Mechanics*, have a steady following.

■ **Intelligentsia.** Some magazines, sometimes called **highbrow slicks,** work at being on the cutting edge of thinking and observation of political, economic, social, artistic and cultural issues. In 1945, almost 50 years before Tim Berners-Lee invented the World Wide Web, intellectual Vannevar Bush wrote his thoughts in the *Atlantic* on the possibility of a worldwide web. The *New Yorker* prides itself on regularly breaking ground on significant issues in articles that run as long as editors think necessary, sometimes the length of a small book.

Ideological magazines like the *New Republic*, *National Review* and *Nation* frequently are cerebral, although partisanship clouds their focus sometimes.

■ **Store-Exclusive Titles.** Herself a mother of four, Bella Price might seem a typical Wal-Mart shopper. Well, yes and no. Price created a Time Inc. weekly, *All You*, a women's title, in 2004 for sale exclusively at the 3,100-plus stores of Wal-Mart. The creation of a one-outlet, nonsubscription magazine was an innovation that was closely watched, then imitated by competing publishers. American Media, publisher of *Star*, launched its own Wal-Mart title, *Looking Good Now*, in 2005. Hachette Filipacchi created newsstand-only *For Me*.

Bella Price's formula for *All You* was no accidental magic. Time Inc. research had identified an unserved audience niche—everyday,

● *Esquire*
The first classy men's magazine

● **Hugh Hefner**
Playboy founder, created modern Q-A

● *Playboy*
A widely imitated girlie/lifestyle men's magazine

● **highbrow slicks**
Cerebral magazines edited for the intelligentsia

Eustace Tilley. The New Yorker *remembers its origins with an annual anniversary cover featuring Eustace Tilley, a character created by Rea Irvin to capture the sophistication of the magazine on its first cover in 1925. The New Yorker remains an intelligent, witty and often irreverent weekly whose substantive coverage of political, social, cultural and other issues has maintained its respect among devoted readers.*

budget-conscious young mothers who didn't relate easily to the svelte models, designer clothes and $100,000 kitchens of haughty women's magazines. Price fitted models of all shapes with clothes you'd find at Wal-Mart. Her recipes included the cost per serving. How-to items included the mundane. About a piece on how to unplug a toilet, Price told a *Business Week* interviewer: "Even if they have a man around, chances are he's not doing it for them." Price has moved on with her career, but *All You* remains a testimony to a strategy of gearing a magazine to price-conscious women who dominate the traffic at Wal-Marts, about 138 million people a week.

In many ways, the *All You* formula makes sense. Magazine industry scholar Samir Husni estimated the start-up costs at $25 million, about half the average, because Time Inc. needed no costly campaign to lure subscribers. Further, no distributors took a cut. Time ships *All You* directly to Wal-Marts. Some cost savings are passed on to customers with a Wal-Mart-type cover price—$1.47, less than a third of competing women's titles.

Early *All You* issues sold 500,000 copies, not bad for a start-up. More important to Time's bottom line, issues soon were bulging with 70 pages of advertising, exceeding projections by 30 percent.

LEARNING CHECK ◄ ···

▸ **What are the major genres of consumer magazines?**

NON-NEWSRACK MAGAZINES

Many organizations publish magazines for their members. Although these **sponsored magazines,** including *National Geographic, AARP The Magazine* and *Smithsonian,* resemble consumer magazines, they generally are not available at newsracks. In fact, consumer magazines are far outnumbered by sponsored magazines and by trade journals.

■ **Sponsored Magazines.** The founders of the National Geographic Society decided in 1888 to put out a magazine to promote the society and build membership. The idea was to entice people to join by bundling a subscription with membership and then to use the dues to finance the society's research and expeditions. Within a few years the *National Geographic* had become a phenomenal success both in generating membership and as a profit center for the National Geographic Society. Today, more than 100 years old and with U.S. circulation at 6.7 million, the *Geographic* is the most widely recognized sponsored magazine in the nation. Other sponsored magazines include *AARP The Magazine,* published by the American Association of Retired Persons for its members. Its circulation exceeds 20 million. Other major membership magazines include *Smithsonian,* published by the Smithsonian Institution; *VFW,* by the Veterans of Foreign Wars; *American Legion;* and *Elks,* by the Elks lodge.

Many sponsored magazines carry advertising and are financially self-sufficient. In fact, the most successful sponsored magazines compete aggressively with consumer magazines for advertising. It is not unusual for an issue of *Smithsonian* to carry 100 pages of advertising.

While advertising has made some sponsored magazines into profit centers for their parent organizations, others come nowhere near breaking even. Typical is *Quill,* which the Society of Professional Journalists publishes as an organizational expense for the good of its membership. The society seeks advertising for *Quill,* but the magazine's relatively small readership has never attracted as much volume or the same types of advertising as *National Geographic, Smithsonian* or *AARP The Magazine.*

Many sponsored magazines do not seek advertising. These include many university magazines, which are considered something that a university should publish

● **sponsored magazine**
Generally a non-newsrack magazine, often member supported

Sara Hale, widowed with five children, decided to write a novel to put her kids through college. *Northwood*, published in 1826, was one of the first books with America as its setting. The book attracted national attention, and all kinds of literary offers came Hale's way. She decided on the editorship of the new Boston-based *Ladies' Magazine*. Although some magazines of the time had women's sections, no previous magazine had wholly devoted itself to women's interests. Hale's innovations and sensitivities made the magazine and its successor a familiar sight in households throughout the nation for half a century. During her tenure Hale defined women's issues and in indirect ways contributed importantly to women's liberation.

As editor of *Ladies' Magazine*, Hale departed from the frothy romance fiction and fashion coverage in the women's sections of other magazines.

Women's Magazine Pioneer. *Sara Josepha Hale edited the first magazine designed for women, but just as important was the distinctive content. Whereas many magazines recycled articles from other magazines, mostly from England, Hale prided herself on original content.*

Her focus was on improving women's role in society. She campaigned vigorously for educational opportunities for women. When Matthew Vassar was setting up a women's college, she persuaded him to include women on the faculty—a novel idea for the time.

No fashion plate, Sara Hale encouraged women to dress comfortably yet attractively—no frills. For herself she preferred black for almost all occasions. When the owners of the magazine thought enthusiastic fashion coverage would boost circulation—and advertising—she went along, but in her own way. She pointed out how impractical

and ridiculous the latest fashions were, and some she dismissed as trivial diversions.

Unlike other magazine editors of the time, she disdained reprinting articles from other publications. Hence, *Ladies' Magazine* created opportunities for new writers, particularly women, and enriched the nation's literary output. One issue, in 1843, was produced entirely by women. In her heyday, from the mid-1830s through the 1840s, Hale attracted the best writers to her pages: Ralph Waldo Emerson, Nathaniel Hawthorne, Oliver Wendell Holmes, Washington Irving, Henry Wadsworth Longfellow, Edgar Allan Poe, Harriet Beecher Stowe.

Hale edited *Ladies' Magazine* from 1828 until 1837, when it was merged into the weaker *Godey's Lady's Book*. She moved to Philadelphia to become editor of the new magazine, which retained the *Godey* title. Circulation reached 150,000 in 1860.

WHAT DO YOU THINK?

▶ How would Sara Josepha Hale's disdain for frilly fashions go over in the magazine industry today?

▶ Sara Josepha Hale courted the best writers of her era as contributors. How much of this legacy do you see in magazines today?

as an institutional expense to disseminate information about research and scholarly activities and, not incidentally, to promote itself. Other sponsored magazines that typically do not carry advertising include publications for union members, in-house publications for employees, and company publications for customers. These publications do not have the public recognition of consumer magazines, but many are as slick and professional as consumer magazines. Altogether, they employ far more editors, photographers and writers than consumer magazines do.

■ Trade Journals. Many trade magazines are parts of companies that produce related publications, some with overlapping staffs. McGraw-Hill, the book publisher, produces more than 30 **trade journals,** including *Chemical Week* and *Modern Hospital*. Another trade magazine company is Crain Communications, whose titles include *Advertising Age, AutoWeek, Electronic Media* and two dozen others. Many trade magazine companies, including McGraw-Hill and Crain, are recognized for honest, hard-hitting reporting of the industries they cover, but the

● **trade journal**
Keeps members of a profession or trade informed

trades have a mixed reputation. Some trade magazines are loaded with puffery exalting their advertisers and industries.

Responsible trade journals are embarrassed by some of their brethren, many of which are upstarts put out by people with no journalistic experience or instincts. Because of this, and also because it takes relatively little capital to start a trade magazine, many bad trade magazines thrive. Several professional organizations, including the American Business Press and the Society of Business Press Editors, work to improve both their industry and its image. Even so, as former ABP President Charles Mill said, trades continue to be plagued "by fleabag outfits published in somebody's garage."

■ **Newsletters.** Even more focused than trade journals are subscription newsletters, a billion-dollar industry. These newsletters are expensive, generally $600 to $1,000 a year, with some as much as $5,000. Why do people pay that much? Where else could Chamber of Commerce executives find the information that's in *Downtown Promotion Reporter?* And no other publications duplicate what's in *Food Chemical News, Beverage Digest* and *Inside Mortgage Finance.* John Farley, vice president of the largest newsletter company, Phillips Publishing, contends that newsletters are the purest form of journalism because they carry little or no advertising: "We're answerable to no one but our subscribers."

LEARNING CHECK ◄

▶ **What are some of the audiences to which non-newsrack magazines are aimed? Give examples.**

▶ **Why are some trade journals less reputable and reliable for straight news than others?**

Magazine Industry

STUDY PREVIEW

The largest, most profitable segment of the U.S. magazine industry is concentrated in a few magazine chains. Some of these chains are engaged in other media enterprises, some of them global. These companies seek synergies among their diverse properties, one promoting the other. This synergy strategy worries media critics because this shifts content away from serving the readers in a broad cultural sense to serving corporations' narrow economic interests.

OWNERSHIP CONCENTRATION

Like other mass media, the magazine industry is concentrated in a few major companies. Some have cross-media interests, like Time Inc., which is part of Time Warner, whose subsidiaries include movies, cable television, recorded music, and online enterprises. In magazines, Time has 64 titles. Here are major magazine companies and their most recognizable titles, although most readers have no idea who owns what:

Time: *Entertainment Weekly, Fortune, InStyle, Money, People Weekly, Sports Illustrated, Time*

Hachette Filipacchi: *Car & Driver, Cycle World, Elle, Premiere, Road & Track, Woman's Day*

Condé Nast: *Allure, Bride's, Glamour, GQ, House & Garden, New Yorker, Self, Vanity Fair, Vogue, Wired*

Bertelsmann: *Child, Family Circle, Fitness, Parents, YM*

Hearst: *Cosmopolitan, Esquire, Good Housekeeping, Marie Claire, O: The Oprah Magazine, Popular Mechanics, Redbook, Seventeen*

Meredith: *Better Homes and Gardens, Ladies' Home Journal*

Primedia: *American Baby, Automobile, Hot Rod, Motor Trend, Snowboarder, Soap Opera Digest*

Historically, going back to Andrew Bradford and Benjamin Franklin and the first colonial magazines in 1741, magazines have been part of other enterprises. Bradford and Franklin were, first of all, newspaper printers. When the book industry took form in the 1800s, publishers created magazines as a vehicle to draw interest to their primary product—books. Those titles bore publishers' names like *Collier's* and *Scribner's*. Today *Harper's* has roots in former book company ownership. After acquiring his fortune in chain newspaper ownership in the late 1800s, William Randolph Hearst went into the magazine business.

Cross-media ownership continues. Condé Nast magazines are part of a company that also owns Newhouse newspapers. Hearst remains in both the magazine and the newspaper business, as well as in television. When these companies consider acquiring other media companies, they factor in possible **synergy** with the existing enterprises. What interaction or cooperation would create an effect greater than the sum of the components?

● **synergy**
A combination that creates more than the sum of the parts

Also, the stretch of parent companies is global. Hachette, based in Paris, has more than 200 titles worldwide, besides 20 in the United States. Bertelsmann, a German company, is one of the world's largest publishers of books, magazines and recorded music.

LEARNING CHECK ◀ •••

▶ **Name the largest U.S. magazine chains. How many of their titles can you name?**

▶ **How did magazines become chain enterprises?**

SELF-SERVING CONTENT

Chain and cross-media ownership pose problems. Do parent companies manipulate their magazines' content to promote their corporate interests? Yes, says media critic Ben Bagdikian. Talking about big media companies, Bagdikian says, "The aim is to control the entire process from an original manuscript or a new series to its use in as many forms as possible. A magazine article owned by *the company* becomes a book owned by *the company*. That becomes a television program owned by *the company*, which then becomes a movie owned by *the company*. It is shown in movie theaters owned by *the company*, and the movie sound track is issued on a record label owned by *the company*, featuring the vocalist on the cover of one of *the company* magazines. It does not take an angel from heaven to tell us that the company will be less enthusiastic about outside ideas and production it does not own, and more and more we will be dealing with closed circuits to control access to most of the public."

Is it coincidence when *Time* has a cover story on a new Warner movie? How about when Time Warner was in the book business and *Time* excerpted major sections of one of the company's new books? To be fair, magazine editors are quick to defend their content decisions as being based on the merits of the work. Even so, that an explanation is even necessary suggests the thin ice on which magazines tread in reader confidence because of corporate connections.

Time Warner uses *Time's* subscription lists to promote its mail-order music sales. The company's local cable television distribution systems tout Warner movies. Home and lifestyle magazine publisher Meredith has a lucrative book unit that dovetails with the readership of its magazines. In one year, on-screen pop-ups on Time Warner's America Online subsidiary generated 1.1 subscriptions for the company's magazines.

LEARNING CHECK ◀ •••

▶ **Is it fair to readers, who don't realize what's going on, when media conglomerates use their control of magazine content to support business for sibling enterprises?**

▶ **Is Ben Bagdikian right about media conglomeration working against diversity in content and the public interest? Explain.**

INDEPENDENT MAGAZINES

Despite concentrated ownership, most of the 12,000 magazines in the United States are owned by institutions for their own purposes. Universities, for example, publish alumni magazines. Large companies publish magazines for shareholders, employees and other constituencies. Too, there are niche publications with audiences too narrow to interest a Bertelsmann, Hachette or Time. Not on their radars are titles like *Railroad Model Craftsman*.

Niches can be profitable. Kalmbach Publishing of Waukesha, Wisconsin, dominates the railroad field and related hobbies. McGraw-Hill, the giant business and textbook publisher, is firmly ensconced with *Business Week*, a major magazine, but also in a wide range of narrow-focus business publications. Crane of Chicago has a competitive array of specialty publications.

LEARNING CHECK ◄ ·······································

▶ What independently published magazines are received in your household? How do you know they're not from a chain magazine publisher?

Magazines as Niche Media

STUDY PREVIEW

Today's magazine industry took form in a dramatic crisis that began in the 1950s when network television lured away advertisers. The networks suddenly offered a bigger audience at less cost. The big magazines, including the archetype *Life*, all were out of business by 1972. What followed was demassification as the surviving magazines sought slices of the mass audience, not the whole.

MASS-AUDIENCE MAGAZINES

Henry Luce got a lot of things right. He coined the term *the American century* to describe the ascendancy of the United States as a dominant world power in the 1900s. Most of all, though, Luce's life was magazines, first with *Time*, the weekly newsmagazine in 1923, then spectacularly with *Life*, also weekly, in 1936. *Life* exceeded Luce's expectations.

These magazines, edited for general audiences, were perfect advertising vehicles for nationally marketed products. Unlike network radio, the magazines were visual. People could see the products. There was no more efficient medium for advertisers to reach large audiences. These were magazines that epitomized the era. At its peak *Life* claimed a circulation of 8.5 million, a real deal for advertisers. Then came television.

● **CPM**
Cost per thousand

The villain for magazines was **CPM**, advertising jargon for cost per thousand readers, the *M* for the Roman numeral meaning thousand. The television networks nibbled, even gobbled at the big magazines' CPMs. In 1970 a full-page advertisement in *Life* ran $65,000, a $7.75 CPM at the time. The networks' CPM was $3.60. It's not hard to see why advertisers shifted to television.

One by one the big magazines folded. *Collier's*, whose rich legacy went back to the muckraking period, published its final issue in 1956, in the first decade of the networks' existence. Hemorrhaging money despite a circulation of 4 million, *Saturday Evening Post*, which claimed a lineage going back to Benjamin Franklin, ceased publication in 1969. In 1971 *Look* died. *Life* hung on one more year.

Doomsayers predicted the end of magazines. The fact, however, was that the prognosis wasn't so severe. It was just that the Henry Luce model for magazine success needed to be rethought.

LEARNING CHECK ◄ ·······································

▶ What happened to the Henry Luce model for magazines, as epitomized by *Life*?

▶ What characteristics distinguish *Life* at its heyday from, say, the magazine *Snowboarding* today?

Seeing the News. *Henry Luce's* Life *magazine pioneered photojournalism, beginning with Margaret Bourke-White's haunting shadows of the giant new Fort Peck Dam in Montana for the inaugural issue. When World War II came,* Life *dispatched Bourke-White and other photographers to capture the story, even the horrific details. With people eager for war news, circulation soared.*

DEMASSIFICATION

Categories of magazines, like the weekly newsmagazines, survived the assault of television. Newsmagazines provided content that audiences could not find easily on television, which had not yet emerged as a competitive news medium. The quick-read *Reader's Digest*, portable and easy to pick up, was unshaken. Also surviving were special-interest magazines focusing on niche topics that the television networks ignored as they tried to build mass audiences.

By and large, magazines needed to reinvent themselves. And they did through a process called **demassification.** The survivors delivered potential customers to narrowly focused advertisers. For manufacturers of high-end audio systems, *Stereo Review* made CPM sense. These demassified audiences were large, and the magazines continued to be vehicles of mass communication; but these were defined audiences—in contrast to Henry Luce's broader formula that sought to deliver something for everyone in every issue.

Although a successful financial and survival tactic, demassification has critics. These critics, of the elitist camp of social studies, say the traditional role of magazines to help readers come to understandings of broad and important issues has been lost. As the critics see it, the social and cultural importance of magazines has largely been lost in a drive to amass narrow slices of readership that will attract a narrow range of advertisers. The result is a frothy mix of light, upbeat features with little that is thoughtful, hard-hitting or broadly illuminating. Norman Cousins, once editor of the highbrow *Saturday Review*, put it this way: "The purpose of a magazine is not to tell you how to fix a faucet but to tell you what the world is about."

● **demassification**
Pursuit of narrow segments of the mass audience

Calvin and Hobbes

by Bill Watterson

Magazine Demassification. *Advertisers favor magazines that are edited to specific audience interests that coincide with the advertisers' products. Fewer and fewer magazines geared to a general audience remain in business today.*

CALVIN AND HOBBES © 1992 Watterson. Dist. by Universal Press Syndicate. Reprinted with permission. All rights reserved.

Look, for example, at a cat fancier magazine. The message is on what great people cat fanciers are, interspersed with advertising touting products and services on how to become even greater as a cat fancier. This, as Norman Cousins would say, is self-indulgent and superficial and contributes nothing to helping people understand what the world is about.

Scholar Dennis Holder put this "unholy alliance" of advertisers and readers this way: "The readers see themselves as members of small, and in some sense, elite groups—joggers, for example, or cat lovers—and they want to be told that they are terribly neat people for being in those groups. Advertisers, of course, want to reinforce the so-called positive self-image too, because joggers who feel good about themselves tend to buy those ridiculous suits and cat lovers who believe lavishing affection on their felines is a sign of warmth and sincerity are the ones who purchase cute little cat sweaters, or are they cat's pajamas." Magazine editors and writers, Holder said, are caught in the symbiotic advertiser-reader alliance and have no choice but to go along.

LEARNING CHECK ◄

▶ **What magazines have survived demassification and still seek broad audiences?**

▶ **How do you respond to Norman Cousins' point that magazines have forfeited an important role in society?**

▶ **Would you categorize women's magazines as demassified?**

▶ **How would you rank these magazine pairs on a scale of demassification?** *Sports Illustrated* and *Runner; MacAddict* and *Wired; Better Homes and Gardens* and *Wine Aficionado; Prevention* and *Diabetes Forecast*

New Competition

STUDY PREVIEW

Television again is challenging magazines, this time with demassified programming on satellite and cable systems. The Web also offers a wealth of information organized for tiny slivers of the mass audience that magazines earlier had carved out as their province.

DEMASSIFIED ALTERNATIVES

The so-called 500-channel universe, with narrowly focused programming on satellite and cable television channels, is the latest challenge to magazines. This time television has followed magazines' lead in demassification. The Home and Garden television channel, for example, covers the same content as the home-lifestyle magazine genre. With recording and playback devices, viewers easily can call up whatever they want whenever they want it.

Sensing that their exclusive turf is facing a challenge, some magazines have established a television presence but generally only as a single program. These play among other programs on the 24/7 demassified channels.

Magazines have done better with the Web. One of the first forays into digital delivery was by Time Warner, which in the mid 1990s created a massive Web site, **Pathfinder,** for *Time, Sports Illustrated, Fortune* and the company's other magazines. Pathfinder wasn't merely an online version of the magazines but a distinctive product. There were hopes that advertisers would flock to the site and make it profitable, but ad revenue only trickled in. In 1998 Pathfinder went to subscriptions to supplement the meager advertising revenue. All in all, the Pathfinder exercise was not a success, but lessons were learned.

Today almost every magazine, including all of Time Warner's, has a namesake Web site with access to the content from the latest issue and usually bonus content that doesn't appear in print issues. Some Web magazines charge subscriptions, but most don't. And advertisers have become comfortable with the sites as part of their mix for reaching potential customers.

● **Pathfinder**
An early Time Warner initiative to place magazines online

LEARNING CHECK ◄ ·······································

▶ **How is television challenging magazines today as a demassified medium?**

▶ **Can magazines meet the challenge of the new demassified competition?**

DIGITAL DELIVERY

For advertisers there is lots of confusion about what their advertising budgets buy. Indeed, is $100,000 better spent on HGTV or on *Better Homes & Gardens*? It's the old CPM question, but the issue is more complex than simply dividing dollars by eyes.

A new way of measuring a magazine's value, the **Reader Usage Measure,** or RUM, was introduced in 2003 to ascertain positive and negative reader reactions. Thirty-nine statements are put to readers in carefully controlled surveys to ascertain positive and negative reactions. The statements are direct. Answering Yes to these statements contributes to a strong RUM score:

● **Reader Usage Measure (RUM)**
A scale for measuring reader satisfaction

- I get value for my time and money.
- It makes me smarter.
- I often reflect on it.

Conversely, answering yes to the following statements lowers the RUM score:

- It disappoints me.
- I dislike some of the ads.
- It leaves me feeling bad.

Ellen Oppenheim, a marketing executive with the Magazine Publishers Association, said RUM data provide "a quantitative measure of qualitative information" that transcends circulation, ad pages and ad revenue—all of which are advertising-rooted measures. RUM is a reader-rooted measure that points to a magazine's connectedness to its audience.

The first RUM study included 4,347 readers of 100 leading magazines, which was a large enough sample to provide demographic breakdowns. Black readers, for

Magazines and the Internet

Bye, Jane. *Battered by circulation shortfalls and advertiser defections, Jane Pratt's namesake magazine is among dozens of glossies that have said good-bye. Where have readers gone? In a word, the Web. In response, surviving magazines are gravitating to the Web. Industry executives, however, are of many minds on finessing the transition. A modest tactic is a site that draws readers to the latest print editions. In contrast, full-blown sites are offering more content than could possibly fit between two covers.*

Remember *Teen People* on the magazine rack? Or *FHM, Jane, Cargo, Premiere, Elle Girl* or *Celebrity Living*? All these mainstream magazines and dozens of others folded over the past couple years.

The competition is stiff among glossies. But Jane Pratt, founder of *Jane*, says it was another medium, the Internet, that largely caused the downfall of her self-titled women's magazine. "With so many women going online, it's possible that there isn't much need for it." Pratt's point is clear: Readers don't need to wait for a monthly when the Internet is always available with convenient, reliable content.

So how can magazines survive in a volatile market where the World Wide Web always wins at getting information to consumers the fastest?

If you can't beat 'em, join 'em. Many magazines have extended their presence to the Web. For several years Condé Nast, a major magazine publisher with numerous titles, has attempted to do this through general Web sites like epicurious.com. The site carries material from the company's food magazines. Condé Nast's brides.com includes material from the bridal magazines, Although these sites are sponsored by the magazines, they are purposefully not named after any of the company's magazines. The goal for the sites is to reach readers who might not typically pick up an issue of *Modern Bride* or *Bon Appetit*.

Some magazines are going a step further with detailed Web sites specifically to accompany their monthlies. *Portfolio*, a new business magazine, has a free Web site with articles from the magazine as well as breaking news, video, blogs and other interactive features.

Steven Newhouse, the Condé Nast executive who oversees the company's Web sites, believes in magazine companion sites: "You gain a broader audience and more loyalty from your subscribers if you extend the experience into the Web."

Many publications still shy away from putting too much free information on the Web, but others have created exhaustive sites. Time Inc. made a distinctive move in 2007 in the belief that the magazine market is in a fundamental change. The company cut nearly 300 employees in order to invest more money into Web sites. Larry Hackett, the managing editor of Time Inc.'s ever-popular *People*, says the layoffs were "brought upon us by some real cold hard facts when it comes to how this business is run, and how media is changing."

DEEPENING YOUR MEDIA LITERACY

EXPLORE THE ISSUE
Search the Web and find a site that is either generally associated or specifically connected with a magazine that you regularly read.

DIG DEEPER
Analyze the content of the Web site. Do you think the Web site is aimed at subscribers or readers who are unfamiliar with the magazine? As a reader of the magazine, do you think you can search the site more easily and/or understand the content better? Do you think a non-reader would be encouraged to pick up the magazine after searching this site?

WHAT DO YOU THINK?
Do magazines need to embrace the Internet in order to survive in today's market? Are there any other ways for them to strengthen market share and increase readership?

example, wanted magazines about which they could say, "It touched me" and "It grabbed me visually." Generation Y women, who came of age in the 1990s, gravitate to magazines that help them share experiences. Historically, the great magazines have been edited by people with an intuitive sense for their audiences. With RUM there is concrete information to supplement instinctive knowledge about what attracts an audience.

LEARNING CHECK ◄ ·······························

▶ **How does RUM differ from CPM? As an advertiser, would RUM merely add to confusion? Or would it help you make better decisions on where to place your ads?**

Chapter Wrap-Up

Influence of Magazines (Page 106)

■ In the formative period of the American republic, magazines made works by the first American authors available at an affordable price. This contributed to a self-recognition by Americans that they indeed possessed a distinct culture. It helped make the American identity. When transportation improvements, mostly railroads, facilitated mass distribution of manufactured goods, magazines were an ideal vehicle for manufacturers to reach national audiences to build a bigger-than-ever customer base. Today about 12,000 magazines are published in the country.

Magazine Innovations (Page 108)

■ Magazines found a huge audience at the start of the 1900s for stories on horrific abuses of power in government and corporations that grew out of rapid economic growth over the previous quarter century. The revelations shocked the country, prompting new regulatory policies, governmental reforms and citizen protections. These magazine stories, called muckraking, were forerunners of modern investigative reporting. Magazines also pioneered other long-form journalism. Another magazine innovation was illustrations, then photography, which made magazines a visual medium long before television.

Magazine Products (Page 109)

■ About 1 in 10 magazines published in the United States appears on newsracks. These 1,200 titles, called consumer magazines, are led by *Reader's Digest*. Women's titles historically have been a major genre. Less visible are non-newsrack magazines issued by institutions. These include association magazines, like *AARP* and *Elks;* union magazines for members; and corporate magazines for shareholders. Trade journals for specific professions and crafts are important in their niches.

Magazine Industry (Page 116)

■ Time Warner epitomizes the ownership of the most prominent U.S. magazines. The company has 64 titles, not to mention its movie and television studios, cable television distribution systems, recorded music, America Online and, until recently, books. Time Warner and other media conglomerates came together with the goal of finding synergies through which various corporate elements would fuel each other's growth. Critics say this synergetic mentality doesn't coincide with what should be the primary goal—serving the audience's interests by bringing enlightenment and understanding and by enriching our culture.

Magazines as Niche Media (Page 118)

■ The modern magazine industry was born in a crisis caused by the advent of network television in the 1950s. National advertisers shifted to television. It wasn't so much that television had more glitz but that the networks could deliver a larger audience for ads at significantly less cost per unit. The big magazines, dependent on advertising, didn't survive, including icons like *Life, Look, Saturday Evening Post* and *Collier's*. Other magazines adapted, the most successful focusing on niches in the audience that network television wasn't much interested in. Today the U.S. magazine industry comprises mostly titles that deliver slivers of the mass audience efficiently to advertisers peddling focused products and services. What has occurred since the 1950s is called demassification.

New Competition (Page 120)

■ Magazines demassified to survive half a century ago. They carved out under-served segments of the mass audience and offered specialized coverage that attracted advertisers that wanted to target those audience segments. These audience slices are now being pursued also by cable and satellite television channels and online services. The new challenge for magazines is keeping their hard-earned audiences and advertisers. Among magazines' answers is a new readership measure, RUM, which tries to ascertain reader satisfaction.

REVIEW QUESTIONS

1. How have magazines contributed to an American identity and shaped the culture?

2. Theodore Roosevelt ran hot and cold on muckraking. When was he right? When was he wrong?

3. What were the contributions of Ida Tarbell? Harold Ross? Henry Luce? Hugh Hefner?

4. What are the major genres in magazines?

5. Does the corporate shape of the magazine industry serve society well?

6. What forced the magazine industry into its current demassified state?

7. How is television encroaching again, as it did in the 1950s and 1960s, on magazine advertising?

CONCEPTS

demassification (Page 119)
long-form journalism (Page 108)
synergy (Page 117)

TERMS

CPM (Page 118)
highbrow slicks (Page 113)
muckraking (Page 108)
Reader Usage Measure (RUM) (Page 121)
trade journal (Page 115)

PEOPLE

Gilbert Grosvenor (Page 108)
Hugh Hefner (Page 113)
Henry Luce (Page 110)
Harold Ross (Page 108)
Ida Tarbell (Page 108)

MEDIA SOURCES

- The trade journal *Folio* tracks the magazine industry. *Advertising Age* and *AdWeek* also provide ongoing coverage.

- Myrna Blyth. *Spin Sisters*. St. Martin's, 2005. Blyth, a former *Ladies' Home Journal* editor, criticizes women's service magazines for forsaking their traditional role. Now, she says, they offer a steady diet of shallow content.

- John Tebbel and Mary Ellen Zuckerman. *The Magazine in America, 1741–1990*. Oxford University Press, 1991. Tebbel and Zuckerman make the case that magazines have been a major shaper of American life.

In this chapter you have deepened your media literacy by revisiting several themes. Here are thematic highlights from the chapter:

Media Technology

Magazines took firm root in American national life by piggybacking on a phenomenon facilitated by perhaps the most powerful product of the Industrial Revolution—railroads. Most U.S. commerce until the mid-1800s was by sea and river, but then railroads were built to link population centers efficiently by land. This put markets within range for goods were mass-produced in faraway places. Trains moved the goods. To capitalize on these newly accessible markets, manufacturers turned to magazines as advertising vehicles to tout their products. It all was part of the emerging national market economy. The magazines, also shipped by the growing web of rail lines, took on a stronger role as national media. (Pages 106–107)

Media Economics

The most visible component of the U.S. magazine industry, the titles available on newsracks, is advertising-dependent. In fact, advertising subsidizes magazine readers. The cover price represents only a fraction of the cost of producing an issue. It's a system that generally has worked well for the magazine industry, advertisers and readers. But there is a downside. In the mid-20th century, when major national advertisers shifted to network television, many magazines went into a financial tailspin. Some disappeared. The industry recovered, but the perilous dependence continues. (Pages 120–123)

Magazine Slump. As slick and fancy as they come, Jane couldn't overcome the rapid shift of readers to the Internet. When readership slipped, advertisers quickly jumped to alternate vehicles. A growing number of magazine titles have disappeared.

Muckraking. Ida Tarbell dug up the bad stuff on Standard Oil with the noble goal of reforms to prevent monopolistic abuses.

Media and Democracy

Magazines were no more vibrant in public policy than in the muckraking period, when deep-digging reporters unearthed wrongdoing and injustices. Magazine exposés led to public policy reforms. Perhaps most notably, Ida Tarbell's marathon 1902 series on the Standard Oil monopoly was a factor in the government breaking up the company. The muckraking tradition continues with intense examinations of the institutions of society. You need look no further than Seymour Hersh's investigative work in recent years in the *New Yorker* on U.S. military policy. Magazines like the *Atlantic* are significant forums for thinkers on political and social issues. *Time* and other newsmagazines offer shocking revelations that regularly rattle the cages of the Powers That Be. (Pages 108–113)

Media and Culture

Through much of U.S. history, magazines fulfilled the media role of binding the culture together. More affordable than books, magazines brought the great early American authors to large numbers of people. These were stories that reflected the unique American culture back to itself, creating a

national identity without which a people lack cohesiveness. The role continued into the mid- to late 20th century as leading magazines worked at reaching the greatest number of readers possible. This culture-creating role has diminished with the shift of many magazines to serve narrow audience segments. It can be argued that magazines today are a factor in the fragmentation of American society and culture. **(Pages 106–107 and Pages 118–120)**

The American Century. *With his* Time *and* Life, *Henry Luce was unabashed in his enthusiasm for growing U.S. world dominance. It was, he said, "the American Century."*

Elitism and Populism

Magazines have become fertile turf for elitists to argue that the mass media are failing in their responsibility to enrich society. The trend of magazines to seek readers within narrow frameworks of personal interest panders to narcissistic self-indulgence, which isn't among the most desirable human characteristics. Not much in a cooking or a sports or a celebrity or a hobbyist magazine is about the common good, moving toward a better society, or illuminating enduring issues. The criticism is overstated, of course, but the elitists' point has validity in the sheer numbers of narrowly focused if not sybaritic magazines that are designed primarily to bring together readers who are a desirable target for advertisers with specialized products and services. Populists are unconcerned. Their position is that the marketplace is giving people what they want. **(Pages 119–120)**

A New View. *Photojournalists like Margaret Bourke-White gave readers a new perspective on the world and their role in it.*

Self-Indulgence. *Bella Price's* All You *may have value in how to make cheaper family meals, but, say elitists, that's a pale contribution to promoting human understanding and enlightenment.*

Media Future

Television is wielding a new specter over magazines. The growth of cable and satellite networks has spawned dozens of narrowly focused channels. There are 24/7 networks on cooking, speed sports, travel, home living, rural life, you name it. These networks, as well as specialized Internet sites, are nibbling at the turf that the U.S. magazine industry established for itself in the 1950s and 1960s when the early television networks, ABC, CBS and NBC, decimated the advertising base of general interest magazines. Those losses forced magazines largely to surrender the huge mass audiences they had amassed over more than a century. To survive, magazines focused on segments of the audience in a process called demassification. Now may be the time for magazines again to reinvent themselves. **(Page 120–121)**

6

Sound Recording

Power of Recorded Music

In Iraq, soldiers rig the intercom systems on tanks and personnel carriers to blast music directly into their helmets. "You have to listen to music before you go out on a mission and get real hyped," Sergeant Junelle Daniels said in a *Rolling Stone* magazine survey. Psyching themselves for combat, soldiers in Iraq go for high-energy niche tracks. Among them: Drowning Pool's *Bodies*, Linkin Park's *Numb*, 2Pac's *Hit 'Em Up* and DMX's *Ruff Ryders Anthem*.

As always in war, patriotic music rises in popularity. Toby Keith's flag-waving *American Soldier* has its place in Iraq. But also there is an anti-war strain, just as in previous wars, that illustrates music's role in issues by which we define our values.

Released in 1985, *We Are the World* right away was the fastest-selling record of the decade. Four million copies were sold within six weeks. Profits from the record, produced by big-name entertainers who volunteered, went to the USA for Africa project. The marketplace success paled, however, next to the social impact. The record's message of the oneness of humankind inspired one of the most massive outpourings of donations in history. Americans pumped $20 million into USA for Africa in the first six weeks the record was out. Within six months, $50 million in medical and financial support was en route to drought-stricken parts of Africa. *We Are the World*, a single song, had directly saved lives.

The power of recorded music is not a recent phenomenon. In World War I, *Over There* and other songs reflected an enthusiasm

Media Ubiquity. *Music is not far from combat. Most U.S. soldiers in Iraq carry MP3 devices and computers full of music.*

for U.S. involvement in the war. Composers who felt strongly about the Vietnam War wrote songs that put their views on vinyl. *The Ballad of the Green Berets* cast U.S. soldiers in a heroic vein, *An Okie from Muskogee* glorified blind patriotism and there were dozens of anti-war songs.

Early in the 2008 presidential campaign, candidates were casting for theme songs. At one point Hillary Clinton picked Celine Dion's *You and I*. In his 1988 State of the Union message, President Bill Clinton borrowed from Paul Simon's *Boy in the Bubble* to make a point about the economy: "If this age of miracles and wonders has taught us anything, it's that if we can change the world we can change America." Popular music, lyrics too, form a communication bridge with mass audiences—something shared. The ongoing role of music that catches on in the public's mind is no better demonstrated than by *Happy Days Are Here Again*, first used by Franklin Roosevelt in the Depression and a musical standard-bearer for Democratic candidates since.

In short, music has tremendous effects on human beings, and the technology of sound recording amplifies these effects. The bugle boy was essential to Company B in earlier times, but today reveille is on tape to wake the troops. Mothers still sing Brahms' lullaby, but more babies probably are lulled to sleep by Brahms on CD. For romance, lovers today rely more on recorded music than their own vocal cords. The technology of sound recordings gives composers, lyricists and performers far larger audiences than would ever be possible through live performances.

Besides explicit advocacy and its immediate, obvious effects, recorded music can have subtle impacts on the course of human events. **Elvis Presley,** "the white boy who sang colored," hardly realized in the mid-1950s that his music was helping to pave the way for U.S. racial integration. It was the black roots of much of Presley's music, as well as his suggestive gyrations, that made him such a controversial performer. Whatever the fuss, white teenagers liked the music, and it blazed a trail for many black singers who became popular beyond the black community. A major black influence entered mainstream U.S. culture. There was also a hillbilly element in early rock, bringing the concerns and issues of poor, rural whites—another oppressed, neglected minority—into the mainstream consciousness. Nashville ceased to be an American cultural ghetto.

● **Elvis Presley**
Pivotal performer in emergence of rock 'n' roll

Recording Industry

The recording industry works mostly in the background of the mass media to which we are exposed daily. Ever heard of Bertelsmann? EMI? Most people haven't. Most music fans know artists and perhaps their labels, but the industry is in fact dominated by four global companies with corporate tentacles also in other media enterprises.

PERVASIVENESS OF MUSIC

When urban sophisticates in earlier eras wanted music, they arranged to attend a concert. Many middle-class people went to the parlor and sat at the piano. Rural folks had their music too—a fiddle on the front porch in the evening, a harmonica at the campfire. Music was a special event, something to be arranged. To those people, life today would seem like one big party—music everywhere all the time. Yes, we arrange to see concerts and major musical events, but we also wake to music, shop to music and drive to music. Many of us work to music and study to music. In fact, the recording industry has products in so many parts of our lives that many people take most of them for granted.

LEARNING CHECK ◄··

▸ **How has the role of music changed with recording technology?**

SCOPE OF THE RECORDING INDUSTRY

The recording industry that brings music to mass audiences, both the flashy stuff and everything else, is gigantic. Global sales in 2004 were estimated at $33.6 billion, with $12.9 billion in the United States alone. These totals don't include symbiotic industries like fan magazines, music television and radio that, all together, claim revenues approaching $17 billion a year. Then there are concerts, performers' merchandise, sponsorships and a miscellany of related enterprises.

Political Theme Song. *Presidential candidate Hillary Clinton chose Celine Dion's* You and I *as the theme song of her 2008 campaign. Music has been part of American politics going back to folk ditties in the 1800s. And who can forget Franklin Roosevelt's* Happy Days Are Here Again? *It still rings out at Democratic conventions.*

David Geffen. *He parlayed drive and an ear for talent into a music fortune through Geffen Records, becoming Hollywood's first billionaire. Later Geffen joined Jeffrey Katzenberg and Steven Spielberg for a 12-year run with their own movie studio, Dreamworks. The studio produced one acclaimed movie after another, starting with* Saving Private Ryan.

● **David Geffen**
Recording, movie entrepreneur; first self-made billionaire in Hollywood

The stakes are big. The first billionaire in Hollywood history, **David Geffen**, became rich by building Geffen Records from scratch. He sold the enterprise for three-quarters of a billion dollars.

Even in leaner times, with major losses to online music swapping, recordings from major acts sell well. Anglo-Dutch recording conglomerate EMI sold 5 million copies of pop singer Robbie Williams' greatest-hits collection. The Beastie Boys' *Hello Nasty* and Janet Jackson's *All for You* both topped 5 million. Two EMI albums by rapper Chingy have approached 4 million copies.

LEARNING CHECK ◄ ···

▶ **What are some measures of the size of the recording industry?**

RECORDING LABELS

The recording industry is concentrated in four major companies known as the Big Four, which have 84 percent of the U.S. market and 75 percent of the global market. Each of these companies, in turn, is part of a larger media conglomerate.

■ **Majors.** The Napster-induced crisis in the early part of the 21st century shook up the industry's corporate landscape. Sony and Bertelsmann merged their music units. Bertelsmann, the German company that is the world's fifth-largest media company, runs the combined Sony BMG. Alarmed at declining sales in the new file-swapping era, Time Warner sold its Warner Music in 2004 to Edgar Bronfman Jr. and fellow investors. Bronfman, heir to the Seagram liquor fortune from Canada, earlier had run the Universal movie and recording empire but had sold it to the French media conglomerate Vivendi. Although Vivendi, financially overextended, sold off many holdings to solve its own crisis in 2003, it decided to stay the course with Universal Music. There were no buyers anyway. Times were tough in the industry, and prospects for a recovery were cloudy at best.

These are the companies that dominate the recording industry, with their major acts by label and their percentage of the global market:

- **Universal Music (French)**   **25.5 percent**
  Guns N' Roses (Universal), Jay-Z (Def Jam), Brian McKnight
  (Motown), George Strait (MCA Nashville), Snoop Dogg
  (Geffen), Gwen Stefani (Interscope), The Killers (Island)

- **Sony BMG (German)**   **21.5 percent**
  Bruce Springsteen (Columbia), Jennifer Lopez (Epic),
  Santa (Legacy), Travis Tritt (Sony Nashville),
  OperaBabes (Odyssey)

- **EMI (Anglo-Dutch)**   **13.1 percent**
  Beastie Boys (Capitol), Janet Jackson (Virgin),
  Tina Turner (Capitol)

- **Warner Music (U.S.)**   **11.3 percent**
  Doors (Elektra), Boyz N Da Hood (Bad Boy),
  Twisted Sister (Lava), Lil' Kim (Atlantic)

● **Big Four**
Major recording companies—
Universal, Sony BMG, EMI,
Warner

The **Big Four** may become three. Warner and EMI have been in a merger dance, trying to find a way to sidestep objections from the European Union about market domination. The European Union also has kept the Sony-Bertelsmann arrangement under scrutiny.

Besides the majors, recording companies called indies are a small but not unimportant industry arrangement. Typically indies claim about 15 percent of U.S. sales.

● **indies**
Independently owned record-making
companies; not part of the Big Four

■ **Indies.** For decades a secondary tier of independent recording companies, **indies,** as they were known in industry jargon, struggled against the majors and occasionally produced a hit. When an indy amassed enough successes, it invariably was bought out by a major. The most famous of the indies, Motown, whose name became synonymous with a black Detroit style, maintained its independence for 30 years. In 1988, however, founder Berry Gordy received an offer he could not refuse—$61 million. Soon Motown was subsumed into the MCA empire, which later became Universal Music.

While struggling indies remain part of the record industry landscape, the latter-day indies are well-funded labels created by major artists who decide to go their own

His Own Label. The cost and risk of launching a record label once were unthinkable, even for a major artist, but digital recording technology has loosened the control that well-financed record companies had on the industry. Queens-born James Todd Smith, professionally LL Cool J, short for "Ladies Love Cool James," helped to propel rap label Def Jam into the big time among indies in the 1980s. Now, still strong in popularity, LL Cool J has launched his own label, P. O. G. Records.

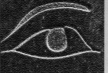

SOUND RECORDING MILESTONES

PIVOTAL EVENTS

1800s

Phonograph
Thomas Edison introduced a recording-playback device (1877)

Mass Production
Multiple copies possible with Emile Berliner invention (1887)

Early phonograph

1900–1949

Buzz
Electricity added to recording and playback (1920s)

Juke Box
Nickel a tune (1930s–)

Microgrooves
Long-play vinyl records (1948)

1950–1999

Rockabilly
Hybrid musical form became rock 'n' roll (1950s)

A&R? What A&R?
Record companies lost tight control of pop music (1960s–)

Protest music has roots in Vietnam period

Digitization
Compact discs (1983)

Streaming
Downloading from Web feasible (1998)

Rap takes place among pop

2000s

MP3
Handheld iPod on market; Apple iTunes store followed (2001)

Podcasting
Adam Curry invented podcasting (2004)

Grokster
U.S. Supreme Court outlawed online music-swap services (2005)

Music anywhere, any time, personalized

Napster-type music-swaps outlawed

- U.S. middle class with discretionary time emerges (1870s–)

- Dance craze (1913–)
- Music added to movies (1927)
- Great Depression (1930s)
- Rhythm 'n' blues a firm musical genre (1940s)

- Radio shifted to recorded music programming (1950s)
- President Truman ended race segregation in federal hiring, military (1948)
- U.S. Supreme Court banned segregated schools (1954)
- Elvis Presley transformed pop music (1956)
- Beatles led British Invasion (1964)
- Vietnam War generated peace movement (1964–1973)
- Rap a major pop music genre (1990s)
- Internet emerged as commercial medium (late 1990s)

- 9/11 terrorist attacks (2001)
- Iraq War (2002–)
- Hurricane Katrina (2005)

way, with themselves in charge, rather than dealing with cumbersome big-studio bureaucracies and machinery. The Beatles did it with Apple. Minnesota-based Prince did it. The Dixie Chicks used it as a negation tactic. Today it's a common route.

LEARNING CHECK ◄ ···

▶ **What are the largest recording companies and the country in which each is based?**

▶ **Historically, what becomes of successful, independent record companies?**

Downloads

STUDY PREVIEW

Napster and other file-sharing technology that facilitates music swapping seriously eroded music sales and record industry viability until 2005, when the U.S. Supreme Court intervened. An older problem, pirate dubbing, continues to be a drain on music industry profitability.

FILE SWAPPING

Shawn Fanning's Napster technology ushered in a frenzy of free music swapping on the Internet in 2000. Suddenly, record stores found themselves unable to move inventory. Major music retailer Best Buy shut down its Sam Goody's, Musicland and other brand-name stores that had seemed sure moneymakers only a few months earlier. The free fall continued. For the first time in its history, the record industry was not in control of new technology—unlike the earlier adjustments, when companies exploited developments to spur sales, like switches to high-fidelity and stereo and the introduction of eight-tracks, cassettes and CDs.

The Recording Industry Association of America, which represents recorded music companies, went to court against Napster. A federal judge bought the argument that Napster was participating in copyright infringement by facilitating illicit copying of protected intellectual property. Napster was toast. But other **file-swapping** mechanisms remained, some harder to tackle. Kazaa, for example, kept moving its operations from one offshore site to another, where legal actions were impossible.

In a surreal initiative in 2003, RIAA began legal action against individuals who **downloaded** music without paying. The association's goal was a few hundred highly publicized lawsuits, perhaps some showcase trials, to discourage download piracy. In one respect, the strategy backfired, only engendering hard feelings among people who were the industry's greatest consumers.

In another legal maneuver, the industry challenged Grokster and other music-swapping services. The argument was that Grokster was not passively involved in copyright infringements by music-swappers but had actively encouraged the infringements. In 2005 the U.S. Supreme Court agreed in what was quickly hailed as a landmark gain for the recording industry. The decision did not end music swapping immediately but so hobbled business as usual among swap services that RIAA was confident it had largely stopped the free-swapping drain on its revenues.

● **file swapping**
Sharing music, usually individual songs, over Internet

● **downloading**
Installing a file on a computer from an Internet source

LEARNING CHECK ◄ ···

▶ **How did Shawn Fanning shake the recording industry out of its new-technology blindspot?**

▶ **How did the U.S. Supreme Court settle the recording industry's file-sharing disaster?**

PIRATE DUBBING

● **pirate dubbing**
Illegal duplication of music and movies for black-market sale

Until the recorded music industry's crisis with downloading, the biggest drain on sales had been criminal music dubbing. **Pirate dubbing** operations, well financed and organized, have been estimated by the industry to account for 20 to 30 percent

Shawn Fanning grew up in a welfare family. Brothers and sisters were in and out of foster homes. His break came when an uncle brought Shawn to his Cape Cod computer game company and gave him a computer. Fascinated, the teenager found new direction. It didn't make him rich, though. When it came time for college, Fanning, with only $80, could afford to apply to only two colleges.

In freshman year at Northeastern University in Boston, Fanning listened to his roommates' complaints that they couldn't find the music they wanted to download from the Internet, Fanning decided to write a program to help. He obsessed about the project. He wrote code day and night until he had a system that would allow people to tap into each other's hard drives for MP3 downloads.

That was in 1998. The rest is history. Fanning dropped out of college, found a venture capitalist, moved to Silicon Valley and went into business. His program, called **Napster** after his childhood nickname, almost instantly attracted thousands of music fans, who began trading millions of songs online. Napster let it all happen automatically, listing every song that every participant had on a hard drive and enabling file swaps with the click of a mouse button.

At age 19, to many, Shawn Fanning was a cyberhero. He was also the recording industry's worst nightmare. Record sales tumbled at campus-area record shops. Alarmed, the **Recording Industry Association of America** sued Fanning's company, charging that Napster enabled people to undermine the whole intellectual property legal apparatus that allowed music creators and owners to profit from their work. People, mostly college students, were acquiring music free, eliminating the economic incentive for composers and lyricists to create new works and for record companies to package and market them.

Fanning responded that Napster was nothing more than an electronic way for people to swap their favorite music—an age-old practice. The recording industry prevailed in federal court. Soon Napster was out of business. Still, other P2P software, short for **peer-to-peer sharing**, continued in operation. In one particularly bad week in 2005, CD sales were down 28 percent from a year earlier. The number of people in the United States who were on one or more file-sharing networks was 4.6 million. Meanwhile, the industry's attorneys continued pressing the courts to shut down all the P2P drain on their sales. In 2005 the U.S. Supreme Court spoke on the issue, in effect shutting down Grokster and other software operations that facilitated free downloading.

Even so, Shawn Fanning's impact has been indelible and enduring. His Napster innovation and its imitators

Napster Guy. *Shawn Fanning introduced free-for-all online music-swapping technology that he dubbed Napster. The incredible popularity of swapping threatened the recording industry's traditional profit model. Why pay $15 for a CD? The industry went to court claiming that swap services were facilitating copyright infringements and won.*

prodded the record industry to rethink its retailing practices and move to online delivery of digitized music. Fanning, the college freshman who obsessed over computer code rather than going to classes, brought about a transformation of the shape of the record industry.

WHAT DO YOU THINK?

▶ How did Shawn Fanning's Napster innovation work?

▶ How would you respond to someone who claims that nobody needs a college degree to be successful, and cites Shawn Fanning to make the point?

● **Shawn Fanning**
Inventor of Napster

● **Napster**
First online music-swapping software

● **Recording Industry Association of America (RIAA)**
Trade association of music recording companies

● **peer-to-peer sharing (P2P)**
Music-swapping software without a central server

of CD sales in the United States. There are no firm figures, but RIAA estimates that the loss globally is $5 billion a year.

The dubbed CDs are from shadowy sources, mostly in Asia but also in other countries, including Saudi Arabia. It is not uncommon for a back-alley Third World pirate operation to have 100 "slave" copying machines going simultaneously 24 hours a day. These pirate operations have no artistic, royalty or promotion expenses. They dub CDs produced by legitimate companies and sell them through black-market channels. Their costs are low, their profits high. Pirate dubs even end up in retail channels, including Wal-Mart at one time.

The Recording Industry Association of America, along with the Motion Picture Association of America, spends millions of dollars a year on private investigators in Bangkok and other piracy centers. They also pressure foreign governments to crack down, as does the U.S. government, but with limited success.

LEARNING CHECK ◄

▶ How are profits made in the pirate dubbing of recorded music for the black market?

▶ Why do many foreign governments avert their eyes to illegal dubbing on their soil?

Authorized Downloads

STUDY PREVIEW

The recorded music industry has moved to get on top of downloading technology with new retailing models. These include the iPod–iTunes distribution structure introduced by Apple, as well as imitators. This shift in retailing has hurt bricks-and-mortar stores, whose sales have slipped. Some chains have gone out of business.

iTUNES

● **Steve Jobs**
The driving force behind the Apple Computer revival, iPod and iTunes

● **iTunes**
Apple-owned online retail site for recorded music

The recording industry, comfortable and immensely profitable, was caught unawares by Napster-inspired online swapping. When the industry finally woke up to the threat, a tremendous floundering occurred on how to tap into the new technology. Numerous stabs at a new business model fell apart—until **Steve Jobs** of Apple Computer presented himself as a rescuing knight in shining armor with the online **iTunes** music store. From the iTunes site people can sample songs with a single click and then download with another click for 99 cents a song. In iTunes' first week, more than 1 million songs were downloaded, juicing a 27 percent spike in Apple stock.

Unlike download-swapping, iTunes wasn't free. But it had advantages. The sound quality was exceptional. Apple used a new format that compressed music efficiently, downloaded faster and consumed less disk space. It was a clean system, without the annoying viruses that affected swap systems like Kazaa, Morpheus and Grokster. Apple benefited too from the guilt trip that RIAA was trying to lay on illegal downloaders.

Jobs began iTunes with huge repertoires from some major labels. Other labels begged to sign on as soon as the iPod–iTunes success was clear. By 2005, 62 percent of all music downloads were from iTunes. To be sure, copycat services spawned quickly. Wal-Mart created WAM. The Napster name was resurrected as a subscription service with unlimited access to downloads, the whole collection playable as long as the subscription was kept current.

LEARNING CHECK ◄

▶ How does iTunes generate profits for both Apple and recording companies?

▶ Despite many products coming along to challenge iPod and iTunes, none have come close. Why?

Download Solution. *Steve Jobs of Apple Computer gave the recording industry an on-line retailing outlet with his iTunes store, from which music could be downloaded into incredibly popular Apple iPod listening devices at 99 cents a song. Downloaders could feel good that they weren't violating the intellectual property rights of recording companies or performers, lyricists or composers. And recording companies, desperate to stem revenue losses from illegal but free downloading, could derive income from the sales.*

RETAILING

The iTunes concept drastically changed the retailing of recorded music. Record shops, once the core outlet for recording companies, already were under siege by retailers like Sam Goody and Musicland. With iTunes, even the chains were in trouble. Bankruptcies followed. The new retailing structure is largely iTunes-like download services, online retailers like Amazon.com, and giant retailers like Wal-Mart and Best Buy.

LEARNING CHECK ◄ ···

▶ **Who have been the losers in the retailing change introduced by iTunes?**

▶ **Who are the survivors?**

Math Challenge. *Apple's iTunes has not been without challengers. A resuscitated Napster, operating within copyright law, made a case in ads aimed at Apple that it had a better idea—a $15-a-month subscription for access to its entire library, rather than iTunes' 99 cents to purchase a song. Hardware rivals, meanwhile, have introduced one device after another to derail Apple. None has come close.*

Podcasting Evolution

Bands used to send their singles on a 45-rpm record to radio stations across the country, hoping for airplay. Today, musicians who want to reach a global audience send their music on a digital file to podcasters. These are the people who put together their own Internet audio shows, typically an MP3 file, that is delivered to a listener with an iPod, or other audio player, or a computer with an Internet connection and speakers. Listeners can access the podcast at their convenience, and it's free.

As of 2006 there were more than 4,750 podcasters in the music/radio category at Podcast Alley, a directory of podcasts for every type of music from jazz to metal. Chris McIntyre started Podcast Alley to index all the podcasts he could find. Music is only part of what his site indexes. "I truly believe that podcasting is a powerful communication tool and will have a profound effect on the way we communicate in the future," says the Purdue University graduate.

While musicians are hoping for exposure from the new medium, PodShow Inc. founder **Adam Curry** is poised to make big bucks from it. "Podfather" Curry and software pioneer Dave Winer developed the computer programs that make podcasting possible. Curry founded PodShow Inc. in 2005. The same venture capital companies that invested in Yahoo! and Google invested $9 million in PodShow.

The mainstream media "are so diluted, so packaged, so predictable. There's so very little that is new or interesting," Curry told Martin Miller of the Los Angeles *Times*. "We've lost a lot of social connectedness that used to come from that. And what we're building here is a social media network for human beings." Curry's critics claim the former MTV VJ "promotes himself as a would-be revolutionary for the little guy, but he's actually as profit mad as the corporate giants."

Other companies are jumping on the podcast wagon. Nokia announced in 2006 that some of its new phones would include a podcasting client featuring the PodShow top 10, Podcast Alley Picks and podcasts from Digital Podcast.

"Thousands of bands are submitting their songs to the Podsafe Music Network. They're connecting with podcasters and listeners, and now they're figuring out that it makes sense to promote shows together and share their audience with each other," said Curry. "This is another way bands are benefiting from the DIY/digital revolution in music."

Adam Curry. He invented podcasting, which he sees as a revolutionary vehicle for just about anybody to assemble radio-like programs for indeed global listening. What's it cost? Not much more than a computer, a modem, and easy-to-use podcast software.

● **Adam Curry**
Pioneer in podcasting technology

DEEPENING YOUR MEDIA LITERACY

EXPLORE THE ISSUE

Canvass 10 people around you on whether podcasts have become a part of their media habit. Ask what they seek from podcasts. Video stories? News? Music? And which podcasts seem most popular?

DIG DEEPER

Visit the most popular podcast sites. Rank them for ease of access. What are the access charges, if any?

WHAT DO YOU THINK?

Does music content available on podcasts comprise a significant shift in the retail delivery of recorded music? Or is it a blip in the music retailing landscape?

Artistic Autonomy

STUDY PREVIEW

Major labels once dominated the nation's music with expensive talent and recording operations that neither indies nor individual performers could match. Digital recording equipment in the 1980s loosened the majors' artistic control.

A&R STRUCTURE

● **A&R (artist and repertoire)**
Units of a recording company responsible for talent

The heart of the recording industry once was the powerful **A&R** units, short for **artist and repertoire,** at major labels. In an arrogant tyranny over artists, A&R executives manufactured countless performers. They groomed artists for stardom, chose their music, ordered the arrangements, controlled recording sessions and even chose their wardrobes for public performances.

In his book *Solid Gold* Serge Denisoff quotes a Capitol executive from the 1950s explaining how the A&R system worked: "The company would pick out 12 songs for Peggy Lee and tell her to be at the studio Wednesday at 8, and she'd show up and sing what you told her. And she'd leave three hours later and Capitol'd take her songs and do anything it wanted with them. That was a time when the artist was supposed to shut up and put up with anything the almighty recording company wanted."

The muscle of the major record companies, aiming for mass market sales, contributed to a homogenizing of U.S. culture. Coast to coast, everybody was humming the same new tunes from Peggy Lee and other pop singers, who served a robotlike role for A&R managers. The A&R structure was a top-down system for creating pop culture. A relatively small number of powerful A&R executives decided what would be recorded and marketed. It was the opposite of grassroots artistry.

A&R Revolution. Unlike the era when major labels controlled every aspect of the work of performers like Peggy Lee, low-cost recording equipment today has reduced artist dependence on big recording companies. Among performers who have bucked the Big Label domination of music have been the Dixie Chicks, whose threat to start their own label gave them negotiating leverage.

LEARNING CHECK ◄ ....

▶ How would the Dixie Chicks respond if recording company A&R staffs tried to dictate their repertoire, even their style, as they did Peggy Lee?

▶ Has the culture been enriched or damaged by the diminished A&R role today?

Peggy Lee

Dixie Chicks

PERFORMER INFLUENCES

● **garage bands**
A term coined for upstart performers without a studio contract

In the 1980s sophisticated low-cost recording and mixing equipment gave individual artists and **garage bands** a means to control their art. The million-dollar sound studio, controlled by major labels and their A&R people, became less important. As little as $15,000 could buy digital recorders and 24-channel mixing boards, plus remodeling the garage, to do what only a major studio could have done a few years earlier. The upshot was liberation for creativity. Artists suddenly had an independence that big recording companies were forced to learn to accommodate. Linda Ronstadt, for example, shifted her recording to a home studio in her basement. Some artists, like LL Cool J, went so far as to create their own labels. The ability of artists to go out on their own gave them clout that was not possible in the A&R heyday. The Dixie Chicks, among others, used this new leverage in negotiating with their labels.

Another result has been greater diversity. A rap fan might never have heard the Dixie Chicks. The music of Barry Manilow is obscure to most Green Day fans. In this sense, recorded music has become less of a unifying element in the whole society. The unification, rather, is in subsets of the mass audience.

LEARNING CHECK ◄•••

▶ **How has technology enabled artistic creativity?**

▶ **What is a cultural downside to the demassification that has come with greater artistic autonomy?**

Regulatory Pressure

••

STUDY PREVIEW

The recording industry has been a scapegoat for social ills. To stay one step ahead of government censorship, the industry has taken a cue from other media groups and introduced self-regulation to head off First Amendment crises.

OBJECTIONABLE MUSIC

Campaigns to ban recorded music are nothing new. In the Roaring 20s some people saw jazz as morally loose. White racists of the 1950s called Bill Haley's rock "nigger music." War protest songs of the Vietnam period angered many Americans.

Government attempts to censor records have been rare, yet the Federal Communications Commission indirectly keeps some records off the market. The FCC can take a dim view of stations that air objectionable music, which guides broadcasters toward caution. Stations do not want to risk their FCC-awarded licenses, which are subject to periodic renewal and can be yanked.

The FCC has been explicit about obnoxious lyrics. In 1971 the commission said that stations have a responsibility to know "the content of the lyrics." Not to do so, said the commission, would raise "serious questions as to whether continued operation of the station is in the public interest." The issue at the time was music that glorified drugs.

LEARNING CHECK ◄•••

▶ **What form have objections to music lyrics taken?**

▶ **Has the government ever banned a song?**

LABELING

● **Parents Music Resource Center**
Crusaded for labels on "objectionable" music

In the 1980s complaints about lyrics focused on drugs, sexual promiscuity and violence. **Parents Music Resource Center,** a group led by wives of influential members of Congress, claimed links between explicit rock music and teen suicide, teen pregnancy, parental abuse, broken homes and other social ills. The group objected to lyrics like those in Prince's *Sister*, which extol incest; Mötley Crüe's *Live Wire,* with its psychopathic enthusiasm for strangulation; Guns N' Roses' white racism; and rap artists' hate music.

The Parents Music Resource Center argued that consumer protection laws should be invoked to require that records with offensive lyrics be labeled as dangerous, like cigarette warning labels or the movie industry's rating system. After the group went to the FCC and the **National Association of Broadcasters,** record companies voluntarily began labeling potentially offensive records: "Explicit Lyrics—Parental Advisory." In some cases the companies printed lyrics on album covers as a warning.

Online retailers, including iTunes, put a label of "explicit" on songs that might raise prudish eyebrows.

On a quadrennial schedule, some presidential candidates resurrect the idea that song lyrics are a corrupting influence of the nation's youth. These concerns can be traced to jitterbug music in the 1940s, rockabilly in the 1950s and rap today. Some is mere grandstanding against new music and performance genres that unsettle some people, like early rock's hip-grinding and excessive stage gestures. Some objections, however, focus on antisocial messages, like Prince's celebration of incest, Ice T's *Cop Killer* and Eminem's misogyny. Bizarre costuming and makeup by Alice Cooper and David Bowie in their early years didn't help. Nor did Jim Morrison's indecent exposure in a Miami concert.

No one doubts the sincerity of some critics, like Senator Joseph Lieberman, the Connecticut Democrat. Strident on the right is William Bennett, who once went after Warner Music: "Are you folks morally disabled?" Once the election passes, however, the political rhetoric cools.

LEARNING CHECK ◄••

▸ **Why did recording companies embrace the idea of labeling music with objectionable lyrics? Was this a good thing?**

▸ **What is the purpose of labeling objectionable music? Does labeling accomplish its purpose?**

ARTISTIC FREEDOM

The usual defense against would-be censors is that artistic freedom merits protection, no matter how objectionable the art's content. When rapper Ice T seemed to push the envelope on acceptability with his song *Cop Killer* on a Warner Music label, police groups and others called for a ban. It was no wonder, with lyrics such as "I got my 12-gauge sawed-off/And I got my headlights turned off/I'm about to dust some cops off." Some defended the album as misunderstood. **Gerald Levin,** chief executive at Time Warner, catapulted the defense of Ice T to another level with an eloquent defense for artistic liberties as an essential value in a free society. Free expressionists were enthusiastic that Levin had taken a pro-artist stance over a financially safer bottom-line position.

A few months later, however, Levin waffled. He called on Warner artists to begin a dialogue on standards. Fervid support for Levin waned as his position shifted to safer ground for Time Warner: corporate well-being. In the end Levin cut loose Ice T's label from the Warner collection—a more typical, albeit less heroic, action for a media executive. Ever-mindful of potential threats to their industry's autonomy, media executives almost always try to finesse their way out of confrontations that have the potential to precipitate serious calls for government censorship.

LEARNING CHECK ◄••

▸ **How would you evaluate the Gerald Levin defense of Ice T's *Cop Killer* lyrics?**

▸ **Would you consider Gerald Levin a hero of free expression?**

● **National Association of Broadcasters**
Radio, television and trade organization

● **Gerald Levin**
Time Warner chief executive who defended artists' free expression

Curtis Jackson. *Ambitious hustling.*

Curtis Jackson epitomizes all that critics see as right and wrong about the culture of rap that has erupted into a dominant element in pop music, if not pop culture. At 22, after jail time for drug dealing in the roughest section of Queens, Jackson lucked out through rap friends and landed a contract with Columbia Records. In two weeks he sketched out 36 songs, including his career-launching *How to Rob.*

Yes, this is the Curtis Jackson who performs as 50 Cent. But despite the promise of the underground bite of his early Columbia music, his rap career took a hit when he did—9mm bullets in his face, legs and a hand in front of his grandmother's place in Queens. Such is the life of a dealer, a career in itself that allowed the prepubescent kid to buy Air Jordans that his grandma, who reared him, could never afford.

Jackson was months recovering in the hospital. Columbia dropped his contract. But Jackson kept writing, the shooting adding grist to his creative mill. He got back to recording and mixing tapes and caught the ear of Eminem, the reigning king of rap, and Dr. Dre, master-rap producer. Other gangsta labels suddenly were on to 50 Cent too. A bidding war erupted, with 50 Cent going with the new Eminem and Dr. Dre label Aftermath/Shady.

Multiple hits followed, all authentically flowing from Jackson's experience. *Need Love*, a heroin addict yearning desperately for a fix, is pop pap. More explicit is the title *When the Guns Come Out, Somebody's Going to Die Tonight*. He made a fortune, with 11 million recordings sold by 2005. Critics say 50 Cent glorifies the drug life. That's not how he sees it: "I was poor for much longer than I been rich, so what do you think I'm going to talk about."

His anthem now is best captured in the title of his superhit *Get Rich or Die Tryin'*. His sense of business, honed from age 8 on the streets of Queens, has served Curtis Jackson well. For Reebok he designed G-unit sneakers and earned $20 million. A clothing line brought in $50 million. He has expanded into the Glaceau vitamin water. Hollywood beckoned, teaming *Sopranos* screenwriter Terence Winter and *In America* director Jim Sheridan for a thinly fictionalized biographical movie, *Hustler's Ambition*, with Curtis Jackson as himself, err, as 50 Cent.

WHAT DO YOU THINK?

▶ Is 50 Cent an authentic artist with an enduring cultural contribution?

▶ Can you name recording artists who, like 50 Cent, have parlayed their music into additional profitable enterprises?

Dependence on Radio

STUDY PREVIEW

The recording industry relies on radio for free advertising of its wares. Airplay has been essential for recordings to sell. This has led to legal issues, like under-the-table payments to decision makers at influential stations for airtime.

RADIO PARTNERSHIP

The radio and record industries have been connected since the mid-1920s, when the bottom fell out of the record business. To stay afloat, record companies looked to advantageous partnerships with radio. The Victor Talking Machine Company began courting with the fledgling RCA radio network. In 1929 they merged. Columbia Phonograph Company acquired another network, which later became CBS. Over time the value of radio to record makers became clearer in another context. In the 1940s, when records by performers like Bing Crosby and Frank Sinatra were promoted over the radio, sales soared.

● airplay
Radio time devoted to a particular recording

● payola
Under-table payments to plug a product in the mass media

When radio shifted mostly to playing recorded music in the 1950s, **airplay** became essential for a new recording to succeed. Radio, in effect, became free advertising. To win airtime, record companies began bribing prominent disc jockeys to play their music. This gave rise to a **payola** scandal. One audit found that $230,000 in "consulting fees" had been paid to radio stations in 23 cities. The Federal Trade Commission issued charges of unfair competition.

Radio station managers, worried that their licenses would be rescinded by the Federal Communications Commission, began demanding signed statements from disc jockeys that they had not accepted payola. Dozens of disc jockeys in major markets quietly left town. The scandals demonstrated that the recording industry's partnership with radio had become dependence.

LEARNING CHECK ◄ ···

▶ Radio needs music, and the music recording industry needs radio. Is this a mutual interdependence? Or is one party more dependent than the other?

▶ If payola is a crime, who is the victim?

MARKETING THROUGH RADIO

The dependence has created a series of payola issues over the years. There were indictments in the 1980s for buying airtime under the table. In 1988 two independent promoters were charged with paying $270,000 to program directors at nine stations whose playlists were widely imitated by other stations. One station executive was charged with receiving $100,000 over two years. Some payola bribery involved drugs.

Although radio has declined in importance for promoting records, with young people opting for iPods and similar devices, nothing beats free advertising. Record makers still supply stations with new music in hopes it finds its way on the air. In an imaginative step, country duo Montgomery Gentry recorded their single

Localizing Lyrics. To curry favor with local fans, country duo Montgomery Gentry recorded 81 versions of Lucky Man. *It was new-style marketing. The lyrics of each variation named a different local sports team.*

The Grammy Bounce. *In the two days after the 2005 Grammy Awards tribute to Ray Charles, sales of his* Genius Loves Company *album spiked 875 percent at the Tower Records chain. The Grammy Bounce is a perennial phenomenon. In 2003 Norah Jones'* Come Away With Me *zoomed to Number One within a week. Sales soon topped 9.2 million.*

Lucky Man 81 times, each time with a different college or professional athletic team in the lyrics. The idea was to attract station music directors in markets key to the song and encourage airplay. At the very least, figured Montgomery Gentry promoters, the local tie-in would prolong airplay more than normal.

LEARNING CHECK ◄ ···

▶ **New payola schemes allow recording companies not to get their hands dirty directly. How do they work?**

MEASURES OF SUCCESS

It would be wrong to suggest that successful recordings can result only from manipulation. Once new music crosses the threshold to exposure, its commercial success rests with public acceptance. Exposure, however, is key. The publicity that comes with a Grammy Award, for example, inevitably boosts sales, usually dramatically.

The most often-cited measure of success is sales. Once a single sells 1 million copies or an album sells 500,000 copies, the RIAA confers a **gold record** award. A **platinum record** is awarded for 2 million singles or 1 million albums. The measure of success for shareholders who own the conglomerates that own the record companies, however, is profit. A gold record for 1 million albums doesn't translate into profit if the artist has a lavish multimillion-dollar deal whose break-even point is 2 million records.

● **gold record**
The award for sales of 500,000 albums or 1 million singles

● **platinum record**
The award for sales of 1 million albums or 2 million singles

LEARNING CHECK ◄ ···

▶ **What does it mean when a record goes gold? Platinum?**
▶ **What is the Grammy Bounce?**
▶ **What noneconomic measures can be used to score a recording's success?**

Chapter Wrap-Up

Recording Industry (Page 131)

■ The recording industry produces products that surround us. Recorded music is almost everywhere, all the time. The industry is dominated by four major companies: Bertelsmann, EMI, Universal and Warner. All are international players, although invisible even to people who buy recorded music, because their products are issued as labels—a kind of brand marketing. Despite the dominance of the Big Four, independent record companies have a strong history of innovation in music.

Downloads (Page 135)

■ The recording industry has been "technologically challenged." Focused on its traditional distribution channels, the industry missed the impact of the Internet for people to swap music until it was almost too late. Through legal action, the industry has stemmed some revenue losses, but the problem is not over. The leading industry trade organization, RIAA, in seeking relief through the courts, has a mantra about looming doom. The industry's customers are of mixed mind. Many feel they've been gouged for years by overpriced CDs. The industry, also, has struggled to combat an older form of piracy—dubbing copies for black-market sales. This is mostly an overseas activity in countries with governments that largely ignore the practice.

Authorized Downloads (Page 137)

■ In desperation the recording industry attempted numerous online distribution mechanisms to combat unauthorized downloading. None worked. Then Apple introduced the iPod device and the iTunes music store, which gave recording companies a 21st-century distribution system through which they could draw revenue. Apple, in effect, became an industry retailer. So did iTunes imitators. Traditional retailers, particularly small, independent record shops that had long been squeezed by chain stores, disappeared almost entirely.

Artistic Autonomy (Page 140)

■ Performers once were beholden to record companies, which owned complex production studios that were essential for recording. The companies also controlled the distribution system. This gave the companies tight control on popular music. No more, or at least less so. With low-cost digital recording equipment, performers now can turn out CDs and podcasts themselves to build a fan base. Also, performers are less dependent on the companies for revenue. They organize their own tours, which can be lucrative revenue streams.

Regulatory Pressure (Page 141)

■ With control by recording companies diminished, artists have gained artistic latitudes. These have included lyrics that are objectionable to some people but that also have resonated well in segments of the marketplace. Recording companies once had the power to obviate the issue by banning the lyrics. But performers now have independent access to audiences and, for better or worse, the objectionable music has a following. Record companies are in a bind between issuing products with strong profit potential and issuing products that draw condemnation, even boycott threats, from organized opposition. Boycotts are especially worrisome to companies, like Time Warner, whose interests extend far beyond music. Also, government leaders rumble about censorship possibilities, especially during election periods.

Dependence on Radio (Page 143)

■ The recording industry relies on radio to play new music. Airtime, basically free advertising, is essential for a single to become popular. This dependence of the recording industry on radio led to payola scandals in the 1950s, with under-the-table payments to decision makers at influential stations for airtime. The problem has persisted, albeit sometimes in subtler forms.

REVIEW QUESTIONS

1. How is the music industry integrated into our daily lives?

2. What is the corporate structure of the music recording industry?

3. How was the recording industry threatened by Napster and similar software?

4. What has transformed the retailing of recorded music?

5. What has happened to the artist and repertoire units at major record companies?

6. How has the recording industry answered threats to censor objectionable lyrics?

7. What's wrong with payola?

CONCEPTS

pirate dubbing (Page 135)

downloading (Page 135)

file swapping (Page 135)

payola (Page 144)

TERMS

A&R (Page 140)

garage bands (Page 141)

iTunes (Page 137)

Parents Music Resource Center (Page 141)

PEOPLE

Adam Curry (Page 139)

Shawn Fanning (Page 136)

David Geffen (Page 132)

Steve Jobs (Page 137)

Gerald Levin (Page 142)

MEDIA SOURCES

● The biweekly *Rolling Stone* is the leading periodical for fans who want to track the music business.

● Ethan Brown. *Queens Reigns Supreme*. Anchor, 2005. Brown traces the roots of many big-name rappers to the 1988 shooting death of rookie cop Edward Byrne, which spurred a police crackdown on Queens drug barons. Many left the drug trade, turning to creating music about what they knew best. Although writing in a detached, neutral journalistic tone, Brown is unsympathetic.

● Barry Truax. *Acoustic Communication*, second edition. Greenwood, 2001. Truax, a Canadian scholar, draws on interdisciplinary studies to create a model for understanding acoustic and aural experiences.

● James Miller. *Flowers in the Dustbin: The Rise of Rock'n' Roll, 1947–1977*. Simon & Schuster, 1999. Miller, an academic who also is a book and music critic, traces rock to earlier origins than most scholars.

In this chapter you have deepened your media literacy by revisiting several themes. Here are thematic highlights from the chapter:

Media Technology

A pattern among established mass-media companies is to miss transformational opportunities from new technology until it's almost too late. The recording industry, as an example, was caught unawares by Napster and offspring technology like Grokster. The technology allowed fans to swap music free. Revenue plummeted. Rather than embrace the fact that the new technology wouldn't go away, the industry resisted it. Unable to get a grip on the new technology, record makers began filing lawsuits, including dozens against fans, many of them college students. This was no way to make friends. The industry also won a copyright-infringement case against Grokster that put swap-facilitating services out of business. What next? A slightly different retailing model, Apple iTunes, has been widely accepted. But iTunes is far short of the dramatic transformation of which we obtained a glimpse with Napster. **(Pages 135–139)**

Monster Unleashed. *The industry almost buckled at the impact of Shawn Fanning's Napster and its file-swap-enabling successors.*

Media Economics

Low-cost sound recording equipment, which gave rise to garage bands in the 1980s, has democratized music. Musicians no longer need support from a studio to produce marketable CDs. Marketing, indeed, remains a problem for upstart performers, but the stranglehold of record companies on the direction of music has been broken. Their multimillion-dollar facilities and staffs have become anachronisms. **(Pages 139–141)**

Independent Labels. *Rappers mostly emerged through off-brand indie labels.*

Media and Democracy

Early in her highly organized 2008 presidential campaign, Hillary Clinton solicited online nominations for a campaign theme song. Ironically, it was a Canadian, Celine Dion, who won with her song *You and I.* Clinton swayed and rocked to Dion at rallies nationwide, a demonstration of the role that recorded music, almost omnipresent in modern society, has in often-dry politics. Ditties, of course, have long been part of political campaigns, but we've come a long way from Franklin Roosevelt's *Happy Days Are Here Again.* **(Pages 131–132)**

Celine Dion

Elitism and Populism

Nothing wrong with a hoedown, but a barn dance hardly requires the sophistication to appreciate that a Rossini opera at La Scala does. Elitists are bothered that the recording industry has built its success on a frenzied issuance of music that is new—pop. This is stuff that is catchy but mostly forgettable after a short run in the manipulatable marketplace of fickle mass taste. Replacement stuff is always in the pipeline. To elitists, the question is: What is this endless parade of pop displacing? What better stuff is not finding its way to market? Is the recording industry failing in its responsibility to make signifcant, enduring contributions with the next Rossini by pushing the Monkeys, Hootie and the Blowfish, and Milli Vanilli? Milli who? **(Page 145)**

Media Effects

The effect of music on individuals is profound. Since the fife and bugle, armies have taken music to battle. Today soldiers in Iraq amp themselves with tough pop. Whose parental instincts aren't stirred by a lullaby? Or patriotism by John Philip Sousa? Think about love songs, varsity fight songs, even advertising ditties. In a broader sense, cultural sociologists look at what music says about a culture. Music from the enslaved U.S. black culture reflected hardship and misery and also, through hymns, a strong sense of a better hereafter. Pop music from the 1950s was a post-war exuberant innocence. The Vietnam-era folk revival was a product of anti-war sentiment. Music flowing from the coinciding Flower Child period was no less revealing. What does pop music today say about the new generation? **(Pages 129–131)**

Armed with an MP3. *Soldiers carry more than their M16 semi-automatics.*

Individualism Reigns. *Download and playback devices, like iPods, have cut into traditional retail outlets. For recorded music. Been to a mom-and-pop music shop lately? Independent shops are hard to find these days, right? And why be a slave to a radio-station playlist when, with no waiting, you can do your own programming and play what you want when you want?*

Audience Fragmentation

Music has always fallen into genres—classical and folk. As a genre, pop was the creation of the recording industry—a stream of commercially promoted music with an emphasis on new, new, new. Although other genres co-existed with it, pop music became dominant in the 1920s. Pop was a socially unifying factor through national radio play well into the 1950s. Then when radio switched almost entirely to recorded music for programming, stations sought to distinguish themselves from one another, and other genres established themselves in a fragmenting music universe. **(Pages 140–141)**

149

7

Motion Pictures

Her Movies Her Way

Julie Dash

For the first 20 years of her career as a moviemaker, Julie Dash shunned Hollywood. She called herself a "film outlaw." She was hooked on innovative movies by independent directors whom her professors lionized. Hollywood slickness was not for Julie Dash. She wanted to make personal films, her stories her way. That she did in all kinds of little-noted projects.

Then, at age 38, after a decade of working on the concept and rounding up $800,000 for production, Dash came up with *Daughters of the Dust*. Hollywood gave the movie a pass at the Sundance Film Festival in 1991 as too surreal, too convoluted, too personal, but *Daughters* caught on with black audiences and gathered momentum that propelled it into national theatrical release. Awards flooded Dash. *Daughters* had made her the first African-American woman to have a full-length theatrical release. After seven years in release, *Daughters* was named the best African-American film of the century.

Daughters of the Dust was indeed Julie Dash's story. Her father, an airport luggage carrier, had roots in the Sea Islands off Georgia and South Carolina. On family trips from Harlem as a kid, her intrigue with the islands grew. Slowly *Daughters* took form in her mind as a story—about a family's painful decision to uproot itself from its impoverished ancestral roots and cross over to the mainland.

Finally Hollywood took notice. But there was a caveat. In Hollywood, a director's self-indulgence needs to be held in check

LEARNING AHEAD

- Movies are most powerful viewed uninterrupted in a darkened auditorium.

- Besides feature films, there are subgenres including animated and documentary films.

- The movie industry is dominated by a handful of major studios.

- The exhibition component of the movie industry is in rapid transition.

- Blockbusters can be spectacular but carry high risk.

Julie Dash's Masterpiece. *In the climatic scene from Dash's* Daughters of the Dust, *set in 1902, Eula struggles to reconcile generational differences between Nana and her children before the children leave Ibo Island. Nana is staying behind.*

so a movie never loses the audience—and Dash's work sometimes pressed the border, as in *Daughter's* nonlinear story line and dialect-heavy script. Dash acknowledges this pressure in telling the story of a Universal executive who, in discussing a possible future project, said: "We loved *Daughter of the Dust*. Don't do that."

Dash's most noted work from her Hollywood period has been *The Rosa Parks Story*, a CBS television movie. Critics praised the film as not just another biopic that heroized a civil rights figure but a deeply personal portrayal. Dash's other long-form features include *Love Song* for MTV, the romantic thriller *Incognito* and the television movie *Funny Valentines*. Among her fortes: music videos.

Still, Dash plays at the cutting edge of filmmaking. Her *Brothers of the Borderland*, which shows at the National Underground Railroad Freedom Center, is a sensory experience like few people have experienced. Viewers feel the spray during river scenes, smell the deep woods and feel drafts and blasts of wind as they are led through the story.

Significance of Movies

STUDY PREVIEW

Movies can have a powerful and immediate effect, in part because theaters insulate moviegoers in a cocoon without distractions. By some measures, the powerful effect is short-lived. Nonetheless, movies can sensitize people to issues and have a long-term effect in shifting public attitudes on enduring issues.

MOVIE POWER

As Dan Brown's thriller *The Da Vinci Code* picked up steam en route to becoming a mega-selling book, the debate intensified on his account of Catholic church history. It was a big deal—but nothing compared to the fury that occurred when Sony moved Ron Howard's movie adaptation toward release. The full crescendo came when the movie premiered. The unprecedented dialogue demonstrates the impact of movies as a storytelling and myth-making medium, which, for mass audiences, can far exceed the impact of other media for at least short windows of time.

Movies with religious themes can strike loud chords, as did Mel Gibson's *Passion of the Christ* and Martin Scorsese's *Last Temptation of Christ*. But movies have an impact on other hot-button issues. Consider *Brokeback Mountain*, which catapulted homosexual affections into a new territory of public dialogue. The short story in the *New Yorker* magazine on which *Brokeback* was based had made merely a ripple in the mass consciousness. Al Gore's documentary *An Inconvenient Truth* gave new urgency in 2006 to finding solutions for global warming. Michael Moore and other docu-ganda producers have stirred significant issues far beyond what magazine and newspaper articles had been doing for years. *Guess Who's Coming to Dinner*, with a theme that was interracially edgy for the 1960s, moved the public toward broader acceptance.

LEARNING CHECK ◄

▸ What impact, perhaps indelible, have the movies mentioned here had on audiences?

▸ What recent movies would you add to the list? Why?

Suspension of Disbelief.
People are carrying their experiences and realities with them when they sit down for a movie. As a story-teller, a movie director needs quickly to suck the audience into the plot—to suspend disbelief, as novelists call it. Master directors, like James Cameron, best known for Titanic, *strive to create this new reality in opening scenes to engross viewers in the story as it unfolds.*

● **suspension of disbelief**
Occurs when you surrender doubts about the reality of a story and become caught up in the story

COCOON EXPERIENCE

Why the powerful and immediate effect of movies? There may be a clue in one of Thomas Edison's first shorts, which included ocean waves rolling toward a camera on a beach. Audiences covered their heads, such was their **suspension of disbelief.** Instinctively they expected to be soaked. Natural human skepticism gets lost in the darkened cocoon of a movie-house auditorium, compounding the impact of what's on-screen.

Although moviegoers are insulated in a dark auditorium, the experience is communal. You're not the only one sobbing or terrified or joyous. Among your fellow viewers is a reinforcement of emotions that other media can't match. A newspaper article, for example, may be read by thousands, but the experience is individual and apart. The emotional impact is less. Television, watched at home, often alone, is similarly disadvantaged, although television has most of the accoutrements of movies—visuals, motion and sound.

At their most potent, movies need to be seen in a theater. A movie may be good on a DVD at home, as computer downloads or as pay-per-view on television—but nothing compares to the theater phenomenon.

LEARNING CHECK ◄···

▸ **In what situation are movies most likely to encourage suspension of disbelief?**

MOVIES AND MORES

As an especially powerful medium, movies have been targets of censors and the moral police from almost the beginning. In retrospect, some concern has been darkly comical—like attempts in 1896 to ban *Dolorita in the Passion Dance.* Provocative or not, nobody has ever made the case that *Dolorita* corrupted anybody. Movies can be successful at moving emotions at the moment, but as for changing fundamentals in lifestyle or triggering aberrant behavior, the jury remains out.

More clear is that movies can sensitize people to issues with sympathetic or deleterious portrayals. Such was the case in 2005 with *Brokeback Mountain.* A generation

Culture Wars. *Director Ang Lee's sympathetic treatment of homosexual commitment amid social obstacles in* Brokeback Mountain *remained such a divisive issue in 2005 that President Bush felt compelled to deny seeing the film to fend off what would have been the natural follow-up question: "Did you like the movie?" The argument can be made that filmic treatments help break taboos. The Sidney Portier film* Guess Who's Coming to Dinner *on interracial relationships was so credited in the 1960s.*

● **Hollywood**
A Los Angeles enclave that was the early center of U.S. filmmaking, now more a metaphor for the industry

earlier, *Guess Who's Coming to Dinner* had done the same. Conversely, terrorists have received no slack in the ever-growing volume of action movies. Knowing the value of on-screen portrayals, special-interest groups have worked to eliminate negative stereotypes. It's wrong, say Italian-American organizers, for organized-crime characters always to carry Italian surnames. Feminists have gone after lopsided portrayals of women in homemaker and subordinate roles. Minority groups have leveled similar charges. The result, although hard to prove, has been a new **Hollywood** sensitivity to these issues that probably is playing out slowly in general attitudes in society.

LEARNING CHECK ◀ ⋯⋯⋯⋯⋯⋯⋯⋯⋯⋯⋯⋯⋯⋯⋯⋯⋯⋯⋯⋯

▶ **What is the difference in the immediate and long-term effects of a movie theater experience?**

▶ **In fiction, what is the significance of suspension of disbelief?**

GLOBAL ROLE

After Europe and its promising young film industry were devastated by World War I, Hollywood filled a void by exporting movies. Thus began Hollywood's move toward global pre-eminence in filmmaking. It happened again in World War II. The U.S. government declared movies an essential wartime industry for producing military training and propaganda films. After the war, Europe again in ruins, Hollywood was intact and expanded its exports.

Today, movies are among the few products that contribute positively to the balance of trade for the United States. More movies are exported than imported. Indeed, the potential for foreign box office presence is essential for Hollywood in working out the financial details for film projects. Movie proposals with good prospects for a foreign box office revenue are more likely to get a green light. Consider this mid-2006 snapshot of leading Hollywood films:

	U.S. Box Office	Foreign Box Office
X-Men: Last Stand	$231.2 billion	$205.5 billion
The Da Vinci Code	213.2 billion	515.1 billion
Cars	205.9 billion	64.6 billion
Ice Age: The Meltdown	194.3 billion	446.9 billion
Superman Returns	141.6 billion	35.8 billion
Pirates of the Caribbean: Dead Man's Chest	135.6 billion	48.6 billion
Mission: Impossible III	133.0 billion	219.4 billion

About 60 percent of U.S. film exports go to Europe, 30 percent to Asia. It is action films that do best abroad. There usually is minimal dialogue to impede the transcultural experience. Media scholar George Gerbner once explained it this way: "Violence travels well."

Although Hollywood historically has been globally dominant in filmmaking, significant film industries have emerged elsewhere. In India, the film capital Mumbai, formerly Bombay and nicknamed Bollywood, outproduces Hollywood with 900 to 1,200 films a year, compared to 700 or so from U.S. studios. China and Hong Kong each put out more than 100 films a year. In Africa the Nigerian film industry has come to be called Nollywood.

LEARNING CHECK ◀

▶ **How did Hollywood establish itself as a global moviemaking center?**

▶ **About Hollywood movie exports, scholar George Gerbner once said, "Violence travels well." What did he mean?**

Movie Products

STUDY PREVIEW

To most people, the word *movie* conjures up the feature films that are the Hollywood specialty. Subspecies include animated films and documentaries. Also, the historic distinction between Hollywood and television as rivals is melding.

FEATURE FILMS

● **narrative films**
Movies that tell a story

Movies that tell stories, much in the tradition of stage plays, are **narrative films.** These are what most people think of as movies. They're promoted heavily, their titles and actors on marquees. Most are in the 100-minute range.

A French magician and inventor, Georges Méliès, pioneered narrative films with fairy tales and science-fiction stories to show in his movie house in 1896. Méliès' *Little Red Riding Hood* and *Cinderella* ran less than 10 minutes—short stories, if you will. In 1902 Edwin Porter directed *Life of a Fireman*, the first coherent narrative film in the United States. Audiences, accustomed to stage plays and being a distance away from the actors, were distressed, some shocked, at his close-ups, a new

● **film literacy**
Ability to appreciate artistic
techniques used for telling
a story through film

technique. They felt cheated at not seeing "the whole stage." Gradually, audiences learned what is called **film literacy,** the ability to appreciate moviemaking as an art form with unique-to-the-medium techniques that add impact or facilitate the telling of a story. Porter's next significant film, *The Great Train Robbery*, was shocking, too, for cutting back and forth between robbers and a posse that was chasing them—something, like close-ups, that film can do and the stage cannot. Slowly movies emerged as a distinctive art form.

■ **Talkies.** At Thomas Edison's lab, the tinkerer William Dickson came up with a sound system for movies in 1889, but it didn't go anywhere. The first successful commercial application of sound was in Movietone newsreels in 1922. But it was four upstart moviemakers, the **Warner brothers,** Albert, Harry, Jack and Sam Warner, who revolutionized **talkies,** movies with sound. In 1927 the Warners released ***The Jazz Singer*** starring Al Jolson. There was sound only for two segments, 354 words total, but audiences in movie houses the Warners had equipped with loudspeakers were enthralled. The next year, 1928, the Warners issued ***The Singing Fool,*** also with Jolson, this time with a full-length sound track. The Warners earned 25 times their investment. For 10 years no other movie attracted more people to the box office.

● **Warner brothers**
Introduced sound

● **talkies**
Movies with sound

● ***The Jazz Singer***
The first feature sound movie

● ***The Singing Fool***
The first full-length sound movie

■ **Color.** Overtaking *The Singing Fool* in 1939 was a narrative movie with another technological breakthrough, *Gone with the Wind* with color. Although *Gone with the Wind* is often referred to as the first color movie, the technology had been devised in the 1920s, and ***The Black Pirate*** with Douglas Fairbanks was far earlier, in 1925. But *GWTW*, as it's called by buffs, was a far more significant film. *GWTW* marked the start of Hollywood's quest for ever-more-spectacular stories and effects to attract audiences—the blockbuster.

● ***The Black Pirate***
The first feature movie in color

■ **Computer-Generated Imagery.** You can imagine why early moviemaker Alfred Clark used a special effect for his 1895 movie *The Execution of Mary Queen of Scots.* "Illusion" was what special effects were called then. Although audiences were amazed, the effects were nothing like today's *CGI*, the shoptalk abbreviation that movie people use for three-dimensional **computer-generated imagery.**

● **computer-generated imagery (CGI)**
The application of three-dimensional computer graphics for special effects, particularly in movies and television

Bryan Singer

Super Heroics. *The 2006* Superman *sequel was budgeted by Warner Bros. for a stratospheric $184.5 million, including special effects. Director Bryan Singer, fresh from his two effects-heavy* X Men *movies, needed more, including $2.3 million for visual FX for one sequence. In all, Singer ran the production budget to $204 million.*

The first use of three-dimensional CGI in movies was *Futureworld* in 1976. University of Utah grad students Edwin Catmull and Fred Parke created a computer-generated hand and face. There were CGI scenes in *Star Wars* in 1977, but the technology remained mostly an experimental novelty until 1989 when the pseudopod sea creature created by Industrial Light & Magic for *The Abyss* won an Academy Award.

Photorealistic CGI was firmly in place with the villain's liquid metal morphing effects in *Terminator 2*, also by Industrial Light & Magic and also recognized by a 1991 Oscar for special effects.

Computer-generated imagery soon became the dominant form of special effects with technology opening up new possibilities. For stunts, CGI characters began replacing doubles that were nearly indistinguishable from the actors. Crowd scenes were easily created without hiring hundreds of extras. This raised the question of whether movie actors themselves might be replaced by pixels.

Movie commentator Neil Petkus worries that some filmmakers may overuse their toy. "CGI effects can be abused and mishandled," Petkus says. "Directors sometimes allow the visual feasts that computers offer to undermine any real content a movie may have had." Petkus faults director George Lucas for going too far in later *Star Wars* movies: "Any interesting character developments that could have occurred in these movies were overwhelmed by constant CGI action sequences."

Movies that overdo CGI can lack the depth of character and nuance that human actors bring to the screen, says Petkus: "How can we relate to a character made up of pixels and mathematical algorithms and not flesh, blood and emotion? Sure, CGI movies are flashy, but they don't convey the sense of reality that we look for in a good cinematic story."

Another commentator, Matt Leonard, has made the point this way: "There are hundreds of Elvis impersonators in the world, some of which are very good, but none of them are good enough to fool us into thinking Elvis has returned. The closer we get to creating a completely digital character the more our senses seem to alert us to the fact that something is not completely right and therefore we dismiss it as a cheap trick or imitation."

So while CGI characters can make sense for stunt stand-ins or for humanly impossible, only-from-Hollywood contortions and feats, they probably don't spell doom for the Screen Actors Guild. About replacing actors, Dennis Muren of Industrial Light & Magic is clear: "Why bother! Why not focus on what doesn't exist as opposed to recreating something that is readily available."

Faster computers and massive data storage capacities have added efficiencies to computer-generated movie imagery, but offsetting the efficiencies has been pressure for greater detail and quality. CGI is labor-intensive. A single frame typically takes two to three hours to render. For a complex frame, count on 20 hours or more. The Warner Bros. budget for the 2006 *Superman Returns*, a record $204 million, was eaten up largely with CGI effects.

LEARNING CHECK ◄ ·······························

▸ **How would you define feature films?**

▸ **How has technology shaped feature films?**

● **Walt Disney**
Pioneer in animated films

● **animated film**
Narrative films with drawn scenes and characters

● ***Steamboat Willie***
Animated cartoon character that became Mickey Mouse

ANIMATED FILMS

The 1920s were pivotal in defining genres of narrative films. In his early 20s, **Walt Disney** arrived in Los Angeles from Missouri in 1923 with $40 in his pocket. Walt moved in with his brother Roy, and they rounded up $500 and went into the **animated film** business. In 1928 ***Steamboat Willie*** debuted in a short film to accompany feature films. The character Willie eventually morphed into Mickey Mouse.

Al Gore. *His documentary*
An Inconvenient Truth
*turned former Vice President
Al Gore into a movie star of
sorts. Suddenly he had riveted public attention on climatic issues that environ-
mentalists as far back as
Rachel Carson in the 1950s
have been arguing threaten
the habitat of the planet for
humans and other species.*

In-Your-Face Documentaries

Not so long ago, moviegoers deemed documentaries dreary, dull
and dry. Today some documentaries are the hottest money-makers
in Hollywood. Michael Moore's in-your-face *Fahrenheit 9/11*
grossed $100 million its first month.

As with all his documentaries, including *Sicko* in 2007,
Moore has critics who say he's neither fair nor balanced. Moore
stands by his accuracy but explains that his documentaries are his
take on issues. He sees them as "balancing" to dominant inter-
pretations offered in the mainstream media.

That contrarian thrust, says television writer Debi Enker, is
addressing a void in general media coverage of issues: "The current interest suggests people are seeking not just immediacy but
also context and the kind of perspective that time, research,
thoughtful analysis, and intelligent storytelling can bring." Dawn
Dreyer of the Center for Documentary Studies at Duke University
puts it this way: "It's narrative. It's storytelling. It's becoming engaged with people's lives."

Dreyer's characterization of documentaries explains, also,
the success of former Vice President Al Gore's *An Inconvenient
Truth*. The movie grossed more than $41 million worldwide.
A documentary typically has a far lower budget than other
movies, which can mean higher profits even if there is only a
limited theatrical release. *Inconvenient Truth*, the first carbon-
neutral documentary, started as a low-tech slide show. Filming
took six months and a little more than $1 million—pocket
change by Hollywood standards.

One of *Inconvenient Truth*'s producers, Lawrence Bender, said: "Everything about
this movie was a miracle." Not only did the film rake in cash, it earned two Oscars. Also,
it made Al Gore a movie star. "When we took Gore to Sundance and Cannes, people
just went crazy around him," said Bender. "It was really amazing. He doesn't sing or act,
but he actually is kind of a rock star. He has this message that's drawing people to him,
making him larger than life."

The British government purchased 3,385 DVDs to distribute to every secondary
school. In the United States, 50,000 copies were given to teachers. The Documentary
Organization of Canada launched a new green code of ethics for documentary filmmakers.
Paramount Classics donated 5 percent of all box office receipts to The Alliance for Climate
Protection. The Alliance also received 100 percent of Gore's proceeds from the film.

DEEPENING YOUR MEDIA LITERACY

EXPLORE THE ISSUE

Pick a new muckraking documentary and a television news report on the same subject.

DIG DEEPER

What makes the documentary different from the way a television news report might
treat the same subject? Would the documentary resonate as well with the audience if
the filmmaker did not feel passionately about the subject and it was completely fair and
balanced?

WHAT DO YOU THINK?

Do you think these new documentaries fill a need? How have they contributed to the
movie industry? To society?

Disney took animation to full length with **Snow White and the Seven Dwarfs** in 1937, cementing animation as a subspecies of narrative films.

Animated films were labor-intensive, requiring an illustrator to create 1,000-plus sequential drawings for a minute of screen time. Computers changed all that in the 1990s, first with digital effects for movies that otherwise had scenes and actors, notably the *Star Wars* series by George Lucas, then animated features. Disney's *Toy Story* in 1995 was the first movie produced entirely by computers. The new technology, brought to a high level by Lucas' Industrial Light & Magic and Steve Jobs' Pixar, has led to a resurgence in the issuance of animated films after a relatively dormant period.

Recent years have seen huge audiences for *Shrek, Finding Nemo* and *Cars,* among others.

LEARNING CHECK ◄

▶ **What were pioneer successes in animated films?**

▶ **How can you explain the resurgence of animated films?**

DOCUMENTARIES

Nonfiction film explorations of historical or current events and natural and social phenomena go back to 1922 and **Robert Flaherty's** look into Eskimo life. With their informational thrust, early **documentaries** had great credibility. Soon, though, propagandists were exploiting the credibility of documentaries with point-of-view nonfiction. Propagandist films found large audiences in World War II, including **Frank Capra's** seven 50-minute films in the **Why We Fight** series.

■ **Television Network Documentaries.** Television journalists righted the tilt of documentaries in the 1950s. In part it was that journalists of the just-the-facts mold were doing the documentaries. Also, it was the television networks that underwrote the budgets of these documentaries. Their purpose was to build corporate prestige, not propagandize. A factor in the neutral thrust of most of these documentaries also was the Federal Communications Commission's licensing dictum on stations for fairness in whatever was broadcast.

■ **Docu-Ganda.** The FCC's **Fairness Doctrine** was withdrawn in 1987, setting in motion a new rationale for documentaries that, in many cases, seeks not so much to inform as to influence the audience. What emerged was a new-form genre that critics call **docu-ganda,** which plays not on the major television networks but in movie houses and niche outlets. Independent filmmaker Michael Moore has epitomized the new generation of documentary-makers, first with *Roger and Me*, a brutal attack on General Motors. Moore was no less savage in *Bowling for Columbine*, this time aiming at gun access advocates, and *Fahrenheit 9/11*, aimed during the 2004 elections at President Bush and his Iraq War motivations. *Fahrenheit* was the largest-grossing documentary in history—a demonstration of the economic viability of documentaries.

Relatively inexpensive digital filmmaking equipment has also driven the new documentaries. For his *Super Size Me*, linking fast food and obesity, Morgan Sperlock could never have persuaded a major studio to cover the budget, several million dollars upfront, for a documentary attacking an American icon like McDonald's. But with a $3,000 digital camera, $5,000 in software and an Apple computer, Sperlock created his personal statement on fast food. So compelling was *Super Size Me* that 200 theaters showed it and grossed $7.5 million in a month. In all, Sperlock had spent only $65,000 to create the movie.

Sicko. *Michael Moore taunted the pharmaceutical industry with his 2007 documentary* Sicko. *In one sense, Moore's documentaries, although fact-based, carry slants and use rhetorical techniques that short-circuit what could be honest persuasion. The techniques leave Moore an easy target for responses from those whom his films attack.*

■ **Single Point of View.** Critics fault many recent documentaries for usurping the detached, neutral tone of earlier documentaries while delivering only a single point of view. Guilty as charged, respond the new documentary-makers. David Zieger, who raised eyebrows with his *Sir! No Sir!* on the anti-war movement within the military during the Vietnam war, says: "If you make a film with both sides, you're going to make a boring film." Film is not journalism, Zieger says. Prolific documentary-maker Robert Greenwald says he covers a subject as he sees it, albeit one-sided. Viewers, he says, need to accept responsibility for weighing his portrayal against what they pick up elsewhere.

In other words, a docu-ganda requires viewers to have a higher level of media literacy than in the heyday of television network documentaries that laid out competing viewpoints within a single package. A Canadian media executive, Christopher Ian Bennett, is less benign about the effect of point-of-view treatments. Bennett says that the contemporary documentaries that make the biggest splash are, in fact, dangerous because they can dupe viewers into accepting them as the whole truth.

LEARNING CHECK ◄••

▶ **What are historically important documentaries?**

▶ **Who are significant current documentary producers? What are their signature works?**

▶ **Some documentaries are journalistic explorations. Others are highly opinionated. How can moviegoers recognize the difference?**

Nanook of the North. *The documentary became a film genre with explorer Robert Flaherty's* Nanook of the North *in 1922. This film was an attempt to record reality— no actors, no props. The film was especially potent not only because it was a new approach and on a fascinating subject but also because, coincidentally, Nanook died of starvation on the ice around the time that the film was released.*

Arctic Explorer

Explorer Robert Flaherty took a camera to the Arctic in 1921 to record the life of an Eskimo family. The result was a new kind of movie: the documentary. While other movies of the time were theatrical productions with scripts, sets and actors, Flaherty tried something different: recording reality.

His 57-minute *Nanook of the North* was compelling on its own merits when it started on the movie-house circuit in 1922, but the film received an unexpected macabre boost a few days later when Nanook, the father of the Eskimo family, died of hunger on the ice. News stories of Nanook's death stirred public interest—and also attendance at the movie, which helped to establish the documentary as an important new film genre.

Flaherty's innovative approach took a new twist in the 1930s when propagandists saw reality-based movies as a tool to promote their causes. In Germany the Nazi government produced propaganda films, and other countries followed. Frank Capra directed the vigorous seven-film series *Why We Fight* for the U.S. War Office in 1942.

After World War II there was a revival of documentaries in Flaherty's style—a neutral recording of natural history. Walt Disney produced a variety of such documentaries, including the popular *Living Desert* in the 1950s.

Today, documentaries are unusual in U.S. movie houses, with occasional exceptions such as movies built around rock concerts and *March of the Penguins.*

The CBS television network gained a reputation in the 1950s and 1960s for picking up on the documentary tradition with *Harvest of Shame,* about migrant workers, and *Hunger in America.* In the same period the National Geographic Society established a documentary unit, and French explorer Jacques Cousteau went into the television documentary business.

Such full-length documentaries are mostly relegated to the Public Broadcasting Service and cable networks today. The major networks, meanwhile, shifted most documentaries away from full-length treatments. Typical is CBS's *60 Minutes,* a twice-weekly one-hour program of three mini-documentaries. These new network projects combine reality programming and entertainment in slick packages that attract larger audiences than traditional documentaries.

WHAT DO YOU THINK?

▶ How would Robert Flaherty have felt about the use of the documentary style in later propaganda films?

▶ Are reality television shows, like the *Amazing Race* and *Survivor,* true to the Flaherty legacy?

MOVIE MILESTONES

1700s

Discovery
Scientists darkened silver nitrate with light, fundamental to photographic technology for movies (1727)

1800s

Openers
Thomas Edison lab invented movie cameras, projectors; followed up by producing movies for exhibition (1888)

1900–1949

Palaces
Strand in New York, first of the opulent movie palaces (1912)

Paramount
Hollywood studio system took form (1912–)

First Documentary
Nanook of the North (1922)

Sound
Fox introduced sound in newsreels (1922)

Color
Black Pirate with Douglas Fairbanks, first color movie (1927)

Talkies
Warner distributed first talkie, *The Jazz Singer* (1927)

Popularity
U.S. box office peaked at 90 million tickets a week (1946)

Breakup
U.S. Supreme Court ruled against Hollywood's vertical integration (1948)

1950–1999

Television
Network television eroded movie attendance (1950s)

Disney
Disney produced weekly television show (1954)

Ratings
G through NC-17 (née X) rating system (1968)

Multiplex
Multiscreen theaters attempted to recover audience (1970s)

VHS
Home movie rentals deteriorated theater attendance (1990s)

2000s

Digitization
Theaters began 10-year conversion to digital projection (2006)

Major studios concentrate in Hollywood

Nanook dead but alive on-screen

Walt Disney

Computer-assisted special effects

PIVOTAL EVENTS

- Age of Reason encouraged ongoing scientific experimentation

- U.S. middle class with discretionary time for amusement emerged (1870s–)

- World War I (1914–1918)
- Great Depression (1930s)
- World War II (1941–1945)

- U.S. Supreme Court extended First Amendment to movies (1952)
- Vietnam War (1964–1973)
- Internet emerged as commercial medium (late 1990s)

- 9/11 terrorist attacks (2001)
- Iraq War (2003–)
- Hurricane Katrina (2005)

Hollywood Studios

STUDY PREVIEW

Hollywood is dominated by six movie studios, all engaged in both producing and distributing movies. These studios, all parts of conglomerates, are enmeshed with the television industry through corporate connections.

STUDIO SYSTEM

● **studio system**
A mass production, distribution and exhibition process for movies

The structure of the U.S. movie industry is rooted historically in a few major companies that tightly controlled everything beginning in the 1920s. In this **studio system,** a handful of companies produced, distributed and exhibited movies. The companies had oligarchic control, successfully excluding outsiders and using their power to coerce the marketplace. No studio better illustrates the system than Paramount under Adolph Zukor.

PARAMOUNT

● **Adolph Zukor**
Innovative creator of Paramount as a major movie studio

Hungarian immigrant **Adolph Zukor** started poor in Hollywood, but in a series of innovations, none of them artistic, he invented the movie business as we know it. Before Zukor there were no movie stars, nothing approaching mass production and only a loose distribution and exhibition structure. Zukor changed all that, becoming the stereotypical Hollywood mogul.

■ **Star System.** When Zukor started in the movie business in 1912, moviemakers kept the names of their actors secret. The idea was to dead-end a nascent fan base that might give actors a star complex and calls for better pay. Fifteen dollars a day was tops then. Zukor saw things differently. He tracked fan letters for mentions of actors. Those most mentioned he signed to exclusive contracts. So to speak, Zukor put their names in lights. It cost him. Mary Pickford was soon at $15,000 a week. The payoff for Zukor was that Mary Pickford's name attracted repeat customers just to see her, even in lackluster movies.

● **star system**
Making actors into celebrities to increase the size of movie audiences

The **star system,** as it was called, was imitated by competing studios, which had no choice. Meanwhile, Zukor had a head start. Soon his enterprise took on the name Paramount.

Hollywood Survivor. Most studios sold their huge sound lots to real estate developers for cash to see them through revenue slumps after big-budget flops. Today only Paramount has retained its facilities in Hollywood.

Adolph Zukor

■ **Production Efficiencies.** Zukor brought mass production to moviemaking, in part because he needed to have projects to keep his stars productive, as well as other contract employees, including hundreds of directors, writers, editors and technicians. Paramount movies became factory-like products. On tight mass-production schedules with programmed progress, Paramount eventually was issuing a movie a week. So were competitors in what came to be called the studio system.

By the mid-1930s, the big movie companies—Columbia, MGM, Paramount, RKO, 20th Century-Fox, Universal and Warner—owned acre upon acre of studios and sets. These were money machines but only as long as production kept moving. So whether scripts were strong or weak, the movie factories needed to keep churning out products on predictable schedules to meet what at the time seemed an insatiable public demand for films at movie houses. The movie houses were part of the studio system, many owned by the big studios.

■ **Vertical Integration.** Studios like Paramount, which controlled the production, distribution and exhibition of movies, squeezed out independent operators. **Block booking** was an example. Zukor booked his Paramount movies into his Paramount-owned theaters. Paramount indeed also provided movies to independent movie houses but only in packages that included overpriced clunkers. Profits were immense, funding the lifestyle and other excesses that gave Hollywood its gilded reputation.

The major studios, controlling the whole process from conception of a movie to the box office, had put the industry into what businesspeople call **vertical integration**. Their control, including coercive practices like block booking, in time attracted the anti-trust division of the U.S. Justice Department. In a case decided by the U.S. Supreme Court in 1948, the studios were told to divest. As a result of the so-called **Paramount decision,** studios gave up their ownership of movie houses. It was a setback for the studio system. Suddenly the studios had to compete for screen time in movie houses. Without a guaranteed outlet for movies, including proverbial B movies, the studios had no choice but to scale back on payrolls and facilities. The lavish excesses of Hollywood's gilded age were over.

Studios, including Paramount, turned more to outside directors. Ongoing contracts for big-name stars disappeared. Instead, actors, directors and others were hired project by project. Those acres of sound studios, as movie sets were called, were sold in lucrative real estate deals in the booming Los Angeles area. Some studios found new business in producing television programs in the 1950s.

■ **After Zukor.** The end of the studio system came when large conglomerates bought the studios and imposed new bottom-line expectations. Zukor continued, though, still chair of the board at Paramount until 1976, when at age 103 he died.

Today Paramount is a unit of the U.S. media conglomerate Viacom, whose interests also include the CBS television network. In a typical year Paramount produces a dozen movies but distributes many more for independent producers. The company also produces television programs. Paramount prides itself as the only major studio still located in Hollywood.

LEARNING CHECK ◄ •••

▶ What were Adolph Zukor's enduring contributions to the U.S. movie business?

▶ How did the U.S. Supreme Court reshape Hollywood?

DISNEY

Disney isn't just Mickey Mouse anymore. It was Disney's unmatched animated cartoons, however, that launched the company and propelled it into a distinctive role among major Hollywood studios. Although ranking studios is tricky because one megahit or one clunker can upset a listing, Walt Disney Studio Entertainment is consistent among the leaders of the major studios.

● **block booking**
A rental agreement through which a movie house accepts a batch of movies

● **vertical integration**
One company owning multiple stages of production, to the detriment of competition

● **Paramount decision**
U.S. Supreme Court breakup of movie industry oligarchy in 1948

■ **Classic Disney.** Although not realizing it, illustrator Walt Disney created the Disney franchise with a squeaky mouse in a synch-sound cartoon in 1928. Although the cartoon, *Steamboat Willie*, was only a short, intended to run with previews of coming attractions, audiences couldn't get enough. For a follow-up, Disney fine-tuned the character Willie with more likable, rounded features and the trademark white gloves. Mickey Mouse was born.

As revenue rolled in, Disney experimented with symphonies and cartoons—and in 1937 risked it all with a full-feature animated film, *Snow White and the Seven Dwarfs*. There was a new wrinkle. Not only did characters move but there was unprecedented personality detail, like Snow White crinkling her nose. Disney also used new multiplane cameras for a realistic depth of field.

Audiences wanted more. Disney responded with *Pinnochio, Dumbo* and *Bambi*. Only one Disney film in this period, the culturally highbrow *Fantasia* in 1940, fumbled at the box office. But no matter. Disney saw a timelessness in his animations and tweaked them for new release to a new generation of kids generally on a seven-year cycle. Even *Fantasia* broke into black ink in the recycling.

While other studios were fighting a losing battle with network television in the 1950s, Disney embraced the enemy. He struck a deal with the ABC network in 1954 to produce an original television series. In effect, he recycled his film content for television. The program *Disneyland*, a Sunday-night ritual for millions of television viewers, accounted for almost half of ABC's billing the first year.

Disney also launched the *Mickey Mouse Club* on ABC in the afternoons, with kids singing and dancing and acting in episodic serials. Those serials gave rise to a new Disney enterprise—family feature films with live characters. The most enduring was *Mary Poppins* in 1964. Others included *The Shaggy Dog* and *The Absent-Minded Professor*.

Not only did Disney cross-fertilize his corporate growth with television, in 1955 he opened the Disneyland amusement park in Los Angeles. The term *theme park* was coined. The Disney park theme? All the movie characters. Talk about cross-promotion. When Disney died in 1966 he was still on the rise. What next?

■ **Disney Brand.** For the next 20 years the mandate at Disney was to cultivate the brand. Indeed, Disney had become a brand name for family-oriented entertainment. Corporate managers worked to exploit the synergies, reissuing the earlier films in cycles, creating new ones in the Disney spirit, and building more theme parks, first in Orlando and then laying the groundwork for parks in Paris, Tokyo and elsewhere around the globe. Disney was indeed an international franchise, but without Walt the luster was fading.

● **Michael Eisner**
Post-Walt Disney executive who expanded Disney while protecting its wholesome cachet; engineered a merger with ABC

■ **Eisner Era.** To jump-start the company, Disney shareholders in 1984 brought in an energetic executive from Paramount, **Michael Eisner.** In a 20-year run Eisner indeed rejuvenated the company. Before he was ousted in a byzantine power struggle in 2005, Eisner had became second only to Walt as the most important character in Disney history. Eisner also came to be known as the most powerful person in Hollywood. Eisner continued recycling classic Disney products and expanding the theme parks. Importantly, Eisner engineered a merger with ABC to create in-house outlets for Disney products.

Eisner moved Disney beyond family fare with cutting-edge and niche movies, like *Powder* and *Dangerous Minds*, but buffered the projects under subsidiary units and partnerships to shield the wholesome Disney aura. Films were produced through Touchstone, Caravan, Hollywood Pictures and Miramax. Meanwhile, Disney's distribution unit, Buena Vista, the largest in the world, moved into producing Broadway plays.

■ **Post-Eisner.** Not all was perfect under Eisner. After *Lion King*'s success in 1995, Disney had a run of animated feature flops. Profits slumped occasionally, which, although typical of the vagaries of the movie business, raised shareholder concerns. Too, there was Eisner's growing compensation, which, good years or bad, had kept growing. During one five-year period Eisner made $737 million—$149 million a year on average. Disney's net income shrank an average of 3.1 percent yearly during that period, compared to 6 percent-plus annual growth for other leading U.S. companies. Eventually Disney's governing board split over the compensation issue. In a messy shareholder battle, Eisner was thrown out.

The post-Eisner leadership, concerned that Disney had lost its edge in animation, offered $7.4 billion to Steve Jobs, the genius behind Apple's resurgence, for his Pixar animation studio. It was Pixar that had stolen Disney's animation pre-eminence with blockbusters like *Toy Story, Finding Nemo* and *The Incredibles*. The deal, in 2006, made Jobs the largest Disney shareholder and put him on the Disney board of directors. Within days, Apple's iTunes Store added ABC and Disney video for downloading to its iPods. Disney seemed well positioned for new realities in media content delivery—the traditional movie theaters, its ABC television access and Internet downloads.

Michael Eisner. *He's the second-most-important person in Disney corporate history. Before being ousted, Eisner's accomplishments included the 1995 merger with ABC that gave Disney a new outlet for its creative output.*

OTHER MAJOR STUDIOS

The Big Six studios, besides Paramount and Disney, are Columbia, 20th Century-Fox, Universal and Warner.

■ **Columbia.** Columbia has moved through high-visibility ownership, including Coca-Cola and the Japanese electronics company Sony. Movies are produced and distributed under brand names Columbia and TriStar and through frequent partnerships with Phoenix and Mandalay. The company also is in television production and distribution, including the venerable game show *Jeopardy.*

■ **20th Century-Fox.** This studio is part of the global media empire of Rupert Murdoch's News Corp., whose roots are in Australia. Corporate siblings include Rupert's Fox television network.

■ **Universal.** The conglomerate General Electric bought Universal from the financially overextended French media giant Vivendi in 2002. Earlier, Universal was part of Canadian-based Seagram, known mostly as a distiller. The GE acquisition put the NBC television network and Universal under the same corporate umbrella. The goal was to create profitable synergies between the entities. Universal, like other major studios, is both a movie producer and a distributor.

■ **Warner.** Warner Bros. became part of the Time Inc. media empire in a 1989 acquisition, prompting the parent company to rename itself Time Warner. The company produces and distributes movies and television programs mostly through units carrying the Warner name but also the names Castle Rock, New Line and Lorimar. The CW television network is a joint Warner and Paramount venture.

LEARNING CHECK ◄ ••

▶ **The movie industry once saw television as a rival but no more. What happened?**

▶ **What is the extent of foreign ownership in the U.S. movie industry?**

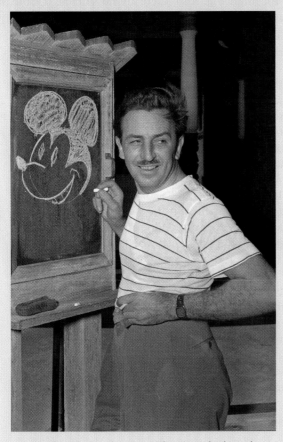

Avuncular Walt. *The personification of a brand.*

After studying art at night school in Chicago and working a series of odd jobs, Walt Disney at age 22 headed for Los Angeles with $40 in his pocket. That was in 1923. Armed only with ink and pencils and a vision for animated films, Disney moved in with his older brother, and set up shop in an uncle's garage. It was a rough start, but a contract came through from a New York company and got them going. The movie, *Alice in Cartoonland*, was forgettable.

Working at Paramount to make ends meet, Disney penned *Oswald the Lucky Rabbit* in 1927. The cartoon was a hit. Disney and Paramount had a falling-out, however. Disney quit. Paramount, of course, owned the rights to *Oswald*. On his own, Disney created a remarkably similar character, this one a mouse, for a 1928 film, *Steamboat Willie*. The mouse talked and sang. Walt himself intoned the mouse's falsetto squeak. Disney soon became a household name. Importantly, the movie was a pioneer in synch-sound technology. Then Willie morphed in subsequent shorts into the iconic Mickey Mouse.

Disney was a genius at converging the evolving technology of moviemaking with cross-generation storytelling. There was an appeal to children in Disney's work, but it wasn't all for kids. As he once put it: "Over at our place we're sure of just one thing—everybody in the world was once a child."

The Disney enterprise grew into an empire and flourished but was always personified in Walt. He was awarded the Presidential Medal of Freedom, in part for his World War II propaganda films. Over Disney's career his studio's films won 31 Oscars and six Emmys. Once he was on the short list for the Nobel Peace Prize. After Disney died in 1966, at age 65, the momentum was carried on with a corporate intensity that built on what had become a mythical cultural entity—the magical Disney touch.

After *Steamboat Willie*, Disney put out animated shorts called *Silly Symphonies*, which although intended as sideshows sometimes played better than the main feature. His breakout sensation was *Three Little Pigs* in 1933. The success inspired Disney to round up the cash, an incredible $1.5 million in the Depression, and put artists to work on Hollywood's first feature-length animated movie, *Snow White and the Seven Dwarfs*. After two years in production *Snow White* came out in 1937, cementing Disney's reputation.

World War II was a hiatus of sorts. With Hollywood declared an essential wartime industry, Disney threw his resources into military training films as well as propaganda pieces to sustain public enthusiasm for victory.

When the war was over, Disney, ever the entrepreneur, expanded his franchise. In 1954 he launched a weekly television series first called *Disneyland*, a weekly anthology. A year later he unlocked the turnstiles at a new kind of amusement park, the squeaky-clean, family-oriented Disneyland, which, like the television series, parlayed Disney into new heights as a brand name.

Not all, however, was hunky-dory and peachy keen. Unhappy cartoonists went on strike in 1941. Disney, who bore an autocratic streak, busted the union. The negative publicity didn't slow him down, though. Nor did his 1947 cooperation with the grand-standing House Un-American Activities Committee's investigation into Communist influences in Hollywood as a internal threat to the country. Disney named names to the delight of Parnell Thomas, the committee's demagogic chair.

When Disney died in 1966, his successors widened the Disney scope beyond family-friendly fare with cutting-edge, sometimes racy movies—but under other names, including Touchstone Films. People didn't make the connection, or chose not to, and the Disney name continued unsullied.

WHAT DO YOU THINK?

▶ What were transforming breakthroughs in cultivating Disney as a brand?

▶ Who were the most important persons in the history of the Disney movie studio? Why were they the most important?

INDEPENDENTS

Besides the major studios that dominate Hollywood, independent studios and producers come and go—often with a single breakthrough film, then not much that attracts attention. The term *independent* is misleading in a sense because these indies frequently lean on majors for financing. Also, there are no suitable options for distribution other than through the corporate siblings and subsidiaries of the major studios. The history of independents is that those that establish a track record end up being acquired by a major studio. A notable exception is United Artists.

■ **United Artists.** Unhappy with profit-obsessed studios limiting their creativity, friends Charlie Chaplin, Douglas Fairbanks, D. W. Griffith and Mary Pickford broke away in 1919. They created United Artists. With full creative control, they produced movies that scored well among critics and attracted huge audiences. United Artists has been among only a few insurgent movie companies to make a long-term mark on Hollywood after the giants established themselves early on.

Despite box office successes, United Artists has had its share of movies in red ink. After Michael Cimino's costly *Heaven's Gate* in 1980, United needed a white knight. The Transamerica insurance company bought the studio, then unloaded it on MGM. The new company, MGM/UA, produced one disaster after another. Among the ups and downs, the question long has been whether the company can crack into the Hollywood Big Six to make it the Big Seven.

■ **Dreamworks.** In the United Artists spirit, three Hollywood legends—David Geffen, Jeff Katzenberg and Steven Spielberg—founded a new studio, Dreamworks, in 1994. The three founders were connected and seasoned Hollywood people, each with a fortune from successful entertainment industry careers. They were called the Hollywood dream team. Spielberg's *Saving Private Ryan* in 1998 established an early Dreamworks benchmark for filmic excellence. Then came *Gladiator*, named 2000's best picture at the Academy Awards. Like most upstarts, even the most successful ones, Dreamworks has disappeared. Geffen, Katzenberg and Spielberg sold the enterprise in 2005 to Paramount for $1.6 billion.

■ **Miramax.** Brothers Bob and Harvey Weinstein blew into Hollywood in 1979, introducing themselves as concert promoters from Buffalo, New York. They set up a movie distribution company, Miramax, with a simple premise: Find low-budget, independently produced movies and buy them cheap, then promote them lavishly. After 10 years of struggling, the Weinsteins hit gold with the biopic *My Left Foot*, on Irish writer-painter Christy Brown. An Academy Award nomination as best picture stirred the box office. So did Daniel Day-Lewis' winning the Oscar for best actor.

Other hits followed, prompting Disney to buy into Miramax in 1993. The deal left creative control with the hands-on Weinsteins, whose magic seemed to be a deft touch for cultural edginess that Disney lacked. The arrangement produced Quentin Tarantino's certainly edgy *Pulp Fiction* in 1994, an $8 million film that grossed $200 million worldwide and earned an Oscar.

More financial and critical successes followed, including *Kill Bill*, *Scary Movie 3* and *Shakespeare in Love*; but then came *Cold Mountain* and *Gangs of New York*, which never earned back their $100 million production budgets. With bigger projects, Miramax had increased its risks—a perilous course that had done in earlier indies.

■ **Lions Gate.** Founded in 1997 by a Canadian investor, Lions Gate found early financial success in acquiring and producing tight-budget movies and then promoting them aggressively and imaginatively. Typical was *Crash*. Production cost $3.3 million, and marketing sextupled that—$21 million. The U.S. and global box office generated $254 million. To create buzz for the Academy Awards, Lions Gate sent 110,000 DVDs to members of the Screen Actors Guild. The movie subsequently

Although born in 1946, Steven Spielberg couldn't have made films like *Jaws, E.T.* and *Indiana Jones* if he weren't still a kid himself. At the dinner table when his seven kids were growing up, Spielberg used to start with a few lines from a story that popped into his head, then each of the kids would add a few lines. Where it would go, nobody knew, but everybody kept the story moving.

Spielberg loves stories, especially with ordinary characters meeting extraordinary beings or finding themselves in extraordinary circumstances. Another theme is that of lost innocence and coming-of-age. A persistent theme is parent-child tensions, which has been attributed to Spielberg's own distress as a child at his parents divorcing.

Critics, however, see unrealistic optimism and sentimentalism in Spielberg films although they admit exceptions. Certainly *Indiana Jones* is not all that has earned Spielberg his reputation as one of history's great moviemakers. One ranking has him Number One. Twice he has won Academy Awards as best director for *Schindler's List* and *Saving Private Ryan*, both gritty films set in wartime misery. *Schindler* took an Oscar for best picture.

As a kid Spielberg was infected with a love for making movies. At 12 he put two Lionel toy trains on a collision course, turned up the juice to both engines and made a home movie of the crash. By that time he already had shot dozens of short films. For one of them, he coaxed his mother into donning a pith helmet and an Army surplus uniform, and then rolled the film as she bounced the family Jeep through backhill potholes near Phoenix. That was his first war movie.

Compelling Storyteller. *Spielberg makes a point with cinematographer Janusz Kaminski and actor Diego Luna for* The Terminal. *Since* Jaws *in 1975, he has directed movies involving history and science, including many on issues that kids deal with.*

Later, on a family trip to Los Angeles he lined up an unpaid summer job on the Universal Studios lot. He enrolled at California State University in Long Beach in 1965 but interrupted his studies to take a television director job at Universal before finishing his degree. Ironically, Spielberg tried three times for admission to the prestigious film program at the University of Southern California and failed—although in 1994 he was awarded an honorary USC degree.

His films, although wide-ranging in subject matter, include family-friendly themes with a childlike wonderment. There also are strong emotions, as in the *Schindler* depiction of the horrors of the Holocaust, social and sexual injustice in *The Color Purple*, slavery in *Amistad* and terrorism in *Munich*. But amid the heavy-duty treatments he mixes in rollicking adventures, like yet another in the *Indiana Jones* series or *Jurassic Park* sequel.

Spielberg's financial success, $250 million alone for the first *Jurassic Park*, has given him the wherewithal to make whatever movie he wants.

In 1994 he teamed with Hollywood legendaries David Geffen and Jeffrey Katzenberg to create Dreamworks, a stand-alone movie studio outside of Hollywood's Big Six. *Amistad* and *Saving Private Ryan* set a benchmark for achievement for the enterprise, which produced acclaimed movies although not in huge numbers. Twelve years later, Geffen, Katzenberg and Spielberg sold Dreamworks to Paramount for $1.6 billion. Before then Spielberg had made the *Forbes* magazine ranking of the richest people in the United States with a net worth at $2.7 billion, second among Hollywood figures only to his buddy George Lucas at $3.5 billion.

The sale of Dreamworks, however, didn't mean an end to Spielberg's moviemaking. A fourth in the *Indiana Jones* series was released in 2008. An Abraham Lincoln bio-pic is coming along. Might we meet the thoroughly ugly but oh-so-lovable E.T., the extraterrestrial, at least one more time?

WHAT DO YOU THINK?

▶ What do Steven Spielberg movies have in common?

▶ What did Dreamworks have in common with earlier independent Hollywood studios?

On the Set. *Terrence Howard and Bernie Mac hang out on the set of* Pride. *Indie studio Lions Gate had earlier profitable projects, also aimed at black audiences, including* Diary of a Mad Black Woman *and* Madea's Family Reunion. *The studio also has found profits in the horror flick niche, including the* Saw *series and* Hostel.

won the 2005 Academy Award for best picture. That generated the predictable bump for *Crash* in movie attendance and rentals.

Lions Gate releases fewer than 20 pictures in a typical year. In 2005 there were 18, of which 15 were profitable, an unusually high ratio in Hollywood. To see itself through slumps, Lions Gate invested in film libraries and gradually amassed an archive of 5,500 titles that generate continuing revenue. The catalog includes *Basic Instinct*, *Total Recall*, *Dirty Dancing* and the lucrative *Leprechaun* horror series.

Will Lions Gate survive as an indie? Paramount twice has considered making an offer. Investor Carl Icahn, known for savvy timing in his stock purchases, has bought a stake in the company.

LEARNING CHECK ◄ ••

▸ **What is the role of independent studios in the U.S. movie industry?**

Exhibition Shift

STUDY PREVIEW

The 90-million-tickets-a-week heyday of U.S. movie houses in 1946 is ancient history. It's been a bumpy road since. The exhibition business has problems with the continuing erosion of box office revenue. Attempts to address the declines include spiffier theaters, enforced audience conduct codes and new technology—d-cinema.

THEATERS: RISE AND DECLINE

● **exhibition**
What local movie houses do

The movie **exhibition** business has been boom and bust. The beginnings, early in the 1900s, were modest. Images were projected onto a white sheet spread across a wall in low-rent storefronts and onto white-washed plywood hoisted upright in circus tents. By 1912, there was a new standard—the Strand in New York, an opulent 3,300-seat theater that rivaled the world's best opera houses. Nattily groomed and uniformed doormen and ushers made moviegoing an experience. So did

Movie Palaces. *The 3,300-seat Strand, which opened in 1912, became the model for opulent downtown movie theaters. Many featured elaborate Roman, Oriental and other themes, with lavish lobbies and furnishings and doormen groomed to fit the fantasy of a night at the movies.*

expansive lobbies, lavish promenades, columns and colonnades and plush velvet wall upholstery. The first air-conditioning was in theaters, using technology invented at Chicago meatpacking plants. Downtown movie palaces were built throughout the land.

■ **Attendance Peak.** To capitalize on the popularity of movies, and to keep access affordable, less ostentatious movie houses were built in neighborhoods and small towns. These were the core of the exhibition part of the movie industry at its peak. Although neither as large nor as lavish as the downtown palaces, the neighborhood movie houses were the heart of moviegoing when attendance peaked in 1946. Ninety million movie tickets a week were sold in the United States, at a time when the nation's population was only 141 million. People even watched movies from automobiles parked row upon row in front of huge outdoor screens with clunky loudspeakers hooked into car windows. Movies were handy and affordable. For many people they were a habit two or three times a week.

The advent of network television in the 1950s cut into movie attendance. Families justified the purchase of their first television set, a major item in household budgets back then, by saving quarters and half-dollars that otherwise would have gone toward movies. A lot of marquees went dark, some permanently, some at least a few nights a week.

● **multiplex**
Movie theater with multiple screens

■ **Multiplexes.** The exhibition business adapted. Beginning in the 1970s, moviehouse chains followed their customers to the suburbs and built a new form of movie house—the multiscreen **multiplex.** Attendance revived, although far short of the 1946 peak and also dependent on what was showing. People, newly discriminating, turned out mostly for movies that had received good reviews—unlike in the heyday of the Strands and the neighborhood theaters, when even weak movies drew crowds. People by the 1970s had many alternatives for entertainment.

The multiplexes addressed the unevenness in attendance. With multiple auditoriums, each with different seating capacity, movies could be switched among auditoriums to coincide with demand. Boffo films could be shown simultaneously in several auditoriums. With multiplexes the new measure of a movie's success was not in how many theaters it was booked but onto how many screens it was projected.

LEARNING CHECK ◄··

▶ Trace the history of movie exhibition from the earliest days to the multiplex.

EXHIBITION CONSTRICTION

In the 1990s, sensing better days ahead, major movie-house chains went on a spending spree to expand and spiff up theaters. Attendance was strong at multiplexes, some with as many as 30 screens. State-of-art sound systems were installed. Some auditoriums were outfitted with plush stadium seating.

■ **Overexpansion.** The expansion and upgrades, however, overextended some chains financially. Bankruptcies followed. Then came a wave of consolidations that eliminated some chains and left Regal dominant with 5,800 screens, followed by Carmike at 3,700 and AMC at 3,300.

The situation worsened with continued box office slippage, down 7 percent in 2005, further reflecting competition from DVD sales and rentals for home viewing on television sets. Pay-per-view home satellite and cable options also hurt. So did video games, which particularly attracted young men who had been core movie-house patrons.

The movie-house crisis is no better illustrated than in these 2005 figures:

Box office revenue	$9.5 billion
DVD revenue	24.5 billion

■ **Release Windows.** The exhibition segment of the movie business became increasingly uneasy over whether Hollywood was its friend. There were deepening doubts. Ever since Hollywood had begun releasing movies to television in the 1950s, there had been a window of exclusivity for movie houses. Studio-owned distribution also kept a protective window for movie houses as home videotapes became more popular, but distributors kept shrinking the window. What had been a window of six months in 1994 shrank to 4 1/2 months by 2004, with studios talking about possibly going to simultaneous release. Clearly, Hollywood was coming to see that its best profit potential was not in staggering the release of new movies in different channels but in maximizing a single promotional burst with simultaneous theatrical and DVD releases.

The future doesn't bode well for exhibitors either, with the expansion of home broadband access making an era of home downloading of feature-length movies possible.

LEARNING CHECK ◄··

▶ Discuss how the interests of Hollywood and movie exhibition companies once coincided but now do so less.

▶ What is the effect of broadband on movie attendance at theaters?

REVIVING THE THEATER EXPERIENCE

Different exhibition companies have responded to the crisis differently. Some have tried holding the line on ticket prices, fearing that hikes to offset revenue declines would further erode attendance. In 2005 tickets averaged $6.34 nationwide, up only 2 percent from the year before. The hidden admission, at the confection counter, included popcorn going up to $8 at some chains, buttered or unbuttered, your choice. Other chains, sensing price sensitivity, held back. The Regal and AMC chains experimented with discounted tickets at $7 through the American Automobile Association and Costco stores. Another experiment was discount admission with memberships in chain-sponsored movie clubs.

■ **Pre-Show Advertising.** Overall, the theater industry has gone after advertising more aggressively. Revenue from pre-feature ads rose 9 percent in 2007. Other exhibitors took an opposite tack. ArcLight Cinemas in Los Angeles and Bridge Cinema de Lux in Philadelphia went with $14 tickets but promised a pure movie experience— no ads. In another variation, pushed by National OneMedia, pre-show ads were screened to be sure they were entertaining. Mixed with ads were behind-the-scenes shorts on moviemaking, sports events or other fresh content in a 20-minute pre-show.

■ **Audience Deportment.** There has been a general effort to restore class to the theater experience. Behavior had become a problem, with a new generation of moviegoers unschooled in theater etiquette and assuming that at-home distractions while watching a video were acceptable in a theater too, like a cell phone buzzing and background chatter. Some, it seems, never outgrew the carnival-like atmosphere of PG-13 action flicks and campy horror flicks like *Rocky Horror Picture Show* where it was OK even to throw objects at the screen at certain cues. To correct moviegoers' bad behavior, new on-screen reminders about theater etiquette have stressed as inoffensively as possible that silence is golden. Ushers have a new duty— checking cell phones at the door. Some theaters have considered cell phone jamming devices with an intercept message that the person being called is in a theater and unavailable. To that, the Federal Communications Commission had objections, but the point is that theater owners saw a problem. In another corrective step, ushers have been trained in effective ways to discourage rowdiness and told to roam the aisles with instructions to escort noncompliant patrons out and refund the price of admission.

LEARNING CHECK ◄

▶ **What problems face the movie exhibition industry?**

▶ **How are movie exhibition companies trying to stem audience losses? Will they succeed?**

D-CINEMA

The exhibition business, with a financial boost from Hollywood, is planning to outfit theaters with digital projectors. Owners had resisted because of the cost, at least $100,000 minimum per screen, but finally decided there was no choice. **Mark Cuban** of the 270-screen Landmark chain was first. Cuban began converting

● **Mark Cuban**
Early advocate of converting to digital exhibition

Mark Cuban. Although known mostly as the excitable owner of the Dallas Mavericks, Mark Cuban, who made his fortune in software, is an advocate of digital video. He owns the pioneering HDNet television movies network. His Landmark movie-house chain has been a leader in switching to digital projection. Cuban also is an advocate of plush furnishing to make a night at the movies a memorable experience.

his theaters in 2005, saying that once people saw their first digital movie on a big screen, they would settle for nothing less. With **d-cinema,** as it is called, colors are more vivid, graininess is gone and projection-room goofs, like reels out of sequence, are no more. Nor will there be any more distracting focus adjustments or scratchy reels that have been pulled over the sprockets too many times.

In 2006, taking a cue from Cuban, the entire movie industry recognized the obvious—that people are becoming more enamored of digital images on computer screens, a trend that is sure to accelerate with the pending television shift to digital transmission. With Hollywood advancing the money, movie-house chains began a 10-year project to convert to digital projection equipment at all of the 36,700 screens in the United States and thousands of screens around the world.

D-cinema also has economic benefits. Digital movies don't require transportation in bulky film canisters, some weighing 85 pounds. One estimate was that $568 million a year could be saved in transportation and handling. Meanwhile, Hollywood studios have begun issuing movies in double versions, on film and digitally, through a transition period.

LEARNING CHECK ◄

▸ **What is d-cinema?**

▸ **How likely is the conversion of movie houses to digital projection to draw audiences back?**

THE NEXT PLATFORM

Hollywood distributors have been keen on DVD sales and rentals, which had buoyed their revenues as box office revenue declined. But by 2007 the DVD market had plateaued. Concerned that the industry may have maxed out the potential of both theatrical and DVD releases, studios earnestly pondered what their next delivery platform might be. Computer downloads remained broadband hogs with little appeal. Downloads to handheld and other devices were mostly short features, not movies, and they were competing with all kinds of other Internet content for attention.

Confronted with the possibility that Hollywood may have reached the end of its cycle as a growth industry, major studios turned cautious. Disney reduced its output in 2006 and laid off 650 employees. Studios cut back on deals with independent producers. The situation was put in startling financial terms by a Kagan Research study that found studios recouped only 84 percent of production and domestic marketing costs from domestic theatrical releases and home video sales in 2005. The shareholder-sensitive corporations that own the studios ordered more scrutiny on spending until bottom lines improve. The trade journal *Variety* put it this way: "In the eyes of Wall Street, studios are now seen as bloated entities."

Blockbuster Quest

STUDY PREVIEW

Massive profits from a runaway movie success lure studio executives into big-budget epics and spectaculars, but some flop. The big stakes and also the risk are encouraged by conglomerate ownership, which pressures studios to outdo their profits season after season. To offset the risk, studios issue low-budget films. Studios are worried long term that the growth cycle of the industry may have peaked.

ESCALATION OF EXPECTATIONS

Early directors, including **D. W. Griffith,** tested the storytelling potential of the new film medium. Growing public enthusiasm was the proof of what worked. Griffith's 1915 Civil War epic *Birth of a Nation* was cinematically innovative and a

Birth of a Nation. *In a dramatic moment in D.W. Griffith's 1915 Civil War epic, Josephine Crowell and Lillian Gish are distressed over Henry Walthall. The powerful and cinematically innovative movie was the blockbuster of its time.*

D. W. Griffith. *On set with Billy Bitzer for* Way Down East *in 1920.*

● **blockbuster**
A movie that is a great commercial success; also used to describe books

commercial success. By the standards of the time, it was a **blockbuster.** The movie fueled Griffith's imagination to push the envelope further in a more complex project, *Intolerance*. In the new movie Griffith wanted to examine social justice through all of human history. He built huge sets and hired hundreds of actors. In all, he spent an unprecedented $2 million. In 1916, when *Intolerance* debuted, the critics were ecstatic at Griffith's audacity and artistry as a director. With audiences, however, the movie bombed. People were baffled by the movie's disparate settings, including ancient Babylon, Renaissance France and the Holy Land at the time of Christ.

Broke, Griffith had to obtain outside financing to make further movies. This meant that bankers and financiers sent agents to look over Griffith's shoulders, always with a pencil and balance sheet in hand, to control expenses. Not infrequently the money men overruled Griffith's creative impulses. The second-guessing involved not only cost issues. Sometimes the on-site agents of the bankrollers imposed their assessment of what would work with audiences. In effect, accountants gained a pivotal role in storytelling.

The *Intolerance* experience demonstrated a dynamic that continues to play out in Hollywood—the tension that erupts not infrequently between financiers and directors. A second lesson from *Intolerance* was another Hollywood reality—boom or bust. The quest for super-earning blockbusters has escalated, often with risky big budgets. There are spectacular payoffs, like *Titanic* of 1997, the reigning box office triumph, and *Gone with the Wind* in 1939, which in inflation-adjusted dollars has done even better.

On the other hand, blockbuster disasters can haunt a studio or production company for years. MGM, once a reigning studio, slipped with miscalculations.

United Artists almost went under with the costs of Michael Cimino's obsession with historical details in *Heaven's Gate* in 1980.

Even so, with the conglomerate structure of the movie industry, involving all major U.S. studios as part of larger corporate structures, there is growing pressure to produce spectacular moneymakers. A spectacular blockbuster will satisfy the bosses at corporate headquarters—and thus the quest to outdo *Titanic* spirals upward with bigger and bigger production and promotion budgets. With great expectations can come great risk.

RISK REDUCTION

To balance the risk of blockbusters, studios look for safe bets. There can be profits if production costs can be contained. The result is a preponderance of formulaic movies that offer little in creative storytelling and don't advance the art of moviemaking but that turn a profit. Called **B movies,** these include sequels, remakes and franchises that, although hardly great movies, are almost sure to outearn their expenses.

- **B movie**
Low-budget movie; usually with little artistic aspiration

Fast action, which doesn't require fine acting and which is cheap to produce, has figured heavily into low-budget and mid-budget movies. So too have violence and sex. Dialogue is minimal in many of these movies, which makes them easily adaptable for distribution to non-English-speaking audiences abroad.

Studios, also, have hedged their bets by building product names into scripts for a fee. This is called **product placement.** Some New York and Los Angeles advertising agencies specialize in product placement, as do talent agencies such as Creative Artists. No, it was no accident that Tom Hanks' character in *Cast Away* worked for FedEx. Or that hulky Chrysler 300s appeared in so many 2005 movies or Cadillacs appeared in MGM's *Be Cool.* In 2006 product placement worked its way into movie titles—*How Starbucks Saved My Life* and *The Devil Wears Prada.* Universal changed *Flight 93* to *United 93.*

- **product placement**
Including a product into a script for a fee

Studios have found revenue too in **merchandise tie-ins,** including trinkets at Burger King and entire lines of toys.

- **merchandise tie-in**
Products spun off from a movie, usually trinkets and toys

RISE OF LITTLE MOVIES

New structures have evolved for moviemaking newcomers to interest the distribution units of major studios in their work.

■ **Film Festivals.** Every January in Park City, Utah, Hollywood dispatches teams to audition films by independent filmmakers at the Sundance Film Festival. These are low-budget projects that sometimes have substantial returns on investment. *The Blair Witch Project*, by a team of University of Central Florida grads, is classic. The movie cost $35,000 to produce. The young colleagues on the project made a killing when scouts from Artisan Entertainment watched a Sundance screening of it in 1998 and paid $1.1 million for distribution rights. For Artisan, the movie generated $141 million at the box office.

■ **Exhibition Niches.** For half a century, major cities and college towns have had **arthouses,** small movie houses that show mostly foreign films. In recent years the theater chains have booked niche films onto a few multiplex screens. Since 1999 Regal has played only specialty titles on 70 of its 546 screens. In 2006 AMC designated 72 of its 3,232 screens for its AMC Select program.

- **arthouses**
Movie houses specializing in artistic films, often from abroad, for high-brow niche audiences

The fare isn't just foreign art films anymore. The AMC Select program included *Little Miss Sunshine* from the Sundance Film Festival, Robert Altman's *Prairie Home Companion* and Al Gore's environmental documentary *An Inconvenient Truth.* For specialty screens, the chains are nurturing potentially major films to build up word-of-mouth promotion. These included *March of the Penguins* and *Brokeback Mountain* in 2005. Neither would have survived long in the usual make-it-or-break-it frenzy of opening-weekend competition.

■ **Demographic Niches.** Hollywood has an uneven history of gearing movies to demographic niches, except for teen flicks, whose low budgets consistently yield solid returns. Many niches are tricky and fickle. The optimistic civil rights films of Sidney Poitier had strong crossover appeal in the 1960s, then faded. So-called blaxploitation films had a brief run with black audiences in the 1970s, only to be succeeded by urban action films like *New Jack City*. The main lesson has been that racial pandering has less box office appeal than good movies that have broader appeal regardless of racial theme.

A 2005 Nielsen study renewed interest in ethnic niches. The study found that Hispanics average 7.6 movies a year, considerably ahead of whites at 6.5 and blacks at 6.4. After the study, Universal, Warner and other studios launched low-budget projects aimed at Hispanics. But as earlier experience with black-themed films suggested, Hollywood sees Hispanic audiences attracted mostly to mainstream movies. In 2005, film advertisements placed in Hispanic media were led by $1.1 million for *Legend of Zorro*, which although shot in Mexico had mainstream appeal. Other leading movies pumped in Hispanic media all were decidedly of cross-ethnic appeal—*Bad News Bears*, $1.7 million; *King Kong*, $1.6 million; *Jarhead*, $1.5 million; and *Chicken Little*, $1.4 million.

■ **Foreign Movies.** Abroad, local-language movies are taking a large slice of home markets. The result: More homegrown competition for Hollywood-produced films in foreign countries. Hit hardest have been mid-range U.S. pictures that once had a sure market abroad. Part of the plight for Hollywood pictures is that the growing number of homemade foreign movies has squeezed the availability of opening weekends and screens.

Beyond the foreign box office, the competition also is for financing. Commercial investors that once financed only Hollywood productions now are recognizing the investment potential in other countries. The result: More producers in more countries are vying for funding to do movies.

While U.S. movies are losing audience to local fare abroad, the U.S. movie industry is protecting itself financially. Several Hollywood studios are putting money into foreign endeavors. Sony has provided financing for foreign studios. In an unusual twist, one of them, *Crouching Tiger, Hidden Dragon*, became a U.S. import with a fairly strong U.S. box office. Twentieth Century-Fox has invested in British and Russian projects, one of them the smash trilogy *Night Watch*. Also, Fox owner Rupert Murdoch has put money into projects by emerging Middle East media giant Rotana, which is producing 20-plus movies a year and accounts for almost 50 percent of the Arab film market. Since 2005 Warner has been in joint-production projects with Chinese studios, which gives the movies favored status for screens and opening dates that are not available for not-made-in-China films.

LEARNING CHECK ◄••

▶ **Why have little movies become a growing segment in Hollywood?**

Chapter Wrap-Up

Significance of Movies (Page 152)

■ For more than a century, movies have been an important element of U.S. culture. Movies can be great entertainers that also sensitize people to issues and have a long-term effect in shifting public attitudes on enduring issues. Measuring the cultural impact is difficult, but conventional wisdom, almost certainly over-stated, is that Hollywood can change fundamental values. This notion has made Hollywood a target in the culture wars that have divided American society in recent years. Comedian Bill Maher has challenged the idea that movies threaten traditional values with a quip that Hollywood is not geared to Red States or Blue States but to green—whether a movie will attract audiences. Producers, he says, don't sit around and work at conceiving movie projects that people in Iowa will really hate.

Movie Products (Page 155)

■ Although most people associate movies with heavily promoted Hollywood feature films, the medium lends itself to a wide range of content besides escapist fiction. Documentaries, a nonfiction genre, have a long tradition. The popularity of documentaries has peaks and ebbs. Propagandist films were a growth industry for Hollywood in World War II. Rock concert documentaries peaked in the 1980s. Today documentaries range from journalistic explorations to opinionated docu-ganda. Another genre that comes and goes in popularity is the animated film. Animation production has changed in recent years with digital technology, which makes production less labor-intensive than in the Disney heyday.

Hollywood Studios (Page 163)

■ Six studios, all parts of conglomerates, dominate Hollywood movie production and distribution. These studios are enmeshed with the television industry through corporate connections. A growing component in movie distribution channels is independent films, which originate outside the Hollywood structure but which the directors sell to studio-owned distribution companies to market them.

Exhibition Shift (Page 170)

■ The exhibition component of the industry, presenting movies to audiences, is in transition. Movie-house attendance and box office revenue have slipped dramatically. Video rentals and sales have offset the revenue decline from Hollywood's perspective, although there are signs that video revenue has peaked. Movie houses have responded with a wide range of tactics, but they seem mostly to be floundering. D-cinema is one new initiative to improve the visual experience in a movie house and also to reduce exhibition costs. Still to be felt is the coming technology that will allow home downloading of feature-length movies.

Blockbuster Quest (Page 174)

■ Massive profits from a runaway movie success lure studio executives into big-budget epics and spectaculars, but some bomb. Historically, studios have issued a mix of big-budget, mid-budget and low-budget movies, but in tight times the emphasis has shifted to caution.

REVIEW QUESTIONS

1. What is required for movies to have their great impact on viewers?

2. What are Hollywood's primary products? Give examples of each.

3. What has happend to Hollywood's studio system?

4. Would you invest your money in a movie exhibition chain? Explain.

5. Can you equate the quest for blockbusters with the goose that laid a golden egg? Explain.

CONCEPTS

exhibition (Page 170)

Hollywood (Page 154)

star system (Page 163)

studio system (Page 163)

suspension of disbelief (Page 153)

TERMS

B movie (Page 176)

blockbuster (Page 175)

d-cinema (Page 174)

computer-generated imagery (CGI) (Page 156)

vertical integration (Page 164)

PEOPLE

Walt Disney (Page 157)

Mark Cuban (Page 173)

D. W. Griffith (Page 174)

Robert Flaherty (Page 159)

Adolph Zukor (Page 163)

MEDIA SOURCES

- Colin McGinn. *The Power of Movies*. Pantheon, 2006. McGinn, a philosopher, builds an easy-to-follow case for the long-analyzed Dream Theory of Cinema to explain the compelling nature of the medium.

- David L. Robb. *Operation Hollywood: How the Pentagon Shapes and Censors Movies*. Prometheus, 2004. Robb, a veteran Hollywood reporter, chronicles the coerciveness of the government in providing and denying technical support for war movies.

- Dade Hayes and Jonathan Bing. *Open Wide: How Hollywood Box Office Became a National Obsession*. Miramax, 2004. Hayes and Bing, both editors at the movie trade journal *Variety*, examine the role of marketing with *T3, LB2* and *Sinbad*, each from a different studio, as case studies. They provide a historical context of movie marketing back to the 1950s.

In this chapter you have deepened your media literacy by revisiting several themes. Here are thematic highlights from the chapter:

Media Technology

Digital technology has enhanced the movie-going experience. Special effects are awe-inspiring. Imagine an action movie without computer-generated imagery. Hard to do, isn't it? For the exhibition component of the movie industry, however, digital technology has been a mixed development. Home DVD rentals, a digital product, have seriously dented movie-house attendance. At the same time the two other industry components, production and distribution, have capitalized on the shift in how people watch movies. Home video revenue today far outdistances revenue from the traditional box office. **(Pages 155–157 and Pages 173–174)**

Superman. *Computer-generated imagery makes him more than super.*

Media Economics

Hollywood suffers from a blockbuster syndrome. Under shareholder pressure to increase profits, studio executives always are mining for high-return projects—smash hits. They put themselves into high-budget, high-risk projects. The payoff from a *Titanic* can be huge. But when a major project bombs, losses can be devastating. Over the industry's history, some studios never recovered from big-budget flops. Studios try to offset risks with a quotient of low-budget projects that have little promise as big earners but also have little risk. The goal is a steady stream of revenue to balance the risk of the blockbuster quest. For low-cost movies, the studios' distribution arms scout aggressively for low-cost movies at film festivals and elsewhere. They look for gems, sometimes called *little movies*, that, skillfully promoted, can produce many multiples of the investment. **(Pages 174–177)**

Indies. *Independent studio Lions Gate, whose productions include Terrence Howard and Bernie Mac's* Pride, *specializes in niche movies that the distribution units of big-name studios put into circulation and market. Some indie projects become incredible money-makers. The big studios cash in as distributors and also sometimes as financers.*

Media and Culture

Movies can ignite fads among impressionable youngsters. The influence of movies on fundamental societal values, however, is less clear. There is agreement, though, that movies can put issues on the public policy agenda and keep them there. Witness Sidney Poitier's *Guess Who's Coming to Dinner*, Jane Fonda's *China Syndrome* and Michael Moore's *Sicko*. The notion that movies have immediate pivotal influence

Brokeback Mountain. *Placing homosexual commitment on the public agenda.*

on the ballot box is overstated. The notion probably derives from the immediate impact of movies in the movie-house experience, but the flow of tears and adrenaline dissipates even as people are exiting the auditorium. Even so, Hollywood finds itself vilified in today's divisive culture wars as promoting causes with the unfair advantage of the medium's potency. The fact, though, is that most movies make it through the selection process for production based on entertainment potential, not ideological value. In a capitalistic system, studios need to make money to satisfy their shareholders. The ideology of almost all shareholders is the bottom line. (Pages 152–154)

Elitism and Populism

The quest for audiences drives studios mostly to choose scripts for mass appeal. Despite this populist incentive, the industry always has issued movies with narrower appeals. This is no more true than it is today, with so-called *little movies*, many from obscure directors, that are being booked into a few screens in multiplexes. This is a continuation of a tradition that dates to *arthouses*, as they were called, that featured European directors' works dating to the 1960s. (Pages 168–170)

Michael Moore. *Love 'em or hate 'em, Moore's documentaries ignite passions about public issues.*

Audience Fragmentation

The largest U.S. movie audience is young people, to whom Hollywood caters. Slasher flicks are big draws among teenagers. So are some truly sappy romances. Other niche audiences with which studios have found financial success are racial and ethnic minorities. The growing U.S. Hispanic audience and its heavy movie-going pattern have given scripts with built-in Hispanic themes a leg up in the selection process. There also was a time when films with black themes had a niche draw. The most successful movies, however, are crossovers that go over big with a wide range of moviegoers—the true blockbusters: *Gone with the Wind, Titanic, Star Wars*. (Pages 154–155 and Pages 174–177)

Movies in War. *Walt Disney mobilized patriotically for World War II.*

Media and Democracy

In World War II the government declared Hollywood an essential war industry. Such was the importance attached to movies at the time as a means to sway people. The government financed propaganda pieces to sustain public enthusiasm for victory. Hollywood also cranked out scripts that built on public enthusiasm for the war cause and tried to notch up patriotism. Of course, Germany also was producing propagandist movies. In a period when audiences were in awe of motion picture technology, these efforts probably were more effective than they would be now. Today's audiences have far greater filmic sophistication. In part this is because people today have far more sources of information and entertainment to weigh in coming to their individual and collective conclusions. (Pages 159–160)

8

Radio

Mobilizing Audiences

Tom Joyner grew up during the Civil Rights Movement. He remembers well the 1960s when Montgomery, Alabama, blacks boycotted merchants in an early display of collective economic power. In his native Tuskegee, 50 miles away, he remembers the weekly unity marches. Joyner got his first peek inside radio while protesting against a white-owned station that refused to play "black music." Joyner prevailed. The station manager left.

After college, majoring in sociology, Joyner landed a radio job in Montgomery. He moved from station to station in the 1960s in the burgeoning of black radio, by then 800-plus stations nationwide, honing his mix of music, guests and goofy comedy and appeals for donations to worthy causes. Even on incendiary issues with which he dealt, Joyner maintained his dulcet cool.

By 1985 Joyner was in demand. When KKDA in Dallas offered him a morning slot and WGCI in Chicago offered him an afternoon slot, he took both. The daily commute made Joyner the first frequent-flyer disc jockey and earned him the nickname "Fly Jock." In 1994 he went into syndication on the ABC network and was eventually piped through 95 stations and stayed home more.

Joyner knows the power of radio. When Christie's auction house in New York decided to auction off items from the slave trade, Joyner and buddy Tavis Smiley were quick to note that Christie's had a policy against trafficking in Holocaust items. Day after day, Joyner and Smiley called on listeners to jam Christie's phone lines in protest. Christie's canceled the auction.

Joyner has courage. For weeks he urged listeners to jam the lines at CompUSA, which didn't advertise on black radio. The company

LEARNING AHEAD

- Radio is easily accessible, but audience for traditional stations is slipping.
- Music, news and talk are the primary radio content.
- Regulation relies on the idea of government and stations as trustees of the public airwaves.
- Chains have reshaped the radio industry.
- Public radio has filled a niche abandoned by commercial stations.
- Satellite radio has shaken the infrastructure of the radio industry.
- To recover audience, commercial terrestrial radio needs to reinvent itself.

"Fly Jock." A daily Dallas–Chicago commute for Tom Joyner.

complained to ABC, which carried Joyner's show. In a decision that the network later regretted, ABC lawyers ordered Joyner to lay off. Joyner read the corporate ultimatum on the air, sparking a massive listener protest to the network. ABC backed off. So did CompUSA, which dispatched a representative for a guest appearance on the Joyner show to make nice.

When Hurricane Katrina devastated New Orleans, Joyner canvassed stations still on the air for the earliest comprehensive accounts of the damage. It was he who coined the catchy term *black folks' tsunami.* Joyner raised $1.5 million to provide housing for the displaced.

In the tradition of black radio generating money for social causes, Joyner has created a foundation to help students who have run out of money at historically black colleges. To his listeners, Joyner says, these students are our future.

Influence of Radio

STUDY PREVIEW

Radio has become a ubiquitous mass medium, available everywhere, anytime. As an industry, however, there are troubling signs. Radio's primary programming, music, has become available through other devices, many with no advertising. A key radio audience, the segment aged 18 to 24, has fallen off dramatically.

UBIQUITY

Radio is everywhere. The signals are carried on the electromagnetic spectrum to almost every nook and cranny. Broadband is a new delivery means. So is direct-to-listener programming from satellite. Hardly a place in the world is beyond the reach of radio.

There are 6.6 radio receivers on average in U.S. households. Almost all automobiles come with radios. People wake up with clock radios, jog with headset radios, party with boomboxes and commute with car radios. People listen to sports events on the radio even if they're in the stadium. Thousands of people build their day around commentators like Paul Harvey. Millions rely on hourly newscasts to keep up to date. People develop personal attachments to their favorite announcers and disc jockeys.

Statistics abound about radio's importance:

● **Arbitron**
Radio listener survey company

- **Arbitron,** a company that surveys radio listenership, says that teenagers and adults average 22 hours a week listening to radio.
- People in the United States own 520 million radio sets. Looked at another way, radios outnumber people 2:1.
- More people, many of them commuting in their cars, receive their morning news from radio than from any other medium.

Although radio is important, cracks are developing in the medium's reach. The audience is slipping from the traditional, federally licensed local stations to iPods, direct-to-listener satellite services, webcasts and cell phones. Yes, 200 million people, a sizable number, still tune in at least once a week, but the audience is shifting. The important 18- to 24-year-old listener block fell 22 percent from 1999 to 2004.

LEARNING CHECK ◄

▶ What are some measures of radio's audience reach?

▶ Is the radio audience expanding or constricting?

RADIO MILESTONES

1800s

Radio
Guglielmo Marconi transmitted first radio message (1895)

1900–1949

Voice
Lee De Forest created audion tube for voice transmission (1906)

Titanic
David Sarnoff's relays of news of the mid-Atlantic tragedy established radio in public mind (1912)

Commercial Radio
KDKA, Pittsburgh, became first licensed commercial station (1920)

Regulation
Congress created Federal Radio Commission to regulate radio (1927)

FCC
Congress replaced FRC with Federal Communications Commission (1934)

FM
Edwin Armstrong put first FM station on air (1939)

1950–1999

Television
TV networks drew audiences, advertisers from radio (1950s)

Recorded Music
Radio shifted to niche audience segments, mostly recorded music (1950s)

Public Broadcasting
Congress established Corporation for Public Broadcasting, a national noncommercial system (1967)

Deregulation
Congress relaxed many regulations on broadcasting, including ownership caps (1996)

2000s

Satellite Radio
Sirius and XM began signal delivery via satellites directly to listeners (2001)

Newspapers put radio on everyone's tongue

Gordon McLendon: Reinventing Radio

Only from satellite: Snoop Dogg

PIVOTAL EVENTS

- Congress created Interstate Commerce Commission, first regulatory agency (1887)

- Right to vote extended to women (1920)
- Great Depression (1930s)
- Franklin Roosevelt presidency (1933–1945)
- World War II (1941–1945)
- Russian–Western rivalry triggered Cold War (1945)

- Television networks (1950s–)
- Nixon presidency (1969–1977)
- Humans reached moon (1969)
- Ronald Reagan presidency (1981–1988)
- Soviet empire imploded (1989)
- Internet emerged as commercial medium (late 1990s)

- 9/11 terrorist attacks (2001)
- iPod introduced (2002)
- Iraq War (2003–)

SCOPE OF THE INDUSTRY

More than 13,000 radio stations, each licensed by the federal government as a local business, are on the air in the United States. Communities as small as a few hundred people have stations.

Although radio is significant as a $19.1-billion-a-year industry, its growth seems to have peaked. Revenue, almost entirely from advertising, grew only 1.2 percent in one recent year—less than the other major mass media. Big radio chains, like Clear Channel with 1,200-plus stations, remain hugely profitable. The profits, however, are due less to audience and advertising growth, which are stagnant at best, than to the chains' economies of scale and radical cost-cutting.

Too, the big revenue growth of the big chains has been fueled by their acquisitions. When federal caps on chains at 40 stations were dropped in 1996, there was massive consolidation. Chains bought up individually owned stations, and chains bought other chains. In effect, the chains now all have bigger shares of a pie that's not growing and may be diminishing. How much is the disparity between big operators and the others? The 20 largest chains, which together own 2,700 stations, brought in $10 billion in advertising in 2003. The remaining 10,000-some stations split the other $9 billion.

LEARNING CHECK ◄

▶ **How has chain ownership masked a softening in radio advertising?**

Radio Content

STUDY PREVIEW

Radio programming falls mostly into three categories: entertainment, mostly music; news; and talk. In addition, public radio has created a growing audience for its rich mixture of news and information programming, most originating with National Public Radio and freelance producers.

RADIO ENTERTAINMENT

The comedies, dramas, variety shows and quiz shows that dominated network-provided radio programming in the 1930s and 1940s moved to television in the 1950s. So did the huge audience that radio had cultivated. The radio networks, losing advertisers to television, scaled back what they offered to affiliates. As the number of listeners dropped, local stations switched to more recorded music, which was far cheaper than producing concerts, dramas and comedies. Thus, radio reinvented itself, survived and prospered.

The industry found itself shaken again in the 1970s when the listeners flocked to new FM stations. Because FM technology offered superior sound fidelity, these became the stations of choice for music. AM listenership seemed destined to tank until, in another reinvention, most AM stations converted to nonmusic formats. From its roots in 1961 with programming genius **Gordon McLendon,** who beamed the first 24/7 news into southern California from XTRA across the border in Tijuana, all-news took off as a format in major cities. So did listener call-in shows with colorful, sometimes bombastic hosts.

● **Gordon McLendon**
Reinvented radio with narrow formats in the 1950s

Music, however, dominates radio, although the popularity of genres is always in flux as stations jockey among shifting public tastes for more lucrative niches.

LEARNING CHECK ◄

▶ **How did radio content change dramatically in the 1950s? And why?**

A crisis hit U.S. radio stations in the 1950s. As comedies, dramas and quiz shows moved to television, so did the huge audience that radio had cultivated. The radio networks, losing advertisers to television, scaled back what they offered to stations. As the number of listeners dropped, local stations switched more to recorded music, which was far cheaper than producing programs.

To the rescue came Gordon McLendon, who perfected a new format, the Top 40, which repeated the day's most popular new music in

RADIO STATION FORMATS

Country music still dominates U.S. radio today, but the number of country stations is slipping.

Country	2,041 stations	Losing
News/talk/sports	1,579 stations	Gaining
Adult contemporary	1,213 stations	Losing
Religious	1,019 stations	Gaining
Golden oldies	822 stations	Steady
Classic rock	639 stations	Gaining
Top 40	444 stations	Gaining
Alternative/modern rock	334 stations	Gaining
Urban contemporary	312 stations	Gaining

rotation. McLendon developed the format at KLIF in Dallas, Texas, by mixing the music with fast-paced newscasts, disc jockey chatter, lively commercials and promotional jingles and hype. It was catchy, almost hypnotizing—and widely imitated.

With the portable transistor radios that were coming onto the market and a growing number of automobiles outfitted with radios, Top 40 was right for the times. People could tune in and tune out on the go. Most tunes last only three minutes or so. It was not programming designed for half-hour blocks. It reshaped radio as a medium that began a recovery in a new incarnation even as some observers were writing the medium's epitaph.

McLendon was no one-shot wonder. He also designed so-called beautiful music as a format at KABL, San Francisco, in 1959; all-news at XTRA, Tijuana, Mexico, aimed at southern California, in 1961; and all-classified ads at KADS, Los Angeles, in 1967. In all of his innovations, McLendon was firm about a strict structure. In Top 40, for example, there were no deviations from music in

Gordon McLendon. McLendon was a programming genius who devised many niche formats, including all-news, Top 40 and beautiful music.

rotation, news every 20 minutes, naming the station by call letters twice between songs, upbeat jingles and no deadpan commercials. McLendon's classified-ad format bombed, but the others have survived.

WHAT DO YOU THINK?

▶ How would Gordon McLendon judge the advent of satellite radio?

▶ What advice would Gordon McLendon offer commercial stations about losing audience to public radio?

RADIO NEWS

Radio news preceded radio stations. In November 1916, Lee De Forest arranged with a New York newspaper, the *American*, to broadcast election returns. With home-built receivers, hundreds of people tuned in to hear an experimental transmission and heard De Forest proclaim: "Charles Evans Hughes will be the next president of the United States." It was an inauspicious beginning. De Forest had it wrong. Actually, Woodrow Wilson was re-elected. In 1920 KDKA signed on as the nation's first licensed commercial station and began by reporting the Harding-Cox presidential race as returns were being counted at the Pittsburgh *Post*. This time, radio had the winner right.

■ **Radio News Forms.** Radio news today has diverse forms, some taken from the De Forest notion of drawing listeners to reports on breaking events as they happen, some more focused on depth and understanding. Mostly, though, radio news is known for being on top of events as they happen.

- **Breaking News.** Radio news came into its own in World War II, when the networks sent correspondents abroad. Americans, eager for news from Europe, developed the habit of listening to the likes of **Edward R. Murrow** and other giants of mid-20th-century journalism, including Walter Cronkite. As a medium of instantaneous reporting, radio offered news on breakthrough events even before newspapers could issue special extra editions. The term **breaking news** emerged to describe something to which radio was uniquely suited.

- **Headline Service.** In the relatively tranquil period after World War II, with people less intent on news, the radio industry recognized that listeners tuned away from lengthy stories. News formats shifted to shorter stories, making radio a **headline service.** Details and depth were left to newspapers. Gordon McLendon's influential rock 'n' roll format in the 1960s epitomized the headline service, generally with three-minute newscasts dropped every 20 minutes amid three-minute songs, with no story more than 20 seconds, most only two sentences.

- **All-News.** As contradictory as it may seem, Gordon McLendon also invented **all-news radio,** also in the 1960s. For the Los Angeles market, McLendon set up a skeletal staff at XTRA across the border in Tijuana to read wire copy nonstop. When XTRA turned profitable, McLendon took over a Chicago station, renamed it WNUS, and converted it to all-news. This was a dramatic departure from the idea of radio as a mass medium with each station trying for the largest possible audience. McLendon's WNUS and later all-news stations sought niche listenerships, finding profitability in a narrow part of the larger mosaic of the whole radio market. Today all-news stations prosper in many large cities, some going far beyond McLendon's low-cost rip-and-read XTRA with large reporting staffs that provide on-scene competitive coverage that goes beyond a headline service.

- **News Packages.** When National Public Radio went on the air in 1970, its flagship *All Things Considered* set itself apart with long-form stories that ignored two premises that had become traditional in radio. These were stories that didn't necessarily fit the news peg of breaking news. Also, the stories ran as long as the reporter or producer felt necessary to tell the story, ignoring the premise that radio listeners had extremely short attention spans. The stories, called **news packages,** were slickly produced and reflected a commitment of time and energy in reporting that other news formats lacked. Many personified issues. News packages typically are full of sounds and recorded interviews and are often marked by poignant examples and anecdotes and powerful writing.

■ **Decline of Radio News.** Despite the ascendancy of all-news radio and National Public Radio, news is hardly a core element of radio programming anymore. By the 1990s, after the Federal Communications Commission dropped public service as a condition for license renewal, many stations eliminated their expensive news

● **Edward R. Murrow**
Pioneer broadcast journalist

● **breaking news**
Reports, often live, on events as they are occurring

● **headline service**
Brief news stories

● **all-news radio**
A niche format that delivers only news and related informational content and commentary

● **news packages**
Carefully produced, long-form radio stories that offer depth; the hallmark of NPR

Not long out of college, Edward R. Murrow had a job arranging student exchanges for the Institute of International Education, including a summer seminar for American students and teachers in the Soviet Union. That was in 1932, and it seemed a good job—lots of travel, meeting interesting people, doing something worthwhile. In the early 1950s, though, the demagogic Red Scare-meisters tried to discredit Murrow as somehow being tied to the communist ideology on which the Soviet Union had been founded.

By that time Murrow had established his reputation as a broadcast journalist and was a CBS executive. Though personally offended at being branded a communist sympathizer, Murrow was even more outraged by the anticommunist hysteria that some members of Congress, notably Wisconsin Senator Joseph McCarthy, were stirring up. Many of his network colleagues had been blacklisted. A close friend committed suicide after being falsely accused. In 1954, on his weekly CBS television program *See It Now*, Murrow went after McCarthy, combining his narrative with film clips that exposed the senator's hypocrisy.

Many analysts say that was a pivotal moment in McCarthy's career. His innuendoes and lies, which had caused such great damage, were exposed to the public. Some say that Marconi's program, in bringing down one of most recognized members of the Senate, clearly demonstrated television's powerful potential for public affairs.

Murrow had begun with CBS as its representative in Europe, where he covered Adolf Hitler's arrival in Vienna in 1938 when Germany invaded Austria. Realizing that war was imminent in Europe, Murrow persuaded CBS to hire more staff to cover it. He devised the format for the CBS *World*

Radio News Icon. *Edward R. Murrow's World War II coverage from Europe, with bombs in the background during his reports, gave CBS listeners the feeling of being there.*

News Roundup, rotating from correspondent to correspondent around Europe for live reports. During World War II he became known for his gripping broadcasts from London. Standing on rooftops with the sounds of sirens, antiaircraft guns and exploding German bombs in the background, he would describe what was happening around him. His reporting had poignancy, color and detail. Here is his description of an Allied air drop over Holland: "There they go. Do you hear them shout? I can see their chutes going down now. Everyone clear. They're dropping just beside a little windmill near a church, hanging

there very gracefully. They seem to be completely relaxed like nothing so much as khaki dolls hanging beneath a green lamp shade."

One of Murrow's television signatures was an ever-present cigarette. His habit, however, didn't get in his way of his examining the dangers of smoking on *See It Now*. Murrow developed cancer and died in 1965 at age 57.

WHAT DO YOU THINK?

▶ Edward R. Murrow died in 1965 but remains an icon in broadcasting. Why?

departments and emphasized low-cost programming based on playing recorded music. Many metropolitan stations, once major players in news, have cut to just one or two people who anchor brief newscasts during commuting hours. Global and national headlines are piped in from a network, if at all. Some stations don't even commit one full-time person to local news.

LEARNING CHECK ◄ ·····································

▶ **What are the different formats for radio news?**

▶ **What stations and networks feature each of these formats?**

TALK RADIO

Talk formats that feature live listener telephone calls emerged as a major genre in U.S. radio in the 1980s. Many AM stations, unable to compete with FM's sound quality for music, realized that they were better suited to talk, which doesn't require high fidelity.

Call-in formats were greeted enthusiastically at first because of their potential as forums for discussion of the great public issues. Some stations, including WCCO in Minneapolis and WHO in Des Moines, were models whose long-running talk shows raised standards. So did *Talk of the Nation* on NPR. However, many talk shows went in other directions, focusing less on issues than on wacky, often vitriolic personalities. Much of the format degenerated into advice programs on hemorrhoids, psoriasis, face-lifts and psychoses. Sports trivia went over big. So did pet care. Talk shows gave an illusion of news but in reality were low-brow entertainment.

● **talkers**
Talk shows

● **Rush Limbaugh**
The most listened-to talk-show host in the 1990s

Whatever the downside of **talkers,** as they're known in the trade, they have huge followings. **Rush Limbaugh** was syndicated to 660 stations at his peak, reaching an estimated 20 million people a week. Although down to 600 stations by 2003, Limbaugh remained a strong influence among his politically conservative audience until 2003, when it was revealed, incredible as it seemed considering his on-air derision of drug addiction, that Limbaugh himself had a drug habit. Since returning to the air, Limbaugh's ratings are down in some markets, partially because overwhelmingly conservative talk has become a crowded genre. Also, there is some ideological competition.

Liberals are also talking. The alternatives to conservative talkers, however, have never attracted as many listeners. The most aggressive left-wing effort, the network Air America, has been floundering in financial difficulties since going on the air in 2004.

■ **Talk Listenership.** The influence of talkers can be overrated. A 1996 Media Studies Center survey of people who listen to political talk shows found that they are hardly representative of mainstream Americans.

The political talk-show audience is largely white, male, Republican and financially well-off. It is much more politically engaged than the general population but on the right wing. Also, these people distrust the mainstream media, which they perceive as biased to the left.

■ **Effect on News.** Many stations with music-based formats used the advent of news and talk stations to reduce their news programming. In effect, many music stations were saying, "Let those guys do news and talk, and we'll do music." The rationale really was a profit-motivated guise to get out of news and public affairs, which are expensive. Playing recorded music is cheap. The result was fewer stations offering serious news and public affairs programming.

To many people, talk formats leave the perception that there is more news and public affairs on radio than ever. The fact is that fewer stations offer news. Outside of major markets with all-news stations, stations that promote themselves as newstalk are really more talk than news, with much of the talk no more than thinly veiled entertainment that trivializes the format's potential.

LEARNING CHECK ◄ ·····································

▶ **What technology was catalytic in creating talk radio as a major format?**

▶ **How is talk radio different from news radio?**

ONE

Civility on the Airwaves

Listeners never knew quite what Don Imus would say next. That's part of the lure of radio shock jocks. Rapping one morning with his producer, with probably 2 million people tuned in, Imus was customarily demeaning. He referred to the Rutgers women's basketball team, comprising mostly black athletes, as "nappy-headed hos." It was typical Imus—crude, racist and sexist. A furious backlash erupted. Media commentators and politicians fueled the outrage. Big advertisers, including Staples, American Express and Procter & Gamble, began pulling their sponsorships. Finally, his show's financial base crumbling, Imus became less than golden to his corporate superiors at CBS. They fired him.

Even so, Imus, who is white, had fans. Some detractors, however, said there oughta be a law. In fact, there is a law. The Federal Communications Commission prohibits "obscene, indecent or profane language by means of radio communication." But Imus' Rutgers comment, no matter how vulgar, tasteless and hurtful, didn't meet the legal definition of any of those things. The FCC has no civility requirement.

Even so, what happened with Imus heated the debate over a shifting tide in the federal regulation of over-the-air radio. The Federal Communications Commission, which issues licenses to radio stations and can also deny licenses, has been under pressure from conservative lawmakers to police Imus and Howard Stern and other shock jocks, including Opie and Anthony. Fines have grown beyond pocket change for stations that carry shock jock programs. Howard Stern, whose fines totaled $2.5 million, finally in 2006 moved his show to Sirius satellite radio, which doesn't transmit on the legally defined "public airwaves" regulated by the FCC. Stern called it liberation.

So, what to do about Imus and on-air offensiveness? If anything? Online columnist j. brotherlove, who is both gay and African American, sees the issues not in legal but in human terms. The problem of bigotry and insulting language, says brotherlove, can be solved only by confronting all forms of bigotry, setting positive examples and policing ourselves: "Labeling people as racist, homophobic, and sexist only reveals that we have varying definitions of what those words mean," he says. "Instead of getting hung up on the terms, we should address the actual actions. Our selective political correctness doesn't show the rest of the world how to treat us. Setting better examples will do more than firing Imus ever will."

Keep in mind that not everyone agrees that Imus, Stern and their ilk are all bad. *Time* magazine columnist James Poniewozik says that Imus crossed a line. "But where is that line nowadays?" he asks. "In a way, the question is an outgrowth of something healthy in our society: the assumption that there is a diverse audience that is willing to talk about previously taboo social distinctions more openly, frankly and daringly than before."

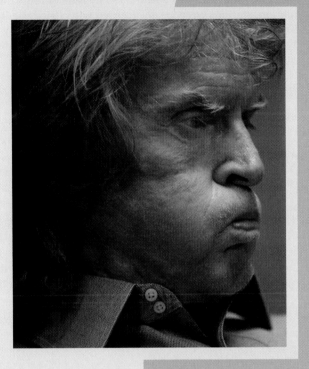

Don Imus. *Dont like what shock jocks sometimes say? Only limited recourse is available in the law. The constitution forbids government interference with citizen expression. Federal broadcast law forbids obscenity, indecency and profanity but they're narrowly defined.*

DEEPENING YOUR MEDIA LITERACY

EXPLORE THE ISSUE

Select a modern day shock jock.

DIG DEEPER

What makes this shock jock controversial? Has the jock ever been fined by the FCC? If so, what action has the station taken? A reprimand? Dismissal?

WHAT DO YOU THINK?

How far should the FCC's jurisdiction reach on decency issues? Should satellite radio be allowed to continue to be a bastion of outlandish expression for shock jocks like Howard Stern? How can the FCC best regulate over the public airwaves radio without infringing on the First Amendment?

Commercial Terrestrial Radio

STUDY PREVIEW

The U.S. radio industry was shaped by federal regulation in the late 1920s. By regulation, stations were locally licensed with strictly limited range for their signals. The system assumed that stations would be financially self-sufficient from advertising. Networks soon bound major stations into a national system, blunting the localism envisioned in regulations.

TRUSTEESHIP CONCEPT

● **First Amendment**
Provision in U.S. Constitution against government interference with free citizen expression, including media content

Unlike the print media, broadcasting is regulated by the federal government. This is something the government isn't supposed to do under terms of the **First Amendment** to the U.S. Constitution. The First Amendment's wording is unambiguous: "Congress shall make no law . . . abridging the freedom of speech or the press." But an impossible situation, wrought by new radio technology, presented itself in the 1920s. Too many stations were on the air than could fit on the available frequencies. The fledgling radio industry could not solve the problem and begged the government for regulation to sort out the problem.

■ **Airwave Cacophony.** Everyone recognized wonderful possibilities for the nascent radio industry in the 1920s. Stations were signing on the air and establishing revenue streams from advertising not only to meet expenses but also to propel the industry's growth. With more stations, however, came a problem. There were not enough frequencies to accommodate all the signals. The airwaves became a deafening cacophony. A station finding itself drowned out would boost its signal to keep

David Sarnoff

Radio a Household Word.
When the Titanic sank in 1912, newspapers relied on young radio operator David Sarnoff for information on what was happening in the mid-Atlantic. For 72 hours Sarnoff sat at his primitive receiver, which happened to be on exhibit in a department store, to pick up details from rescue ships. The newspaper coverage of the disaster credited Sarnoff and radio, demonstrating the potential importance of this new medium for news.

listeners, in effect turning up the volume to drown out competing signals in a kind of king-of-the-mountain competition. To be heard, stations were forever jumping to frequencies that were less cluttered at the moment, asking listeners to follow. It was chaos. And without a consistent place on the dial, stations could offer advertisers little assurance about the size of their audience. This impeded the economics for sustaining and growing the industry.

■ **Regulation.** Station owners called on the federal government for a solution. In 1927 Congress established the **Federal Radio Commission.** The commission had authority to specify frequency, power and hours of operation through licenses. But that was not enough to solve the problem. The commission found that 732 stations were on the air, but the technology of the time allowed room for only 568. Through clever sandwiching of signals, daytime-only and nighttime-only operations, the Federal Radio Commission eventually found room for 649 stations.

But therein rested a problem: There still were not enough channels to allow all existing stations to remain in operation. A government agency, through media licensing, had no choice but to take away the megaphone of some stations and deny a megaphone to others who might want to start a station. This was a constitutional issue. The government was de facto interfering in press freedom, in effect putting some stations out of business. Although the First Amendment, written in 1789, used the word "press," everyone assumed that the founders of the republic, had they been able to project themselves 150 years into the future, would have chosen a more inclusive word.

■ **Public Airwaves.** To sidestep the First Amendment issue, Congress embraced the concept that the airwaves, which carried radio signals, were a public asset and therefore, somewhat like a public park, were subject to government regulation for

● **Federal Radio Commission**
Agency to regulate U.S. radio; created in 1927; predecessor of Federal Communications Commission

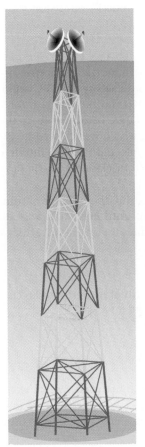

THE SHAPE OF RADIO

Federal regulation of radio made assumptions and established rules that gave the U.S. industry the following historic characteristics, some of which have been shaken in recent years:

Private Sector. Historically the industry has been privately owned in the U.S. capitalistic tradition. This was in contrast to most other countries, which used the concept of the airwaves being public to create government-sponsored national, not local, broadcast structures.

Advertising Supported. The industry is financially self-supporting through advertising, also in the U.S. capitalistic tradition. There are, however, exceptions. In recognition of radio's potential as an educational tool that might not be commercially sustainable, several frequencies are reserved for noncommercial licenses.

Engineering Regulation. The government holds licensees strictly accountable to broadcasting precisely within their assigned space on the electromagnetic spectrum to avoid the pre-1927 chaos. This has allowed for as many stations as possible to be squeezed into available spectrum.

Ownership. Stations are licensed for local communities to encourage diverse content, including news and ideas. Some group ownership was permitted, for years a maximum of seven stations, but until recent years it was strictly limited.

Content. The government never has had agents sitting at radio stations to keep things off the air, but the FCC is willing to consider listener complaints. The possibility of having their licenses yanked, although it rarely happens, is sufficient to keep stations from wandering too far from mainstream social acceptability and business practices.

Networks. Although not licensed, networks conform to government expectations for affiliates. The FCC clearly maintains that affiliates are responsible for whatever they retransmit from networks.

the public good. The **public airwaves** concept was useful for justifying regulation of the 1927 chaos on the airwaves, but it also was problematic. What criteria would the government use in issuing and denying licenses? Congress came up with another concept: The Federal Radio Commission should award licenses to applicants who best demonstrated that they would broadcast in the **public interest, convenience and necessity.** Today, 80 years later, that standard remains in effect. Government regulates as a trustee for the public good, and station owners, as licensees, are also trustees.

Although the **trusteeship concept** phraseology was high-sounding, some already on-the-air stations that lost licenses cried foul and used the ugly word "censorship." A quack doctor in Kansas, who used his station to sell cure-all potions, went to court on First Amendment grounds. So did a hate-monger preacher who used his church-owned station in Los Angeles as a pulpit. The federal courts ruled glibly that the Federal Radio Commission was acting within its authority, leaving the First Amendment issue for another day.

LEARNING CHECK ◄ ••

▸ Why is radio, unlike print media, regulated by government?

▸ Why did early radio station operators embrace government regulation?

▸ Explain the trusteeship concept. Who is the trustee? Trustee of what? Trustee for whom?

LOCALLY LICENSED STATIONS

The Federal Radio Commission used several mechanisms to guard against broadcasting becoming a one-voice government mouthpiece. There would be no powerful national stations. Stations were licensed to local service areas with local ownership. Further, there were strict limits on how many stations a single person or corporation could own. The goal of **localism** was a diversity of voices.

The law that established the Federal Radio Commission stated explicitly that stations would have First Amendment protection. The fact, however, was that the commission needed to assess station programming in deciding what was in the public interest, convenience and necessity. This inherent contradiction was glossed over during most of U.S. radio history because station license-holders were more than pleased to program whatever it took to satisfy the FRC and its successor, the Federal Communications Commission. That was the trade-off for stations to retain their licenses and stay in what, by and large, became one of the 20th century's most lucrative businesses. Also, the FCC, which was created in 1934, was gingerly about regulating content. Never, for example, did the FCC interfere with format issues, no matter how loud the protests from classical music fans when their favorite station shifted to rock.

Content regulation was mostly measuring the number of minutes per hour of news and public-service announcements, until even that was abandoned in the 1980s. Before shock jock Howard Stern, fines for on-air vulgarities were mere wrist-slaps.

LEARNING CHECK ◄ ••

▸ How did Congress try to avoid the growth of powerful radio chains, like those in the newspaper industry in the 1920s? Did it work?

NETWORKS

Congress did not foresee the impact of radio networks, which were in their infancy when the Federal Radio Commission was created in 1927. By the 1930s NBC and CBS were piping programs to local stations, called **affiliates,** throughout the land.

Although the networks gave local exclusivity to affiliates, one per market, the high quality of the programming amassed unprecedented audiences. Then in 1924 came the Mutual Broadcasting System, which allowed any station to pick up any or all of its programming. Stations became less the forums of local issues and culture that Congress had intended with local licensing. For better or worse, local stations were becoming mere conduits for a powerful, emerging national culture.

Localism was further weakened in the 1950s when the networks shifted their emphasis to television and took much of radio's audience with them. Radio stations went almost entirely to recorded music, in effect displacing the original ideal of local talent with music geared for a national audience from the major music recording centers of New York, Los Angeles and Nashville.

LEARNING CHECK ◄ ⋯⋯⋯⋯⋯⋯⋯⋯⋯⋯⋯⋯⋯⋯⋯⋯⋯⋯⋯⋯⋯

▶ **How did radio networks weaken the idea of local stations geared to serving local audiences?**

MARKETPLACE CONCEPT

● **deregulation**
A trend in the 1980s and later to reduce government regulation of business

Ronald Reagan proclaimed that his presidency would "get government off the backs of business." In 1996, seven years after Reagan left office, it seemed that his **deregulation** dream had come true—at least in broadcasting. With the 1996 Telecommunications Act the age-old limits were relaxed on how many radio stations a single company could own. Right away, radio companies began gobbling one another up in mergers. Today the FCC has no limits on ownership except for a maximum of eight stations in a single market.

The change in the corporate structure of U.S. radio represented a weakening of the trusteeship concept. No longer did the government see its role as an intermediary for the public as necessary to ensure that the industry performed in the public interest. The trusteeship concept had led to requirements like the Fairness Doctrine, which required stations to air all sides of controversial issues and to air public-service announcements, and even micromanagement details like requiring the identification of a station by call letters and location on the hour and the half-hour. Those requirements were mostly gone by 1996 because one of the premises necessitating the trusteeship role for government, **channel scarcity,** had disappeared. Technology had found ways to squeeze 13,000 stations onto the available electromagnetic spectrum, which was plenty.

● **channel scarcity**
An insufficiency of radio frequencies that necessitated government regulation in the 1920s

● **marketplace concept**
Allowing people through marketplace mechanisms to determine the fate of a business; a successor in broadcasting to the trusteeship concept

In place of the trusteeship concept had emerged a **marketplace concept,** in which the marketplace would have a far greater role in deciding the shape of radio broadcasting. If people were dissatisfied with a station, they had many other stations to go to—in effect voting with a turn of the dial or the press of a preset button. Stations that didn't meet public expectations would, given time, lose listeners and advertisers and cease to be viable businesses. The concept was simple: Let marketplace mechanics serve as a regulator, the people acting directly.

Rarely, however, has government regulation been obviated. There just isn't as much of it. Also, the regulatory mechanisms that were a cocoon that protected the infrastructure of the industry from change is being shed. Even so, the National Association of Broadcasters, which represents radio station owners, as well as television owners, continues to lobby for government maintenance of the status quo to protect its interests. For example, the industry delayed for years the approval for XM and Sirius to use orbiting satellites as platforms for direct-to-listener broadcasting. On that issue, however, the FCC eventually applied the marketplace concept, allowed the satellites to go up, and let the people decide.

LEARNING CHECK ◄ ⋯⋯⋯⋯⋯⋯⋯⋯⋯⋯⋯⋯⋯⋯⋯⋯⋯⋯⋯⋯⋯

▶ **How do the trusteeship and marketplace concepts differ?**

▶ **Can the trusteeship and marketplace concepts co-exist?**

Corporate Radio

STUDY PREVIEW

A few corporations dominate the U.S. radio industry, using mostly centralized music and other programming geared to mass tastes. The approach, however, has earned the disapproving moniker "corporate radio" for its bland sameness. The chains have taken steps to win back listeners who had left for alternative sources of music, news and information.

CHAIN OWNERSHIP

Pressured by broadcasters to relax the limits in how many stations a single company could own, Congress in 1996 eliminated any cap. The only limit was that a chain could not own more than eight stations in a large market. Right away radio chains began buying up stations and also other chains. The 1999 merger of Clear Channel and AMFM created an 838-station group. The FCC then relaxed the limit further. By 2003, Clear Channel owned 1,200-plus stations. A new era of *corporate radio* had arrived.

● **playlist**
A list of songs that a radio station plays

To cut costs and thus maximize profits, these chains consolidated their new properties in the post-1996 era and centralized not only **playlists** but also disc jockeys. Most stations owned by Clear Channel, Viacom and other chains went to formulaic computerized scheduling, with stations each drawing from libraries of only 300 to 400 titles with the same 30 or 40 songs playing most of the time. Through a system called **voice tracking**, a handful of announcers at central sites played the songs over multiple stations in different markets. This robo-programming was efficient.

● **voice tracking**
A few announcers who prerecord music intros and outros for multiple stations to create a single personality for stations

Also to maximize profits, programming was larded with advertising. Some stations were running 22 minutes of ads an hour, some packages of ads going on for 10 minutes straight. A 2004 study by the investment banking firm J. P. Morgan found an average of 15 minutes an hour of advertising.

LEARNING CHECK ◄

▶ What has happened to the goal of the 1927 Federal Radio Act to prevent radio chains?

▶ How has programming changed under the big radio chains?

NEW CORPORATE TUNE

Shifting a few gears, Clear Channel began striking deals with stations outside its ownership to pick up revenue from advertisers that were following listeners to alternative stations. An example is unorthodox Indie 103, a Los Angeles station whose music mix is personality-driven—pretty much whatever suits a disc jockey at the moment. It's quirky, but it also inspires about 700 listener calls a day. That's an intensity of listener loyalty that robo-radio can't match even with massively larger audiences. Hedging its course for the future, Clear Channel bought every minute of Indie 103's available advertising airtime. The deal allowed the station to meet expenses, and Clear Channel made money reselling the time at a premium with the advertising staff that served the chain's existing eight robo-programmed Los Angeles stations.

Clear Channel crafted another deal with the Bush-bashing liberal network Air America that kept the financially failing operation in business. It's a strange deal indeed for a company whose Texas management strongly supported Bush in the 2004 election. Political ideology, it seemed, was less critical than stopping the leaks of listeners and ad revenue, even small ones, that were breaking out all over the Clear Channel landscape.

● **Jack**
An eclectic, somewhat unpredictable musical radio format

Some stations with robo-programming shifted gears in 2005 with **Jack,** a format developed by Rogers Media of Canada that has a decidedly more eclectic mix of music. Jack playlists typically include 1,200 songs. Unlike robo-formulas, few songs get played even once a day in Jack's unlikely patterns, with none of the segues that slide from one tune seamlessly into another. Eight U.S. stations licensed

Jack from Rogers in 2005. Others are imitating it. At KSJK in Kansas City, which calls itself 105.1 Jack FM, program director Mike Reilly prides himself on "train wrecks," a collision of unlikely music in sequence: "If you hear MC Hammer go into the Steve Miller Band, I've done my job." It's the kind of programming excitement that people can create on an iPod. In fact, KSJK's print advertising shows an iPod with the line: "I guess you won't be needing this anymore, huh?"

Jack, say critics, is less than it seems. The playlists don't venture beyond what is familiar to listeners. A Jack consultant, Mike Henry, put it this way in a *Wall Street Journal* interview: "You're only challenging them on a stylistic level. You're not challenging them on a familiar/unfamiliar level." Nirvana grunge may butt up against Village People disco, but both are proven pop.

The big chains also have begun trimming commercials, a recognition that they had overdone it and driven listeners away. Radio companies don't like to talk about how much advertising they carry, but a brokerage firm, Harry Nesbitt, said Clear Channel was down to an average 9.4 minutes per hour at its 1,200 stations in 2004. Also, advertisers were encouraged to shorten their spots.

LEARNING CHECK ◄ ···

▶ **How have radio chains backed off their original goal of one-size-fits-all programming?**

▶ **What do you see as problems ahead for radio chains?**

Public Radio

STUDY PREVIEW

For 40 years the noncommercial component of the U.S. radio industry, called *public radio*, has grown steadily with distinctive programming. A 1967 law provided federal funding—a response to a vision that radio could do better in serving the public good. A major gift from Joan Kroc, the widow of McDonald's founder, has secured the future for the backbone of the system, the network National Public Radio.

CORPORATION FOR PUBLIC BROADCASTING

● **Carnegie Commission for Educational Television**
Proposed a government-funded educational TV and radio system

● **Public Broadcasting Act**
Established the Corporation for Public Broadcasting

● **Corporation for Public Broadcasting**
Quasi-government agency that administers federal funds for noncommercial radio and television

● *All Things Considered*
Pioneer NPR afternoon news magazine

From its beginnings in the 1920s, the U.S. radio industry was built around government licenses assigned to local communities and a financial advertising structure. In the backwaters were noncommercial stations, conceived originally as testbeds for experimentation. Many were licensed to universities, many to the physics departments. There also were noncommercial licenses for educational purposes. These stations, barred from raising revenue through advertising, were merely a blip in the radio landscape until the privately funded blue-ribbon **Carnegie Commission for Educational Television** began rethinking noncommercial broadcasting. The influential commission concluded that noncommercial broadcasting was an undeveloped national resource.

Congress followed through on the Carnegie recommendations for a government-funded television and radio system to meet "the full needs of the American public." The enabling legislation, the 1967 **Public Broadcasting Act,** was a slap at commercial broadcasting, whose content was mostly entertaining at a low and vapid level. The idea was for broadcasting to do better. Only a few years earlier, in 1961, FCC Chair Newton Minow had chastised broadcast executives at a convention as responsible for a "vast wasteland." The term stuck. So did the sting. But nothing changed in content.

The new law established the **Corporation for Public Broadcasting**, a quasi-government agency to channel federal funds into noncommercial radio and television. Right away, National Public Radio (NPR), which had been founded in 1970, created *All Things Considered,* a 90-minute newsmagazine for evening drive time. Many noncommercial stations offered *ATC*, as it's called in the trade, as an

Terry Gross. *Her probing interviews on* Fresh Air, *marked by a disarming truth-seeking honesty, are among radio's longest running programs. On 330 NPR affiliates, the daily show typically has 2.9 million listeners.*

alternative to the headline services on commercial stations. The program picked up an enthusiastic albeit small following but grew steadily. In 1979 an early drive-time companion program, ***Morning Edition,*** was launched.

● ***Morning Edition***
NPR's morning newsmagazine

LEARNING CHECK ◄

▶ **What motivated Congress to act on the Carnegie recommendations?**

▶ **How was the new *public radio* different from commercial radio? Have these distinctions survived?**

MCDONALD'S FORTUNE

● **Joan Kroc**
Single handedly sextupled NPR's endowment

● **National Public Radio**
Network for noncommercial stations

Joan Kroc, widow of the founder of the McDonald's fast-food chain, was a faithful radio listener. She especially enjoyed programs from **National Public Radio.** When she died in 2003, Kroc bequeathed $200 million to NPR, sextupling its endowment. The gift is transforming NPR into a powerhouse in radio in ways reminiscent of the commercial networks in their heyday.

Today NPR claims more listeners than ratings-leader Rush Limbaugh does on commercial radio. Limbaugh's is the number-one stand-alone program at 22 million listeners a week, but NPR does better overall. *Morning Edition* has 13.1 million listeners, and *ATC* has 11.5 million. In news, NPR has a lot to offer. With the Kroc gift and steeper charges to affiliates, the network has built a news staff of 300 in its Washington and Los Angeles bureaus and in 23 U.S. and 14 foreign bureaus. The programs are carried on 773 stations.

Although much of the Kroc endowment has underwritten NPR's growing news operations, the network prides itself on cultural programming too, much of it innovative and experimental, sometimes offbeat. The greatest audience that has evolved, however, has been news-related.

● **American Public Media**
Program provider for noncommercial stations

● **Garrison Keillor**
Long-running host of *A Prairie Home Companion*

Although NPR is the most visible component of U.S. noncommerical radio, its programs constitute only about one-quarter of the content on its affiliate stations. These stations originate 49 percent of their own programming. Stations also buy about 19 percent of their programming from a competing program service, **American Public Media.** PRI, a creation of the Minnesota Public Radio network, has the folksy **Garrison Keillor** live-audience variety show *A Prairie Home Companion,* which dates to 1974.

LEARNING CHECK ◄

▶ **Trace the growth of public radio into a formidable second component of the U.S. radio industry.**

Satellite Radio

STUDY PREVIEW

Satellite radio, transmitting directly from national networks to individual listeners, is squeezing traditional locally licensed stations. Satellite networks Sirius and XM offer 100-plus channels, some commercial free, some duplicating what's available on over-air stations.

SIRIUS AND XM

● **satellite radio**
Delivery method of programming from a single source beamed to an orbiting satellite for transmission directly to individual end users

Two **satellite radio** operations, the first national U.S. radio stations, went on the air in 2001. Both Sirius and XM beamed multiple programs from multiple satellites, providing digital-quality sound, much of it commercial free, for a monthly fee ranging between $10 and $13. The companies tried to build an immediate audience by lining up automobile manufacturers to install receivers into new vehicles—about 12 million a year. Both Sirius and XM offered at least a hundred channels—pop, country, news, sports and talk—but also specialized programming like chamber music, Broadway hits, NPR, audiobooks and gardening tips.

● **shock jock**
Announcer whose style includes vulgarities, taboos

In 2004 Sirius and XM raised the stakes against each other and against traditional over-the-air radio. Sirius signed Howard Stern to a five-year deal worth $500 million, which began in 2006 when his previous contract expired with a terrestrial station. Stern's **shock jock** act on Sirius is beyond the jurisdiction of the FCC, which licenses only the technical parameters of satellite radio. Signals downlinked from satellites are not considered use of the public's air.

Not to be outdone, XM signed a deal with Major League Baseball to broadcast every big-league game played through 2011, with an option for 2012 to 2014. That deal may be worth as much as $650 million to baseball. Raising their programming bar represents a huge gamble by both satellite firms, which, going into 2008, were hemorrhaging money.

LEARNING CHECK ◄ ···

▶ How has satellite radio diversified the infrastructure of the U.S. radio industry?

▶ Why doesn't the concept for government regulation of public airwaves apply to XM and Sirius?

ASSAULT ON TERRESTRIAL RADIO

● **terrestrial radio**
The industry based on audio transmission from land-based towers, as opposed to transmission via satellite

While XM and Sirius duke it out, a larger battle is shaping up between satellite radio and what's come to be called **terrestrial radio.** The term was devised to identify the traditional radio industry built around local stations that transmit from towers, in contrast to satellite transmission. Language purists object that *terrestrial radio* is a retronym like *print newspapers* and *broadcast television*. But boosted derisively by Howard Stern in hyping his 2006 move to Sirius, the term caught on.

Shock Jock. *Howard Stern made oodles of money for the Viacom-owned Infinity radio chain, but his bosses were uneasy at the possibility of a Federal Communications Commission crackdown on decency. Not liking the pressure, Stern decided against renewing his Infinity contract. Instead, he left "terrestrial radio," as he called it, and went to satellite service Sirius. The government claims no jurisdiction over direct-to-listener satellite services that bypass local FCC-licensed stations.*

Whatever the semantics tiff, the reality is that locally licensed commercial stations are under unprecedented competition for listeners. Among alternatives:

■ **Public Alternative.** National Public Radio and its local affiliates have skimmed off the listenership whose demographics, including educational attainments and income, are coveted by advertisers. Although public stations cannot carry advertising, they are allowed to acknowledge supporters on the air, including purveyors of high-end products and services. These acknowledgments can sound like advertising as long as they don't exhort listeners to action.

■ **Satellite Alternative.** Every listener that local commercial stations lose to Sirius and XM makes these stations less attractive to advertisers. The exodus has been major. Together Sirius and XM have 14 million subscribers.

Other technologies also are working against the traditional radio industry.

■ **iPod.** Handheld MP3 players, epitomized by the Apple iPod, are siphoning listeners from over-air local radio. With these devices and music downloaded from the Internet or ripped from their own CDs, people are able to create their own playlists—no inane disc jockey patter, no commercials, no waiting through less-than-favorite tunes for the good stuff.

■ **Podcasting.** Almost anybody who wants to create a show can prerecord a batch of favorite music, complete with narration, as an audio file on a personal computer. Then, by adding a hyperlink on a Web server, they can let the world download the show for playback on a computer or MP3 player. Whenever the listener links to the server again, a new show from the same source will be downloaded automatically. Podcasting has the potential to make everybody a disc jockey. This too has cut into the audience of traditional radio.

■ **On-Demand Radio.** Like the earlier TiVo device for television, on-demand radio devices are available for recording programs for later playback. The leading service, RadioTime, offers a real-time database of 35,000 stations from 140 countries for a $39 annual subscription. Some RadioTime models include an AM-FM tuner to grab local shows that aren't webcast.

LEARNING CHECK ◀
▶ Locally licensed terrestrial commercial radio is beleaguered. How has this happened?

Snoop Dogg. *Satellite radio services have shared exclusive talent in their competition for listeners, including Snoop Dogg on XM and Howard Stern on Sirius. Satellite audiences are growing, but neither Sirius nor XM have found profitability and are in a merger dance.*

Whither Radio?

STUDY PREVIEW

With deregulation, radio programming has become more populist, formulaic and bland. Many stations are devoid of local identity. Even so, some stations set themselves apart with local and distinctive content.

■ **High-Definition.** Happy with the heady profits in the 1990s, the radio industry missed an opportunity to upgrade with digital transmission technology. The technology, which would have improved clarity, was deemed too costly at $100,000 a station. What a mistake. Joel Hollander, who came in as chief executive at the Infinity chain in 2005, is frank: "If we had invested three to five years ago, people would be thinking differently about satellite." By 2005, only 300 stations had gone digital.

● **IBOC (in-band, on-channel)**
A radio industry standard for digital transmission; allows multiple programming on the same channel

● **multiplexing**
Sending multiple messages in bundles on the same channel

The largest chains now have all committed to digital conversion. About 2,000 stations will be sending digital signals by 2008. The system requires two transmitters, one for the traditional analog signal and one for the new digital signal, but a new industry-adopted standard, called **IBOC,** short for "in-band, on-channel," allows old-style analog and new-style digital receivers to pick up either signal at the same spot on the dial.

■ **Bundled Transmission.** Unlike analog radio, digital signals are encoded as binary 1s and 0s, which means that multiple programs can be **multiplexed** on the same channel. Segments of multiple programs are sent in packets, each coded to be picked out at the receiving end as a single unit and the others ignored. The company that holds the patents on high-definition radio, iBiquity Digital, has a system with which stations can spray six simultaneous messages to listeners, which opens opportunities for stations to regain listeners. Imagine a commuter setting a receiver to a music station with instructions to interrupt for traffic updates embedded in the same signal.

Receivers can be designed to store programs, TiVo-like. NPR's *All Things Considered* can be waiting on a commuter's car radio no matter what time the workday ends and the commute home begins.

LEARNING CHECK ◄ ···

▶ **What are possibilities for technological innovation for terrestrial radio?**

REINVENTING RADIO

The structure of the U.S. radio industry that resulted from the 1927 Radio Act has had a long run. No one predicts a quick end to radio as we have come to know it—locally licensed, advertising-supported, over-air signals, and mostly lowbrow, middlebrow at best. But alternatives are coming on strong. Public radio, satellite services and iPod-enabled personal playlists are not friends of the old-line radio industry. They are taking away listeners, eroding bottom lines even for highly efficient chains like Clear Channel.

Radio has had doomsayers before, as when network television stole the audience and advertisers in the 1950s. Radio reinvented itself then. Gordon McLendon, the low-budget niche programming innovator, led radio into a survival mode. Will a new knight in shining armor come along to reinvent terrestrial commercial radio again?

Local radio stations have assets to reposition themselves. These include local news, which stations have largely abandoned but which could be revived. News is much costlier to program than recorded music, but it's a niche that is open in most markets—although public stations have established a small stake in local news and newspapers are moving into online delivery with audio.

Another unfilled niche is local culture. Stations spend little airtime on local concerts, drama, poetry and dialogue. All are labor-intensive compared with piping in pop culture from Nashville, New York and Los Angeles in the form of recorded music. Piped-in network programming, by its nature, is hardly local.

When is the last time you heard a city council meeting live on radio? Or a poetry reading from a campus coffee shop? Or an intelligent interview with a local author? You're more likely to find a faraway Major League Baseball game than a local Legion game. Local content may not be riveting stuff for the large mass audiences that radio once garnered, but all signs point to those audiences continuing to dwindle. Radio's reinvention may be into niches even narrower than those to which McLendon was gearing programs in the 1950s. Even so, there indeed are things that radio can do that competitors don't or can't.

Ironically, local programming would be nearer to what Congress envisioned in the **1927 Radio Act**—local stations recording and playing back their communities to themselves.

● **1927 Radio Act**
Established the Federal Radio Commission

LEARNING CHECK ◄ ···

▶ **What threatens the future of commercial terrestrial radio?**

▶ **How can commercial terrestrial radio survive?**

Chapter Wrap-Up

Influence of Radio (Page 184)

■ Radio is everywhere with a growing multiplicity of portable listening devices. Although large, the audience is fragmenting. Alternatives include iPods with individually customized playlists that no station can match. Within the radio industry itself, a fragmentation is occurring that especially threatens commercial terrestrial stations that the government has licensed for local service throughout the country since 1927. Noncommercial stations have built a loyal, growing audience, mostly by piping in programs from the NPR network and independent sources. Also, satellite radio with low-cost subscriptions to 100-plus channels has cut into the drive-time commute audience of local stations.

Radio Content (Page 186)

■ Most radio programming is entertainment, primarily recorded music created in Nashville, Los Angeles and New York. Not much indigenous creative programming is offered. Although news once was a major component of radio programming, it's now been replaced with piped-in music. Talk programs are a significant programming mainstay at many stations but are mostly imported from faraway network sources and are not local.

Commercial Terrestrial Radio (Page 192)

■ The structure of U.S. radio was created by Congress in 1927—a system of stations almost all with strict limits on signal strength to serve local communities. It was a system based financially on advertising. For three-quarters of a century, the industry's core has been commercial terrestrial radio.

Corporate Radio (Page 196)

■ The 1927 regulatory legislation sought to avoid chain ownership in radio. Congress, indeed the American people, were leery about the possibility of an equivalent to the powerful newspaper chains of the time. Gradually limits on ownership were relaxed. In 1996 limits were scrapped altogether, albeit for a provision against a single company buying up all the stations in large markets. The result has been exactly the chain ownership that Congress once sought to prevent. The largest chain, Clear Channel, operates 1,200 stations, with as many as eight in some markets. Three chains have 200 or so stations. A pattern at these stations has been new efficiencies that include centralized programming, albeit with occasional exceptions.

Public Radio (Page 197)

■ A segment of the radio spectrum set aside in 1927 for educational broadcasting has evolved into a strong component of the industry—public radio. These noncommercial stations have long been resented by owners of advertising-based mainstream stations for taking even a sliver of the audience and treated as outsiders. Antagonism has grown since 1967 when Congress, tacitly criticizing commercial radio for not living up to public service, expectations, channeled major funding into the noncommercial system. Today noncommercial stations have a growing, loyal audience for news and public affairs that commercial stations had neglected. The public radio audience is growing even as the commercial audience is shrinking.

Satellite Radio (Page 199)

■ The technology for national stations to beam signals directly to listeners, bypassing local stations, was available long before the Sirius and XM satellite services went live in 2001. But the commercial terrestrial radio industry had fought successfully against the authorization of satellite services. The industry preferred the regulated infrastructure in which it found financial comfort. The industry's self-serving objections turned out to be well rooted. When authorization finally came, Sirius and XM lured a large part of the audience away from terrestrial stations. Neither Sirius nor XM have made back their huge investments in technology and programming, but no one doubts that satellite-direct radio is here to stay.

Whither Radio? (Page 200)

■ The near-myopic focus on pop music may be the comeuppance of commercial terrestrial stations. Think iPod. How can a radio station compete with handheld devices that facilitate individual playlists? These devices put listeners in control. People no longer have to wait for songs they want to hear. Nor do they have to wait through commercial breaks. Where can commercial radio go from here? Narrower, local-oriented niches are a possibility, like miking civic events, concerts and other cultural events. Stronger local news and public affairs is another niche that commercial radio has largely forsaken. This alternative would require bigger budgets and new business models. Locally originated programming is costlier than playing recorded music.

REVIEW QUESTIONS

1. What is happening to the number of people who listen to traditional radio?

2. How has the mix of entertainment and information changed through the course of radio's history in the United States?

3. How has the trusteeship model for broadcast regulation given way to a marketplace model?

4. How has the 1966 Telecommunications Act reshaped the U.S. radio industry?

5. What has contributed to the growth of public radio audiences?

6. How has satellite radio shaken the historic infrastructure of U.S. radio?

7. What is radio's future?

CONCEPTS
deregulation (Page 195)
marketplace concept (Page 195)
public airwaves (Page 194)
public interest, convenience and necessity (Page 194)
terrestrial radio (Page 199)

TERMS
corporate radio (Page 196)
affiliate (Page 194)
1927 Radio Act (Page 201)
playlist (Page 196)
satellite radio (Page 199)

PEOPLE
Don Imus (Page 191)
Joan Kroc (Page 198)
Gordon McLendon (Page 186)
Edward R. Murrow (Page 188)
Howard Stern (Page 199)

MEDIA SOURCES

● The biweekly *Rolling Stone* is the leading authority for fans who want to track the music business.

● Gerald Eskenazi. *I Hid It Under the Sheets: Growing Up with Radio.* University of Missouri, 2006. Eskenazi, a New York *Times* sports reporter, reminisces about the so-called Golden Era of Radio. His focus is the comedies, quiz shows, soap operas, dramas, mysteries, Westerns and thrillers of the 1930s and 1940s, as well as early radio sports.

● Thomas Doherty. "Return with Us Now to Those Thrilling Days of Yesteryear: Radio Studios Rise Again," *Chronicle of Higher Education* (May 21, 2004), Pages B12–B13. Doherty, a broadcast scholar, sees new interest in radio as a social phenomenon, in this report on the state of recent scholarship in radio.

● Robert L. Hilliard and Michael C. Keith. *Dirty Discourse: Sex and Indecency in American Radio.* Iowa State Press, 2003. Hilliard and Keith, both communication scholars, trace the course of radio deregulation and changes in FCC decency standards.

RADIO: A Thematic Chapter Summary

In this chapter you have deepened your media literacy by revisiting several themes. Here are thematic highlights from the chapter:

Media Technology

The technology of terrestrial radio, beaming signals from towers on high points in the landscape, has been refined over the past century but fundamentally is unchanged. Satellite delivery is no different except that the towers are hundreds of miles out in orbit. The transformational aspect of satellite radio is not so much the technology, but rather in delivering signals directly to listeners. Signals are not relayed through local terrestrial stations, which had been the infrastructure of the industry. **(Pages 192–195 and Page 199)**

News Icon. *Where would Edward R. Murrow find airtime today?*

Media Economics

In one of its deregulation moves in the late 1900s, the Federal Communications Commission eased license requirements on radio stations for public affairs and news. Soon commercial stations shifted in great numbers to more music. Not only was music more of an audience draw, which translated into advertising revenue, but music also was less costly than staffs of news reporters and public affairs producers. The shift was dramatic evidence of the fact that media companies are capitalistic enterprises that seek the least expensive routes to the greatest financial return. So secondary was promoting citizen participation in the life of the community and public affairs that it was all but forgotten. **(Pages 186–190)**

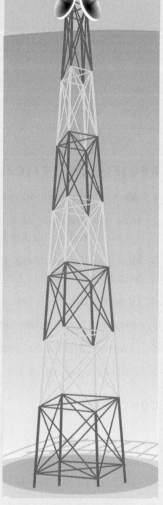

Terrestrial Radio. *Earthbound transmitters.*

Media and Democracy

The potential of radio as a medium for news has a long history. Returns in the 1916 presidential election were reported by radio. Franklin Roosevelt used radio in the Great Depression to comfort the nation and in World War II to mobilize patriotism. Television took over much of this role in the latter 20th century, but parts of the radio industry have continued the medium's role as a forum for discussing public issues. Today this role is mostly on talk stations, although much of the content is more showmanship and bluster than enlightening. Noncommercial public stations, meanwhile, grew as a contributor to public affairs dialogue. **(Pages 190–191 and Pages 197–198)**

Tom Joyner. *Showing the power of radio to mobilize people.*

Media and Culture

Radio networks were a culturally binding influence that contributed to a common American identity through the mid-1900s. The networks had a major role with comedies, dramas and concerts that played coast-to-coast.

When radio switched mostly to recorded music in the 1950s, the homogenizing effect continued. The music was almost entirely out of Nashville, New York and Los Angeles, albeit with occasional blips from Motown and the British Invasion. Some stations, it is true, occupied niches, like jazz and country, but the culture being promoted was imported and hardly local. (Pages 194–195)

Elitism and Populism

The extremes of media content on the elitist-populist continuum are no more readily apparent than they are in radio. Compare the news snippets in a Howard Stern program with the discussion led by the Diane Rehm show on National Public Radio. An interview by NPR's Terry Gross is a class apart from anything Imus ever offered, even though in his heyday, Imus attracted powerful political leaders to his microphone. (Pages 197–200)

Titanic. *Through young David Sarnoff, an eager nation learned what had happened at sea.*

Don Imus. *This critics say he dumbed down public affairs for audience segments who weren't very interested otherwise.*

Audience Fragmentation

The 1950s radio programming whiz Gordon McLendon saw the hopelessness of fighting television after the networks took over the dramas, comedies and other programs that radio had pioneered. McLendon went for new formats, designed for narrower but still significant audience segments. These were mostly with low-cost recorded music, ranging from pop to a syrupy quasi-classical mix called *beautiful music.* McLendon also invented all-news stations. In short, McLendon reinvented radio to address the reality that television had pre-empted radio's earlier attraction. (Pages 186–190)

Demassification. *Gordon McLendon pioneered niche programming.*

Satellite Radio. *Bypassing any terrestrial relay.*

Media Future

The backbone of the U.S. radio industry, commercial terrestrial radio—stations licensed by the government—may be breaking. Perhaps the biggest threat is from the iPod and similar devices that allow people to create their own commercial-free playlists. With an iPod, why is there any need for a music aficionado to listen to the radio? Audience also is being siphoned away by public stations and satellite channels. Commercial terrestrial radio will need to reinvent itself with distinctive programming, probably more niche-driven and local, to stem its audience losses. (Pages 200–201)

9

Television

Satcom Prospects

They started calling **John Malone** the Space Cowboy in 2007. That's when, in an $11 billion swap of media properties, Malone took control of DirecTV, the largest U.S. satellite television provider. The deal gave Malone new distribution muscle for programming from his giant Liberty Media production companies. But the deal also raised the question anew about whether the future of television was indeed in home delivery via satellites. Most media analysts had written off satellites as dead-end technology. Was Malone a Lone Ranger moving into a falling orbit? Or did the Space Cowboy have a vision that others were missing?

Satcoms, as satellite companies are called, once were seen as having advantages over both local cable systems and over-air television for delivering programming. The greatest advantage was satcoms' capacity for hundreds of channels. But, as technology evolved, the cable industry closed the gap on channel capacity. More seriously, a major obstacle showed itself for satcoms: Interactive messages are not feasible. The cable television industry has begun a giant shift to offering bundled services to consumers, including telephone and Internet, both with easy two-way capability. Conventional wisdom led people to the conclusion that satcoms couldn't compete long term. Some called it a failing technology.

Or is it? What does Malone know that others don't?

Malone is no dummy. He built the huge TCI into the nation's largest owner of local cable systems. In 1999 he sold TCI to AT&T for $50 billion. But he kept TCI's program-producing unit, Liberty

LEARNING AHEAD

- The television industry is under siege from new technology.
- U.S. television was built on the same dual infrastructure as radio.
- Cable television grew to challenge the affiliate-network monopoly.
- Satellite delivery has further fragmented the television-delivery industry.
- New technology offers video on demand, which is reconfiguring the industry.
- Public television is an alternative to commercial television.
- Advertisers are eyeing alternatives created by time-shift devices and portable devices.

● **John Malone**
Television entrepreneur; interests include DirecTV, Liberty Media

● **satcom**
Short for "satellite company" that delivers television

Flying Way High. *A question for the television industry is what the future of delivery systems will be. Satellite home delivery has limitations as far as interactive communication, but John Malone, chair of Liberty Media, sees possibilities for overcoming the obstacles.*

207

John Malone. *He built Liberty Media into a television programming powerhouse. Now with the satellite-delivery company DirecTV, he has a platform for delivery. But can DirecTV compete successfully against new telco services and beefed-up cable companies?*

Media, and built it into a new media juggernaut whose interests include Discovery, QVC, other cable channels, Web sites and the Starz pay-per-view movie service. With DirecTV he now controls a significant platform for delivering his programs, 15.5 million subscribers in the United States.

Malone is a deal maker. And although he admits he has details to work out, he says that emerging systems for television delivery, notably those being devised by telephone and Internet companies, need Liberty. Malone talks about forming "a warmer and cozier relationship" with AT&T, BellSouth and Verizon. They're hungry for content, he says. Liberty can be their answer or at least part of the answer.

DirecTV, and also competing satcom Dish Network, have only clunky mechanisms for interactivity that are pretty much limited to phone hookups for subscribers to order pay-per-view programs. That capacity is far short of what **telcos** and cable companies are racing pell-mell to offer with billions of dollars of investments.

● **telco**
Short for "telephone company"

Besides deals with telcos, Malone talks about joint projects with even Dish his most direct competitor. He sees the two satcoms together engineering a common high-definition platform. Also, he hints at joint programming.

Too, Malone already has a stake in Internet delivery, albeit a narrow slice of the market—rural areas where people don't have access to cable. His WildBlue Communications delivers broadband to rural subscribers by satellite. His Current Communications delivers rural Internet services over power lines.

So does John Malone know something that others don't? If so, he has one up on global media player Rupert Murdoch. It was from

Murdoch that Malone bought the controlling interest in DirecTV in 2007. Only three years earlier, when Murdoch had taken control of DirecTV, Murdoch had seen the company as a vital U.S. component in his global satellite-delivery network. In selling to Malone, Murdoch gave it up in the face of the "triple play" of services—television, telephone and Internet—that cable companies and telcos were putting together.

Profound changes are ahead not only in video-delivery systems. Media literacy means understanding that multiplicity is a step toward seeing our future in a radically different media landscape.

Television in Transition

STUDY PREVIEW

Once, television was so influential that its cultural influence was described as "a molder of the soul's geography." The question now is whether television as a medium can retain its social role amid a changing technological environment.

TELEVISION INDUSTRY IN CRISIS

Television transformed the mass media. In the 1950s, television, the new kid on the block, forced its media elders, notably movies, radio and magazines, to reinvent themselves or perish. Year by year television entrenched itself in the latter 20th century, first as a hot new medium, then as the dominant medium. Now the industries that developed around television technology are themselves in crisis. They have been overtaken by innovations in delivering video through other channels. Can the television industry reinvent itself? Can the industry get on top of the new technology? Or will television as an industry find itself subsumed, perhaps even replaced, by new competition? High drama is being played out even as you read this chapter.

CULTURAL ROLE OF TELEVISION

Despite questions about how the U.S. television industry will adapt to an era of iPods, blogs and online gaming, the medium itself is hardly on its deathbed. Almost every U.S. household has at least one television set. On average, television is playing about seven hours a day in those households. Many people, sometimes millions, still shape their leisure time around when CBS runs *CSI*. Somewhere around 134 million people assemble ritual-like for the Super Bowl.

As a medium, television can create cultural icons, as Budweiser has demonstrated time and again. A generation remembers the Bud frog, then "Whazzup?" became an icon greeting. Even though many advertisers are shifting their spending to alternative media, Procter & Gamble spends $1.7 billion touting its wares on television, General Motors $1.3 billion.

For important messages to U.S. citizens, President Bush, even though visibly uncomfortable with television, has no more effective pulpit. It is rare for a candidate for public office not to use television to solicit support. For information, millions of people look to network news—and also Jon Stewart, Oprah Winfrey, David Letterman and Conan O'Brien.

Fictional television characters can capture the imagination of the public. Perry Mason did wonders for the reputation of the legal profession in the 1960s.

Barney and Friends. *At what price does a child's screen time displace physical exercise? Has Barney been a factor in the new obesity epidemic?*

Television as Babysitter

The scene is typical. Dad plunks the kids in front of the television so he can do laundry. Mom does the same while cooking dinner. In school, kids also find themselves being babysat by television. Teachers use it to give students a break from real learning or just to settle them down.

A 2005 study by the Kaiser Family Foundation found that 83 percent of children under age 6 use what's called screen media (television, video or computers) about two hours a day. And media use increases with age. Sixty-one percent of babies watch screen media in a typical day. For 4-year-olds to 6-year-olds it's 90 percent. Other studies have found that in lower-income homes, kids watch more television and are more likely to have a television set in their bedrooms, a practice discouraged by pediatricians.

Strong cases can be made that too much television isn't good for kids. Why aren't they out exercising? And nobody would prescribe watching violence. At the same time, shows like *Sesame Street, Blue's Clues* and *Dora* can teach spelling, arithmetic, problem-solving and social skills. These shows employ experts with doctoral degrees to work with writers to set goals and review scripts. *Sesame Street* tests its shows in day-care centers. In the early 1970s, researcher and psychologist Daniel Anderson watched kids watching *Sesame Street* and found that "television viewing is a much more intellectual activity for kids than anybody had previously supposed."

Demand for quality children's shows increased after Congress passed the Children's Television Act in 1990. The PBS network, creator of *Sesame Street,* launched *Barney & Friends. Sesame*-derived merchandise flew off the shelves.

According to Joseph Blatt, of the Harvard Graduate School of Education, *Dora,* created by Nickelodeon's Brown Johnson, proved that it is possible to do quality programming for kids in a commercial environment. Now marketers spend a lot of money trying to convince parents that their shows will help children's brains develop. It has worked. The Kaiser study found that many parents are enthusiastic about the use of television. Two-thirds say their child imitates positive behavior, such as helping or sharing, as seen on television.

The phenomenon of using television as a babysitter has been debated since the first picture flickered on the small screen. "Like alcohol or guns, TV will be used sensibly in some homes and wreak havoc in others," writes Daniel McGinn in *Newsweek.* "Debating its net societal value will remain a never-ending pursuit."

DEEPENING YOUR MEDIA LITERACY

EXPLORE THE ISSUE
Check out the PBS Kids: Sesame Street—Caregivers Web page and the Playhouse Disney Guide for Grownups Web page.

DIG DEEPER
What do you notice about these pages? What do you think their message is to parents?

WHAT DO YOU THINK?
Does the quality of children's shows matter in the debate about television as a babysitter? Are shows without commercials or merchandise marketing inherently better than commercialized shows?

Then Mary Tyler Moore's role as a television news producer showed that women could succeed in a male-dominated business. Roles played by Alan Alda were the counter-macho model for the bright, gentle man of the 1970s. The sassy belligerence of Bart Simpson still makes parents shudder.

LEARNING CHECK ◄·······························

▶ **What are some measures of television's role in our culture?**

▶ **What are examples of this role? Include some from your own experience.**

ENDURING TELEVISION EFFECTS

Although television can be effective in creating short-term impressions, there also are long-term effects. Social critic Michael Novak, commenting on television at its heyday, called television "a molder of the soul's geography." Said Novak: "It builds up incrementally a psychic structure of expectations. It does so in much the same way that school lessons slowly, over the years, tutor the unformed mind and teach it how to think." Media scholar George Comstock made the point this way: "Television has become an unavoidable and unremitting factor in shaping what we are and what we will become."

Whether the influence ascribed to television by Novak and Comstock will survive the fast-changing media landscape of the 21st century remains to be seen. Nobody, however, is predicting the imminent disappearance of television. The question is whether the television industry will lose its legacy as a mass medium to technological innovations from new media of mass communication.

LEARNING CHECK ◄·······························

▶ **What did Michael Novak mean by calling television "a molder of the soul's geography"?**

Over-Air Delivery

···

STUDY PREVIEW

The regulatory mechanism created by Congress for television in the 1930s resulted in a two-tier U.S. television system. Corporate entities that entered television comported with the regulatory infrastructure. The original television industry comprised local stations, generally with the most successful carrying network programs from NBC, CBS and ABC.

DUAL INFRASTRUCTURE

● **Federal Radio Act**
Original law in 1927 for government regulation of U.S. broadcasting

● **Federal Communications Act**
Revision of Federal Radio Act in 1935 to include television

● **David Sarnoff**
Broadcast visionary who built RCA, NBC

● **Philo Farnsworth**
Invented the electronic technology for television

● **coaxial cable**
A high-capacity wire with dual electric current conductors

With television on the horizon in the 1930s, Congress looked at how its regulation of radio had worked. Congress was pleased with the **Federal Radio Act** of 1927. If the regulatory system worked for radio, why wouldn't it work for television? The **Federal Communications Act** of 1934 tidied up the 1927 law and expanded the scope to television.

The powerhouse in making television technology viable commercially was **David Sarnoff.** He had parlayed his fame as the kid picking up signals from the Titanic rescue drama in 1912 into leadership at the Radio Corporation of America. With a patent from **Philo Farnsworth,** the inventor of television, Sarnoff demonstrated television—"radio with pictures," some called it—at the 1939 World's Fair in New York. People marveled. The FCC licensed the first station in 1941, but World War II interrupted Sarnoff's plan to replicate the successful NBC radio network as a television system.

After the war more stations were licensed. By 1948 heavy-duty **coaxial cables** that were necessary to carry television signals had been laid out to the Midwest, and NBC began feeding programs to local stations. The coaxial linkup, with some stretches covered by microwave relays, connected the East and West coasts in 1951.

LEARNING CHECK ◄ ⋯⋯⋯⋯⋯⋯⋯⋯⋯⋯⋯⋯⋯⋯⋯⋯⋯⋯⋯⋯⋯⋯⋯⋯

▶ **How did David Sarnoff create the structure of the early U.S. television industry?**

LOCAL STATIONS

The backbone of the national television system was local stations. The first stations, all in larger cities, took affiliations with the fledgling NBC, CBS, ABC and short-lived Dumont networks. Larger cities also had unaffiliated, independent stations. Noncommercial stations were licensed for educational programming, mostly operated by school districts.

The largest:

Sinclair, 63 stations

Paxson, 61 stations

Viacom, 39 stations

Fox, 37 stations

Univision, 36 stations

LEARNING CHECK ◄ ⋯⋯⋯⋯⋯⋯⋯⋯⋯⋯⋯⋯⋯⋯⋯⋯⋯⋯⋯⋯⋯⋯⋯⋯⋯⋯⋯⋯⋯⋯⋯⋯⋯

▶ **What is the role of a station as a network affiliate?**

NETWORKS

For most of television's history, three networks, ABC, CBS and NBC, provided programming to local stations in prime time at night and parts of daytime. NBC dominated early on, but the **Big Three,** as they were called, came to be evenly matched with about 200 affiliates each. Their programs reached the whole country. As with radio earlier, the infrastructure of television became a **two-tier system.** Stations, licensed for local communities by the government, were one tier. The networks provided a national tier of infrastructure.

● **Big Three**
ABC, CBS, NBC

● **two-tier system**
Original U.S. broadcast infrastructure had two tiers, one of locally licensed stations, the other of national networks

■ **NBC Television.** The genius who had built the NBC radio network within the RCA empire, David Sarnoff, moved into television as soon as the government resumed licensing local stations after World War II. For early programming NBC raided its radio repertoire of shows and stars. Then came innovations. **Pat Weaver,** an ad executive recruited by NBC as a vice president in 1951, created a late-night comedy-variety talk show, precursor to the venerable *Tonight Show.* Weaver also created a wake-up show, the still-viable *Today.* With those shows NBC owned the early morning and late-night audience for years.

● **Pat Weaver**
NBC program innovator, 1950s

■ **CBS Television.** Sarnoff's longtime rival in radio, **William Paley** of CBS, was not far behind in moving soap operas and other programs from radio to television. Soon CBS was fully competitive with its own innovations, which included the *Twilight Zone* science-fiction anthology. By 1953 the *I Love Lucy* sitcom, which eventually included 140 episodes, was a major draw. Paley worked at creating a cachet for CBS, which he relished calling the "Tiffany network" after the ritzy New York jewelry store.

● **William Paley**
CBS radio, television founder

CBS established a legacy in public affairs when **Edward R. Murrow,** famous for his World War II radio reporting from Europe, started *See It Now.* Three years later, in 1954, when Senator Joseph McCarthy was using the prestige of his office to smear people as communists even though they weren't, it was Murrow on *See It*

● **Edward R. Murrow**
Pioneer broadcast journalist

Making Fox. *The* Simpsons *was among a handful of programs that helped Fox, a Johnny-come-lately television network, establish itself with a young audience. Some early Fox programs floundered, like* Married . . . with Children, *which faded after a few seasons. The Simpson brood, however, maintained its following, spawning a profitable movie version in 2007.*

● **Roone Arledge**
ABC sports programming innovator, 1960s, 1970s

● **Rupert Murdoch**
His media empire includes Fox television and 20th Century Fox movies

● **Barry Diller**
Creator of early, profitable Fox network programming

● **CW**
Upstart network owned by Viacom, Time Warner formed from each company's failed earlier efforts

Now who exposed the senator's dubious tactics. Many scholars credit Murrow not only for courage but also for undoing McCarthy and easing Red Scare phobias.

■ **ABC Television.** ABC established its television network in 1948 but ran a poor third. Two programs, though, gave ABC some distinction—*Disneyland* in 1954 and the *Mickey Mouse Club* in 1955. ABC picked up steam in 1961 with *Wide World of Sports,* a weekend anthology that appealed to more than sports fans. **Roone Arledge,** the network's sports chief, created *Monday Night Football* in 1969. Network television was a three-way race once again. In 1976 ABC was leading by a hair.

■ **Fox. Rupert Murdoch,** the Australian-born media magnate, made a strategic decision in 1986 to become a major media player in the United States. He bought seven non-network stations in major markets and also the 20th Century Fox movie studio. The stations gave Murdoch a nucleus for a fourth network. With 20th Century Fox, Murdoch had production facilities and a huge movie library to fill airtime. Murdoch also recruited **Barry Diller,** whose track record included a series of ABC hits, to head the new network; Murdoch called it Fox.

There were doubts that Fox would make it, but Diller kept costs low with low-budget shows like *Married . . . with Children,* which featured the crude, dysfunctional Bundy family. The *Simpsons* attracted young viewers, whom advertisers especially sought to reach. Fox outbid CBS to televise half of the Sunday National Football League games in 1994. Soon some CBS affiliates defected to Fox.

The Murdoch strategy worked. With almost 200 affiliates, Fox made network television into the Big Four.

■ **CW.** Two upstarts in the Fox mold went on the air in 1995—Time Warner's WB and Viacom's UPN, but neither caught on much with viewers or advertisers. They were merged in 2006 into the **CW** network for another try. The *C* in CW comes from the Viacom corporate subsidiary CBS, and the *W* comes from Warner.

LEARNING CHECK ◄ ••••••••••••••••••••••••••••••••••••

▶ List the programming innovators who shaped each of the major networks. What were their contributions?

Cable Delivery

STUDY PREVIEW

The television industry began experiencing a slow fragmentation with the growth of cable delivery. Early cable companies were small-town enterprises that merely relayed signals from over-air stations to townspeople, but in the 1970s networks were formed to provide exclusive programming to these local cable companies. Explosive growth followed.

CABLE SYSTEMS

Entrepreneurs in mountainous sections of Oregon, West Virginia and western Pennsylvania figured out how to bring television to their communities in the late 1940s even though mountains blocked the signals. The only stations at the time were in big cities. By hoisting a reception tower on a nearby mountain top, these entrepreneurs caught the faraway signals and strung a cable down to town. Voila, places like Astoria, Oregon, had television. Gradually every small town beyond the reach of over-air television signals had a local cable system—all low-cost distribution systems. None offered local-origination programming, however.

Urban television stations and the networks too were pleased with the upstart **CATV** enterprises, short for *community antenna television*. With no investment, the big-city stations picked up additional viewers, which permitted the stations to charge more to advertisers. Small-town people were enthusiastic to be able to watch Jack Benny.

Although not a technological leap, the locally owned small-town cable systems were a new wrinkle in television delivery. The systems were a minor, relatively passive component in the U.S. television industry. Even into the 1970s nobody sensed what a sleeping giant they had become.

● **CATV**
Early local cable television systems. Short for *community antenna television*

LEARNING CHECK ◄

▶ Why was cable television only a small-town phenomenon for a quarter century?

CABLE NETWORKS

● **Gerald Levin**
Used orbiting satellite to relay exclusive programs to local cable systems in 1975

A young executive at Time Inc. in New York, **Gerald Levin,** put two and two together and came up with a new direction for television in the early 1970s. His idea was to create a network exclusively for local cable systems to augment what they were picking up from over-air stations. The network, built on a floundering Time entity called Home Box Office, HBO for short, would send programming via orbiting satellites.

With only 265,000 households at its 1975 launch, the first cable network, HBO, barely dented the viewership of over-air stations. But HBO grew. A year later Atlanta station owner Ted Turner put his WTBS on satellite as mostly a movie channel for local cable systems. Turner called WTBS a "superstation," and it quickly became a money machine. Leveraging the revenue, Turner then created CNN, then bought a fledgling competitor and started Headline News, a second 24/7 news service. Then Turner created TNT, a second movie channel.

These networks avoided most government regulation because their programming was delivered to viewers by cable. The new delivery system bypassed FCC-regulated airwaves. It was an alternative that shook up the over-air television industry, siphoning viewers.

Sopranos Attraction. Since its inception, HBO has hastened the fragmentation of television programming. Beginning in 1975 with post-release movies, HBO was an exclusive network for cable systems, then became a power to be reckoned with in original programming. Series like The Sopranos *built HBO as a brand and attracted more subscribers. The torments of Carmela Soprano, a tough, dependent, religious yet rationalizing mob wife, played by Edie Falco, made irresistible viewing for millions of HBO subscribers until the 2007 finale.*

In Astoria, Oregon, downriver from Portland at the mouth of the Columbia, **Ed Parsons** had tinkered with radio since he was a kid. Nobody was surprised when he put a local radio station on the air. In 1946 Ed and his wife Grace saw a demonstration of television in Chicago—and Grace was hooked. Two years later, when they heard that a station was going on the air in Seattle, Grace told Ed that if anybody could figure out how to get the television signal from Seattle, 125 miles north it was him.

There were problems. One was that television signals travel straight rather than follow the earth's curvature. Reception is chancy beyond 50 miles. Another problem was the 4,000-foot coastal range, which further impeded reception from Seattle.

Parsons, a pilot, took a modified FM receiver and flew around the county to find the Seattle station's audio signal. He also roamed back roads to find a place to raise an antenna, but none was practicable. Then he discovered that a suitable signal came in at the roof of the eight-story John Jacob Astor Hotel downtown—a bit more than a stone's throw from his and Grace's apartment.

Parsons jury-rigged an antenna, mounted it on the hotel roof, and strung a line to his living room. On Thanksgiving Day 1948, Grace turned on the set in their living room while

● **Ed Parsons**
Built first CATV system in Astoria, Oregon, in 1949

Ed, listening to her reports on a walkie-talkie, adjusted the antenna on the Astor Hotel roof until, eventually, the Seattle station came in.

Ed and Grace were little prepared for what happened next. "We literally lost our house. People would drive for hundreds of miles to see television," he said. "You couldn't tell them no." But the situation got so bad on Christmas Eve that Parsons chased everybody out and locked the door.

To regain household peace Parsons arranged with the manager of the Astor Hotel to drop a cable down the elevator shaft of the hotel and make a television set available in the lobby. The manager thought it would be good for business. Little did he realize that the television would draw so many people to the hotel lobby that guests wouldn't be able to squeeze their way to the registration desk.

Next Parsons persuaded a music store down the street to put a set in a display window. It, too, seemed like a good idea—until traffic jams prompted the police chief to urge Parsons to try something else. At that

First Cable System. *Small-town entrepreneur Ed Parsons brought big-city television to isolated Astoria, Oregon.*

point, however, in March 1949, Parsons made history, using cable to connect a television reception antenna with a customer: Cliff Poole's music store.

To alleviate congestion at the store windows, Parsons extended the cable to more stores and taverns and to homes. Within a year Parsons had 25 places hooked up. Six months later there were 75. He charged $125 for installation, then $33 a month.

WHAT DO YOU THINK?

▶ How do you explain the mania that Ed Parsons stirred in Astoria, Oregon?

▶ Were people as excited about the Playstation 3 release in 2006? What about the iPhone in 2007?

Seeing the potential, other cable channels soon were competing for space on local cable systems—ESPN for sports, a weather network, music video networks, home shopping networks. By 2008 there were more than 330 national cable networks.

LEARNING CHECK ◀

▶ What transformed cable into a major player in the television industry?

▶ How did Gerald Levin transform cable? How did Ted Turner do likewise?

MULTISYSTEM OPERATORS

● **multisystem operator (MSO)**
A company that owns several local cable television delivery units in different, usually far-flung, communities

The potential of the cable television industry that Gerald Levin had recognized did not go unnoticed on Wall Street. For investors, cable suddenly was hot. CATV systems were gobbled up in hundreds of acquisitions. What emerged were **multisystem operators,** called MSOs in the industry. These companies, many of them subsidiaries of larger media companies, simultaneously were raising money from investors to wire big cities so that cable programming could be offered for a monthly subscription. Today, more than 90 percent of U.S. households have access to cable, although only about two-thirds of them subscribe.

The company Comcast catapulted into becoming the largest multisystem operator in 2002 by buying AT&T Broadband and claiming, with earlier acquisitions, more than 21 million subscribers. Time Warner is second at 11 million. The consolidation of cable systems into large ownerships has reduced the number of MSOs nationwide to 25—a far cry from the individual local systems that began in the late 1940s.

LEARNING CHECK ◄ ....

▶ **What has happened to all those CATV systems?**

OWNERSHIP MELD

● **ownership meld**
When a company is subsumed into the ownership of a competing company

For years, over-air networks resented the intrusion of cable networks as a competitor for national advertising, but the tension cooled as media conglomerates added cable networks to their bevy of holdings. It was an **ownership meld.** Advertising revenue that the over-air networks lose to cable may still end up in the parent company's coffers. For 2005, for example, NBC's advance revenue guarantees from advertisers were about the same as the year before, but stablemate Bravo's upfront advertising commitments doubled. Senior sales executives cut deals with advertisers to buy time on both the networks serving over-air affiliates and on the network-owned cable services. Consider that the five major network companies have cable siblings:

	Over-Air Networks	Among Cable Networks
Disney	ABC	ABC Family Channel, Disney Channel, ESPN, SoapNet
NBC Universal	NBC, Telemundo	Bravo, CNBC, MSNBC, Mun2TV, SciFi Channel, Trio, USA Networks
News Corp.	Fox	Fox Movie, Fox News, Fox Sports, Fuel, National Geographic Channel
Time Warner	CW	Cartoon Network, CNN, TBS, Turner Classic Movies, TNT
Viacom	CBS, CW	BET, MTV, MTV2, The N, Nickelodeon, Nick at Nite, Noggin, Spike, VH1

LEARNING CHECK ◄ ....

▶ **How have major television networks hedged their bets against cable as a competitor?**

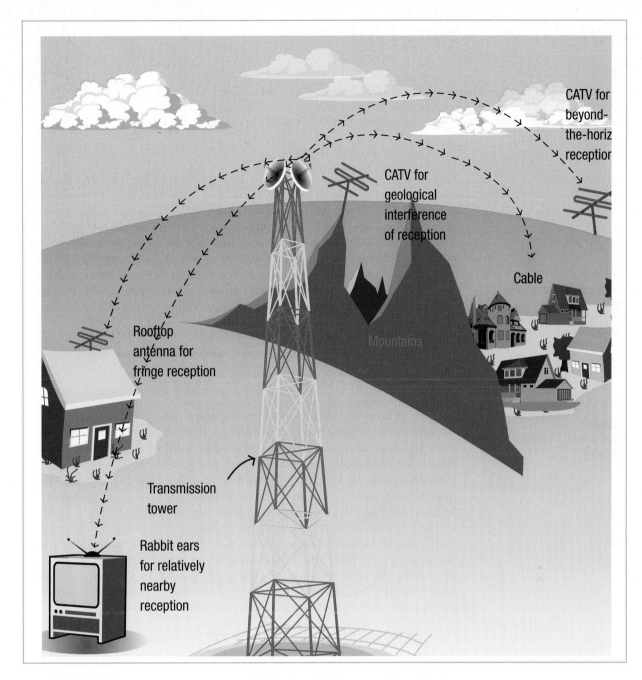

Television Signals

Signals transmitted by AM radio stations ricochet off the upper atmosphere and thus follow the curvature of the earth. FM radio and television signals, however, go in straight lines, which gives relatively short range. So while rabbit ears will pick up television within a few miles of a television station, farther away it takes rooftop antennas. Even farther distances require a tall tower, which gave rise to community antenna systems in faraway places beginning in 1949. Eventually CATV grew into the national cable television industry.

Satellite-Direct Delivery

STUDY PREVIEW

Television delivery fragmented further with satellite signals delivered directly to viewers via their own reception dishes. This so-called satcom system bypassed the federally licensed system of over-air local stations as well as cable distributors.

STANLEY HUBBARD

● **Stanley Hubbard**
Pioneer of direct-to-viewer satellite television

The possibilities for satellite delivery were not lost on **Stanley Hubbard,** who owned television station KSTP in Minnesota. Like almost all network-affiliated stations, KSTP was incredibly profitable, but Hubbard believed it might become a dinosaur in the age of satellite communication. Why should people tune into local stations, which picked up network signals from satellite for retransmission to viewers, when the technology was available for viewers to pick up the signals directly from satellite? Skeptics scoffed, but in 1984 Hubbard joined General Motors, which was in a diversification mode, to offer a **direct broadcast satellite** service. People could pick up signals from almost anyplace with home dishes the size of a large pizza.

● **direct broadcast satellite (DBS)**
Transmission of television signals directly from orbiting satellite to viewers without a local station or cable system as intermediary

LEARNING CHECK ◄

▶ **What television delivery innovation did Stanley Hubbard champion?**

SATCOMS

● **DirecTV**
Larger of two U.S. satellite-direct companies

The cost of entry for satellite-direct transmission has limited the number of U.S. satcom operators to two. **DirecTV,** the larger, has 15.5 million subscribers. For several years media mogul Murdoch controlled DirecTV with 34 percent ownership. He sold his interest in 2006 but continues with similar satellite services on other continents—Star TV in Asia, B-Sky-B in Britain, Sky Italia in Italy and Foxtel in Australia. The Dish Network, the trade name for EchoStar, has 11 million subscribers. EchoStar has a fleet of nine satellites in orbit, DirecTV eight.

Both DirecTV and EchoStar are growing, taking subscribers away from cable. In 2003 Dallas became the first major city with more satellite than cable customers. The growth accelerated when the Federal Communications Commission cleared the way for the satellite-delivery companies to include local over-air stations and their network programs among their array of cable channels. Both services also carry pay-per-view movies, pornography and sports packages.

LEARNING CHECK ◄

▶ **What is a satcom?**

▶ **How many satcoms serve the United States? Name them.**

▶ **How big a factor are satcoms in the U.S. television industry? Globally?**

Video on Demand

STUDY PREVIEW

Time-shifting devices enable viewers to decide when they watch television. Portable devices let them decide where. These video-on-demand devices, as well as content designed for watching on the go, are undermining some long-term attractions of networks, stations, cable systems and satcoms as advertising vehicles.

TIME SHIFTING

● **video on demand (VOD)**
Mechanisms that allow viewers to tune in to programs any time they choose

Devices that allow people to watch what they want when they want, **video on demand,** date to Betamax videotape players introduced by Sony in 1976. Later devices, like **TiVo** digital recorders, provide other options for what's called

● TiVo
Digital recording and playback device for television

● time shifting
Audience control of time for viewing a chosen program.

time shifting. People don't have to schedule their activities around a channel's schedule. It's possible to program a TiVo to record the news at 6 p.m. and then watch it whenever. The same is true with *Jericho* or Leno.

Time shifting has dramatically reduced the tyranny that network and station programmers once had over people's lives. A troubling upshot of the technology for networks and stations is that they are losing their power to amass great numbers of people in front of the screen at the same time. That had been a selling point to advertisers. An advertiser for time-of-day products like Subway sandwiches wants to reach viewers at mealtime—not when viewers decide to watch a show. What good is an advertisement designed to stir excitement for the weekend introduction of the new Dodge Challenger if viewers don't see the spot until a week later?

Also, those TiVo devices allow viewers to skip commercials entirely.

LEARNING CHECK ◄ ┄┄┄┄┄┄┄┄┄┄┄┄┄┄┄┄┄┄┄┄┄┄┄┄

▸ **How was Betamax revolutionary?**

▸ **How did TiVo further empower viewers?**

PORTABLE DEVICES

● video iPod
A handheld Apple device for playing not only music but video at the viewer's choice of time and place

In 2005 a video-playing Internet device introduced by Apple fully liberated viewers from planting themselves before large and stationary television sets. The Apple **video iPod** suddenly splintered television as an industry. By 2008 handheld iPods could store as many as 150 hours of video and display the images on a 2 1/2-inch color screen. People could watch television shows on the road or wherever—and whenever. It was true video on demand, with people downloading programs from the Internet to catch any time they wanted. Next Apple came up with iPhone, which had video-on-demand capabilities, followed by upgrades with greater capabilities.

Not to be left out, the major television networks, ABC, CBS, Fox and NBC, scrambled to sell archived programming for iPods. The one-time monopoly of the big networks providing programming through over-air local affiliates was further fractured.

Mobile Television. Comic-strip detective Dick Tracy of the 1950s would love cell phone television. All Tracy had was a two-way wrist radio. Today for $15 a month, the telephone company Verizon's V Cast offers newscast snippets and clips from the previous night's Jon Stewart show. Longer programs are available from the iTunes store and other sources for downloading.

Webisodes. *CBS news producer Susan Zirinsky takes the proverbial busman's holiday. From the CBS drama* Jericho *she looks for possible news angles, arranges news interviews with subject-area experts, and weaves them into five-minute items for Web delivery.*

As a television news producer, Susan Zirinsky has done it all. In college she took a job answering phones in the CBS Washington bureau one day a week. By her senior year she was typing scripts for the evening news. After graduation she became a researcher, at age 24 an associate producer. In 1980 she took a producing assignment at journalism's premier beat of the era—the White House. She was on the road with Ronald Reagan and a CBS crew for the 1984 presidential campaign. More recently she's been executive producer of the CBS newsmagazine *48 Hours*.

Most people would find themselves fully occupied with responsibilities like Zirinky's at *48 Hours*, but in her odd time she is dabbling with a new form of television—webisodes. These are brief episodic stories for Web delivery. Zirinsky, with her newsgathering skills honed covering Washington, will pick up a story line from the post-apocalyptic network drama *Jericho* and mix it with live interviews. A term hasn't come up yet for these webisode hybrids with news angles. Zirinsky calls them webumentaries.

Are webisodes the future of television? Certainly they are a departure from the prime-time bread and butter of television networks—ongoing episodes mostly in 30-minute or 60-minute blocks. Those formats have worked for generations. But the industry has cause to be uneasy about whether the young audience, hooked with on-the-go media, will sit still for 30 minutes, let alone 60. The new generation is going for Web-style snippet drama and amusement.

Time will tell whether Zirinsky is on the ground floor of a reinvention of television programming.

WHAT DO YOU THINK?

▶ Is the future of television in webisodes?

▶ What are the cultural implications of cutting television drama from 60-minute blocks to 5-minute blocks? What about 30-minute sitcoms? Soap operas?

Meanwhile, cell phone providers led by Verizon added VOD capabilities to their phones. Verizon's subscription service, rolled out in 2006, offered snippets, then longer video features, some truncated from programs to which rights had been purchased from the big networks and other television program creators.

LEARNING CHECK ◀ •

▶ **How has television viewing become untethered?**

media timeline

TELEVISION MILESTONES

1900–1949

First Tube
Philo Farnsworth invented a tube to capture and transmit moving images (1927)

World's Fair
RCA demonstrated television at New York World's Fair (1939)

Technology
FCC adopted standards for U.S. television (1941)

Networks
NBC began network feeds, followed by CBS, ABC (1948)

CATV
Ed Parsons introduced cable television in Astoria, Oregon (1949)

Philo Farnsworth, image dissector inventor

Rooftop Antennas, Rabbit Ears picked up over-air signals

1950–1999

Public Television
Congress established Corporation for Public Broadcasting (1967)

HBO
First satellite-delivered programming to cable systems (1975)

Fourth Network
Rupert Murdoch launched Fox network (1986)

Dishes
DirecTV began satellite-direct programming (1994)

Digital
FCC adopted digital standards for gradual phase-in (1996)

Flying way high

2000s

iPod
Apple introduced video iPod (2005)

Digital
FCC required stations to complete conversion to digital (2009)

Television anywhere, any time

PIVOTAL EVENTS

- Prohibition (1920–1933)
- Right to vote extended to women (1920)
- Great Depression (1930s)
- Franklin Roosevelt presidency (1933–1945)
- World War II (1941–1945)
- Russian–Western rivalry triggered Cold War (1945)

- FCC chair Newton Minow characterized television as "vast wasteland" (1961)
- Telstar in orbit (1961)
- Nixon presidency (1969–1977)
- Humans reached moon (1969)
- Ronald Reagan presidency (1981–1988)
- Soviet empire imploded (1989)
- Internet emerged as commercial medium (late 1990s)

- George W. Bush presidency (2001–2009)
- 9/11 terrorist attacks (2001)
- iPod introduced (2002)

221

VOD CHALLENGES

VOD is the great unknown in the future of television as we know it. Apple has positioned itself with the handheld video iPod and its Disney ABC connection. In 2006 Warner made a deal to put 14,000 free episodes of vintage shows, including *Welcome Back, Kotter*, *Wonder Woman* and *Kung Fu*, on the America Online subscription service owned by its parent company, Time Warner. AOL started with a drama channel, a comedy channel and four others. By 2006 about half of U.S. households had fast broadband connections to accommodate larger-than-ever-before downloads from the Internet, including ever-longer videos.

The VOD revolution has only begun. The cost of entry is so low that almost anyone with a few hundred dollars in software can create videos for VOD distribution. Just about everyone has easy access to post on YouTube.

LEARNING CHECK ◄

▶ **How do affiliate stations view network forays into VOD?**

▶ **Who owns massive inventory assets of programming for VOD?**

▶ **How can a case be argued that VOD is democratizing television?**

Economics of Television

STUDY PREVIEW

The backbone of television economics historically has been the 30-second spot. Even with audience numbers slipping in recent years, 30-second spots have remained popular enough with advertisers that the networks have kept charging more. Some observers, however, see a softening in demand.

NETWORK ADVERTISING

The big television networks have become an enigma. While cable networks have nibbled steadily at the audience once devoted to ABC, CBS, Fox and NBC, these major networks still have been able to continue raising their advertising rates. Strange as it seems, advertisers are paying the networks more money than ever to reach fewer viewers.

■ **30-Second Spot.** Even so, there are signs that advertiser demand for 30-second spots may be softening. Big Four networks are not filling slots as far in advance as they once did. Why? Cable channels, many with relatively low-cost programming, have eased the demand with cut-rate pricing while also opening up manifold more slots, albeit for smaller audience slices. Also, doubts have arisen among advertisers about whether pricey 30-second spots on the Big Four are as cost-effective as cable, the Internet and other emerging advertising platforms. In short, the 30-second spot as the economic engine of the television industry may be an endangered species.

■ **Upfront.** Drama is intense every spring when the networks ask big advertisers to commit themselves upfront to spots in the future year's programming. The networks list shows that they plan to continue, as well as a sample of new programs, and announce their asking price per 30-second spot based on audience projections. Then begins jockeying and bidding between the networks and the agencies that represent advertisers. The **upfront,** as the process is called, locks sponsors into specific shows three to five months ahead of the new season—although contracts generally have options that allow an advertiser to bail out.

For the 2005 season, the networks serving over-air stations obtained $9.1 billion in the upfront. Cable networks, which use the same process, lined up $6.3 billion in commitments.

● **upfront**
Advance advertiser commitments to buy network advertising time

Eighty percent of a year's commercial time typically gets spoken for in the up-front process. If a show misses the network's projected audience numbers, advertisers are given **make-goods,** the industry's term for additional spots to compensate. If a show turns into a smash hit and exceeds audience forecasts, the price per spot gets jacked higher or, in some cases, if there is no escalation clause, the advertisers end up with a real deal.

LEARNING CHECK ◄ ···

▶ **What has happened to the 60-second television commercial?**

▶ **Does the 30-second spot have a future?**

▶ **What happens when a network doesn't deliver an audience to an advertiser as promised?**

CABLE REVENUE STREAMS

Cable systems, going back to CATV, have a core revenue stream from subscribers, who are charged a monthly access fee. Cable networks tap into that revenue stream by charging the local systems to carry their programming. Fees for many cable channels are modest. The Travel Channel is lowest at 7 cents per subscriber per month. These are the highest:

> ESPN, 76 cents
>
> TNT, 64 cents
>
> Nickelodeon, 55 cents
>
> CNN, 43 cents
>
> MTV, 42 cents

When cable networks emerged in the late 1970s, some sought national advertising in competition with the over-air networks. Also, local cable systems went head-to-head with local over-air stations for local advertising.

LEARNING CHECK ◄ ···

▶ **How do cable networks and systems finance themselves?**

Public Television

··

STUDY PREVIEW

Government financial support of a national noncommercial television system grew out of concern in the 1960s that television was a "vast wasteland" of low-brow content. Programming at the time came mostly from the three networks. Then PBS came into being as an alternative. Today, with a great array of programming available, a question is whether public funding is necessary anymore.

NONCOMMERCIAL STATIONS

Many universities and school districts set up stations as noncommercial operations in the 1950s and 1960s as part of their mission to broaden their reach. These stations, as a condition of their licenses from the Federal Communications Commission, could not sell time to advertisers. As educational experiments, the **ETV** stations, as they were called, had mixed results. Most programs were dull lectures. The following was small. In some cities, meanwhile, citizen groups obtained licenses for noncommercial stations. By the late 1960s there were 300 of these stations, but viewership was sparse.

Meanwhile, commercial television was drawing unprecedented audiences nightly. Lifestyles changed dramatically, as barkeeps and movie-house operators nationwide could attest. Many lodges surrendered their charters because of membership declines. The big draws were local news and network entertainment. While popular, the entertainment fare was criticized by elitists as downscale and a horrible default on television's potential to make positive and enduring contributions. In a notable 1961 speech, the chair of the Federal Communications Commission, **Newton Minow,** accused the industry of presiding over a "vast wasteland."

LEARNING CHECK ◄ ·····································

▶ Put Newton Minow's 1961 "vast wasteland" indictment of television in a modern context. Is it still true?

▶ Where would you put Minow on an elitist-populist scale?

▶ What was the original purpose of noncommercial television stations?

PUBLIC BROADCASTING SERVICE

In 1967 a blue-ribbon group, the **Carnegie Commission on Educational Television,** examined the situation and saw a grossly underdeveloped national resource. The commission recommended an alternate concept and used the term **public television** to "serve the needs of the American public." Within months, Congress responded by creating the **Corporation for Public Broadcasting** to develop a national noncommercial broadcasting system for both television and radio. The goal was high-quality programming distinct from that of the commercial networks, which, by their nature, pandered to mass audiences. Thus was born the **Public Broadcasting Service** as a network serving the former ETV stations, most of which shifted to the new public television model.

To pay the bills, public television has cobbled together motley sources of revenue. Until recent years, congressional appropriations buffered from political control through a quasi-government agency, the Corporation for Public Broadcasting, were a

PBS and News. The Public Broadcasting Service has established a following for public affairs programs, albeit relatively small compared to that of commercial networks. Judy Woodruff, whose career has included time with commercial networks, frequently hosts Frontline *documentaries that are often noted for breakthrough reports. PBS, whose affiliates are barred from carrying advertisements, portrays itself as a quality-focused alternative that functions free of commercial entanglements.*

● **Newton Minow**
FCC chair who called television a "vast wasteland"

● **Carnegie Commission on Educational Television**
Recommended ETV be converted to the public television concept

● **public television**
Noncommercial television with an emphasis on quality programs to meet public needs

● **Corporation for Public Broadcasting (CPB)**
Quasi-government agency that channels tax-generated funds into the U.S. noncommercial television and radio system

● **Public Broadcasting Service (PBS)**
Television network for noncommercial over-air stations

The War. *Documentary producer Ken Burns drew more viewers to PBS with his 1990 Civil War series than any other program in the network's history. His 10-part series* Jazz, *which tracked the history of the distinctive U.S. musical genre, was in the same spirit in 2001, as is his most recent documentary that explores World War II from the perspectives of the soldiers on the ground and the loved ones they left behind.*

mainstay. As federal funding has declined, the public television system has stepped up its drive for donations from public-spirited corporations and viewers themselves. Although prohibited from selling advertising time, stations can acknowledge their benefactors. These acknowledgments, once bare-bones announcements, have become more elaborate over the years and sometimes seem close to advertising.

Public television has never been much liked by the commercial television industry. Public stations take viewers away, even though relatively few. Also, that public television receives what amounts to government subsidies seems unfair to the commercial stations. The upside of the arrangement for commercial television is that the presence of high-quality programming on public television eases public and government pressure on them to absorb the cost of producing more high-culture fare as a public service that would attract only niche audiences and few advertisers.

LEARNING CHECK ◄ •

▶ **What did the founding of PBS say about the quality of television programming at the time?**

▶ **What happened to educational television?**

▶ **Somebody has to pay the bills to keep public television on the air. Who?**

Future for Television

STUDY PREVIEW

Fundamental changes in the role of television in people's lives are occurring. Time shifting, possible with video on demand, is eroding the social tradition of gathering around the television. A related phenomenon, possible through television's growing portability, is space shifting. People can carry television with them to anywhere— any space—they choose.

TIME SHIFTS

Television as a centerpiece in people's lives in the evening for half a century is waning, even in prime time. With TiVo-like playback devices, people don't need to tune in at 8 for a favorite sitcom. To be sure, events like sports playoffs, elections and the *American Idol* finale will draw huge, live prime-time audiences. But the end may be in sight for prime-time scheduling for ongoing network series, the historic foundation of network programming.

A fundamental paradigm shift is occurring. Instead of people adapting their daily routines to television's scheduling, people are watching television when it suits them. This is audience empowerment.

LEARNING CHECK ◄ •

▶ **More than ever, television networks are scouting for big events that will attract a real-time audience. Why?**

SPACE SHIFTS

● **New Television**
A catchall term that variously includes cable, satellite, handheld and other delivery and reception technology

● **space shifts**
The change in where people watch television

● **mobisodes**
Mini-episodes, some a mere minute, to fit into the short time frames that mobile television viewers have available

The portability of **New Television,** as it might be called, signals a transformation in programming. The old 30-minute blocks assumed an audience being in one place, seated for a whole program, and hence the coinage *couch potato.* Thirty-minute blocks were also useful for affiliate breakaways and local patching of programming into network structures. On-the-move audiences, with handheld screens, are neither in place nor freed from other activities in neat 30-minute segments.

With **space shifts,** the changes in where people watch television, programming is bound to change. Expect to see more **mobisodes,** short episodes for mobile viewers. For Verizon's V Cast service, geared for mobile devices, Fox has created one-minute episodes of its program *24*, something to watch between checking for new e-mail messages or a new online video game.

LEARNING CHECK ◄ •••

▶ **Are couch potatoes an endangered species? Explain.**

ADVERTISING SHIFTS

Once the darling of almost every national brand for marketing, 30-second spots on network television are losing luster.

■ **Webisodes.** One brand-name advertiser that's shifted away from 30-second spots is American Express. In the mid-1900s AmEx put 80 percent of its advertising budget on network spots. By 2005, however, the amount was down to 35 percent. Where have AmEx and other brand-name advertisers diverted their dollars? Some AmEx dollars have stayed with the networks through product mention in scripts. But much has gone into Web initiatives, concert sponsorships, and experiments like stocking blue-labeled bottled water at trendy health clubs to promote American Express's blue card. There have been blue popcorn bags at movie houses and AmEx-sponsored museum exhibits. AmEx has been a leader with **webisodes,** those four-minute mini-movies on the Web. In another alternative to television, blue-card logos were everywhere for an AmEx-sponsored concert with Elvis Costello, Stevie Wonder and Counting Crows at the House of Blues in Los Angeles, renamed the House of Blue for the event.

● **webisodes**
Mini-movies, generally four minutes, on the Web; usually sponsored and sometimes with the advertiser part of the story line

■ **Product Placement.** Mindful that advertisers are scouting for alternative media, television networks have gone to selling plugs for products and services in

Product Placement. *It was no mistake that contestants on the Game Show Network's* American Dream Derby *swilled Diet Dr. Pepper while discussing strategy. Nor that JellO and other brand names are frequent props built into scripts and stunts for a fee. Product placements, sometimes subtle, sometimes not, have become a vehicle for advertisers to get in your face even if you zap the usual commercials with TiVo or other record-replay devices.*

scripts. It's not so unlike early radio and 1950s television, when hosts for sponsored programs touted products. For Arthur Godfrey, no tea was as good as Lipton's—and viewers never knew when to expect a plug. This was a leftover from an era when radio advertisers produced their own programs. As the networks took over programs, selling commercial slots to the highest bidder, a purist distinction between creative control of programming content and advertising became a given. Now the wall has been breached between commercials and pure, pristine, untainted entertainment and drama as creative arts.

In the 1980s Hollywood began selling product mentions in movie scripts. The result was a continuing boiling controversy. The controversy now is back in television, with networks, facing the TiVo drain of viewers who skip the ads, weaving product names into scripts. The presence of Coca-Cola as an *American Idol* prop and Pepsi products in *Survivor* were major-league examples. Despite protests from some producers and calls in Congress for on-air notices, the practice seems destined to stay.

LEARNING CHECK ◄••

▶ **What screen media alternatives to television are advertisers finding?**

▶ **What is the upside of product placement? The downside?**

Chapter Wrap-Up

Television in Transition (Page 209)

■ Television transformed lifestyles in the United States beginning in the 1950s. It's hard to imagine the Super Bowl without television. Lodge meetings, Wednesday-night vespers and evening socializing at neighborhood taverns suddenly were relegated to something from the not-so-much-regretted good ol' days. Today, however, that huge audience is fragmenting. The fragmentation began with the arrival of cable networks in the 1970s and accelerated with satellite-direct delivery systems. Video on demand via the Internet is the latest technology to beleaguer the traditional structure of television. For clarity, perhaps the term today should be *screen media* instead of *television*. Even so, the medium has had a powerful influence. Social critic Michael Novak calls television "a molder of the soul's geography."

Over-Air Delivery (Page 211)

■ The original U.S. television system was modeled on radio—local stations licensed by the national government. As with radio, national networks soon were providing local stations with their most popular programming, particularly in the evening. The evening hours came to be called prime time because that's when networks could charge advertisers premium rates for the biggest audiences. The first television network was created by radio pioneer David Sarnoff, who applied lessons from radio to organize NBC. Not far behind was rival William Paley at CBS. ABC was a late arrival, but by the mid-1950s the industry was dominated by the Big Three. The truly late arrival was Fox in 1986.

Cable Delivery (Page 213)

■ Cable television sat in the backwaters of the television industry for its first quarter century. Originally, cable systems were merely mechanisms for relaying big-city and Big Three over-air television programming to faraway communities beyond the reach of over-air signals. That changed dramatically in 1975 when HBO began offering exclusive programming to cable systems, followed by Ted Turner's WTBS superstation, then CNN. Today, 330 cable networks compete for viewers. Those small-town CATV systems, short for "community antenna television," now have been absorbed by giant multisystem cable companies that have wires in big cities. Cable is no longer a small-town business.

Satellite-Direct Delivery (Page 218)

- With satellite communication, dating to the Telstar satellite in 1961, the technology was at hand to deliver television directly to individual home receivers—dishes, they're called. The television industry opposed satellite-direct delivery because it would bypass local stations and cable too. But in 1984 DirecTV won authorization to establish the satcom business, followed by EchoStar's Dish Network. This further fragmented the television industry. In some cities today there are more satellite than cable subscribers, an additional drain on viewers for over-air stations. That eats into the rates that the Big Four networks can charge for national advertising.

Video on Demand (Page 218)

- The Internet's impact on television has been just as great as its impact on other media. With portable devices, including advanced cell phones, people can pick up video programming on the go. Because of technical download issues, live programs tend to be short—like five-minute webisodes. But long-form programs can be downloaded in advance for viewing any time, anywhere. This is another challenge for older over-air and cable delivery and even newer satellite-direct delivery to deal with. Other technology also is giving traditional television fits. Devices that allow time shifting, like TiVo recording and playback machines, are cutting into the massive audiences that networks and their over-air affiliates once could rely on to sit down and watch *I Love Lucy* simultaneously, along with the interspersed ads. With TiVo, viewers can even skip the ads.

Economics of Television (Page 222)

- As Congress conceived of television in the 1930s, even when the technology was in its infancy, stations would be limited to local broadcasting and be self-sufficient financially with advertising. This was unlike many countries in which government operated the national television system. The financial structure of the U.S. industry indeed became dependent, entirely, on advertising—notwithstanding the few educational stations that attracted hardly any viewers.

Public Television (Page 223)

- Responding to the television industry's focus on programming that appealed to the widest possible audience, necessarily a lowbrow strategy, Congress in 1967 established a structure for federal funding to develop noncommercial stations as an alternative. The result was a financial base for programming that otherwise would not be aired for want of sufficient advertising revenue. Noncommercial stations that had been licensed for educational purposes redubbed themselves *public television* and built their programming around a new network, the Public Broadcasting Service. Public funding always has been controversial. One severe critic, radio talk-show host Rush Limbaugh, epitomized the opposition this way: "Why should tax dollars fund broadcasting that people don't want to watch?" The fact is that with the proliferation of cable and satcom channels, PBS and its affiliates' programming is less distinctive than it was originally.

Future for Television (Page 225)

- Increasingly advertisers are less enchanted with the major television networks that service local over-air stations—and also cable and satcom channels. The audience is dwindling, siphoned off by competing new media. Time-shift devices like TiVo and portable video devices raise questions among advertisers about a new mushiness in network audiences. No surprise, more advertising dollars are going into these alternates, at least experimentally. The traditional networks have responded with deals to work product plugs into scripts, a controversial step. Over the objections of affiliates, the traditional networks are selling programs through iStore and other outlets to offset softening advertising revenue. In short, the face of the U.S. television industry is in flux.

REVIEW QUESTIONS

1. What technological innovations are beleaguering the original television industry?

2. Why did a two-tier system develop for U.S. television? How well has it worked?

3. What ended the happy relationship between CATV operators and over-air stations?

4. How is the cable television industry receiving a comeuppance from satcoms?

5. What are examples of video on demand?

6. Has public television addressed the 1961 observation of FCC chair Newton Minow that television is a "vast wasteland"?

7. Will advertisers abandon over-air, cable and satcom television channels because of time-shift and portable devices? Explain.

CONCEPTS

ownership meld (Page 216)

public television (Page 224)

space shifts (Page 225)

time shifting (Page 219)

two-tier system (Page 212)

TERMS

CATV (Page 214)

Corporation for Public Broadcasting (CPB) (Page 224)

multisystem operator (MSO) (Page 216)

upfront (Page 222)

video on demand (Page 218)

PEOPLE

Stanley Hubbard (Page 218)

Gerald Levin (Page 214)

John Malone (Page 207)

Newton Minow (Page 224)

Ed Parsons (Page 215)

MEDIA SOURCES

- Bill Carter. *Desperate Networks*. Doubleday, 2006. Carter, a television reporter for the New York *Times,* tracks network television programming for a season.

- J. D. Lasica. *Darknet: Hollywood's War Against the Digital Generation.* Wiley, 2005. Lasica draws on a wide range of interviews in making a case that the framework for U.S. broadcasting is outdated for the digital age.

- Roger P. Smith. *The Other Face of Public Television: Censoring the American Dream.* Algora, 2002. Smith, a widely recognized television producer, argues that U.S. public television is substantively the same as commercial television, only in a cosmetically different wrapping. He rhetorically asks whether public television can be truly independent as long as it is dependent on government funding. He concludes with a call for an alternative television production organization endowed with a nongovernment trust fund.

In this chapter you have deepened your media literacy by revisiting several themes. Here are thematic highlights from the chapter:

Satcom. *Is satellite programming delivered directly to viewers the future of television? Ask Rupert Murdoch. Ask John Malone. You'll find different takes on the question.*

Media Technology

For half a century television was a fast-growth industry built on a technology that marveled people. "Radio with pictures," it was called. Networks supplied programming to local affiliates for relay to anyone within a signal's reach. Now that's all old technology. The new technology, digital and Internet-based, delivers video any time, anywhere. One result is a challenge to the traditional U.S. television infrastructure and the program forms built around it—30-second spots and 30-minute and 60-minute scheduled programs. On-the-go people with access to a cell phone won't sit down for an hour-long drama. So now we have five-minute webisodes and newscasts. On the Internet, people download an item or two and move on, with the idea of tuning in later when they have another couple minutes. **(Pages 211–220 and 225–227)**

Media Effects

While some researchers focus on whether television and other media affect public attitude and opinion, cultural sociologists focus on lifestyle effects that lend themselves to firmer conclusions. The effect of early television was obvious. Wednesday-night boxing, an early program fixture, kept people home and dented the attendance at older venues for out-of-home activities. And who in America in the 1950s would have missed the *$64,000 Question?* In a reversal of sorts, people today are adapting to television less than television is adapting to them. Devices that enable time shifting and on-the-go video pickups are putting the audience in charge. Theoretically the latest *Survivor* series is available 24/7. Some 60-minute programs are being divided into five-minute

Too Much TV? *Ongoing issue for researchers is effects on kids.*

segments, some self-contained, some with their own cliff-hangers to entice viewers back for the next installment. **(Pages 209–211 and 218–220)**

Webisodes. *How far is our fast-paced 21st-century existence taking us? No more sitting down for 60-minute television shows? Thirty minutes too long, too? How about Susan Zirinsky's five-minute webisode news items taken from Jericho scripts?*

Media Economics

Television for the networks and their affiliates once was money-making bliss. Advertisers lined up to buy every spot available, particularly in prime time. The whole industry was built on charging advertisers what the market would bear, which was on a roll with double-digit annual growth. Today the economic structure is fracturing. Advertisers have options galore in which to make visual appeals to consumers, not only on cable and satcom channels but also via Internet venues and a dizzying array of digital-based alternative media. Where the unraveling of the traditional economic infrastructure will end is for clairvoyants to predict. In the meantime, the major over-air networks are testing other venues, like selling programs for Internet viewing. **(Pages 222–223 and 226–227)**

Elitism and Populism

The new medium of television, quickly engaging millions of viewers in the 1950s, seemed to have great potential as a force for cultural enlightenment and for encouraging public participation in the great issues. A decade later FCC chair Newton Minow had, in effect, given up on this potential. He called television a "vast wasteland," a label that has stuck ever since. The networks pandered to low tastes with programming that neither excited the mind nor motivated political engagement. In the main, television was narcoticizing, lowbrow stuff—comedy geared to momentary chuckles, drama with predictable outcomes, and superficial takes on news. Whether television overall is less a wasteland today can be debated, but at least public stations are in existence as an alternative. Also, the narrow range of program offerings in the 1950s, broadcast by three largely duplicative New York-based networks, has increased by several hundred cable and satcom channels and myriad Internet-delivered video sources. Television is still mostly the same, just more of it. Or is something going on that would satisfy Newton Minow? **(Pages 223–225)**

PBS. *A little good history, anyone? Documentary producer Ken Burns has drawn big audiences on public television. His 2007 series on World War II outdrew a large audience in terms of numbers. However, most PBS offerings draw a mass-audience yawn. Is there a place for serious-minded works on television?*

"Tracy, Here." *The miniaturization of electronics envisioned for comic-strip detective Dick Tracy more than half a century ago has arrived—with unanticipated consequences. The way that television content is delivered, for example, is being transformed even as you read this. Seen Jon Stewart on an iPod? How about on a Tracy-like wristwatch screen? Oh, that's next week.*

Audience Fragmentation

The explosion of television as a new medium ruined the magazine, radio and movie industries, at least for a while, and took away time that people had spent with books. The consolidation of audiences around the new medium was phenomenal. Magazines and radio demassified to survive, seeking segments of their former audiences. No question about it, the magazine and radio industries surrendered large segments of their audiences to television. In a comeuppance, the television audience itself now is fragmenting. The core network-affiliate over-air system has lost audience to hundreds of channels available on cable systems and by satcom delivery. These are mostly niche channels seeking profitable segments of the singular mass audience that the original networks and their over-air affiliates had amassed over a period of 50 years. The fragmentation is being accelerated by thousands of entertainment and information sources on the Internet. **(Pages 213–220 and 225–227)**

Media and Democracy

Video-on-demand technology has liberated people from being tied down to a television set. The control that networks once had over lifestyles with their tantalizing prime-time and other fare is breaking down. People can watch television at their convenience with recording and playback devices. Portable devices enable people to choose not only when to watch but where. This has been called the democratization of television, the power shifting from national network program schedulers at corporate offices in New York to individual viewers. **(Pages 218–220)**

Liberation Tool. *Portable video viewing is freeing people from half a century of lifestyle tyranny by television network executives, who schedule when programs will air.*

231

10

Internet

French Grammar, Breezy and Online

Who better to offer French lessons than somebody from France? That's me, figured Sebastian Babolat, who was doing college studies in California when he learned about podcasting. He gave it a try. Babolat had fun creating his FrenchPodClass, which took a breezy tack with the grammar. Within months the 26-year-old French guy from Monterey had 10,000 listeners. Babolat was among podcast leaders. Babolat is among millions of people who have capitalized on readily available digital tools—a PC and a few bucks' worth of gear—to create digital audio programs on whatever they want and post them on the Web. Subjects cover the spectrum—grunge music and commentary, politics of every stripe, vegan cooking, and, yes, having fun learning French.

Podcasting first was a self-expression tool that grew out of the political blogs that proved to be a low-cost, high-yield communication tool in the 2004 U.S. elections. Inspired by the potential, bloggers devised sites on all kinds of subjects. In 2005 Apple began promoting podcast shows on its iTunes online music store. That's about the time that Babolat started podcasting for people to brush up on their *bonjours*.

Early podcasting had a pristine, noncommercial quality, but the growing audience inevitably took on a commercial cast. Georgia-Pacific, the huge timber company and papermaker, set up Mommycast on parenting with plugs for its Dixie products. Google and others created podcast search engines with sponsored links. Sirius satellite radio hired a former MTV video jock, Adam Curry, to create a program with his podcast highlights du jour.

LEARNING AHEAD

- The Internet emerged suddenly in the 1990s as a major mass medium.
- The Internet resulted from a confluence of technological advancements.
- The World Wide Web links individual computers with the Internet.
- Subscriptions and advertising are becoming the Internet's foundation.
- The shape of the Internet industry is still taking form.
- The Internet is democratizing mass communication, albeit with side effects.
- Internet technology is blurring distinctions among traditional media.

Sebastian Babolat. *His breezy lessons in French became a podcast hit with 10,000 listeners.*

Nobody sees a clear course yet for podcasting or whatever next month will bring as the new marvel of the Digital Age. In this chapter you will learn about dynamics that have brought us to where we're at with the Internet, the Web and, of course, podcasting. This knowledge will give you tools to keep abreast and perhaps ahead of where it is all going.

Influence of the Internet

STUDY PREVIEW

The Internet has emerged as the eighth major mass medium, with a range of content, especially through Web coding, that exceeds that of traditional media in many ways.

NEW MASS MEDIUM

From a dizzying array of new technologies, the Internet emerged in the mid-1990s as a powerful new mass medium. What is the Internet? It's a jury-rigged network of telephone and cable lines and satellite links that connects computers. Almost anybody on the planet with a computer can tap into the network. A few clicks of a mouse button will bring in vast quantities of information and entertainment that originate from all over the world.

Although in some ways the Internet resembles a traditional mass medium that sends messages from a central transmission point, it is much more. Message recipients are able to click almost instantly from one source to another—from an L.L. Bean catalog to a Disney movie to *USA Today*. In another significant difference from other mass media, the Internet is interactive. It has the capacity to allow people to communicate outward, not just receive messages, and to do it in real time. Try doing that with a Spielberg movie or the latest *Harry Potter* sequel.

LEARNING CHECK ◄

▶ **How is the Internet unique as a medium of mass communication?**

SCOPE OF THE INTERNET

Every major mass-media company has put products on the Internet. Thousands of start-up companies are establishing themselves on the ground floor. The technology is so straightforward and access is so inexpensive that millions of individuals have set up their own sites.

How significant is the Internet as a mass medium? Estimates are that the number of users in the United States is well past 200 million—75 percent of the population. In only a few years the Internet has become a major medium for advertising. In 2005 advertisers spent $12.9 billion for space on Internet Web sites, up 34 percent from the year before and wholly one-fifth of what was spent on television. More than half of new-car buyers based their choice on information they had found on the Internet.

The significance of the Internet is measurable in other ways too. There are people who have given up reading the print edition of newspapers and instead browse through the Internet edition. Some of the news sites are updated constantly. Almost every U.S. magazine and newspaper has an **Internet site,** from the venerable but tech-savvy New York *Times* to local papers in the hinterlands.

● **Internet site**
Where an institution or individual establishes its Web presence

LEARNING CHECK ◄

▶ **List examples of the scope of the Internet. Include examples from your own experience.**

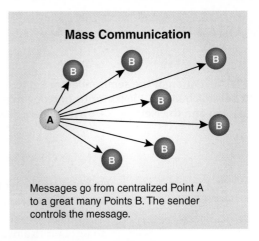

Linear Communication

Point
A

Point
B

The telegraph moves messages from Point A to Point B. The sender controls the message.

Mass Communication

A
B B B B B B B

Messages go from centralized Point A to a great many Points B. The sender controls the message.

Whither Mass Communication?

Web communication shifts much of the control of the communication through the mass media to the recipient, turning the traditional process of mass communication on its head. Receivers are no longer hobbled to sequential presentation of messages, as on a network television newscast. Receivers can switch almost instantly to dozens, hundreds even, of alternatives through a weblike network that, at least theoretically, can interconnect every recipient and sender on the planet.

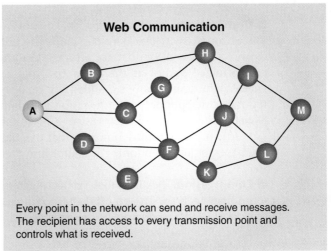

Web Communication

Every point in the network can send and receive messages. The recipient has access to every transmission point and controls what is received.

NEW TERMINOLOGY

The terms *Internet* and *Web* are often tossed around loosely, leading to lots of confusion. The fundamental network that carries messages is the Internet. It dates to a military communication system created in 1969. The early Internet carried mostly text.

The Web is a structure of codes that permits the exchange not only of text but also of graphics, video and audio. Web codes are elegantly simple for users, who don't even need to know them to tap into the Web's content. The underlying Web codes are accepted universally, which makes it possible for anyone with a computer, a modem and an Internet connection to tap into anything introduced from anywhere on the global Web. The term *Web* comes from the spidery links among millions of computers that tap into the system—an ever-changing maze that not even a spider could visualize and that becomes more complex all the time.

Internet technology led to many attempts at a name to set this new medium, its technological offspring and its siblings apart from traditional media. In a 2001 book, Lev Manovich made a case for *new media,* which caught on. Even so, there was confusion over products that spanned older and newer technologies, such as digitally delivered newspapers. *New media* was further blurred when it became an advertising buzzword for anything more sophisticated than a flashing neon sign. We are still searching for the right term to describe the revolutionary transformation of the media of mass communication.

LEARNING CHECK ◄••

▸ **What is meant by the terms *Internet* and *Web*? How is each different?**

▸ **Why is the term *new media* problematic?**

Internet Origins

STUDY PREVIEW

The 1947 invention of the semiconductor led to digitization and compression, which became building blocks for technology that made the Internet possible. Web coding and the Netscape browser widened access.

UNDERLYING TECHNOLOGIES

Researchers Walter Brattain, Jack Bardeen and William Shockley at AT&T's Bell Labs knew they were on to something important for telephone communication in 1947. They had devised glasslike silicon chips—pieces of sand, really—that could be used to respond to a negative or positive electrical charge.

● **semiconductor**
Silicon chips that are used in digitization

■ **Digitization.** The tiny chips, called **semiconductors,** functioned very rapidly as on-off switches. With the chips the human voice could be reduced to a stream of digits—1 for on, 0 for off—and then transmitted as rapid-fire pulses and reconstructed so fast at the other end that they sounded like the real thing. Digitization dramatically expanded the capacity of telephone systems and revolutionized telephone communication. Brattain, Bardeen and Shockley won a Nobel Prize.

Little did they realize, however, that they had laid the groundwork for revolutionizing not just telephonic communication but all of human communication.

● **compression**
Technology that makes a message more compact by deleting nonessential underlying code

■ **Compression.** Bell Labs took semiconductors to a new level with **compression** technology in 1965. The on-off digital technology had so compacted messages for transmission that, suddenly, it was possible to break calls into spurts and transmit them simultaneously on a single line, each spurt like a railroad car joining a train on a track and then leaving the train to go to its own destination. People marveled that 51 calls could be carried at the same time on a single wire.

The capacity of the nation's telephone system was dramatically increased without a single new mile of wire being laid.

■ **Miniaturization.** Semiconductors gradually replaced electrical tubes in broadcast equipment. The idea of a radio as a piece of furniture disappeared with semiconductor-equipped portable radios in the 1950s. But that was only the beginning of miniaturization of all kinds of electrical and mechanical functions. In the emerging field of computers, early models used electrical tubes and were housed in entire buildings. Now the movement is toward central units with footprints of less than four square feet. Laptops are a marvel of miniaturization.

There seems no end to miniaturization. The Marquandt Corporation estimates that all the information recorded in the past 10,000 years can be stored in a cube six feet by six feet by six feet. All the 12 million books in the Library of Congress would take fewer than two cubic inches. IBM expects to produce a computer drive that crams an incredible 2 billion digital characters on a thumbtack-size disk. That's equivalent to 2,000 novels.

LEARNING CHECK ◄ ⋯⋯⋯⋯⋯⋯⋯⋯⋯⋯⋯⋯⋯⋯⋯⋯⋯⋯⋯⋯

▶ **What technology breakthroughs came together to result in the Internet as we know it?**

DECENTRALIZED NETWORK

● **ARPAnet**
Military network that preceded the Internet

Untold numbers of innovations came together to create the Internet. In 1969 the U.S. military created a computer network called **ARPAnet,** which stood for Advanced Research Projects Agency Network. The Pentagon built the network for

National Science Foundation
Developed current Internet to give scholars access to supercomputers

internet
A network of computer networks

data packets
Clumps of digital data broken out of a a larger package for transmission

Vint Cerf, Bob Kahn
Coauthors of TCP, sometimes called the Fathers of the Internet

Transmission Control Protocol (TCP)
Universal system that connects individual computer systems to the Internet

Corning Glass
Company that developed fiber-optic cable

fiber-optic cable
Glass strands capable of carrying data as light

streaming
Technology that allows playback of a message to begin before all the components have arrived

Mead Data Central
Created Lexis, Nexis

Lexis
First online full-text database; carries legal documents

military contractors and universities doing military research to exchange information. In 1983 the **National Science Foundation,** whose mandate is to promote science, took over.

This new National Science Foundation network attracted more and more institutional users, many of which had their own internal networks. For example, most universities that joined the NSF network had intracampus computer networks. The NSF network, then, became a connector for thousands of other networks. As a backbone system that interconnects networks, **internet** was a name that fit.

■ **Data Packets.** The key to the tremendous efficiency of the system was the concept of **data packets,** which was drawn from earlier Bell Labs work for telephone communication. Data were broken into small packets to shoot into the decentralized network. The packets each would seek ways around jams and blockages, then reassemble at their destination—all in less than the blink of an eye when all was working well.

■ **Transmission Protocols.** One of the obstacles to the Internet becoming a universal vehicle for communication was that governments, universities, banks and other institutions had local networks built on a polyglot of computer languages. It was a mishmash of incompatibility. In 1974 two University of California at Los Angeles researchers, **Vint Cerf** and **Bob Kahn,** introduced a common language, **Transmission Control Protocol,** TCP for short, to allow the local networks to talk to each other.

For his contribution, Cerf has come to be called the Father of the Internet. The title also goes sometimes to Kahn. Both are uncomfortable with the appellation. Says Cerf: "None of this was happening in a vacuum."

■ **Fiber Optics.** While AT&T was building on its off-on digital technology to improve telephone service in the 1960s, **Corning Glass** developed a cable that was capable of carrying light at incredible speeds—theoretically, 186,000 miles per second. It was apparent immediately that this new **fiber-optic cable** could carry far more digitized messages than could the copper wire used for telephones. The messages were encoded as light pulses rather than as the traditional electrical pulses used for transmission.

By the 1980s new equipment to convert data to light pulses for transmission was in place, and long-distance telephone companies were replacing their copper lines with fiber optics, as were local cable television systems. With fiber-optic cable and other improvements, a single line could carry 60,000 telephone calls simultaneously.

Still, the Internet, using the telephone system to carry messages, was limited mostly to text-only messages. Visuals were rare. Video? Forget it. The number of data packets for video was too much for the system to reassemble in a reasonable time.

But when the nation, then the planet, was rewired with fiber-optic cable in one of the greatest construction projects in history, the Internet's capacity to scoot data packets from point to point grew dramatically. Messages that had massive amounts of coding, such as video, became commonplace. The process, called **streaming,** sometimes had reception that was jerky—it still is but is becoming less so.

LEARNING CHECK ◄ ••

▸ What is meant by describing the Internet as a decentralized network?

COMMERCIALIZATION

An Ohio company, **Mead Data Central,** was one of the first to find commercial applications for the Internet. In 1973, before TCP and fiber optics, Mead created **Lexis** with quick access to state and federal statutes, court decisions and other legal documents. Lawyers who subscribed could tap into Lexis for research and cut back on maintaining and updating the traditional expensive office law library. Because Lexis was delivered via telephone lines whose capacity precluded data-intensive graphics, there was nothing fancy about how Lexis looked—simple text on the computer screen. But it was just what lawyers and legal scholars needed, and they paid handsomely for the service.

Building on its Lexis success, Mead launched **Nexis** in 1978. Nexis was the first online database with national news organizations, including the New York *Times*, the Washington *Post*, the Associated Press and *U.S. News & World Report*. Nexis proved invaluable to researchers, who could search not only recent editions of participating newspapers and magazines but also back issues. Today, Nexis includes thousands of publications from around the world.

A new kind of company, **Internet service providers,** went into business in the 1980s to give ordinary folks a portal to the Internet and help in navigating the Internet's inherent complexity and disorganization. CompuServ was the first to provide online service to consumers, but America Online quickly became the leading provider. These companies charged subscription fees for a combination of services—Internet access, e-mail and, most important, a mapping structure to help get to where the user wanted to go among the seemingly infinite number of places on the Internet.

● **Nexis**
First online database with national news

● **Internet service provider**
Company that charges a fee for online service

LEARNING CHECK ◄ ···

▶ How have commercial aspects of the Internet changed since Lexis?

The World Wide Web

STUDY PREVIEW

A breakthrough in Internet communication was a new addressing system for linking each and every computer on the planet. The system, appropriately dubbed the World Wide Web, was created by Tim Berners-Lee. With the Web, anyone anywhere on the planet can connect with any other connected computer.

HYPERTEXT

● **Tim Berners-Lee**
Devised protocols, codes for the World Wide Web

● **World Wide Web**
System that allows global linking of information modules in user-determined sequences

A major breakthrough was developed by English engineer **Tim Berners-Lee,** who in 1991 devised an addressing system that could connect every computer in the world. The name that Berners-Lee came up with for his system sounded audacious, the **World Wide Web,** but it was accurate—a decentralized global network with the potential, theoretically, for everyone at a computer to communicate with everyone else at a computer anywhere on the planet.

Berners-Lee's invention was built on three components:

● **hypertext transfer protocol (HTTP)**
Coding that allows computers to talk with each other to read Web pages

● **hypertext markup language (HTML)**
Language that is used to code for Web pages

- **Universal resource locators (URL).** Berners-Lee devised an addressing system that gives every computer a unique identifier, much like a postal address enables mail to be delivered to the right place. The identifiers, URLs, allow computers connected in a network to exchange messages. Being "universal," it is a comprehensive and standardized system that is the foundation of the World Wide Web.
- **Hypertext transfer protocol (HTTP).** This was a new protocol that carried the Cerf-Kahn TCP idea to a new plane. With HTTP, individuals' computers can read Internet files.
- **Hypertext markup language (HTML).** This is a relatively simple computer language that permits someone creating an Internet message to insert so-called hot spots or links that, if clicked, will instantly switch the on-screen image to something else. For example, a research article could include visible indicators, usually an underline below a term, that with a click of a mouse will move to another article on the subject.

Single-handedly, Tim Berners-Lee invented the World Wide Web. Then, unlike many entrepreneurs who have used the Internet to amass quick fortunes, Berners-Lee devoted his life to refining the Web as a medium of communication open to everyone for free.

Berners-Lee, an Oxford engineer, came up with the web concept because he couldn't keep track of all his notes on various computers in various places. It was 1989. Working at CERN, a physics lab in Switzerland, he proposed a system to facilitate scientific research by letting scientists' computers tap into each other. In a way, the software worked like the brain. In fact, Berners-Lee said that the idea was to keep "track of all the random associations one comes across in real life and brains are supposed to be so good at remembering, but sometimes mine wouldn't."

Working with three software engineers, Berners-Lee had a demonstration up and running within three months. As Berners-Lee traveled the globe to introduce the Web at scientific conferences, the potential of what he had devised became clear. The Web was a system that could connect all information with all other information.

The key was a relatively simple computer language known as HTML, short for "hypertext markup language," which, although it has evolved over the years, remains the

Original Webmaster. *Tim Berners-Lee and his associates at a Swiss research facility created new Internet coding in 1989, dubbing it the World Wide Web. Today the coding is the heart of global computer communication.*

core of the Web. Berners-Lee also developed the addressing system that allows computers to find each other. Every Web-connected computer has a unique address, a universal resource locator (URL). For it all to work, Berners-Lee also created a protocol that actually links computers: HTTP, short for "hypertext transfer protocol."

In 1992, leading research organizations in the Netherlands, Germany and the United States committed to the Web. As enthusiasm grew in the scientific research community, word spread to other quarters. In one eight-month period in 1993, Web use multiplied 414 times. Soon "the Web" was a household word.

As you would expect, Berners-Lee had offers galore from investors and computer companies to build new ways to derive profits from the Web. He said no. Instead, he chose the academic life. At the Massachusetts Institute of Technology he works out of spartan facilities as head of the W3 consortium, which sets the protocol and coding standards that are helping the World Wide Web realize its potential.

It's hard to overstate Berners-Lee's accomplishment. The Internet is the information infrastructure that likely will, given time, eclipse other media. Some liken Berners-Lee to Johannes Gutenberg, who 400 years earlier had launched the age of mass communication with the movable type that made mass production of the written word possible.

WHAT DO YOU THINK?

▶ Would someone else have devised the World Wide Web if Tim Berners-Lee hadn't?

▶ Is Tim Berners-Lee in the same league as Gutenberg, Edison, Marconi, or Farnsworth?

Memex. *After World War II, a leading intellectual, Vannevar Bush, proposed a machine that could hold all of the information accumulated in human history. People using the machine could retrieve whatever they wanted in whatever sequence they wanted. The machine, which Bush called Memex, was never built, but the concept came to fruition three decades later with the Internet.*

● **hypertext**
System for nonsequential reading

The term **hypertext** was devised by technologist Ted Nugent in his 1962 book *Literary Machines* for a system that would allow people to interrupt themselves while reading through material in the traditional linear way, from beginning to end, and transport themselves nonlinearly to related material. Nugent also called it *nonsequential writing*, but the term *hypertext* stuck.

It was a quarter century later when Berners-Lee devised the HTML coding that makes nonsequential reading possible.

LEARNING CHECK ◄ ···

▶ **What sets URLs, HTTP and HTML apart from Vint Cerf and Bob Kahn's TCP?**

WEB BROWSERS

The importance of the Berners-Lee innovations for scientists to find sites all around the Internet was a landmark, but for the rest of us, the content was geeky stuff. In 1993 the Internet as we know it began to come to life. At the University of Illinois, grad student **Marc Andreessen** developed a software program, **Mosaic,** that improved the interconnections that permitted scientists to browse each other's research.

● **Marc Andreessen**
Devised the Netscape browser

● **Mosaic**
Predecessor browser to Netscape

● **browser**
Software that allows access to Web sites

● **Netscape**
Browser that made the Web easily accessible, attractive to personal computer owners

Enthusiasm for the potential of the **browser,** as it was called, quickly swelled. By tweaking Mosaic, Andreessen and a few colleagues created a new browser, **Netscape,** that could connect any of the three disparate computer operating systems that were becoming commonplace: Microsoft's Windows, Apple's Macintosh OS and Unix. Netscape was a point-and-click system by which anyone with a computer could unlock more content than had ever been conceivable in human history. Competing browsers followed and eclipsed Netscape.

Commercialization of the Internet, which had been gradual, moved into high gear. First a few retailers displayed their wares on-screen and took orders online, then shipped their products. The old point-of-purchase concept, catching consumers at the store with displays and posters, took on a whole new meaning. In the new cyberworld the point-of-purchase was not the merchant's shop but the consumer's computer screen. Sites for pitching products and services, some of them complete catalogs, sprouted by the thousands.

INTERNET MILESTONES

PIVOTAL EVENTS

1940–1949

Memex
Intellectual Vannevar Bush proposed a machine to store all information (1945)

Chips
Bell engineers invented the semiconductor (1947)

Why they call it the web

- World War II (1941–1945)
- Russian–Western rivalry triggered Cold War (1945)

1950–1959

- Eisenhower presidency (1953–1962)

1960–1969

ARPAnet
U.S. military linked computers of contractors, researchers (1969)

- Telstar in orbit (1961)
- Vietnam War (1964–1975)
- Humans reached moon (1969)

1970–1979

Lexis
Mead launched for-profit online database (1973)

Nexis
Mead launched news database (1978)

CompuServ
First online service for general-interest users (1979)

Tim Berners-Lee

- Nixon presidency (1969–1974)

1980–1989

Web
Tim Berners-Lee devised coding for World Wide Web (1989)

- Reagan presidency (1981–1988)
- Soviet empire imploded (1989)

1990–1999

Netscape
Marc Andreessen created Netscape browser (1993)

Fiber Optics
Telecommunications Act set off race to expand U.S. fiber-optic infrastructure (1996)

Blogs
Rob Marta created slashdot.org, first blog (1997)

Marc Andreessen, Netscape inventor

- Gulf War (1990–1991)
- Clinton presidency (1993–2000)

2000

Dot-Com Bubble
Internet overexpansion collapsed; economic disaster (2001)

Blogs, giving almost everyone a megaphone

- George W. Bush presidency (2001–2009)
- 9/11 terrorist attacks (2001)
- iPod introduced (2002)

The next stage in Internet commercialization occurred when advertisers began looking for Web sites to carry their pitches for products and services. Web sites whose content attracted large audiences were attractive to advertisers. So were sites that attracted niche audiences whose interests coincided with narrow-market products. These sites were built on the model of newspapers, magazines, radio and television as advertising-financed media. This, of course, drew revenue away from older media products, many of which responded by creating their own Web sites to capitalize on the shift in advertisers' media choices.

LEARNING CHECK ◄ •

▶ **How did Netscape add to the usefulness of the Internet?**

The Internet Industry

STUDY PREVIEW

A gold rush, the Internet drew major investments when it became a vehicle for commercial traffic. The dot-com boom, however, turned into a major bust that derailed the economy. Although there is new stability now, the Internet remains a nascent industry whose eventual shape is a matter of conjecture.

EMERGING COMPANIES

● **dot-com**
Informal general term for Internet commercial sites, most of whose online addresses ended with the suffix *.com*

Early on, entrepreneurs saw the Internet as a mountain of gold waiting to be mined. Investors poured millions into a wide range of ventures beginning in the early 1990s. Most didn't get it right. The financial landscape ended up littered with failed start-ups and bankruptcies by 1999, triggering a prolonged economic recession. The **dot-com** boom was bust, the bubble had burst.

Google was first to figure out how to make massive profits from the Internet. While everyone else was obsessing about creating Web site content that attracted readers, Google trumped them all by indexing the content—all of it, everything that everyone else was posting. As a portal for finding the content, Google captures millions and millions of eyeballs daily. With every search, Google posts sponsored links on-screen, side by side with links to sites of some relevance to the search. Advertisers, eager for the exposure, pay Google for the sponsored links. By 2005 Google was the fastest-growing company in history, with annual revenue topping $6.7 billion.

Google, however, was not the first to make money from the Internet. On a lesser scale, the Lexis and Nexis databases had made money all the way back in the 1970s.

Even today, with the Internet reaching its second quarter century as a medium for commercial traffic, the history on the shape of the industry is still to be written. Until the technology plateaus, the rough-and-tumble of energetic, hopeful new enterprises, followed by disappointments and setbacks amid successes, will mark the industry.

LEARNING CHECK ◄ •

▶ **What has risen from the ashes of the dot-com bust?**

▶ **What twist did Google add to the Internet business?**

PORTALS

● **portal**
Entry point for further Internet access

The original model for Internet fortunes was multipurpose **portals,** which came to be epitomized by America Online and its offering e-mail, access to the Web, and lots of exclusive content. Survivors of the dot-com bust include MSN and Yahoo, but the failures were spectacular, including General Electric's GEnie and an elaborate AT&T venture.

Also, portals have found it harder to sell subscriptions—the original business model. Thanks to the Tim Berners-Lee protocols, people can go directly to a countless number of Web sites on their own. The problem facing traditional portals is no better illustrated than by AOL, which has shifted away from subscriptions to advertising

At his 240-student high school in New Lisbon, Wisconsin, Marc Andreessen didn't play sports or mingle a lot. He recalls those times as "introverted." Recovering from surgery, he spent his time reading up on computer programming. Back at school, he built a calculator on the library computer to do his math homework.

Later, at the University of Illinois, he honed his interest in computer languages. At his $6.85-an-hour campus job writing computer code, he decided that the Web protocols devised by Tim Berners-Lee in Switzerland in 1989 needed a simple interface so that ordinary people could tap in. Marc Andreessen and fellow student Eric Bina spent three months, nights and weekends, writing a program they called Mosaic. It became the gateway for non-nerds to explore the Web. After Andreessen graduated, entrepreneur Jim Clark of Silicon Graphics heard about Mosaic and began some exploratory talks with Andreessen.

Browser Genius. At 21, Marc Andreessen and a geek buddy created Mosaic, which facilitated Web access. Then they trumped themselves by creating Netscape.

At one point, as Internet folklore has it, Andreessen said: "We could always create a Mosaic killer—build a better product and build a business around it." Andreessen hired geek friends from Illinois, and Netscape was born. It was the pioneer browser for the masses. Andreessen and a bunch of fellow 21-year-olds had democratized the Internet.

Netscape's revenues zoomed to $100 million in 1996. Meanwhile, Microsoft introduced the Explorer browser as a competitor, which hurt. But America Online, the giant content provider, bought Netscape in 1998 and folded it into AOL. Andreessen became a chief resident thinker at AOL, but he didn't cotton well to the New Jersey bureaucracy. By 1999 he was back in Silicon Valley, this time with the idea for a robotic site builder called Loudcloud, which quickly attracted multimillion-dollar bids for its emerging product line. Meanwhile, Loudcloud has been reincarnated as Opsware. Andreessen has moved on to other projects.

WHAT DO YOU THINK?

▶ What does it mean when people say Marc Andreessen democratized the Internet?

to keep users. The media conglomerate Time Warner, which acquired AOL at its peak, has the unit up for sale—a far cry from when Time Warner even changed its name to Time Warner AOL. The company, now acknowledging a major acquisition error, has gone back to simply Time Warner.

LEARNING CHECK ◄

▶ What eclipsed the success of the Internet portal AOL?

SEARCH ENGINES

With Google's success, search engine companies have become the darling of Internet investors. Yahoo, MSN and others all have tried rivaling Google.

Search engines dispatch automated crawlers through the Internet to take snapshots of Web pages. With millions of Web sites, it's a massive and time-consuming process, but slowly, massive reference files have been amassed and then updated as the crawlers continue making their rounds.

The original search engines, however, were not good at keeping up to date with blogs. With an estimated 17.1 million blogs, many updated several times a day, the task was too much. Then came blog searchers. Google's, for example, is built on an index of blogs, sending a ping to Google with every update, which then becomes part of a separate blog database for specialized searchers.

LEARNING CHECK ◄····································

▶ How do search engines do what they do?

GAMING

Firmly established in the Internet universe is video gaming. Gaming has grown from the simple games added to software packages with the first generation of home computers even before people had heard of the Internet. These games were hardly mass communication, any more than a Monopoly board. Gradually, though, games went on the Internet, some with thousands of players.

With their huge and growing following, video games have become a natural target for advertising. It's an attractive audience. The Entertainment Software Association says that players average 6.5 hours a week at their games. Players include a broad range of people. Thirty-eight percent are male and 39 percent earn $50,000 a year or more—an attractive group that advertisers have a hard time tapping with other media.

Today, annual sales of gaming hardware, software and accessories have topped $10 billion. The most popular games earn more money faster than the leading movies. The future looks bright, especially with interactive portable games. Game advertising revenue, doubling annually, passed $4.3 million in 2005.

LEARNING CHECK ◄····································

▶ How has gaming come to be seen by advertisers as a mass medium?

Reshaping the Internet

STUDY PREVIEW

Wireless Internet connections, called *wi-fi*, have added to the portability of the Internet. Further untethering from a wired infrastructure is possible through ultrawideband technology.

WI-FI

● **wi-fi**
Wireless fidelity technology

● **muni wireless**
Wi-fi as a public utility

● **digital divide**
The economic distinction between impoverished groups and societal groups with the means to maintain and improve their economic well-being through computer access

Another wrinkle in interactive media is wireless fidelity technology, better known as **wi-fi.** It untethers laptops and allows Internet access anywhere through radio waves. The coffee chain Starbucks made a splash with wi-fi, encouraging people to linger. Hotels and airports were naturals for wi-fi. In 2004 Iowa installed free wi-fi at interstate highway rest stops. San Francisco installed free wi-fi all over its landmark Union Square.

Municipalities large and small have created a wi-fi boom, dubbed **muni wireless,** with wi-fi networks as a utility. In 2005 Mayor Joe Show flicked a switch in Addison, Texas, population 100,000, providing wireless Internet access throughout the Dallas suburb for a subscription fee of $16.95 a month. Three hundred other cities have wireless systems either in place or about to go onstream as a less expensive alternative for consumers hooked up to the Internet by telephone, cable or satellite.

One justification for municipal wi-fi is bridging the **digital divide,** the socioeconomic distinction between people in neighborhoods that can afford Internet access and those in neighborhoods that can't. In Philadelphia the plan is to allow low-income people to subscribe for $10 a month, creating new opportunities to tap into mainstream information that can improve quality of life.

LEARNING CHECK ◄····································

▶ What is different about wi-fi?

▶ How is wi-fi changing Internet usage?

After their wondrous introduction in the 1950s, silicon chips, the basis of digital communication, have become smaller and ever more powerful. In 1965 **Gordon Moore**, sometimes called the godfather of microprocessing, predicted in a technical article that chips would be improved to double their capacity every 18 months. Moore was right. His prediction is now called **Moore's Law.** Silicon flakes have shrunk to mere flecks, 90 nanometers thick, about 1/1,000th of the finest human hair.

But problems loom. The smaller the chips, the hotter they run. The fastest chips today could fry an egg were it not for fans and metal casings to conduct the heat away. The heat not only saps about half of a computer's energy, but smaller and smaller chips become increasingly fragile. The walls of their channels that carry on-off data bits are inclined to leakage, which makes for more errors as the walls are manufactured thinner and thinner.

Numerous labs are working on a silicon replacement: carbon molecules, 100,000th as thick as a human hair, which bond in hexagonal nanotube structures that look like rolled-up chicken wire. **Carbon nanotubes,** their walls no thicker than a single molecule, are stronger than steel, and there is no leakage.

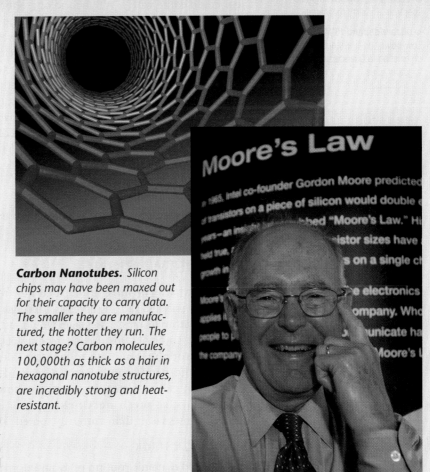

Carbon Nanotubes. *Silicon chips may have been maxed out for their capacity to carry data. The smaller they are manufactured, the hotter they run. The next stage? Carbon molecules, 100,000th as thick as a hair in hexagonal nanotube structures, are incredibly strong and heat-resistant.*

● **Gordon Moore**
Predicted that silicon chips would be refined to double their capacity every 18 months; called Moore's Law

● **Moore's Law**
Silicon chip capacity doubles every 18 months

● **carbon nanotubes**
Hexagon arrangement of carbon molecules into incredibly strong coils for carrying on-off digital bits

Too, their heat resistance means that they can be densely packed.

What do these carbon nanotubes mean for the future? A dramatic improvement in Moore's Law. They could also mean instant boot-ups for personal computers.

The following table is a comparison of nanotech engineering progress.

WHAT DO YOU THINK?

▶ Why is heat a problem in digitized communication equipment?

▶ Can Moore's Law keep working indefinitely? Why or why not?

THINNER AND THINNER

1990	Intel 286 chip	5,000 nanometers
2002	Intel Pentium 3	180 nanometers
2005	IBM PowerPC chip	90 nanometers
2005	Lab carbon nanotube	7 nanometers
2015	Minimum carbon nanotube	1.5 nanometers

ULTRAWIDEBAND

● bandwidth
Space available in a medium, such as cable or the electromagnetic spectrum, to carry messages

● ultrawideband (UWB)
Low-power wi-fi system that rides on existing frequencies licensed for other uses

Short-range wi-fi networks become sluggish as more people tap in. It's an issue of **bandwidth,** not enough capacity to carry a growing number of messages. The problem is being eased with incremental system upgrades. A dramatic improvement could come with UWB technology, short for **ultrawideband,** unless opponents prevail. The technology uses existing frequencies, including commercial broadcast channels, but with such lower power that the primary signals seem to be unaffected. In the United States the Federal Communications Commission authorized developers to proceed working on the technology in 2003, despite protests from the aviation industry, which was concerned that frequencies used by onboard collision-avoidance systems could be compromised by crowding. Air safety stands to be jeopardized, according to some tests by the National Aeronautics and Space Administration. Also, wireless carriers including Sprint and Verizon objected to potential interference with existing spectrum occupants.

LEARNING CHECK ◄

▶ **What is the promise of UWB technology?**

▶ **What is preventing UWB from widespread use?**

MESH NETWORKING

● dynamic routing
Technology that makes every wireless device a vehicle for furthering a message along to its destination, rather than having it move along a structured network

● mesh networking
The ad hoc network created for each single message to reach its destination; also called *dynamic routing*

After wi-fi, what? The most anticipated new technology is **dynamic routing,** in which every wireless gadget serves as a receiver and transmitter to every other wireless device within its range. Messages would just keep moving, hop-skipping invisibly from device to device until each reaches its intended destination. There is no formal network; messages go to whatever device has capacity at the moment—or, rather, the nanosecond. Every wireless device outfitted for dynamic routing would be on call as a stepping stone for however many messages come its way. Engineers say that **mesh networking,** as it is called, using high-speed protocols, will be 15 times faster than currently touted DSL services.

LEARNING CHECK ◄

▶ **How would dynamic routing relay an Internet communication?**

▶ **Would it bother you to be part of a mesh network whenever you had your computer on?**

Internet Issues

STUDY PREVIEW

Blogs hold promise for democratizing mass communication with affordable and technologically easy access. Critics note, however, that there is a polluting element. Blogging has no codes of conduct that require readers to be on guard against irresponsible postings. There are no gatekeepers. Other Internet issues involve privacy. Also, advertisers are susceptible to misleading, even false, claims about the audiences to which they are buying access.

BLOGS AND DEMOCRATIZATION

As a mass communication tool, the Internet has outpaced older media in democratizing mass communication. This has become an era in which the price of entry to media ownership precludes most mortals. But the Internet, although young as a mass medium, is already democratizing mass communication. The rules are new. The most powerful member of the U.S. Senate, Trent Lott, never figured that his career would be sidelined under pressure created by a pip-squeak citizen in the hinterlands. It happened.

■ **People Power.** Joshua Marshall, creator of his own Web site, talking pointsmemo.com, picked up on a speech by Lott that, depending on your view, was either racist or racially insensitive. Lott uttered his comment at the 100th birthday party of Senator Strom Thurmond, once a strong segregationist. Mainstream news media missed the possible implications of Lott's comments. Not Joshua Marshall. In his **blog** on talkingpointsmemo.com, he hammered away at Lott day after day. Other bloggers, also outraged, joined in. Three days later the story hit NBC. Four days later Lott apologized. Two weeks later his Senate colleagues voted him out as majority leader.

As a blogger who made a difference, Joshua Marshall is hardly alone. Best known is Matt Drudge, whose revelations propelled the Bill Clinton-Monica Lewinsky dalliances in the Oval Office into a national scandal. Another blogger, college student Russ Kirk, at his computer in Arizona, looked for information on government refusals to release photographs of caskets of fallen U.S. soldiers in Iraq and Afghanistan, which he regarded as documents to which the public, himself included, had legal access. Kirk filed a request for the documents under the Freedom of Information Act. Then on his Web site thememoryhole.org, he posted the photographs of the flag-draped coffins and also of the astronauts who had died in the Columbia disaster. The photos became front-page news. At one point Kirk's blog was receiving 4 million hits a day—almost twice the circulation of *USA Today*.

■ **Accuracy, Truth.** Both the beauty and the bane of blogs is their free-for-all nature. On the upside, the Web gives ordinary citizens access to mass audiences. It can be a loud and effective megaphone that is outside traditional news media, which have resulted from institutionalized practices and traditions. Joshua Marshall's work on Trent Lott is an example of outside-the-box news reporting.

Blog Fame. Ana Marie Cox was born to blog. Every day at 7 a.m. she wrote 12 items, a self-set quota, on whatever struck her fancy. Though from Nebraska, Cox had transplanted herself to Washington and focused on Capitol gossip. The blog became a must-read in Washington power circles. Cox's satire was funny to some, irritating to others. At Wonkette world headquarters (Cox's spare bedroom), she got "hate mail," as she called it, from both liberals and conservatives. As she saw it, she must be doing something right. She sold the blog in 2007.

ever had **Glenn Reynolds** thought of himself as a media mogul. Although a young man of strong views, he saw his future as a college prof, not a media star. As a sideline lark in 2001, he set up a Web site, Instapundit.com, and tapped out libertarian opinions for anybody who might be interested. At first nobody was.

Then, a month later, came the September 11 terrorism. People by the thousands turned to the Internet, found Reynolds' impassioned commentaries from Knoxville, Tennessee, and made Instapundit a daily routine. *Wired* magazine has declared Reynold's site the world's most popular blog—a shortened word for "Web log" or diary.

At 120,000 visits a day, Reynolds has a larger audience than the average U.S. daily newspaper and more than most cable television pundits. He's prolific, writing 20 to 30 opinion items a day, some fairly long, mostly

● **Glenn Reynolds**
Blogger whose Instapundit.com has attracted a large audience

political. He's also gotten the attention of the traditional media. *Fox News* has posted his stuff on its site. MSNBC gave him a separate blog on its site.

Reynolds' blog is not alone in its success. Thousands exist, created by individuals who have something to say. Blogs fulfill a promise of the Internet to give people of ordinary means a printing press to reach the world, enriching the dialogue in a free society to an extent once possible only to media moguls and those relatively few whom they chose to print and air.

The Internet is transforming the structure of mass communication.

Blogmeister. *He never aspired to a major media career, but his blog site Instapundit attracts more hits a day than the average U.S. newspaper's circulation.*

WHAT DO YOU THINK?

▶ How are blogs democratizing mass communication?

▶ What does this democratization mean for existing mass media industries?

▶ What does this democratization mean for society as a whole?

The easy access that bloggers have to mass audiences is also a problem. Most bloggers are amateurs at news, and their lack of experience with journalistic traditions has a downside. It was bloggers, for example, who kept alive a story that presidential candidate John Kerry and an office intern had carried on an affair. So persistent were the bloggers that neither the mainstream news media nor Kerry could ignore it, although Kerry and the intern denied the allegations and there was no evidence that there was anything to it. Kevin Drum, of calpundit.com, calls himself "unedited and unplugged" Although Drum never touched the Kerry intern story and is respected by his followers, his point that bloggers are "unedited and unplugged" is both the good news and the bad news about the democratizing impact of the Internet.

■ **New Gatekeeping.** So-called mainstream media are introducing an element of old-fashioned, journalistically valued gatekeeping into blogging. The New York *Times*, for example, picks up news generated by bloggers when it meets the paper's standards for what's worth reporting. The imprimatur of being cited in the *Times,* which involves fact-checking and news judgment, lends credibility to a blogger. When mainstream media are silent on blog content, their silence speaks volumes.

Increasingly common are mainstream-media summaries of blog content as a barometer of what's on the minds of participants in this emerging forum. Several times daily, CNN, as an example, reports what's new from the blogs.

How Do Bloggers Know What They Know?

Sean-Paul Kelley's fall from grace was anything but graceful.

The creator of the popular war blog Agonist was caught using as many as six unattributed verbatim reports a day from an Iraq War site operated by the intelligence firm Stratfor. Sometimes Kelley would attribute the Stratfor material to "a Turkish friend" or "a little birdie."

When Kelley was outed, Stratfor's chief analyst, Matthew Baker, said he was surprised at the volume of Stratfor material Kelley used. Stratfor people were also offended by not getting credit. Stratfor's vice president, Aaric Eisenstein, told *Wired* magazine that credit, and also the profit, should accrue to the people actually doing the work. At the time, Stratfor had 150,000 subscribers, who paid from $50 to $600-plus a year for the company's reports on the Iraq War.

Before Kelley's downfall, his site was racking up 120,000 page views a day. Kelley was picking up fame as a war expert. He was interviewed by the New York *Times,* NBC, *Newsweek* and National Public Radio. On NPR, Kelley said readers flocked to his site "based on my reporting and my integrity." After he was accused of plagiarism, Kelley said he lost 40 to 45 percent of the traffic. He eventually agreed to use no more than two Stratfor items per day and always with attribution.

What did other bloggers think of Kelley?

University of Chicago political science professor and blogger Daniel W. Drezner was critical: "As a graduate student in international relations, Kelley knew (or should have known) he was in the wrong as he was lifting Stratfor's content." Also, Drezner said, Kelley was in the wrong when he initially tried to deny the plagiarism.

On his site Instapundit.com Glenn Reynolds noted that he hadn't linked to Kelley's site because most of his posts didn't have links to sources: "I'm generally skeptical of secondhand reports without clear sourcing."

Although Kelley's plagiarism drew critics, others see it as no big deal. Blogs, they say, aren't part of mainstream journalism anyway. Only 23 percent of the 10,230 respondents to a 2006 Globescan survey conducted in 10 countries said they trusted blogs' current-affairs information.

BBC's Paul Reynolds believes, however, that asking people if they trust blogs is asking the wrong question. "Blogs do not really exist to provide people with 'news and information,'" Reynolds said. "More useful questions would be: 'Do you read them and how do you use the information?' Quite often, they just offer you a perspective you might not have thought about. You can use them to test your own judgment."

Trustworthy Sourcing.*
The ease with which material can be picked up from one web site and reused elsewhere has posed questions about plagiarism in a new framework. The people who run the Stratfor site on military intelligence grew tired of the leakage and outed a serial copier.*

DEEPENING YOUR MEDIA LITERACY

EXPLORE THE ISSUE

Write out your definition of a blog.

DIG DEEPER

Visit a blog. How does it compare to your definition of a blog? How would you evaluate a blog? Write down seven to nine questions you should ask yourself when you read a blog.

WHAT DO YOU THINK?

What are valid ways to use the information you gather by reading blogs? Can blogs be part of the mainstream media?

Newsrooms everywhere keep an eye on YouTube and other self-post sites. Oddities worth reporting such as man-bites-dog items are picked up every day. YouTube attained a special status in the 2008 presidential elections when people were invited to upload questions for candidates. Questions were put to the candidates in CNN-hosted debates. Real issues by real people on video was undeniable as a new kind of vehicle for voters to assess candidates. The videos cut through carefully manipulated campaign tactics that had come to mark U.S. elections—staged photo-ops, town-hall meetings with only prescreened participants, and politically calibrated 30-second spots. Not all YouTube-posted questions made the debates, though. As a gatekeeper, CNN used journalistic standards to winnow the chaff.

LEARNING CHECK ◄ ·······································

▶ **Has blogging added a common person's voice to public dialogue on important issues?**

▶ **How is blogging being integrated into mainstream-media news reporting?**

PRIVACY AND THE WEB

The genius of Tim Berners-Lee's original Web concept was its openness. Information could be shared easily by anyone and everyone. Therein was a problem. During the Web's commercialization in the late 1990s, some companies tracked where people ventured on the Internet. The tracking was going on silently, hidden in the background, as people coursed their way around the Internet. Companies gathering information were selling it to other companies. There was fear that insurance companies, health care providers, lenders and others had a new secret tool for profiling applicants.

● **P3P**
A Web protocol that allows users to choose a level of privacy. Short for "Platform for Privacy Preferences"

Government agencies began hinting at controls. Late in 1999, Berners-Lee and the Web protocol-authoring consortium he runs came up with a new architecture, **P3P,** short for "Platform for Privacy Preferences," to address the problem. With P3P people can choose the level of privacy they want for their Web activities. Microsoft, Netscape and other browser operators agreed to screen sites that were not P3P-compliant. In effect, P3P automatically bypasses Web sites that don't meet a level of privacy expectations specified by individual Web users.

Yet to be determined is whether P3P, an attempt at Web industry self-regulation, can effectively protect consumers from third parties sharing private information. If P3P fails, Congress and federal agencies might follow through with backup protections.

LEARNING CHECK ◄ ·······································

▶ **How has the Web concept introduced by Tim Berners-Lee led to privacy issues?**

▶ **Can personal privacy problems on the Internet be solved?**

Internet Future

STUDY PREVIEW

Traditional gatekeeping processes that filter media content for quality are less present in the Internet. Users need to take special care in assessing the material they find.

MEDIA CONVERGENCE

Johannes Gutenberg brought mass production to books. The other primary print media, magazines and newspapers, followed. People never had a problem recognizing differences among books, magazines and newspapers. When sound recording and movies came along, they too were distinctive, and later so were radio and television. Today, the traditional primary media are in various stages of transition to digital form. Old distinctions are blurring.

technological convergence
Melding of print, electronic and photographic media into digitized form

Search Inside
Amazon.com's search engine that can find a term or phrase in every book whose copyright owners have agreed to have it scanned into a database

The cable television systems and the Internet are consolidating with companies in the forefront, such as AT&T. This **technological convergence** is fueled by accelerated miniaturization of equipment and the ability to compress data into tiny digital bits for storage and transmission. And all the media companies, whether their products traditionally relied on print, electronic or photographic technology, are involved in the convergence.

As the magazine *The Economist* noted, once-discrete media industries "are being whirled into an extraordinary whole." Writing in *Quill* magazine, *USA Today*'s Kevin Manay put it this way: "All the devices people use for communicating and all the kinds of communication have started crashing together into one massive megamedia industry. The result is that telephone lines will soon carry TV shows. Cable TV will carry telephone calls. Desktop computers will be used to watch and edit movies. Cellular phone-computers the size of a notepad will dial into interactive magazines that combine text, sound and video to tell stories."

Unanticipated consequences of the new technology are no better illustrated than by Amazon.com. Amazon's site has a growing list of books that people can search internally for the frequency of key terms and phrases. In Scott Ritter's *Solving the Iraq Crises*, Amazon lists 52 pages that contain the term "weapons of mass destruction." A person can call up each of the pages, as well as adjoining pages, to read the paragraphs around the use of the words "weapons of mass destruction," usually several hundred words. Amazon, in the business of selling books, won't let people download whole books, but the service, called **Search Inside,** demonstrates possibilities for the library of the future.

In 2005 Google, the search engine company, began scanning the entire collections of five major libraries to post online. Although copyright-ownership issues in regard to many works created in the last 75 years remain unresolved, the Google project is underway at Harvard University, the New York Public Library, Oxford University, Stanford University and the University of Michigan. When completed, the Google project will allow online access to just about everything ever put between book covers in the history of the English language—15 million titles.

LEARNING CHECK ◄ ·······························

▶ **Which mass media are furthest along in being subsumed into Internet delivery?**

TRANSITION AHEAD

Nobody expects the printed newspaper to disappear overnight or movie houses, video rental shops and over-air broadcasters to go out of business all at once. But all the big media companies have established stakes on the Internet, and in time, digitized messages delivered over the Internet will dominate.

Outside of the Internet itself, major media companies also are trying to establish a future for themselves in reaching audiences in new digital ways. Companies that identify voids in their ability to capitalize on new technology have created joint ventures to ensure they won't be left out. The NBC television network, for example, provides news on Microsoft's MSN online service. All of the regional Bell telephone companies have picked up partners to develop video-delivery systems. Cable companies have moved into telephone-like two-way interactive communication systems that, for example, permit customers not only to receive messages but also to send them.

Some see a dark side to convergence, with a few major companies coming to dominate the Internet and working against the democratization that others see as the fulfillment of the new technology's promise. Media mogul Barry Diller, who's consulted regularly for his visions on media directions, talks about the Internet losing its diversity through ownership consolidation. Citing cable giant Comcast, he said in a *Newsweek* interview: "You can already see at Comcast and others the beginning of efforts to control the home pages that their consumers plug into. It's for one reason: To control a toll bridge or turnstile through which others must pay to go. The inevitable result will be eventual control by media giants of the Internet

The Eyeball as a Screen. *A Seattle company, Microvision, is hoping to market a device that projects images directly onto the human eyeball. This VRD, short for "virtual retina display," is not much more cumbersome to wear than a pair of glasses, and it gives a sharper image than a 70-millimeter IMAX screen. With VRD, people would not need television or computer screens. Microvision says this device can be made for less than $100.*

in terms of independence and strangulation. This is a situation where history is absolutely destined to repeat itself." Most Internet users hope Diller is wrong. He does too.

LEARNING CHECK ◄ ·······································

▶ **What effects has the Internet had on each of the other major mass media?**

GOVERNMENT DEREGULATION

Until recent years a stumbling block to the melding of digital media was the U.S. government. Major components of today's melded media—the telephone, television and computer industries—grew up separately, and government policy kept many of them from venturing into the others' staked-out territory of services. Telephone companies, for example, were limited to being common carriers. They couldn't create their own media messages, just deliver other people's. Cable companies were barred from building two-way communication into their systems.

● **Ronald Reagan**
President who pushed deregulation

● **deregulation**
Government policy to reduce regulation of business

In the 1970s government agencies began to ease restrictions on business. In 1984 President **Ronald Reagan** stepped up this **deregulation,** and more barriers came down. The pro-business Reagan administration also took no major actions against the stampede of media company mergers that created fewer and bigger media companies. George H. W. Bush, elected in 1988, and Bill Clinton, elected in 1992, continued Reagan's deregulation initiatives and also his soft stance on mergers. The Clinton position, however, was less ideological and more pragmatic. Clinton's thinking was based on the view that regulation and anti-trust actions would hamstring U.S. media companies, and other enterprises too, in global competition.

● **Telecommunications Act of 1996**
Repealed many limits on services that telephone and cable companies could offer

In 1996 Congress approved a new telecommunications law that wiped out many of the barriers that heeded full-bore exploitation of the potential of new media. The law repealed a federal ban against telephone companies providing video programming. Just as significant, cable television systems were given a green light to offer two-way local telephone services. The law, the **Telecommunications Act of 1996,**

$100 Laptop. For schools in developing countries, the Media Lab at the Massachusetts Institute of Technology has designed a $100 crank-up laptop. Features include an eight-inch monitor and word processing, Web browsing, e-mail and programming software. M.I.T. sees initial production of 5 to 10 million units and eventually 150 million.

accelerated the competition that had been emerging between telephone and cable television companies to rewire communities for higher-quality, faster delivery of new audio and video services.

LEARNING CHECK ◄ •••

▶ **What industries are in a contest to control Internet delivery systems?**

▶ **What law has shaped this contest?**

GLOBAL INEQUITIES

● **diffusion of innovation**
Process through which news, ideals, values and information spread

The exchange of information facilitated by the Internet boosted the United States into unprecedented prosperity going into the 21st century. One measure of efficiency, **diffusion of innovation,** improved dramatically. The time that innovations take to be widely used, which was once 10 years, dropped to one year. Giga Information Group projected that by 2002, businesses would be saving $1.3 trillion because of Internet commerce—an incredible 765 percent gain over five years.

One problem, though, is that much of the world isn't plugged in. In all of the Middle East and Africa, there are only 7.5 million Web users in total.

In short, the economic advantages of the Internet may be creating new international inequities. If maximum prosperity depends on free trade in a global economy, as many economists argue, then all of the world must be folded fully into the Internet.

LEARNING CHECK ◄ •••

▶ **What effect has the Internet had on diffusion of innovation?**

Chapter Wrap-Up

Influence of the Internet (Page 234)

■ The Internet is transforming mass communication. Traditional origination points for communication, like a book publisher or radio station, suddenly have been joined by millions of additional origination points, all interconnected. An individual with minimal equipment can be an originator. The cost of entry to be a mass communicator is within almost everyone's means. Participation is impossible to measure. Tried counting all the bloggers lately?

Internet Origins (Page 236)

- Radio technology can be traced to Marconi, television to Farnsworth. Not so the Internet, which came into being more as a convergence of technologies that were developed separately. These included the silicon chip, which brought about digitized data, and fiber optics.

The World Wide Web (Page 238)

- The Internet coding protocols devised by Tim Berners-Lee in 1989 were a breakthrough in Internet development. The coding makes it possible for every computer on the planet to be an origination point for communicating and for messages to integrate video and audio with text. Quite appropriately this new layer of coding was called the World Wide Web. Everybody has access to what everybody else is posting. The Web enables people to be their own editors, choosing what to read and watch rather than having those decisions made by faraway editors. Individuals can search among literally millions of items. Navigating the Web has been made seamless by Web browsers, the first of which was Netscape.

The Internet Industry (Page 242)

- As is typical of emerging technology, the Internet industry has taken some dead-end routes. The most obvious is the original America Online concept, a subscription-only site that sought to be a one-stop shop. In recent years AOL has been struggling to reinvent itself. Meanwhile, sites that try to index all Web content, best exemplified by Google, have become industry leaders. Sites designed around viewer uploads, like YouTube and MySpace, have become major players too. In this transition, the Internet has become a commercial vehicle. Retailing has a major Internet presence. So does advertising in the traditional sense of advertisers seeking to piggyback messages on sites that attract the greatest number of eyeballs. Gaming also has become a favorite vehicle for advertisers seeking potential consumers in the young adult male demographic.

Reshaping the Internet (Page 244)

- The Internet was built on telephone networks of landline, microwave and satellite links. You had to plug physically into a jack on the wall. Wi-fi technology has untethered computers, adding new portability to laptops and hand-held devices. Strategically placed wi-fi hubs communicate with computers over short ranges, making it possible to tap in without a jack in a coffee house, for example, or a dorm or hotel or a neighborhood. Technology is on hand for every computer to become a vehicle for relaying messages. This technology, called mesh networking, would be the ultimate decentralization of Internet communication. Messages would invisibly hop, skip and jump their way to a destination via the nearest individual computer, the next, then the next. Meanwhile, work continues to increase capacity of the Internet for higher-quality audio and video.

Internet Issues (Page 246)

- As with predecessor mass media, the Internet was initially hailed for its potential to transform human existence. By the time the World Wide Web and Netscape were in place, it seemed that every human being could have a megaphone. It would be the democratization of mass communication. The enthusiasm has been diminished, however, by the fact that not everybody has much to contribute to our dialogue. The Internet is loaded with junk, some criminal, some just wildly short of being a positive contribution to the marketplace of ideas. It would be a mistake to focus too much on the dark side, but it does exist. Even so, any Netizen, as Internet users are called, can talk about unwanted solicitations. Tales abound about privacy intrusions.

Internet Future (Page 250)

- The Internet's impact on other media has been profound. Newspapers have online editions. Radio stations stream their programs. Television networks sell programs for Internet delivery. There are predictions that all the traditional media will gravitate entirely to the Internet in a kind of convergence. That won't happen overnight, but the fact is that the Internet is an efficient delivery means for mass communication of all sorts. In the meantime, competing industries, notably telephone and cable television companies, are struggling to dominate the delivery mechanisms. Amid all the flux, questions remain about who is being left out. Impoverished parts of the world are missing out on the advantages of Internet communication and exchanges that contribute to prosperity.

REVIEW QUESTIONS

1. How is the Internet being defined as a new and distinctive mass medium?

2. What technology breakthroughs made the Internet possible?

3. How did World Wide Web coding and the Netscape browser change the Internet?

4. Track the changes in successful business models for Internet companies.

5. What technologies are improving the Internet?

6. How well has the Internet fulfilled its potential to democratize mass communication?

7. Are the earlier media of mass communication doomed by the Internet? Explain.

CONCEPTS

compression (Page 236)

digital divide (Page 244)

hypertext (Page 240)

technological convergence (Page 251)

mesh networking (Page 246)

TERMS

blog (Page 247)

dot-com (Page 242)

fiber-optic cable (Page 237)

semiconductor (Page 236)

wi-fi (Page 244)

PEOPLE

Marc Andreessen (Page 240)

Tim Berners-Lee (Page 238)

Vint Cerf, Bob Kahn (Page 237)

Glenn Reynolds (Page 248)

MEDIA SOURCES

- Jack Goldsmith and Tim Wu. *Who Controls the Internet?: Illusions of a Borderless World.* Oxford University Press, 2006. Goldsmith and Wu see cracks in the widespread notion that governments are powerless at controlling Internet content.

- J. Storrs Hall. *Nanofuture.* Prometheus, 2005. Certain that technology challenges can be overcome, Hall, a futurist with a software background, waxes enthusiastically that the manipulation of individual constructs of atoms can be manufactured to create any and everything.

- David Bondanis. *Electric Universe.* Crown, 2005. Bondanis, who teaches mathematical physics at Oxford, offers a parallel to the Internet's quick remaking of the world by chronicling the 19th-century inventions of Michael Faraday, Samuel Morse and Alan Turing.

INTERNET: A Thematic Chapter Summary

In this chapter you have deepened your media literacy by revisiting several themes. Here are thematic highlights from the chapter:

Media Technology

Unforeseen possibilities for the Internet turn up regularly with new developments in the underlying technologies. This happened with the advent of fiber-optic cable networks. What the World Wide Web protocols of Tim Berners-Lee brought was revolutionary. Marc Andreessen's Netscape browser made access so seamless that the Internet moved dramatically toward universal access. Only a fool would pretend to know what's next, but already wi-fi has transformed Internet usage into high portability. Look around at all the untethered laptops and handheld devices. Technology is on hand to increase Internet capacity so that long-form video won't have even occasional jerkiness. **(Pages 236–242 and 244–246)**

Web Giants. *Tim Berners-Lee developed the coding and protocols that he aptly named the World Wide Web. Marc Andreessen came up with the Netscape browser that enabled the least tech-savvy individuals to use the Web, plus open e-mail accounts and get into the rest of the Internet.*

Unlimited Future?
Microprocessing theorist Gordon Moore predicted in 1965 that the capacity of silicon chips would double every 18 months. So far, he's been right. His omniscience has become embedded in Internet lore as Moore's Law.

Media Future

Mass-media forms based on older technology have begun a gravitation to digital delivery. Will we see a convergence of all past media into the Internet? That's a matter of conjecture. But clearly the blurring of old distinctions has yet to run its course. **(Pages 250–253)**

Media Economics

The largely unorganized techies who conceived of the early Internet and brought it into being had a vague awareness of its commercial potential and didn't want anything to do with it. They adamantly resisted anything that would sully their pristine invention. They lost the battle. First came information services like Lexis that sold Internet access to its giant legal database. A second wave of commercialization came with companies like America Online offering humongous volumes of exclusive content, as well as access to e-mail and the larger Web. Meanwhile, retailers created catalog-like sites to pitch their wares and take online orders. The Internet has now entered a new phase with advertisers looking for sites that attract audiences they want to reach. This latest phase of Internet commercialization is moving the Internet toward a financial basis in advertising revenue, competing directly with newspapers, magazines, radio and television. **(Pages 227–235 and 242–244)**

Media and Democracy

With the Internet, all it takes to be a mass communicator is a computer and modem and something to say. Is democracy better for this theoretically universal access to an unprecedented audience? Blogs, those sites created by individuals or groups, have indeed affected political dialogue. Ask Bill Clinton about Matt Drudge. Or Trent Lott about Joshua Marshall. But, also, the marketplace for exchanging information and ideas has been polluted. Rumor and falsity, sometimes malicious, are part of the mix in blogging. There is a high quotient of babble. **(Pages 246–250)**

French, Anyone? Although not everyone is interested in conversational French, Sebastian Babolat has found a following for the lessons on his podcast. Some podcasts have much narrower followings. Would you believe an audience of a handful of people? That's how fragmented mass communication has become.

Elitism and Populism

The unlimited capacity of the Internet for people to post communications is easing the historic tension between elitists and populists about media content. Populists have argued that most people were squeezed out of access to the media because there were too few channels or that access was too costly. Not everybody can afford to build a television station or buy a printing press. Channel scarcity and access, however, are hardly issues with the Internet. The elitist argument that high-quality content was displaced by the quest of media companies to amass the largest possible audiences, thus pandering to low tastes, is less valid with the Internet. The Net has capacity aplenty for stuff for the highest of the high-brows as well as limitless junk—and everything in between. **(Pages 233–253)**

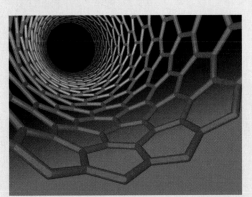

Capacity for Everybody. Technology for manufacturing carbon molecules to replace silicon chips will mean computers can run cooler and faster and carry more stuff. For the Internet this means more capacity for storage and messages. More people can communicate more. Is this a great promise for advancing human knowledge and understanding? Or just more capacity for more babble?

Every point in the network can send and receive messages. The recipient has access to every transmission point and controls what is received.

Communication Revolution. Mass communication traditionally has meant a central source sending messages to numerous recipients, even millions of them. The Internet has turned the masscom model on its head. With the Internet, message originators and recipients can be anyone, and they're all interconnected in a web of channels that they choose.

Audience Fragmentation

The computers on the planet have so much storage capacity that, for practical purposes, there are no limits to what people can do on the Internet. This is the ultimate in audience fragmentation. There is something for every interest and taste, no matter how obscure or arcane. Access is easier and 24/7, which older media cannot match. **(Pages 233–253)**

11

News

When Balanced Reporting Isn't

In a massive study of news coverage on global warming, brothers Jules Boykoff, a political scientist, and Maxwell Boykoff, a geographer, reviewed four leading U.S. newspapers—the New York *Times, Wall Street Journal,* Washington *Post* and Los Angeles *Times*—over 14 years and identified 3,542 news items, editorials and other articles on global warming. Randomly they chose 636 articles for analysis. Fifty-three percent, more than half, gave equal weight to the opposing views. The easily inferred impression, they said, was that the scientific community was "embroiled in a rip-roaring debate on whether or not humans were contributing to global warming." The fact is there was no such debate.

How could the news media in their reporting of science be so out of synch with scientists? It's a question at the heart of this chapter on news, which examines definitions of news and, importantly, how media-literate consumers can decide which reporting to trust.

The Boykoffs have a theory about what was wrong: In a sense, as counterintuitive as it seems, journalists try too hard to be fair.

"The professional canon of journalistic fairness requires reporters who write about a controversy to present competing points of view," the Boykoffs explained. "Presenting the most compelling arguments of both sides with equal weight is a fundamental check on biased reporting. But this canon causes problems when it is applied to issues of science. It seems to demand that journalists

LEARNING AHEAD

- Many news media practices originated during periods of major change in U.S. history.
- The notion of objectivity in news is vexing.
- Journalists bring personal, social and political values to their work.
- Variables affect what ends up being reported.
- Gatekeeping is both essential and hazardous to the news process.
- Journalistic trends include exploratory reporting, soft news, 24/7 coverage.

Counter Science. *Scholars Jules and Maxwell Boykoff see journalists getting trapped in a desire for balance. For too long, journalists gave equal play to sources lined up by big energy companies to downplay the seriousness of global warming despite overwhelming evidence that it was occurring at a pace accelerated by environmentally reckless human activity. The Boykoffs make the point that truth doesn't necessarily come from tit-for-tat balance of opposing views.*

259

present competing points of view on a scientific question as if they had equal scientific weight, when actually they do not."

The fairness chink in journalistic armor has given special interests an opportunity to manipulate news by making misleading and even false information easily available to reporters who, dutifully if not mindlessly, apply the principle of fairness. A legion of spokespersons, many funded by special interests, end up with roles in journalists' stories. The Boykoffs cite many examples, one being the New York *Times* quoting a global-warming skeptic that carbon dioxide emissions aren't a threat to the climate but "a wonderful and unexpected gift from the Industrial Revolution."

Who are these special interests? Former Vice President Al Gore, himself a journalist early in his career, has been blunt: "A relatively small cadre of special interests including Exxon Mobil and a few other oil, coal and utilities companies." Why? "These companies want to prevent any new policies that would interfere with their current business plans that rely on the massive, unrestrained dumping of global-warming pollution of the Earth's atmosphere every hour of every day."

The Boykoffs put it this way: "Balanced reporting has allowed a small group of global warming skeptics to have their views amplified." Balanced coverage, according to the Boykoffs, has not translated into accurate coverage.

Are journalists dishonest? Jules Boykoff doesn't blame the journalists. Boykoff notes that giant media companies, intent on improving profits, have cut back on newsroom staffs and labor-intensive investigative reporting. The result: More and more reporters are called upon to be generalists and are being denied time to build expertise on a complex subject such as climate change.

Journalism Traditions

STUDY PREVIEW

U.S. journalism has evolved through four distinctive eras: the colonial, partisan, penny and yellow periods. Each of these periods made distinctive contributions to contemporary news media practices.

● **colonial period**
From the founding of the colonies to the American Revolution

● **Benjamin Harris**
Published *Publick Occurrences*

● **Publick Occurrences**
First colonial newspaper, Boston, 1690

COLONIAL PRESS

In the American **colonial period, Benjamin Harris** published the first newspaper, **Publick Occurrences,** in Boston in 1690. He was in hot water right away. Harris scandalized Puritan sensitivities by alleging that the king of France had dallied with his son's wife. In the colonies, just as in England, a newspaper needed royal consent. The governor had not consented, and Harris was put out of business after one issue.

● **John Peter Zenger**
Defied authorities in New York
Journal

Even so, Harris' daring was a precursor for emerging press defiance against authority. In 1733 **John Peter Zenger** started a paper in New York in competition with the existing Crown-supported newspaper. Zenger's New York *Journal* was backed by merchants and lawyers who disliked the royal governor. From the beginning, the newspaper antagonized the governor with items challenging his competence. Finally, the governor arrested Zenger. The trial made history. The jury found for Zenger, who had become a hero for standing up to the Crown. He was freed. To the government's chagrin, there was great public celebration in the streets of New York that night.

Zenger Trial. *Printer John Peter Zenger, in the dock, won his 1735 trial for criticizing New York's royal governor. The victory fed a colonial exuberance that culminated 46 years later in winning the revolution against British rule.*

Zenger's success against the Crown foreshadowed the explosive colonial reaction after Parliament passed a stamp tax in 1765. The colonies did not have elected representatives in Parliament, so the cry was a defiant "No taxation without representation." The campaign, however, was less ideological than economic. It was led by colonial printers, who stood to lose from the new tax, which was levied on printed materials. Historian **Arthur Schlesinger** has called it the newspaper war on Britain. The newspapers won. The tax was withdrawn. Having seen their potential to force the government's hand, newspapers then led the way in stirring other ill feelings against England and precipitating the American Revolution.

● **Arthur Schlesinger**
Viewed newspapers as instigating revolution

These traditions from the colonial period remain today:

- The news media, both print and broadcast, relish their independence from government censorship and control.
- The news media, especially newspapers and magazines, actively try to mold government policy and mobilize public sentiment. Today this is done primarily on the editorial page.
- Journalists are committed to seeking truth no matter who is offended.
- The public comes down in favor of independent news media when government becomes too heavy-handed, as demonstrated by Zenger's popularity.
- In a capitalistic system the news media are economic entities that sometimes react in their own self-interest when their profit-making ability is threatened. Newspaper opposition to the stamp tax illustrates this point.

LEARNING CHECK ◂ •••••••••••••••••••••••••••••••••••••

▸ The colonial campaign against the 1765 stamp tax has been called the newspaper war against Britain. What does the campaign tell us about the news media?

▸ Both Harris and Zenger were slapped down by colonial governors for their early newspapers, but the cases were dramatically different. Which of these early printers would you regard as more heroic? More important?

PARTISAN PRESS

After the Revolution, newspapers divided along partisan lines. What is called the Federalist period in U.S. history is also referred to as the partisan period among newspaper historians. Intense partisanship characterized newspapers of the period, which spanned roughly 50 years to the 1830s

Initially, the issue was over a constitution. Should the nation have a strong central government or remain a loose coalition of states? James Madison, Alexander Hamilton, Thomas Jefferson, John Jay and other leading thinkers exchanged ideas with articles and essays in newspapers. The *Federalist Papers,* a series of essays printed and reprinted in newspapers throughout the nation, were part of the debate. Typical of the extreme partisanship of the era were journalists who reveled in nasty barbs and rhetorical excesses. It was not unusual for an ideological opponent to be called a "dog," "traitor," "liar" or "cheat."

After the Constitution was drafted, partisanship intensified, finally culminating lopsidedly when the Federalist party both controlled the Congress and had the party leader, **John Adams,** in the presidency. In firm control and bent on silencing their detractors, the Federalists ramrodded a series of laws through Congress in 1798. One of the things the **Alien and Sedition acts** prohibited was "false, scandalous, malicious" statements about government. Using these laws, the Federalists made 25 indictments, which culminated in 10 convictions. Among those indicted was **David Bowen,** a Revolutionary War veteran who felt strongly about free expression. He put up a sign in Dedham, Massachusetts: "No stamp tax. No sedition. No alien bills. No land tax. Downfall to tyrants of America. Peace and retirement to the president [the Federalist John Adams]. Long live the vice president [the Anti-Federalist **Thomas Jefferson**] and the minority [the Anti-Federalists]. May moral virtues be the basis of civil government." If only criticisms of recent presidents were so mild! But the Federalists were not of a tolerant mind. Bowen was fined $400 and sentenced to 18 months in prison.

Federalist excesses were at their most extreme when **Matthew Lyon,** a member of Congress, was jailed for a letter to a newspaper editor that accused President Adams of "ridiculous pomp, foolish adulation, selfish avarice." Lyon, an Anti-Federalist, was sentenced to four months in jail and fined $1,000. Although he was tried in Rutland, Vermont, he was sent to a filthy jail 40 miles away. When editor Anthony Haswell printed an advertisement to raise money for Lyon's fine, he was jailed for abetting a criminal. The public was outraged at Federalist heavy-handedness. The $1,000 was quickly raised, and Lyon, while still in prison, was re-elected by a two-to-one margin. After his release from prison, Lyon's supporters followed his carriage for 12 miles as he began his way back to Philadelphia, the national capital. Public outrage showed itself in the election of 1800. Jefferson was elected president, and the Federalists were thumped out of office, never to rise again. The people had spoken.

Here are traditions from the partisan period that continue today:

- Government should keep its hands off the press. The First Amendment to the Constitution, which set a tone for this period, declared that "Congress shall make no law . . . abridging freedom . . . of the press."
- The news media are a forum for discussion and debate, as newspapers were in the *Federalist Papers* dialogue on what form the Constitution should take.
- The news media should comment vigorously on public issues.

LEARNING CHECK ◄ ∙∙∙

▶ **What lesson can political leaders of today draw from public reaction to the Alien and Sedition acts?**

PENNY PRESS

In 1833, when he was 22, the enterprising **Benjamin Day** started a newspaper that changed U.S. journalism: the **New York *Sun*.** At a penny a copy, the *Sun* was within reach of just about everybody. Other papers were expensive, an annual subscription costing as much as a full week's wages. Unlike other papers, which were distributed mostly by mail, the *Sun* was hawked every day on the streets. The *Sun's* content was different too. It avoided the political and economic thrust of the traditional papers, concentrating instead on items of interest to common folk.

The writing was simple, straightforward and easy to follow. For a motto for the *Sun*, Day came up with "It Shines for All," his pun fully intended.

Day's *Sun* was an immediate success. Naturally, it was quickly imitated, and the **penny period** began. Partisan papers that characterized the partisan period continued, but the mainstream of American newspapers came to be in the mold of the *Sun*.

Merchants saw the unprecedented circulation of the **penny papers** as a way to reach great numbers of potential customers. Advertising revenue meant bigger papers, which attracted more readers, which attracted more advertisers. A snowballing momentum began that continues today with more and more advertising being carried by the mass media. A significant result was a shift in newspaper revenues from subscriptions to advertisers. Day, as a matter of fact, did not meet expenses by selling the *Sun* for a penny a copy. He counted on advertisers to pick up a good part of his production cost. In effect, advertisers subsidized readers, just as they do today.

Several social and economic factors, all resulting from the Industrial Revolution, made the penny press possible:

- **Industrialization.** With new steam-powered presses, hundreds of copies an hour could be printed. Earlier presses had been hand operated.
- **Urbanization.** Workers flocked to the cities to work in new factories, creating a great pool of potential newspaper readers within delivery range. Until the urbanization of the 1820s and 1830s, the U.S. population had been almost wholly agricultural and scattered across the countryside. Even the most populous cities had been relatively small.
- **Immigration.** Waves of immigrants arrived from impoverished parts of Europe. Most were eager to learn English and found that penny papers, with their simple style, were good tutors.
- **Literacy.** As immigrants learned English, they hungered for reading material within their economic means. Also, literacy in general was increasing, which contributed to the rise of mass-circulation newspapers and magazines.

A leading penny press editor was **James Gordon Bennett,** who, in the 1830s, organized the first newsroom and reporting staff. Earlier newspapers had been either sidelines of printers, who put whatever was handy into their papers, or projects of ideologues, whose writing was in an essay vein. Bennett hired reporters and sent them out on rounds to gather information for readers of his New York *Herald*.

Another penny press editor, **Horace Greeley,** used his newspaper to fight social ills that accompanied industrialization. Greeley's *Tribune*, especially in its editorial section, was a voice against poverty and slums, an advocate of labor unions and an opponent of slavery. It was a lively forum for discussions of ideas. Karl Marx, the communist philosopher, was a *Tribune* columnist for a while. So was Albert Brisbane, who advocated collective living. Firm in Greeley's concept of a newspaper was that it should be used for social good. He saw the *Tribune* as a voice for those who did not have a voice; a defender for those unable to articulate a defense; and a champion for the underdog, the deprived and the underprivileged.

In 1844, late in the penny press period, **Samuel Morse** invented the telegraph. Within months the nation was being wired. When the Civil War came in 1861, correspondents used the telegraph to get battle news to eager readers. It was called **lightning news,** delivered electrically and quickly. The Civil War also gave rise to a new convention in writing news, the **inverted pyramid.** Editors instructed their war correspondents to tell the most important information first in case telegraph lines failed—or were snipped by the enemy—as a story was being transmitted. That way, when a story was interrupted, editors would have at least a few usable sentences. The inverted pyramid, it turned out, was popular with readers because it allowed them to learn what was most important at a glance. They did not have to wade through a whole story if they were in a hurry. Also, the inverted pyramid helped editors to fit stories into the limited confines of a page—a story could be cut off at any paragraph and the most important parts remained intact.

● penny period
One-cent newspapers geared to mass audience and mass advertising

● penny papers
Affordable by almost everyone

● James Gordon Bennett
Organized the first methodical news coverage

● Horace Greeley
Pioneered editorials

● Samuel Morse
Invented the telegraph

● lightning news
Delivered by telegraph

● inverted pyramid
Most important information first

Years later, reflecting on the instant success of his New York *Sun*, Benjamin Day shook his head in wonderment. He hadn't realized at the time that the *Sun* was such a milestone. Whether he was being falsely modest is something historians can debate. The fact is the *Sun*, which Day founded in 1833, discovered mass audiences on a scale never before envisioned and ushered in the era of modern mass media.

Ben Day, a printer, set up a shop in 1833, but business was slow. With time on his hands, he began a little people-oriented handbill with brief news items and, most important, an advertisement for his printing business. He printed 1,000 copies, which he sold for a penny apiece. The tiny paper, four pages of three columns of type, sold well, so Day decided to keep it going. In six months the *Sun*, the first of a new era of penny papers, had the highest circulation in New York. By 1836 circulation had zoomed to 20,000.

Fifty years later Day told an interviewer that the *Sun*'s success was "more by accident than by design." Even so, the *Sun* was the first newspaper that, at a penny a copy, was within the economic means of almost everyone. He filled the paper with the local police court news, which is the stuff that arouses universal interest. True to its masthead motto, "It Shines for All," the *Sun* was a paper for the masses.

At a penny a copy, Day knew he couldn't pay his bills, so he built the paper's economic foundation on advertising. This remains the financial basis of most mass media today—

Mass-Media Pioneer. *When Benjamin Day launched the New York* Sun *in 1833 and sold it for one cent a copy, he ushered in an era of cheap newspapers that common people could afford. Years later his successors pushed circulation past 1 million a week. Today mass media have many of the* Sun's *pioneering characteristics. These include content of interest to a great many people, a financial base in advertising and easy access.*

Ben Day

newspapers, magazines, television and radio. Just as today, advertisers subsidized the product to make it affordable to great multitudes of people.

Today it still is technology that makes the media possible. The *Sun* was a pioneer in using the technology of its time: engine-driven presses. The *Sun*'s messages—the articles—were crafted to interest large, diverse audiences, as are mass messages today. Also like today, advertising drove the enterprise financially. The story of Day's *Sun* also

demonstrates a reality, as true then as now, that the mass media must be businesses first and purveyors of information and entertainment second.

WHAT DO YOU THINK?

▶ What about the New York *Sun*'s content made it different at the time? How much of the *Sun*'s content formula remains part of news reporting today?

▶ What parts of the New York *Sun*'s financial model have survived?

The inverted pyramid remains a standard expository form for telling event-based stories in newspapers, radio and television.

LEARNING CHECK ◀ ∙∙∙

▶ News as we think of it today has roots in the penny press period. What are these roots?

▶ What was the connection between the telegraph and the inverted pyramid?

James Gordon Bennett, a young man seeing the success of Ben Day's penny paper, the New York *Sun*, rounded up $500 and rented a basement. There, in 1835, with a plank across two flour barrels for a desk, a dilapidated press and barely enough type, Bennett produced his own humble penny paper—the New York *Herald*, with pages slightly larger than sheets of a legal pad.

Bennett quickly recognized that being first with news gave him an advantage over competitors. His obsession with getting news to readers quickly brought an emphasis on timeliness as an important element in the concept of news. It also contributed to the fact-oriented telling of news because reporters rushing to get a dispatch together are too pressed to be analytical.

Bennett made a fetish of timeliness. He used small, fast boats to sail out to Sandy Point, on the coast beyond New York, to pick up parcels of newspapers and letters from arriving oceanic ships and then sail back to the city before the ships themselves could arrive and dock. He beat other papers by hours with fresh news.

In one case Bennett himself went to Halifax, Nova Scotia, where many European vessels landed before continuing down the coast. With a news packet in hand he hired a locomotive to take him to Boston, Worcester and New London, where he took a ferry to Long Island, and then another locomotive to New York. That news was days ahead.

The *Herald* was a quick success, surpassing the circulation of Ben Day's *Sun*.

Bennett never relented in his quest for quick news. After Samuel Morse invented the telegraph in 1844, Bennett instructed reporters to use the infant network that was being built around the country to send back their dispatches without delay.

Inventor of News. *Bennett organized the first newsroom with reporters assigned to beats. His* Herald *was known for comprehensive, timely coverage.*

WHAT DO YOU THINK?

▶ It's been said that James Gordon Bennett invented news as we think of it today. How so?

▶ How did Bennett capitalize on the invention of the telegraph?

YELLOW PRESS

● **yellow period**
Late 1800s; marked by sensationalism

● **Joseph Pulitzer**
Emphasized human interest in newspapers; later sensationalized

● **Nellie Bly**
Stunt reporter

The quest to sell more copies led to excesses that are illustrated by the Pulitzer–Hearst circulation war in New York in the 1890s, in what came to be known as the **yellow period**.

Joseph Pulitzer, a poor immigrant, made the St. Louis *Post-Dispatch* into a financial success. In 1883 Pulitzer decided to try a bigger city. He bought the New York *World* and applied his St. Louis formula. He emphasized human interest, crusaded for worthy causes and ran lots of promotional hoopla. Pulitzer's *World* also featured solid journalism. His star reporter, **Nellie Bly,** epitomized the two faces of the Pulitzer formula for journalistic success. For one story Bly feigned mental illness, entered an insane asylum and emerged with scandalous tales about how patients were treated. It was enterprising journalism of great significance. Reforms resulted. Later, showing the less serious, show-biz side of Pulitzer's formula, Nellie Bly was sent

Yellow Journalism's Namesake. *The Yellow Kid, a popular cartoon character in New York newspapers, was the namesake for the sensationalist "yellow journalism" of the 1880s and 1890s. Many newspapers of the period, especially in New York, hyperbolized and fabricated the news to attract readers. The tradition remains in isolated areas of modern journalism, like the supermarket tabloids and trash documentary programs on television.*

● **William Randolph Hearst**
Built circulation with sensationalism

out to circle the globe in 80 days, like Jules Verne's fictitious Phileas Fogg. Her journalism stunt took 72 days.

In San Francisco, Pulitzer had a young admirer, **William Randolph Hearst.** With his father's Nevada mining fortune and mimicking Pulitzer's New York formula, Hearst made the San Francisco *Examiner* a great success. In 1895 Hearst decided to go to New York and take on the master. He bought the New York *Journal* and vowed to "out-Pulitzer" Pulitzer. The inevitable resulted. To outdo each other, Pulitzer and Hearst launched crazier and crazier stunts. Not even the comic pages escaped the competitive frenzy. Pulitzer ran the *Yellow Kid*, and then Hearst hired the cartoonist away. Pulitzer hired a new one, and both papers ran the yellow character and plastered the city with yellow promotional posters. The circulation war was nicknamed "yellow journalism," and the term came to be a derisive reference to sensational excesses in news coverage.

The yellow excesses reached a feverish peak as Hearst and Pulitzer covered the growing tensions between Spain and the United States. Fueled by hyped atrocity stories, the tension eventually exploded in war. One story, perhaps apocryphal, epitomizes the no-holds-barred competition between Pulitzer and Hearst. Although Spain had consented to all demands by the United States, Hearst sent the artist **Frederic Remington** to Cuba to cover the situation. Remington cabled back: "Everything is quiet. There is no trouble here. There will be no war. Wish to return." Hearst replied: "Please remain. You furnish the pictures. I'll furnish the war."

The yellow tradition still lives. The New York *Daily News*, founded in 1919 and almost an immediate hit, ushered in a period that some historians characterize as

Joseph Pulitzer

William Randolph Hearst

Journalistic Sensationalism. *Rival New York newspaper publishers Joseph Pulitzer and William Randolph Hearst tried to outdo each other daily with anti-Spanish atrocity stories from Cuba, many of them trumped up. Some historians say the public hysteria fueled by Pulitzer and Hearst helped to precipitate the Spanish–American War, especially after the U.S. battleship* Maine *exploded in Havana harbor. Both Pulitzer and Hearst claimed that it was a Spanish attack on an American vessel, although a case can be made that the explosion was accidental.*

Stunt Journalism. When newspaper owner Joseph Puliter sent reporter Nellie Bly on an around-the-world trip in 1890 to try to outdo the fictional Phileas Fogg's 80-day trip, stunt journalism was approaching its peak. Her feat took 72 days.

● **Frederic Remington**
News illustrator whose work included Spanish-American War

● **jazz journalism**
Updated yellow journalism, often in tabloid format and featuring photography

jazz journalism. It was just Hearst and Pulitzer updated in tabloid form with an emphasis on photography. Today, newspapers like the commercially successful *National Enquirer* are in the yellow tradition.

LEARNING CHECK ◄ ∙∙∙

▸ **What stunt journalism have you seen in recent months that would make Nellie Bly proud?**

▸ **News that's sensationalized beyond what the facts warrant can be dangerous. Give an example from the yellow press period. Can you cite recent examples from your experience?**

Concept of News

∙∙

STUDY PREVIEW

News is a report on change that survives the competition for reporting other change that is occurring. What ends up being reported is the result of news judgments by reporters and editors who package their regular updates on what they believe their audiences need and want to know.

DEFINITION OF NEWS

Ask anybody: "What's news?" Everybody thinks they know, but press them and you'll hear a lot of fumbling. So why is consensus elusive about something as much a part of everyday life as news? In part it's because the U.S. Constitution forbids government from interfering with almost anything that the media report. This freedom has led to diverse presentations under the label of news. Compare the outrageous tabloid *News of the World*, which reports on alien creatures visiting earthly celebrities weekly, and the New York *Times*, the pillar of U.S. daily journalism. Not even mainstream media report events and issues in lockstep.

A useful definition of news involves two concepts—news and newsworthiness.

● **news**
A report on change

In short, **news** is a report on change. This is no more apparent than in traditional newspaper headlines, which contain a verb—the vehicle in a language to denote change:

> **Obama *wins* Democratic Iowa caucus**
> **Roadside Iraq bombs *kill* four soldiers**
> **Paris Hilton *leaves* jail a "new person"**

Not all change can fit into the limited time in a newscast or the limited space in a newspaper. Nor does all change warrant audience time online. So what change

● **newsworthiness**
A ranking of news that helps decide
what makes it into news packages

makes the news? Journalists apply the concept of **newsworthiness** to rank change. When George Bush sniffles, it's change—and the whole world cares. A lot is at stake. For most of us, when we sniffle, only Mom cares. Applying a newsworthiness test to a series of events that might be reported requires judgment. No two people will assign all priorities the same. See for yourself: Rank these hypothetical events by newsworthiness and ask a friend to do the same:

> **Yankees win World Series**
> **Congress votes to remove Mexico fence**
> **Navy launches new aircraft carrier**
> **Bin Laden found dead in Afghan mountains**
> **Scientology founder returns from dead**
> **Airline crash kills 220 in Kenya**

A lot of factors go into determining newsworthiness—proximity to audience, prominence of people involved, timeliness, impact on society, even the so-called gee-whiz factor. But there is no clinical formula for newsworthiness. A subjective element flowing from journalists' values and sense of the world and sense of audience is at the heart of what is reported and how it's reported.

LEARNING CHECK ◄ ••

▸ News is a report on change, but clearly more change is occurring than is possible to report. What principles do journalists apply to identify change that most merits reporting?

▸ Why is it unavoidable that journalists disagree among themselves on what merits being reported on a given day?

OBJECTIVITY

● **objectivity**
A concept in journalism that
news should be gathered and told
value-free

Despite the high quotient of judgment in deciding what changes to report, a lot of people use the term **objectivity** to describe news. By this they mean a value-free process in making choices about what to tell and how to tell it. It's a self-contradictory concept: Choice, by definition, is never value-free. So how did we end up with this idea that news should be objective when it cannot be? History has the answer.

■ **Penny Press.** Part of the answer goes back to the era of Ben Day and his New York *Sun*, the first of the penny papers with a mass audience. Day looked for stories with mass appeal. Suddenly, what made the paper was not the opinionated ramblings of the preceding partisan press but stories chosen to appeal to the largest possible audience. Opinion was out, storytelling in. The writer became subordinate to the tale, even to the point of near-invisibility. No more first person. Facts carried the story.

■ **Associated Press.** Several cost-conscious New York newspaper publishers agreed in 1848 to a joint venture to cover distant news. The Associated Press, as they called the venture, saved a lot of money. It also transformed U.S. journalism in a way that was never anticipated. Inherent in the AP concept was that its stories needed to be nonpartisan to be usable by all of its member newspapers, whose political persuasions spanned the spectrum. The result was an emphasis, some say fetish, on fact-driven journalism devoid of even a hint of partisanship.

■ **Newspaper Economics.** Another fundamental shift cemented the detached, neutral AP tone, often characterized as objective. News became profitable—highly so. The fortune that Benjamin Day made with the New York *Sun* in the mid-1830s was puny compared with the Pulitzer, Hearst and other news empires that came within 50 years. These super-publishers saw their newspapers as money machines as much as political tools. The bottom line gradually and inevitably gained more weight. The safest route to continue building their mass audiences and enhancing revenue was to avoid antagonizing readers and advertisers. There was money to be made in presenting news in as neutral a tone as possible. Picking up a lesson

NEWS MILESTONES

1700s

Zenger Trial
Colonial jury freed John Peter Zenger (1735)

Stamp Tax
Colonial newspapers campaigned against stamp tax (1760s)

Challenged the crown

1800s

Penny Press
Ben Day founded New York *Sun*, first penny paper (1833)

Modern News
James Gordon Bennett pioneered systematic news coverage (1840s)

Penny Press, unprecedented mass audiences

Editorials
Horace Greeley established editorial page (1841)

Telegraph
Samuel Morse invented the telegraph (1844)

Yellow Press
Sensationalistic excesses (1880s)

James Gordon Bennett, created news as we know it

1900s

Muckraking
Ida Tarbell and journalism aimed at reform (1902–)

Radio
Presidential returns were broadcast (1916)

Watergate
Confidential sources became issue in reporting the Watergate scandal (1972)

Yellow Kid, the cartoon namesake for an era

Televison
CNN introduced 24-hour television news (1980)

Online News
Albuquerque, New Mexico, *Tribune* launched online edition (1982)

2000s

Iraq War
Government manipulation intensified as people took issue with the information used to justify war (2005)

New York Daily News, *reporting Watergate*

PIVOTAL EVENTS

- Puritans established Cambridge Press (1638)
- French and Indian wars (1689–1763)
- *Publick Occurrences*, first colonial newspaper (1690)
- First colonial magazines (1741)
- Revolutionary War (1776–1781)

- Public education took root as a social value (1820s)
- Factory jobs fueled urban growth (1830s–)
- Waves of immigration added to urbanization (1830s–)
- U.S. Civil War (1861–1864)
- Populism widened effective political participation (1880s–)
- Spanish–American War (1898)

- Right to vote extended to women (1920)
- Radio emerged as commercial medium (late 1920s)
- Great Depression (1930s)
- World War II (1941–1945)
- Russian–Western Cold War (1945–1989)
- Television emerged as commercial medium (early 1950s)
- Vietnam War (1964–1973)
- Humans reached moon (1969)
- Internet emerged as commercial medium (late 1990s)

- 9/11 terrorist attacks (2001)
- Iraq War (2003–)
- Hurricane Katrina (2005)

from the AP, but with a different motivation—to make money rather than save money—profit-driven publishers came to favor information-driven news.

By the early 20th century, when news practices became institutionalized in the first journalism textbooks and in the formation of professional organizations, the notion of a detached, neutral presentation was firmly ensconced. Ethics codes, new at the time, dismissed other approaches as unacceptable and unethical, even though they had been dominant only three generations earlier. The word *objectivity* became a newsroom mantra.

To be sure, there are exceptions to the detached, neutral presentation, but traditionalists are quick to criticize the departures. The goal is to keep the reporter, even the reporter's inherently necessary judgment, as invisible in the presentation as possible.

LEARNING CHECK ◄ ···

▶ **How did so many people come to the vexatious opinion that news should be objective?**

Personal Values in News

STUDY PREVIEW

Journalists make important decisions on which events, phenomena and issues are reported and which are not. The personal values journalists bring to their work and that therefore determine which stories are told, and also how they are told, generally coincide with mainstream American values.

ROLE OF THE JOURNALIST

Even with the values-free pretext under which most U.S. journalism functions, values cannot be wished out of existence. The fact is that journalists make choices. NBC newscaster Chet Huntley, after years of trying to come up with a definition of news, threw up his hands and declared: "News is what I decide is news." Huntley wasn't being arrogant. Rather, he was pointing out that there are no clinical criteria for news that sidestep human judgment on what to put in the paper or on the air. Even if an event has intrinsic qualities as news, such as the prominence of the people involved and the event's consequence and drama, it becomes news only when it's reported. Huntley's point was that the journalist's judgment is indispensable in deciding what is news.

Huntley's conclusion underscores the high degree of autonomy that individual journalists have in shaping what is reported. Even a reporter hired fresh out of college by a small daily newspaper and assigned to city hall has a great deal of independence in deciding what to report and how to report it. Such trust is unheard of in most other fields, which dole out responsibility to newcomers in small bits over a lengthy period. Of course, rookie journalists are monitored by their newsroom supervisors, and editors give them assignments and review their stories, but it is the city hall reporter, no matter how green, who is the news organization's expert on city government.

The First Amendment guarantee of a free press also contributes to the independence and autonomy that characterize news work. Journalists know that they have a high level of constitutional protection in deciding what to report as news. While most reporters will agree on the newsworthiness of some events and issues, such as a catastrophic storm or a tax proposal, their judgments will result in stories that take different slants and angles. On events and issues whose newsworthiness is less obvious, reporters will differ even on whether to do a story.

LEARNING CHECK ◄ ···

▶ **What personal values would shape your work as a journalist?**

▶ **In what kinds of situations would you expect your values to be a problem in reporting stories?**

JOURNALISTS' PERSONAL VALUES

The journalistic ideal, an unbiased seeking of truth and an unvarnished telling of it, dictates that the work be done without partisanship. Yet as human beings, journalists have personal values that influence all that they do, including their work. Because the news judgment decisions that journalists make are so important to an informed citizenry, we need to know what makes these people tick. Are they left-wingers? Are they ideological zealots? Are they quirky and unpredictable? Are they conscientious?

As a sociologist who studied stories in the American news media for 20 years, **Herbert Gans** concluded that journalists have a typical American value system. Gans identified primary values, all in the American mainstream, that journalists use in making their news judgments:

- **Herbert Gans**
Concluded that journalists have mainstream values

■ **Ethnocentrism.** American journalists see things through American eyes, which colors news coverage. In the 1960s and 1970s, Gans noted, North Vietnam was consistently characterized as "the enemy." U.S. reporters took the view of the U.S. government and military, which was hardly detached or neutral. This **ethnocentrism** was clear at the end of the war, which U.S. media headlined as "the *fall* of South Vietnam." By other values, Gans said, the communist takeover of Saigon could be considered a *liberation*. In neutral terms, it was a *change in government*.

- **ethnocentrism**
Seeing things on the basis of personal experience, values

This ethnocentrism creates problems as the news media become more global. In the 2003 Iraq War, news reporters embedded with U.S. units advancing toward Iraq used the term "the enemy" for Iraqi resistance, which was hardly neutral considering that many Iraqis regarded the invading army as the enemy. It is hard for all people, including journalists, to transcend their own skins.

■ **Democracy and Capitalism.** Gans found that U.S. journalists favor U.S.-style democracy. Coverage of other governmental forms dwells on corruption, conflict, protest and bureaucratic malfunction. The unstated idea of most U.S. journalists, said Gans, is that other societies do best when they follow the American ideal of serving the public interest.

Gans also found that U.S. journalists are committed to the capitalist economic system. When they report corruption and misbehavior in U.S. business, journalists treat them as aberrations. The underlying posture of the news coverage of the U.S. economy, Gans said, is "an optimistic faith" that businesspeople refrain from unreasonable profits and gross exploitation of workers or customers while competing to create increased prosperity for all. In covering controlled foreign economies, U.S. journalists emphasize the downside.

It may seem only natural to most Americans that democracy and capitalism should be core values of any reasonable human being. This sense itself is an ethnocentric value, which many people do not even think about but which nonetheless shapes how they conduct their lives. Knowing that U.S. journalists by and large share this value explains a lot about the news coverage they create.

■ **Small-Town Pastoralism.** Like most of their fellow citizens, U.S. journalists romanticize rural life. Given similar stories from metropolitan Portland and tiny Sweet Home, Oregon, editors usually opt for the small town.

Cities are covered as places with problems; rural life is celebrated. Suburbs are largely ignored. Gans' understanding of small-town pastoralism helped explain the success of the late Charles Kuralt's *On the Road* series on CBS television.

■ **Individualism Tempered by Moderation.** Gans found that U.S. journalists love stories about rugged individuals who overcome adversity and defeat powerful forces. This is a value that contributes to a negative coverage of technology as something to be feared because it can stifle individuality. Gans again cited the long-running CBS series *On the Road*, in which Charles Kuralt presented pastoral features on rugged individuals. Today the *Everybody Has a Story* series by Steve Hartman serves the same role at CBS.

Seymour Hersh broke a story about U.S. soldiers wiping out a remote village of civilians during the Vietnam war. Finding official denials everywhere he turned, Hersh tracked veterans to their homes after their tours of duty to piece together an account of the horrible incident. Becoming known as the My Lai Massacre, it led, as it should have, to court-martials. But the story so embarrassed the Pentagon that Hersh became a pariah in top Pentagon circles.

Even so, he was so respected for his dogged truth-seeking that knowledgeable sources within the Pentagon and the Central Intelligence Agency continued to feed him leads on other stories.

Hersh was no one-shot wonder with his 1969 My Lai stories. En route to becoming one of the pre-eminent investigative reporters of our time, he focused on clandestine operations of the U.S. government. These included the CIA's covert role in the overthrow of Salvador Allende in Chile. Hersh exposed secret bombing in Cambodia that had been authorized by presidential aide Henry Kissinger.

In 2004 in the *New Yorker* magazine Hersh exposed prisoner abuses at the Abu Ghraib prison in Iraq. Even though the Pentagon's initial response was to label Hersh's Abu Ghraib account "outlandish and conspiratorial," the photos that Hersh showed could not be ignored.

In 1975 when Donald Rumsfeld was President Ford's chief of staff, he and Dick Cheney, a high administration official, exchanged memos on how to contain damaging reporting by Hersh, then with the New York *Times*. In new positions in the second Bush administration—Rumsfeld as secretary of defense, Cheney as vice president—they were no less angry at Hersh. But despite the denials and minimizing reaction statements, the accuracy of Hersh's reporting still was proving unshakable.

No matter how hard the Pentagon tries at the highest levels to make Hersh an outsider, he has become, in fact, an insider. Sources come to him, especially, it seems, mid-level and some senior civilian and military leaders in the defense establishment with grudges against President Bush for ignoring their experience and advice in setting new policy courses, including the Iraq War.

WHAT DO YOU THINK?

▶ For 40 years White House news secretaries have found themselves denying information dug up by Seymour Hersh. In the end, Hersh has always been right. If you were the White House news secretary, how would you respond to a new and embarrassing revelation

Military Beat. *Hersh's scoops began with the My Lai Massacre in the Vietnam War and have continued through the Abu Ghraib prison torture during the War in Iraq.*

from Hersh about secret military operations?

▶ What sets Hersh's reporting apart from that of most other reporters?

Journalists like to turn ordinary individuals into heroes, but there are limits. Rebels and deviates are portrayed as extremists who go beyond another value: moderation. To illustrate this bias toward moderation. Gans noted that "the news treats atheists as extremists and uses the same approach, if more gingerly, with religious fanatics. People who consume conspicuously are criticized, but so are people such as hippies who turn their backs on consumer goods. The news is scornful both of the overly academic scholar and the oversimplifying popularizer. It is kind neither to high-brows nor to low-brows, to users of jargon or users of slang. College students who play when they should study receive disapproval, but so do 'grinds.' Lack of moderation is wrong, whether it involves excesses or abstention."

Because all reporting is investigative in the sense that it seeks truth through inquiry, the term *investigative reporting* is tricky. Here is a useful definition:
- A story that would not have been revealed without the enterprise of a reporter.
- A story that is pieced together from diverse and often obscure sources.
- A story that may be contrary to the version from officials, who might have tried to conceal the truth.

Examples:

St. Louis *Post-Dispatch*	Police routinely write up sex crimes not as official reports but as informal memos, which aren't included in crime statistics.
Seattle *Post-Intelligencer*	Oil companies have sidestepped environment-sensitive regulations imposed after the Exxon Valdez shipwreck disaster that spoiled an Alaska bay.
South Florida *Sun-Sentinel*	Inspectors hired by the government to enter Hurricane Katrina-damaged homes to verify damage claims included criminals convicted of robbery, embezzlement and drug dealing.

Investigative Journalism. *Dogged pursuit of meticulous factual detail became a new wrinkle in 20th-century journalism after Washington* Post *reporters Carl Bemstein and Bob Woodward unearthed the Watergate scandal. For months they pursued tips that a break-in at the Democratic Party national headquarters in the Watergate hotel, office and apartment complex in Washington, D.C., had been authorized high in the Republican White House and that the White House then had tried to cover it up. In the end, for the first time in U.S. history, a president, Richard Nixon, resigned.*

In politics, Gans said, both ideologues and politicians who lack ideology are treated with suspicion: "Political candidates who talk openly about issues may be described as dull; those who avoid issues entirely evoke doubts about their fitness for office."

■ **Social Order.** Journalists cover disorder—earthquakes, hurricanes, industrial catastrophes, protest marches, the disintegrating nuclear family and transgressions of laws and mores. This coverage, noted Gans, is concerned not with glamorizing disorder but with finding ways to restore order. Coverage of a hurricane, for example, lasts not much longer than the storm, but coverage of the recovery goes on for days. The media focus is far more on restoring order than on covering death and destruction.

The journalistic commitment to social order also is evident in how heavily reporters rely on people in leadership roles as primary sources of information. These leaders, largely representing the Establishment and the status quo, are the people in the best position to maintain social order and to restore it if there's disruption. This means government representatives often shape news media reports and thus their audiences' understanding of what is important, "true" or meaningful. No one receives more media attention than the president of the United States, who is seen, said Gans, "as the ultimate protector of order."

LEARNING CHECK ◄··

▶ **Which of the values that Herbert Gans attributed to American journalists do you share?**

▶ **What additional values do you hold?**

JOURNALISTIC BIAS

Critics of the news media come in many flavors. Conservatives are the most vocal, charging that the media slant news to favor Democrats and liberal causes. Numerous studies, some shoddily partisan, others not, fuel the conservatives' accusations.

Although his work is dated, Ken Walsh of *U.S. News & World Report* is often quoted for a survey that found 50 White House correspondents had voted Democratic and only seven Republican in 1996. To be sure, some news organizations offer partisan spin, for years most notably the Washington *Times*. More recently Fox News took a lesson from the most successful talk-radio shows and intentionally positioned itself to appeal to right-wing viewers.

In general, though, most U.S. newsrooms pride themselves on neutral presentation and go to extraordinary lengths to prove it. To avoid confusion between straight news and commentary, newspaper opinion pieces are set apart in clearly labeled editorial sections. Broadcast commentaries are also flagged.

■ **Professional Standards.** Most news reporters, even those with left or right leanings, profess a zealous regard for detached, neutral reporting. In the United States this is the journalistic creed, embodied in every professional code of ethics. Almost all reporters see their truth-seeking as unfettered by partisanship. In self-flagellating postmortems, they are the first to criticize lapses.

Editors and news directors say they have no political litmus test in hiring reporters. They recruit reporters for their skills and intelligence, not their politics. Joe Strupp, who interviewed dozens of editors for the trade journal *Editor & Publisher*, found that editors rely on peer dynamics in the newsroom to keep the focus on complete and thorough reporting, which trumps any ideological bent. At the San Diego *Union-Tribune*, editor Karin Winter said: "We know how to turn off our affiliation when we walk through the door. It does not come up."

The editing process, an elaborate kind of peer review to which virtually all stories are subjected, also works against bias in coverage. Reporters know that the final word on their copy rests with editors, who recognize that the main product a newsroom has to offer the audience is accurate, truthful and believable reporting. The media have an economic incentive to tell news straight. Bruce Bartlett of the National Center for Policy Analysis, noted that people will cancel their subscriptions if they perceive "liberal claptrap."

■ **News as Change.** If the news media indeed are obsessed with avoiding partisan reporting, how do the charges of bias retain currency? A historical reality in the bipolar U.S. political tradition is that the extremes have been conservatives, who by and large prefer things as they are, and liberals, who seek reform and change. Critics who paint the news media as liberal usually are forgetting that news, by its nature, is concerned with change. Everybody, journalists and news media consumers alike, is more interested in a volcano that is blowing its top than in a dormant peak. People are interested congenitally in what is happening, as opposed to what is not happening. Friends don't greet each other: "Hey, what's not new?" News stories on Krakotoa in 1883 hardly meant that journalists favor volcanic eruptions. The fact is that change is more interesting than the status quo, although usually less comforting and sometimes threatening. News is about change—proposed, pending and occurring. And change is not what political conservatism is about.

When journalists write about a presidential candidate's ideas to, for example, eliminate farm subsidies, it's not that journalists favor the proposed change. Rather, it's that the topic is more interesting than stories about government programs that are in place, functioning routinely and unchallenged. In short, to conclude that journalists' concern with change is necessarily born of political bias is to overlook the nature of journalism—and also the natural human interest in what's new.

■ **Watchdog Function.** Some accusations of journalistic bias originate in confusion between message and messenger. Incumbent officeholders often are quick to blame the media when news is less than hunky-dory. The classic case was in 1968 when the White House was beset with unfavorable news. Vice President Spiro Agnew, addicted as he was to fanciful alliteration, called the press "nagging nabobs of negativism." Successive presidential administrations, Democratic and Republican alike, have been no less gentle in charging the media with bias when news is less than flattering.

The news media frequently are whipping boys for performing their constitutionally implied **watchdog function.** Since the founding of the Republic, journalists have been expected to keep government honest and responsive to the electorate by reporting on its activities, especially shortcomings. Unless the people have full reports, they cannot intelligently discuss public issues, let alone vote knowledgeably on whether to keep or replace their representatives.

This is not to suggest that journalists are perfect or always accurate, especially in reporting confusing situations against deadline. Nor is it to suggest that there are no partisans peppered among reporters in the press corps. But critics, usually themselves partisans, too often are reflexive with a cheap charge of bias when reporters are, as one wag put it, doing their job to keep the rascals in power honest. In the process of doing their work, journalists sometimes indeed become facilitators of change—but as reporters, not advocates.

> **watchdog function**
> The news media role to monitor the performance of government and other institutions of society

LEARNING CHECK ◄ ·······························

▶ Most mainstream media in the United States package or label opinion as separate from news. How does this work? Does it work well?

▶ How well do your local news media perform their watchdog function? Give recent examples.

Variables Affecting News

STUDY PREVIEW

The variables that determine what is reported include things beyond a journalist's control, such as how much space or time is available to tell stories. Also, a story that might receive top billing on a slow news day might not even appear on a day when an overwhelming number of major stories are breaking.

NEWS HOLE

> **news hole**
> Space for news in a newspaper after ads are inserted; time in a newscast for news after ads

A variable affecting what ends up being reported as news is called the **news hole.** In newspapers the news hole is the space left after the advertising department has placed all the ads it has sold in the paper. The volume of advertising determines the number of total pages, and generally, the bigger the issue, the more room for news. Newspaper editors can squeeze fewer stories into a thin Monday issue than a fat Wednesday issue.

In broadcasting, the news hole tends to be more consistent. A 30-minute television newscast may have room for only 23 minutes of news, but the format doesn't vary. When the advertising department doesn't sell all seven minutes available for advertising, it usually is public-service announcements, promotional messages and program notes—not news—that pick up the slack. Even so, the news hole can vary in broadcasting. A 10-minute newscast can accommodate more stories than a 5-minute newscast, and, as with newspapers, it is the judgment of journalists that determines which events make it.

LEARNING CHECK ◄ ·······························

▶ Why does the news hole frustrate journalists?

NEWS FLOW AND NEWS STAFFING

> **news flow**
> Significance of events worth covering varies from day to day

Besides the news hole, the **news flow** varies from day to day. A story that might be placed prominently on a slow news day can be passed over entirely in the competition for space on a heavy news day.

On one of the heaviest news days of all time—June 4, 1989—death claimed Iran's Ayatollah Khomeini, a central figure in U.S. foreign policy; Chinese young people and the government were locked in a showdown in Tiananmen Square; the Polish people were voting to reject their one-party communist political system; and a revolt was under way in the Soviet republic of Uzbekistan. That was a heavy news day, and the flow of major nation-rattling events pre-empted many stories that otherwise would have been considered news.

Heavy news days cannot be predicted. One would have occurred if there had been a confluence on a single day of these 2005 events: Hurricane Katrina, the Samuel Alito nomination to the U.S. Supreme Court, the 2,000th U.S. combat death in Iraq, the Michael Jackson acquittal and the Afghanistan-Pakistan earthquake.

● **staffing**
Available staff resources to cover news

Staffing affects news coverage, for example, whether reporters are in the right place at the right time. A newsworthy event in Nigeria will receive short shrift on U.S. television if the network correspondents for Africa are occupied with a natural disaster in next-door Cameroon. A radio station's city government coverage will slip when the city hall reporter is on vacation or if the station can't afford a regular reporter at city hall.

LEARNING CHECK ◄ •

▶ Look at your local newspaper over the past week. Which was the heaviest news day? The slowest news day? Explain.

▶ Which is cheaper for a newspaper or television station to report? A session of the city council or a session of the British Parliament? Explain.

PERCEPTIONS ABOUT AUDIENCE

How a news organization perceives its audience affects news coverage. The *National Enquirer* lavishes attention on unproven cancer cures that the New York *Times* treats briefly if at all. The *Wall Street Journal* sees its purpose as news for readers who have special interests in finance, the economy and business. The Bloomberg cable network was established to serve an audience more interested in quick market updates, brief analysis and trendy consumer news than the kind of depth offered by the *Journal*.

The perception that a news organization has of its audience is evident in a comparison of stories on different networks' newscasts. CNN may lead newscasts with a coup d'état in another country, while Bloomberg leads with a new government economic forecast and MTV with the announcement of a rock group's tour.

LEARNING CHECK ◄ •

▶ How do your expectations differ regarding the news coverage on the *Daily Show* and CNN?

COMPETITION

Two triggers of adrenaline for journalists are landing a scoop and, conversely, being scooped. Journalism is a competitive business, and the drive to outdo other news organizations keeps news publications and newscasts fresh with new material.

Competition has an unglamorous side. Journalists constantly monitor each other to identify events that they missed and need to catch up on to be competitive. This catch-up aspect of the news business contributes to similarities in coverage, which scholar Leon Sigal calls the **consensible nature of news.** It also is called "pack" and "herd" journalism.

● **consensible nature of news**
News organization second-guessing competition in deciding coverage

In the final analysis, news is the result of journalists scanning their environment and making decisions, first on whether to cover certain events and then on how to cover them. The decisions are made against a backdrop of countless variables, many of them changing during the reporting, writing and editing processes.

LEARNING CHECK ◄ •

▶ How can similar content in competing news media be explained?

Confidential Sources

STUDY PREVIEW

Journalists receive story tips all the time, sometimes confidentially. Although usual journalistic practice is to cite sources, some stories based on confidential tips are so vital that reporters decide to tell them and protect their sources' identities. It's a risky practice that raises doubts about a story's credibility, but journalists generally agree that sometimes there is no alternative.

NEWS ON CONDITION

Reporters like to identify their sources in their stories. That makes the stories more credible. But what is a reporter to do when a source says, "I've got some information for you but only if you won't use my name"? The issue becomes critical if a reporter's perception is that the public good would be served by a story.

In the divisive late 1960s in the United States, with many people conflicted by the anti-war and civil rights movements, reporters drew on confidential sources for insightful articles about what was ripping the country apart. In some cases reporters shielded the names of people whom the police were trying to identify for prosecution for acts of violence. Some judges called reporters in and demanded that they divulge their sources or go to jail for defying a judge's order. Journalists claimed that they were bound by a higher calling, noting that important stories could not be told if their sources couldn't count on being shielded.

Finally, the U.S. Supreme Court weighed in, ruling that journalists "are not exempt from the normal duty of all citizens" to cooperate in criminal investigations. In related cases, however, the Court has said that police and the courts should exhaust every other avenue before pressing journalists on their sources. Still, jail can be a reality when journalists try to shield sources if crimes are involved. In a worst-case situation the consensus among journalists is that the right thing to do is go to jail.

LEARNING CHECK ◄ •

▶ Reporters prefer to identify their sources in their stories, but there can be exceptions. Give an example and explain the rationale for the exception. Do you accept the rationale?

SHIELD LAWS

● **shield laws**
Allow journalists to protect the identification of confidential sources

Several states have adopted **shield laws,** which recognize reporter-source confidentiality. A problem with shield laws is that they require government to define who is a journalist. This raises the specter of the government's deciding who is and who is not a journalist, which smacks of authoritarian press licensing and control. As an example, the Ohio shield law protects "bona fide journalists," who are defined as people employed by or connected to newspapers, radio stations, television stations and news services. Not only is it disturbing when government defines who is a journalist in a free society, but such attempts are destined to fail. The Ohio definition, for example, fails to protect freelance journalists and writers who do their work on their own in the hope they will eventually sell it.

A congressional attempt at a federal shield law in 2007, the Free Flow of Information bill, tries to protect reporters, defined as anyone engaged in "the gathering, preparing, collecting, photographing, recording, writing, editing, reporting, or publishing of news or information that concerns local, national or international events or other matters of public interest for dissemination to the public." Although well intentioned, the bill poses the same problem as earlier state-level

Reporter's Choice: Tell or Go to Jail?

Forty-nine states have shield laws or other protections in place that recognize reporters' privilege to protect their sources. But there is no national shield law, which leaves journalists vulnerable to court orders to break promises to their sources. When subpoenaed, journalists must reveal their sources or go to jail for refusing a judge's order.

A 2007 attempt in Congress at a federal shield law, the Free Flow of Information Act, was supported by dozens of media companies and journalistic organizations. Supporters included the Free the Media organization, established by Josh Wolf. The 24-year-old blogger spent almost eight months in prison for not giving the FBI video he shot in San Francisco during a protest facilitated by a group called Anarchist Action against the G-8 Summit in Scotland.

Wolf posted some of his video on his blog. Also, he sold some of the video to television news outlets. A few days later the FBI turned up at his door.

Wolf was subpoenaed by a federal grand jury, which had been called to determine if arson charges should be brought against protestors for damaging a police car, even though it had only a damaged taillight. The federal court circumvented the state's shield law and got involved because the purchase of the police car was funded in part by federal anti-terror money.

"What I caught on videotape was a cop choking a guy," Wolf said, not the car incident, but FBI agents still wanted his video, and they wanted him to identify protestors, who were wearing masks. They wanted all documents, writings and recordings related to the protest, as well as all his cameras and recording devices and his computer. Wolf refused to comply with the subpoena. "There was a trust established between people in the organization that I was covering," he said in one interview. "I wasn't an investigator for the state turning over piles of tape for fishing expeditions."

After Wolf spent 226 days in jail, longer than any other journalist in U.S. history, an agreement was reached. Wolf gave federal prosecutors his tape, and at the same time he published it on his Web site. He answered no to two questions about what he had seen the demonstration. A statement on his site declared victory for "a free press."

U.S. Attorney Kevin Ryan said in a court filing that it was "only in Wolf's imagination that he is a journalist."

The Society for Professional Journalists and the National Newspaper Guild disagreed. The SPJ Northern California chapter honored Wolf as Journalist of the Year and gave him the James Madison Freedom of Information Award. He received the Herb Block Freedom Award from the National Newspaper Guild.

Josh Wolf. *A prosecutor argued that Josh Wolf, as a blogger, had no right to refuse to divulge information about an anti-G-8 demonstration. The prosecutor said it was "only in Wolf's imagination that he is a journalist." Wolf spent 226 days in jail for refusing to divulge information that he said was acquired only because sources trusted him not to rat on them.*

DEEPENING YOUR MEDIA LITERACY

EXPLORE THE ISSUE

Do you think blogger Josh Wolf is a journalist who deserves the protection of a shield law?

DIG DEEPER

Tom Rosentiel of the Project for Excellence in Journalism says the proper question should be not whether you call yourself a journalist but whether your work constitutes journalism. With this definition in mind, analyze the Josh Wolf case.

WHAT DO YOU THINK?

Do you think a federal shield law is necessary? Why? Do you think it should include bloggers and independent journalists? Why?

shield laws: How close does it come to government licensing of journalists when the government defines who is a journalist and who isn't?

LEARNING CHECK ◄ ••

▶ Would you go to jail to protect a confidential source's identity rather than obey a court order to reveal the source's name?

GATEKEEPING

● **gatekeeper**
Person who decides whether to shorten, drop or change a story en route to the mass audience

Although individual reporters have lots of independence in determining what to report and how, news work is a team effort. News dispatches and photographs are subject to changes at many points in the communication chain. At these points, called *gates*, **gatekeepers** delete, trim, embellish and otherwise try to improve messages.

Just as a reporter exercises judgment in deciding what to report and how to report it, judgment also is at the heart of the gatekeeping process. Hardly any message, except live reporting, reaches its audience in its original form. Along the path from its originator to the eventual audience, a message is subject to all kinds of deletions, additions and changes of emphasis. With large news organizations this process may involve dozens of editors and other persons.

The gatekeeping process affects all news. A public relations practitioner who doesn't tell the whole story is a gatekeeper. A reporter who emphasizes one aspect of an event and neglects others is a gatekeeper. Even live, on-scene television coverage involves gatekeeping because it's a gatekeeper who decides where to point the camera, and that's a decision that affects the type of information that reaches viewers. The C-SPAN network's live, unedited coverage of Congress, for example, never shows members of Congress sleeping or reading newspapers during debate, even though such things happen.

Gatekeeping can be a creative force. Trimming a news story can add potency. A news producer can enhance a reporter's field report with file footage. An editor can call a public relations person for additional detail to illuminate a point in a reporter's story. A newsmagazine's editor can consolidate related stories and add context that makes an important interpretive point.

Most gatekeepers are invisible to the news audience, working behind the scenes and making crucial decisions in near anonymity on how the world will be portrayed in the evening newscast and the next morning's newspaper.

LEARNING CHECK ◄ ••

▶ Why is gatekeeping unavoidable in the process of reporting news?

▶ Explain how gatekeeping worked for any recent story from far away in your local news media. How about a local story?

Journalism Trends

STUDY PREVIEW

The explosion of 24/7 news on television and the Internet is transforming news gathering and redefining news practices and audience expectations. Traditional avenues for news, sometimes called mainstream media, were shaken in the 2004 political campaign by individuals, mostly without journalistic training, generally operating alone, who created hundreds of blog sites. Bloggers offer an interconnected web of fascinating reading. Sometimes they score scoops.

NEWSROOMS IN TRANSITION

Two dynamics are reshaping newsrooms. One is the transition into Internet delivery of news, which is pushing editors to find ways to stretch their staffs to produce their traditional products—plus offer competitive Web sites. The other dynamic is financial, primarily at newspapers where recent years have seen drastic staff reductions. Newspaper industry reporter Joe Strupp, writing in the trade journal *Editor & Publisher*, put it this way: "So with newsrooms shrinking and corporate demands growing, the question inevitably may be asked: 'What gives?'" Most television newsrooms face the same issue. How can the extra duty of a 24/7 Web site or perhaps multiple sites, some interactive, be absorbed by existing staff?

Among the new realities:

■ **Less Comprehensive Coverage.** Newsrooms once put lots of energy into catching up on their competitors' scoops and taking the coverage further. Less so now. Ken Paulson, editor of *USA Today*, said he now applauds the New York *Times* and Washington *Post* when they break an exclusive story. Applaud—and forget it. Said Paulson: "We have to make judgment calls on what our priorities are."

The new *USA Today* practice, common in strapped newsrooms, doesn't speak well for the kind of excellence that competition has generated historically in U.S. journalism. The coverage of historically significant stories, like the Pentagon Papers and Watergate in the 1970s, was marked by intense competition. Independent coverage by competing newsrooms led to revelations that no one news organization could have managed single-handedly. Every breakthrough from competing newsrooms in Watergate, for example, further peeled away at the truth and became a stepping stone for new rounds of pursuit.

■ **Less Enterprise.** With smaller, stretched staffs, newsrooms are opting for easier stories. This has meant a greater quotient of stories that chronicle events and fewer stories that require labor-intensive digging. This further means fewer reporters being freed for what David Boardman, executive editor at the Seattle *Times*, calls "two- and three-day stories." There was a time in the lore of the *Wall Street Journal* that editors would work up a promising story possibility with a veteran reporter, give the reporter an American Express card, and say come back with a story in six months. Although the *Journal* still features exhaustive journalistic examinations, they are becoming less common in American journalism.

■ **Less Outlying News.** Many newsrooms have trimmed or shuttered bureaus in outlying areas. Typical is the Memphis, Tennessee, *Commercial Appeal*. The bureaus in Jackson, Mississippi, and Little Rock, Arkansas, have been shut down. The state Capitol bureau in Nashville, once with three reporters, was trimmed to one.

■ **Fewer Beats.** Reporters assigned to cover specialized areas are being given broader beats. Some police beat reporters, for example, now also cover the courts. To cover some beats, editors in some newsrooms have shuffled reporters from general assignment duties to beats, which means there are fewer resources for day-to-day coverage of breaking news that doesn't fall in the bailiwick of one of the surviving beats.

■ **Less Independent Reporting.** Newsrooms are sharing stories among corporate siblings, which fills space cheaply but reduces the traditional value of competitive reporting yielding better coverage overall. Many newspapers and newscasts fill up with a growing percentage of faraway content from the Associated Press, which is far less costly per story than staff-generated local coverage. One upshot is less diversity in content when AP stories, appearing word for word in news packages statewide, even nationwide, displace local coverage.

The trend toward shared stories is most obvious with so-called multimedia newsrooms. One of the first was the integrated newsroom of the Tampa, Florida, *Tribune*, television station WFLA and TBO.com. Some local television stations are sparing themselves the cost of operating a newsroom and contracting with crosstown stations to provide the newscasts. Efficient? Yes. That repackaging is better than fresh content, however, is hard to argue.

LEARNING CHECK ◄•••

▶ The Watergate coverage by Carl Bernstein and Bob Woodward of the Washington *Post* began with a brief, routine account of a break-in at the Democratic Party's national headquarters. Discuss whether Bernstein and Woodward in a newsroom like today's would have had the time to pursue the story. What if their coverage had stopped with a burglary item?

▶ How much duplicate reporting—competing reporters all doing the same stories—do you see in your local news media?

NONSTOP COVERAGE

Reporters for the Associated Press and other news agencies were a breed apart through most of the 20th century. In contrast to most newspaper reporters, who had one deadline a day, agency reporters sent dispatches to hundreds of news organizations, each with its own deadlines. Agency reporters literally had a deadline every minute.

● **nonstop coverage**
News reporting geared to ever-present deadlines, as 24/7 formats

The advent of all-news radio and then CNN expanded **nonstop coverage** beyond the news agencies. This is no better illustrated than at the White House, where CNN reporters race from an event or interview to a camera for a live stand-up report, often ad-libbing from notes scribbled on the run, and then, adrenaline surging, run back to sources for a new angle or event. This is event-based reporting, which emphasizes timely reports but which has a downside. Going on air a dozen times a day, perhaps more when the news flow is heavy or especially significant, stand-up reporters have scant time to think through implications and context. Theirs is a race to cover events more than to provide understanding. This too was a classic criticism of the news agencies.

The pressures of nonstop coverage have emerged poignantly at National Public Radio, which established its reputation in the 1970s with contemplative and in-depth reporting for its daily flagship, *All Things Considered*. Then NPR added *Morning Edition*, then *Day to Day*, then hourly updates. Reporters were being asked somehow to be contemplative and insightful while also doing endless stand-ups. NPR veteran reporter Nina Totenberg bristled at a planning meeting about her schedule: "If you want me to know anything for me to report, you have to leave me alone a few hours to do it."

Quality erosion shows up in small ways. Reporters shudder at their typos making it online because fewer editors are assigned to check copy. At the Baltimore *Sun*, Bill Salganik, the president of the Newspaper Guild, which represents reporters as a collective-bargaining agent, says the new pressures make more mistakes inevitable: "How do we maintain ethical and journalistic standards?"

In short, nonstop coverage, whatever the advantage of keeping people on top of breaking events, has shortcomings. The pressure for new angles tends to elevate the trivial. Also, context and understanding are sacrificed.

LEARNING CHECK ◄•••

▶ How has 24/7 news changed journalism?

▶ Do these changes have a downside?

LIVE NEWS

Over the past 150 years the news media in the United States, elsewhere too, have evolved standard and accepted practices. These practices, taught in journalism schools and institutionalized in codes of ethics, guide reporters and editors in preparing their summaries and wrap-ups. In general the traditional practices worked well when newspapers were the dominant news medium, and they worked well in broadcasting too—until the advent of highly portable, lightweight equipment that enabled broadcasters to carry news events live, bypassing the traditional editing process.

With television cameras focused on the towers of the World Trade Center as they turned into infernos in the 2001 terrorist attack, trapped people began jumping from windows hundreds of feet above ground. The plunges were desperate and fatal, and audiences viewing the scene live were shocked and horrified. Neither the video nor still photographs were included in most later newscasts or newspapers.

Whatever the virtues of live coverage, a significant downside is that the coverage is raw. Nobody is exercising judgment in deciding what to organize and how to present the material. There is no gatekeeper. Live coverage, of course, obviates the criticism of those who, rightly or wrongly, distrust journalism.

Following live coverage is time-consuming for the audience. Compare, for example, the efficiency of reading or listening to a 60-second report on a congressional hearing or watching the whole four-hour session live.

LEARNING CHECK ◄ ·····

▸ **How has the role of gatekeeping been changed by live broadcast coverage?**

UNEDITED BLOGS

When *Columbia Journalism Review* created a Web site for commentary on reporting of the 2004 presidential campaign, the magazine went out if its way to distance the new site from the thousands of Web log sites, called **blogs,** on which amateurs post whatever is on their minds. No, said *CJR*, its campaigndesk.org would be held to the highest journalistic standards. The point was that a lot of irresponsible content gets posted on the Web by people without any journalistic training or sense of journalistic standards. The Web has made it possible for anyone to create a blog that is as easily accessible as are sites from news organizations that consciously seek to go about journalism right.

No gnashing of teeth, however, will make blogs go away—and their impact is substantial. Blog rumors, gossip and speculation, even when untrue, sometimes gain such currency that the mainstream media cannot ignore them. It's become a bromide, drawn from the tail-wags-dog metaphor, that blogs can wag the media.

LEARNING CHECK ◄ ·····

▸ **What do you think of** *Columbia Journalism Review's* **distinction between good blogs and bad blogs?**

EXPLORATORY REPORTING

Although in-depth reporting has deep roots, the thrust of U.S. journalism until the 1960s was a chronicling of events: meetings, speeches, crimes, deaths and catastrophes. That changed dramatically in 1972. Two persistent Washington *Post* reporters, **Bob Woodward** and **Carl Bernstein,** not only covered a break-in at the Democratic national headquarters, at a building called the Watergate, but also linked the crime to the White House of Republican President Richard Nixon. The morality questions inherent in the reporting forced Nixon to resign. Twenty-five aides went to jail. The **Watergate** scandal created an enthusiasm for **investigative reporting** and in-depth approaches to news that went far beyond mere chronicling, which is relatively easy to do and, alas, relatively superficial.

The roots of investigatory reporting extend to the **muckraking** period in U.S. history. **Ida Tarbell,** a leading muckraker, uncovered abusive corporate practices at Standard Oil in 1902, triggering government reforms that broke up the Rockefeller oil monopoly and paved the way for anti-trust legislation. Today's newspapers continue this tradition. But is anybody listening? The New Orleans, Louisiana, *Times-Picayune* won a fistful of awards for John McQuaid and Mark Schleifstein's 2002 series "Washing Away," a chilling prediction of the Hurricane

---

● **blog**
An amateur Web site, generally personal in nature, often focused on a narrow subject, such as politics. Short for "Web log"

● **Bob Woodward**
Bernstein's colleague in the Watergate revelations

● **Carl Bernstein**
Washington *Post* reporter who dug up Watergate

● **Watergate**
Reporting of the Nixon administration scandal

● **investigative reporting**
Enterprise reporting that reveals new information, often startling; most often these are stories that official sources would rather not have told

● **muckraking**
Fanciful term for digging up dirt but that usually is used in a laudatory way for investigative journalism; aimed at public policy reform

● **Ida Tarbell**
Muckraker remembered for her series on monopolistic corruption at Standard Oil

When Ida Tarbell was growing up in the 1870s, her father jobbed wooden oil barrels to the infant western Pennsylvania oil industry. Later he was an independent oilman, who eventually ran into the growing monopoly of John D. Rockefeller's Standard Oil. When Ida went to college, unusual at the time for women, she developed a fascination with science and original research.

After success with researching and writing biographies for *McClure's* magazine, Tarbell was casting around for a new subject. She was aware of growing public skepticism about big business. And she knew from her father that the power-hungry Rockefeller was ruthless in undercutting small-time competitors to turn Standard Oil into a corporate juggernaut. Drawing on her skills at original, detailed research, Tarbell threw herself into two years of research into the company.

The result was a voluminously documented 19-part series that told about the discovery of oil near Titusville, Pennsylvania, in 1859, with petroleum soon replacing whale oil for lamps. Tarbell explained that Rockefeller got into the oil business in Cleveland in 1865 and bought competitors or ran them out of business, finally merging the Rockefeller, Harness and Flagler petroleum empires, which concentrated his control of refining. Then

Rockefeller strong-armed railroads into special rates that undercut his rivals. He also put together the control of pipelines. By 1879 Standard Oil controlled as much as 95 percent of the U.S. refined oil business.

Tarbell's saga was complex, replete with convoluted business arrangements, but she cast the story in easy-to-follow terms of price-fixing, product blockades, and unfair squeezes on competitors.

Tarbell's tone was dispassionate, but, typical of the emerging school of muckraker journalism, she exploited the public abuse angles. Her evidence that Rockefeller used unfair and illegal tactics was compelling, and it made dramatic reading.

With reform-minded Theodore Roosevelt new in the White House, the government was already pressing Rockefeller to change his ways. During Roosevelt's two terms, 44 antitrust suits were started, including one, inspired by Ida Tarbell's series, against Standard Oil. Rockefeller fought the action but lost before the U.S. Supreme Court. Standard Oil of New Jersey was dissolved in 1911. The name *Standard Oil* survived another 90 years only as a multitude of separate companies that, under terms of the 1911 Supreme Court ruling, were geographically limited in where they could do business.

Muckraking. The classic early investigative journalism was Ida Tarbell's 19-part series on abusive monopolistic practices by John D. Rockefeller's Standard Oil. The series began in McClure's magazine in 1902.

WHAT DO YOU THINK?

▶ In what news outlets would Ida Tarbell's muckraking find a home today? Your local newspaper? *Time* or *Newsweek*? CNN? *Mother Jones*? The *Wall Street Journal*?

▶ Muckraking continues to serve public interests as a significant journalism genre. What recent examples can you list?

Katrina disaster that came true three years later. Government didn't do anything at the federal, state or local level.

LEARNING CHECK ◀ ···

▶ **All reporting results from inquiry. What sets investigative reporting apart?**

▶ **List five examples of investigative reporting that have affected history.**

SOFT NEWS

● **soft news**
Geared to satisfying, audience's information wants, not needs

In contrast to hard investigative reporting came a simultaneous trend toward **soft news.** This includes consumer-help stories, lifestyle tips, entertainment news and offbeat gee-whiz items often of a sensational sort. The celebrity-oriented *National Enquirer*, whose circulation skyrocketed in the 1960s, was the progenitor of the trend. Time-Life launched *People* magazine. The staid New York *Times* created *Us*. Newspaper research found that readers like soft stuff. Soon many dailies added "People" columns. The television show *Entertainment Tonight* focuses on glamour and glitz, usually as a lead-in to the evening news on many local stations.

Traditionalists decry the space that soft news takes in many newspapers today, but hard news remains part of the product mix.

LEARNING CHECK ◄···

▶ **In what divergent directions is news moving today?**

▶ **How has live reporting changed journalism, in contrast to eras when newspapers were dominant?**

▶ **How has 24/7 coverage changed news?**

Chapter Wrap-Up

Journalism Traditions (Page 260)

■ In the colonial period the people made a hero of John Peter Zenger, whose newspaper represented an anti-Establishment voice. The tradition continues of U.S. news media as an independent voice apart from government. In 1833, a century after Zenger, fast-growing cities created the first mass audiences. In the new penny papers, facts trumped opinion in vying for space and spawned the idea that news reporting should be values-free. Later came the sensationalism of the so-called yellow press, which continues as part of American journalism.

Concept of News (Page 267)

■ News is a report on change that journalists deem most worth their audience's attention. In the United States there is a high premium on a detached, neutral presentation in which reporters keep their presence as much in the background as they can. The emphasis generally is on the story, not the storyteller, even though the reporter's role in seeking and organizing stories requires judgments that are subjective and flow from personal values.

Personal Values in News (Page 270)

■ Since news cannot be values-free, the question is what values do journalists bring to their work? Values include those that prevail in the society. In the United States these include broad values often taken for granted, like family, education and health. Studies have found other values that flavor American journalism. These include a national ethnocentrism, a commitment to democracy and capitalism, a romanticism about rural and small-town lifestyles, a favoring of individualism tempered by moderation, and a commitment to social order.

Variables Affecting News (Page 275)

■ Practical matters shape much of what appears in the news. How much space is there in an edition? Never enough to tell all that journalists would like to tell. Time on a newscast? Never enough either. Nor does the audience have the time to be engaged in everything that gets reported. Also, more stories are worth telling than any news organization has the staff and resources to pursue.

Confidential Sources (Page 277)

■ Journalists like to attribute their stories to credible sources, telling audiences where their information comes from. Sometimes, though, sources insist on confidentiality. Whistle-blowers, for example, might fear for their jobs. So-called *leakers* can have motivations as divergent as performing a duty as a good citizen to playing dirty-trick politics. Journalists have devised ways to report stories from confidential sources, but these are not without difficulties. Some journalists have gone to jail to shield their sources when instructed by a judge to reveal the names. Great reporting can mean jail time.

Journalism Trends (Page 279)

■ Journalism is going in many directions. Lengthy treatments, typified by *Wall Street Journal* lead stories every day and television network documentaries, are long-form journalism—labor-intensive to produce but often with breakthrough revelations. At another extreme are snippets sometimes only a couple lines long that are packaged in radio newscasts. The advent of 24/7 news on television and the Web has stretched the resources of many newsrooms. With a limited number of reporters being asked to repackage stories for multiple outlets, there has been a shift to stories that are quicker to report. The result: A decline in significant enterprise reporting that takes major commitments of newsroom time and resources.

REVIEW QUESTIONS

1. What contemporary news practices are rooted in the major periods in U.S. journalism history?

2. How are all journalists captives of the personal values they bring to their work?

3. What variables about news gathering and news packaging are beyond the control of reporters and even editors but nonetheless affect what people read, hear and see?

4. What pressures from outside the media affect news reporting?

5. What are good arguments for and against news reporters accepting and using information from confidential sources?

6. Trends in news reporting are going in divergent directions. Why? Evaluate these trends and their long-term prospects.

CONCEPTS

gatekeeper (Page 279)

news (Page 267)

objectivity (Page 268)

soft news (Page 283)

yellow period (Page 265)

TERMS

Alien and Sedition acts (Page 262)

investigative reporting (Page 282)

Watergate (Page 282)

PEOPLE

James Gordon Bennett (Page 263)

Carl Bernstein, Bob Woodward (Page 282)

Benjamin Day (Page 262)

Herbert Gans (Page 271)

John Peter Zenger (Page 261)

MEDIA SOURCES

- Joe Strupp. "What Gives?" *Editor & Publisher* (May 2007), pages 36–44.
- William David Sloan, editor. *The Media in America,* sixth edition. Vision Press, 2005. This textbook is the standard for U.S. media history.
- David Wallkis, editor. *Killed: Great Journalism Too Hot to Print.* Nation, 2004. Wallis has compiled great magazine articles that never made it to print, mostly to avoid litigation or not to offend advertisers or the editors' sensitivities. Among the stricken are works by Betty Friedan, George Orwell and Terry Southern.
- Bob Woodward and Carl Bernstein. *All the President's Men.* Simon & Schuster, 1974. The reporters' own chronicle of the obstacles they overcame in the classic unfolding series of investigative reports in the Nixon Watergate scandal.

In this chapter you have deepened your media literacy by revisiting several themes. Here are thematic highlights from the chapter:

Mass Audience. *Ben Day, publisher of the* Sun, *the best known of the penny papers, chose stories for their broad appeal.*

Media Technology

News as we know it today did not exist before the 1830s and 1840s, when presses were invented to produce thousands of copies an hour. The question became: What content will sell all this product? Stories on current events displaced the opinion thrust that had marked earlier papers. In the 1920s when broadcasting was introduced, stories became briefer. Internet technology is now changing the rules again, with many mainstream news media conventions being ignored in the shaping and exchanging of information. Whether these changes are merely amateur-hour bloggers breaking rules they never knew is unclear. Some changes may have long futures. **(Pages 260–264 and 279–284)**

Media Economics

Because news companies cannot survive without audiences, the quest to deliver content that attracts audiences is never-ending—and also competitive. Recent years have seen a rise in celebrity news, mostly inconsequential but followed avidly. This is an example of news following the dollar. Economics also shapes news in other ways. To varying degrees, news companies are cautious about reporting events and issues that might offend their advertisers. The issue is whether serving the audience or serving advertisers comes first. In some newsrooms, it's an easy call. In others, advertisers usually win out. **(Pages 275–276)**

Celebrity News. *The Associated Press experimented with a blackout on partygoing celebrity Paris Hilton. The blackout lasted one week. Not a single AP subscribing media outlet complained. But other news organizations continued pouring out Paris copy. The AP rejoined the mania but promises a case-by-case assessment of newsworthiness.*

Global Warming. *Al Gore got everyone's attention with* An Inconvenient Truth. *Now global warming and the environment are hot-button issues in the news.*

Media and Democracy

An independent streak has been present in American news media going back to Ben Harris. Government banned Harris' *Publick Occurrences* in 1690 after one issue. Although Ben Harris' paper hardly contributed to the making of public policy, the independence of the news media became an enduring and important element in U.S. democracy. News media convey information, ideas and opinions that enable the people to participate in the creation of public policy. The mechanisms of participation are uneven, but without them the people would be woefully lacking in what they need to know to participate in governance. Democracy needs an independent media. **(Pages 274–275 and 282–283)**

Media Effects

The news media can have powerful effects. The resignation of Alberto Gonzales as attorney general in 2007 was fueled by the news coverage in which he demonstrated continuing ineptness. The 1971 Watergate scandal that sent Richard Nixon packing midterm was the result of news coverage of dirty tricks and deceits that he and his lieutenants committed. Today, news coverage of the pending global-warming disaster is mobilizing public alarm, which is translating into public policy reform. (Pages 282–283)

Watergate. *Richard Nixon did it to himself, but the news media were catalysts that led to his resignation.*

Elitism and Populism

Publications in the early days of the Republic were too expensive for most people. Articles were narrowly focused. These publications were forums where the thinkers and ideologues of the time shared their views. The political, economic and not un-

"It Shines for All." *Ben Day's motto for his New York* Sun *in 1833 captured his innovation—a newspaper for everyone, a true mass audience.*

commonly philosophical thrust was elitist. The commercialization of newspapers, with the mass audience beginning in the 1830s, sparked a shift to news of interest to all strata of society. Ben Day's motto for his New York *Sun* in 1833 said it all: "It Shines for All." The beginning of marketing that relied on advertising, which changed the financial base of newspapers from subscriptions to advertisers, made it essential economically that news be found to attract and keep as many readers as possible. Advertisers went with papers with the largest circulations. (Pages 260–267)

Divergent Paths. *Long-form journalism survives amid the emergence of softer, briefer, less consequential news. The* Wall Street Journal, *for example, has a huge audience for seriousness and depth.*

Media Future

No media maven has all the answers on where the news media are headed. Trends point in no single direction. Faster-pace lifestyles and spare-time diversions are robbing people of time once spent tracking news. The upshot is briefer coverage that's often superficial. At the same time, news junkies abound. Long-form journalism thrives on national and specialized subjects, albeit not so much in local daily coverage. A major change involves the around-the-clock news cycle, particularly with CNN and other cable channels and the Internet. The competition to be first is changing reporting conventions. Not long ago reporters had time, albeit not much, to think and assess their reportage before telling their stories. Today more and more reporting is going live—now. (Pages 279–284)

12

Public Relations

Media Relations

Peter Diamantis envisions the next NASCAR, this time in the air—race pilots firing their rocket engines in spurts, trailing 20-foot flames, as they jockey Star Wars-like mini-planes around a 3-D trackway 5,000 feet up while excited fans, thousands of them, all paying admission, crane their necks to track the aerial dueling. Millions more would follow on television. Years ago Diamantis, a spaceflight enthusiast, founded the $10 million X Prize for suborbital competition. As Diamantis sees it, the next stage for getting the human species into space is to spread his excitement about the prospects. What better model than NASCAR, which stirs the adrenaline of millions of people. For his Rocket Racing League, Diamantis faces new financial and technological hurdles. Those he is solving.

He also needs public relations.

The promotion machine is rolling. At a 2005 media event, Diamantis unveiled the X-Racer, what he calls the planes, at the league's Las Cruces, New Mexico, spaceport. Space shuttle commander Rick Seafoss was there as chief pilot. In 2006, with four prototype racers, the league took off. The pilots, each with only three minutes of fuel, jockeyed to surpass each other by igniting their engines, then gliding, then restarting over and over again as they roared and soared through virtual tunnels in the sky at 200-plus miles an hour. "It's really the mix of NASCAR excitement and spaceflight," Diamantis said. His enthusiasm and sound bites were perfect. So was partner Granger Whitelaw, an Indianapolis 500 veteran: "It is nothing like a NASCAR or Indy car—it's 10 times louder."

LEARNING AHEAD

■ Public relations is a persuasive communication tool that uses mass media.

■ Public relations grew out of public disfavor with big business.

■ Public relations is an important management tool.

■ Public relations includes promotion, publicity, lobbying, fund-raising and crisis management.

■ Advertising and public relations are distinctive undertakings.

■ Public relations usually involves a candid, proactive relationship with mass media.

■ Public relations organizations are working to improve the image of their craft.

Media Relations. *Publicity and media relations are key for bringing attention to the new NASCAR-like sport of rocket racing. The promoters' long-term goal is to generate public enthusiasm for space travel.*

Peter Diamantis.
Jockeys of his X-Racers fire their rocket engines in spurts as they loop a circuit before bleachers of fans.

Seafoss was at no loss for sound bites either, calling the crafts "fire-breathing dragons."

In media event after media event, Diamantis and his partners skillfully built enthusiasm for rocket racing. There were demonstrations of the technology. There were attention-getting announcements, like signing Erik Lindbergh, grandson of pioneer aviator Charles Lindbergh, as a Rocket Racing League pilot. Then came the unveiling of handheld global-positioning tracking devices for spectators to add another dimension to their stadium experience. Onboard cameras compound the verisimilitude. No less spectacular were introductions of the satellite-navigation technology to keep planes from colliding, albeit only a few hundred feet apart. Then came the introduction of virtual X-Racing, a video game for fans to race alongside actual flyers during races—all, as Diamantis explained, to engage public interest in human spaceflight.

In many ways Diamantis is his own best promoter, his passion for space travel a consistent theme. The Rocket Racing League, however, is a complex endeavor. Professionals in public relations, who understand how to attract media attention and to craft media messages, are an essential component.

Importance of Public Relations

STUDY PREVIEW

Public relations is a persuasive communication tool that people can use to motivate other people and institutions to help them achieve their goals.

DEFINING PUBLIC RELATIONS

● **Edward Bernays**
Early public relations practitioner whose practice and scholarship helped define the field

● **public relations**
A management tool to establish beneficial relationships

The public relations pioneer **Edward Bernays** lamented how loosely the term **public relations** is used. To illustrate his concern, Bernays told about a young woman who approached him for career advice. He asked her what she did for a living. "I'm in public relations," she said. He pressed her for details, and she explained that she handed out circulars in Harvard Square. Bernays was dismayed at how casually people regard the work of public relations. There are receptionists and secretaries who list public relations on their résumés. To some people, public relations is glad-handing, backslapping and smiling prettily to make people feel good. Public relations, however, goes far beyond good interpersonal skills. A useful definition is that public relations is a management tool for leaders in business, government and other institutions to establish beneficial *relationships* with other institutions and groups. Four steps are necessary for public relations to accomplish its goals:

■ **Identify Existing Relationships.** In modern society, institutions have many relationships. A college, for example, has relationships with its students, its faculty, its staff, its alumni, its benefactors, the neighborhood, the community, the legislature, other colleges, accreditors of its programs, perhaps unions. The list could go on and on. Each of these constituencies is called a public—hence the term *public relations*.

■ Evaluate the Relationships. Through research, the public relations practitioner studies these relationships to determine how well they are working. This evaluation is an ongoing process. A college may have excellent relations with the legislature one year and win major appropriations, but after a scandal related to the president's budget the next year, legislators may be downright unfriendly.

■ Design Policies to Improve the Relationships. The job of public relations people is to recommend policies to top management to make these relationships work better, not only for the organization but also for the partners in each relationship. **Paul Garrett,** a pioneer in corporate relations, found that General Motors was seen in unfriendly terms during the Great Depression, which put the giant automaker at risk with many publics, including its own employees. GM, he advised, needed new policies to seem neighborly—rather than as a far-removed, impersonal, monolithic industrial giant.

■ Implement the Policies. Garrett used the term **enlightened self-interest** for his series of policies intended to downsize GM in the eyes of many of the company's publics. Garrett set up municipal programs in towns with GM plants and grants for schools and scholarships for employees' children. General Motors benefited from a revised image, and in the spirit of enlightened self-interest, so did GM employees, their children and their communities.

Public relations is not a mass medium itself, but PR often uses the media as tools to accomplish its goals. To announce GM's initiatives to change its image in the 1930s, Paul Garrett issued news releases that he hoped newspapers, magazines and radio stations would pick up. The number of people in most of the publics with which public relations practitioners need to communicate is so large that it can be reached only through the mass media. The influence of public relations on the news media is extensive. Half of the news in many newspapers originates with formal statements or news releases from organizations that want something in the paper. It is the same with radio and television.

LEARNING CHECK ◄ •••

▶ **What does it mean to describe public relations as a management function?**

▶ **What did Paul Garrett mean by the term** *enlightened self-interest?*

PUBLIC RELATIONS IN DEMOCRACY

Misconceptions about public relations include the idea that it is a one-way street for institutions and individuals to communicate to the public. Actually, the good practice of public relations seeks two-way communication between and among all the people and institutions concerned with an issue.

A task force established by the **Public Relations Society of America** to explore the stature and role of the profession concluded that public relations has the potential to improve the functioning of democracy by encouraging the exchange of information and ideas on public issues. The task force said public relations practitioners:

- Communicate the interests of an institution to the public, which broadens and enriches public dialogue.
- Seek mutual adjustments through dialogue between institutions in the society, which benefits the public.
- Create a safety valve for society by helping work out accommodations between competing interests, reducing the likelihood of coercion or arbitrary action.
- Activate the social conscience of organizations with which they work.

LEARNING CHECK ◄ •••

▶ **Draw on your knowledge and experience for examples of public relations serving the democratic ideal of the fullest dialogue on important issues.**

● **Paul Garrett**
Devised the notion of enlightened self-interest

● **enlightened self-interest**
Mutually beneficial public relations

● **Public Relations Society of America**
Professional public relations association

At one of the most precarious times in U.S. history, the Great Depression, Paul Garrett led public relations in new directions to win public support. Amid worries that people—many hungry, all distressed—would see huge corporations as scapegoats and perhaps upend capitalism, Garrett had an unprecedented challenge as General Motors' public relations chief. How precarious was the situation? Sit-down strikes were occurring at GM plants. Discontent was bubbling throughout the country.

Garrett, in the first generation of public relations people who had learned their craft from the government's Creel Committee in World War I, immediately sought to minimize the image of General Motors as some sort of monolithic giant that, being big and distant, was an especially easy target for hate.

To head off problems, Garrett introduced a public strategy: *enlightened self-interest*. It was in GM's self-interest, he argued, to touch the lives of people in personal ways, such as with grants for local schools and scholarships for employees' children. General Motors, of course, nurtured publicity about these corporate good deeds.

Garrett summed it up this way: "The challenge that faces us is to shake off our lethargy and through public relations make the American plan of industry stick. For unless the contributions of

Enlightened Self-Interest. *Paul Garrett, a pioneer in corporate public relations, encouraged General Motors to act both in its corporate interest and in the interest of employees and other constituencies. It is possible to serve multiple masters, Garrett said. He called his approach to public relations enlightened self-interest.*

the system are explained to consumers in terms of their own interest, the system itself will not stand against the storm of fallacies that rides the air."

Garrett also worked on GM's image at a macro level, aiming for consumers

in general to think well of the company. A GM caravan, called the Parade of Progress, traveled from coast to coast in 1936 with a message that new technologies would facilitate progress and social change. In the same spirit, prominent radio announcer Lowell Thomas narrated a feature film, *Previews of Science*, that cast business, big business in particular, in heroic terms. In short, the genius of corporate science and initiative was creating a better tomorrow.

The National Association of Manufacturers caught Garrett's spirit. Garrett worked with the association to tie the public impression of big corporations into warm, albeit fuzzy, notions about Americanism. At a 1939 meeting, the association's public relations division, with Garrett on board, said that its job was to "link free enterprise in the public consciousness with free speech, free press and free religion as integral parts of democracy."

Public relations had become widely embraced as a way to channel the thinking of the country.

WHAT DO YOU THINK?

▶ Paul Garrett's term *enlightened self-interest* has been preserved in the PR lexicon. Why?

▶ Why are behavior and actions as essential to public relations as words?

Origins of Public Relations

STUDY PREVIEW

Many big companies found themselves in disfavor in the late 1800s for ignoring the public good to make profits. Feeling misunderstood, some moguls of industry turned to Ivy Lee, the founder of modern public relations, for counsel on gaining public support.

● **William Henry Vanderbilt**
Embodied the bad corporate images of the 1880s, 1890s with "The public be damned"

MOGULS IN TROUBLE

Nobody would be tempted to think of **William Henry Vanderbilt** as having been good at public relations. In 1882 it was Vanderbilt, president of the New York

Central Railroad, who, when asked about the effect of changing train schedules, said: "The public be damned." Vanderbilt's utterance so infuriated people that it became a banner in the populist crusade against robber barons and tycoons in the late 1800s. Under populist pressure, state governments set up agencies to regulate railroads. Then the federal government established the Interstate Commerce Commission to control freight and passenger rates. Government began insisting on safety standards. Labor unions formed in the industries with the worst working conditions, safety records and pay. Journalists added pressure with muckraking exposés on excesses in the railroad, coal and oil trusts; on meat-packing industry frauds; and on patent medicines.

The leaders of industry were slow to recognize the effect of populist objections on their practices. They were comfortable with **social Darwinism,** an adaptation of **Charles Darwin**'s survival-of-the-fittest theory. In fact, they thought themselves forward-thinking in applying Darwin's theory to business and social issues. It had been only a few decades earlier, in 1859, that Darwin had laid out his biological theory in *On the Origin of Species by Means of Natural Selection.* To cushion the harshness of social Darwinism, many tycoons espoused paternalism toward those whose "fitness" had not brought them fortune and power. No matter how carefully put, paternalism seemed arrogant to the "less fit."

George Baer, a railroad president, epitomized both social Darwinism and paternalism in commenting on a labor strike: "The rights and interests of the laboring man will be protected and cared for not by labor agitators but by the Christian men to whom God in His infinite wisdom has given the control of the property interests of the country." Baer was quoted widely, further fueling sentiment against big business. Baer may have been sincere, but his position was read as a cover for excessive business practices by barons who assumed superiority to everyone else.

Meanwhile, social Darwinism came under attack as circuitous reasoning: Economic success accomplished by abusive practices could be used to justify further abusive practices, which would lead to further success. Social Darwinism was a dog-eat-dog outlook that hardly jibed with democratic ideals, especially not as described in the preamble to the U.S. Constitution, which sought to "promote the general welfare, and secure the blessings of liberty" for everyone—not for only the chosen "fittest." Into these tensions at the turn of the century came public relations pioneer Ivy Lee.

LEARNING CHECK ◄ ••

▶ **How was social Darwinism appealing to religious people who found themselves with massive wealth while others suffered at their expense?**

THE IDEAS OF IVY LEE

Coal mine operators, like railroad magnates, were held in the public's contempt at the start of the 1900s. Obsessed with profits, caring little about public sentiment or even the well-being of their employees, mine operators were vulnerable to critics in the growing populist political movement. Mine workers organized, and 150,000 in Pennsylvania went on strike in 1902, shutting down the anthracite industry and disrupting coal-dependent industries, including the railroads. The mine owners snubbed reporters, which probably contributed to a pro-union slant in many news stories and worsened the owners' public image. Six months into the strike, President Theodore Roosevelt threatened to take over the mines with Army troops. The mine owners settled.

Shaken finally by Roosevelt's threat and recognizing Roosevelt's responsiveness to public opinion, the mine operators began reconsidering how they went about their business. In 1906, with another strike looming, one operator heard about **Ivy Lee,** a young publicist in New York who had new ideas about winning public support. He was hired. In a turnabout in press relations, Lee issued a news release that announced: "The anthracite coal operators, realizing the general public interest in conditions in the mining regions, have arranged to supply the press with all

● social Darwinism
Application to society of Darwin's survival-of-the-fittest theory

● Charles Darwin
Devised survival-of-the-fittest theory

● Ivy Lee
Laid out fundamentals of public relations

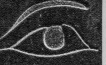

PUBLIC RELATIONS MILESTONES

PIVOTAL EVENTS

1800s

Promotional Excesses
P. T. Barnum made huckster promotion a high art (1870s)

"The Public Be Damned"
Yes, incredibly, railroad titan William Henry Vanderbilt said it (1882)

**1900–
1949**

Ivy Lee
Founder of first public relations agency (1906)

George Creel
Head of first government public relations agency (1917)

Edward Bernays
Wrote *Crystallizing Public Opinion* (1923)

Arthur Page
First corporate public relations vice president (1927)

Paul Garrett
Created term *enlightened self-interest* (1930s)

Office of War Information
Elmer Davis headed federal agency to generate war support (1942)

**1950–
1999**

Ethics
Public Relations Society of America ethics code (1951)

Accreditation
PRSA accreditation system (1965)

Strike-Back PR
Herb Schmertz pioneered adversarial practices (1970s)

Tylenol Crisis
Classic campaign aided recovery from product-tampering crisis (1982)

Integrated Marketing
Attempt to subsume public relations into marketing (1990s–)

2000s

Consolidation
Advertising agencies bought up many public relations agencies to broaden client services (2002)

Dialogics
Scholars applied dialogic theory to public relations (2002)

Lobbying Scandal
Washington master lobbyist Jack Abramoff went to jail (2006)

Large-scale public relations: Government rallies public enthusiasm for World War I

Tylenol scare: Model case study in public relations

Jack Abramoff, lobbyist bad boy gets prison time

- Public education took root as a social value (1820s)
- Charles Darwin wrote *Origin of Species* (1859)
- U.S. Civil War (1861–1864)
- Rise of banks, major corporations (1870s–)
- Populist political movement aimed against monopolies (1880s–)
- Samuel Gompers formed predecessor of American Federation of Labor (1881)
- Social Darwinism used to justify corporate excesses (1890s)
- Labor crisis in coal industry (1902)
- Ludlow Massacre (1914)
- Right to vote extended to women (1920)
- Great Depression (1930s)
- World War II (1941–1945)

- Korean War (1950–1953)
- Vietnam War (1964–1973)
- Humans reached moon (1969)

- 9/11 terrorist attacks (2001)
- Iraq War (2003–)
- Hurricane Katrina (2005)

possible information." Then followed a series of releases with information attributed to the mine operators by name—the same people who earlier had preferred anonymity and refused all interview requests. There were no more secret strike-strategy meetings. When operators planned a meeting, reporters covering the impending strike were informed. Although reporters were not admitted into the meetings, summaries of the proceedings were given to them immediately afterward. This relative openness eased long-standing hostility toward the operators, and a strike was averted.

Lee's success with the mine operators began a career that rewrote the rules on how corporations deal with their various publics. Among his accomplishments:

■ **Institutional Openness.** Railroads had notoriously secretive policies not only about their business practices but even about accidents. When the Pennsylvania Railroad sought Ivy Lee's counsel, he advised against suppressing news—especially on things that inevitably would leak out anyway. When a train jumped the rails near Gap, Pennsylvania, Lee arranged for a special car to take reporters to the scene and even take pictures. The Pennsylvania line was applauded in the press for the openness, and coverage of the railroad, which had been negative for years, began changing. A "bad press" continued plaguing other railroads that persisted in their secretive tradition.

■ **Finding Upbeat Angles.** When the U.S. Senate proposed investigating International Harvester for monopolistic practices, Lee advised the giant farm implement manufacturer against reflexive obstructionism and silence. A statement went out announcing that the company, confident in its business practices, not only welcomed but also would facilitate an investigation. Then began a campaign that pointed out International Harvester's beneficence toward its employees. The campaign also emphasized other upbeat information about the company.

■ **Giving Organizations a Face.** In 1914, when workers at a Colorado mine went on strike, company guards fired machine guns and killed several men. More battling

Ivy Lee

Ludlow Massacre. *Colorado militiamen, called in to augment company guards, opened fire during a 1914 mine labor dispute and killed women and children. Overnight, John D. Rockefeller Jr. became the object of public hatred. It was a Rockefeller company that owned the mine. Even in New York, where Rockefeller lived, there were rallies demanding his head. Public relations pioneer Ivy Lee advised Rockefeller to tour the Ludlow area as soon as tempers cooled to show his sincere concern and to begin work on a labor contract to meet the concerns of miners. Rockefeller ended up a popular character in the Colorado mining camps.*

followed, during which two women and 11 children were killed. It was called the **Ludlow Massacre,** and **John D. Rockefeller Jr.,** the chief mine owner, was pilloried for what had happened. Rockefeller was an easy target. Like his father, widely despised for the earlier Standard Oil monopolistic practices, John Jr. tried to keep himself out of the spotlight, but suddenly mobs were protesting at his mansion in New York and calling out, "Shoot him down like a dog." Rockefeller asked Ivy Lee what he should do. Lee began whipping up articles about Rockefeller's human side, his family and his generosity. Then, on Lee's advice, Rockefeller announced that he would visit Colorado to see conditions himself. He spent two weeks talking with miners at work and in their homes and meeting their families. It was a news story that reporters could not resist, and it unveiled Rockefeller as a human being, not a far-removed, callous captain of industry. A myth-shattering episode occurred one evening when Rockefeller, after a brief address to miners and their wives, suggested that the floor be cleared for a dance. Before it was all over, John D. Rockefeller Jr. had danced with almost every miner's wife, and the news stories about the evening did a great deal to mitigate antagonism and distrust toward Rockefeller. Back in New York, with Lee's help, Rockefeller put together a proposal for a grievance procedure, which he asked the Colorado miners to approve. It was ratified overwhelmingly.

■ **Straight Talk.** Ivy Lee came on the scene at a time when many organizations were making extravagant claims about themselves and their products. Circus promoter **P. T. Barnum** made this kind of **puffery** a fine art in the late 1800s, and he had many imitators. It was an age of *puffed-up* advertising claims and fluffy rhetoric. Lee noted, however, that people soon saw through hyperbolic boasts and lost faith in those who made them. In launching his public relations agency in 1906, Lee vowed to be accurate in everything he said and to provide whatever verification anyone requested. This became part of the creed of good practice in public relations, and it remains so today.

LEARNING CHECK ◄

▸ How did public relations pioneer Ivy Lee help revolutionize they way business conducted itself in the early 1900s?

▸ What are enduring pillars of Ivy Lee's concept of good business practice?

PUBLIC RELATIONS ON A NEW SCALE

The potential of public relations to rally support for a cause was demonstrated on a gigantic scale during World War I and again during World War II.

■ **World War I.** In 1917 President Woodrow Wilson, concerned about widespread anti-war sentiment, asked **George Creel** to head a new government agency whose job was to make the war popular. The Committee on Public Information, better known as the Creel Committee, cranked out news releases, magazine pieces, posters, even movies. A list of 75,000 local speakers was put together to talk nationwide at school programs, church groups and civic organizations about making the world safe for democracy. More than 15,000 committee articles were printed. Never before had public relations been attempted on such a scale—and it worked. World War I became a popular cause even to the point of inspiring people to buy Liberty Bonds, putting up their own money to finance the war outside the usual taxation apparatus.

■ **World War II.** When World War II began, an agency akin to the Creel Committee was formed. Veteran journalist **Elmer Davis** was put in charge. The new Office of War Information was public relations on a bigger scale than ever before.

The Creel and Davis committees employed hundreds of people. Davis had 250 employees handling news releases alone. These staff members, mostly young,

Sidebar terms:

● **Ludlow Massacre**
Colorado tragedy that Ivy Lee converted into a public relations victory

● **John D. Rockefeller Jr.**
Ivy client who had been the target of public hatred

● **P. T. Barnum**
Known for exaggerated promotion

● **puffery**
Inflated claims

● **George Creel**
Demonstrated that public relations works on a mammoth scale; in World War I

● **Elmer Davis**
Led Office of War Information in World War II

War Popular. World War I did not begin as a popular cause with Americans. There were antidraft riots in many cities. This prompted President Woodrow Wilson to ask journalist George Creel to launch a major campaign to persuade Americans that the war was important to make the world safe for democracy. Within months Americans were financing much of the war voluntarily by buying government bonds. This poster was only one aspect of Creel's work, which demonstrated that public relations principles could be applied on a massive scale.

George Creel

carried new lessons about public relations into the private sector after the war. These were the people who shaped corporate public relations as we know it today.

LEARNING CHECK ◄ ··

▶ How did George Creel contribute to the expansion of public relations?

▶ What happened to the thousands of people on George Creel's payroll after World War I?

Structure of Public Relations

STUDY PREVIEW

In developing sound policies, corporations and other institutions depend on public relations experts who are sensitive to the implications of policy on the public consciousness. This makes public relations a vital management function. Besides a role in policymaking, public relations people play key roles in carrying out institutional policy.

POLICY ROLE OF PUBLIC RELATIONS

● **Arthur Page**
Established the role of public relations as a top management tool

When giant AT&T needed somebody to take over public relations in 1927, the president of the company went to magazine editor **Arthur Page** and offered him a vice presidency. Before accepting, Page laid out several conditions. One was that he have a voice in AT&T policy. Page was hardly on an ego trip. Rather, he had seen too many corporations that regarded their public relations arm merely as an executor of policy. Page considered PR itself as a management function. To be effective, Page knew that he must contribute to the making of high-level corporate decisions as well as executing them.

Today, experts on public relations agree with Arthur Page's concept: When institutions are making policy, they need to consider the effects on their many publics. That can be done best when the person in charge of public relations, ideally at the vice presidential level, is intimately involved in decision making. The public relations executive advises the rest of the institution's leaders on public perceptions and the effects that policy options might have on perceptions. Also, the public relations vice president is in a better position to implement the institution's policy for having been a part of developing it.

LEARNING CHECK ◄ ···

▶ **What is the role of public relations at the policymaking level of an institution?**

HOW PUBLIC RELATIONS IS ORGANIZED

No two institutions are organized in precisely the same way. At General Motors 200 people work in public relations. In smaller organizations PR may be one of several hats worn by a single person. Except in the smallest operations, the public relations department usually has three functional areas of responsibility:

■ **External Public Relations.** Public relations helps organizations engage with groups and people outside the organization. These include customers, dealers, suppliers, community leaders and policymakers.

■ **Internal Public Relations.** Organizations need internal communication for optimal relations among employees, managers, unions, shareholders and other internal constituencies. In-house newsletters, magazines and brochures are common elements in internal public relations.

■ **Media Relations.** For communication with large groups, organizations rely largely on mass media. It is media relations people who respond to news reporters' queries, arrange news conferences, issue statements to the news media and often serve as an organization's spokespersons.

LEARNING CHECK ◄ ···

▶ **Would you classify media relations more as an external or an internal public relations function?**

PUBLIC RELATIONS AGENCIES

● **public relations agencies**
Companies that provide public relations services

Even though many organizations have their own public relations staff, they may go to **public relations agencies** for help on specific projects or problems. In the United States today, hundreds of companies specialize in public relations counsel and related services. It is a big business. Income at global PR agencies like Burson-Marsteller runs about $200 million a year.

The biggest agencies offer a full range of services on a global scale. These agencies will take on projects anywhere in the world, either on their own or by working with local agencies.

These are the largest agencies with significant U.S. accounts:

	Global Income	Employees Worldwide
Edelman	$261 million	1,800
Ruder Finn	92 million	600
Waggener Edstrom	84 million	600
APCO	73 million	400
Text 100	52 million	500

Some agencies bill clients only for services rendered. Others charge clients just to be on call. Hill & Knowlton, for example, has a minimum $5,000-a-month retainer fee. Agency expenses for specific projects are billed in addition. Staff time usually is charged at an hourly rate that covers the agency's overhead and allows a profit margin. Other expenses are usually billed with a 15 to 17 percent markup.

LEARNING CHECK ◀ ....

▶ When does an organization with its own public relations operation need also to hire an outside public relations agency?

Public Relations Services

STUDY PREVIEW

Public relations deals with publicity and promotion, but it also involves less visible activities. These include lobbying, fund-raising and crisis management. Public relations is distinct from advertising.

PUBLICITY AND PROMOTION

● **publicity**
Brings public attention to something

● **promotion**
Promoting a cause, idea

Full-service public relations agencies provide a wide range of services built on two of the cornerstones of the business: **publicity** and **promotion.** These agencies are ready to conduct media campaigns to rally support for a cause, create an image or turn a problem into an asset. Publicity and promotion, however, are only the most visible services offered by public relations agencies.

LOBBYING

● **lobbying**
Influencing public policy, usually legislation or regulations

No doubt about it, **lobbying** is a growth industry. Every state capital has hundreds of public relations practitioners whose speciality is representing their clients to legislative bodies and government agencies. In North Dakota, hardly a populous state, more than 300 people are registered as lobbyists in the capital city of Bismarck. The number of registered lobbyists in Washington, D.C., exceeds 10,000 today. In addition, there are an estimated 20,000 other people in the nation's capital who have slipped through registration requirements but who nonetheless ply the halls of government to plead their clients' interests.

In one sense, lobbyists are expediters. They know local traditions and customs, and they know who is in a position to affect policy. Lobbyists advise their clients, which include trade associations, corporations, public interest groups and regulated utilities and industries, on how to achieve their goals by working with legislators and government regulators. Many lobbyists call themselves "government relations specialists."

LEARNING CHECK ◀ ....

▶ Why does lobbying have a bad name? Is it deserved? Undeserved?

POLITICAL COMMUNICATION

● **political communication**
Advising candidates and groups on public policy issues, usually in elections

Every capital has political consultants whose work is mostly advising candidates for public office in **political communication.** Services include campaign management, survey research, publicity, media relations and image consulting. Political consultants also work on elections, referendums, recalls and other public policy issues.

LEARNING CHECK ◀ ....

▶ Is it näive to think a candidate for federal or statewide office can succeed without political consultants?

In college Jack Abramoff was smitten with politics. From his base at Brandeis University, Abramoff rallied Massachusetts college students statewide for Ronald Reagan's presidential bid in 1980. Reagan took the state in an upset. On to Washington, Abramoff rose quickly in the national College Republicans, moving the organization into right-wing activism.

Not all went well. The College Republicans vastly overspent their budget with a poorly conceived direct-mail campaign in 1982. The party elders threw out the free-spending Abramoff. Unsuppressible, Abramoff found a spot running the privately funded Citizens for America, which campaigned for conservative causes. Under the group's banner Abramoff organized some audacious projects. His climactic accomplishment—a convention in a remote part of Angola for a motley bunch of anticommunist guerrillas from disparate Afghanistan, Laos and Nicaragua. The project was costly. The sugar daddy who financed Citizens for America fired Abramoff for taking too many liberties with the group's $3 million budget.

In all this, and in a checkered résumé of more Republican-related jobs, mostly in Washington, the young, energetic Abramoff made contacts. His reputation grew rapidly as one of the

Free-Spending Lobbyist.

most influential lobbyists on Capitol Hill and in numerous executive branch agencies.

By 2000, with Republicans controlling the federal government, Abramoff had amassed the biggest lobbying portfolio in Washington. For the right ambiance to make pitches to members of Congress and top aides and also to acknowledge favors, Abramoff opened two posh restaurants down the street from the Capitol. He bought a fleet of casino boats. He leased four arena and stadium skyboxes. He sponsored golf outings to exclusive

St. Andrews in Scotland and to the South Pacific.

The party began imploding in 2003 with revelations by Susan Schmidt of the Washington *Post*. Schmidt tracked $45 million in lobbying fees from Indian tribes that were desperate to protect their casino revenue from possible taxation. There were irregularities galore, including massive overbilling. Abramoff told one aide, for example, to find some way to bill a Choctaw band $150,000 one month: "Be sure we hit the $150k minimum. If you need to add time for me, let me know." The aide responded: "You only had two hours." Abramoff fired back: "Add 60 hours for me."

An avalanche of other revelations followed in what became one of the biggest congressional corruption scandals in history. The scandal was a centerpiece issue in the 2006 elections. Abramoff went to jail. It was not only a few members of Congress and their aides who worried about subpoenas for accepting Abramoff's largesse. For lobbyists who conduct themselves honorably, it all was an embarrassing sullying of their craft.

WHAT DO YOU THINK?

▶ If you were the judge, how would you have sentenced Jack Abramoff? Would you have set him free?

▶ Would you require public relations students to study Jack Abramoff's practices? Which lessons would you want them to learn?

IMAGE CONSULTING

A growing specialized branch of public relations has been image consulting. In the first energy crisis of the 1970s, oil companies realized that their side of the story wasn't getting across. These companies turned to image consultants to groom corporate spokespersons, often chief executives, to meet reporters one on one and go on talk shows. The groomers did a brisk business, and it paid off in countering the stories and rumors that were blaming the oil companies for skyrocketing fuel prices.

LEARNING CHECK ◄ . . . .

▶ What would Ivy Lee think of image consulting for top executives?

Crisis Management at *Time*

When *Time*'s cutting-edge journalism brings heat on the magazine, the Time Inc. senior vice president for corporate communications finds herself trying to set the facts straight from the company's perspective. In her job of handling media relations for the company, Dawn Bridges finds herself frequently put to the test.

In 2005, when *Time*'s editor decided to comply with a federal prosecutor's demand for reporter Matt Cooper's notes in the Valerie Plame spy-outing scandal, everyone was clamoring for an explanation. In effect, Cooper's notes revealed his confidential source. People wanted to know how *Time* could break the journalism standard of shielding confidential sources. Reporters were pounding at Bridges' door for answers.

The crisis was a career challenge for Bridges. Many supporters of the Iraq War shuddered that Matt Cooper's notes would put the leak close to President Bush himself. The journalism community was outraged at the handover of the notes. At the same time, many people in the judicial system were pleased. There was court pressure for the notes.

Too, there was the drama of New York *Times* reporter Judith Miller gaining heroic martyrdom for refusing to give up notes for her Plame stories. Miller had gone to jail in the name of good journalism. How could *Time* have sold out?

To new reporters, Bridges made her points on behalf of *Time:*

• **Unfair Comparison.** Bridges explained to reporters that critics were taking shortcuts with the facts in equating the Judith Miller and Matt Cooper subpoenas. The New York *Times* was never asked for Judith Miller's notes. Miller's decision to go to jail was hers alone—not that of the newspaper as her employer. In the Cooper case, *Time* magazine was subpoenaed. Although the distinction was not at the heart of the criticism of *Time*, Bridges called the situations apples and oranges: To lionize the New York *Times* and to pillory *Time*, she said, was misleading.

• **Unique Situation.** The journalistic standard to shield whistleblowers, she argued, was less the issue than dirty politics. The allegation under federal investigation was that a political partisan had leaked Plame's name to discredit revelations from her husband. He had criticized the rationale for the U.S. war against Iraq and angered the White House. "This," said Bridges, "was allegedly a case of a political partisan breaking a law about national security in a time of war for political gain." Bridges said the case was far from a typical whistleblowing confidential source issue.

Dawn Bridges. *Public relations challenges include explaining decisions that may not be popular with everyone.*

DEEPENING YOUR MEDIA LITERACY

Crisis management is one of the greatest challenges for public relations. By definition, crises are unexpected. Each has twists that could not have been anticipated and require sharp analytical and communication skills to address the crisis.

EXPLORE THE ISSUE

Go to your library or online to brief yourself on the facts of the case.

DIG DEEPER

Next, tap into the wealth of commentary on both sides of the issue. Online search terms include *Valerie Plane, Judith Miller,* and *Matt Cooper.*

WHAT DO YOU THINK?

If you were a journalist with grave doubts about *Time*'s decision to surrender Matt Cooper's notes, what questions would you put to Dawn Bridges in an interview to expand on the points she made in her statement? If you were in Bridges' position, how would you respond to these questions? And what further questions would those answers beg be asked?

Leslie Unger was there at the beginning, when in 1992 the Academy of Motion Picture Arts & Sciences created an in-house communication unit. In her early 20s, after a couple of entry-level public relations jobs, Unger found herself helping run logistics for the Academy Awards. Now, even after so many times through the annual Hollywood extravaganza, Unger at moments can't believe what she's in the middle of. She pinches herself in a reality check: "I'm at the Academy Awards!"

Working up to Oscar night occupies Unger full time-plus for five months beginning in November. Her usual seven-person staff is bulked up to 12 to handle news media requests for credentials. In recent years there have been 500 to 600 requests. Only about half are cleared.

For the audience, much of Unger's media-support work is invisible. She decides where individual reporters will be placed so they don't stumble over each other, at least not too much. Interview rooms need to look good on television. Even often-ratty pressrooms must be presentable. And are there enough jacks for bloggers and all the laptops?

Academy Awards Preparation. *Making Oscar night work right, look good.*

There are countless meetings with fire and security experts and art directors. The network covering the event has its own marketing and publicity team with which Unger must coordinate. To do it all, Unger has to bring in outside public relations help, most recently from the Dobbin/Bolgla agency in New York.

Unger learned publicity and event management out of college in the public affairs department of the Los Angeles County Public Works Department. Then for a year she was a junior account executive at Ruder Finn, a public relations agency, in Los Angeles. Ruder Finn had handled the Academy Awards account until 1992 when the Academy created an internal communications unit—and Unger joined the Academy payroll.

The five-month buildup to the climactic Oscar night hardly ends Unger's work. Countless queries come in for days, like, she says, "What was the instrument Sting played?" After a while, though, she moves into less hectic months, an interlude of sorts. She works on Academy programs to promote film appreciation and literacy and the Academy's film archives, and to encourage student moviemaking. Those activities include Unger generating a couple of new releases a week—although nothing like the two-a-day rate in the pre-Oscar months.

WHAT DO YOU THINK?

▶ Would college alone have prepared Leslie Unger to be the event coordinator of the Academy Awards?

▶ What career-building advice do you infer from Leslie Unger's experience?

FINANCIAL PUBLIC RELATIONS

In the 1920s and 1930s the U.S. Securities and Exchange Commission cracked down on abuses in the financial industry. Regulations on promoting sales of securities are complex. It is the job of people in financial PR to know not only the principles of public relations but also the complex regulations governing the promotion of securities in corporate mergers, acquisitions, new issues and stock splits.

CONTINGENCY PLANNING

● **contingency planning**
Developing programs in advance of an unscheduled but anticipated event

Many organizations rely on public relations people to design programs to address problems that can be expected to occur, known as **contingency planning.** Airlines, for example, need detailed plans for handling inevitable plane crashes—situations requiring quick, appropriate responses under tremendous pressure. When a crisis occurs, an organization can turn to public relations people for advice on dealing with it. Some agencies specialize in **crisis management,** which involves picking up the pieces either when a contingency plan fails or when there was no plan to deal with a crisis.

LEARNING CHECK ◄ ∙∙∙

▶ **If you were hired by an airline to design a contingency plan for an eventual inevitability of an accident, what would you lay out?**

POLLING

Public opinion sampling is essential in many public relations projects. Full-service agencies can either conduct surveys themselves or contract with companies that specialize in surveying.

EVENTS COORDINATION

Many public relations people are involved in coordinating a broad range of events, including product announcements, news conferences and convention planning. Some in-house public relations departments and agencies have their own artistic and audio-visual production talent to produce brochures, tapes and other promotional materials. Other agencies contract for these services.

Public Relations and Advertising

∙∙

STUDY PREVIEW

Although public relations and advertising both involve crafting media messages for mass audiences, public relations is involved in creating policy. Advertising is not. Even so, there has been a recent blending of the functions, some under the umbrella concept of integrated marketing.

DIFFERENT FUNCTIONS

Both public relations and advertising involve persuasion through the mass media, but most of the similarities end there.

■ **Management Function.** Public relations people help to shape an organization's policy. This is a management activity, ideally with the organization's chief public relations person offering counsel to other key policymakers at the vice presidential level. **Advertising,** in contrast, is not a management function. The work of advertising is much narrower. It focuses on developing persuasive messages, mostly to sell products or services, after all the management decisions have been made.

● **advertising**
Unlike public relations, advertising
seeks to sell a product or service

■ **Measuring Success.** Public relations "sells" points of view and images. These are intangibles and therefore are hard to measure. In advertising, success is measurable with tangibles, such as sales, that can be calculated from the bottom line.

■ **Control of Messages.** When an organization decides that it needs a persuasive campaign, there is a choice between public relations and advertising. One advantage of advertising is that the organization controls the message. By buying space or time in the mass media, an organization has the final say on the content of its advertising messages. In public relations, by contrast, an organization tries to influence the media to tell its story a certain way, but the message that actually goes out is up to the media. For example, a news reporter may lean heavily on a public relations person for information about an organization, but the reporter also may gather information from other sources. In the end, it is the reporter who writes the story. The upside of this is that the message, coming from a journalist, has a credibility with the mass audience that advertisements don't. Advertisements are patently self-serving. The downside of leaving it to the media to create the message that reach the audience is surrendering control over the messages that go to the public.

LEARNING CHECK ◀ ·····································

▶ **What are the similarities of advertising and public relations? The differences?**

INTEGRATED MARKETING

● **integrated marketing communication (IMC)**
Comprehensive program that links public relations and advertising

For many persuasive campaigns, organizations use both public relations and advertising. Increasingly, public relations and advertising people find themselves working together. This is especially true in corporations that have adopted **integrated marketing communication,** which attempts to coordinate advertising as a marketing tool with promotion and publicity of the sort that public relations experts can provide. Several major advertising agencies, aware of their clients' shift to integrated marketing, have acquired or established public relations subsidiaries to provide a wider range of services under their roof.

It is this overlap that has prompted some advertising agencies to move more into public relations. The WWP Group of London, a global advertising agency, has acquired both Hill & Knowlton, the third-largest public relations company in the United States, and the Ogilvy PR Group, the ninth largest. The Young & Rubicam advertising agency has three public relations subsidiaries: Burson-Marsteller, the largest; Cohn & Wolf, the 13th; and Creswell, Munsell, Fultz & Zirbel, the 50th. These are giant enterprises that reflect the conglomeration and globalization of both advertising and public relations.

To describe IMC, media critic James Ledbetter suggests thinking of the old Charlie the Tuna ads, in which a cartoon fish made you chuckle and identify with the product—and established a brand name. That's not good enough for IMC. "By contrast," Ledbetter says, "IMC encourages tuna buyers to think about all aspects of the product. If polls find that consumers are worried about dolphins caught in tuna nets, then you might stick a big 'Dolphin Safe' label on the tins and set up a web site featuring interviews with tuna fishermen." The new wave of IMC, according to one of its primary texts, is "respectful, not patronizing; dialogue-seeking, not monologic; responsive, not formula-driven. It speaks to the highest point of common interest—not the lowest common denominator."

● **institutional advertising**
Paid space and time to promote an institution's image and position

Public relations and advertising crossovers are hardly new. One area of traditional overlap is **institutional advertising,** which involves producing ads to promote an image rather than a product. The fuzzy, feel-good ads of agricultural conglomerate Archer Daniels Midland, which pepper Sunday morning network television, are typical.

LEARNING CHECK ◀ ·····································

▶ **Interagency competition among advertising agencies has blurred some distinctions between public relations and advertising. How so? And why?**

Media Relations

STUDY PREVIEW

Public relations people generally favor candor in working with the news media. Even so, some organizations opt to stonewall journalistic inquiries. An emerging school of thought in public relations is to challenge negative news coverage aggressively and publicly.

OPEN MEDIA RELATIONS

The common wisdom among public relations people today is to be open and candid with the mass media. It is a principle that dates to Ivy Lee, and case studies abound to confirm its effectiveness. A classic case study on this point is the Tylenol crisis.

Johnson & Johnson had spent many years and millions of dollars to inspire public confidence in its painkiller Tylenol. By 1982 the product was the leader in a crowded field of headache remedies with 36 percent of the market. Then disaster struck. Seven people in Chicago died after taking Tylenol capsules laced with cyanide. James Burke, president of Johnson & Johnson, and Lawrence Foster, vice president for public relations, moved quickly. Within hours, Johnson & Johnson:

- Halted the manufacture and distribution of Tylenol.
- Removed Tylenol products from retailers' shelves.
- Launched a massive advertising campaign requesting people to exchange Tylenol capsules for a safe replacement.
- Summoned 50 public relations employees from Johnson & Johnson and its subsidiary companies to staff a press center to answer media and consumer questions forthrightly.
- Ordered an internal company investigation of the Tylenol manufacturing and distribution process.
- Promised full cooperation with government investigators.
- Ordered the development of tamper-proof packaging for the reintroduction of Tylenol products after the contamination problem was resolved.

Investigators determined within days that an urban terrorist had poisoned the capsules. Although exonerated of negligence, Johnson & Johnson nonetheless had a tremendous problem: how to restore public confidence in Tylenol. Many former Tylenol users were reluctant to take a chance, and the Tylenol share of the analgesic market dropped to 6 percent.

To address the problem, Johnson & Johnson called in the Burson-Marsteller public relations agency. Burson-Marsteller recommended a media campaign to capitalize on the high marks the news media had given the company for openness during the crisis. Mailgrams went out inviting journalists to a 30-city video teleconference to hear James Burke announce the reintroduction of the product. Six hundred reporters turned out, and Johnson & Johnson officials took their questions live.

James Burke

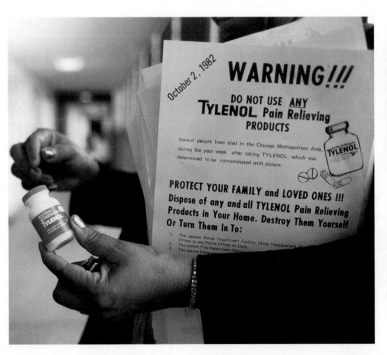

Product-Tampering Crisis. *When cyanide-laced Tylenol capsules killed seven people in Chicago, the manufacturer, Johnson & Johnson, responded quickly. Company President James Burke immediately pulled the product off retailers' shelves and ordered company publicists to set up a press center to answer news media inquiries as fully as possible. Burke's action and candor helped to restore the public's shaken confidence in Tylenol, and the product resumed its significant market share after the crisis ended. It turned out that it probably was somebody outside Johnson & Johnson's production and distributing system who had contaminated the capsules rather than a manufacturing lapse.*

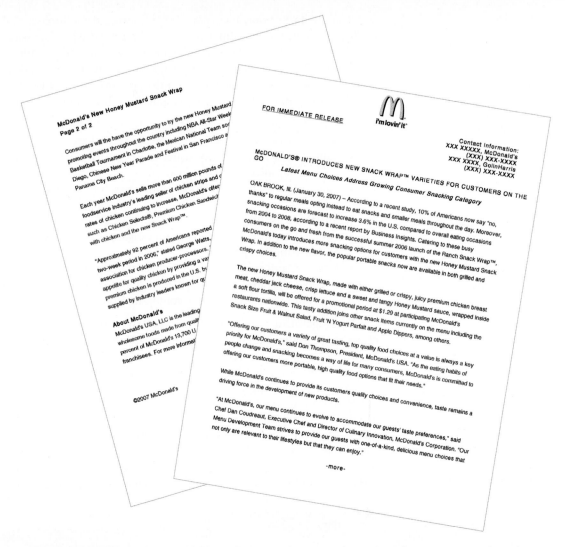

News Release. *The workhorse of media relations is the news release, issued to newspapers, broadcast stations and other media to stir reporter interest in covering an event or developing a story or in hope of getting a point of view included in news stories. Studies have found that as many as 90 percent of news stories rely to some extent on information in news releases. Some releases even are reported verbatim, particularly in small-market, low-budget newsrooms.*

● **media kit**
A packet provided to news reporters to tell the story in an advantageous way

To stir even wider attention, 7,500 **media kits** had been sent to newsrooms the day before the teleconference. The kits included a news release and a bevy of supporting materials: photographs, charts and background information.

The resulting news coverage was extensive. On average, newspapers carried 32 column inches of copy on the announcement. Network television and radio as well as local stations also afforded heavy coverage. Meanwhile, Johnson & Johnson executives, who had attended a workshop on how to make favorable television appearances, made themselves available as guests on the network morning shows and talk shows. At the same time Johnson & Johnson distributed 80 million free coupons to encourage people to buy Tylenol again.

The massive media-based public relations campaign worked. Within a year Tylenol had regained 80 percent of its former market share. Today, in an increasingly crowded analgesic field, Tylenol is again the market leader with annual sales of $670 million, compared with $520 million before the cyanide crisis.

LEARNING CHECK ◀ ••

▶ **Is there anything Ivy Lee would have done differently than Tylenol executives did after a terrorist replaced Tylenol with cyanide in Chicago drugstores?**

PROACTIVE MEDIA RELATIONS

Although public relations campaigns cannot control what the media say, public relations people can help to shape how news media report issues by taking the initiative. In the Tylenol crisis, for example, Johnson & Johnson reacted quickly and decisively and took control of disseminating information, which, coupled with full disclosure, headed off false rumors that could have caused further damage. This is a good example of **proactive media relations.**

● **proactive media relations**
Taking the initiative to release information

■ **Crisis Response.** For successful crisis management, public relations people need strong, ongoing relationships with their organization's top management. Otherwise, when crisis strikes, public relations people will face delays in rounding up the kind of breaking information they need to deal effectively with the news media. This was shown when President Bush, his popularity at an all-time low in 2006, brought in Tony Snow as White House news secretary to try to get media relations back on at least a less hostile track. Snow was a respected newsman and commentator in whom the White House reporting corps had confidence.

A principle in crisis management is to seize leadership on news reporting of the event. For public relations people, this means anticipating what news reporters will want to know and providing it even before the reporters have time to formulate their questions. Ivy Lee invented this technique. Johnson & Johnson applied the technique with great success in 1982. At the White House in 2006, reporters saw Tony Snow as a spokesperson they could trust as a straight-shooter who had the ear of the president.

LEARNING CHECK ◄ ••

▶ Why are so many public relations jobs filled by people with journalism degrees and backgrounds?

● **media relations**
Component of public relations that deals with press and other media

■ **Ongoing Media Relationships.** Good **media relations** cannot be forged in the fire of a crisis. Organizations that survive a crisis generally have a history of solid media relations. Their public relations staff people know reporters, editors and news directors on a first-name basis. They avoid hyping news releases on routine matters, and they work hard at earning the trust of journalists.

Many public relations people, in fact, are seasoned journalists themselves, and they understand how journalists go about their work. It is their journalistic background that made them attractive candidates for their PR jobs.

■ **Sound Operating Principles.** An underlying strength that helped to see Johnson & Johnson through the Tylenol crisis was the company's credo. The credo was a written vow that Johnson & Johnson's first responsibility was to "those who use our products and services." The credo, which had been promoted in-house for years, said, "Every time a business hires, builds, sells or buys, it is acting *for the people* as well as *for itself*, and it must be prepared to accept full responsibility."

With such a sound operating principle, Johnson & Johnson's crisis response was, in some respects, almost reflexive. Going silent, for example, would have run counter to the principles that Johnson & Johnson people had accepted as part of their corporate culture for years.

Wal-Mart to the Rescue.
While the federal emergency response agency was spinning bureaucratic wheels in hopeless confusion and disarray, Wal-Mart dispatched 2,400 truckloads of relief supplies to victims of Hurricane Katrina. Wal-Mart scored mightily with the public, although the rescue caravans were more a demonstration of the company's adroit delivery system than a sound public relations strategy. In public relations, Wal-Mart flies mostly blind.

AMBIVALENCE IN MEDIA RELATIONS

Despite the advantage of open media relations, not all companies embrace the approach. Giant retailer Wal-Mart, as an example, long resisted putting resources into public relations. Founder Sam Walton saw PR as a frill. It didn't fit his keep-costs-minimal concept. By 2005, even with Walton dead, his philosophy remained in place. The company had only a 17-member public relations staff—minuscule in business. How minuscule? Wal-Mart sales exceeded $285 billion, yet the company had but one public relations staffer per $16 billion in earnings. Put another way, the company had one public relations person per 76,000 employees.

Wal-Mart's spectacular growth, with a new store opening every day in 2005, masked problems. The company was generating legions of critics, whose mantra was epitomized in Anthony Bianco's choice of a title for his Wal-Mart-bashing book in 2006—*The Bully of Bentonville*. In Irvine, California, voters killed a planned store. Public opposition undid plans in the Queens section of New York City for another store. Reflecting growing employee discontent, there were rumblings to unionize—anathema in the Wal-Mart culture. There was a scandal about illegal aliens doing overnight cleanup work. A class-action suit alleging gender discrimination was filed by some women employees.

Wal-Mart's attempts at damage control were clumsy. Occasional spectacular public relations successes flowed more from a corporate conscience in crisis than a methodical public relations strategy. In 2005, for example, Wal-Mart upstaged federal agencies in moving relief supplies to the Gulf Coast after Hurricane Katrina. More than 2,400 truckloads of merchandise were dispatched to stricken communities, the first 100 loads of donated merchandise arriving before the fumbling federal mobilization. Wal-Mart drivers also transported water and other essentials.

Occasional image successes, however, weren't doing the job. With a vague sense that something methodical in the public relations spirit was needed, Wal-Mart created an executive position in 2006 with the curious title "senior director stakeholder engagement." The job description had some earmarks of public relations, albeit not quite at the vice presidential level. Strangely, perhaps in homage to Sam Walton, the words *public relations* appeared nowhere in the job description's 3,000 words. You could, however, read a lot into wording like "an innovative out-of-the-box thinker" and "fundamental changes in how the company does business" and "social responsibility."

LEARNING CHECK ◄ •

▶ **These companies have notorious histories for weak media relations, often snubbing reporter queries—Amerada Hess, IBM, Texas Instruments, Wal-Mart, Winn-Dixie. Would you defend the practice? Why or why not?**

ADVERSARIAL PUBLIC RELATIONS

● **adversarial public relations**
Attacking critics openly

● **Herb Schmertz**
Pioneered advertorials

● **advertorial**
A public relations message, taking an editorial position, that appears in paid space or time; a term contrived from *advertisement* and *editorial*

● **information boycott**
A policy to ignore news coverage and reporter queries

Public relations sometimes takes on aggressive even, feisty tactics. A pioneer in **adversarial public relations,** a vice president at Mobil Oil in the 1970s, **Herb Schmertz,** launched an assault on the ABC television network for a documentary critical of the U.S. oil industry. Schmertz bought full-page newspaper and magazine space for **advertorials,** a contrived word splicing *advertising* and *editorial,* for word-heavy, point-by-point rebuttals. Schmertz gave six Mobil executives a crash course on becoming spiffy interviewees and sent them on the talk-show circuit. They appeared on 365 television and 211 radio shows and talked with 85 newspaper reporters, not only tackling the ABC show but spinning Mobil practices in an upbeat light.

Another adversarial approach is the corporate pout. Upset with the *Wall Street Journal,* carmaker General Motors once launched an **information boycott** of the newspaper. Contact with *Journal* reporters was cut off. So was GM advertising in the *Journal.* General Motors eventually came to its senses, after learning that information boycotts carry great risks:

- By going silent, an organization loses avenues for conveying messages to mass audiences.
- Yanking advertising is perceived by the public as coercive wielding of economic might.
- Because advertising is designed to boost sales, discontinuing ads is counter-productive.

Thirty years later, the jury is still out on Schmertz's adversarial public relations. Certainly, though, it has not been widely adopted, perhaps because more sophisticated tools have emerged for getting institutional messages across in society's ever-richer media mix. Glossy magazines are rife with paid content deliberately intended to blend with articles. Spokespersons are more practiced in avoiding a bite as they counter detractors in media forums.

LEARNING CHECK ◄ ·····································

▶ **If you were president of a major corporation, would you hire Herb Schmertz as your public relations vice president? Why or why not?**

Directions for Public Relations

STUDY PREVIEW

New sensitivity about the ethical practice of public relations is being generated by theorists who favor open, honest dialogue with publics. Although not without risks, dialogic thinking has the potential to move public relations closer to ethical high ground. Ethics discussions and accreditation also aim to improve the practice of public relations.

A TARNISHED IMAGE

● **whitewashing**
Covering up

Unsavory elements in the heritage of public relations remain a heavy burden. P. T. Barnum, whose name became synonymous with hype, attracted crowds to his stunts and shows in the late 1800s with extravagant promises. Sad to say, some promoters still use Barnum's tactics. The claims for snake oils and elixirs from Barnum's era live on in commercials for pain relievers and cold remedies. The early response of tycoons to muckraking attacks, before Ivy Lee came along, was **whitewashing**—covering up the abuses but not correcting them. It is no wonder that the term *PR* is sometimes used derisively. To say something is "all PR" means that it lacks substance. Of people whose apparent positive qualities are a mere façade, it may be said that they have "good PR."

LEARNING CHECK ◄ ·····································

▶ **Will contemporary public relations people ever live down the legacy of P. T. Barnum? Of Jack Abramoff?**

STANDARDS AND CERTIFICATION

● **APR**
Indicates PRSA accreditation

The Public Relations Society of America, which has grown to 28,000 members in 114 chapters, has a different approach: improving the quality of public relations work, whatever the label. In 1951 the association adopted a code of professional standards. In a further professionalization step, PRSA has established a certification process. Those who meet the criteria and pass exams are allowed to place **APR,** which stands for "accredited public relations," after their names. About 5,000 PRSA members hold APR status.

Since 1998 the APR program has been operated by the Universal Accreditation Board, which was created for that purpose by PRSA and a consortium of nine other public relations organizations. It is a rigorous process. Nationwide, only 80 to 90 practioners a year earn the right to use APR with their signatures.

LEARNING CHECK ◄ ··

▶ If you were in a capacity to hire someone for an entry-level public relations position in your organization, would you make a journalism degree a requirement? How about APR?

▶ How about for a senior public relations position?

DIALOGIC PUBLIC RELATIONS

● **dialogic theory**
Dialogue-based approach to negotiating relationships

Among scholars an enthusiasm has developed for applying **dialogic theory** for a kinder, gentler practice of public relations. Advocates draw on the concept of genuine dialogue, which is deeply rooted in philosophy, psychology, rhetoric and relational communication. Rather than communication to publics, the traditional public relations model, dialogic theory insists on genuine listening in a true exchange. The theoretical shift is from managing communication to using communication as a tool for negotiating relationships without any manipulative or Machiavellian tricks.

Scholars Michael Kent and Maureen Taylor have summarized five major features of dialogic theory in operation:

- **Mutuality.** A corporation or other institution engaged in public relations must recognize a responsibility to engage in communication on an even playing field. This means not taking advantage of financial might to talk down or push ideas without also listening.
- **Propinquity.** For communication to be genuine, interaction with publics must be spontaneous.
- **Empathy.** The institution must have a sincere sympathy in supporting and confirming public goals and interests.
- **Risk.** Dialogic theory can work only if there is a willingness to interact with individuals and publics on their own terms.
- **Commitment.** An institution must be willing to work at understanding its interactions with publics. This means that significant resources must be allocated not only to the dialogue but also to interpretation and understanding.

Dialogic theory offers a framework for a highly ethical form of public relations, but it is not without difficulties. As Kent and Taylor have noted, institutions have many publics, which makes dialogue a complex process. Participants in dialogic public relations put themselves in jeopardy. When publics engage in dialogue with organizations, they run the risk that their disclosures will be used to exploit or manipulate them.

Even so, discussion about dialogic theory is sensitizing many people in public relations to honesty and openness as ideals in the democratic tradition of giving voice to all. The theory is based on principles of honesty, trust and positive regard for the other rather than simply a conception of the public as a means to an end.

LEARNING CHECK ◄ ··

▶ How could dialogic theory improve the practice of public relations?

TECHNOLOGY AND PUBLIC RELATIONS

The workhorse of public relations, the news media, made an easy transition to the Internet in the 1990s but pretty much only the medium changed—a mass-delivered e-mail of the standard release that once was snailed. In 2006 a Boston public relations agency, Shift Communications, reinvented the news release for the digital age. Shift's Todd Defren, who devised the new release, called it one-stop shopping for journalists to whom releases are targeted. The release includes tech-rich

After graduation from college in 1912, Edward Bernays tried press agentry. He was good at it, landing free publicity for whoever would hire him. Soon his bosses included famous tenor Enrico Caruso and actor Otis Skinner. Bernays felt, however, that his success was tainted by the disdain in which press agents were held in general. He also saw far greater potential for affecting public opinion than his fellow press agents did.

From Bernays' discomfort and vision was born the concept of modern public relations. His 1923 book *Crystallizing Public Opinion* outlined a new craft he was the first to call public relations.

Bernays saw good public relations as counsel to clients. He called the public relations practitioner a "special pleader." The concept was modeled partly on the long-established lawyer–client relationship in which the lawyer, or counselor, suggests courses of action. Because of his seminal role in defining what public relations is, Bernays sometimes is called the "Father of PR," although some people say the honor should be shared with Ivy Lee.

No matter, there is no question of Bernays' ongoing contributions. He

Edward Bernays. *Integrity was important to public relations pioneer Edward Bernays. When he was asked by agents of fascist dictators Francisco Franco and Adolf Hitler to improve their images in the United States, he said no. "I wouldn't do for money what I wouldn't do without money," Bernays said.*

taught the first course in public relations in 1923 at New York University. Bernays encouraged firm methodology in public relations, a notion that was captured in the title of a book he edited in 1955: *The Engineering of Consent.*

He long advocated the professionalization of the field, which laid the groundwork for the accreditation of the sort the Public Relations Society of America has developed.

Throughout his career Bernays stressed that public relations people need a strong sense of responsibility. In one reflective essay, he wrote, "Public relations practiced as a profession is an art applied to a science in which the public interest and not pecuniary motivation is the primary consideration. The engineering of consent in this sense assumes a constructive social role. Regrettably, public relations, like other professions, can be abused and used for anti-social purposes. I have tried to make the profession socially responsible as well as economically viable."

Bernays became the Grand Old Man of public relations, still attending PRSA and other professional meetings past his 100th birthday. He died in 1993 at age 102.

WHAT DO YOU THINK?

▶ Edward Bernays liked to call himself the Father of Public Relations. Who deserves the accolade more—Bernays or Ivy Lee? Explain your choice.

▶ Bernays likened the relationship of public relations practitioners and their clients to lawyer–client relationships. Is it a fair comparison?

● **social media news release**
Internet-based news releases with links to related material and interactive opportunities for news reporters

features, such as links to blogs that relate to the subject, links to related news releases and sites, downloadable company logos, and videos.

Defren calls it the **social media news release** because it encourages interactive and ongoing communication. With a Shift release posted to the DIGG consumer-generated news site, journalists and bloggers and anyone else can click to sites that add to the dialogue. "This gives journalists everything they need in one place," Defren said.

The basis of Defren's invention is the Web 2.0 bevy of Internet services that facilitate the creation of content and exchange of information online. Within months of the Shift creation, which was downloadable free as a template, larger public relations agencies were on to the concept. Giant Edelman unveiled its variation by the end of the year.

Chapter Wrap-Up

Importance of Public Relations (Page 290)

■ Public relations is a tool of leaders in business, government and other institutions to create beneficial relationships with other institutions and groups. Used well, public relations facilitates discussion that otherwise might not occur on issues of importance to constituent groups within society. This is discussion that affects the interests of the organization that has a stake in the issues—a kind of honest advocacy. This all puts public relations in an important role in the functioning of a democratic society. Key in public relations is the crafting of messages for mass audiences. The messages are delivered largely by mass media.

Origins of Public Relations (Page 292)

■ Modern public relations was the concept of Ivy Lee, who in 1906 began providing counsel to corporate clients that were under siege because of a wide range of abusive practices. These practices included exploitation of labor and unfair monopolistic policies against consumers and competitors. Lee urged corporations to soften their closed-door and arrogant practices. Lee also recommended an end to cover-ups when things go badly and facing issues publicly, honestly and openly. Lee had disdain for misleading, circus-like publicity excesses of the P. T. Barnum variety. These not only were less than honest but also were wearing thin with the public.

Structure of Public Relations (Page 297)

■ A revised model for corporate structures emerged in the late 1920s, putting an executive in charge of public relations. Typically a vice president, this executive provides input in corporate policies that would serve the interests not only of the organization but also of various constituencies. These constituencies are called publics, hence the term *public relations*. These executives head in-house public relations operations. Many organizations also draw on outside public relations agencies for special needs. Most public relations activities are either external communication, which is aimed at external publics, or internal communication, which is aimed at employees, shareholders and other groups within the organization.

Public Relations Services (Page 299)

■ Public relations covers a wide range of activities. These include lobbying on public policy and providing advocacy on organizational and public interests to legislators and other government officials. Lobbying done dishonestly can be against the public interest, as attested in occasional scandals about bribes and improper attempts to influence public policy. Done properly, however, lobbying is important in creating good public policy. Public relations also involves fund-raising, image management, crisis management and events coordination.

Public Relations and Advertising (Page 303)

■ Although public relations and advertising both involve crafting media messages for mass audiences, public relations is involved in creating policy. Advertising is not. Even so, there has been a recent blending of the functions, some under the umbrella concept of *integrated marketing*. This blending has blurred some traditional distinctions between public relations and advertising, especially as major advertising agencies have bought up public relations agencies to offer their clients a broader range of services.

Media Relations (Page 304)

■ The news media are especially important for public relations because they are the primary venue for distributing an organization's messages to groups in the public.

The workhorse of media relations is the news release—a statement from an organization sent to newspapers, magazines and broadcasters. Newspeople decide what to pick up from these statements and how to integrate them into their news packages. Some studies have found that as much as 90 percent of news in U.S. media has roots in information from public relations sources. Media relations, however, is more than news releases. Most public relations involves making an organization accessible to the news media. Such open relations are valuable in emergencies because they help public relations people handle communication in crisis situations.

Directions for Public Relations (Page 309)

■ New sensitivity about the ethical practice of public relations is being generated by theorists who favor open, honest dialogue with publics. Although not without risks, dialogic thinking has the potential to move public relations closer to ethical high ground. Ethics discussions and accreditation also aim to improve the practice of public relations.

REVIEW QUESTIONS

1. What is public relations? How is public relations connected to the mass media?

2. Why did big business become interested in the techniques and principles of public relations beginning in the late 1800s?

3. How is public relations a management tool?

4. What is the range of activities in which public relations people are involved?

5. What is the difference between public relations and advertising? What are the similarities?

6. What kind of relationship do most PR people strive to have with the mass media?

7. Why does public relations have a bad image? What are public relations professionals doing about it?

CONCEPTS

dialogic theory (Page 310)
enlightened self-interest (Page 291)
integrated marketing communication (Page 304)
public relations (Page 290)
social Darwinism (Page 293)

TERMS

adversarial public relations (Page 308)
advertorial (Page 308)
lobbying (Page 299)
media relations (Page 307)
public relations agencies (Page 298)

PEOPLE

Edward Bernays (Page 290)
George Creel (Page 296)
Paul Garrett (Page 291)
Ivy Lee (Page 293)
Herb Schmertz (Page 308)

MEDIA SOURCES

● The industry's dominant trade journal is *PRWeek*.

● Michael L. Kent and Maureen Taylor. "Toward a Dialogic Theory of Public Relations," *Public Relations Review* (February 2002), pages 21–27. Kent and Taylor, both scholars, draw on a wide range of disciplines to argue for genuine dialogue as a basis for the moral practice of public relations.

● George S. McGovern and Leonard F. Guttridge. *The Great Coalfield War.* Houghton Mifflin, 1972. This account of the Ludlow Massacre includes the success of the Ivy Lee-inspired campaign to rescue the Rockefeller reputation but is less than enthusiastic about Lee's corporate-oriented perspective and sometimes shoddy fact gathering.

● Ray Eldon Hiebert. *Courtier to the Crowd: The Story of Ivy Lee and the Development of Public Relations.* Iowa State University Press, 1966. Professor Hiebert's flattering biography focuses on the enduring public relations principles articulated, if not always practiced, by Ivy Lee.

PUBLIC RELATIONS: A Thematic Chapter Summary

In this chapter you have deepened your media literacy by revisiting several themes. Here are thematic highlights from the chapter:

Media Economics

The dark side of capitalism, unmitigated greed, marked the rise of corporations into unprecedented wealth and power in the latter 1800s. Abusive practices, often from monopolies, included the pursuit of profit over and above any sense of social responsibility. The Populist movement, led by underclass farmers and laborers, caught the ear of government. Public policy reforms followed, forcing industry to find new ways to conduct itself. Public relations, following a model devised by Ivy Lee in 1906, guided corporations toward behavior that served their own good and also took note of the needs and interests of society's other constituency groups. **(Pages 292–297)**

To the Rescue. *Ivy Lee helped major corporations out of dilemmas resulting from their economic success.*

Media and Democracy

Sullied Reputation. *Jack Abrahamoff's excesses hurt public relations.*

Public relations ensures more diversity in public dialogue by giving an articulate voice to organizations. The best practice of public relations seeks win-win solutions on issues not only for the organization being represented but also for other constituencies with stakes in the issues. Public relations, practiced well, is honest advocacy in society's marketplace of ideas. One public relations activity, lobbying, goes to the heart of public policy by providing information and arguments to legislators in the creation of public policy. Lobbyists also work with government officials who put public policy into effect. Unethical and illegal lobbying activities, which sometimes make headlines, malign an otherwise honorable public relations activity that helps democracy work. **(Page 291)**

Elitism and Populism

The Industrial Revolution that transformed U.S. society in the decades following the Civil War created a two-tiered society—the Haves and the Have-Nots. Many in the upper class, panged to varying degrees with guilt about their unprecedented wealth, drew on the survival-of-the-fittest theory of Charles Darwin, the new rage of the time, to justify their privileged position. They called it social Darwinism, which meant they had acquired their advantage of superior status by being the most fit. The theory was cast in terms of a religious theme. It wasn't the fault of rich people that the Creator had imbued them with special gifts at amassing fortunes that enabled extravagant lifestyles. The notion was insulting to laborers, farmers and other ordinary blokes, and a new political movement, Populism, arose to give voice to the underprivileged "inferiors" who, according to social Darwinism, had been left behind. The Populist movement inspired public policy changes that shook industry. Into this environment came public relations, as a way for industry to both listen to and communicate with the whole range of society's constituent groups. **(Pages 292–293)**

Enlightened Self-Interest. *At General Motors in the 1930s, Paul Garrett pioneered the concept of sensitivity to public needs and interests as an element in high-level corporate decision making.*

Media Future

Public relations has a bum rap in many quarters. Take, for example, the derogatory application of the term "It's only PR" to suggest something illusory and less than honest. The public relations profession has been working at the tarnished image, encouraging good practice through codes of ethics and accreditation. Scholars are working on new theories to guide public relations practitioners. These include dialogics, which emphasizes genuine listening before developing positions on issues.**(Pages 309–311)**

Two Tiers. *The fragmentation of society into thousands of subgroups offers new challenges for public relations communication.*

Audience Fragmentation

The concept of publics, groups within society that are identifiable and addressable, has grown more complex with the proliferation of special-interest groups. People once identified themselves mostly as members of large groups, like political parties, religious denominations, ethnic communities and geographic areas. The old categories today have subcategories and subcategories within them, most with articulate leadership and their own channels of communication. This all adds layers of challenge for public relations practitioners in listening to the growing diversity of voices and designing campaigns to build support for mutually beneficial goals.

(Pages 290–291)

Michael J. Fox. *Special-interest groups can personify their messages and broaden their appeals through celebrity support for the cause. Michael J. Fox not only drew support for stem-cell research funding, he also drew more people into the debate.*

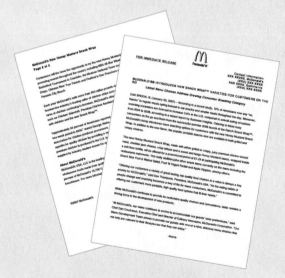

News Releases. *To encourage news coverage, public relations people prepare statements to the press.*

Media Technology

Not being a mass medium itself but relying on media to carry its messages, public relations has no technology unique to itself. But technology for other media, particularly the Internet, has opened fascinating new wrinkles for the conduct of public relations. One is online news releases with links to blogs and a wide range of related sites. Called the *social media news release*, the innovation encourages interactive and ongoing communication. It makes public relations more than ever a two-way street for communication.

(Pages 310–311)

13

Advertising

Advertising Outside the Box

If advertising had a guru it would be Bob Greenberg. He was the first to talk about cell phones as a new advertising medium—the "third screen," he called it, coming after movies and television. In the fast-changing media environment, those insights were ages ago—at least a couple years. Now Greenberg is into massive outdoor signage becoming even more massive. Think Times Square.

Greenberg shares his observations freely, but, no mere armchair commentator, he practices post-mass media advertising at his R/GA agency in New York, part of the global Interpublic agency chain. R/GA designed the Nikeid Web site, where footwear freaks can spend hours designing their own. That's customer interactivity that sells products, he says.

The era of entertainment that brought massive audiences to advertising messages is fast-fading, Greenberg says. It's time to think outside the box.

Greenberg pities those ad agency execs who still pitch the 30-second television spot to clients because it's all they know. It's not that television, radio, magazines and newspapers are dead but that their heyday is past and their near-monopoly as carriers of advertising is fading fast. As Greenberg tells it, ad agencies that don't find new models to reach consumers are setting themselves up for extinction.

Greenberg's answer: Rather than ads being sandwiched into entertainment products, the ads themselves must be the entertainment. He's been called a media futurist, but there is evidence

LEARNING AHEAD

- Advertising is key in consumer economies, democracy and the mass media.
- Most advertising messages are carried through the mass media.
- Advertising agencies create and place ads for advertisers.
- Advertisements are placed with care in media outlets.
- Advertisers are experimenting with new platforms.
- Brand names as an advertising strategy are in transition.
- Advertising tactics include lowest common denominators, positioning, redundancy and testimonials.
- New advertising tactics include encouraging word-of-mouth testimonials.
- Challenges ahead for advertisers include ad clutter and creative excesses.

Bob Greenberg. *His crystal ball sees advertising not in packaging ads inside entertainment and news but in advertising so compelling that it's why people tune in.*

that the future is now. Samsung and Verizon have tripled their Internet ad budgets. American Express has shifted away from network television.

At R/GA Greenberg has integrated information technologists, data analysts and what he calls "experience designers" into his staff. He must be doing something right. In 2005 he added 85 people to bring the R/GA staff to 400.

Importance of Advertising

STUDY PREVIEW

Advertising is vital in a consumer economy. Without it people would have a hard time even knowing what products and services are available. Advertising, in fact, is essential to a prosperous society. Advertising also is the financial basis of important contemporary mass media.

CONSUMER ECONOMIES

Advertising is a major component of modern economies. In the United States the best estimates are that advertisers spend about 2 percent of the gross domestic product to promote their wares. When the nation's production of goods and services is up, so is advertising spending. When production falters, as it did in the early 2000s, many manufacturers, distributors and retailers pull back their advertising expenditures.

The essential role of advertising in a modern consumer economy is obvious if you think about how people decide what to buy. If a shoe manufacturer were unable to tout the virtues of its footwear by advertising in the mass media, people would have a hard time learning about the product, let alone knowing whether it is what they want.

LEARNING CHECK ◄
▶ Could a consumer economy work without advertising? Explain.

ADVERTISING AND PROSPERITY

Advertising's phenomenal continuing growth has been a product of a plentiful society. In a poor society with a shortage of goods, people line up for necessities like food and clothing. Advertising has no role and serves no purpose when survival is the main concern. With prosperity, however, people have not only discretionary income but also a choice of ways to spend it. Advertising is the vehicle that provides information and rationales to help people decide how to enjoy their prosperity.

Besides being a product of economic prosperity, advertising contributes to prosperity. By dangling desirable commodities and services before mass audiences, advertising can inspire people to greater individual productivity so that they can have more income to buy the things that are advertised.

Advertising also can introduce efficiency into the economy by allowing comparison shopping without in-person inspections of all the alternatives. Efficiencies also can result when advertising alerts consumers to superior and less costly products and services that have displaced outdated, outmoded and inefficient offerings.

Said Howard Morgens when he was president of Procter & Gamble: "Advertising is the most effective and efficient way to sell to the consumer. If we should ever find better methods of selling our type of products to the consumer, we'll leave advertising and turn to these other methods." Veteran advertising executive David Ogilvy once made the point this way: "Advertising is still the cheapest form of selling. It would cost you $25,000 to have salesmen call on a thousand homes. A television commercial can do it for $4.69." McGraw-Hill, which publishes trade magazines, has offered research showing that a salesperson's typical call costs $178, a letter $6.63 and a phone call $6.35. For 17 cents, says McGraw-Hill, an advertiser can reach a prospect through advertising. Although advertising does not close a sale for all products, it introduces products and makes the salesperson's job easier and quicker.

Here are estimates of how much the leading advertisers spend in U.S. mass media:

General Motors	$4.0 billion
Procter & Gamble	3.9 billion
Time Warner	3.3 billion
Pfizer	3.0 billion
SBC Communications	2.7 billion
DaimlerChrysler	2.5 billion
Ford Motor	2.5 billion
Walt Disney	2.2 billion
Verizon	2.2 billion
Johnson & Johnson	2.2 billion

LEARNING CHECK ◄ ·

▶ **What is the link between advertising and prosperity?**

ADVERTISING AND DEMOCRACY

Advertising first took off as a modern phenomenon in the United States, which has given rise to the theory that advertising and democracy are connected. This theory notes that Americans, early in their history as a democracy, were required by their political system to hold individual opinions. They looked for information so that they could evaluate their leaders and vote on public policy. This emphasis on individuality and reason paved the way for advertising: Just as Americans looked to the mass media for information on political matters, they also came to look to the media for information on buying decisions.

In authoritarian countries, by contrast, people tend to look to strong personal leaders, not reason, for ideas to embrace. This, according to the theory, diminishes the demand for information in these nondemocracies, including the kind of information provided by advertising.

Advertising has another important role in democratic societies in generating most of the operating revenue for newspapers, magazines, television and radio. Without advertising, many of the media on which people rely for information, for

A Society of Choices. *By presenting choices to consumers, advertising mirrors the democratic ideal of individuals choosing intelligently among alternatives. The emphasis is on individuals making up their own minds: Clinton or Obama? Nike or Reebok? Chevrolet or Ford?*

entertainment and for the exchange of ideas on public issues would not exist as we know them.

LEARNING CHECK ◄

▶ How does advertising dovetail with the democratic ideal of individual decision making?

PERSUASION VERSUS COERCION

Advertising has critics who point out that almost all ads are one-sided. Ads don't lay out options, which violates the principle of honesty that is essential in persuasive communication. Persuasiveness requires a full presentation of available options and then argumentation based on all the evidence and premises. Ads don't do that. The argument in advertisements, sometimes screaming, often emotional, is direct: "Buy me." What an ad doesn't say speaks volumes. This makes advertising, say the critics, a type of coercive communication—far short of honest persuasion.

Whatever the criticism, advertising is a major element in mass communication. The financial base of newspapers, magazines, radio, television—and more and more the Internet—depends on advertising. The role of advertising both in the media as we know them today as well as in our consumer economy cannot be denied.

LEARNING CHECK ◄

▶ What is the difference between coercive and persuasive communication?

▶ Can you find any ads that meet the criteria of being persuasive rather than coercive?

Origins of Advertising

STUDY PREVIEW

Advertising is the product of great forces that have shaped modern society, beginning with Gutenberg's movable type, which made mass-produced messages possible. Without the mass media there would be no vehicle to carry advertisements to mass audiences. Advertising also is a product of the democratic experience; of the Industrial Revolution and its spin-offs, including vast transportation networks and mass markets; and of continuing economic growth.

STEPCHILD OF TECHNOLOGY

● **Johannes Gutenberg**
Progenitor of advertising media

Advertising is not a mass medium, but it relies on media to carry its messages. **Johannes Gutenberg**'s movable type, which permitted mass production of the printed word, made mass-produced advertising possible. First came flyers. Then advertisements, as newspapers and magazines were introduced. In the 1800s, when technology created high-speed presses that could produce enough copies for larger audiences, advertisers used these media to expand markets. With the introduction of radio, advertisers learned how to use electronic communication. Then came television.

● **William Caxton**
Printed first advertisement

● **John Campbell**
Published first ad in British colonies

Flyers were the first form of printed advertising. The British printer **William Caxton** issued the first printed advertisement in 1468 to promote one of his books. In America publisher **John Campbell** of the Boston *News-Letter* ran the first advertisement in 1704, a notice from somebody wanting to sell an estate on Long Island. Colonial newspapers listed cargo arriving from Europe and invited readers to come, look and buy.

LEARNING CHECK ◄

▶ How is advertising dependent on media technology?

▶ How is advertising efficient for selling products and services?

INDUSTRIAL REVOLUTION

● **Benjamin Day**
His penny newspaper brought advertising to new level

The genius of **Benjamin Day**'s New York *Sun*, in 1833 the first penny newspaper, was that it recognized and exploited so many changes spawned by the Industrial Revolution. Steam-powered presses made large pressruns possible. Factories drew great numbers of people to jobs in cities that were geographically small areas to which newspapers could be distributed quickly. The jobs also drew immigrants who were eager to learn—from newspapers as well as other sources—about their adopted country. Industrialization, coupled with the labor union movement, created unprecedented wealth, with laborers gaining a share of the new prosperity. A consumer economy was emerging, although it was primitive by today's standards.

A key to the success of Day's *Sun* was that, at a penny a copy, it was affordable for almost everyone. Of course, Day's production expenses exceeded a penny a copy. Just as the commercial media do today, Day looked to advertisers to pick up the slack. As Day wrote in his first issue, "The object of this paper is to lay before the public, at a price within the means of everyone, all the news of the day, and at the same time afford an advantageous medium for advertising." Day and imitator penny press publishers sought larger and larger circulations, knowing that merchants would see the value in buying space to reach so much purchasing power.

National advertising took root in the 1840s as railroads, another creation of the Industrial Revolution, spawned new networks for mass distribution of manufactured goods. National brands developed, and their producers looked to magazines, also delivered by rail, to promote sales. By 1869 the rail network linked the Atlantic and Pacific coasts.

LEARNING CHECK ◄ ·······································

▸ **What was the genius of Benjamin Day?**

Advertising Agencies

STUDY PREVIEW

Central in modern advertising are the agencies that create and place ads on behalf of their clients. These agencies are generally funded by the media in which they place ads. In effect, this makes agency services free to advertisers. Other compensation systems are also emerging.

PIONEER AGENCIES

● **Wayland Ayer**
Founded first ad agency

By 1869 most merchants recognized the value of advertising, but they grumbled about the time it took away from their other work. In that grumbling, a young Philadelphia man sensed opportunity. **Wayland Ayer,** age 20, speculated that merchants, and even national manufacturers, would welcome a service company to help them create advertisements and place them in publications. Ayer feared, however, that his idea might not be taken seriously by potential clients because of his youth and inexperience. So when Wayland Ayer opened a shop, he borrowed his father's name for the shingle. The father was never part of the business, but the agency's name, N. W. Ayer & Son, gave young Ayer access to potential clients, and the first advertising agency was born. The Ayer agency not only created ads but also offered the array of services that agencies still offer clients today:

- Counsel on selling products and services.
- Design services, that is, actually creating advertisements and campaigns.
- Expertise on placing advertisements in advantageous media.

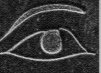

ADVERTISING MILESTONES

PIVOTAL EVENTS

1400s–
1600s

First Ad
In England William Caxton promoted a book with first printed advertisement (1468)

1700s

Colonial Ad
Joseph Campbell included advertisements in his Boston *News-Letter* (1705)

1800s

Penny Press
Benjamin Day created New York *Sun* as combination news, advertising vehicle (1833)

Ad Agency
Wayland Ayer opened first advertising agency, Philadelphia (1869)

Ben Day's one-cent New York Sun *was dependent on advertising*

1900–
1949

Ethics
Edward Bok of *Ladies' Home Journal* established advertising code (1919)

Regulation
Congress created Federal Trade Commission to combat unfair advertising (1914)

Broadcast Code
NBC established code of acceptable advertising (1929)

Ad Council
Media industries created predecessor to Ad Council (1942)

David Ogilvy championed a first-class image for branded products

1950–
1999

Brands
David Ogilvy devised brand imaging (1950s)

TV Ads
Network television surpassed magazines as national advertising medium (1960s)

USP
Rosser Reeves devised unique selling proposition (1960s)

Regulation
Federal crackdown on misleading claims (1980s)

Dave Balter has freelanced buzzing with agents to whom he issues sample products

2000s

Store Brands
Store brands emerged as major challenge to brand names (2000s)

Viral
Ongoing story lines used to generate buzz (2000s)

Super Bowl
Thirty-second spot on televised game reached record $2.6 million (2006)

Hybrid branding, like Paris Hilton fragrances, integrates implied testimonials and celebrity names

- Gutenberg invented movable metal type (1440s)
- First colonial newspaper (1690)

- Civil War (1861–1865)
- Penny Press period (1833–)
- Mass production, railroads contribute to creation of national market economy (1870s–)

- Women's rights movement succeeds in suffrage (1920)
- Great Depression (1930s)
- World War II (1941–1945)

- Korean War (1950–1953)
- Vietnam War (1964–1973)
- Humans reached moon (1969)
- Carter presidential administration (1981–1984)

- 9/11 terrorist attacks (2001)
- Iraq War (2003–)
- Hurricane Katrina (2005)

Full-service advertising agencies conduct market research for their clients, design and produce advertisements and choose the media in which the advertisement will run. The 500 leading U.S. agencies employ 120,000 people worldwide. In the United States they employ about 73,000.

These are U.S. agencies, ranked by revenue from their core domestic clients:

JWT (a unit of WPP)	$469 million
McCann Erickson (Interpublic)	436 million
Leo Burnett (Publicis)	353 million
BBDO (Omnicom)	281 million
Ogilvy & Mather (WPP)	278 million
DDB (Omnicom)	267 million
Grey (WPP)	251 million
FCB (Interpublic)	201 million
Publicis (Publicis)	196 million

LEARNING CHECK ◄ ·······

▶ **What services of a modern advertising agency can be traced to Wayland Ayer?**

AGENCY COMPENSATION

Advertising agencies once earned their money in a standard way—15 percent of the client advertiser's total outlay for space or time. On huge accounts, like Procter & Gamble, agencies made killings.

● **commission contract**
An advertising agency earns an agreed-upon percentage of what the advertising client spends for time and space, traditionally 15 percent

■ **Commissions.** The 15 percent **commission contract** system broke down in the 1990s when U.S. businesses scrambled to cut costs to become more competitive. Today, according to a guesstimate by the trade journal *Advertising Age*, only 10 to 12 percent of agency contracts use a standard percentage. Agency compensation generally is negotiated. Big advertisers, like P&G, are thought to be paying 13 percent on average, but different agencies handle the company's brands, each with a separate contract. For competitive reasons all parties tend to be secretive about actual terms.

In one sense, advertising under the commission system is free for advertisers. Most media companies offer a 15 percent discount for ads placed by agencies. In effect, media companies induce agencies to place their clients' messages with them. Media companies and agencies prefer, however, to explain the discount as compensation for bulk purchases of time and space.

● **performance contract**
An advertising agency earns expenses and an agreed-upon markup for the advertising client, plus bonuses for exceeding minimal expectations

■ **Performance.** Commission contracts have been replaced largely by **performance contracts.** The advertiser pays an agency's costs plus a negotiated profit. In addition, if a campaign works spectacularly, agencies land bonuses.

● **equity contract**
An advertising agency is compensated with shares of stock in an advertising client

■ **Equity.** In the 1990s dot-com boom, a performance contract variation was to pay agencies with shares in the company. **Equity contracts** are chancy for agencies because an advertiser's success hinges on many variables, not just the advertising, but the return for an agency with a soaring client can be stratospheric.

LEARNING CHECK ◄ ·······

▶ How does the commission system in advertising work?

▶ What has forced changes in the commission system? What are the changes?

Picking the worst gas company? That's no problem at all. It's Esso.* For ten years, Esso has worked hard to stop any real action on global warming. And unlike BP and Shell, Esso does not invest in renewable energy research.

ESSO

We boycott you.

* and its entire family of brands - Exxon Mobil, Imperial Oil, ExxonGeneral

Tactical Media. *One response in other countries to imported cultural values and icons has been called tactical media. Organzations like Adbusters and Autolabs turn loose their creative talent to ridicule slick intrusions.*

Countering Cultural Imperialism

Cultural imperialism occurs when indigenous cultures are displaced, lost forever, by cultural icons and values from more powerful countries and societies. Movies, television shows and newspapers carry the messages of cultural imperialism. So does advertising. The concept was articulated well in a 1971 book, *Para leer al pato Donald,* which translates as "How to Read Donald Duck." Authors Armand Mattelart, a professor of mass communications and ideology at the University of Chile, and Ariel Dorfman, a literary critic and novelist, saw cultural threat in a growing Walt Disney global popularity that "forces us Latin Americans to see ourselves as they see us." The book went through more than 15 editions and was translated into several languages.

Pure cultural exportation, a la the Disney to which Mattelart and Dorfman objected, doesn't work quite the same anymore. U.S.-based MTV customizes contents regionally for 14 different 24-hour feeds around the world. Still, there is commonality. Tellingly, MTV calls the feeds "all different and all similar."

Also, some home-country media themselves are accelerating the loss of their own distinctive cultures. In India the news media have been so influenced by Western media contents that European fashion design and American-style beauty queens get big play. Outside influences also are affecting Bollywood, India's domestic film industry. In other places too, the spread of Western culture has lessened enthusiasm for homegrown works.

This insidious imperialism has become a target of pirate or tactical media that try to undermine the imported influence, sometimes through ridicule. Patricia Aufderheide, professor of communication at American University, defines tactical media as "projects that people do opportunistically—seizing temporarily available or unclaimed resources—to claim or reclaim some communicative channels or some expressive space." One example is billboard "pirating" by Adbusters, a global network of artists, activists, writers, pranksters, students, educators and entrepreneurs. Another example is Autolabs in Brazil.

Autolabs teaches cheap, do-it-yourself tactics to young people in poor districts and slums in Sao Paulo, using free software and open-source operational systems. In workshops the students, 17 to 21, recycle discarded computers, learn how to use them, and produce their own media: Web sites, movies, music, radio programs and a storytelling archive. After a year of workshops, the network of interlinked community media centers totaled about 200 countrywide. The plan was to create as many as 1,000 centers.

DEEPENING YOUR MEDIA LITERACY

EXPLORE THE ISSUE

The television shows *CSI, The Price Is Right* and soap operas are popular around the world. Watch one of these shows.

DIG DEEPER

Make a list of the American values featured and the messages the show subtly or overtly promotes. Look for unstated and underlying messages. What kind of lifestyle is being presented? Is it glamorized? How? What values are expressed? Is the promotion of these values a product of commercialism? Is there any benefit for local cultures?

WHAT DO YOU THINK?

Do you think projects like Autolabs or Adbusters can be effective?

Placing Advertisements

The placement of advertisements is a sophisticated business. Not only do different media have inherent advantages and disadvantages in reaching potential customers, but so do individual publications and broadcast outlets.

MEDIA PLANS

● **media plans**
Lay out where ads are placed

Agencies create **media plans** to ensure that advertisements reach the right target audience. Developing a media plan is no small task. Consider the number of media outlets available: 1,400 daily newspapers in the United States alone, 8,000 weeklies, 1,200 general-interest magazines, 13,000 radio stations and 1,200 television stations. Other possibilities include direct mail, banners on Web sites, billboards, blimps, skywriting and even printing the company's name on pencils.

Media buyers use formulas, some very complex, to decide which media are best for reaching potential customers. Most of these formulas begin with a factor called **CPM,** short for cost per thousand. If airtime for a radio advertisement costs 7.2 cents per thousand listeners, it's probably a better deal than a magazine with a 7.3-cent CPM, assuming that both reach the same audience. CPM by itself is just a starting point in choosing media. Other variables that media buyers consider include whether a message will work in a particular medium. For example, radio wouldn't work for a product that lends itself to a visual pitch and sight gags.

● **CPM**
Cost per thousand; a tool to determine the cost effectiveness of different media

● **Audit Bureau of Circulations**
Verifies circulation claims

Media buyers have numerous sources of data to help them decide where advertisements can be placed for the best results. The **Audit Bureau of Circulations,** created by the newspaper industry in 1914, provides reliable information based on independent audits of the circulation of most dailies. Survey organizations like Nielsen and Arbitron conduct surveys of television and radio audiences. Standard Rate and Data Service publishes volumes of information on media audiences, circulations and advertising rates.

LEARNING CHECK ◄

▶ Why are media plans necessary in advertising?

▶ Why is CPM an essential advertising tool?

▶ How do advertisers know they are getting the audience to which they buy access?

Global Marketing. *Knowing the following that Houston Rockets star Yao Ming has in his China homeland, the distributor for the Chinese beer Yanjing paid $6 million for Chinese-language billboards at the Rockets' arena. When Rockets games were broadcast in China, millions of viewers saw Yanjing signs. Also, the imported Yanjing beer picked up customers in Houston.*

TRADITIONAL CHOICES

Here are pluses and minuses of major advertising vehicles:

■ **Newspapers.** The hot relationship that media theorist Marshall McLuhan described between newspapers and their readers attracts advertisers. Newspaper readers are predisposed to consider information in advertisements seriously. Studies show that people, when ready to buy, look more to newspapers than to other media. Because newspapers are tangible, readers can refer back to advertisements just by picking up the paper a second time, which is not possible with ephemeral media like television and radio. Coupons are possible in newspapers. Newspaper readers tend to be older, better educated and higher-earning than television and radio audiences. Space for newspaper ads usually can be reserved as late as 48 hours ahead, and 11th-hour changes are possible.

The Geico Spurt. *Discount insurer Geico credits its rapid growth to heavy advertising geared to different market segments. For young buyers, the Martin Agency of Richmond, Virginia, created the hilarious cavemen series with cavemen sighing and making their way through tony lifestyle situations—airports, psychotherapy, ritzy restaurants. For the older set, Geico has performers like Little Richard in campy self-mockery. Then there's the chatty gecko. Over five years Geico moved from 4.6 percent of the competitive U.S. insurance market to 6.3 percent. Industry insiders say Geico spent $499 million for advertising time and space in 2006.*

● **shelf life**
How long a periodical remains in use

● **pass-along circulation**
All the people who see a periodical

However, newspapers are becoming less valuable for reaching young adults. To the consternation of newspaper publishers, there has been an alarming drop in readership among these people in recent years, and it appears that, unlike their parents, young adults are not picking up the newspaper habit as they mature.

Another drawback to newspapers is printing on newsprint, a relatively cheap paper that absorbs ink like a slow blotter. The result is that ads do not look as good as they do in slick magazines. Slick, stand-alone inserts offset the newsprint drawback somewhat, but many readers pull the inserts out and discard them as soon as they open the paper.

■ **Magazines.** As another print medium, magazines have many of the advantages of newspapers plus longer **shelf life,** an advertising term for the amount of time that an advertisement remains available to readers. Magazines remain in the home for weeks, sometimes months, which offers greater exposure to advertisements. People share magazines, which gives them high **pass-along circulation.** Magazines are more prestigious, with slick paper and splashier graphics. With precise color separations and enameled papers, magazine advertisements can be beautiful in ways that newspaper advertisements cannot. Magazines, specializing as they do, offer more narrowly defined audiences than do newspapers.

On the downside, magazines require reservations for advertising space up to three months in advance. Opportunities for last-minute changes are limited, often impossible.

■ **Radio.** Radio stations with narrow formats offer easily identified target audiences. Time can be bought on short notice, with changes possible almost until airtime. Comparatively inexpensive, radio lends itself to repeated play of advertisements to drive home a message introduced in more expensive media like television. Radio also lends itself to jingles that can contribute to a lasting image.

However, radio offers no opportunity for a visual display, although the images that listeners create in their minds from audio suggestions can be more potent than those set out visually on television. Radio is a mobile medium that people carry with them. The extensive availability of radio is offset, however, by the fact that people tune in and out. Another negative is that many listeners are inattentive. Also, there is no shelf life.

■ **Television.** As a moving audio-visual medium, television offers special impact for advertising messages. Throughout its history, dating to the 1950s until recently, television has outpaced the growth of other media as an advertising vehicle. Today, the Web is growing faster but remains a mere blip compared with network, cable and local television.

Drawbacks to placing ads on television include production costs. Because of cost, many advertisers have gone to shorter and shorter commercials. The resulting **ad clutter** overwhelms many viewers and diminishes the punch of the ads.

● **ad clutter**
So many competing ads that all lose impact

Limited inventory is also a problem for advertisers considering television. The networks, for example, have only so many ad slots available within and between programs. Historically, demand for slots has outstripped availability. Slots for some hours are locked up months, even whole seasons, in advance. The networks historically have used the short supply of slots to push rates to what every year seems to be even more astronomical levels. The demand, however, appears to be softening with the fragmentation of television's audiences and the advent of new media.

Because of the television audience's diversity, especially at local stations and major networks, targeting potential customers with any precision is difficult. Narrowly focused cable services are an exception.

■ **Online.** Hesitation about using the Internet for advertising has yielded to the advantages. Literally thousands of sites serve niche audiences, enhancing the likelihood of reaching people with an inherent interest in specific products. For advertisers that choose the right sites, there is less waste than with traditional mass media, like the television networks that seek massive heterogeneous audiences.

For mail-order products, orders can be placed over the Internet right from the ad. With older media, ads only whet the consumer's appetite. A phone call or a visit to a showroom is necessary—and lots of otherwise likely customers frequently don't take that next step.

Another advantage of Internet advertising is cost. Except for high-demand sites, space is relatively inexpensive.

Some advertisers have experimented with consumer-created content on sponsored blog sites. An advantage of these post-your-own-clip sites is the consumer interest created by the bizarre stuff that people post. The sites have a high level of credibility because of their free-for-all nature. But there is also great risk. General Motors, for example, invited homemade clips about its Chevrolet Tahoe, a large sport-utility. The site ended up hosting TV spot-like messages about the Tahoe contributing to global warming. An advertiser that edits or shuts off negative input runs the risk of losing credibility.

Heavy consumer traffic on social networking sites like MySpace, YouTube and Facebook attracts advertising. But these sites also carry risk because people can post pretty much whatever they want on their pages, including negative stuff on a product that works against the effectiveness of the paid-for sponsored ads.

Among the five major media, here is how U.S. advertising spending was divided, both nationally and locally, according to a 2005 projection:

Television	$65.8 billion
Newspapers	49.6 billion
Magazines	13.0 billion
Radio	20.0 billion
Online	12.9 billion

LEARNING CHECK ◄ ●

▶ **What are the advantages of each of the advertising-funded mass media? The disadvantages?**

New Advertising Platforms

STUDY PREVIEW

Internet search engines are a growing advertising vehicle not only because of their high traffic but also because they organize the audience into subject categories. What better place to advertise skin-care products than on an index page for dermatology sites? Game sites attract advertisers because of their young, male audience, which has always been hard to reach.

SEARCH ENGINES

The Internet search engine Google, capitalizing on its super-fast hunt technology, has elbowed into the traditional placement service provided by advertising agencies. Google arranges for advertising space on thousands of Web sites, many of them narrowly focused, like blogs, and places ads for its clients on the sites. Every blog visitor who clicks a **sponsored link** placed by Google will go to a fuller advertisement. Google charges the advertiser a **click-through fee.** Google pays the site for every click-through. Google matches sites and advertisers—so a search for new Cadillacs doesn't display ads for muffler shops.

Google also places what it calls "advertiser links" on search screens. The New York *Times,* for example, has a license to use Google technology when readers enter search terms on the *Times* site. The license allows Google to display ads of likely interest whenever a *Times* site reader conducts an internal site search. A search for *Times* coverage of Jamaica news, for example, will also produce links to *Times* stories on Jamaica, as well as to advertisements for Caribbean travel elsewhere on the Internet. If a *Times* reader clicks on an ad, Google pays the *Times* a click-through fee—from the revenue the advertiser paid to Google to place its ads.

Google has quickly become a major player in Web advertising. Of the estimated $10 billion spent by advertisers for online messages in 2004, Google had $1.9 billion. No other site was earning more advertising revenue from the Internet.

LEARNING CHECK ◄

▸ **Why are search engines a hot new medium for advertising?**

GAMING

To catch consumers who spend less time with television and more time with video games, advertisers have shifted chunks of their budgets to gaming. The potential is incredible. Half of Americans 6 and older play games, and that elusive target for advertisers, men 18 and older, makes up 26 percent of the gamers.

For an on-screen plug, advertisers pay typically $20,000 to $100,000 for a message integrated into the game. In gaming's early days, game makers and product markets worked directly with each other, but now many ad agencies have gaming divisions that act as brokers.

Game ads have advantages, particularly for online games. Messages can be changed instantly—a background billboard with a Pepsi ad can become a Chevy Cobalt ad or a movie trailer. One company, Massive, uses unseen interactive coding to identify gamers and adjust plugs that, for example, list stores near specific players and make geographic and other ad content adjustments. Nielsen, known mostly for television ratings, and game publisher Activision have an interactive system for tracking how many players see advertiser impressions—how many gamers see an ad and even how many recall an ad.

Although online gaming has advantages for advertisers, there are downsides. Online gaming ads, although generally cost-effective, are problematic. Games can take months to develop, requiring far more lead time than advertisers usually have for rolling out a comprehensive multimedia campaign. For simple billboard messages, however, games have the advantage of being instantly changeable.

sponsored link
On-screen hot spot to move to an online advertisment

click-through fee
A charge to advertisers when an online link to their ads is activated; also, a fee paid to Web sites that host the links

Game Platform. *Jeep has found video games a new advertising platform. Background billboards on Tony Hawk's Pro Skater 2 can be updated with new products either as new DVD editions are issued or with downloads for internet-connected games.*

● **advergame**
A sponsored online game, usually for an established brand at its own site

Established brands have created their own games, which appear on their Web sites. In an early **advergame,** as these ads are called, the shoe manufacturer Nike created a soccer game at Nikefootball.com. Kraft Foods had an advergaming race at Candyland.com. A downside: Because advergames are accessible only through a brand's site, they don't make sense for emerging brands.

LEARNING CHECK ◄ ·····························

▶ **What are the attractions of Internet-based games for advertisers?**

PRE-MOVIE ADVERTISING

Although around a long time, advertising as a lead-in for movies is taking off. Why? Because it works. The research company Arbitron surveyed moviegoers as they left theaters and found that 80 percent remembered ads shown at the beginning of the movie. Other media aren't close, recently spurring a 37 percent increase in movie ad revenue to $356 million in one year. Also, according to Arbitron, the notion that most people resent ads is mythical. Of viewers between ages 12 and 24, 70 percent weren't bothered by the ads.

Brand Strategies
···

STUDY PREVIEW

Branding is a time-proven advertising strategy for establishing a distinctive name among consumers to set a product apart from competitors. The recent history of branding has moved beyond products into arrays of unrelated products. Special K is no longer just a breakfast cereal. Now it's an extensive line of diet products. Branding now includes building lines of products around celebrity images.

BRAND NAMES

A challenge for advertising people is the modern-day reality that mass-produced products intended for large markets are essentially alike: Toothpaste is toothpaste is toothpaste. When a product is virtually identical to the competition, how can one toothpaste maker move more tubes?

By trial and error, tactics were devised in the late 1800s to set similar products apart. One tactic, promoting a product as a **brand** name, aims to make a product a household word. When it is successful, a brand name becomes almost the generic identifier, like Coke for cola and Kleenex for facial tissue.

Techniques of successful brand-name advertising came together in the 1890s for an English product, Pears' soap. A key element in the campaign was multimedia saturation. Advertisements for Pears' were everywhere—in newspapers and magazines and on posters, vacant walls, fences, buses and lampposts. Redundancy hammered home the brand name. "Good morning. Have you used Pears' today?" became a good-natured greeting among Britons that was still being repeated 50 years later. Each repetition reinforced the brand name.

LEARNING CHECK ◄

▶ **What brand names would you list as household words?**

▶ **How effective are brand names with you personally?**

▶ **Do you resent the manipulation that is part of brand-name advertising?**

BRAND IMAGES

David Ogilvy, who headed the Ogilvy & Mather agency, developed the **brand image** in the 1950s. Ogilvy's advice: "Give your product a first-class ticket through life."

Ogilvy created shirt advertisements with the distinguished Baron Wrangell, who really was a European nobleman, wearing a black eye patch—and a Hathaway shirt. The classy image was reinforced with the accoutrements around Wrangell: exquisite models of sailing ships, antique weapons, silver dinnerware. To some seeing Wrangell's setting, the patch suggested all kinds of exotica. Perhaps he had lost an eye in a romantic duel or a sporting accident.

Explaining the importance of image, Ogilvy once said: "Take whisky. Why do some people choose Jack Daniels, while others choose Grand Dad or Taylor? Have they tried all three and compared the taste? Don't make me laugh. The reality is that these three brands have different images which appeal to different kinds of people. It isn't the whisky they choose, it's the image. The brand image is 90 percent of what the distiller has to sell. Give people a taste of Old Crow, and tell them it's Old Crow. Then

First-Class Ticket. In one of his most noted campaigns, advertising genius David Ogilvy featured the distinguished chair of the company that bottled Schweppes in classy locations. Said Ogilvy, "It pays to give products an image of quality—a first-class ticket." Ogilvy, realized how advertising creates impressions: "Nobody wants to be seen using shoddy products."

How many can afford to buy Schweppes Ginger Ale?

David Ogilvy

give them another taste of Old Crow, but tell them it's Jack Daniels. Ask them which they prefer. They'll think the two drinks are quite different. They are tasting images."

LEARNING CHECK ◄ •

▸ **What twist did David Ogilvy put on brand names?**

WHITHER BRAND NAMES?

Perhaps prematurely, perhaps not, obituaries are being written for brand names—and brand-name advertising.

● **store brands**
Products sold with a store brand, often manufactured by the retailer. Also called *house brands* and *private labels*

■ **Store Brands.** Retailers are pushing **store brands,** on which they typically score 10 percent higher profits. Every time somebody buys Wal-Mart's Ol' Roy dog chow, Purina and other brand-name manufacturers lose a sale. Wal-Mart spends virtually nothing other than packaging costs for in-store displays to advertise Ol' Roy, which has knocked off Purina as top-seller. The store-brand assault has struck at a whole range of venerable brand names: Kellogg's, Kraft, Procter & Gamble and Unilever. Forrester Research, which tracks consumer trends, said in a 2002 report: "Wal-Mart will become the new P&G."

Some brands remain strong, like automobile lines, but many manufacturers of consumer goods, whose advertising has been a financial mainstay of network television and magazines as well as newspapers and radio, have had to cut back on ad spending. P&G spent $13.9 million advertising its Era detergent in 2001, only $5.4 million in 2002. Some manufacturers have dropped out of the brand-name business. Unilever has only 200 brands left, compared to 1,600 in the mid-1990s.

Retail chains, led by Wal-Mart, have the gigantic marketing channels to move great quantities of products without advertising expenses. Some retailers even own the factories. The Kroger chain owns 41 factories that produce 4,300 store-brand products for its grocery shelves.

Sam Walton

Store Brands. *Changes in retailing to one-stop superstores have diluted the value of traditional brand names. Chains, meanwhile, have introduced their own brands. Wal-Mart's Ol' Roy pet food and related pet products pick up on the name of company founder Sam Walton's favorite dog.*

Celebrity Branding. *Hybrid branding, like for Paris Hilton productions, integrates implied testimonials and celebrity names. For her namesake hair extensions, Hilton showed off the product at a hyped launch.*

Before the mega-retailers, brand names gave products an edge—with network television and national magazines carrying the messages. In those days the major networks—ABC, CBS and NBC—delivered messages to millions of consumers with greater effect than could small retailers. Not only are small retailers disappearing, but the networks also can't deliver what they used to. Television systems with 500 channels and the highly diverse Web have divided and subdivided the audience into fragments. In a 2003 newsletter to clients, the ad agency Doremus noted, despairingly, that "it's almost impossible to get your name in enough channels to build substantial awareness." Willard Bishop Consulting came to a similar conclusion from a study on network television, noting that three commercials could reach 80 percent of one target audience, 18- to 49-year-old women, in 1995. That penetration level required 97 ads in 2000.

In an analysis of the phenomenon, *Fortune* magazine writer Michael Boyle said the big superstores are displacing brand-name advertising as the new direct connection to consumers. The new mass channel, he said, is the superstore.

■ **Branding.** Brand names have taken on a new dimension. Today the concept includes lending a recognized name to an array of unrelated products: a Paris Hilton handbag, a Paris Hilton wristwatch, a Paris Hilton whatever. It's called **branding.** Originally, brand names were for products from a particular company, but the concept now includes unconnected products whose only connection is a name. Celebrities willing to objectify their image lend their names to arrays of products, giving the products a marketing cachet.

● **branding**
Enhancing a product image with a celebrity or already-established brand name, regardless of any intrinsic connection between the product and the image

LEARNING CHECK ◄ ·······································

▶ Is there evidence that brand names are losing their luster? Explain.

▶ How has branding drifted from the original brand-name concept?

Advertising Tactics

STUDY PREVIEW

When the age of mass production and mass markets arrived, common wisdom in advertising favored aiming at the largest possible audience of potential customers. These are called lowest common denominator approaches, and such advertisements tend to be heavy-handed so that no one can possibly miss the point. Narrower pitches, aimed at segments of the mass audience, permit more deftness, subtlety and imagination.

LOWEST COMMON DENOMINATOR

● lowest common denominator
Messages for broadest audience possible

Early brand-name campaigns were geared to the largest possible audience, sometimes called an LCD, or **lowest common denominator,** approach. The term *LCD* is adapted from mathematics. To reach an audience that includes members with IQs of 100, the pitch cannot exceed their level of understanding, even if some people in the audience have IQs of 150. The opportunity for deft touches and even cleverness is limited by the fact they might be lost on some potential customers.

● unique selling proposition
Emphasizes a single feature

● Rosser Reeves
Devised unique selling proposition

■ **Unique Selling Proposition.** LCD advertising is best epitomized in contemporary advertising by USP, short for **unique selling proposition,** a term coined by **Rosser Reeves** of the giant Ted Bates agency in the 1960s. Reeves' prescription was simple: Create a benefit of the product, even if from thin air, and then tout the benefit authoritatively and repeatedly as if the competition doesn't have it. One early USP campaign boasted that Schlitz beer bottles were "washed with live steam." The claim sounded good—who would want to drink from dirty bottles? However, the fact was that every brewery used steam to clean reusable bottles before filling them again. Furthermore, what is "live steam"? Although the implication of a competitive edge was hollow, it was done dramatically and pounded home with emphasis, and it sold beer. Just as hollow as a competitive advantage was the USP claim for Colgate toothpaste: "Cleans Your Breath While It Cleans Your Teeth."

A unique selling proposition need be neither hollow nor insulting, however. Leo Burnett, founder of the agency bearing his name, refined the USP concept by insisting that the unique point be real. For Maytag, Burnett took the company's slight advantage in reliability and dramatized it with the lonely Maytag repairman.

● Jack Trout
Devised positioning

● positioning
Targeting ads for specific consumer groups

■ **Positioning.** Rather than pitching to the lowest common denominator, advertising executive **Jack Trout** developed the idea of **positioning.** Trout worked to establish product identities that appealed not to the whole audience but to a specific audience. The cowboy image for Marlboro cigarettes, for example, established a macho attraction beginning in 1958. Later, something similar was done with Virginia Slims, aimed at women.

Positioning helps to distinguish products from all the LCD clamor and noise. Advocates of positioning note that there are more and more advertisements and that they are becoming noisier and noisier. Ad clutter, as it is called, drowns out individual advertisements. With positioning, the appeal is focused and caters to audience segments, and it need not be done in such broad strokes.

Campaigns based on positioning have included:

- Johnson & Johnson's baby oil and baby shampoo, which were positioned as adult products by advertisements featuring athletes.
- Alka-Seltzer, once a hangover and headache remedy, which was positioned as an upscale product for stress relief among health-conscious, success-driven people.

LEARNING CHECK ◄

▶ What is lowest common denominator advertising?

▶ What is a **unique selling proposition** in advertising? Give examples from your own experience.

▶ How has the concept of positioning added dimension to advertising commodities?

REDUNDANCY TECHNIQUES

Advertising people learned the importance of redundancy early on. To be effective, an advertising message must be repeated, perhaps thousands of times. Redundancy is expensive, however. To increase effectiveness at less cost, advertisers use several techniques:

● **flight (or wave)**
Intense repetition of ads

- **Barrages.** Scheduling advertisements in intensive bursts called **flights** or **waves.**
- **Bunching.** Promoting a product in a limited period, such as running advertisements for school supplies in late August and September.
- **Trailing.** Running condensed versions of advertisements after the original has been introduced, as automakers do when they introduce new models with multipage magazine spreads and follow with single-page placements.
- **Multimedia trailing.** Using less expensive media to reinforce expensive advertisements. Relatively cheap drive-time radio in major markets is a favorite follow-through to expensive television advertisements created for major events like the Super Bowl.

Repetition can be annoying, especially with heavy-handed, simplistic messages. Hardly any American has escaped the repeated line for a roll-on headache remedy: "Head-On: Apply directly to the forehead." A follow-up ad series acknowledged the irritation with users proclaiming: "I hate your ads, but I love your product." And then repeating the annoying line. Annoying or not, redundancy can work. The chairman of Warner-Lambert, whose personal products include Rolaids gastric-relief tablets, once joked that the company owed the American people an apology for insulting their intelligence with the redundant line that "R-O-L-A-I-D-S spells relief." Warner-Lambert, however, has never been apologetic to shareholders about Rolaids maintaining its market dominance.

Marshall McLuhan, the media theorist prominent in the 1960s, is still quoted as saying that advertising is important after the sale to confirm for purchasers that they made a wise choice. McLuhan's observation has not been lost on advertisers that seek repeat customers.

LEARNING CHECK ◄

▶ **If repeating an advertisement annoys people, why do advertisers do it?**

Over and Over. The redundancy of Head-On ads, hammering away at the unique roll-on application, is enough to give you a headache. But the redundancy establishes a product in the minds of consumers. When a headache strikes, consumers reach for heavily promoted Head-On. No matter how annoying, redundancy has proven to work to propel a product to success and maintain sales.

TESTIMONIALS

Celebrity endorsements have long been a mainstay in advertising. Testimonials can be less than classy, though. Actress Rita Hayward offered testimonials to a denture adhesive, quarterback Joe Montana to a jock-itch potion, former presidential candidate Bob Dole to an erectile-dysfunction prescription, former Surgeon General Everett Koop to an emergency-call device. Professional fund-raising, a growth industry, includes pleas from celebrity volunteers. For commercial products, however, testimonials are given only for compensation.

During Jimmy Carter's presidential administration in the 1980s, the Federal Trade Commission was among the federal agencies that cracked down on excessive business practices. The FTC saw testimonials getting out of hand and required that endorsers actually be users of the product. The commission also clamped down on implied expert endorsements, like actors wearing white coats to suggest they were physicians while they extolled the virtues of over-the-counter remedies. That led to one laughable FTC-ordered disclaimer that has endured as a comedy line: In the interest of full disclosure, one soap-opera star in a white frock opened an ad: "I'm not really a doctor but I play one on TV." Then he made the spiel.

LEARNING CHECK ◄ ·································

▶ **How has the government policed testimonial advertising?**

New Advertising Techniques

STUDY PREVIEW

What goes around comes around. The original pre-media advertising, word of mouth, has new currency in techniques that go by the name "buzz communication." The goal is to create buzz about a product. Many buzz campaigns originate on the Internet with the hope of something virus-like. The term *viral advertising* **has come into fashion.**

Viral Advertising. *Automakers have experimented with what's called "viral advertising," producing compelling action stories on the Web that viewers will want to pass on, virus-like, to friends. Embedded in story lines, like Ford's* Evil Twin *for its SportKa in Europe, are product messages. BMW estimates that 55.1 million people have seen its* For Hire *series. Honda couldn't be more pleased with its* Cog *ministory. A Honda executive said, "I have never seen a commercial that bolted around the world like* Cog *in two weeks."*

WORD-OF-MOUTH ADVERTISING

A problem in advertising is credibility. Consumers are hardly blotters who absorb any line laid on them through the mass media. Far more credible are stories from friends and acquaintances who have had a favorable experience with a product.

■ **Buzz Advertising.** Word-of-mouth testimonials, friends talking to friends, is strong advertising. But how does word-of-mouth advertising get the buzz going? And how can the buzz be sustained? In the advertising industry's desperation in recent years to find new avenues for making pitches, buzzing has turned into an art. Several agencies specialize in identifying individuals with a large circle of contacts and introducing them to a product. These agents sample the product, generally being able to keep the samples for their help in talking them up with family, coworkers and anyone else in earshot. The agents file occasional reports, with the incentive of being eligible for prizes.

How does buzz stack up against traditional advertising media? Nobody knows, but it's cheap enough that advertisers have seen it as worth trying.

■ **Viral Advertising.** Another word-of-mouth tactic is **viral advertising,** so called because, when successful, it

viral advertising
Media consumers pass on the message, like a contagious disease, usually on the Internet

spreads contagion-like through the population. Advertisers create clever clips that they hope will prompt visitors to pass on to friends. People open messages from friends, which tangentially increases an ad's reach at low cost. Viral advertising works particularly well on the Web. Automakers were among the first to experiment with viral techniques. Ford promoted its SportKa in Europe with story lines designed to stir conversation and draw people in for other installments. BMW estimated that 55.1 million people saw its *For Hire* series. Honda could not have been happier with its *Cog* mini-story. Said a Honda executive: "I have never seen a commercial that bolted around the world like *Cog* in two weeks."

On the downside, however, advertisers can't cancel viral ads, which have a life of their own and can float around the Internet for months, even years. An advertisement for beach vacations in Beirut would have been fine in 2005 but grotesquely inappropriate a year later with Israeli air attacks on Hezbollah targets in the city, mass evacuations and hundreds of casualties.

stealth ads
Advertisements, often subtle, in nontraditional, unexpected places

product placement
Writing a brand-name product into a television or movie script

LEARNING CHECK ◄ ··

▸ **Who in your group of friends would make a good buzz agent? Why? How about you?**

▸ **Where did the term *viral advertising* come from?**

▸ **What are examples of viral advertising?**

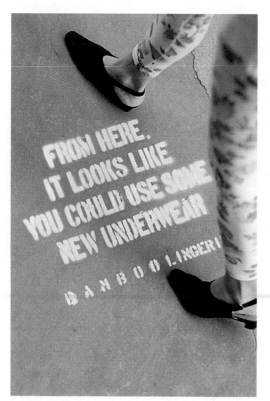

Omnipresent Ads. *Bamboo Lingerie's stenciled sidewalk messages may have been unsettling to some folks, but they sold underwear. Like many advertisers worried that their messages are lost in ad-crammed traditional media, Bamboo has struck out for nontraditional territory to be noticed. Regina Kelley, director of strategic planning for the Saatchi & Saatchi agency in New York, said: "Any space you can take in visually, anything you can hear, in the future will be branded."*

UNDER-THE-RADAR ADVERTISING

Inundated with advertisements, 6,000 a week on network television, double since 1983, many people tune out. Some do it literally with their remotes. Ad people are concerned that traditional modes are losing effectiveness. People are overwhelmed. Consider, for example, that a major grocery store carries 30,000 items, each with packaging that screams "buy me." More commercial messages are there than a human being can handle. The problem is ad clutter. Advertisers are trying to address the clutter in numerous ways, including stealth ads, new-site ads and alternative media. Although not hidden or subliminal, stealth ads are subtle—even covert. You might not know you're being pitched unless you're attentive, really attentive.

■ **Stealth Ads.** So neatly can **stealth ads** fit into the landscape that people may not recognize they're being pitched. Consider the Bamboo lingerie company, which stenciled messages on a Manhattan sidewalk: "From here it looks like you could use some new underwear." Sports stadiums like FedEx Field outside of Washington, D.C., work their way into everyday dialogue, subtly reinforcing product identity.

■ **Product Placement.** In the 1980s advertisers began wiggling brand-name products into movie scripts, creating an additional although minor revenue stream for moviemakers. The practice, **product placement,** stirred criticism about artistic integrity, but it gained momentum. Fees zoomed upward. For the 2005 release of *The Green Hornet*, Miramax was seeking an automaker willing to pay at least $35 million for its products to be written into the script, topping the $15 million that Ford paid for its 2003 Thunderbird, Jaguar and Aston Martin lines to be in the James Bond movie *Die Another Day*.

Out of Skidmore College with a psych degree, Dave Balter set out to be a romance author. Sidetracked, he instead landed jobs on the periphery of advertising in direct marketing and promotion. In time, seeing the slipping effectiveness of traditional advertising, Balter toyed in his mind with word of mouth. Today at his marketing company in Boston, he's known around the office as buzz-agent Dave.

The company, BzzAgent, is at the vanguard of the explosive word-of-mouth segment of the advertising industry—WOM, for short. BzzAgent handles about 300 campaigns simultaneously. Clients include Levi's Dockers, Anheuser-Busch and Cadbury-Schweppes.

By age 40 Balter, an absolute believer in buzz, had founded the Word-of-Mouth Marketing Association and chaired the association's ethics committee. Balter was in the process of securing a patent on the buzz schemes he had devised at BzzAgent. In 2005 he cemented his place in the evolution of advertising with a book fittingly titled *Grapevine*.

The premise of Balter's system is the universally acknowledged fact that people are more influenced by people around them, no matter how much they're also immersed in traditional advertising messages. BzzAgent

Buzzmeister. *They call Dave Balter the master of buzz. His BzzAgent company stirs up word-of-mouth promotion for products through networks of people he calls "influentials." These people are given a product to try and to talk up to friends and associates.*

signs up volunteers who meet a profile of "influentials," as they're called, and matches them up with a client's products—jeans, perfumes, cheese goodies, you name it—to sample and then chat up the products among family, friends, associates and anybody else. The buzzing is unscripted, mostly just everyday conversation,

although some agents use the Internet to spread the word. The buzz agents file reports on their buzzing and earn buzz points that can be redeemed for rewards. iPods go over well. So do cameras and books.

Balter's agents constitute an army, as many as 117,000 at any one point.

Does buzz marketing work? Measures are elusive, but WOM is so cheap compared to buying space and time in traditional media that advertisers figure, what's to lose?

Anecdotal evidence of the effectiveness abounds. For example, the influential book-retailing trade journal *Publishers Weekly*, after receiving advance proofs of Balter's book *Grapevine*, issued a negative review that normally would be a death knell: "Balter's gee-whiz, narcissistic writing voice won't help win converts." But Balter also had put 2,000 copies into the hands of buzz agents. The book became a best-selling business title.

WHAT DO YOU THINK?

▶ Which products lend themselves to buzz promotion? Which do not?

▶ If you were an executive at on automobile manufacturer, how much of your advertising budget would you risk on buzz tactics? Explain your reasoning.

▶ What if the product were a new book? A new toothpaste? Or new athletic shoe aimed at pre-teens? An iPhone competitor?

● **TiVo**
A television recording and playback device that allows viewers to edit out commercials. A competing device is ReplayTV

● **infomercial**
Program-length broadcast commercial

● **'zine**
Magazine whose entire content, articles and ads, pitches a single product or product line

Later, placing products into television scenes gained importance with the advent of **TiVo** and other devices that allow people to record shows and replay them commercial-free at their convenience. By 2004 about 1 million people owned these devices. Their growing popularity worried the television industry, whose business model was dependent on revenue from advertisers to which it guaranteed an audience for ads. With TiVo, audiences no longer were trapped into watching commercials. Was the 30-second spot commercial doomed? The television and advertising industries struck product placement deals that went beyond

Product Placement. *A financial linchpin for the CBS adventure series* Survivor *was integrating identifiable brand-name products into the story lines for a price. Advertisers have gravitated to product placement to counter viewership that's lost to fast-growing options such as TiVo and Replay that viewers can use to bypass commercial messages.*

anything seen before. For a fee, products are being built into scripts not only as props but also for both implicit and explicit endorsement.

■ **Infomercials.** Less subtle is the **infomercial**, a program-length television commercial dolled up to look like a newscast, a live-audience participation show or a chatty talk show. With the proliferation of 24-hour television service and of cable channels, airtime is so cheap at certain hours that advertisers of even offbeat products can afford it. Hardly anybody is fooled into thinking that infomercials are anything but advertisements, but some full-length media advertisements, like Liz Taylor wandering through CBS sitcoms, are cleverly disguised.

A print media variation is the **'zine**—a magazine published by a manufacturer to plug a single line of products with varying degrees of subtlety. 'Zine publishers, including such stalwarts as IBM and Sony, have even been so brazen as to sell these wall-to-wall advertising vehicles at newsstands. One example was a splashy new magazine called *Colors*, for which you paid $4.50. Once inside, you probably realized it was a thinly veiled ad for Benetton casual clothes. *Guess Journal* may look like a magazine, but guess who puts it out as a 'zine: The makers of the Guess fashion brand.

Stealth advertisements try "to morph into the very entertainment it sponsors." wrote Mary Kuntz, Joseph Weber and Heidi Dawley in *Business Week*. The goal, they said, is "to create messages so entertaining, so compelling—and maybe so disguised—that rapt audiences will swallow them whole, oblivious to the sales component."

LEARNING CHECK ◄ •

▶ **How do advertisers try to avoid being lost in ad clutter?**

Problems and Issues

STUDY PREVIEW

People are exposed to such a blur of ads that advertisers worry that their messages are being lost in the clutter. Some advertising people see more creativity as the answer so that people will want to see and read ads, but there is evidence that creativity can work against an ad's effectiveness.

ADVERTISING CLUTTER

Leo Bogart of the Newspaper Advertising Bureau noted that the number of advertising messages doubled through the 1960s and 1970s. Except for the recession at the start of the 1990s, the trend continues. This proliferation of advertising creates a problem: too many ads. The problem has been exacerbated by the shortening of ads from 60 seconds in the early days of television to today's widely used 15-second format.

At one time the National Association of Broadcasters had a code limiting the quantity of commercials. The Federal Communications Commission let station owners know that it supported the NAB code, but in 1981, as part of the Reagan administration's deregulation, the FCC backed away from any limitation. In 1983 a federal court threw out the NAB limitation as a monopolistic practice.

Ad clutter is less of an issue in the print media. Many people buy magazines and newspapers to look at ads as part of the comparative shopping process. Even so, some advertisers, concerned that their ads are overlooked in massive editions, such as a seven-pound metro Sunday newspaper or a 700-page bridal magazine, are looking to alternative means to reach potential customers in a less cluttered environment.

The clutter that marks much of commercial television and radio today may be alleviated as the media fragment further. Not only will demassification create more specialized outlets, such as narrowly focused cable television services, but there will be new media. The result will be advertising aimed at narrower audiences.

One measure of network television ad clutter is the average number of messages per commercial break, here including network program promotions:

ABC	7.1
CBS	6.3
NBC	6.2
Fox	6.0

LEARNING CHECK ◄ ··

▸ **Why is ad clutter more of a problem in broadcast than in print media?**

▸ **How might demassification ease the ad clutter problem?**

CREATIVE EXCESSES

● **Harry McMahan**
Dubious about ad creativity

● **Clio Award**
Award for advertising creativity

Advertisers are reviewing whether creativity is as effective an approach as hard sell. **Harry McMahan** studied **Clio Awards** for creativity in advertising and discovered that the 36 agencies that produced 81 winners of the prestigious awards for advertisements had either lost the winning account or gone out of business.

Predicts advertising commentator E. B. Weiss: "Extravagant license for creative people will be curtailed." The future may hold more heavy-handed pitches, perhaps with over-the-counter regimens not only promising fast-fast-fast relief but also spelling it out in all caps and boldface with exclamation marks: **F-A-S-T! F-A-S-T!! F-A-S-T!!!**

A London agency, Naked Communications, set up a New York office in 2005 and became the talk of the industry for eschewing creativity. Rather than catchy slogans and clever jingles, Naked focuses first on strategy, identifying the audience for a product or service, then identifying how to reach that audience. Only then does Naked begin work on the message. As Naked executives put it, the rest of the advertising industry for too long has let the tail wag the dog by going for creative glitz before devising strategy. Naked worked wonders for early clients, including Heineken beer and Honda cars.

LEARNING CHECK ◄ ··

▸ **Does creativity in advertising translate into sales successes? Explain.**

Chapter Wrap-Up

Importance of Advertising (Page 318)

■ Modern consumer economies are driven by the demand stirred by advertising for products. The demand contributes to economic growth and prosperity. Also, because advertising brings attention to consumer choices, it fits well with the democratic notion of people making decisions individually on what serves their interests. Questions can be asked whether advertising is a negative in consumer decision making because it is aimed at selling products and not at promoting the common good. Conversely, it can be argued that prosperity is the common good. Also, advertising messages are one-sided and often filled with emotional appeals.

The messages thus are more coercive communication than persuasive communication. Despite the critics, the role of advertising is undeniable. Some estimates put advertising spending at 2 percent of the U.S. gross domestic product.

Origins of Advertising (Page 320)

■ The printing technology that developed from Johannes Gutenberg's movable metal type made possible the mass production of advertising messages. Actual advertising evolved slowly, but some 400 years later, when the Industrial Revolution was in full swing, advertising became integral in the nascent U.S. national consumer economy. Mass-produced products for far-flung markets were promoted through national advertising with ads in national magazines and in hundreds of local newspapers. Later, radio and television became part of the media mix through which manufacturers, distributors and retailers promoted their wares nationally and locally—and increasingly globally.

Advertising Agencies (Page 321)

■ Retailers and other advertisers tried managing their own promotions in the growing U.S. consumer economy in the 1870s. Gradually they farmed out the advertising to new agencies that specialized in creating advertising. These agencies also chose media outlets for reaching the most potential customers efficiently. Agencies charged for the services, generally as a percentage of the cost of the time or space purchased from media companies to carry the ads. More variations on this so-called commission system have been introduced in recent years.

Placing Advertisements (Page 325)

■ Advertisements don't appear magically in the mass media. Media companies, dependent on advertising revenue, energetically court agencies and advertisers. Also, agencies and advertisers conduct extensive research before buying space and time to reach target consumers. Each type of media outlet has advantages.

New Advertising Platforms (Page 328)

■ Advertisers covet the millions of eyeballs that browse the Internet. But how to reach the right ones? The hottest Internet advertising vehicle has become search engines, which help people find sites they're interested in. The search engine Google lines up sites with advertisers seeking likely cohorts of consumers for their products. It's ads for high-end products on sites that attract upper-crust visitors. You won't find Mercedes ads on a skateboarding site. Nor muffler shop ads on a site for luxury vacations. Another new advertising platform is video game sites that attract the young male audience that advertisers have always found elusive.

Brand Strategies (Page 329)

■ Brand names became a vehicle for distinguishing a product from competitors in the late 1800s. Brand names have endured as an advertising strategy. For commodities, with products largely the same, advertisers linked brands with extraneous qualities—like excitement with Pontiacs, daring and adventure with Hathaway shirts, class with Grand Dad whisky. Today, it seems, everything is branded. Does a Paris Hilton watch keep better time than a Timex? In the media, CNN is promoted as a brand. So is Fox News. Each has its own cachet. Less glamorous than branding in promoting products are hard-sell pitches, especially those that refrain from going over anyone's head by using lowest common denominator messages that hammer away. Redundancy works in selling, which makes those hard-sell messages annoying but no less effective.

Advertising Tactics (Page 332)

■ Like all mass messages advertising has the potential to reach the largest possible audience when it appeals to a lowest common denominator. Tactics include often-grating, heavy-handed messages and repetition.

New Advertising Techniques (Page 335)

■ The original pre-media advertising, word-of-mouth, is back. This time it's called buzz communication. The goal is to get people talking about a product. Many buzz campaigns originate on the Internet with the hope of spreading virus-like. The term viral advertising has come into favor.

Problems and Issues (Page 338)

■ Modern life has become advertising saturated. On prime-time network television, dozens of 15-second spots drown each other out. Inundated, viewers zone out. The problem, called ad clutter, is a critical challenge for the advertisers that need somehow to get their messages across. Is creativity the answer, with ads that stand out for their cleverness? Evidence suggests, counterintuitive though it may seem, that the creativity may get attention but not move products. One answer seems to be more research to target audiences and to craft ads that rise above the clutter.

REVIEW QUESTIONS

1. What is advertising's role in a capitalistic society? In a democracy? In the mass media?

2. Trace the development of advertising since Johannes Gutenberg.

3. What is the role of advertising agencies? How do agencies work?

4. Why do some ads appear in some media products and not in others?

5. What new platforms are advertisers trying? What are long-term prospects for each?

6. How is brand-name advertising morphing?

7. What are major tactics in advertising? Who devised each one?

8. What new advertising tactics are being devised? Why?

9. What unanswered issues face the advertising industry? What answers do you see?

CONCEPTS

ad clutter (Page 327)
branding (Page 332)
pass-along circulation (Page 326)
lowest common denominator (Page 333)
shelf life (Page 326)

TERMS

commission contract (Page 323)
media plans (Page 325)
Audit Bureau of Circulations (Page 325)
stealth ads (Page 336)

PEOPLE

Wayland Ayer (Page 321)
Benjamin Day (Page 321)
David Ogilvy (Page 330)
Rosser Reeves (Page 333)
Jack Trout (Page 333)

MEDIA SOURCES

● Tom Reichert and Jacqueline Lamblase, editors. *Sex in Consumer Culture: The Erotic Content of Media and Advertising.* Erlbaum, 2006. Reichert and Lamblase, both professors, have collected quantitative and qualitative articles on gender differences and representation in mass media.

● Helen Katz. *Media Handbook: A Complete Guide to Advertising, Media Selection, Planning, Research and Buying,* third edition. Erlbaum, 2006. Katz, a media-buying executive, assesses categories of media for advertising choices.

● Dave Balter and John Butman. *Grapevine: The New Art of Word-of-Mouth Marketing.* Portfolio, 2005. With chatty enthusiasm, Balter and Butman extol the cost-efficiency and also fun of buzz marketing as the next wave in advertising.

ADVERTISING: A Thematic Chapter Summary

In this chapter you have deepened your media literacy by revisiting several themes. Here are thematic highlights from the chapter:

Media Technology

As a form of media message, advertising didn't take off quickly after Johannes Gutenberg's invention of movable metal type. But by the time the Industrial Revolution was transforming economies 400 years later, advertising became key to drawing customers to new mass-produced products. Printing technology was advanced to the point that thousands of copies of a message could be distributed. Broadcasting, particularly the networks, augmented the audience. **(Pages 320–321)**

Media Economics

Of all the messages that use mass media to reach huge audiences, advertising is the most obvious. It's in-your-face, sometimes shouting: "See me. Buy this." The core message of advertising smacks of a circus sideshow barker, but the media magnification adds potency of which a circus barker could only dream. In the United States it's estimated that 2 percent of the gross domestic product goes to advertising. When advertising succeeds in exciting consumer demand and spending, it contributes to prosperity. Not unimportantly, advertising is the economic engine for the newspaper, magazine, radio and television industries and increasingly the Internet. It is from these media outlets that advertisers buy time and space for their spiels. **(Pages 318–319)**

Create Demand. *Advertising spurs economic growth by encouraging people to spend. How about another can of Pringles? When consumer purchases increase, so does prosperity. In a more abstract sense, advertising dazzles consumers with products beyond their means—like a teenage boy on a $10-a-week allowance coveting a 600-horsepower Corvette. To attain the dream promoted enticingly in advertising, the kid may do what's necessary, like go to college and study for a career. Advertising thus encourages financial achievement. Critics fault advertising for encouraging materialistic values.*

Choices. *A premise for democracy is that citizens will make intelligent decisions about public policy if competing ideas are afloat in what's called the marketplace of ideas. Individual choice is a key element. Choice also is a premise in advertising. The goal of an advertisement is to convince consumers to choose a particular product over competitors or to give a new product a try.*

Media and Democracy

When democracy works well, people choose their common course through informed decision making. This conceptually dovetails with the societal role of advertising, which provides people with information to make choices as consumers. The emphasis is on individuals reasoning their own way to conclusions about what's best. In some ways, however, advertising falls short. Ads seldom are aimed at even-handed and intelligent discourse but rather at a quick sell, often with emotional and one-sided appeals. **(Pages 319–320)**

Audience Fragmentation

Advertisers see no point in buying time and space in media outlets that don't deliver the likeliest customers. The American Association of Retired Persons, for example, doesn't recruit members through the magazine *Seventeen*. To deliver the audiences that advertisers want, media companies have narrowed the focus of their products to coincide with what advertisers are seeking. The mutual interests of media companies and advertisers have led to fragmentation of the mass audience into countless subsets. Even the media products that continue in the tradition of seeking mega-audiences with something for everyone are dissected by advertisers and advertising agencies for modicums of difference. Demographically there are differences between CBS and Fox prime-time audiences. Advertisers know whether the New York *Times* or the New York *Daily News* is better for delivering the customers they seek. (Pages 325–329)

Media Future

Newspaper and magazine publishers delight when ads comprise 70 percent of the space in their publications. That's the max allowed by the U.S. Postal Service to qualify for discount mail rates. In television, networks can run six to seven ads in sequence during single prime-time breaks. Consumers, overwhelmed by the quantity, tune out. This ad clutter, as it's called, is a major problem that the advertising industry needs to solve. A message lost in the clutter is wasted. One answer has been to find alternate media with better chances for ads to get attention. New tactics also include word-of-mouth campaigns. Another tactic, called viral advertising, offers compelling story lines continued through a series of ads. Stealth advertising is a tactic that puts messages where people least expect them, sometimes as time-proven as skywriting and chalked messages on sidewalks. (Pages 328–329 and 335–339)

Elitism and Populism

Advertising messages generally are brief. A rule of thumb for billboards is no more than seven words. Any more than that, motorists going 60 mph will miss the message. The requirement for ads to be compact can make for cleverness, but it also can lead to simplistic "Buy me" exhortations that not only lack cleverness but are downright annoying. Worse is "buy me" in all caps, bold type and italics and followed by multiple exclamation marks. These are appeals to the lowest common denominator among consumers. On a populist-elitist scale, these LCD appeals, repeated to the point of being annoying, are at the populist extreme. (Pages 332–335)

Over and Over. Head-On ads hammer away at the unique roll-on application. It's enough to give you a headache. But the redundancy establishes a product in the minds of consumers. When a migraine strikes, consumers reach for heavily promoted Head-On. No matter how annoying, redundancy can propel a product to success and maintain sales.

14

Entertainment

His Action Packed Leap

One of Hollywood's top-grossing movie producers, Jerry Bruckheimer, is on his way to becoming a top-grossing television producer as well.

Bruckheimer has produced fast-paced, swashbuckling, exploding films like *The Rock, Con Air, Pearl Harbor, Pirates of the Caribbean* and *Black Hawk Down* and films about people who made a difference like *Remember the Titans* and *Veronica Guerin*.

Before 1980, the average shot in a mainstream film lasted 8 to 11 seconds, according to film scholar David Bordwell. In Bruckheimer's *Top Gun*, made in 1986, the shots shrank to 3 to 4 seconds. In 1998's *Armageddon* they were 2 to 3 seconds. Jeanine Basinger, historian and chair of film studies at Wesleyan University, says Bruckheimer may have been the first filmmaker to understand how quickly audiences can assimilate images and their meaning: "Bruckheimer movies are the opposite of what his critics say. They're not mindless—they engage a different part of the mind."

Not many people can make the leap from movies to television, but Bruckheimer brought his action-packed brand to shows like *CSI* and its spin-offs, the *Amazing Race* reality shows, and *Without a Trace*. Bruckheimer says he just wants to keep the story moving, and to do that he "takes the air out," just as in his movies, although he likes being able to develop a character through a season of shows.

He came to Hollywood in 1972 with a degree in psychology and a career as an advertising art director. In 2003 his films earned $12.5 billion in worldwide box office receipts.

Jerry Bruckheimer. *The signature cinematic feature of his movies and television shows, including* CSI, *is the pace. Shots average 2 to 3 seconds, compared to 8 to 11 only 20 years earlier.*

LEARNING AHEAD

- Mass-media technology has magnified the audience for storytelling and entertainment.
- Pure performance and mediated performance are different.
- Mass media powerfully extend the reach of literature.
- Technology has accelerated music as a social unifier.
- Mass media feed an insatiable demand for sports.
- Gaming has become a mass medium with advertisers pursuing gamers.
- Mass media have championed the right of adult access to sexual content.
- Mass-media entertainment quality is compromised by factory-style production.
- Mass media often fall short in elevating cultural sensitivity.

345

Bruckheimer is "able to make the world's best B movies without condescending to the audience," *Time*'s Joel Stein stays. "His instinct for what excites audiences is eerily perfect."

"We are in the transportation business," says Bruckheimer. "We transport audiences from one place to another." And he does it at high speed.

Entertainment in History

STUDY PREVIEW

The mass media, during their 550-year existence, have magnified the audience for entertainment. Technology has wrought many refinements, but the core categories of media entertainment remain storytelling and music.

PRE-MASS-MEDIA ROOTS

Entertainment predates the written history of the human species. Around the prehistoric campfire there was music. We know this from Neolithic animal hide drums that archaeologists have unearthed. Certainly, the cave dwellers must have told stories. Who knows when the visual arts began? The record goes back to paintings on cave walls. Through the eons, entertainment became higher and higher art. Archaeologists know that the elites of ancient civilizations enjoyed lavish banquets that included performing entertainers—acrobats, musicians and dancers. Sports and athletics became institutionalized entertainment by the time of ancient Greece with the Olympic games and large stadiums. Then came ancient Rome with athletics and competition on an even larger scale. Circus Maximus in Rome could hold 170,000 spectators for chariot races and gladiator games.

Entertainment that has survived the ages includes music, literature, sports and sex. Other breakdowns can be made, like performing arts and visual arts. Some people distinguish entertainment from art, relegating entertainment to a somehow less worthy category. On close examination these distinctions blur, however. Art is in the eye of the beholder, a highly personal and subjective issue.

LEARNING CHECK ◄

▶ **What are categories into which entertainment can be sorted for analysis?**

TECHNOLOGY-DRIVEN ENTERTAINMENT

What distinguished the Age of Mass Communication, which began with Gutenberg's movable type in the 1440s, was that messages, including entertainment, could be mass-produced to reach audiences of unprecedented size. The post-Gutenberg press gave literature wider and wider audiences. But even 200 years after Gutenberg the audience for John Milton's *Paradise Lost*, to take one example, was remarkable for the time but minuscule compared to the audience for every book now on the New York *Times* weekly list of leading titles. Too, literature has taken on diverse forms today, from academic tomes in the Milton tradition to pulp romances and Westerns—and it's not all in printed form.

As media technology leapfrogged into photographic and electronic forms, literature adapted to the new media. Movies extended the reach and the artistic form of books. So did radio and then television. Music, a rare treat in people's lives before audio recording was invented, is everywhere today. Indeed, the impact of the entertainment content of today's mass media is hard to measure. With television turned on seven hours a day in U.S. homes on average, most of it tuned to

Perennial Cop Shows. *The police story, almost always a who-dun-it, is an enduring story genre that spikes periodically in popularity. The latest generation is led by the prime-time CBS series* CSI *and its spinoffs. Here, true to the series' title, characters played by William Petersen and Jorja Fox are at a crime scene investigation.*

entertainment content, it's obvious that people are being entertained more than ever before in history.

LEARNING CHECK ◄••

▶ **What is the role of media technology in entertainment?**

ENTERTAINMENT GENRES

● **genres**
Broad thematic categories of media content

To make sense of the gigantic and growing landscape of entertainment in the mass media, people have devised **genres** that are, in effect, subdivisions of the major categories of storytelling and music.

■ **Storytelling.** Whether novels, short stories, television drama or movies, literature can be divided into genres. Popular genres include suspense, romance, horror, Westerns, fantasy, history and biography. Further slicing and dicing are possible. There are subgenres, such as detective stories. Also, some subgenres cut across two or more genres, such as sci-fi Westerns: Remember the 1999 movie *Wild Wild West?* Some genres are short-lived. In the 1960s a movie genre dubbed *blaxploitation* emerged, for better or worse, with a black racist appeal to black audiences. The genre culminated in the Shaft series, which, although updated in 2003, had been eclipsed by the ongoing racial integration of society.

■ **Music.** A lot of crossover makes for genre confusion in music. Wanting to define their tastes, aficionados keep reinventing thematic trends. The array of subgenres is dizzying. How is acid rock different from hard rock, from solid rock, from

Nancy Tellum can be tough. When *CSI* stars George Eads and Jorja Fox threatened to leave the show unless they were paid more, Tellum said: "Walk." They did, only to come back, tails between their legs, after the reality set in that Tellum was at her max. As president of CBS Paramount television entertainment, she controlled the leverage.

Tellum learned her negotiation skills in law school and honed them at a Los Angeles law firm in the 1980s, tracking the truth about people claiming to be heirs of multibillionaire Howard Hughes.

In 1982 she took a turn as a legal expert for celebrity attorney F. Lee Bailey's television show *Lie Detector.* When the Bailey show flopped, Tellum went to *Wheel of Fortune.* There in 1987 she met erstwhile actor Les Moonves. Together they went to Warner television, where they created the hits *Friends* and *ER.* Thus began their reputation for sensing hot shows.

Later they rose together at CBS, where Moonves became chief executive and Tellum the president responsible for shows on the $14.5 billion CBS and CW networks.

It isn't unusual for Tellum to shepherd 15 pilots into the networks' schedules. She runs auditions for the long-running *Survivor* reality series, a CBS franchise. The participants all have passed her test. Tellum negotiates with agents, decides budgets and scheduling and jockeys between

Prime-Time Boss. *At CBS, Nancy Tellum's greatest gift is a knack for sensing what shows will attract mega-audiences. Although her budget is huge by most standards, Tellum needs to contain costs in a highly competitive business. Her law school-honed negotiation skills have made her a force for program producers to reckon with. Actors too.*

Los Angeles and New York to pull it together.

Tellum has tried doing it from home after the 1992 birth of her third son. Like her husband, big-time sports agent Arn Tellum, she decided she needed be in the action to do the job. It was in that period that the Federal Communications Commission relaxed

its ban on networks producing their own programs. It was Tellum who persuaded Sony to let CBS buy a 50-50 stake in production and, of course, to share profits 50-50. *The King of Queens,* a big moneymaker, followed.

As budget manager, Tellum deals with big bucks but is attentive to detail. When *CSI* producers needed to go over budget by $50,000 for Kid Rock to appear as a *CSI* guest star, the decision was hers. It was yes.

Tellum is no lone ranger. She's on the phone two or three times a day with Moonves, her boss. She also has two women as her key lieutenants, Nine Tassler at CBS and Dawn Ostroff, whom she inherited from UPN when it was folded into CW. Together they're a rarity in Hollywood's male-dominated executive suites.

WHAT DO YOU THINK?

► As more women break the glass ceiling and enter the executive suites in the entertainment industry, what kind of role model is Nancy Tellum?

► What in her professional background helped prepare Nancy Tellum for the pivotal role of determining the CBS prime-time television lineup?

progressive rock, from alternative rock, from power rock, from metal rock? Don't ask. Categorizing is not a neat, clinical task.

■ **Sports.** Genres are clearest in sports because the rules, although not set in granite, have been agreed on, as have the procedures for revising the rules. Nobody confuses baseball with soccer or the shot put with Formula One auto racing. Attempts at crossover genres, like the wrestling-inspired XFL football experiment, don't do well.

LEARNING CHECK ◄ ···

▸ What are major genres of media-delivered entertainment?

Performance as Media Entertainment

STUDY PREVIEW

The mass media's entertainment content is performance, but it's not pure performer-to-audience. The media change the performance. Authentic performance is live and eyeball-to-eyeball with the audience. Mediated performance is adapted for an unseen and distant audience.

AUTHENTIC PERFORMANCE

When liberal commentator Al Franken used to do a routine before a live audience, before entering politics as a candidate himself, it was uproariously funny unless his bite hit a raw ideological nerve. That's why conservatives avoided his shows. But in 2004, when Franken took his humor to radio in a talk show on the new Air America network, his humor and bite didn't translate well. On radio he was flat. The fact is that the media change performance. There are many reasons for this.

● authentic performance
Live with on-site audience

■ **Audience.** At a play, whether on Broadway or in a high school auditorium, the audience is assembled for one purpose. It's **authentic performance,** live with the audience on-site. Everyone is attentive to the performance. Nuances are less likely to be missed.

■ **Feedback.** Performers on stage are in tune with their audience's reactions. There can be reaction and interplay. For the same performance through a mass medium, performers guess—some better than others—at how they are coming across. The fact is, taking television as an example, what resonates in one living room does not necessarily resonate in another. Some performers are more gifted at maximizing their impact, but to reach the massive, scattered, heterogeneous mass audience requires pandering to some extent to common denominators. There is less edge.

■ **Technology.** The equipment that makes mass communication possible is what sets it apart from interpersonal and group communication. Technology imposes its own requirements on performance. The aural beauty of operatic trills in an acoustically optimal concert hall cannot be duplicated by a home stereo, no matter how many woofers it has. Andrew Lloyd Webber's stage musical *Starlight Express*, with roller-skating singers on ramps in front of, behind and above the audience, would be a different audience experience in a movie or on television. Media transform a performance. In ways large and small, it becomes a **mediated performance.**

● mediated performance
A performance modified and adjusted for delivery to an audience by mass media

By definition purists prefer pure, unmediated performance. There will always be a following for Broadway, live concerts and ghost stories around the campfire.

LEARNING CHECK ◄ ··

▶ **What are advantages of live performances over mediated performances?**

MEDIATED PERFORMANCE

In ways we don't always realize, media technology affects and sometimes shapes the messages the media disseminate. The changes necessary to make a **mediated message** work are a function of the technology that makes it possible to reach a mass audience.

● mediated message
Adjusted to be effective when carried by the mass media

■ **Music.** Edison's mechanical recording technology, which captured acoustic waves in a huge horn, picked up no subtleties. Brass bands and loud voices recorded best. Scratchy background noise drowned out soft sounds. It's no wonder that the late 1800s and early 1900s were marked by the popularity of martial music and marching bands. High-pitched voices came through best, which also shaped the popular music of the period.

Live Earth. *Live performance has become rooted in mediated performance. When top-tier entertainers took to stages on every continent for the 2007 Live Earth concert, the repertoire was almost wholly music from their recordings. Even the live performances were mediated. One million people attended in person, but 19 million watched on television and 10 million on the Internet. The mega-event was designed to exploit the power of music to elevate global warming on public policy agendas globally and generate long-term reforms.*

When Joseph Maxwell's electrical technology was refined in the 1920s, subtle sounds that now could survive the recording and playback processes came into vogue. Rudy Vallee and Bing Crosby were in, John Philip Sousa was out. Improvements in fidelity beginning in the 1950s meant that music could be played louder and louder without unsettling dissonance—and many rockers took to louder renditions.

■ **Movies.** Media technology profoundly affects art. When audio and film technology were merged to create talkies, moviemakers suddenly had all kinds of new creative options for their storytelling. Directors had more new possibilities when wide screens replaced squarish screens in movie houses. When technology changes the experience for the moviemaker, it also changes the experience for moviegoers.

■ **Sports.** Technology has dazzled sports fans. Instant replays on television, tried first during an Army-Navy football game in the early 1960s, added a dimension that in-stadium fans could not see. Then came miniature cameras that allow viewers to see what referees see on the field. Putting microphones on referees, coaches and players lets the mass audience eavesdrop on the sounds of the playing field that no one in the stands or sidelines can pick up.

Some digital cable channels allow viewers to select various static camera angles during a game. Viewers, in effect, can participate in creating the media coverage they see. This is a profound development. Watching television, once a largely passive activity, now can involve the viewer at least to some degree.

LEARNING CHECK ◄ ••

▶ **What are advantages of mediated performances over live performances?**

Storytelling

STUDY PREVIEW

The media are powerful vehicles for exponentially extending the reach of literature. The most enduring include romances and mysteries, but variations and hybrids come and go in popularity.

GENRES OF LITERATURE

Some of literature's storytelling genres have lasted through the centuries. Shakespeare was neither the first to do romances and mysteries, nor the last. Genres help us make sense of literature, giving us a basis for comparison and contrast. Literature can be categorized in many ways, one as basic as fiction and nonfiction, another being prose and poetry. There are periods: Medieval, Antebellum, Postmodern. There are breakdowns into geographic, ethnic and cultural traditions: Russian, Hispanic and Catholic. Ideologies comprise genres: Marxist, fascist and libertarian. Bookstores use thematic genres to sort their inventory, including mysteries, romances, sports, biographies and hobbies.

LEARNING CHECK ◄ •

▶ **What genres of media content can you identify besides those mentioned here?**

MEDIA-DEFINED TRENDS

Genres rise and fall in popularity. Early television was awash with variety shows, which featured a range of comedy, song and dance, and other acts. Then came the wave of 1950s quiz shows, then Westerns, then police shows. Going into the 21st century, the television programming fads were talk shows in the style pioneered by Phil Donahue and sustained by Oprah Winfrey, reality shows epitomized by the unending CBS *Survivor* series, and yet another rush of who-done-it police shows.

Some categories are short-lived. A wave of buddy movies was ushered in by *Butch Cassidy and the Sundance Kid* in 1969. Later *Thelma and Louise* spawned girlfriend movies.

Genre trends are audience-driven. People flock to a particular book, song, film or television show and then to the thematic sequels until they tire of it all. Although a lot of genre content is derivative rather than original art, new twists and refinements can reflect artistic fine-tuning by authors, scriptwriters and other creators. People may quibble about whether Francis Ford Coppola's *Godfather* or *Godfather, Part II*, was the better, but almost everyone, including the critics, concur that both were filmic masterpieces. At the same time, nobody serious about creative media content is looking forward to Sylvester Stallone in *Rocky XXXIII*. At some point the possibilities for fresh treatments within a theme are exhausted.

Genre du Jour. *Television series built around complex female characters—antiheroines, they could be called— have been a recent genre rage. Kyra Sedgwick's character on* The Closer *was squarely in the genre. Minnie Driver played an ex-con drug addict in FX's* The Riches. *Other edgy lead portrayals of flawed and nonstereotypical women included Mary-Louise Parker, a drug-dealing widow on Showtime's* Weeds, *Courteney Cox on FX's* Dirt, *Glenn Close on FX's* Damages, *and Holly Hunter on TNT's* Saving Grace. *As with all genres, no one knows when this one will run its course.*

LEARNING CHECK ◄ •

▶ **What genres of media content have you seen come and go?**

Music

STUDY PREVIEW

Audio technology accelerated the effect of music as a social unifier. This is no better illustrated than by the integration of traditional black music and white hillbilly music into rock 'n' roll, a precursor to the furthering of racial integration of U.S. society. The potency of music has been enhanced by its growing role in other media forms, including movies and television.

ROCKABILLY REVOLUTION

Most music historians trace contemporary popular music to roots in two distinctive types of American folk music. There was the black music emanating from the enslaved black culture. Another form was hillbilly music, also from the South but with roots in rural Appalachia.

● **black music**
Folk genre from American black slave experience

■ **Black Music.** Africans who were brought to the colonies as slaves used music to soothe their difficult lives. Much of the music reflected their oppression and hopeless poverty. Known as **black music,** it was distinctive in that it carried strains of slaves' African roots and at the same time reflected the black American experience. This music also included strong religious themes, expressing the slaves' indefatigable faith in a glorious afterlife. Flowing from the heart and the soul, this was folk music of the most authentic sort.

After the Civil War, black musicians found a white audience on riverboats and in saloons and pleasure palaces of various sorts. That introduced a commercial component into black music and fueled numerous variations, including jazz. Even with the growing white following, the creation of these latter-day forms of black music remained almost entirely with African-American musicians. White musicians who picked up on the growing popularity of black music drew heavily on black songwriters. Much of Benny Goodman's swing music, for example, came from black arranger Fletcher Henderson.

● **rhythm and blues**
Distinctive style of black music that took form in 1930s

In the 1930s and 1940s a distinctive new form of black music, **rhythm and blues,** emerged. The people who enjoyed this music were all over the country, and these fans included both blacks and whites. Mainstream American music had come to include a firm African-American presence.

● **hillbilly music**
Folk genre from rural Appalachian, Southern white experience

■ **Hillbilly Music.** Another authentic American folk music form, **hillbilly music,** flowed from the lives of Appalachian and Southern whites. Early hillbilly music had a strong colonial heritage in English ballads and ditties, but over time hillbilly music evolved into a genre in its own right. Fiddle playing and twangy lyrics reflected the poverty and hopelessness of rural folk, "hillbillies" as they called themselves. Also like black music, hillbilly music reflected the joys, frustrations and sorrows of love and family. However, hillbilly music failed to develop more than a regional following—that is, until the 1950s, when a great confluence of the black and hillbilly traditions occurred. This distinctive new form of American music, called **rockabilly** early on, became rock 'n' roll.

● **rockabilly**
A splicing of rock 'n' roll and hillbilly, used for early rock music

LEARNING CHECK ◄

▶ **What distinctive American musical genres melded in rockabilly?**

● **rock 'n' roll**
A popular dance music characterized by a heavy beat, simple melodies, and guitar, bass and drum instrumentation, usually on a 12-bar structure

ROCK 'N' ROLL

If **rock 'n' roll** as a musical genre has a single progenitor, it may be Memphis disc jockey and promoter **Sam Phillips.** In 1951 Phillips recorded a cars and girls song, *Rocket 88,* an ode to a new Oldsmobile. The recording itself was technically flawed. Willie Kizart's guitar had a cracked amp, but, folded into a boogie-woogie

● **Sam Phillips**
A Memphis music producer who recorded and promoted early rock music

FIRST TIME IN MEMPHIS!

W.C. HANDY THEATRE

2 DAYS ONLY - SAT. & SUN. APRIL 7 - 8

ON STAGE! ----- IN PERSON

JACKIE BRENSTON

★ ★

THE
TERRIFIC **ROCKET "88"** SENSATION

WITH

IKE TURNER

" THE KING OF THE PIANO "

AND

★ **— " HIS KING OF RHYTHM "—** ★

JACKIE IS GONNA TEAR THE HOUSE DOWN

ADMISSION_____ 60c Tax. Incl.

Birth of Rock 'N' Roll. *A strong claim can be made that a two-minute ode to a powerful new Oldsmobile,* Rocket 88, *with a firm backbeat, launched rock 'n' roll as a musical genre in 1951. Other claimants: Louis Jordan's* Caledonia, *Fats Domino's* Fat Man, *and Lloyd Price's* Lawdy Miss Clawdy.

piano, a blues sax and Jackie Brenston's rhythm and blues vocals, the fuzzy guitar sounds seemed to fit. Right away *Rocket 88* was atop the R&B charts.

Rock 'n' roll was hardly calculated. *Rocket 88* came from four buddies, Ike Turner and His Kings of Rhythm. Infatuated with the new Oldsmobile and driving to a recording session in Memphis, they scribbled rhymes about the Oldsmobile. A blown tire, a rainstorm and a night in jail later, they were in Sam Phillips' recording studio and jamming impromptu—Turner boogie-woogieing his piano, Raymond Hill blowing his blues sax, Willie Kizart hitting wuzzy chords on his failing guitar, and Jackie Brentson intoning those on-the-fly lyrics from the trip.

Sam Phillips was pleased that *Rocket 88*, from a black group, caught on with white as well as black teenagers. But Phillips realized that this emerging hybrid musical genre needed a white face in order to find an enduring place in mainstream pop. In 1954 a white crooner, Elvis Presley, was in the studio recording ballads. During a break Presley belted out a variation of black composer Arthur Crudup's *That's All Right*. Phillips knew he had found what he called, at least apocryphally, his "white boy who sang colored."

Elvis wasn't the first, but he put a white face on rock 'n' roll. A cultural race barrier was transcended on an unprecedented scale. It can be argued that the racial integration of music paved the way for the accelerated civil rights movement in the 1960s that profoundly changed U.S. society.

LEARNING CHECK ◄ ···

▶ **How did Elvis Presley personify the music traditions that fused into rock 'n' roll?**

MUSIC OF DISSENT

Entertainment can be political, potently so. A folk revival was a centerpiece of the anti-Vietnam anti-war movement of the late 1960s into the 1970s. There were countersingers too, who sold lots of vinyl. *The Ballad of the Green Berets* cast soldiers in a heroic vein. *An Okie from Muskogee* glorified blind patriotism.

This was nothing new. Stephen Foster's *Nothing but a Plain Old Soldier* kept the legend of George Washington going; *The Battle Hymn of the Republic* still moves people. The Civil War generated a spate of patriotic music. The catchy *Over There* did the same in World War I.

It was an offhand remark, not their music, that made the sassy Dixie Chicks the bad girls among George W. Bush loyalists. In 2003 at the height of enthusiasm for the Iraq War, lead singer Natalie Maines told a London audience that she was "ashamed" that the president was from Texas. Despite the popularity of their music, the Chicks were banned by many radio stations whose managements were cowed by the volume of listener outrage. The Chicks had the last word, however.

In 2006, with public sentiment shifted against the war, the group rebuffed the angry reaction with *Not Ready to Make Nice* on a CD that opened at Number 28 on *Billboard*'s Hot 100.

Classic rockers Pearl Jam added to the anti-war revival with an album that included *World Wide Suicide*, which opened with a newspaper casualty report. Then came the dark lyrics: "Now you know both sides / Claiming killing in God's name / But God is nowhere to be found, conveniently." The new anti-Iraq War repertoire was perhaps most strident with Neil Young's track *Let's Impeach the President,* in

Mixing Music and Politics. *The Dixie Chicks were no friend of the Iraq War even before Bush-bashing became a national pastime in the waning months of his presidency. After Natalie Maines lashed out at the President in an aside at a London performance, Bush supporters pressured radio stations to stop playing their music. Sales of their music fell, but the group, unapologetic, didn't back off. Within months, record sales rebounded. The saga demonstrated how the role of music and performers is perceived in public policy.*

which he sings "flip" and "flop" amid Bush quotes. Paul Simon, whose popularity, like Young's, dated to the Vietnam period, entered the anti-war revival in 2006 with the politically tinged album *Surprise*.

Political leaders know the power of incorporating popular music into their campaign personas. Can you imagine a documentary on Franklin Roosevelt without Jack Yellen and Milton Ager's *Happy Days Are Here Again*? The first President Bush paraphrased the Nitty Gritty Dirt Band on the campaign trail, then borrowed from Paul Simon's *Boy in the Bubble* to make a point about the economy: "If this age of miracles has taught us anything, it's that if we can change the world, we can change America."

The mobilizing power of recorded music was demonstrated with *We Are the World,* the fastest-selling record of the 1980s. Four million copies were sold in six weeks. Profits from the recording, produced by big-name entertainers who volunteered, went to the USA for Africa project. In six months $50 million was raised for medical and financial support for drought-stricken people. *We Are the World,* a single song, had directly saved lives.

Willie Nelson has done the same with recordings from his Farm Aid concerts. The worldwide Live Aid and Live Earth concerts were in the same spirit.

In short, music has tremendous effects on human beings, and the technology of sound recording amplifies these effects. The bugle boy was essential to World War II's Company B, but today reveille is digitized to wake the troops. Mothers still sing Brahms' *Lullaby,* but more babies are lulled to sleep by Brahms on disc. For romance, lovers today rely more on recorded music than on their own vocal cords. The technology of sound recording gives composers, lyricists and performers far larger audiences than would ever be possible through live performances.

LEARNING CHECK ◄

▶ **What has historically been the role of protest music?**

RAP

● **rap**
Dance music with intense bass, rhyming riffs, the lyrics often with antiestablishment defiance

As transforming as rock was, so too 40 years later was **rap.** Born in the impoverished Bronx section of New York, this new style of music had an intense bass for dancing and rhyming riffs, often a strong and rapid-fire attitude, overlaid on the music. Slowly rap spread to other black urban areas. Indie-produced *Run-D.M.C.* and *King of Rock* were the first black rap albums to break into the U.S. music mainstream. Major record companies soon were signing up rap acts. Controversial groups Public Enemy and N.W.A., with violence and racism as themes of their songs, made rap a public issue in the 1990s, which only fanned diehard enthusiasm.

Like rock 'n' roll, major labels missed the significance of early rap, scrambling to catch up only after the catchy lyrics were siphoning sales from older pop genres. A maxim in media studies is that large enterprises become mired in tradition with an aversion for risk taking.

LEARNING CHECK ◄ ••

▸ **What was the role of independent labels in the rise of rap?**

▸ **Why was significant innovation, such as rock 'n' roll and rap, a business challenge for major media companies?**

MUSIC AS MULTIMEDIA CONTENT

Although music often is studied as the content issued by the recording industry, music is hardly a one-dimensional form of media message. Even in pre-mass-media eras, going back to prehistoric times, music was integrated with dance and theater. When movies were establishing themselves, music was an important component. Even before movie sound tracks were introduced with the "talkies," many movie houses hired a piano player who kept one eye on the screen and hammered out supportive music. D. W. Griffith's *The Birth of a Nation* of 1915 had an accompanying score for a 70-piece symphony.

Some movies are little more than musical vehicles for popular performers, going back to Bing Crosby and continuing through Elvis Presley and the Beatles. Rare is the modern movie without a significant musical bed. Just count the number of songs in the copyright credits at the end of today's movies.

Early radio recognized the value of music. Jingles and ditties proved key to establishing many brand names. Today many composers and lyricists derive significant income from their work being built into advertisements for television, radio and online. Think about the Intel and NBC tones or the grating "Hey, Culligan Man."

LEARNING CHECK ◄ ••

▸ **What is the difficulty of separating music from other forms of entertainment?**

Hit Jingles. *Jingle houses typically charge national advertisers $20,000 to $40,000, with undiscovered musicians earning a few hundred dollars for a few hours' work to pay the rent. The dynamics of jingles, however, are changing. With CD sales plummeting, big-name artists are cashing in on their names for radio and television ads. A talent service that promotes top-name ad music, Sound Proof, says the costs to advertisers is less than the $10 million it can cost to license already-existing music. In some cases, top-name jingles have an afterlife as hit music. A Christina Aguilera jingle was later released in fuller form as* Hello *on the RCA record label.*

Christina Aguilera

Sports as Media Entertainment

STUDY PREVIEW

Early on, mass-media people sensed the potential of sports to build their audiences, first through newspapers, then through magazines, radio and television. The media feed what seems an insatiable demand for more sports. Why the huge public intrigue with sports? One expert suggests it's the mix of suspense, heroes, villains, pageantry and ritual.

MASS AUDIENCE FOR SPORTS

● **James Gordon Bennett**
New York newspaper publisher in 1830s; first to assign reporters to sports regularly

● **Joseph Pulitzer**
New York newspaper publisher in 1880s; organized the first newspaper sports department

● **KDKA**
Pittsburgh radio station that pioneered sports broadcasting in 1920s

● **Henry Luce**
Magazine publisher known for *Time, Life, Sports Illustrated* and others

● **Roone Arledge**
ABC television executive responsible for *Wide World of Sports* in 1961

The brilliant newspaper publisher **James Gordon Bennett** sensed how a public interest in sports could build circulation for his New York *Herald* in the 1830s. Bennett assigned reporters to cover sports regularly. Fifty years later, with growing interest in horse racing, prizefighting, yacht racing and baseball, **Joseph Pulitzer** organized the first separate sports department at his New York *World*. Sportswriters began specializing in different sports.

Audience appetite for sports was insatiable. For the 1897 Corbett-Fitzsimmons heavyweight title fight in remote Nevada, dozens of writers showed up. The New York *Times* introduced celebrity coverage in 1910 when it hired retired prizefighter John L. Sullivan to cover the Jeffries-Johnson title bout in Reno.

Sports historians call the 1920s the Golden Era of Sports, with newspapers glorifying athletes. Heroes, some with enduring fame, included Jack Dempsey in boxing, Knute Rockne and Jim Thorpe in football, and Babe Ruth in baseball. The 1920s also marked radio as a medium for sports. In 1921 **KDKA** of Pittsburgh carried the first play-by-play baseball game, the Davis Cup tennis matches and the blow-by-blow Johnny Ray versus John Dundee fight. Sportswriter Grantland Rice, the pre-eminent sportswriter of the time, covered the entire World Series live from New York for KDKA, also in 1921.

Sports magazines have their roots in *American Turf Register*, which began a 15-year run in Baltimore in 1829. The *American Bicycling Journal* rode a bicycling craze from 1877 to 1879. Nothing matched the breadth and scope of *Sports Illustrated*, founded in 1954 by magazine magnate **Henry Luce.** The magazine, launched with 350,000 charter subscribers, now boasts a circulation of 3.3 million a week.

Although television dabbled in sports from its early days, the introduction of *Wide World of Sports* in 1961 established that television was made for sports and, conversely, that sports was made for television. The show, the brainchild of ABC programming wizard **Roone Arledge,** covered an unpredictable diversity of sports, from Ping-Pong to skiing. In this period, professional athletic leagues agreed to modify their rules to accommodate television for commercial breaks and, eventually, to make the games more exciting for television audiences.

Television commentator Les Brown explains sports as the perfect program form for television: "At once topical and entertaining, performed live and suspensefully without a script, peopled with heroes and villains, full of action and human interest and laced with pageantry and ritual."

The launching of ESPN as an all-sports network for cable television systems prompted millions of households to subscribe to cable. The success of ESPN spawned sibling networks. Regional sports networks have also emerged, including many created by Fox as major revenue centers.

LEARNING CHECK ◄ ∙∙∙∙∙∙∙∙∙∙∙∙∙∙∙∙∙∙∙∙∙∙∙∙∙∙∙∙∙∙∙∙∙∙∙∙∙∙

▶ **What have been landmarks in the growth of media sports for amusement?**

AUDIENCE AND ADVERTISER CONFLUENCE

The television networks and national advertisers found a happy confluence of interest in the huge audience for televised sports. This goes back at least to *Friday Night Fights,* sponsored by Gillette, and *Wednesday Night Fights*, sponsored by Pabst beer, in the 1950s. Today, sports and television are almost synonymous. Not only does the Super Bowl pack a stadium, but 90 million U.S. households tune in. The World Cup soccer tournament draws the largest worldwide television audiences.

In part to keep their names on screen, some firms have bought the rights to put their name on sports stadiums. The value of brand-name exposure at places like the Target Center in Minneapolis, the Bank One Ballpark in Phoenix and Coors Field in Denver is impossible to measure.

Advertiser interest flows and ebbs, as do audiences. The 1950s audience for Wednesday-night fights, for example, grew fickle. The phenomenal success of the World Wrestling Federation lost steam after the September 11 terrorist attacks in 2001. Too, there seems to be a saturation point. The WWF's colorful promoter, Vince McMahon, bombed with his new XFL professional football league in 2001. Even with its own rules, designed to add excitement for television audiences, and even with tireless promotion by NBC, it seemed that football fans already had their plates full.

LEARNING CHECK ◄··

▶ **Why are advertisers attracted to sports?**

COST OF SPORTS BROADCASTING

Sports attracts huge audiences to television. Roughly 71 percent of U.S. households tuned in to the 2004 Olympics from Athens. For the 2005 Super Bowl it was 70 percent. Advertisers pay millions of dollars for commercial time to reach these audiences. Anheuser-Busch spent $222.8 million on sports advertising in one recent year, Chevrolet $182 million, and Coca-Cola $131.2 million. Even so, the networks generally lose money in broadcasting major sports. With the exception of NBC and recent Olympics, the networks have not found ways to generate enough advertising revenue to offset the licensing fees negotiated by sports leagues. Broadcast rights exceeded $6.9 billion in 2004 for the Big Four professional leagues and NASCAR.

Here are some recent bottom lines for U.S. television networks:

2004 Athens Olympics	$65 million
2003 College football	10 million
2003 Major League baseball	-370 million
2003 National Football League	-270 million
2004 National Basketball Ass'n	-246 million
2003–2004 NASCAR	-106 million
2003–2004 National Hockey League	-77 million
2003–2004 College basketball	-55 million

Considering the economics, the networks occasionally retreat from the bidding frenzy for broadcast rights. NBC opted out of bidding to renew its four-year $1.6 billion National Basketball Association contract after losing $100 million in 2003. What happened? ESPN won the rights for $2.4 billion.

Madness, you say? Maybe not. Consider the experience of CBS, which was the leading sports network in 1994. CBS executives, trying to make the numbers work to continue its National Football League coverage, was outbid by Fox. Six local affiliates switched to Fox. CBS fell to fourth among the networks with male viewers, an important demographic group for advertisers. Smarting at the setbacks, CBS was not to be outdone. When CBS regained the NFL rights in 1998, the network resumed leadership in terms both of total viewers and of men 18 and older. Now CBS and Fox have bid $8 billion for NFL games from 2007 to 2010, 25 percent more than the previous deal.

The networks have adjusted their business model from seeing sports as a profit center. Instead, sports has become recognized as a **loss leader.** The goal now is to

● **loss leader**
A product sold at a loss to attract customers

use sports programs to promote other network programming, to enhance the network as a brand, and to deny coverage to competing networks—and at the same time to generate enough in advertising and in some cases subscription revenue to minimize the loss. Les Moonves, president of CBS, explained the new thinking this way: "Broadcast networks must look at sports as a piece of a much larger puzzle and not focus on the specific profits and losses of sports divisions."

Culturally the Moonves mindset has negative effects. The sports drain has forced CBS and other networks to emphasize more low-cost programming, like reality shows, for the rest of their schedules. The question: After the sports, what's worth watching? Also, critics note that the huge licensing fees paid in broadcast rights make possible the mega-salaries of top athletes.

LEARNING CHECK ◄ ···

▶ **Why do broadcast companies compete to air sports even though the programming generally is a money loser?**

Sex as Media Content

···

STUDY PREVIEW

Despite the risk of offending some people's sensitivities, the media have long trafficked in sexual content. Undeniably, there is a market. The media have fought in the U.S. courts for their right to carry sexually explicit content and for the right of adults to have access to it.

ADULT ENTERTAINMENT

Sexually oriented content has bedeviled the mass media in the United States for longer than anyone can remember. Clearly, there is a demand for it. Sales of banned books soared as soon as the courts overruled government restrictions, no better illustrated than by the Irish classic **Ulysses** by James Joyce in 1930. Firm data on the profitability of sexual content are hard to come by, partly because definitions are elusive. *Ulysses*, as an example, is hardly a sex book to most people, yet its sexual content is what once prompted a federal import ban. The difficulty of a definition gives partisans the opportunity to issue exaggerated estimates of the scope of the sexual media content.

● **Ulysses**
James Joyce novel banned in the United States until 1930 court decision

Even so, there is no denying that sex sells. Although revenues are difficult to peg precisely, most estimates are in the range of $8 billion to $10 billion annually for the entire U.S. sex industry, a major part of which is media content. About 8,000 adult movie titles a year are released. Pay-per-view adult movies on satellite and cable television generate almost $600 million in revenue a year.

It was no sleazy outfit that first imported *Ulysses* but the venerable publisher Random House. Today the major purveyors of adult content include Time Warner's HBO and Cinemax, which pipe late-night adult content to multiple-system cable operators including Time Warner. Satellite providers DirecTV and Dish Network offer porn to their subscribers. Big-name hotel chains pipe adult movies into rooms. In addition, moralists periodically picket Barnes & Noble and other mainstream bookstores to protest the books and magazines they stock.

LEARNING CHECK ◄ ···

▶ **What has been government's role in curbing sexual content in entertainment?**

▶ **Why is government regulation of sexual media content difficult?**

DECENCY REQUIREMENTS

Most media companies have found comfort in the definition of sexually acceptable content that has evolved in free expression cases in the U.S. courts. Today the courts

Margin glossary

● **obscenity**
Sexually explicit media depictions that the government can ban

● **pornography**
Sexually explicit depictions that are protected from government bans

● **Miller Standard**
Current U.S. Supreme Court definition of sexually explicit depictions that are protected by the First Amendment from government bans

● **Sam Ginsberg**
Figure in U.S. Supreme Court decision to bar sales of pornography to children

● **George Carlin**
Comedian whose satires on vulgarities prompted rules on radio programming to shield children

● **Pacifica case**
U.S. Supreme Court ruling to keep indecency off over-air broadcast stations at times when children are likely to be listening or watching

---

make a distinction between **obscenity,** which is not allowed, and **pornography,** which the courts find to be protected by the First Amendement guarantee not only of free expression but also of adult access to other people's expressions.

How are obscenity and pornography different? Since 1973, when the U.S. Supreme Court decided the case *Miller* v. *California*, the courts have followed the **Miller Standard.** In effect, sexual content is protected from government bans unless the material fails all of these tests:

- Would a typical person applying local standards see the material as appealing mainly for its sexually arousing effect?
- Is the material devoid of serious literary, artistic, political or scientific value?
- Is the sexual activity depicted offensively, in a way that violates a state law that explicity defines offensiveness?

The Miller Standard protects a vast range of sexual content. Only material for which the answer is "yes" to all three Miller questions can be censored by government agencies.

The Miller Standard notwithstanding, the Federal Communications Commission fined CBS $550,000 for the Janet Jackson breast flash during the 2004 Super Bowl halftime show. The producer, CBS's Viacom cousin MTV, called the incident a "wardrobe malfunction." About 89 million people were tuned in. Some complained.

LEARNING CHECK ◄ ••

▶ **How are obscenity and pornography different?**

▶ **What is the Miller Standard?**

▶ **How useful do you find the Miller Standard?**

SEXUAL CONTENT AND CHILDREN

Although government limits on sexual content gradually eased in the late 20th century, there remained restrictions on media content for children. State laws that forbid the sale of sexually explicit materials to children are exempted from regular First Amendment rules. The U.S. Supreme Court established the childhood exception in 1968 in a case involving a Bellmore, New York, sandwich shop owner, **Sam Ginsberg,** who had sold girlie magazines to a 16-year-old. The local prosecutor went after Ginsberg using a state law that prohibited selling depictions of nudity to anyone under age 17. The U.S. Supreme Court upheld the constitutionality of the state law.

In broadcasting, the U.S. Supreme Court has upheld restrictions aimed at shielding children. After New York radio station WBAI aired a comedy routine by **George Carlin** with four-letter anatomical words and vulgarities, the Federal Communications Commission, which can yank a station's license to broadcast, took action against the station's owner, the Pacifica Foundation. In the **Pacifica case,** as it came to be known, the U.S. Supreme Court upheld the FCC's limits on indecency during times of the day when children are likely to be listening. Carlin's monologue, *Filthy Words*, had aired at 2 p.m. In response, stations now are careful to keep the raunchiest stuff off the air until late night.

The courts also have upheld laws against sexual depictions of juveniles as exploitative. Many prosecutors come down hard even for the possession of such materials. Child pornography is one of society's last taboos.

Filthy Words. *After Pacifica radio station WBAI in New York aired a 12-minute recorded George Carlin monologue, the U.S. Supreme Court authorized government restrictions on indecency at times of the day when children might be listening.*

LEARNING CHECK ◄ ••••••••••••••••••••••••••••••••••

▶ **Describe attempts by the government to create a double standard, one for adults and one for children, on sexual media content.**

Gaming as Media Content

STUDY PREVIEW

Gaming has grown as a form of mass entertainment. Some games outdraw television. As typical with new media content, gaming has become a whipping boy for society's ills with calls for restriction. The courts have not found compelling reasons to go along with restrictions.

GROWING ENTERTAINMENT FORM

Nobody could doubt the significance of video games as a media form after 2001. Sales in the United States outpaced movies. In 2004 when Microsoft introduced its Halo2, it was a news event. At 6,800 retailers nationwide, the doors opened at midnight on the release date to thousands of fans waiting in line, some for as long as 14 hours. Within 24 hours, sales surpassed $125 million—way ahead of the $70 million opening-weekend box office for the year's leading film, *The Incredibles*.

The time enthusiasts spend with video games is catching up with television. Players of Madden NFL 2004 spend an estimated average of 100 hours a year on the game. With 4 million players, that is 400 million hours. The full season of *The Sopranos*, then at its heyday, was claiming 143 million viewing hours. Do the math: *The Sopranos* averaged 11 million viewers for 13 episodes that year.

To catch consumers who spend less time with television and more time with video games, advertisers have shifted chunks of their budgets to gaming. The potential is incredible. Half of Americans 6 and older play games, and that elusive target for advertisers, men 18 and older, make up 26 percent of the gamers.

LEARNING CHECK ◄

▶ **Why is gaming attractive as an advertising vehicle?**

IMPACT OF GAMING

Although gaming is distinctive as a form of media content, market-savvy executives have extended their franchise to other forms. The 2001 movie *Lara Croft Tomb Raider*, adopted from a 1996 game and six sequels, generated $131 million in U.S. box offices. *Resident Evil* grossed $90 million, *Mortal Kombat* $135 million. There is inverse cross-fertilization too. Games have been based on movies, including *James Bond*, *Matrix*, *Shrek*, *Spider-Man* and *Star Wars*. Gaming shows on television and gaming magazines have proliferated.

Music ranging from orchestral to hip-hop has replaced the blips and bleeps of early generation games. For recorded music companies and artists, landing a spot in a game can provide wider exposure than MTV. For Madden NFL 2005, game manufacturer Electronic Arts auditioned 2,500 songs submitted by recording companies. Twenty-one ended up in the game. The Phoenix band Minibosses plays nothing but Nintendo music, note for note.

Not surprisingly, the integration of gaming into larger media conglomerates is under way. The Warner Brothers movie studio now has a gaming division. So does Disney's Buena Vista. Sumner Redstone, whose media empire includes CBS and MTV, has bought into

Computer Gaming. *Dressed as Lara Croft, the action game heroine, Diana Dorow promotes the latest Tomb Raider at a computer gaming convention in Leipzig, Germany. Game manufacturers work to stir interest in their products with booths at game conventions worldwide.*

the Midway gaming company. Hollywood and New York talent agencies have divisions that look for game roles for their client actors.

LEARNING CHECK ◄ ••
▶ **Why is gaming shedding its status as a niche media?**

CENSORSHIP AND GAMING

Like other entertainment forms, gaming is a lightning rod of concern about the effects of explicit violence and sex on children. The industry devised a voluntary rating system with EC for "early childhood" to AO for "adults only," but critics have called the system a joke among retailers. Three high-visibility U.S. senators, Evan Bayh of Indiana, Hillary Clinton of New York and Joe Lieberman of Connecticut, have proposed $5,000 fines for every time a retailer violates the code for kids under 17.

Similar attempts to codify ratings through law at the state level have not been viewed kindly in the courts. Since 2001 federal judges have found a lack of compelling evidence from opponents who claim that games like Grand Theft Auto: San Andreas cause harm. If anyone ever demonstrates that a game begets violent behavior, the courts may change their stance. Meanwhile, the First Amendment gives constitutional protection to game makers as freedom of expression and to game players as freedom to inquire and explore.

LEARNING CHECK ◄ ••
▶ **How have gaming companies responded to calls to censor violence and sex?**

Artistic Values

STUDY PREVIEW

The mass media are inextricably linked with culture because it is through the media that creative people have their strongest sway. Although the media have the potential to disseminate the best creative work of the human mind and soul, some critics say the media are obsessive about trendy, often silly subjects. These critics find serious fault with the media's concern for pop culture, claiming it squeezes out things of significance.

MEDIA CONTENT AS HIGH ART

● **Andre Bazin**
French film critic who devised the term *auteur* for significant cutting-edge filmmakers

● **auteur**
A filmmaker recognized for significant and original treatments

Mass-media messages can be art of a high order, as was perhaps no better illustrated than by early filmmaker D. W. Griffith. In the 1910s Griffith proved himself a filmmaking author whose contribution to the culture, for better or worse, was original in scale, content and style. Griffith had something to say, and the new mass medium of film was the vehicle for his message.

In the 1950s, when French New Wave directors were offering distinctive stories and messages, film critic **Andre Bazin** devised the term **auteur** to denote significant and original cinematic contributions. Bazin's auteurs included Jean Luc Godard, who made *Breathless*, and François Truffaut, who made *The 400 Blows*. Their work was marked by distinctive cinematic techniques—freeze-frames, handheld cameras and novel angles, many of them common in movies now. Perhaps the most famous of these highbrow filmmakers who developed a global following was the Swedish director Ingmar Bergman, with his *The Seventh Seal* and other dark, moody and autobiographical works.

American filmmakers have also contributed to the auteur movement. Among them is Stanley Kubrick, who directed *2001: A Space Odyssey*. Other notable contemporary American film auteurs include Martin Scorsese, whose films include *Taxi Driver*; David Lynch, who made *Blue Velvet*; and Spike Lee, who focuses on African-American life.

Culturally significant media content is hardly limited to movies. Older media forms, including novels and short stories, have long been home for creative people whose work adds insight to our lives and deepens our understandings and appreciations. The impact of great composers from eras before the mass media has been exponentially extended through recording, film and television. The printing press greatly expanded the audience for religious scriptures, whose messages go back to prehistoric times.

LEARNING CHECK ◄ ···

▶ **Which media content easily ranks as worthy art?**

LESSER ART

To be sure, not all media content is high art.

■ **Production-Line Entertainment.** A television soap opera, whatever its entertainment value, lacks the creative genius of Shakespeare's enduring *Romeo and Juliet*. Why can't all media content rank high on an artistic scale? Besides the obvious explanation that not everyone is born a Shakespeare, the modern mass media are commercial enterprises that must produce vast quantities of material. In the 1920s, for example, an insatiable public demand for movies led to the creation of the Hollywood **studio system,** in effect turning moviemaking into a factory process. Production quotas drove movie production. The studios, awash in money, hired leading authors of the day, including F. Scott Fitzgerald and William Faulkner, for creative story lines and scripts, but inexorable demands for material drained them. It has been said that Hollywood had some of the most gifted writers of the time doing their weakest work.

The factory model, a product of the Industrial Age, extends throughout the media. The Canadian book publisher **Harlequin** grinds out romance novels with their bodice-busting covers. Nobody confuses them with high art. Imagine, also, filling a television network's prime-time obligation, 42 half-hour slots a week. It can't all be great stuff, despite the promotional claims in preseason ramp-ups. Also, many in the mass audience don't want great art anyway.

■ **Copycat Content.** Significant amounts of media content are imitative. Copycat sounds abound in material from the recording industry. In network television a sudden success, like ABC's *Who Wants to Be a Millionaire* in 2001, spawned other, albeit less successful, quiz shows. Alas, even *Millionaire* was hardly original. The concept was licensed from an already-running show in Britain.

■ **Cross-Media Adaptations.** The demand for content creates a vacuum that sucks up material from other media. Movie studios draw heavily on written literature, from best-selling novels to comic books like *Spider-Man* and *The X-Men*. Conversely, fresh movies sometimes are adapted into book form.

Cross-media adaptations don't always work well. Movie versions of book often disappoint readers. Scenes change. So do characters. Inevitably, a lot is left out. Some of the criticism is unfair because it fails to recognize that movies are a distinct medium. How, for example, could a screenwriter pack everything in a 100,000-word novel into a 100-minute script? These are different media. Passages that work brilliantly in a word-driven medium, like a magazine or short story, can fall flat in a medium with visual enhancements. Conversely, the nuances compactly portrayed by a master actor, like Meryl Streep or Jack Nicholson, could take pages and pages in a book and not work as well. Also, movie studio producers, almost always needing to appeal to the widest possible audience, will alter plots, scenes and characters and sometimes even reverse a story line's climactic events.

Some cross-media adaptations are commercial disasters. With limited success, movie studios have tried to cash in on the popularity of video games. Despite high expectations, *Super Mario Bros.* flopped in 1993. The explanation? Some critics cite

● **studio system**
A production-line movie system devised by Hollywood in the 1920s

● **Harlequin**
Canadian publisher known for romances with clichéd characters, settings and themes; the term is applied generically to pulp romances

the same difficulties that occur in transferring messages from books to movies. With video games the audience member plays an active role by exercising some control over the story line. Watching a movie, however, is relatively passive.

LEARNING CHECK ◄ •••
▶ **What mass-media dynamics work against consistent delivery of quality content?**

UNPRETENTIOUS MEDIA CONTENT

Although critics pan a lot of media content as unworthy, the fact is that lowbrow art and middlebrow art find audiences, sometimes large audiences, and have a firm place in the mix that the mass media offer. There is nothing artistically pretentious in **pulp fiction,** including the Harlequin romances, nor their soap-opera equivalents on television. The lack of pretension, however, can have its own campy charm.

ELITIST VERSUS POPULIST VALUES

The mass media can enrich society by disseminating the best of human creativity, including great literature, music and art. The media also carry a lot of lesser things that reflect the culture and, for better or worse, contribute to it. Over time, a continuum has been devised that covers this vast range of artistic production. At one extreme is artistic material that requires sophisticated and cultivated tastes to appreciate. This is called **high art.** At the other extreme is **low art,** which requires little sophistication to enjoy.

One strain of traditional media criticism has been that the media underplay great works and concentrate on low art. This **elitist** view argues that the mass media do society a disservice by pandering to low tastes. To describe low art, elitists sometimes use the German word *kitsch,* which translates roughly as "garish" or "trashy." The word captures their disdain. In contrast, the **populist** view is that there is nothing unbecoming in the mass media's catering to mass tastes in a democratic, capitalistic society.

In a 1960 essay still widely cited, "Masscult and Midcult," social commentator **Dwight Macdonald** made a virulent case that all popular art is kitsch. The mass media, which depend on finding large audiences for their economic base, can hardly ever come out at the higher reaches of Macdonald's spectrum.

This kind of elitist analysis was given a larger framework in 1976 when sociologist **Herbert Gans** categorized cultural work alsong socioeconomic and intellectual lines. Gans said that classical music, as an example, appealed by and large to people of academic and professional accomplishments and higher incomes. These were **high-culture audiences,** which enjoyed complexities and subtleties in their art and entertainment. Next came **middle-culture audiences,** which were less abstract in their interests and liked Norman Rockwell and prime-time television. **Low-culture audiences** were factory and service workers whose interests were more basic; whose educational accomplishments, incomes and social status were lower; and whose media tastes leaned toward kung fu movies, comic books and supermarket tabloids.

Gans was applying his contemporary observations to flesh out the distinctions that had been taking form in art criticism for centuries—the distinctions between high art and low art.

■ **Highbrow.** The high art favored by elitists generally can be identified by its technical and thematic complexity and originality. High art is often highly individualistic because the creator, whether a novelist or a television producer, has explored issues in fresh ways, often with new and different methods. Even when it's a collaborative effort, a piece of high art is distinctive. High art requires a sophisticated audience to appreciate it fully. Often it has enduring value, surviving time's test as to its significance and worth.

Margin glossary terms:

● **pulp fiction**
Quickly and inexpensively produced easy-to-read short novels.

● **high art**
Requires sophisticated taste to be appreciated

● **low art**
Can be appreciated by almost everybody

● **elitist**
Mass media should gear to sophisticated audiences

● *kitsch*
Pejorative word for trendy, trashy, low art

● **populist**
Mass media should seek largest possible audiences

● **Dwight Macdonald**
Said all pop art is kitsch

● **Herbert Gans**
Said social, economic and intellectual levels of audience coincide

● **high-, middle- and low-culture audiences**
Continuum identified by Herbert Gans

Has Hollywood Institutionalized Racism?

Following Hurricane Katrina, filmmaker Spike Lee was commissioned by HBO to create a two-hour documentary about the devastation. After a scouting trip to New Orleans, he told HBO he needed four hours and twice the budget. He got it.

That hasn't always been the case for the controversial, award-winning filmmaker. His breakout film, *She's Gotta Have It,* was made for $175,000 in 12 days at one location and edited in Lee's apartment. It won a best new film award at the 1986 Cannes Film Festival and eventually grossed more than $7 million.

But even after he proved that black films about race relations could be profitable, finding financing has never been easy for Lee.

He spent years looking for the money to make a movie about Jackie Robinson, who broke Major League Baseball's color barrier in 1947. Robert Redford convinced Robinson's wife, now in her 80s, to take back the rights from Lee because Redford had the means to finance the movie, scheduled for completion in 2008. Redford himself will star as Branch Rickey, the Brooklyn Dodgers owner who signed Robinson. Writes commentator Gordon Jackson of the Dallas *Examiner*, "With white writers and producers, will Branch Rickey's character come out more of a hero than Robinson?"

Most Hollywood movies about African-Americans center on "relatively insignificant white people," asserts writer Gabriella Beckles. She points to *Blood Diamond* with the black character relegated to sidekick status.

While Lee acknowledges a rise in the number of African-American actors, such as Halle Berry, who can get $14 million for a movie, and Will Smith and Denzel Washington, who can command more than $20 million, he says that the television and film industries think they "just have to have black people on the screen, and don't care about the images."

For the characterizations of African-Americans on television and in films to change, Lee says, blacks need to achieve positions of power in those industries for some control over the images that are produced.

Spike Lee. *Speaking to a college audience about his movie* Bamboozled, *Lee said that "institutionalized racism" in the entertainment industry can be eradicated only by pressuring gatekeepers who are mostly behind the scenes and who are faceless to audiences: "We have to exert whatever power we can on the people who make these decisions."*

DEEPENING YOUR MEDIA LITERACY

EXPLORE THE ISSUE

Write down what you think makes a black film "black." The story? The actors? The director?

DIG DEEPER

The 2000 census estimated that African-Americans comprise 13 percent of the U.S. population, and black moviegoers are estimated to be 25 to 30 percent of film audiences. Based on these figures, what percentage of films would you expect to be black films?

Get several copies of a publication with more than four ads for current movies. Does the percentage of ads for black films match the percentage of the black population?

WHAT DO YOU THINK?

Do you think Spike Lee's claim of racism in the entertainment industry is true?

The sophistication that permits an opera aficionado to appreciate the intricacies of a composer's score, the poetry of the lyricist and the excellence of the performance sometimes is called **highbrow.** The label has grim origins in the idea that a person must have great intelligence to have refined tastes, and a high brow is necessary to accommodate such a big brain. Generally, the term is used by people who disdain those who have not developed the sophistication to enjoy, for example, the abstractions of a Fellini film, a Matisse sculpture or a Picasso painting. Highbrows generally are people who, as Gans noted, are interested in issues by which society is defining itself and look to literature and drama for stories on conflicts inherent in the human condition and between the individual and society.

■ **Middlebrow. Middlebrow** tastes recognize some artistic merit but don't have a high level of sophistication. There is more interest in action than abstractions—in Captain Kirk aboard the starship Enterprise, for example, than in the childhood struggles of Ingmar Bergman that shaped his films. In socioeconomic terms, middlebrow appeals to people who take comfort in media portrayals that support their status quo orientation and values.

■ **Lowbrow.** Someone once made this often-repeated distinction: Highbrows talk about ideas, middlebrows talk about things, and **lowbrows** talk about people. Judging from the circulation success of the *National Enquirer* and other celebrity tabloids, there must be a lot of lowbrows in contemporary America. Hardly any sophistication is needed to recognize the machismo of Rambo, the villainy of Darth Vader, the heroism of Superman or the sexiness of Lara Croft.

LEARNING CHECK ◄ •

▶ **What kinds of scales can be used to rank creative activity?**

CASE AGAINST POP ART

Pop art is of the moment, including things like body piercings and hip-hop garb—and trendy media fare. Even elitists may have fun with pop, but they traditionally have drawn the line at anyone who mistakes it as having serious artistic merit. Pop art is low art that has immense although generally short-lived popularity.

Elitists see pop art as contrived and artificial. In their view, the people who create **popular art** are masters at identifying what will succeed in the marketplace and then providing it. Pop art, according to this view, succeeds by conning people into liking it. When capri pants were the fashion rage in 2006, it was not because they were superior in comfort, utility or aesthetics but because promoters sensed that profits could be made by touting them through the mass media as new and cashing in on easily manipulated mass tastes. It was the same with pet rocks, Tickle-Me Eimo and countless other faddy products.

The mass media, according to the critics, are obsessed with pop art. This is partly because the media are the carriers of the promotional campaigns that create popular followings but also because competition within the media creates pressure to be first, to be ahead, to be on top of things. The result, say elitists, is that junk takes precedence over quality.

Much is to be said for this criticism of pop art. The promotion by CBS of the screwball 1960s sitcom *Beverly Hillbillies*, as an example, created an eager audience that otherwise might have been reading Steinbeck's critically respected *Grapes of Wrath*. An elitist might chortle, even laugh, at the unbelievable antics and travails of the Beverly Hillbillies, who had their own charm and attractiveness, but an elitist would be concerned all the while that low art was displacing high art in the marketplace and that society was the poorer for it.

LEARNING CHECK ◄ •

▶ **Why do elistists frown on pop art?**

POP ART REVISIONISM

Pop art has always had a few champions among intellectuals, although the voices of **pop art revisionism** often have been drowned out in the din of elitist pooh-poohing. In 1965, however, essayist **Susan Sontag** wrote an influential piece, "On Culture and the New Sensibility," that prompted many elitists to take a fresh look at pop art.

■ **Pop Art as Evocative.** Sontag made the case that pop art could raise serious issues, just as high art could. She wrote: "The feeling given off by a Rauschenberg painting might be like that of a song by the Supremes." Sontag soon was being called the High Priestess of Pop Intellectualism. More significantly, the Supremes were being taken more seriously, as were a great number of Sontag's avant-garde and obscure pop artist friends.

■ **Pop Art as a Societal Unifier.** In effect, Sontag encouraged people not to look at art on the traditional divisive, class-conscious, elitist-populist continuum. Artistic value, she said, could be found almost anywhere. The word "camp" gained circulation among 1960s elitists who were influenced by Sontag. These highbrows began finding a perversely sophisticated appeal in pop art as diverse as Andy Warhol's banal soup cans and ABC's outrageous *Batman*.

■ **High Art as Popular.** While kitsch may be prominent in media programming, it hardly elbows out all substantive content. In 1991, for example, Ken Burns' public television documentary *The Civil War* outdrew low-art prime-time programs on ABC, CBS and NBC five nights in a row. It was a glaring example that high art can appeal to people across almost the whole range of socioeconomic levels and is not necessarily driven out by low art. Burns' documentary was hardly a lone example. Another, also from 1991, was Franco Zeffirelli's movie *Hamlet*, starring pop movie star Mel Gibson, which was marketed to a mass audience yet could hardly be dismissed by elitists as kitsch. In radio, public broadcasting stations, marked by highbrow programming, have become major players for ratings in some cities.

LEARNING CHECK ◄ ∙∙∙

▶ **How do pop art revisionists defend pop art?**

Susan Sontag. *Her defense of less-than-high-brow art earned Susan Sontag the title of High Priestess of Pop Art. Sontag, a thinker on cultural issues, said paintings, music and other art with wide, popular appeal can evoke significant insights and sensitivities for some people.*

● **pop art revisionism**
Pop art has inherent value

● **Susan Sontag**
Saw cultural, social value in pop art

▶Chapter Wrap-Up

Entertainment in History (Page 346)

■ Entertainment far predates its modern eminence as a mass-media enterprise. People always have loved stories and music. Media technology, beginning with printing, dramatically changed entertainment. Master storytellers and musicians, for example, could have audiences whose size could never have been anticipated in earlier times. Entertainment of a high caliber became available widely. People gradually took less responsibility for creating their own entertainment, becoming consumers of entertainment.

Performance as Media Entertainment (Page 349)

■ Mass media affect performance. A stage product transferred to television, for example, needs to be adapted to camera possibilities such as close-ups. The relationship to the audience is far different. So are cutaway possibilities to multiple additional scenes. Audio technology has brought dramatic changes to music. Early acoustic technology was crude, which put a premium on loud if not blaring martial music. Amplification technology brought the crooners. Changes are not entirely wrought by technology, however. The NFL has changed football rules to accommodate television's requirement for commercial breaks.

Storytelling (Page 351)

- Mass-media companies have made storytelling in its various forms a commodity. Always looking for a competitive edge, companies shift in their promoting of different genres of literature programming. A book or program that catches the public's fancy becomes hot and spawns imitators. The public inevitably grows weary of a genre. Having run their course, genres are displaced for what's newly hot.

Music (Page 352)

- The impact of music is impossible to measure. Think about Scottish pipes at a funeral, a love ballad in a romantic tragedy, a patriotic march in a Fourth of July parade. Then there's *Here Comes the Bride*. In a broader sense, music can help society adjust its attitudes, especially when performance is broadened to audiences of millions of people by the mass media. The genius of independent record maker Sam Phillips in the 1950s was apparent when, so goes the story, he recognized Elvis Presley as a "white boy who sang colored." The result was a breakdown in racial divisions in U.S. music. The impact reverberated in the civil rights movement of the 1960s and new laws to end racial segregation.

Sports as Media Entertainment (Page 356)

- Mass media have taken sports beyond the amphitheater, exponentially compounding the audience. The huge fan base created by the mass media is an attractive target for advertisers, especially because male consumers are hard to reach as a demographic cluster. But guys come together for sports, by the millions in front of television receivers for some events. Sports has shaped the media in ways not always recognized. What percentage of the pages of your daily newspaper are devoted to sports? It's easy to argue that sports coverage panders disproportionately to an audience mania. The media also shape sports. Time-outs and period lengths have been adjusted in the rules to accommodate broadcast and advertiser priorities.

Sex as Media Content (Page 358)

- The presence of sexual content in mass-media products has been largely settled by the U.S. Supreme Court. Adults, according to the Court, have constitutional rights to sexual depictions. 'Twasn't always so. The federal government once banned James Joyce's *Ulysses* through import regulations. Postal regulations were also used to stop distribution of other literary works, as well as some works of dubious literary merit. The issue has mostly been settled with the Court saying, in effect, that government should not be allowed to determine the material to which people can and cannot have access. Among major purveyors of sexually explicit material in recent years have been General Motors, when it controlled DirecTV, and Rupert Murdoch, when he controlled the company. Among the last bastions of restrictions is over-air broadcasting. The Federal Communications Commission has statutory controls to keep decency off the public airwaves, although defining *decency* remains contentious.

Gaming as Media Content (Page 360)

- Advertisers have not missed the growing audience, largely male, for Internet games. Advertising takes the form of billboards in game landscapes, scripted plugs and game sponsorship. The popularity of gaming has found critics who focus on violent and sexual elements. To blunt criticism, game makers have followed the lead of the recorded music and movie industries and incorporated product labeling.

Artistic Values (Page 361)

■ Significant creative content can be found in the mass media. In movies there are auteurs. In literature there are Ernest Hemingways, Pearl Bucks and Toni Morrisons. Masterpieces, however, are exceptions in the huge ocean of media content. The economics of modern mass media pressures companies to produce quantities to meet huge demands. It's like zookeepers needing to keep the lions fed. Production lines for television series, romance novels and the latest hot genres are designed to produce quantities to meet low thresholds of audience acceptability.

REVIEW QUESTIONS

1. What categories of entertainment from prehistoric times to now reach people through mass media?

2. Do you prefer live or mediated performance? Why? In which do you participate more?

3. How do genres both clarify and cloud serious discussion of the quality of mass-media content?

4. How has recorded music radically changed the social complexion of U.S. society?

5. How do you explain the exponential growth of sports as a form of entertainment?

6. What is driving gaming into its new status as a mass-media vehicle?

7. What are the legal obstacles facing people who oppose sexual content in mass media?

8. What works against the presence of significant art and creativity in mass-media content?

9. How well do mass media elevate cultural sensitivity? Explain.

CONCEPTS	TERMS	PEOPLE
auteur (Page 361)	genre (Page 347)	Roone Arledge (Page 356)
highbrow (Page 365)	kitsch (Page 363)	George Carlin (Page 359)
mediated performance (Page 349)	rhythm and blues (Page 352)	Dwight Macdonald (Page 363)
popular art (Page 365)	rockabilly (Page 352)	Sam Phillips (Page 352)
pornography (Page 359)	studio system (Page 362)	Susan Sontag (Page 366)

MEDIA SOURCES

● Steven Johnson. *Everything Bad Is Good for You*. Riverhead, 2005. Johnson, a thinker and essayist, draws on neuroscience, economics and media theory to present the contrarian perspective that media content that's often maligned as lowbrow, middlebrow at best, actually is intellectually enriching.

● Glenn C. Altschuler. *All Shook Up: How Rock 'n' Roll Changed America*. Oxford University Press, 2004. Altschuler, a writer specializing in the media, explores the social effects, including racial integration, of rock from the 1950s on.

● Guthrie P. Ramsey Jr. *Race Music: Black Culture from Bebop to Hip-Hop*. University of California Press, 2003. Ramsey, a scholar, sees popular music in the United

States from the 1940s to the 1990s as a window into the diverse black American culture, society and politics.

- Steven L. Kent. *The Ultimate History of Video Games: From Pong to Pokemon—The Story Behind the Craze That Touched Our Lives and Changed the World.* Random House, 2001. Kent, drawing on hundreds of interviews, offers a comprehensive history of video games, starting from the first pinball machines.
- Dolf Zillmann and Peter Voderer. *Media Entertainment: The Psychology of Its Appeal.* Erlbaum, 2000.

In this chapter you have deepened your media literacy by revisiting several themes. Here are thematic highlights from the chapter:

Fan Base. *The global sports industry is built on media coverage and attention. It's hard to imagine the World Cup or the NFL without the mass media. The Olympics? Sure, the Athenians had the Olympics, but how dull the ancient games must have been compared to today's sequenced quadrennial winter and summer games. On radio and television, sports is a big draw. Sports is the second largest section in most daily newspapers. The Internet game Madden NFL earns more for Electronic Arts, its corporate parent, than Hollywood studios take in from most leading movies.*

Media Technology

Entertainment's role has been amplified in human existence by media technology. Amusement and diversion are available any time, anywhere. Consider background music. How about 24/7 sports channels? Then there's handheld access to news and YouTube. Technology also shapes entertainment. Actors once needed strong voices that could carry to the back of the theater. Now audiences hear even hushed whispers from the lips of miked actors. With movies, screen tests are part of the audition process. Book publishers, too, want to know whether the author of a prospective book will look good during talk-show interviews. **(Pages 346–347)**

Elitism and Populism

The interplay between mass-media content and public tastes may never be understood fully. Do media reflect public tastes and values? Or are media reshaping tastes and values? No one denies that mass media have the potential to put values to rigorous tests. Great authors have done this for centuries, posing and examining issues through fictional situations. Nonfiction can be just as influential. But lots of media content is not driven to help audiences seek understandings and appreciations. The goal instead is to attract audiences of sufficient size and variety to be platforms for advertisers to reach potential customers. This is true of books, magazines, radio, television and more and more the Internet. Book and movie companies work to satisfy shareholders with direct sales, the more the better. Elitists fault media as failing in their responsibility to leave the world a better place by focusing too much on audience building, in contrast to promoting human knowledge and understanding. **(Pages 361–366)**

Peaking Genre? *Quick, can you name the spin-offs of the successful CSI series plus copycat variations that have created a major prime-time genre? As with all entertainment genres, the high-rolling crest of these dramas surely will peak and fade—only to be replaced by another genre that catches the ever-shifting fancy of mass audiences and advertisers.*

Media and Culture

The elitist-populist tension is apparent in merit ratings of art. High art requires sophisticated and cultivated tastes to appreciate. Sergey Rachmaninoff was no rockabilly composer. This doesn't mean rockabilly is without value, but it falls into a category like pop art and folk art. Whether middlebrow or lowbrow on a merit rating, rockabilly is easy to appreciate. Anyone can get the message. A school of thought defends media on the lower rungs of rating scales if they bridge the gaps among the abilities of audience segments. Disney's *Fantasia* may be as close as some people get to a symphony hall. It's the same with Richard Strauss' or Wagner's prominence in space movie soundtracks. (Pages 363–366)

Media Economics

Factory-like production lines are among the techniques that mass-media companies use to keep costs down. The factory model works well to increase profits for products that are imitative and attract audiences, which explains in part the rise of genres of media content. Imitative stuff lends itself to expanding a genre until it runs its course. In television, horse operas had their day in the 1960s *(Wagon Train)*. So have police dramas *(Cagney and Lacey)*, prime-time soaps *(Dallas)*, talk shows *(Donahue)* and reality shows *(Survivor)*. But audiences, ever fickle, tire of old stuff. Even the long-running sitcom genre seems in a fall from grace. If nobody's buying, further production is pointless, no matter the efficiency. Media companies then need to create a hot new genre or glom onto somebody else's next hot genre. (Pages 351 and 362–363)

Not So Quick. *Although lots of mass-media content is easy to dismiss as second-rate, essayist Susan Sontag cautioned against being too quick to judge. An often-quoted line from a Sontag essay is: "The feeling given off by a Rauschenberg painting might be like that of a song by the Supremes." Also, Sontag made the point that pop art has social value in broadening the common experience of a society.*

Audience Fragmentation

Entertainment is easily dissected into genres, but the mass media have created such a massive audience that subgenres and sub-subgenres also are economically viable. Consider music formats in radio a half century ago. What once was country now is splintered into country rock, bluegrass, urban country, and a half-dozen others. Rock 'n' roll, once dominant in radio, is no less fragmented. (Pages 347–348)

Natalie Maines. *Her off-hand slap at President Bush during a 2003 Dixie Chicks concert was in the vein of a long-running history of protest music. Politics and music can mix potently.*

Media and Democracy

Mediated entertainment can give voice and feeling to ideas and build pressure for political and social change. Powerful sympathy for the mentally ill, as an example, has been generated in novels, movies and television in recent years, manifesting itself in growing pressure for public policy reforms. One all-time classic was Upton Sinclair's novel *The Jungle* in 1906, which led to government setting health standards for the meat-processing industry. Organized crime has been done no favors by Mario Puzo or Francis Ford Coppola. The debate over public policies is acted out through entertainment, no better illustrated than by Merle Haggard's *An Okie from Muskogee*, extolling blind patriotism, and the rising tide of anti-war music in the Vietnam War period. (Pages 353–354 and 358–359)

15

Media Research

Making and Breaking Television Programs

Susan Whiting had critics waiting when, after 26 years at the Nielsen audience rating service, she was named president. Media mogul Rupert Murdoch was irate. He accused Nielsen of underrating the audience of his Fox television network. Nielsen data, he said, were costing him millions in advertising revenue. Reverend Al Sharpton was storming that urban blacks were underrepresented in Nielsen ratings. Then there were advertisers, which rely on Nielsen. They complained that the data were insufficient to help them make intelligent decisions in negotiating with networks on what to pay for 30-second spots.

Whiting, 47 at the time, had her hands full. The fact is that a lot is at stake in Nielsen television data. It is hardly an overstatement to say that Nielsen is called the most influential company in the television industry. Nielsens are used to determine the price of some $60 billion in television commercials a year. Network shows depend on the Nielsens for renewal. Ad agencies pay for access to Nielsen data. Time Warner itself pays more than $20 million a year. NBC, Viacom and Disney pay much more.

Whiting, from Quaker roots, joined Nielsen at 21 as a trainee. In 2004, when she was put in charge, Whiting immediately set out to double the number of Nielsen "families," the 5,000 households nationwide that Nielsen taps to measure network viewership. Because the television audience was fragmenting with the growth of cable and satellite television, a larger sample was needed for detailed information on proliferating niche networks.

LEARNING AHEAD

- Surveys of mass audiences factor into media content.
- Mass audience size is measured by pressruns, sales, surveys.
- Audience measuring companies have gone electronic to track media habits.
- Reactions of mass audiences are part of media content decision making.
- Audience analysis includes demographics, geodemographics, psychographics.

Susan Whiting. *The president of Nielsen stands behind the company's television viewership tracking.*

373

A perennial complaint against Nielsen is that networks and advertisers have no alternative. There is no competitor. In the 1990s, upset at slipping viewership data from Nielsen, NBC threatened to form a separate service. Nothing came of the grumbling, but later Murdoch, displeased with the Nielsens for his Fox network, decried Nielsen as a monopoly. Murdoch's claim was that Nielsen undercounted urban blacks, which he said were a substantial 25 percent of Fox's audience. Murdoch went so far as to place an ad in the New York *Times*, "Don't Count Us Out," the ad shouted, claiming that "flawed" Nielsen numbers could have "a dramatic effect on the diversity of television programming."

Quietly but firmly, Whiting methodically defended Nielsen methodology. Black viewers, she demonstrated, were as accurately represented in new meters being introduced in major cities as they had been by earlier methods. Simultaneously, she stepped up plans to reduce statistical margins of error and to track where viewers were going in the fragmented universe of television choices.

Public Opinion Sampling

STUDY PREVIEW

The effectiveness of mass-media messages is measured through research techniques that are widely recognized in the social sciences and in business. These techniques include public opinion polling, which relies on statistical extrapolation that can be incredibly accurate. Sad to say, less reliable survey techniques also are used, sullying the reputation of serious sampling.

SURVEY INDUSTRY

● **George Gallup**
Introduced probability sampling

● **Institute of American Public Opinion**
Gallup polling organization

Public opinion surveying is a $5 billion-a-year business whose clients include major corporations, political candidates and the mass media. Today, just as in 1935 when **George Gallup** founded it, the **Institute of American Public Opinion** cranks out regular surveys for clients. Major news organizations hire survey companies to tap public sentiment regularly on specific issues.

About 300 companies are in the survey business in the United States, most performing advertising and product-related opinion research for private clients. During election campaigns, political candidates become major clients. There are dozens of other survey companies that do confidential research for and about the media. Their findings are important because they determine what kinds of advertising will run and where, what programs will be developed and broadcast, and which ones will be canceled. Some television stations even use such research to choose anchors for major newscasts.

The major companies:

■ **Nielsen.** Nielsen Media Research, owned by Dutch publisher VNU, is known mostly for its network television ratings although it does local television ratings in major markets and other sampling too.

■ **Arbitron.** Arbitron measures mostly radio audiences in local markets.

■ **Gallup.** The Gallup Organization studies human nature and behavior and specializes in management, economics, psychology and sociology.

■ **Pew.** The Pew Research Center is an independent opinion research group that studies attitudes toward the press, politics and public policy issues.

■ **Harris.** Market research firm Harris Interactive Inc. is perhaps best known for the Harris Poll and for pioneering and engineering Internet-based research methods.

LEARNING CHECK ◄ ·······························

▶ **Name as many major public opinion sampling companies as you can.**

▶ **To whom do polling companies sell their information?**

PROBABILITY SAMPLING

● **probability sampling**
Everyone in the population being surveyed has an equal chance to be sampled

Although polling has become a high-profile business, many people do not understand how questions to a few hundred individuals can indicate the mood of 250 million Americans. In the **probability sampling** method pioneered by George Gallup in the 1940s, four factors figure into accurate surveying:

■ **Sample Size.** To learn how Layne College students feel about abortion on demand, you start by asking one student. Because you can hardly generalize from one student to the whole student body of 2,000, you ask a second student. If both agree, you start developing a tentative sense of how Layne students feel, but because you cannot have much confidence in such a tiny sample, you ask a third student and a fourth and a fifth. At some point between interviewing just one and all 2,000 Layne students, you can draw a reasonable conclusion.

● **sample size**
Number of people surveyed

● **384**
Number of people in a properly selected sample for results to provide 95 percent confidence that results have less than a 5 percent margin of error

How do you choose a **sample size?** Statisticians have found that **384** is a magic number for many surveys. Put simply, no matter how large the **population** being sampled, if every member has an equal opportunity to be polled, you need ask only 384 people to be 95 percent confident that you are within 5 percentage points of a precise reading. For a lot of surveys, that is close enough. Here is a breakdown, from Philip Meyer's *Precision Journalism*, a book for journalists on surveying, on necessary sample sizes for 95 percent confidence and being within 5 percentage points:

● **population**
Group of people being studied

Population Size	Sample Size
500,000 or more	384
100,000	383
50,000	381
10,000	370
5,000	357
3,000	341
2,000	322
1,000	278

At Layne, with a total enrollment of 2,000, the sample size would need to be 322 students.

● **sample selection**
Process for choosing individuals to be interviewed

■ **Sample Selection.** Essential in probability sampling is **sample selection**, the process of choosing whom to interview. A good sample gives every member of the population being sampled an equal chance to be interviewed. For example, if you want to know how Kansans intend to vote, you cannot merely go to a Wichita street corner and survey the first 384 people who pass by. You would need to check a list of the state's 675,000 registered voters and then divide by the magic number, 384:

$$\frac{675,000}{384} = 1,758$$

You would need to talk with every 1,758th person on the list. At Layne College, 2,000 divided by 322 would mean an interval of 6.2. Every sixth person in the student body would need to be polled.

George Gallup was excited. His mother-in-law, Ola Babcock Miller, had decided to run for secretary of state. If elected, she would become not only Iowa's first Democrat but also the first woman to hold the statewide office. Gallup's excitement, however, went beyond the novelty of his mother-in-law's candidacy. The campaign gave him an opportunity to pull together his three primary intellectual interests: survey research, public opinion and politics. In that 1932 campaign George Gallup conducted the first serious poll in history for a political candidate. Gallup's surveying provided important barometers of public sentiment that helped Miller to gear her campaign to the issues that were most on voters' minds. She won and was re-elected twice by large margins.

Four years after that first 1932 election campaign, Gallup tried his polling techniques in the presidential race and correctly predicted that Franklin Roosevelt would beat Alf Landon. Having called Roosevelt's victory accurately, Gallup had clients knocking at his door.

Gallup devoted himself to accuracy. Even though he had predicted Roosevelt's 1936 victory, Gallup was bothered that his reliability had not been better. His method, quota sampling, could not call a two-way race within 4 percentage points. With quota sampling, a representative percentage of women and men was surveyed, as was a representative percentage of Democrats and Republicans, Westerners and Easterners, Christians and Jews, and other constituencies.

In 1948 Gallup correctly concluded that Thomas Dewey was not a shoo-in for president. Nonetheless, his preelection poll was 5.3 percentage points off. So he decided to switch to a tighter method, probability sampling, which theoretically gives everyone in the population being sampled

● **statistical extrapolation**
Drawing conclusions from a segment of the whole

Probability Sampling. *Data collection has become more sophisticated since George Gallup began polling in the 1930s. Polls today track changes in public attitudes over the several decades that data have been accumulated.*

Gallup and aide

an equal chance to be surveyed. With probability sampling, there is no need for quotas because, as Gallup explained in his folksy Midwestern way, it was like a cook making soup: "When a housewife wants to test the quality of the soup she is making, she tastes only a teaspoonful or two. She knows that if the soup is thoroughly stirred, one teaspoonful is enough to tell her whether she has the right mixture of ingredients." With the new method, Gallup's **statistical extrapolation** narrowed his error rate to less than 2 percentage points.

Even with improvements pioneered by Gallup, public opinion surveying has detractors. Some critics say that polls influence undecided voters toward the front-runner—a bandwagon effect. Other critics say that polls make elected officials too responsive to the momentary whims of the

electorate, discouraging courageous leadership. George Gallup, who died in 1984, tirelessly defended polling, arguing that good surveys give voice to the "inarticulate minority" that legislators otherwise might not hear. Gallup was convinced that public opinion surveys help to make democracy work.

WHAT DO YOU THINK?

▶ What variables determine how close is close enough in probability sampling?

▶ Explain George Gallup's metaphor of polling and making soup.

▶ Do you trust election polls? What do you need to know to have confidence in a poll?

Besides the right sample size and proper interval selection, two other significant variables affect survey accuracy: margin of error and confidence level.

■ **Margin of Error.** For absolute precision, every person in the population must be interviewed, but such precision is hardly ever needed, and the process would be prohibitively expensive and impracticable. Pollsters must therefore decide what is an acceptable **margin of error** for every survey they conduct. This is a complex matter, but in simple terms, you can have a fairly high level of confidence that a properly designed survey with 384 respondents can yield results within 5 percentage points, either way, of being correct. If the survey finds that two candidates for statewide office are running 51 to 49 percent, for example, the race is too close to call with a sample of 384. If the survey says that the candidates are running 56 to 44 percent, however, you can be reasonably confident who is ahead in the race because, even if the survey is 5 points off on the high side for the leader, the candidate at the very least has 51 percent support (56 percent minus a maximum 5 percentage points for possible error). At best, the trailing candidate has 49 percent (44 percent plus a maximum 5 percentage points for possible error).

Increasing the sample size will reduce the margin of error. Meyer gives this breakdown:

Population Size	Sample Size	Margin of Error
Infinity	384	5 percentage points
Infinity	600	4 percentage points
Infinity	1,067	3 percentage points
Infinity	2,401	2 percentage points
Infinity	9,605	1 percentage point

Professional polling organizations that sample U.S. voters typically use sample sizes between 1,500 and 3,000 to increase accuracy. Also, measuring subgroups within the population being sampled requires that each subgroup, such as men and women, Catholics and non-Catholics or Northerners and Southerners, be represented by 384 properly selected people.

■ **Confidence Level.** With a sample of 384, pollsters can claim a relatively high 95 percent **confidence level,** that is, that they are within 5 percentage points of being on the mark. For many surveys, this is sufficient statistical validity. If the confidence level needs to be higher, or if the margin of error needs to be decreased, the number of people surveyed will need to be increased. In short, the level of confidence and margin of error are inversely related. A larger sample can improve confidence, just as it also can reduce the margin of error.

LEARNING CHECK ◄ •

▸ **How does probability sampling work?**

▸ **Does probability sampling necessarily yield accurate results with samples of 384?**

▸ **What is margin of error?**

▸ **What could make an election race too close to call?**

QUOTA SAMPLING

Besides probability sampling, pollsters survey cross-sections of the whole population. This quota sampling technique gave Gallup his historic 1936 conclusions about the Roosevelt-Landon presidential race. With **quota sampling,** a pollster checking an election campaign interviews a sample of people that includes a quota of men and women that corresponds to the number of male and female registered voters. The sample might also include an appropriate quota of Democrats, Republicans and independents; of poor, middle-income and wealthy people; of Catholics,

● **margin of error**
Percentage that a survey may be off mark

● **confidence level**
Degree of certainty that a survey is accurate

● **quota sampling**
Demographics of the sample coincide with those of the whole population

Jews and Protestants; of Southerners, Midwesterners and New Englanders; of the employed and unemployed; and other breakdowns significant to the pollster.

Both quota sampling and probability sampling are valid if done correctly, but Gallup abandoned quota sampling because he could not pinpoint public opinion more closely than 4 percentage points on average. With probability sampling, he regularly came within 2 percentage points.

LEARNING CHECK ◄ ···

▶ **How does quota sampling differ from probability sampling?**

▶ **What attracted George Gallup to probability sampling?**

EVALUATING SURVEYS

Sidewalk interviews cannot be expected to reflect the views of the population. The people who respond to such polls are self-selected by virtue of being at a given place at a given time. Just as unreliable are call-in polls with 800 or 900 telephone numbers. These polls test the views only of people who are aware of the poll and who have sufficiently strong opinions to go to the trouble of calling in.

Journalists run the risk of being duped when special-interest groups suggest that news stories be written based on their privately conducted surveys. Some organizations selectively release self-serving conclusions.

To guard against being duped, the Associated Press insists on knowing methodology details before running poll stories. The AP tells reporters to ask:

- **How many people were interviewed and how were they selected?** Any survey of fewer than 384 people selected randomly from the population group has a greater margin for error than is usually tolerated.
- **When was the poll taken?** Opinions shift over time. During election campaigns, shifts can be quick, even overnight.
- **Who paid for the poll?** With privately commissioned polls, reporters should be skeptical, asking whether the results being released constitute everything learned in the survey. The timing of the release of political polls to be politically advantageous is not uncommon.
- **What was the sampling error?** Margins of error exist in all surveys unless everyone in the population is surveyed.
- **How was the poll conducted?** Whether a survey was conducted over the telephone or face-to-face in homes is important. Polls conducted on street corners or in shopping malls are not worth much statistically. Mail surveys are flawed unless surveyors follow up on people who do not answer the original questionnaires.
- **How were questions worded and in what order were they asked?** Drafting questions is an art. Sloppily worded questions yield sloppy conclusions. Leading questions and loaded questions can skew results. So can question sequencing.

Polling organizations get serious when someone misuses their findings. In 1998 the Gallup organization publicly told the tobacco industry to stop saying that a 1954 Gallup poll found that 90 percent of Americans were aware of a correlation between smoking and cancer. Not so, said Gallup. The question was "Have you heard or read anything recently that cigarette smoking may be a cause of cancer of the lung?" Ninety percent said that they were aware of a controversy, but, says Gallup, that doesn't necessarily mean those people believed there was smoking-cancer correlation. Gallup threatened to go to court to refute the flawed conclusion if a tobacco company used it again in any wrongful-death lawsuit. Lydia Saad of Gallup told the *Wall Street Journal* that her organization gives people lots of latitude in interpreting its surveys. But this, Saad added, "really crosses the line."

It is with great risk that a polling company's client misrepresents survey results. Most polling companies, concerned about protecting their reputations, include a

In college **Andy Kohut** learned polling from the experts. He first had a part-time job with the Gallup organization in Princeton, New Jersey, Polling fascinated Kohut more than his graduate studies, so he went full time with Gallup and eventually worked his way up to president. What drew him to Gallup? Kohut, who has a strong sense of civic responsibility, liked Gallup's continuing work on public opinion on the great issues.

Something bad, from Kohut's perspective, happened in 1988. Gallup was bought by a market research company whose interest was providing data to corporations to push their goods and services more efficiently. Social polling issues were sure to take a backseat.

Eventually, Kohut joined the Los Angeles *Times'* quasi-independent polling organization, the Times Mirror Research Center for People and the Press. Times Mirror had created the center to find how the public perceived the media, what interests people in the news, and to assess the relationship among the people, press and politics. In many ways it was like the old Gallup. The Times Mirror studies provided scholars, as well as the media, with new baselines of understanding.

● **Andy Kohut**
Director of widely cited Pew public policy polls

But like the old Gallup, it changed. Times Mirror, with a new bottom-line-focused management, let it be known in 1995 that Kohut's operation was on a cut list. Was there no place left for public policy polling? A philanthropic organization, Pew Charitable Trusts, was concerned about the loss of the Times Mirror polling unit and offered to take it over.

Today, Kohut's work generally is called the *Pew polls*. They are the most widely cited studies on U.S. public opinion. Robert Strauss, in a biographical article, said that the Los Angeles *Times* cites Pew polls every five days on average and the Washington *Post* cites them every six days. Said James Beninger, when he was president of the American Association for Public Opinion: "It is reported in all of the places where people of influence seem to look, the New York *Times* and the like."

What separates Pew polls from others?

● **Impartiality.** Nobody can accuse Pew of being the hireling of special interests.
● **Distribution.** Pew findings are distributed free.
● **Independence.** Unlike news media-sponsored surveys, Kohut isn't driven by deadlines. The polls sometimes make news, but that's residual.
● **Social and political thrust.** Kohut and his staff don't need to

Andy Kohut. *He opted for public opinion polling that's pristine from commercial underpinnings.*

weigh whether to do a lucrative marketing survey or an issues poll. Because their focus is on public issues alone, their focus is never diluted.

WHAT DO YOU THINK?

▶ Is a high confidence level warranted in Pew polls?

---

clause in their contracts with clients that gives the pollster the right to approve the release of findings. The clause usually reads: "When misinterpretation appears, we shall publicly disclose what is required to correct it, notwithstanding our obligation for client confidentiality in all other respects."

LEARNING CHECK ◄ ••••••••••••••••••••••••••••••••••••

▶ **What information do you need to assess what a survey purports to have found?**

▶ **How can survey outcomes be manipulated?**

LATTER-DAY STRAW POLLS

The ABC and CNN television networks and other news organizations dabble, some say irresponsibly, with phone-in polling on public issues. The vehicle is the

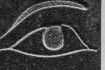

MEDIA RESEARCH MILESTONES	PIVOTAL EVENTS

1900–1949

Pressruns
Audit Bureau of Circulations created to verify circulation claims (1914)

Radio
Archibald Crossley conducted first listenership survey (1929)

Gallup Poll
George Gallup used quota sampling in Iowa election (1932)

Quota Sampling
Gallup used quota sampling in presidential election (1936)

Demographics
A. C. Nielsen conducted demographic listenership survey (1940s)

Probability Sampling
Gallup used probability sampling in presidential election (1948)

George Gallup

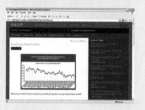

Polls trace changing attitudes

PIVOTAL EVENTS

- Radio emerged as commercial medium (late 1920s)
- Great Depression (1930s)
- World War II (1941–1945)
- Russian–Western Cold War (1945–1989)

1950–1999

VALS
Psychographics introduced (1970s)

Geodemographics
Jonathan Robbin introduced PRIZM geodemographics (1979)

Psychographics

- Television emerged as commercial medium (early 1950s)
- Vietnam War (1964–1973)
- Humans reached moon (1969)
- Internet emerged as commercial medium (late 1990s)

2000s

Bigger Samples
Nielsen committed to double the number of homes for television ratings (2004)

More Media
Nielsen added measures of Internet, iPod, cell phone devices (2006)

Billboards
Nielsen introduced cell phone-based Go Meters (2008)

Visceral news judgment

- 9/11 terrorist attacks (2001)
- Iraq War (2003–)
- Hurricane Katrina (2005)

900 telephone number, which listeners dial at 50 cents a call to register yea or nay on a question. These **straw polls** are conducted on the Internet too. While they can be fun, statistically they are meaningless.

Just as dubious are the candid-camera features, popular in weekly newspapers, in which a question is put to people on the street. The photos of half a dozen individuals and their comments are then published, often on the editorial page. These features are circulation builders for small publications whose financial success depends on how many local names and mug shots can be crammed into an issue, but it is only coincidental when the views expressed are representative of the population as a whole.

These **roving photographer** features are at their worst when people are not given time to formulate an intelligent response. The result too often is contributions to the public babble, not public understanding. The result is irresponsible pseudojournalism.

LEARNING CHECK ◄ •

▸ **Why are listener call-in polls statistically suspect?**

Measuring Audience Size

STUDY PREVIEW

To attract advertisers, the mass media need to know the number and kinds of people they reach. This is done for the print media by audits and for the broadcast media by surveys. Although surveying is widely accepted for obtaining such data, some approaches are more reliable than others.

NEWSPAPER AND MAGAZINE AUDITS

The number of copies a newspaper or magazine puts out, called **circulation,** is fairly easy to calculate. It is simple arithmetic involving data like pressruns, subscription sales and unsold copies returned from news racks. Many publishers follow strict procedures that are checked by independent audit organizations, like the **Audit Bureau of Circulations,** to assure advertisers that the system is honest and circulation claims comparable.

The Audit Bureau of Circulations was formed in 1914 to remove the temptation for publishers to inflate their claims to attract advertisers and hike ad rates. Inflated claims, contagious in some cities, were working to the disadvantage of honest publishers. Today, most magazines and daily newspapers belong to ABC, which means that they follow the bureau's standards for reporting circulation and are subject to the bureau's audits.

LEARNING CHECK ◄ •

▸ **How do advertisers know how much circulation they are buying in print media?**

BROADCAST RATINGS

Radio and television audiences are harder to measure, but advertisers have no less need for counts to help them decide where to place ads and to know what a fair price is. To keep track of broadcast audiences, a whole **ratings** industry, now with about 200 companies, has developed. **Nielsen Media Research** tracks network television viewership.

Radio ratings began in 1929 when advertisers asked pollster **Archibald Crossley** to determine how many people were listening to network programs. Crossley checked a small sample of households and then extrapolated the data into

MONDAY

Time	ABC	CBS	NBC	FOX	Univision	Telemundo	myTV	CW
8:00	1 Dancing With the Stars 14.1/21	53 How I Met/Mother 4.8/7	57 Chuck 4.3/6	67 House 3.9/6	103 Amar Sin Limites 1.6/2	128 Madre Luna 0.7/1	134 Celebrity Exposé 0.6/1	100 Evrybdy Hates Chris 1.7/3
8:30		45 Big Bang Theory 5.3/8						114 Aliens in America 1.4/2
9:00		16 Two and a Half Men 8.5/12	32 Heroes 6.1/9	86 K-Ville 2.7/4	82 Destilando Amor 3.0/4	134 La Esclava Isaura 0.6/1	134 Celebrity Exposé 0.6/1	103 Girlfriends 1.6/2
9:30	19 Samantha Who? 9.8/14	27 Rule/Engagement 6.7/10						100 The Game 1.7/2
10:00	25 The Bachelor 6.9/11	20 CSI: Miami 9.8/16	71 Journeyman 3.7/6		89 Cristina 2.5/4	174 Pecados Ajenos 0.3/1		
10:30								

TUESDAY

Time	ABC	CBS	NBC	FOX	Univision	Telemundo	myTV	CW
8:00	29 It's the Great Pumpkin, Charlie Brown 6.6/10	7 NCIS 10.4/16	71 Singing Bee 3.7/6	41 Bones 5.7/9	103 Amar Sin Limites 1.6/3	134 Madre Luna 0.6/1	103 Breaking the Magician's Code 1.6/2	103 Beauty and the Geek 1.6/2
8:30								
9:00	3 Dancing With the Stars Results 12.3/18	26 The Unit 6.8/10	61 The Biggest Loser 4.1/6	8 House 10.3/15	79 Destilando Amor 3.1/5	128 La Esclava Isaura 0.7/1	122 Iron Mask 0.8/1	100 Reaper 1.7/3
9:30								
10:00	22 Boston Legal 7.7/13	22 Cane 5.5/9	40 Law & Order: SVU 5.8/10		109 Como Ana Una Mujer 1.5/3	160 Pecados Ajenos 0.4/1		
10:30								

WEDNESDAY

Time	ABC	CBS	NBC	FOX	Univision	Telemundo	myTV	CW
8:00	43 Pushing Daisies 5.6/10	57 Kid Nation 4.3/8		77 Back to You 3.4/6	114 Amar Sin Limites 1.4/2	134 Madre Luna 0.6/1	134 Decision House 0.6/1	93 America's Next Top Model 2.2/4
8:30			67 Phenomenon 3.9/7	78 'Til Death 3.2/6				
9:00	20 Private Practice 7.8/13	13 Criminal Minds 9.5/15		89 Kitchen Nightmares 2.5/4	83 Destilando Amor 2.8/4	134 La Esclava Isaura 0.6/1	134 Decision House 0.6/1	121 Gossip Girl 1.1/2
9:30								
10:00	41 Dirty Sexy Money 5.7/10	15 CSI: NY 8.7/15	71 Life 3.7/6		93 Don Francisco Presents 2.0/4	174 Pecados Ajenos 0.3/1		
10:30								

THURSDAY

Time	ABC	CBS	NBC	FOX	Univision	Telemundo	myTV	CW
8:00	27 Ugly Betty 6.7/11	16 Survivor: China 8.5/14	54 My Name is Earl 4.6/7	47 Are You Smarter Than a 5th Grader? 5.2/8	98 Amar Sin Limites 1.8/3	128 Madre Luna 0.7/1	124 My Thursday Night Movie—Hot Shots! Part Deux 0.8/1	86 Smallville 2.7/4
8:30								
9:00	2 Grey's Anatomy 12.6/19	4 CSI 11.9/18	50 The Office 4.9/7	47 Are You Smarter Than a 5th Grader? 5.3/8	79 Destilando Amor 3.1/5	128 La Esclava Isaura 0.7/1		95 Supernatural 2.0/3
9:30			67 Scrubs 3.9/6					
10:00	48 Big Shots 5.1/9	12 Without a Trace 9.7/15	38 ER 5.9/10		97 Aquí y Ahora 1.9/3	160 Pecados Ajenos 0.4/1		
10:30								

FRIDAY

Time	ABC	CBS	NBC	FOX	Univision	Telemundo	myTV	CW
8:00	65 Men in Trees 4.0/7	34 Ghost Whisperer 6.0/11	34 Deal or No Deal 6.0/1	109 Next Great American Band 1.5/3	114 Amar Sin Limites 1.6/3	134 Madre Luna 0.7/1	124 My Friday Night Movie—Rocky 0.8/1	83 Friday Night Smackdown 2.8/5
8:30								
9:00	30 Women's Murder Club 6.5/11	50 Moonlight 4.9/9	74 Friday Night Lights 3.6/6		83 Destilando Amor 3.1/5	134 La Esclava Isaura 0.6/1		
9:30								
10:00	48 20/20 5.1/9	32 Numb3rs 6.1/11	50 Las Vegas 4.9/9		93 La Familia P Luche 2.2/4	174 Pecados Ajenos 0.4/1		
10:30						98 Retro P Luche 1.8/3			

SATURDAY

Time	ABC	CBS	NBC	FOX	Univision	Telemundo	myTV	CW
8:00		(nr) College Football—LSU vs. Alabama 4.0/8	89 Bionic Woman 2.5/5	74 Cops 3.6/7		174 Cine de Impacto—Enter the Dragon 0.3/1	174 NFL Network Total Access 0.3/1	
8:30			67 Cops 3.9/7					
9:00	61 Saturday Night Football 4.1/8		92 Chuck 2.3/4	65 America's Most Wanted: Amer Fights Back 4.0/7	117 Sábado Gigante 1.3/2		160 IFL Battleground 0.4/1	
9:30		61 Crimetime Saturday 4.1/7				134 Cine de Impacto—The Fast and the Furious 0.6/1		
10:00			76 Law & Order: SVU 3.5/6					
10:30		54 Crimetime Saturday 4.6/8						

SUNDAY

Time	ABC	CBS	NBC	FOX	Univision	Telemundo	myTV	CW
7:00	(nr) NASCAR Nextel Cup 3.7/7	(nr) NFL Game 2 20.1/36	Football Night Pt. 1 Sustaining	83 The Simpsons 2.8/4				134 CW Now 0.6/1
7:30	57 Amer Fun Home Vid 4.3/7		61 Football Night Pt. 2 4.1/7	56 The Simpsons 4.5/7	117 Festival Mariachi Disney 1.3/2	174 Marav Mundo Disney—Spy Kids 3: Game Over 0.3/1		134 Aliens in America 0.6/1
8:00	20 Extreme Makeover: Home Edition 7.8/12	4 60 Minutes 11.9/19	61 F'ball Night Pt. 3 5.9/10	31 The Simpsons 6.4/10				
8:30				34 Family Guy 6.0/9				124 Life is Wild 0.8/1
9:00	6 Desperate Housewives 11.8/18	18 The Amazing Race 8.3/12	9 NFL Sunday Night Football—Dallas Cowboys vs. Philadelphia Eagles 10.2/16	34 Family Guy 6.0/9				122 America's Next Top Model 0.9/1
9:30				60 American Dad 4.2/6	117 Cine Especial—Tonta, Tonta. Pero no Tonta 1.3/2	149 Cine Millonario—The Hulk 0.5/1		
10:00	19 Brothers & Sisters 8.1/14	14 Cold Case 9.0/14						
10:30		23 Shark 7.6/14						

Nielsen Ratings. *Every prime-time network show is ranked by audience in weekly Nielsens. ABC's* Dancing with the Stars *at 8 p.m. Monday led this week. Second, also on ABC, was* Grey's Anatomy. *Thursday night at 9 p.m.*

<u>Ratings:</u> *One measure of audience is the rating. This is the percentage of television-equipped households viewing a program. Because 97 million U.S. households have television sets, each percentage point represents 970,000 households.* Dancing's *rating was 14.1.*

<u>Shares:</u> *A second audience measure, share, is a show's percentage of all television sets that are turned on,* Dancing *had a 21 share, far outdistancing CBS's* How I Met Your Mother *with 7, NBC's* Chuck *and Fox's* House, *both with 6. Univision, Telemundo, MyTV and CW all picked up splinters.*

Source: Nielsen Media Research, adapted from Broadcasting & Cable, *November 12, 2007, 24.*

● **A. C. Nielsen**
Founder of broadcast survey firm bearing his name

● **demographic**
Characteristics of groups within a population being sampled, including age, gender, affiliations

national ratings, the same process that radio and television audience-tracking companies still use, though there have been refinements.

In the 1940s **A. C. Nielsen** showed up in the broadcasting ratings business. Nielsen began telling advertisers which radio programs were especially popular among men, women and children. Nielsen also divided listenership into age brackets: 18 to 34, 35 to 49 and 50 plus. These were called **demographic** breakdowns. When Nielsen moved into television monitoring in 1950, it expanded audience data into more breakdowns. Today breakdowns include income, education, religion, occupation, neighborhood and even which products the viewers of certain programs use frequently.

While Archibald Crossley's early ratings were sponsored by advertisers, today networks and individual stations also commission ratings to be done. The television networks pass ratings data on to advertisers immediately. Local stations usually recast the raw data for brochures that display the data in ways that put the stations in the most favorable light. These brochures are distributed by station sales representatives to advertisers. While advertisers receive ratings data from the stations and networks, major advertising agencies have contracts with Nielsen, Arbitron and other market research companies to gather audience data to meet their specifications.

LEARNING CHECK ◄ ·······················

▶ **How did Nielsen advance broadcast ratings from Crossley's early approach?**

▶ **Why are advertisers interested in broadcast audience ratings?**

▶ **How do television networks and stations use ratings?**

▶ **How have broadcast ratings improved since Archibald Crossley's telephone calls?**

Audience Measurement Techniques

STUDY PREVIEW

Traditional polling techniques include interviews and diaries, both of which are being eclipsed by meters. Some devices even track which billboards a person passes and how often. These new devices track usage of new media forms, including the Internet, and the extension of television viewing beyond the living room and also playback viewing with TiVo and similar devices.

BASIC TOOLS

The primary techniques, sometimes used in combination, for measuring broadcast audiences are interviews, diaries and meters.

■ **Interviews.** In his pioneer 1929 listenership polling, Archibald Crossley placed telephone calls to randomly selected households. Although many polling companies use telephone **interviews** exclusively, they're not used much in broadcasting anymore. Also rare in broadcasting are face-to-face interviews.

● **interviews**
Face-to-face, mail, telephone survey technique

Although eyeball-to-eyeball interviewing can elicit fuller information, it is labor-intensive and relatively expensive.

● **diaries**
Sampling technique in which respondents keep their own records

■ **Diaries.** Nielsen began using **diaries** in the 1950s. Instead of interviews, Nielsen mailed forms to selected families in major markets for them to list program titles, times and channels and who was watching. This was done in major sweep periods: February, May, July and November. Although diaries were cost-efficient, viewers would forget their duty and then try to remember days later what they had watched. The resulting data were better than no data but were rather muddy.

■ **Meters.** Meters were introduced in the 1970s as a supplement to diaries to improve accuracy. Some Nielsen families had their TV sets wired to track what channel was on. Some were issued meters that household members could click so that Nielsen could determine for whom programs have their appeal—men, women, children, oldsters. Some set-top meters even traced who was watching by sensing body mass.

● **people meters**
Devices that track individual viewers

■ **People Meters.** In 1987 Nielsen introduced **people meters.** These were two-function units, one on the television set to scan the channels being watched every 2.7 seconds and a handheld remote that monitored who was watching. With data flowing in nightly to Nielsen's central computers, the company generates next-day reports, called **overnights,** for the networks and advertisers.

● **overnights**
Next-morning reports on network viewership

■ **Portable Meters.** In 2001 Nielsen and Arbitron, which focuses on radio audiences, jointly tested portable meters that people can carry around. The pager-size meters, weighing 2 1/2 ounces, are set to pick up inaudible signals transmitted with programs. The goal: to track away-from-home audiences at sports bars, offices and airports and, in the case of radio, cars. ESPN estimates that 4 million people watch its sports away from home in a typical week. The "walking meters," as they are called, also track commuter radio habits for the first time.

LEARNING CHECK ◄ ....

▸ **What methods do ratings companies use to measure broadcast audiences?**

INTERNET AUDIENCE MEASURES

● **Media Metrix**
A service measuring Internet audience size

The leading Internet audience measuring company, **Media Metrix,** uses a two-track system to determine how many people view Web sites. Media Metrix gathers data from 40,000 individual computers whose owners have agreed to be monitored. Some of these computers are programmed to track Internet usage and report data back by e-mail. In addition, Media Metrix has lined up other computer users to mail in a tracking disc periodically. In 1998 the Nielsen television ratings company set up a similar methodology. Other companies also are in the Internet ratings business.

How accurate are Internet ratings? Some major content providers, including CNN, ESPN and Time Warner, claim that the ratings undercount their users. Such claims go beyond self-serving comments because, in fact, different rating companies come up with widely divergent ratings. The question is: Why can't the ratings companies get it right? The answer, in part, is that divergent data flow from divergent methodologies. Data need to be viewed in terms of the methodology that was used. Also, the infant Internet ratings business undoubtedly is hobbled by methodology flaws that have yet to be identified and corrected.

LEARNING CHECK ◄ ....

▸ **How accurate are ratings of commercial Internet sites?**

MULTIMEDIA MEASURES

Recognizing that television viewers were increasingly mobile and less set-bound, Nielsen began remaking its ratings system in 2006 to measure the use of personal computers, videogame players, iPods, cell phones and other mobile devices. Nielsen said the program, called **Anytime Anywhere Media Measurement,** or **A2/M2** for short, represented a commitment to "follow the video" with an "all-electronic measurement system that will deliver integrated ratings for television viewing regardless of the platform." Nielsen's chief researcher, Paul Donato, put it this way: "The plan is to try to capture it all."

An initial step was creating a panel of 400 video iPod users to track the programs they download and watch. Nielson also began fusing data from its television-tracking unit and its Nielsen/Net Ratings unit to measure the relation between conventional television viewing and Web surfing with meters on both televisions and personal computers.

● **Anytime Anywhere Media Measurement (A2/M2)**
Nielsen plan to integrate audience measurements on a wide range of video platforms

LEARNING CHECK ◄ ···

▶ **What is A2/M2? Why is it important?**

MOBILE AUDIENCE MEASURES

Over-air networks tried addressing the audience leakage to DVD and TiVo-like devices when the Nielsen rating service introduced its Live Plus Seven measure in 2006. The new measure tracked live viewing plus any viewing within seven days. The networks built the extended period into their audience guarantees with advertisers. The network argument was that DVD and TiVo viewers are more affluent as a group and therefore worth more to advertisers. Advertisers balked. Advertisers argued that ads viewed after the fact have diminished value. Also, the new Nielsen gizmo for recording viewers didn't record ads that were skipped, which TiVo facilitates. Advertisers were more comfortable with Nielsen's live-plus-same-day counts, which included DVD viewing before the next morning.

Despite the issue over the counting period being spread out, Nielsen continued to install the new measuring devices. By 2007 about 18 percent of measured U.S. households were included.

Billboard Meter. To measure the number of people who pass electronically tagged billboards, Nielsen Media Research issues palmsize devices that tell when participants pass an electronically coded billboard. Data are uploaded from the device to a satellite, then down to Nielsen data keepers who score billboards. Competitor Arbitron has a similar device.

Number-Crunching Center. Every night, ratings of every network television show in the country are tabulated at Nielsen's facility in Oldsmar, Florida. The same facility also tracks billboard traffic generated by new meters that track people who pass by coded billboards.

CRITICISM OF RATINGS

However sophisticated the ratings services have become, they have critics. Many fans question the accuracy of ratings when their favorite television program is canceled because the network finds the ratings inadequate. Something is wrong, they say, when the viewing preferences of a few thousand households determine network programming for the entire nation. Though it seems incredible to someone who is not knowledgeable about statistical probability, the sample base of major ratings services like Nielsen generally is considered sufficient to extrapolate reliably on viewership in the 97 million television-equipped U.S. households.

It was not always so. Doubts peaked in the 1940s and 1950s when it was learned that some ratings services lied about sample size and were less-than-scientific in choosing samples. A congressional investigation in 1963 prompted the networks to create the **Broadcast Ratings Council** to accredit ratings companies and audit their reports.

● Broadcast Ratings Council
Accredits ratings companies

Rating have problems, some inherent in different methodologies and some attributable to human error and fudging.

■ **Discrepancies.** When different ratings services come up with widely divergent findings in the same market, advertisers become suspicious. Minor discrepancies can be explained by different sampling methods, but significant discrepancies point to flawed methodology or execution. It was discrepancies of this sort that led to the creation of the Broadcast Ratings Council.

■ **Slanted Results.** Sales reps of some local stations, eager to demonstrate to advertisers that their stations have large audiences, extract only the favorable data from survey results. It takes a sophisticated local advertiser to reconcile slanted and fudged claims.

■ **Sample Selection.** Some ratings services select their samples meticulously, giving every household in a market a statistically equal opportunity to be sampled. Some sample selections are seriously flawed: How reliable, for example, are the listenership claims of a rock 'n' roll station that puts a disc jockey's face on billboards all over town and then sends the disc jockey to a teenage dance palace to ask about listening preferences?

● sweeps
When broadcast ratings are conducted

● hyping
Intensive promotion to attract an audience during ratings periods

● black weeks
Periods when ratings are not conducted

■ **Hyping.** Ratings-hungry stations have learned how to build audiences during **sweeps** weeks in February, May and November when major local television ratings are compiled. Consider these examples of **hyping:**

- Radio giveaways often coincide with ratings periods.
- Many news departments promote sensationalistic series for the sweeps and then retreat to routine coverage when the ratings period is over.
- Besides sweeps weeks, there are **black weeks** when no ratings are conducted. In these periods some stations run all kinds of odd and dull serve-the-public programs that they would never consider running during a sweeps period.

■ **Respondent Accuracy.** With hand-written diaries, respondents don't always answer honestly. People have an opportunity to write that they watched *Masterpiece Theatre* on PBS instead of less classy fare. For the same reason, shock radio and trash television probably have more audience than the ratings show.

In a project to tighten measurement techniques, Nielsen gradually began eliminating diaries in local television markets in 2006. In the 10 largest markets, Nielsen redesigned its people meters, which measure both what network shows are being watched and who is in the room watching. The new meters also track

Tracking Technology

At first, research companies collected data on television audiences by asking people to fill out a paper diary. Then Nielsen began using its electronic People Meter, which automatically recorded what channel a television set was tuned to.

Now Nielsen is planning to provide ratings for television regardless of the platform on which it is viewed. Its Anytime Anywhere Media Measurement (A2/M2) will assess the new ways that people are watching television, including on the Internet, outside the home and via personal mobile devices.

Nielsen also is developing and testing new personal meters to measure television viewership away from home, including at work and in bars, restaurants, hotels and airports. The Go Meters are designed to collect audio signatures. One device places metering technology in cell phones, and the other is a customized meter that resembles an MP3 player. Nielsen expects to introduce these meters by the end of 2008. The company also plans to expand the use of electronic metering to smaller television markets and by 2011 to have replaced paper diaries and logs with electronic meters in smaller cities.

The Solo Meter that the company is developing can be used with any portable media system. For wireless connections, Nielsen is working on a tiny wireless meter that will passively listen to communication between mated devices. For wired systems, Nielsen is building a diminutive in-line meter that will be physically inserted between the device and its earphones. These Solo Meters also will identify viewing by collecting audio signatures.

For advertisers, Nielsen plans to adopt a measure of engagement for television. Engagement assesses how deep an impression an ad or program has made on a viewer. As audiences for programming and advertising grow narrower, the need to make a deeper impression on a smaller group of people becomes more important than the conventional focus on reaching as many people as possible. Recent research points toward the possibility of a link between media engagement and advertising engagement.

As the techonology of the mass media continues to progress, audience measurement companies must find ways to keep up. Sometimes that could mean dramatic changes in the way viewership figures are tallied. And that could result in major shifts in the way advertising dollars are spent and received. Stay tuned.

Jogging Viewers.
Television watching in a Mankato State University, Mankato, workout gym misses the radar of Nielsen audience tracking. New audience tracking devices will cast their nets wider to recognize the reality that television is no longer only an at-home activity. Nielsen had been missing sports bars, airport waiting lounges, luxury SUVs and other non-living room audiences.

DEEPENING YOUR MEDIA LITERACY

EXPLORE THE ISSUE

Find someone who has been asked to participate in a public opinion poll. Does that person know why he or she was chosen?

DIG DEEPER

Ask about the reliability of the information given to the polling company. Were answers based on recollection? Ask the person how completely he or she collected the information. Was it merely from memory or recollection?

WHAT DO YOU THINK?

Will consumers benefit as much as advertisers from the newest audience tracking technology?

local viewing choices. Gradually Nielsen sought to eliminate diaries in smaller markets too.

■ **Zipping, Zapping and Flushing.** Ratings services measure audiences for programs and for different times of day, but they do not measure whether commercials are watched. Advertisers are interested, of course, in whether the programs between which their ads are sandwiched are popular, but more important to them is whether people are watching the ads.

This vacuum in audience measurements was documented in the 1960s when somebody with a sense of humor correlated a major drop in Chicago water pressure with the Super Bowl halftime, in what became known as the **flush factor.** Football fans were getting off the couch by the thousands at halftime to go to the bathroom. Advertisers were missing many people because although viewers were watching the program, many were not watching the ads.

This problem has been exacerbated with the advent of handheld television remote controls and systems like TiVo. Viewers can **zip** from station to station to avoid commercials, and when they record programs for later viewing, they can **zap** out the commercials.

● **flush factor**
Viewers leave during commercials to go to refrigerator, bathroom, etc

● **zipping**
Viewers change television channels to avoid commercials

● **zapping**
Viewers record programs and eliminate commercial breaks

LEARNING CHECK ◄ ••

▶ How are broadcast ratings susceptible to manipulation?

▶ Besides deliberate manipulations, what vulnerabilities beset ratings?

Measuring Audience Reaction

STUDY PREVIEW

The television ratings business has moved beyond measuring audience size to measuring audience reaction. Researchers measure audience reaction with numerous methods, including focus groups, galvanic skin checks and prototypes.

FOCUS GROUPS

● **focus groups**
Small groups interviewed in loosely structured ways for opinion, reactions

Television consulting companies measure audience reaction with **focus groups.** Typically, an interview crew goes to a shopping center, chooses a dozen individuals by gender and age, and offers them cookies, soft drinks and $25 each to sit down and watch a taped local newscast. A moderator then asks these individuals for their reactions, sometimes with loaded and leading questions to open them up. It is a tricky research method that depends highly on the skill of the moderator. In one court case an anchor who had lost her job as a result of responses to a focus group complained that the moderator had contaminated the process with prejudicial assertions and questions:

- "This is your chance to get rid of the things you don't like to see on the news."
- "Come on, unload on those sons of bitches who make $100,000 a year."
- "This is your chance to do more than just yell at the TV. You can speak up and say I really hate that guy or I really like that broad."
- "Let's spend 30 seconds destroying this anchor. Is she a mutt? Be honest about this."

Even when conducted skillfully, focus groups have the disadvantage of reflecting the opinion of the loudest respondent.

LEARNING CHECK ◄ ••

▶ What is the role of analysis in focus group research?

▶ What is the role of a focus group moderator?

If It Bleeds, It Leads.
Audience researchers have found newscast ratings go up for stations that consistently deliver graphic video. This has prompted many stations to favor fire stories, for example, even if the fire wasn't consequential, if graphic video is available. The ratings quest also prompts these stations to favor crimes and accidents over more substantive stories, like government budgets, that don't lend themselves to gripping graphics.

● **galvanic skin checks**
Monitor pulse, skin responses to stimuli

GALVANIC SKIN CHECKS

Consulting companies hired by television stations run a great variety of studies to determine audience reaction. Local stations, which originate news programs and not much else, look to these consultants for advice on news sets, story selection and even which anchors and reporters are most popular. Besides surveys, these consultants sometimes use **galvanic skin checks.** Wires are attached to individuals in a sample group of viewers to measure pulse and skin reactions, such as perspiration. Advocates of these tests claim that they reveal how much interest a newscast evokes and whether the interest is positive or negative.

These tests were first used to check audience reaction to advertisements, but today some stations look to them in deciding whether to remodel a studio. A dubious use, from a journalistic perspective, is using galvanic skin checks to determine what kinds of stories to cover and whether to find new anchors and reporters. The skin checks reward short, photogenic stories like fires and accidents rather than significant stories, which tend to be longer and don't lend themselves to flashy video. The checks also favor good-looking, smooth anchors and reporters, regardless of their journalistic competence. One wag was literally correct when he called this "a heartthrob approach to journalism."

LEARNING CHECK ◄••

▶ **How would you as a television program executive use physiological indicators from galvanic skin checks?**

PROTOTYPE RESEARCH

Before making major investments, media executives seek as much information as they can obtain in order to determine how to enhance a project's chances for success or whether it has a chance at all. This is known as **prototype research.**

● **prototype research**
Checks audience response to a product still in development

■ **Movie Screenings.** Movie studios have previewed movies since the days of silent film. Today the leading screening contractors are units of Nielsen and OTX. Typically about 300 people, selected carefully to fit a demographic, watch the movie and fill out comment cards. Were they confused at any point? Did they like the ending? What were their favorite scenes? Would they recommend the movie to a friend? The audience usually is filmed watching the movie, and producers and

richard schwartz

Creepy, slithery? Yes. A great movie? A kind and gentle way to put it is that *Snakes on a Plane* wasn't on anybody's short list for an Oscar. But the low-budget 2006 movie crept into the public's consciousness as firmly as the best pictures of the year—and with hardly any promotional spending by distributor New Line Cinema. The buzz, spontaneous, was from the Internet.

The chilling title helped. Screenwriter Josh Friedman called it a gobstopper.

The domestic marketing president at New Line, Richard Schwartz, was puzzling over how to promote the film early in its planning. It was then that Friedman, who had been brought in to work on the script, mentioned the project on his blog. Soon the snake was out of the bag, so to speak. Every film blogger, it seemed, was talking about the project.

Snakes on a Plane. *Movie distributor New Line Cinema, a unit of Time Warner, let bloggers carry the load in promoting the low-budget thriller. It was a technique pioneered for the* Blair Witch Project *seven years earlier.*

Movie Marketer. *Richard Schwartz.*

Schwartz wasn't pleased—at least not at first. He saw himself losing control of promotion for the movie and all kinds of unpredictable troubles ahead. But what to do? Then scenes from raw footage somehow ended up being posted on Web sites. Bloggers couldn't get enough. Attorneys at Time Warner, parent company of New Line, contemplated suing bloggers for copyright infringement. After all, the bloggers had no legal right to be posting the scenes.

Schwartz, however, decided to do nothing. It seemed best to let the blogging run its course. Then, he figured, on the eve of the movie's release he would launch promotions that reflected lessons from focus groups that would be called in to look at a near-final version—a typical Hollywood approach. But bloggers were unsated. Then Schwartz's worst fears came to be when mainstream media picked up advance information on the film. Word-of-mouth about the film had escaped completely beyond his control.

Although he had doubts during the course of these events, Schwartz had been wise to let the blogging go. The publicity far outreached whatever hype an orchestrated promotional campaign could have had.

As for focus groups, they weren't necessary. Director David Ellis monitored the blogs and, taking cues from the exchanges, reshot some scenes to include what the enthusiasts, mostly young men, seemed to want—more sex, violence and profanity.

WHAT DO YOU THINK?

▶ Are blog leaks a good idea in general to promote a new movie?

▶ Would movie-makers be wise to sue for leaks of copyright-protected advance information about movies?

studio executives later look for reactions on a split screen with the movie running. Usually 20 or so testers are kept after a screening as a sit-down focus group with the studio people listening in.

Screenings make a difference. How a movie is promoted can be shaped by the test audience's reactions. Some endings have been changed. Astute moviegoers noticed that Vince Vaughn seemed thinner toward the end of *The Break Up*. The fact is that Universal executives had decided for a happier ending and ordered Vaughn and a crew back to Chicago to reshoot. He had lost weight in the meantime. More widely known is that Paramount took the advice of a Nielsen screener and had Glenn Close's character in *Fatal Attraction* be murdered rather than commit suicide.

Many directors don't like their creative control contravened by test screenings. Some directors, indeed, have the clout to refuse screenings. Steven Spielberg famously forsakes them. The usual objection from directors is that they don't want to surrender creative control. Put another way, some directors see screenings as a way for studio executives to cover their backsides by claiming to their supervisors, if a movie flops, that they did all they could to ensure its success.

In recent years, screenings have been squeezed out of tighter and tighter production schedules, especially when computer-generated imaging plays a big role in a movie. For *The Da Vinci Code, Superman Returns* and *Pirates of the Caribbean: Dead Man's Chest,* all big 2006 summer releases, there were no screen tests. There was no time to line up preview audiences, let alone make any changes that might have bubbled up through the process.

Some studio execs also have cooled to screenings because of negative leaks that can derail promotion plans. In 2006 a blogger had posted a review of Oliver Stone's *World Trade Center* within hours of a screening in Minneapolis. One site, Ain't It Cool News, works at infiltrating screenings. Drew McSweeney, a site editor, defends the crashing as a way to stunt executive interference in movies and return power to directors.

■ **Publication Protoypes.** When Gannett decided to establish a new newspaper, *USA Today,* it created prototypes, each designed differently, to test readers' reactions. Many new magazines are preceded by at least one trial issue to sample marketplace reaction and to show to potential advertisers.

Advertising agencies, too, often screen campaigns before launch to fine-tune them.

● **pilot**
A prototype television show that is given an on-air trial

■ **Television Pilots.** In network television a prototype can even make it on the air in the form of a **pilot.** One or a few episodes are tested, usually in prime time with a lot of promotion, to see whether the audience goes for the program concept. Some made-for-television movies actually are test runs to determine whether a series might be spun off from the movie.

LEARNING CHECK ◄ •

▶ Why do strong-willed screenwriters and directors bristle at prototype research to adjust story lines?

▶ What role should an audience have in determining the mass media's literary content? What about a Hemingway novel? A James Cameron movie? A Ken Burns documentary? The *Sopranos* finale?

Audience Analysis

STUDY PREVIEW

Traditional demographic polling methods divided people by gender, age and other easily identifiable population characteristics. Today, media people use sophisticated lifestyle breakdowns such as geodemographics and psychographics to match the content of their publications, broadcast programs and advertising to the audiences they seek.

DEMOGRAPHICS

Early in the development of public opinion surveying, pollsters learned that broad breakdowns had limited usefulness. Archibald Crossley's pioneering radio surveys, for example, told the number of people who were listening to network programs, which was valuable to the networks and their advertisers, but Crossley's figures did not tell how many listeners were men or women, urban or rural, old or young. Such breakdowns of overall survey data, called demographics, were developed in the 1930s as Crossley, Gallup and other early pollsters refined their work.

Today, if demographic data indicate that a presidential candidate is weak in the Midwest, campaign strategists can gear the candidate's message to Midwestern concerns. Through demographics, advertisers keen on reaching young women can identify magazines that will carry their ads to that audience. If advertisers seek an elderly audience, they can use demographic data to determine where to place their television ads.

While demographics remains valuable today, newer methods can break the population into categories that have even greater usefulness. These newer methods, which include cohort analysis, geodemography and psychographics, provide lifestyle breakdowns.

LEARNING CHECK ◄

▸ **What are common demographic breakdowns in survey research?**

COHORT ANALYSIS

● **cohort analysis**
Demographic tool to identify marketing targets by common characteristics

Marketing people have developed **cohort analysis,** a specialized form of demographics, to identify generations and then design and produce products with generational appeal. Advertising people then gear media messages to the images, music, humor and other generational variables that appeal to the target cohort. The major cohorts are dubbed:

- **Generation X,** who came of age in the 1980s.
- **Baby Boomers,** who came of age in the late 1960s and 1970s.
- **Postwar Generation,** who came of age in the 1950s.
- **World War II Veterans,** who came of age in the 1940s.
- **Depression Survivors,** who came of age during the economic depression of the 1930s.

Cohort analysis has jarred the traditional thinking that as people get older, they simply adopt their parents' values. The new 50-plus generation, for example, grew up on Coke and Pepsi drinks and, to the dismay of coffee growers, may prefer to start the day with cola—not the coffee their parents drank.

The Chrysler automobile company was early to recognize that Baby Boomers aren't interested in buying Cadillac-type luxury cars even when they have amassed the money to afford them. In 1996 Chrysler scrapped plans for a new luxury car to compete with Cadillac and instead introduced the $35,000 open-top 1997 Plymouth Prowler that gave Baby Boomers a nostalgic feel for the hot rods of their youth. Chrysler also determined that graying Baby Boomers preferred upscale Jeeps to the luxo-barge cars that appealed to the Postwar Generation.

Advertising people who use cohort analysis know that Baby Boomers, although now in their 50s, are still turned on by pizzas and the Rolling Stones. In short, the habits of their youth stick with a generation as it gets older. What appealed to the 30-something group a decade ago won't necessarily sail with today's 30-something set. David Bostwick, Chrysler's marketing research director, puts it this way: "Nobody wants to become their parents."

When the guerrilla war in Iraq began hurting U.S. military recruiting, the Pentagon desperately needed to fine-tune its message to reach the young men and women who were the most likely prospects to enlist. Applying analytical tools to its own existing data, the Pentagon identified ethnic, geographical and income cohorts that are more receptive to the military. The analysis also identified media for reaching these cohorts. Prospective Army recruits, for example, listen more to Spanish radio than the general population does. *Bassmaster* magazine is more the style of Air Force prospects. Marine prospects lean to *Car Craft, Guns & Ammo* and *Outdoor Life.*

Here are 18 cohorts that the Pentagon identified to target their recruiting pitches:

Cohort	Urbanization	Ethnicity	Income
Upward Bound	Small city	White/Asian	Upscale
Beltway Boomers	Suburban	White/Asian	Upper-middle
Kids and Cul de Sacs	Suburban	White/Asian/Hispanic	Upper-middle
Fast-Track Families	Town/rural	White	Upscale
New Homesteaders	Town/rural	White	Midscale
Big Sky Families	Town/rural	White	Midscale
White Picket Fences	Small city	White/black/Hispanic	Midscale
Blue-Chip Blues	Suburban	White/black/Hispanic	Midscale
Sunset City Blues	Small city	White	Lower-middle
Young and Rustic	Town/rural	White	Downscale
Kid Country USA	Town/rural	White/Hispanic	Lower-middle
Shotguns and Pickups	Town/rural	White	Lower-middle
Suburban Pioneers	Suburban	White/black/Hispanic	Lower-middle
Mobility Blues	Small city	White/black	Downscale
Multicultural Mosaic	Urban	black/Hispanic	Lower-middle
Old Milltowns	Town/rural	White/black	Downscale
Family Thrifts	Small city	Black/Hispanic	Downscale
Bedrock America	Town/rural	White/black/Hispanic	Downscale

LEARNING CHECK ◄••••••••••••••••••••••••••••••••••••

▶ **How can cohort analysis help mass communicators craft their messages?**

▶ **What kind of cohort would be useful for analysis by an advertiser for toothpaste? The Marine Corps? An automobile?**

▶ **Do you like being pigeonholed as a target for advertising and other media messages?**

GEODEMOGRAPHICS

While demographics, including cohort analysis, remain valuable today, new methods can break the population into categories that have even greater usefulness. These newer methods, which include geodemography, provide lifestyle breakdowns.

Computer whiz **Jonathan Robbin** provided the basis for more sophisticated breakdowns in 1974 when he began developing his **PRIZM** system for **geodemography.** From census data Robbin grouped every zip code by ethnicity, family life cycle, housing style, mobility and social rank. Then he identified 34 factors that statistically distinguished neighborhoods from each other. All this information was cranked through a computer programmed by Robbin to plug every zip code into 1 of 40 clusters. Here are the most frequent clusters created through PRIZM, which stands for Potential Rating Index for Zip Markets, with the labels Robbin put on them:

● **Jonathan Robbin**
Devised PRIZM geodemography system

● **PRIZM**
Identifies population characteristics by zip code

● **geodemography**
Demographic characteristics by geographic area

- **Blue-Chip Blues.** These are the wealthiest blue-collar suburbs. These Blue-Chip Blues, as Robbin calls them, make up about 6 percent of U.S. households. About 13 percent of these people are college graduates.

- **Young Suburbia.** Childrearing outlying suburbs, 5.3 percent of the U.S. population; college grads, 24 percent.
- **Golden Ponds.** Rustic mountain, seashore or lakeside cottage communities, 5.2 percent; college grads, 13 percent.
- **Blue-Blood Estates.** Wealthiest neighborhoods; college grads, 51 percent.
- **Money and Brains.** Posh big-city enclaves of townhouses, condos and apartments; college grads, 46 percent.

Geodemographic breakdowns are used not only by advertisers on ad placement decisions but also for editorial content. At Time Warner magazines, geodemographic analysis permits issues to be edited for special audiences. *Time*, for example, has a 600,000 circulation edition for company owners, directors, board chairs, presidents, other titled officers and department heads. Among others are editions for physicians and college students.

LEARNING CHECK ◄••

▸ **How is geodemographics different from demographics?**

▸ **Geodemographics cubbyholes people. In what cubbyholes do you fit more or less?**

PSYCHOGRAPHICS

● **psychographics**
Breaking down a population by lifestyle characteristics

● **VALS**
Psychographic analysis by values, lifestyle, life stage

A refined lifestyle breakdown introduced in the late 1970s, **psychographics**, divides the population into lifestyle segments. One leading psychographics approach, the Values and Life-Styles program, known as **VALS** for short, uses an 85-page survey to identify broad categories of people:

- **Belongers.** Comprising about 38 percent of the U.S. population, these people are conformists who are satisfied with mainstream values and are reluctant to change brands once they're satisfied. Belongers are not very venturesome and fit the stereotype of Middle America. They tend to be churchgoers and television watchers.
- **Achievers.** Comprising about 20 percent of the population, these are prosperous people who fit into a broader category of inner-directed consumers. Achievers pride themselves on making their own decisions. They're an upscale audience to which a lot of advertising is directed. As a group, achievers aren't heavy television watchers.
- **Societally Conscious.** Comprising 11 percent of the population, these people are aware of social issues and tend to be politically active. The societally conscious also are upscale and inner-directed, and they tend to prefer reading to watching television.
- **Emulators.** Comprising 10 percent of the population, these people aspire to a better life but, not quite understanding how to do it, go for the trappings of prosperity. Emulators are status seekers, prone to suggestions on what makes the good life.
- **Experientials.** Comprising 5 percent of the population, these people are venturesome, willing to try new things in an attempt to experience life fully. They are a promising upscale audience for many advertisers.
- **I-Am-Me's.** Comprising 3 percent of the population, these people work hard to set themselves apart and are susceptible to advertising pitches that offer ways to differentiate themselves, which gives them a kind of subculture conformity. SRI International, which developed the VALS technique, characterized a member of the I-Am-Me's as "a guitar-playing punk rocker who goes around in shades and sports an earring." Rebellious youth, angry and maladjusted, fit this category.
- **Survivors.** This is a small downscale category that includes pensioners who worry about making ends meet.
- **Sustainers.** These people live from paycheck to paycheck. Although they indulge in an occasional extravagance, they have slight hope for improving

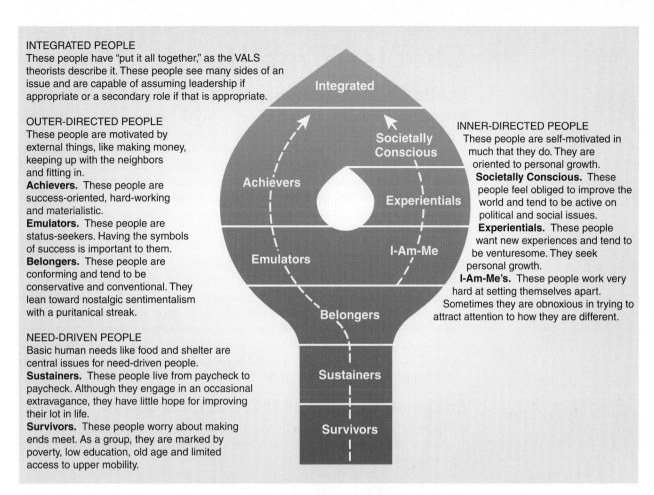

INTEGRATED PEOPLE
These people have "put it all together," as the VALS theorists describe it. These people see many sides of an issue and are capable of assuming leadership if appropriate or a secondary role if that is appropriate.

OUTER-DIRECTED PEOPLE
These people are motivated by external things, like making money, keeping up with the neighbors and fitting in.
Achievers. These people are success-oriented, hard-working and materialistic.
Emulators. These people are status-seekers. Having the symbols of success is important to them.
Belongers. These people are conforming and tend to be conservative and conventional. They lean toward nostalgic sentimentalism with a puritanical streak.

NEED-DRIVEN PEOPLE
Basic human needs like food and shelter are central issues for need-driven people.
Sustainers. These people live from paycheck to paycheck. Although they engage in an occasional extravagance, they have little hope for improving their lot in life.
Survivors. These people worry about making ends meet. As a group, they are marked by poverty, low education, old age and limited access to upper mobility.

INNER-DIRECTED PEOPLE
These people are self-motivated in much that they do. They are oriented to personal growth.
Societally Conscious. These people feel obliged to improve the world and tend to be active on political and social issues.
Experientials. These people want new experiences and tend to be venturesome. They seek personal growth.
I-Am-Me's. These people work very hard at setting themselves apart. Sometimes they are obnoxious in trying to attract attention to how they are different.

VALS Hierarchy. *Developmental psychologists have long told us that people change their values as they mature. Today, many advertisers rely on the Values and Life-Style model, VALS for short, which was derived from developmental psychology, to identify potential consumers and to design effective messages. Relatively few advertising messages are aimed at survivors and sustainers, who have little discretionary income. However, belongers and people on the divergent outer-directed or inner-directed paths are lucrative advertising targets for many products and services.*

their lot in life. Sustainers are a downscale category and aren't frequent advertising targets.

- **Integrateds.** Comprising only 2 percent of the population, integrateds are both creative and prosperous—willing to try different products and ways of doing things, and they have the wherewithal to do it.

Applying psychographics is not without hazard. The categories are in flux as society and lifestyles change. SRI researchers who chart growth in the percentage of I-Am-Me's, experientials and the societally conscious project that they total one-third of the population. Belongers are declining.

Another complication is that no person fits absolutely the mold of any one category. Even for individuals who fit one category better than another, there is no single mass medium to reach them. VALS research may show that achievers constitute the biggest market for antihistamines, but belongers also head to the medicine cabinet when they're congested.

LEARNING CHECK ◄

▶ **Think about a person your grandparents' age and plug them into the VALS category that today fits them best. Discuss how you came to your conclusion.**

▶ **Into what category did this same individual best fit 40 years ago?**

▶ **Compare where you are on the VALS system with where you expect to be in 20 years.**

Chapter Wrap-Up

Public Opinion Sampling (Page 374)

■ Surveying for opinions plays a growing role in our society's public life, in public policy and in decisions about advertising and other media content. Survey techniques have become increasingly complex and statistically more reliable. Generally the best surveys use probability sampling, which statistically chooses respondents whose responses will coincide with the whole group. All surveys have caveats, however. Some surveys are hocus-pocus with no statistical reliability, including 800 and 900 number call-ins and man-on-the-street interviews.

Measuring Audience Size (Page 381)

■ Advertisers long were victims of bogus circulation claims by newspapers and magazines, whose advertising rates were based on unverified audience rates. The Audit Bureau of Circulations largely cleaned up false claims beginning in 1914. ABC checked pressruns. Radio, then television audiences were not so easily measured. In 1929 Archibald Crossley used extrapolations from small samples to see how many people were tuned to network radio programs. The networks, of course, wanted the information to guide programming decisions. Today Nielsen is the largest player in television ratings.

Audience Measurement Techniques (Page 383)

■ Traditional polling techniques include interviews and diaries. Meters have added new precision in recent years. Some new devices even track which billboards a person passes and how often.

Measuring Audience Reaction (Page 388)

■ Special techniques have been devised to measure how audiences react to media messages. This includes focus groups to generate feedback on media content, like a television program, a publication redesign, and advertisements. Visceral effects can be tracked by charting heartbeat, brain activity and other physiological reactions as a message is being presented. The fate of a pilot for a program can hang on these measures. So can an advertising campaign. Some movies are adjusted by analyzing audience reactions to pre-final cuts. Advisers to large-budget political candidates also use these techniques to hone messages to various blocs of voters.

Audience Analysis (Page 391)

■ The imperative to match messages with audience has created a relatively new component of analysis. The historical breakdowns—demographics like age, gender and affiliations—have become much more sophisticated. Some analysis looks at media habits in highly defined neighborhoods in assessing how to craft media messages, particurlarly advertising and political spots. Called geodemographics, the method clusters people by income, education and geography. Psychographics looks at lifestyles and motivations. Some groupings include high achievers, followers, and convention-defiers.

REVIEW QUESTIONS

1. What variables determine whether surveys based on probability sampling can be trusted?

2. How is the size of newspaper audiences measured? Radio? Television?

3. What lifestyle and media changes have prompted media survey companies to update their techniques? What are these new techniques?

4. How are audience reactions to mass-media content measured? What results from these measurements?

5. What are techniques of audience analysis? How are data from these analyses used?

CONCEPTS

cohort analysis (Page 392)

geodemography (Page 393)

probability sampling (Page 375)

statistical extrapolation (Page 376)

VALS (Page 394)

TERMS

Audit Bureau of Circulations
  (Page 381)

margin of error (Page 377)

quota sampling (Page 377)

ratings (Page 381)

Anytime Anywhere Media
  Measurement (A2/M2) (Page 385)

PEOPLE

Archibald Crossley (Page 381)

George Gallup (Page 374)

Andy Kohut (Page 379)

A. C. Nielsen (Page 383)

Jonathan Robbin (Page 393)

MEDIA SOURCES

- James Webster, Patricia Phalen and Lawrence W. Lichty. *Ratings Analysis: The Theory and Practice of Audience Research,* third edition. Erlbaum, 2006. The authors, all professors, discuss how to conduct audience research and how to make use of the findings.

- Kenneth F. Warren. *In Defense of Public Opinion Polling.* Westview, 2001. Warren, a pollster, acknowledges that bad polling exists but explains and defends good practices and notes their growing role in democracy.

- Dan Fleming, editor. *Formations: 21st Century Media Studies.* Manchester University Press, 2001. In this collection of essays, Fleming lays out the groundwork for students interested in advanced media studies.

MEDIA RESEARCH: A Thematic Chapter Summary

In this chapter you have deepened your media literacy by revisiting several themes. Here are thematic highlights from the chapter:

Following the viewers

The Go Meter

Media Technology

Traditional techniques to measure media audiences focused on the advertising-supported mass media of newspapers, magazines, radio and television. For broadcast media these techniques have fallen short over time. The proliferation of television to follow people out of their homes—to dentists' waiting rooms and pizza joints, for example—left millions of viewing hours untracked. VCRs and DVDs complicated the tracking of audiences. And what of Web browsing? Advertisers wanted wider and better measuring techniques to help them find the right media for their messages and to weigh competing advertising rates. Survey companies are introducing gizmos to provide more detailed media usage data. These include A2/M2 devices, short for Anytime Anywhere Media Measurement, to track television viewing regardless of platform—over-air stations, cable, satellite, even the Web. Some devices even count how many billboards a person passes. **(Pages 381–388)**

Media Economics

John Wanamaker, the department store magnate of 100 years ago, said he recognized that half of his advertising budget was wasted on reaching people who had no interest in shopping at his stores. Alas, he added, he didn't know which half. Today a major industry exists to help advertisers make informed decisions on where to place their advertising. For a fee, these survey companies provide data on audience size and breakdowns of demographics and lifestyle. Media companies use these data in choosing content that will attract the kinds of audiences that advertisers covet. **(Pages 391–395)**

Nielsen Headquarters. *Home of a leading company in a major industry.*

Media and Democracy

Techniques for measuring media audiences were pioneered and honed by George Gallup's political polling in the 1930s. His core contribution, probability sampling, is the backbone of surveying today. The data are important for political candidates in shaping campaign strategies and tactics.

News reports based on these surveys also help citizens track shifting moods in the country. These reports are an important part of the nation's grassroots dialogue on the direction of public policy. (Pages 374–381)

George Gallup. Pioneer pollster.

Audience Fragmentation

Recent refinements in surveying have yielded data that provide advertisers with incredible tools for designing messages and then buying media time and space to reach their most likely customers. The Army, for example, has breakdowns to match its media buys with specific targets for recruiting ads on scales of an urban-rural lifestyle, ethnicity and socioeconomics. This goes beyond the broad categories of traditional demographics like age and gender. The use of these data, from techniques like geodemographics and psychographics, have prompted media companies to shape their products more precisely to match slivers of the mass audience with advertisers. This has furthered media demassification—the Cartoon Network for kids' breakfast cereals and HGTV for Home Depot, for example. (Pages 391–395)

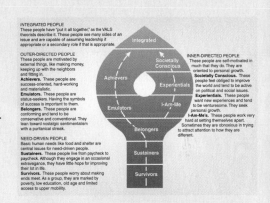

Psychographic Audience Analysis. The VALS model.

Media Effects

More Action, Less Substance. Visceral news judgment.

Media companies that seek the biggest possible audiences, including over-air television stations, use research to identify what goes over with the most people. The result, say critics, has been a coarsening of what's on the air and a trend away from news and information that contributes to public understanding and participation in significant issues. Research has found, for example, that a roaring house fire with its visceral visuals attracts more viewers than a report on a municipal budget crisis. Wags have said of TV news: "If it bleeds it leads." The obsession of many media products on celebrities is a reflection of offering what draws the largest viewership. Celeb news displaces what's more important. A proliferation of violence in movies and television also reflects what survey data say about audience preferences. (Pages 388–391)

16

Mass-Media Effects

Orson Welles

The boy genius Orson Welles was on a roll. By 1938, at age 23, Welles' dramatic flair had landed him a network radio show, *Mercury Theater on the Air*, at prime time on CBS on Sunday nights. The program featured adaptations of well-known literature. For their October 30 program, Welles and his colleagues decided on a scary 1898 British novel, H. G. Wells' ***War of the Worlds.***

Orson Welles opened with the voice of a wizened chronicler from some future time, intoning an unsettling monologue. That was followed by an innocuous weather forecast, then hotel dance music. Then the music was interrupted by a news bulletin. An astronomer reported several explosions on Mars, propelling something at enormous velocity toward Earth. The bulletin over, listeners were transported back to the hotel orchestra. After applause the orchestra started up again, only to be interrupted by a special announcement: Seismologists had picked up an earthquake-like shock in New Jersey. Then it was one bulletin after another.

The story line accelerated. Giant Martians moved across the countryside spewing fatal gas. One at a time, reporters at remote sites vanished off the air. The Martians decimated the Army and were wading across the Hudson River. Amid sirens and other sounds of emergency, a reporter on a Manhattan rooftop described the monsters advancing through the streets. From his vantage point he described the Martians felling people by the thousands and moving in on him, the gas crossing Sixth Avenue, then Fifth Avenue, then 100 yards away, then 50 feet. Then silence.

LEARNING AHEAD

- Scholars today believe that the effects of mass communication generally are cumulative over time.

- Mass messages are significant in helping children learn society's expectations.

- Most of the effects of mass communication are difficult to measure and predict.

- Mass communication binds large audiences culturally but also can reinforce cultural fragmentation.

- Some notions about the effects of mass messages, including subliminal messages, have been overstated.

- Scholars differ on whether media-depicted violence triggers aggressive behavior.

War of the Worlds. *Young Orson Welles scared the living daylights out of several million radio listeners with the 1938 radio drama* War of the Worlds. *Most of the fright was short-lived though. All but the most naïve listeners quickly realized that Martians really had not had the time within a one-hour real-time drama to devastate the New Jersey militia en route to wading the Hudson River to destroy Manhattan.*

To the surprise of Orson Welles and his crew, the drama triggered widespread mayhem. Neighbors gathered in streets all over the country, wet towels held to their faces to slow the gas. In Newark, New Jersey, people—many undressed—fled their apartments. Said a New York woman, "I never hugged my radio so closely. . . . I held a crucifix in my hand and prayed while looking out my open window to get a faint whiff of gas so that I would know when to close my window and hermetically seal my room with waterproof cement or anything else I could get a hold of. My plan was to stay in the room and hope that I would not suffocate before the gas blew away."

Researchers estimate that one out of six people who heard the program, more than 1 million in all, suspended disbelief and braced for the worst.

The effects were especially amazing considering that:

■ An announcer identified the program as fiction at four points.

■ Almost 10 times as many people were tuned to a popular comedy show on another network.

■ The program ran only one hour, an impossibly short time for the sequence that began with the blastoffs on Mars, included a major military battle in New Jersey and ended with New York's destruction.

Unwittingly, Orson Welles and his *Mercury Theater* crew had created an evening of infamy and raised questions about media effects to new intensity. In this chapter you will learn what scholars have found out about the effects of the mass media on individuals.

Effects Theories

STUDY PREVIEW

Early mass communication scholars assumed that the mass media were so powerful that ideas and even ballot-box instructions could be inserted as if by hypodermic needle into the body politic. It's called the magic bullet theory. Doubts arose in the 1940s about whether the media were really that powerful, and scholars began shaping their research questions on the assumption that media effects are more modest. Recent studies are asking about long-term, cumulative media effects.

MAGIC BULLET THEORY

The first generation of mass communication scholars thought the mass media had a profound, direct effect on people. Their idea, called **powerful effects theory**, drew heavily on social commentator **Walter Lippmann**'s influential 1922 book *Public Opinion*. Lippmann argued that we see the world not as it really is but as "pictures in our heads." The "pictures" of things we have not experienced personally, he said, are shaped by the mass media. The powerful impact that Lippmann ascribed to the media was a precursor to the powerful effects theory that evolved among scholars over the next few years.

● **Harold Lasswell**
His mass communication model assumed powerful effects

● **magic bullet model**
Another name for the overrated powerful effects theory

Yale psychologist **Harold Lasswell,** who studied World War II propaganda, embodied the effects theory in his famous model of mass communication: *Who, says what, In which channel, To whom, With what effect.* At their extreme, powerful effects theory devotees assumed that the media could inject information, ideas and even propaganda into the public consciousness. The theory was explained in terms of a hypodermic needle model or **magic bullet model.** Early powerful effects scholars would agree that newspaper coverage and endorsements of political candidates decided elections.

The early scholars did not see that the hypodermic metaphor was hopelessly simplistic. They assumed, wrongly, that individuals are passive and absorb uncritically and unconditionally whatever the media spew forth. The fact is that individuals read, hear and see the same things differently. Even if they did not, people are exposed to many, many media—hardly a single, monolithic voice. Also, there is a skepticism among media consumers that is manifested at its extreme in the saying "You can't believe a thing you read in the paper." People are not mindless, uncritical blotters.

● **third-person effect**
One person overestimating the effect of media messages on other people

● **W. P. Davison**
Scholar who devised third-person effect theory

A remnant of now-discredited perceptions that the media have powerful and immediate influence is called **third-person effect.** In short, the theory holds that people overestimate the impact of media messages on other people. Scholar **W. P. Davison,** who came up with the concept in 1983, told a story about a community film board that censored some movies because they might harm people who watch them—even though the board members denied that they themselves were harmed by watching them. The theory can be reduced to this notion: "It's the other guy who can't handle it, not me."

Davison's pioneering scholarship spawned many studies. Most of the conclusions can be boiled down to these:

- Fears about negative impact are often unwarranted.
- Blocking negative messages is often unwarranted.

LEARNING CHECK ◀ ••

▸ **Explain the ink-blotter metaphor for mass audiences in the early thinking about mass communication effects.**

▸ **What evidence supports the conclusion that the magic bullet theory simplistically overstates the effects of mass communication?**

MINIMALIST EFFECTS THEORY

Scholarly enthusiasm for the hypodermic needle model dwindled after two massive studies of voter behavior, one in Erie Country, Ohio, in 1940 and the other in Elmira, New York, in 1948. The studies, led by sociologist **Paul Lazarsfeld** of Columbia University, were the first rigorous tests of media effects on an election. Lazarsfeld's researchers went back to 600 people several times to discover how they developed their campaign opinions. Rather than citing particular newspapers, magazines or radio stations, as had been expected, these people generally mentioned friends and acquaintances. The media had hardly any direct effect. Clearly, the hypodermic needle model was off base, and the powerful effects theory needed rethinking. From that rethinking emerged the **minimalist effects theory,** which includes:

● **Paul Lazarsfeld**
Found voters are more influenced by other people than by mass media

● **minimalist effects theory**
Theory that media effects are mostly indirect

● **two-step flow**
Media affects individuals through opinion leaders

● **opinion leaders**
Influence friends, acquaintances

■ **Two-Step Flow Model.** Minimalist scholars devised the **two-step flow** model to show that voters are motivated less by the mass media than by people they know personally and respect. These people, called **opinion leaders,** include many clergy, teachers and neighborhood merchants, although it is impossible to list categorically all those who are opinion leaders. Not all clergy, for example, are influential, and opinion leaders are not necessarily in authority roles. The minimalist scholars' point is that personal contact is more important than media contact. The two-step flow model, which replaced the hypodermic needle model, shows that whatever effect the media have on the majority of the population is through opinion leaders. Later, as mass communication research became more sophisticated, the two-step model was expanded into a **multistep flow** model to capture the complex web of social relationships that affects individuals.

■ **Status Conferral.** Minimalist scholars acknowledge that the media create prominence for issues and people by giving them coverage. Conversely, neglect relegates issues and personalities to obscurity. Related to this **status conferral** phenomenon is **agenda-setting**. Professors **Maxwell McCombs and Don Shaw,** describing the agenda-setting phenomenon in 1972, said the media do not tell people *what to think* but tell them *what to about*. This is a profound distinction. In covering a political campaign, explain McCombs and Shaw, the media choose which issues or topics to emphasize, thereby helping set the campaign's agenda. "This ability to affect cognitive change among individuals," say McCombs and Shaw, "is one of the most important aspects of the power of mass communication."

■ **Narcoticizing Dysfunction.** Some minimalists claim that the media rarely energize people into action, such as getting them to go out to vote for a candidate. Rather, they say, the media lull people into passivity. This effect, called **narcoticizing dysfunction,** is supported by studies that find that many people are so overwhelmed by the volume of news and information available to them that they tend to withdraw from involvement in public issues. Narcoticizing dysfunction occurs also when people pick up a great deal of information from the media on a particular subject—poverty, for example—and believe that they are doing something about a problem when they are really only smugly well informed. Intellectual involvement becomes a substitute for active involvement.

LEARNING CHECK ◄ ···

▶ **What layers of complexity did Paul Lazarsfeld add to our understanding of the effects of mass communication?**

CUMULATIVE EFFECTS THEORY

In recent years some mass communication scholars have parted from the minimalists and resurrected the powerful effects theory, although with a twist that avoids the simplistic hypodermic needle model. German scholar **Elisabeth Noelle-Neumann,** a leader of this school, concedes that the media do not have powerful, immediate effects but argues that effects over time are profound. Her **cumulative effects theory** notes that no-body can escape either the media, which are ubiquitous, or the media's messages, which are driven home with redundancy. To support her point, Noelle-Neumann cites multimedia advertising campaigns that hammer away with the same message over and over. There's no missing the point. Even in news reports there is a redundancy, with the media all focusing on the same events.

Noelle-Neumann's cumulative effects theory has troubling implications. She says that the media, despite surface appearances, work against diverse, robust public consideration of issues. Noelle-Neumann bases her observation on human psychology, which she says encourages people who feel they hold majority viewpoints to speak out confidently. Those views grow in credibility when they are carried by the media, whether they really are dominant or not. Meanwhile, says Noelle-Neumann, people who perceive that they are in a minority are inclined to speak out less, perhaps not at all. The result is that dominant views can snowball through the media and become consensus views without being sufficiently challenged.

To demonstrate her intriguing theory, Noelle-Neumann has devised the ominously labeled **spiral of silence** model, in which minority views are intimidated into silence and obscurity. Noelle-Neumann's model raises doubts about the libertarian

---

● **multistep flow**
Media affects individuals through complex interpersonal connections

● **status conferral**
Media attention enhances attention given to people, subjects, issues

● **agenda-setting**
Media tell people what to think about, not what to think

● **Maxwell McCombs and Don Shaw**
Articulated agenda-setting theory

● **narcoticizing dysfunction**
People deceive themselves into believing they're involved when actually they're only informed

● **Elisabeth Noelle-Neumann**
Leading cumulative effects theorist

● **cumulative effects theory**
Theory that media influence is gradual over time

Elisabeth Noelle-Neumann.
Her spiral of silence theory sees people with minority viewpoints being discouraged into silence by louder majority views. These majority views sometimes come into dominance through media amplification. The more the dominance, the less these views are subject to continuing review and evaluation.

● **spiral of silence**
Vocal majority intimidates others
into silence

concept of the media providing a marketplace in which conflicting ideas fight it out fairly, all receiving a full hearing.

LEARNING CHECK ◄ ••

▶ Explain the way that Elisabeth Noelle-Neumann and most contemporary scholars see mass communication as having effects on people.

▶ Do you have an example of the spiral of silence model from your own experience? Explain.

Lifestyle Effects

STUDY PREVIEW

Mass media have a large role in initiating children into society. The socialization process is essential in perpetuating cultural values. For better or worse, mass media have accelerated socialization by giving youngsters access to information that adults kept to themselves in earlier generations. While the mass media affect lifestyles, they also reflect lifestyle changes that come about for reasons altogether unrelated to the mass media.

SOCIALIZATION

Nobody is born knowing how to fit into society. This is learned through a process that begins at home. Children imitate their parents and brothers and sisters. From listening and observing, children learn values. Some behavior is applauded, some is scolded. Gradually this culturization and **socialization** process expands to include friends, neighbors, school and at some point the mass media.

● **socialization**
Learning to fit into society

In earlier times the role of the mass media came into effect in children's lives late because books, magazines and newspapers require reading skills that are learned in school. The media were only a modest part of early childhood socialization. Today, however, television is omnipresent from the cradle. A young person turning 18 will have spent more time watching television than in any other activity except sleep. Television, which requires no special skills to use, has displaced much of the socializing influence that once came from parents. *Sesame Street* imparts more information on the value of nutrition than does Mom's admonition to eat spinach.

● **prosocial**
Socialization perpetuates positive values

By definition, socialization is **prosocial.** American children learn that motherhood, baseball and apple pie are valued; that buddies frown on tattling; that honesty is virtuous; and that hard work is rewarded. The stability of a society is ensured through the transmission of such values to the next generation.

LEARNING CHECK ◄ ••

▶ Why is mass communication a growing issue in child development?

LIVING PATTERNS

The mass media both reflect lifestyles and shape them. The advent of television in the mid-1950s, for example, kept people at home in their living rooms in the evening. Lodge memberships tumbled. Wednesday-night vespers became an anachronism of earlier times. Television supplanted crossroads taverns in rural areas for socializing and keeping up to date.

Media and lifestyle are intertwined. To find and keep audiences, media companies adjust their products according to the changes caused by other changes. Department stores, a phenomenon in the 1880s, put shopping into the daily routine of housewives, giving rise to evening newspapers carrying store ads so that women could plan their next day's shopping expeditions. Newspapers previously were almost all in morning publication.

MASS-MEDIA EFFECTS MILESTONES

PIVOTAL EVENTS

1900–1949

Powerful Effects Theory
The media shape the pictures in our heads (1922)

Minimalist Effects Theory
Paul Lazarsfeld tested media effects on elections (1940s)

Aristotle: Nothing to worry about

- Right to vote for women (1920)
- Radio emerged as commercial medium (late 1920s)
- Great Depression (1930s)
- World War II (1941–1945)
- Russian–Western rivalry triggered Cold War (1945–1989)

1950–1999

Bobo Doll Studies
Albert Bandura concluded media cause violence (1960)

Cognitive Dissonance
Media depictions cause overt racism to fade (1960s)

Cultural Imperialism
Herbert Schiller examined media's impact on indigenous cultures (1969)

Agenda Setting
Maxwell McCombs and Don Shaw showed that media set agendas, not opinions (1972)

Cumulative Effects Theory
Elisabeth Noelle-Neumann theorized media effects (1973)

Intergenerational Eavesdropping
Joshua Meyrowitz observed that television was eroding childhood innocence (1985)

Offensive Mascots Debated
Nebraska *Journal Star* banned offensive sports mascots (2005)

Orson Welles' radio drama stirred panic—or did it?

Elisabeth Noelle-Neumann says media effects are seldom sudden 180-degree reversals

- Television emerged as commercial medium (early 1950s)
- Vietnam War (1964–1973)
- Humans reached moon (1969)
- Internet emerged as commercial medium (late 1990s)

- 9/11 terrorist attacks (2001)
- Iraq War (2003–)
- Hurricane Katrina (2005)

A century later, with the growing influx of women into full-time, out-of-the-house jobs, newspapers dropped their evening editions. Today almost all U.S. newspapers have only morning publication. Other societal changes also contributed to the demise of evening newspapers. In the old industrial economy, most jobs were 7 a.m. to 3 p.m., which allowed discretionary evening time to spend with a newspaper. With the emergence of a service economy, with 9 a.m. to 5 p.m. jobs coming into dominance, the market for evening newspapers withered. Television, as an alternative evening activity, also squeezed into the available time for people to read an evening paper.

LEARNING CHECK ◄••

▶ **Can you offer examples from your own experience of mass media reflecting lifestyles?**

▶ **How about examples of lifestyles reflecting mass media?**

INTERGENERATIONAL EAVESDROPPING

The mass media, especially television, have eroded the boundaries between the generations, genders and other social institutions that people once respected. Once, adults whispered when they wanted to discuss certain subjects, like sex, when children were around. Today, children "eavesdrop" on all kinds of adult topics by seeing them depicted on television. Though meant as a joke, these lines ring true today to many squirming parents:

Father to a friend: My son and I had that father-and-son talk about the birds and the bees yesterday.
Friend: Did you learn anything?
Joshua Meyrowitz, a communication scholar at the University of New Hampshire, brought the new socialization effects of intergenerational eavesdropping to wide attention with his 1985 book, *No Sense of Place*. In effect, the old socially recognized institution of childhood, which long had been protected from "grown-up issues" like money, divorce and sex, is disappearing. From television sitcoms, kids today learn that adults fight and goof up and sometimes are just plain silly. These are things kids may always have been aware of in a vague sense, but now they have front-row seats.

Television also cracked other protected societal institutions, such as the "man's world." Through television many women enter the man's world of the locker room, the fishing trip and the workplace beyond the home. Older mass media, including books, had dealt with a diversity of topics and allowed people in on the "secrets" of other groups, but the ubiquity of television and the ease of access to it accelerated the breakdown of traditional institutional barriers.

● **Joshua Meyrowitz**
Noted that media have reduced generational and gender barriers

LEARNING CHECK ◄••

▶ **Has modern media content eroded the innocence of childhood? Explain.**

Attitude Effects

STUDY PREVIEW

When media messages rivet people's focus, public opinion can take new forms almost instantly. These quick cause-and-effect transformations are easily measured. More difficult to track are the effects of media messages on opinions and attitudes that shift over time—like customs and social conventions. Studies on role models and stereotype shifts seek to address these more elusive effects and how media messages can be manipulated to influence opinions and attitudes.

INFLUENCING OPINION

How malleable are opinions? People, in fact, change their minds. In politics, the dominance of political parties shifts. Going into the 2008 election, polls found a growing disaffection with the Democratic and Republican parties. More people were calling themselves independents. Enthusiasm for products can spiral to success overnight and collapse just as fast. We know that people adjust their opinions, sometimes gradually, sometimes suddenly. Also, we know that media messages are important in these processes.

Some cause and effect is tracked easily. A horrendous event, like the unexpected Japanese attack on U.S. Navy facilities at Pearl Harbor in 1941, instantly transformed American public opinion. Before the attack, sentiment had been against armed resistance to Japanese and German expansionism. In an instant, a massive majority decided to go to war. In 2005 public confidence in the federal government bottomed with the failure to deal with the hurricane devastation in New Orleans and the Gulf Coast. Such sudden shifts result from information carried by mass media, including statements from opinion leaders.

Causal explanations for gradual opinion shifts are elusive, although mass messages are a factor. What puts a company atop lists of most-admired brands? What makes the rest of the country view California as it does? Or New York? Or New Jersey? Many institutions, including state tourism agencies, budget millions of dollars to promote an image that they hope will be absorbed over time. One concentration of corporate image messages airs weekly on Sunday-morning television talk shows.

Scholars have puzzled for decades over how to measure the effects of media content on opinion. Except for major events that trigger sudden turnarounds, media effects on opinion are gradual.

LEARNING CHECK ◄ ···

▸ **Give an example of sudden and drastic changes in public opinion based on media information and other content.**

▸ **How frequently do mass media trigger turnarounds in public opinion?**

ROLE MODELS

The extent of media influence on individuals may never be sorted out with any precision, in part because every individual is a distinct person and because media exposure varies from person to person. Even so, some media influence is undeniable. Consider the effect of entertainment idols as they come across through the media. Many individuals, especially young people casting about for an identity all their own, groom themselves in conformity with the latest heart-throb. Consider the Mickey Mantle butch haircuts in the 1950s and then Elvis Presley ducktails, Beatle mopheads in the 1960s and punk spikes in the 1980s. Then there were all the Spice Girls look-alikes in high school some years ago. This imitation, called **role modeling**, even includes speech mannerisms from whoever is hip at the moment—"Show me the money," "Hasta la vista, baby" and "I'm the king of the world." Let's not forget "yadda-yadda-yadda" from *Seinfeld*.

No matter how quirky, fashion fads are not terribly consequential, but serious questions can be raised about whether role modeling extends to behavior. Many people who produce media messages recognize their responsibility for role modeling. Whenever Batman and Robin leaped into their Batmobile in the campy 1960s television series, the camera always managed to show them fastening their seat belts. Many newspapers have a policy of mentioning in accident stories whether seat belts were in use. In the 1980s, as concern about AIDS mounted, moviemakers went out of their way to show condoms as a precaution in social situations. For example, in the movie *Broadcast News*, the producer character slips a condom into her purse before leaving the house on the night of the awards dinner.

● **role modeling**
Basis for imitative behavior

Asics Revival. *When Uma Thurman slashed her way through Quentin Tarantino's movie* Kill Bill, *the 1949-vintage Asics sneakers she wore, the Onitsuka Tiger model, were suddenly a hit again. In the first quarter after the movie, Asics net profits outperformed $1.8 billion in expectations to $2.6 billion. The question was whether Thurman would wear Asics in the sequel in 2004 and whether interest in the Tiger model could be sustained.*

If role modeling can work for good purposes, such as promoting safety consciousness and disease prevention, it would seem that it could also have a negative effect. Some people linked the Columbine High School massacre in Littleton, Colorado, to a scene in the Leonardo DiCaprio movie *The Basketball Diaries*. In one scene, a student in a black trench coat executes fellow classmates. An outbreak of shootings followed other 1990s films that glorified thug life, including *New Jack City, Juice* and *Boyz N the Hood*.

LEARNING CHECK ◄ ···

▶ **From your experience, cite examples of role modeling on issues more consequential than fashion and fads.**

STEREOTYPES

Close your eyes. Think "professor." What image forms in your mind? Before 1973 most people would have envisioned a harmless, absent-minded eccentric. Today, *The Nutty Professor* movie remake is a more likely image. Both the absent-minded and later nutty professor images are known as stereotypes. Both flow from the mass media. Although neither is an accurate generalization about professors, both have long-term impact.

● **stereotyping**
Using broad strokes to facilitate storytelling

Stereotyping is a kind of shorthand that can facilitate communication. Putting a cowboy in a black hat allows a movie director to sidestep complex character exploration and move quickly into a story line because moviegoers hold a generalization about cowboys in black hats: They are the bad guys—a stereotype.

Newspaper editors pack lots of information into headlines by drawing on stereotypes held by readers. Consider the extra meanings implicit in headlines that refer to the "Castro regime," a "Southern belle" or a "college jock." Stereotypes paint broad strokes that help create impact in media messages, but they are also a problem. A generalization, no matter how useful, is inaccurate. Not all Scots are tightfisted, nor are all Wall Street brokers crooked, nor are all college jocks dumb—not even a majority.

By using stereotypes, the mass media perpetuate them. With benign stereotypes there is no problem, but the media can perpetuate social injustice with stereotypes. In the late 1970s the U.S. Civil Rights Commission found that blacks on network television were portrayed disproportionately in immature, demeaning or comic roles. By using a stereotype, television was not only perpetuating false generalizations but also being racist. Worse, network thoughtlessness was robbing black people of strong role models.

Feminists have leveled objections that women are both underrepresented and misrepresented in the media. One study by sociologist Eve Simson found that most female television parts are decorative, played by pretty California women in their 20s. Worse are the occupations represented by women, said Simson. Most frequent are prostitutes, at 16 percent. Traditional female occupations—secretaries, nurses, flight attendants and receptionists—represent 17 percent. Career women tend to be man-haters or domestic failures. Said Simson: "With nearly every family, regardless of socioeconomic class, having at least one TV set and the average set being turned on seven hours per day, TV has emerged as an important source for promulgating attitudes, values and customs. For some viewers it is the only major contact with outside 'reality,' including how to relate to women. Thus, not only is TV's sexism insulting, but it is also detrimental to the status of women."

Media critics like Simson call for the media to become activists to revise demeaning stereotypes. Although often right-minded, such calls can interfere with accurate portrayals. Italian-Americans, for example, lobbied successfully against Mafia characters being identified as Italians. Exceptions like HBO's Soprano family remained irritants, however. In general, activists against stereotyping have succeeded. Simson would be pleased with the women and black and Latino characters in nonstereotypical roles in popular shows like NBC's *Law & Order* and CBS's *CSI*.

LEARNING CHECK ◄ •

▶ Why are stereotypes an essential element in mass communication?

▶ What media-perpetuated stereotypes do you see that are false, misleading and damaging?

AGENDA-SETTING AND STATUS CONFERRAL

Media attention lends a legitimacy to events, individuals and issues that does not extend to things that go uncovered. This conferring of status occurs through the media's role as agenda-setters. It puts everybody on the same wavelength, or at least a similar one, which contributes to social cohesion by focusing our collective attention on issues we can address together. Otherwise, each of us could be going in separate directions, which would make collective action difficult if not impossible.

Examples of how media attention spotlights certain issues abound. An especially poignant case occurred in 1998 when a gay University of Wyoming student, Matthew Shepard, was savagely beaten, tied to a fence outside of town and left to die. It was tragic gay-bashing, and coverage of the event moved gay rights higher on the national agenda. Coverage of the gruesome death was an example of the media agenda-setting and of status conferral.

LEARNING CHECK ◄ •

▶ How does mass communication wield power through status conferral on some issues and neglect others?

To people who criticize the mass media for trafficking in misleading sterotypes, Kathleen Rutledge is a hero. Rutledge, editor of the Lincoln, Nebraska, *Journal Star*, has banned references to sports mascots and nicknames that many American Indians consider insulting. Readers of the *Journal Star*, circulation 74,000, no longer read about the Washington Redskins, just Washington. Instead of the Fighting Sioux, it's just North Dakota. The Cleveland Indians' mascot, Chief Wahoo, whose weird grin irked Indians, doesn't appear in the newspaper either.

Rutledge acknowledges that the policy change rankled some readers when it was announced. In 500-some letters and e-mail messages, readers accused the newspaper of abandoning tradition and succumbing to the leftist politically correct agenda. Leftist? Hardly, responds Rutledge, noting that the *Journal Star* endorsed the self-proclaimed "compassionate conservative" George Bush for president in 2000.

Rather, she says, the newspaper is working hard to recognize diversity. Influxes of people from Latin America, Africa and Asia have changed the Lincoln area. "We've just become more aware of other cultures, other ethnicities," Rutledge said.

Banned in Lincoln. *Kathleen Rutledge, editor of the Lincoln* Journal Star *in Nebraska, doesn't allow nicknames and mascots that offend many American Indians to appear in the newspaper. Chief Wahoo, mascot of the Cleveland professional baseball team, doesn't appear in the newspaper. Nor does the tribal name Fighting Illini for the University of Illinois athletic teams. In 2005 the National Collegiate Athletic Association stepped up pressure on other college teams to drop Indian nicknames like the Fighting Sioux at North Dakota and the Savages at Southeastern Oklahoma State.*

Kathleen Rutledge

WHAT DO YOU THINK?

▶ Should sports teams be required to choose kinder, gentler mascots and nicknames so as not to offend?

▶ Can a media ban on references to a controversial mascot be effective in reducing stereotyping?

Cultural Effects

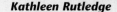

STUDY PREVIEW

Mass-media messages to large audiences can be culturally unifying, but media demassification, with messages aimed at narrower audiences, has had a role also in the fragmentation of society. On a global scale, media have imposed U.S. and Western values on the traditional values of other cultures. Even in countries with emerging media systems, the indigenous media continue to be influenced by media content from dominant cultures.

VALUES

■ **Historical Transmission.** Human beings have a compulsion to pass on the wisdom they have accumulated to future generations. There is a compulsion, too, to learn from the past. In olden times, people gathered around fires and in temples to hear storytellers. It was a ritual through which people learned the values that governed their community. This is a form of **historical transmission.**

Five thousand years ago, the oral tradition was augmented when Middle Eastern traders devised an alphabet to keep track of inventories, transactions and rates of exchange. When paper was invented, clay tablets gave way to scrolls and eventually books, which became the primary vehicle for storytelling. Religious values were passed on in holy books. Military chronicles laid out the lessons of war. Literature provided lessons by exploring the nooks and crannies of the human condition.

Books remain the primary repository of our culture. For several centuries it has been between hard covers, in black ink on paper, that the experiences, lessons and wisdom of our forebears have been recorded for posterity. Other mass media today share in the preservation and transmission of our culture over time. Consider these archives:

- **Museum of Television and Radio** in New York, with 1,200 hours of television documentaries; great performances, productions, debuts and series; and a sample of top-rated shows.
- **Library for Communication and Graphic Arts** at Ohio State University, whose collection includes editorial cartoons.
- **Vanderbilt Television News Archive** in Nashville, Tennessee, with 7,000 hours of network nightly news programs and special coverage such as political conventions and space shots.

■ **Contemporary Transmission.** The mass media also transmit values among contemporary communities and societies, sometimes causing changes that otherwise would not occur. This is known as **contemporary transmission.** Anthropologists have documented that mass communication can change society. When Edmund Carpenter introduced movies to an isolated New Guinea village, the men adjusted their clothing toward the Western style and even remodeled their houses. This phenomenon, which scholars call **diffusion of innovations,** occurs when ideas move through the mass media. Consider the following:

- **American Revolution.** Colonists up and down the Atlantic seaboard took cues on what to think and how to act from newspaper reports on radical activities, mostly in Boston, in the decade before the Declaration of Independence. These included inflammatory articles against the 1765 Stamp Act and accounts of the Boston Tea Party in 1773.
- **Music, fashion and pop culture.** In modern-day pop culture, the cues come through the media, mostly from New York, Hollywood and Nashville.
- **Third World innovation.** The United Nations creates instructional films and radio programs to promote agricultural reform in less developed parts of the world. Overpopulated areas have been targets of birth control campaigns.
- **Democracy in China.** As China opened itself to Western tourists, commerce and mass media in the 1980s, the people glimpsed Western democracy and prosperity, which precipitated pressure on the Communist government to westernize and resulted in the 1989 Tiananmen Square confrontation. A similar phenomenon was a factor in the glasnost relaxations in the Soviet Union in the late 1980s.
- **Demise of Main Street.** Small-town businesses are boarding up throughout the United States as rural people see advertisements from regional shopping malls, which are farther away but offer greater variety and lower prices than Main Street.

Scholars note that the mass media can be given too much credit for the diffusion of innovations. Diffusion almost always needs reinforcement through interpersonal

● **historical transmission**
Communication of cultural values to later generations

● **contemporary transmission**
Communication of cultural values to different cultures

● **diffusion of innovations**
Process through which news, ideas, values, information spread

communication. Also, the diffusion is hardly ever a one-shot hypodermic injection but a process that requires redundancy in messages over an extended period. The 1989 outburst for democracy in China did not happen because one Chinese person read Thomas Paine one afternoon, nor do rural people suddenly abandon their local Main Street for a Wal-Mart 40 miles away. The diffusion of innovations typically involves three initial steps in which the mass media can be pivotal:

- **Awareness.** Individuals and groups learn about alternatives, new options and possibilities.
- **Interest.** Once aware, people need to have their interest further whetted.
- **Evaluation.** By considering the experience of other people, as relayed by the mass media, individuals evaluate whether they wish to adopt an innovation.

The adoption process has two additional steps in which the media play a small role: the trial stage, in which an innovation is given a try, and the final stage, in which the innovation is either adopted or rejected.

LEARNING CHECK ◄ ···

▶ **What is the role of mass communication in connecting us to the past?**

▶ **How does mass communication resolve diverse values in contemporary society?**

CULTURAL IMPERIALISM

Nobody could provoke debate quite like Herbert Schiller, whether among his college students or in the whole society. He amassed evidence for a pivotal 1969 book, *Mass Communications and American Empire.* His argument: U.S. media companies were coming to dominate cultural life abroad. He called it **cultural imperialism.**

Schiller sensitized readers to the implications of exporting movies and other U.S. media products. He also put leading media companies on notice that Mickey Mouse in Borneo, no matter how endearing, had untoward implications for the indigenous culture. U.S. corporate greed, he said, was undermining native cultures in developing countries. He described the process as insidious. People in developing countries found U.S. media products so slickly produced and packaged that, candy-like, they were irresistible no matter the destruction they were causing to the local traditions and values that were fading fast into oblivion.

Plenty of evidence supported Schiller's theory. In South Aftica, robbers have taken to shouting, "freeze," a word that had no root in either Afrikaans or other indigenous languages. The robbers had been watching too much American television. A teen fashion statement in India became dressing like *Baywatch* characters, a fashion hardly in subcontinent tradition. In India, too, television talk shows began an American-like probing into private lives. Said media observer Shailja Bajpai: "American television has loosened tongues, to say nothing of our morals."

Schiller's observations were a global recasting of populist-elitist arguments. Populists, whose mantra is "Let the people choose," called Schiller hysterical. These populists noted that Hollywood and other Western media products weren't being forced on anyone. People wanted the products. Some elitists countered that traditional values, many going back centuries, were like endangered species and needed protection against Western capitalistic instincts that were smothering them pell-mell. Elitists noted too that the Western media content that was most attractive abroad was hardly the best stuff. *Rambo* was a case in point at the time that Schiller was becoming a best-selling author with his ideas.

■ **Post-Schiller Revisionism.** Schiller's ideas took firmer hold in the 1990s as major U.S. and European media companies extended their reach. MTV and ESPN turned themselves into global brands. The Murdoch empire was flying high as his SkyTV satellite serviced virtually all of Asia plus similar ventures in Europe and Latin America. Hollywood was firmly in place as a reigning international icon. The largest U.S. newspaper, *USA Today,* launched editions in Europe and Asia.

● **cultural imperialism**
One culture's dominance over another

Herbert Schiller. *Schiller sounded the alarm that Western culture, epitomized by Hollywood, was flooding the planet. The result, he said, was that traditions and values in other cultures were being drowned out. The phenomenon, called cultural imperialism, has been offset somewhat by the growth in media content originating in other countries and targeted at U.S. and other Western audiences.*

Devi. *In an attempt to stop Bala, a fallen god, the other gods each place a part of themselves into a warrior woman to create Devi. The manga comic book is part of an exploding mix of transcultural media content from East to West and every other direction on the globe.*

At the same time, cracks were appearing in Schiller's model. Homegrown television production powerhouses in Latin America, like TV Globo in Brazil and Televisa in Mexico, were pumping programs into the United States. In Asia and the Middle East, Western programming ideas were being adapted to local cultures. Countless variations of *American Idol,* for example, from a growing number of independent companies in the Middle East, went on the air in Arabic countries. Pokémon wasn't invented in America. Nor Hello Kitty. Manga comics from Japan have mushroomed into $180 million in U.S. sales, roughly a third of comic sales.

Too, Western media products are adapted to local cultures. Profanities are edited from movies exported to Malaysia. For India, Spider-Man switched his crotch-hugging tights for the traditional billowing Hindu dhoti. He also wears pointy sandals.

By the first decade of the 21st century, the idea of a monolithic Western culture displacing everything else on the globe needed rethinking. Yes, Hollywood was still big globally, but other players were emerging.

Richard Branson. *The aviation entrepreneur and adventurer sees a future in exporting Indian legends, complete with underlying Hindu themes, to global audiences.*

■ **Transcultural Enrichment.** Turning the cultural imperialism model on its head has been the British-based Virgin Comics, a Johnny-come-lately to the comic book business. With London capital and Bangalore studios, comics with story lines from Indian religion and mythology were launched in U.S. and other markets in 2007. Other themes were drawn from the epic Sanskrit poem *Ramayana.* Could this be called cultural counterimperialism?

Adventurer-entrepreneur Richard Branson, who is masterminding Virgin Comics, has set his sights far beyond just another product on magazine racks. Aware that the sources for franchise movie series like *Superman, Batman, Spider-Man* and *X-Men* are nearing exhaustion, Branson is looking to Indian mythology as a Next Big Thing. The comic *Sudhu,* about a Brit who discovers he was a Hindu holy man in a previous life, will become a Virgin movie. Self-help author Deepak Chopra has been contracted to write the screenplay, actor Nicolas Cage to play the lead. John Woo, whose action films include *Mission: Impossible 2,* cocreated a China-themed story, *Seven Brothers,* for Virgin. For other story lines, Branson is leaning on movie director Guy Ritchie.

The Virgin Comics phenomenon is hardly isolated. Think Al-Jazeera, the Middle Eastern news channel that went global in 2006. Think the Chinese policy to become a global player in motion pictures. This can be seen as enriching. Scholar George Steiner has made the point that U.S. and European cultures are the richer for, not corrupted by, the continuing presence of Greek mythology from over 2,000 years ago. Sociologist Michael Tracey points to silent-movie comedian Charlie Chaplin, whose humor traveled well in

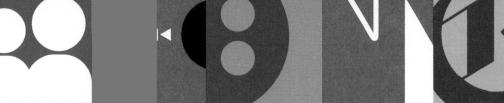

Media Agenda-Setting

A few years ago hardly anyone cared, but pick up any newspaper today and you'll find a story about immigration. It's a hot-button issue filled with emotion, conflict and drama. Many claim the immigration debate parallels the debate about black civil rights.

Just as 50 years ago, the news media kept the immigration story to the forefront of American consciousness, and today's media advocacy mirrors the role of the media in the older civil rights movement.

In California in 2006 a few advocacy groups wanted to organize a protest to a bill in Congress that would criminalize millions of unauthorized workers and punish those who helped them, including social and religious groups. It also called for the construction of a wall along the U.S.–Mexico border.

About 10 groups wanted to organize a protest in Los Angeles, said Noé Hernández, an immigrant rights activist. "Then they invited members of the Spanish press, and everything changed." Spanish-language DJs spread the word. So did television stations with information on how to participate.

The stunned mainstream news media stepped up coverage. An estimated 500,000 people took to the streets of Los Angeles. About 300,000 participated in Chicago. Similar protests were held in other cities across the country. In Atlanta 80,000 Latinos did not show up for work one day as part of a citywide boycott.

The media were criticized, mostly by those who leaned to the right politically. They charged that the news coverage was advocacy. Critics on the left criticized the words used in the media to frame the debate. Saurav Sarkar of Fairness & Accuracy in Reporting said: "The mainstream media helped to set the terms of the debate by endlessly repeating catchphrases and buzzwords like *porous borders* and *comprehensive immigration reform.*"

The words most often criticized were *illegal* and *alien*. The National Association of Hispanic Journalists said their use dehumanized people and stereotyped them as having committed a crime. An estimated 40 percent of the group referred to as *illegal immigrants* initially had valid visas but did not return to their native countries when their visas expired. Some former students fell into this category. However it was worded, the media set the country's agenda to debate the immigration question.

DEEPENING YOUR MEDIA LITERACY

EXPLORE THE ISSUE

Check a major news site lite CNN or *USA Today* for a recent story on illegal immigration in which a special-interest group is a source for information or opinion.

DIG DEEPER

What can you find out about this group and its leadership, financing, positions, activism and lobbying?

WHAT DO YOU THINK?

Does media coverage of the group help set the agenda for national debate on immigration policy? Should media coverage be setting the agenda? If not the media, who?

Immigration Demonstration. An estimated 500,000 people took to the streets in Los Angeles to protest a proposal in Congress to criminalize millions of unauthorized workers in the United States from other countries. Critics faulted the news media for picking up the protesters' arguments in the coverage. What all sides agreed on was that news coverage kept the issue on the public agenda.

415

other cultures: "Was it not Chaplin's real genius to strike some common chord, uniting the whole of humanity?"

LEARNING CHECK ◄ ··

▸ Why was Herbert Schiller alarmed by what he called cultural imperialism?

▸ Was Schiller's concern about cultural imperialism warranted?

▸ Can transcultural communication be enriching even if also imperialist? Why or why not?

Behavioral Effects

STUDY PREVIEW

The overstated magic bullet theory on how mass communication affects people has been perpetuated by advertising. The message is "buy me" or "test me" either immediately or soon. Manipulative advertising can have behavioral effects, although some techniques, like subliminal messages, are overrated and dubious.

MOTIVATIONAL MESSAGES

The 1940s marked the beginning of a confusing period about the effects of mass communication that remains with us. Early magic bullet theories, challenged by Lazarsfeld and others, were falling apart. Even so, as World War II progressed, people had a growing uneasiness about how media might be affecting them. Sinister possibilities were evident in the work of Joseph Goebbels, the Minister of Propaganda and Public Enlightenment in Nazi Germany. His mantra for using the media: Tell lies often enough and loud enough, and they'll be believed. In the Pacific the Japanese beamed the infamous Tokyo Rose radio broadcasts to GIs to lower morale. Then during the Korean War in the early 1950s, a macabre fascination developed with so-called brainwashing techniques used on U.S. prisoners of war. In this same period, the work of Austrian psychiatrist **Sigmund Freud,** which emphasized hidden motivations and repressed sexual impulses, was being popularized in countless books and articles.

● **Sigmund Freud**
Austrian neurologist who theorized that the human mind is unconsciously susceptible to suggestion

● **Ernest Dichter**
Pioneered motivational research

● **motivational research**
Seeks subconscious appeals that can be used in advertising

No wonder, considering this intellectual context, that advertising people in the 1950s looked to the social sciences to find new ways to woo customers. Among the advertising pioneers of this period was **Ernest Dichter,** who accepted Freud's claim that people act on motivations that they are not aware of. Depth interviewing, Dichter felt, could reveal these motivations, which could then be exploited in advertising messages.

Dichter used his interviewing, called **motivational research,** for automotive clients. Rightly or wrongly, Dichter determined that the American male is loyal to his wife but fantasizes about having a mistress. Men, he noted, usually are the decision makers in purchasing a car. Then, in what seemed a quantum leap, Dichter equated sedans, which were what most people drove, with wives. Sedans were familiar, reliable. Convertibles, impractical for many people and also beyond their reach financially, were equated with mistresses—romantic, daring, glamorous. With these conclusions in hand, Dichter devised advertisements for a new kind of sedan without a center door pillar. The hardtop, as it was called, gave a convertible effect when the windows were down. The advertisements, dripping with sexual innuendo, clearly reflected Dichter's thinking: "You'll find something new to love every time you drive it." Although they were not as solid as sedans and tended to leak air and water, hardtops were popular among automobile buyers for the next 25 years.

Dichter's motivational research led to numerous campaigns that exploited sexual images. For Ronson lighters, the flame, in phallic form, was reproduced in extraordinary proportions. A campaign for Ajax cleanser, hardly a glamourous product, had a white knight charging through the street, ignoring law and regulation with a great phallic lance. Whether consumers were motivated by sexual imagery is hard to establish. Even so, many campaigns based on motivational research worked.

To some extent, mass communication can move people to action—at least to sample a product. This, of course, is far short of brainwashing. Also, the effect is uneven—not everybody buys. And the effect can be short-lived if an advertised product fails to live up to expectations. Seen many pillarless sedans lately?

LEARNING CHECK ◄ •

▸ **What in the mid-century American experience contributed to the belief that mass messages can force people to change their behavior radically?**

SUBLIMINAL MESSAGES

● **Jim Vicary**
Made dubious subliminal advertising claims

Some concern, stirred by market researcher **Jim Vicary,** about mass communication as a hidden persuader was wacky. He claimed in 1957 that he had inserted messages like "Drink Coca-Cola" and "Eat Popcorn" into movies. The messages were flashed too fast to be recognized by the human eye, but, Vicary claimed, were nonetheless recognized by the brain. Prompted by the **subliminal message,** as he called it, people flocked midmovie to the snack bar. Vicary had impressive numbers from his experiments, supposedly conducted at a New Jersey movie house. Coke sales increased 18 percent, popcorn almost 60 percent. Vicary's report stirred great interest, and also alarm, but researchers who tried to replicate his study found no evidence to support his claim.

● **subliminal message**
Cannot be consciously perceived

Despite doubts about Vicary's claims, psychologists have identified a phenomenon they call **subception,** in which certain behavior sometimes seems to be triggered by messages perceived subliminally. Whether the effect works outside laboratory experiments and whether the effect is strong enough to prod a consumer to go out and buy are uncertain. Nevertheless, there remains a widespread belief among the general population that subliminal advertising works, and fortunes are being made by people who peddle various devices and systems with extravagant claims that they can control human behavior. Among these are the "hidden" messages in stores' sound systems that say shoplifting is not nice.

● **subception**
Receiving subconscious messages that trigger behavior

David Ogilvy, founder of the Ogilvy & Mather agency, once made fun of subliminal effects claims, pointing out the absurdity of "millions of suggestible consumers getting up from their armchairs and rushing like zombies through the traffic on their way to buy the product at the nearest store." The danger of "Go Taliban" being flashed during the *NBC Nightly News* is remote, and whether it would have any effect is dubious.

LEARNING CHECK ◄ •

▸ **Why does the fraudulent research of Jim Vicary continue as urban legend?**

▸ **To what extent can subliminal messages be effective?**

Media-Depicted Violence

STUDY PREVIEW

Some individuals mimic the aggressive behavior they see in the media, but such incidents are exceptions. Some experts argue, in fact, that media-depicted violence actually reduces real-life aggressive behavior.

LEARNING ABOUT VIOLENCE

● **observational learning**
Theory that people learn behavior by seeing it in real life, in depictions

The mass media help to bring young people into society's mainstream by demonstrating dominant behaviors and norms. This prosocial process, called **observational learning,** turns dark, however, when children learn deviant behaviors from the media. In Manteca, California, two teenagers, one only 13, lay in wait for a friend's father in his own house and attacked him. They beat him with a fireplace poker, kicked him and stabbed him, and choked him to death with a dog chain. Then they poured salt in his wounds. Why the final act of violence—the salt in the wounds? The 13-year-old explained that he had seen it on television. While there is no question that people can learn about violent behavior from the media, a major issue of our time is whether the mass media are the cause of aberrant behavior.

Individuals on trial for criminal acts occasionally plead that "the media made me do it." That was the defense in a 1974 California case in which two young girls playing on a beach were raped with a beer bottle by four teenagers. The rapists told police they had picked up the idea from a television movie they had seen four days earlier. In the movie a young woman was raped with a broom handle, and in court the youths' attorneys blamed the movie. The judge, as is typical in such cases, threw out media-projected violence as an unacceptable scapegoating defense and held the young perpetrators responsible.

Although the courts have never accepted transfer of responsibility as legal defense, it is clear that violent behavior in the media can be imitated. Some experts, however, say that the negative effect of media-depicted violence is too often overstated and that media violence actually has a positive side.

LEARNING CHECK ◀ •••

▶ **Why do the courts refuse to excuse violent criminals who blame their behavior on media-depicted violence?**

MEDIA VIOLENCE AS POSITIVE

● **cathartic effect**
People release violent inclinations by seeing them portrayed

● **Aristotle**
Defended portrayals of violence

● **Seymour Feshbach**
Found evidence for media violence as a release

People who downplay the effect of media portrayals of blood, guts and violence often refer to a **cathartic effect.** This theory, which dates to ancient Greece and the philosopher **Aristotle,** suggests that watching violence allows individuals vicariously to release pent-up everyday frustration that might otherwise explode dangerously. By seeing violence, so goes the theory, people let off steam. Most advocates of the cathartic effect claim that individuals who see violent activity are stimulated to fantasy violence, which drains latent tendencies toward real-life violence.

In more recent times, scholar **Seymour Feshbach** has conducted studies that lend support to the cathartic effect theory. In one study, Feshbach lined up 625 junior high school boys at seven California boarding schools and showed half of them a steady diet of violent television programs for six weeks. The other half were shown nonviolent fare. Every day during the study, teachers and supervisors reported on each boy's behavior in and out of class. Feshbach found no difference in aggressive behavior between the two groups. Further, there was a decline in aggression among boys who had been determined by personality tests to be more inclined toward aggressive behavior.

Opponents of the cathartic effect theory, who include both respected researchers and reflexive media bashers, were quick to point out flaws in Feshbach's research methods. Nonetheless, his conclusions carried a lot of influence because of the study's unprecedented massiveness—625 individuals. Also, the study was conducted in a real-life environment rather than in a laboratory, and there was a consistency in the findings.

LEARNING CHECK ◀ •••

▶ **How did Aristotle defend violence as a spectator activity?**

▶ **How is the cathartic effect theory controversial?**

PRODDING SOCIALLY POSITIVE ACTION

Besides the cathartic effect theory, an argument for showing violence is that it prompts people to engage in socially positive action. This happened after NBC aired *The Burning Bed*, a television movie about an abused woman who could not take any more and set fire to her sleeping husband. The night the movie was shown, battered-spouse centers nationwide were overwhelmed by calls from women who had been putting off doing something to extricate themselves from relationships with abusive mates.

On the negative side, one man set his estranged wife afire and explained that he was inspired by *The Burning Bed*. Another man who beat his wife senseless gave the same explanation.

LEARNING CHECK ◄••

▶ Offer an example from your experience of media-depicted violence having a positive effect on an individual.

MEDIA VIOLENCE AS NEGATIVE

● **aggressive stimulation**
Theory that people are inspired to violence by media depictions

● **Bobo doll studies**
Kids seemed more violent after seeing violence in movies

● **Albert Bandura**
Found that media violence stimulated aggression in children

● **catalytic theory**
Media violence is among factors that sometimes contribute to real-life violence

The preponderance of evidence is that media-depicted violence has the potential to cue real-life violence. However, the **aggressive stimulation** theory is often overstated. The fact is that few people act out media violence in their lives. For example, do you know anybody who saw a murder in a movie and went out afterward and murdered somebody? Yet you know many people who see murders in movies and *don't* kill anyone.

We need to be careful when we talk about aggressive stimulation. Note how scholar Wayne Danielson, who participated in the 1995–1997 National Television Violence Study, carefully qualified one of the study's conclusions: "Viewing violence on TV *tends* to increase violent behavior in viewers, more *in some situations* and less in others. For whatever reason, *when the circumstances are right*, we *tend* to imitate what we see others doing. Our inner resistance to engage in violent behavior *weakens*."

The study concluded that children may be more susceptible than adults to copying media violence, but that too was far, far short of a universal causal statement.

Why, then, do many people believe that media violence begets real-life violence? Some early studies pointed to a causal link. These included the 1960 **Bobo doll studies** of **Albert Bandura,** who showed children a violent movie and then encouraged them to play with oversize, inflated dolls. Bandura concluded that kids who saw the film were more inclined to beat up the dolls than were other kids. Critics have challenged Bandura's methodology and said that he mistook childish playfulness for aggression. In short, Bandura and other aggressive stimulation scholars have failed to prove their theory to the full satisfaction of other scholars.

When pressed, people who hold the aggressive stimulation theory point to particular incidents they know about. A favorite is the claim by serial killer Ted Bundy that *Playboy* magazine had led him to stalk and kill women. Was Bundy telling the truth? We will never know. He offered the scapegoat explanation on his way to the execution chamber, which suggests that there may have been other motives. The Bundy case is anecdotal, and anecdotes cannot be extrapolated into general validity.

An alternative to aggressive stimulation theory is a theory that people whose feelings and general view of the world tend toward aggressiveness and violence are attracted to violence in movies, television and other media depictions of violence. This alternative theory holds that people who are violent are predisposed to violence, which is far short of saying that the media made them do it. This leads us to the **catalytic theory,** which sees media-depicted violence as having a contributing role in violent behavior, not a triggering one.

Scapegoating. *On the eve of his execution, serial killer Ted Bundy claimed that his violence had been sparked by girlie magazines. Whatever the truth of Bundy's claim, scholars are divided about whether media depictions precipitate violent behavior. At one extreme is the view that media violence is a safety valve for people inclined to violence. At the other extreme is the aggressive stimulation theory that media violence causes real-life violence. The most prevalent thinking, to paraphrase a pioneer 1961 study on television and children, is that certain depictions under certain conditions may prompt violence in certain people.*

LEARNING CHECK ◄••

▶ What evidence supports the theory that media-depicted violence leads to real-life violence?

▶ How are catalytic effects of media-depicted violence different from causal effects?

CATALYTIC THEORY

Simplistic readings of both cathartic and aggressive stimulation effects research can yield extreme conclusions. A careful reading, however, points more to the media having a role in real-life violence but not necessarily triggering it and doing so only infrequently—and only if several nonmedia factors are also present. For example, evidence suggests that television and movie violence, even in cartoons, is arousing and can excite some children to violence, especially hyperactive and easily excitable children. These children, like unstable adults, become wrapped up psychologically with the portrayals and are stirred to the point of acting out. However, this happens only when a combination of other influences are also present. Among these other influences are:

- **Whether violence portrayed in the media is rewarded.** In 1984 David Phillips of the University of California at San Diego found that the murder rate increases after publicized prizefights, in which the victor is rewarded, and decreases after publicized murder trials and executions, in which, of course, violence is punished.
- **Whether media exposure is heavy.** Researcher Monroe Lefkowitz studied upstate New York third-graders who watched a lot of media-depicted violence. Ten years later, Lefkowitz found that these individuals were rated by their peers as violent. This suggests cumulative, long-term media effects.
- **Whether a violent person fits other profiles.** Studies have found correlations between aggressive behavior and many variables besides violence viewing. These include income, education, intelligence and parental child-rearing practices. This is not to say that any of these third variables cause violent behavior. The suggestion, rather, is that violence is far too complex to be explained by a single factor.

Most researchers note too that screen-triggered violence is increased if the aggression:

- Is realistic and exciting, like a chase or suspense sequence that sends adrenaline levels surging.
- Succeeds in righting a wrong, like helping an abused or ridiculed character get even.
- Includes situations or characters similar to those in the viewer's own experience.

● **Wilbur Schramm**
Concluded that television has minimal effects on children

All these things would prompt a scientist to call media violence a catalyst. Just as the presence of a certain element will allow other elements to react explosively but itself is not part of the explosion, the presence of media violence can be a factor in real-life violence but not be a cause by itself. This catalytic theory was articulated by scholars **Wilbur Schramm,** Jack Lyle and Edwin Parker, who investigated the effects of television on children and came up with this statement in their 1961 book *Television in the Lives of Our Children*, which has become a classic on the effects of media-depicted violence on individuals: "For *some* children under *some* conditions, *some* television is harmful. For *other* children under the same conditions, or for the same children under *other* conditions, it *may* be beneficial. For *most* children, under *most* conditions, *most* television is *probably* neither particularly harmful nor particularly beneficial."

LEARNING CHECK ◄ •

▶ **Why is it difficult to demonstrate that media-depicted violence directly causes real-life violence?**

▶ **What variables may contribute to a person's proneness for violence after an experience with media-depicted violence?**

SOCIETALLY DEBILITATING EFFECTS

● **George Gerbner**
Speculated that democracy is endangered by media violence

Media-depicted violence scares far more people than it inspires to commit violence, and this, according to **George Gerbner,** a leading researcher on screen violence, leads some people to believe the world is more dangerous than it really is. Gerbner calculated that 1 in 10 television characters is involved in violence in any given week. In real life the chances are only about 1 in 100 per *year*. People who watch a lot of television, Gerbner found, see their own chances of being involved in violence nearer the distorted television level than their local crime statistics or even their own experience would suggest. It seems that television violence leads people to think they are in far greater real-life jeopardy than they really are.

The implications of Gerbner's findings go to the heart of a free and democratic society. With exaggerated fears about their safety, Gerbner said, people will demand greater police protection. They are also likelier, he said, to submit to established authority and even to accept police violence as a trade-off for their own security.

LEARNING CHECK ◄······························

▶ **Does media-depicted violence misrepresent the extent of real-life violence in society?**

▶ **Does media-depicted violence lead people to unwarranted concern for their personal safety?**

MEDIA VIOLENCE AND YOUTH

Nobody would argue that Jerry Springer's television talk show is a model of good taste and restraint. In fact, the conventional wisdom is that such shows do harm. But do they? Two scholars at the University of Pennsylvania, Stacy Davis and Marie-Louise Mares, conducted a careful study of 292 high school students in North Carolina, some from a city and some from a rural area, and concluded from their data: "Although talk shows may offend some people, these data do not suggest that the youth of the U.S. is corrupted by watching them."

One issue was whether talk-show viewing desensitizes teenagers to tawdry behavior. The conventional wisdom, articulated by many politicians calling for television reform, is that teenagers are numbed by all the anti-social, deviant and treacherous figures on talk shows. Not so, said Davis and Mares: "Heavy talk-show viewers were no less likely than light viewers to believe that the victims of antisocial behavior had been wronged, to perceive that the victim had suffered, or to rate the antisocial behavior as immoral."

Do talk shows undercut society's values? According to Davis and Mares, "In fact, the world of talk shows may be quite conservative. Studio audiences reinforce traditional moral codes by booing guests who flout social norms, and cheering those who speak in favor of the show's theme. So, actually, it looks almost as though talk shows serve as cautionary tales, heightening teens' perceptions of how often certain behaviors occur and how serious social issues are."

LEARNING CHECK ◄·····························

▶ **How can it be argued that media portrayals of deviant behavior discourage real-life deviance?**

TOLERANCE OF VIOLENCE

● **desensitizing theory**
Tolerance of real-life violence grows because of media-depicted violence

An especially serious concern about media-depicted violence is that it has a numbing, callousing effect on people. This **desensitizing theory,** which is widely held, says not only that individuals are becoming hardened by media violence but also that society's tolerance for such anti-social behavior is increasing.

Media critics say that the media are responsible for this desensitization, but many media people, particularly movie and television directors, respond that it is the desensitization that has forced them to make the violence in their shows even more graphic. They explain that they have run out of alternatives to get the point across when the story line requires that the audience be repulsed.

Some movie critics, of course, find this explanation a little too convenient for gore-inclined moviemakers and television directors, but even directors who are not

George Gerbner

George Gerbner worried a lot about media violence. And when he died in 2005, he had been doing this longer than just about anybody else. In 1967 Gerbner and colleagues at the University of Pennsylvania created a television violence index and began counting acts of violence. Today, more than three decades later, the numbers are startling. Gerbner calculated that the typical American 18-year-old has seen 32,000 murders and 40,000 attempted murders at home on television.

In a dubious sense, there may be good news for those who fear the effects of media violence. Gerbner's index found no significant change in the volume of violence since the mid-1970s. Maybe it maxed out.

Gerbner theorized that the media violence has negative effects on society. It's what he called "the mean-world syndrome." As he saw it, people exposed to so much violence come to perceive the world as a far more dangerous place than it really is. One of his concerns was that people become overly concerned for their own safety and, in time, may become willing to accept a police state to ensure their personal security. That, he said, has dire consequences for the free and open society that has been a valued hallmark of the American lifestyle.

Are there answers? Gerbner pointed out that the global conglomeration of mass-media companies works against any kind of media self-policing. These companies are seeking worldwide outlets for their products, whether movies, television programs or music, and violence doesn't require any kind of costly translations. "Violence travels well," he said. Also, violence has low production costs.

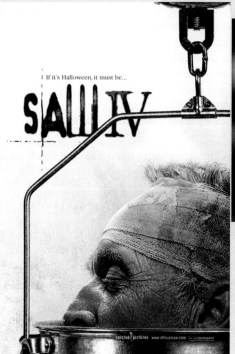

It's a Mean World. *Scholar George Gerbner, who began tracking television violence in 1967, found that the typical American child sees 32,000 on-screen murders before age 18. The result, he said, is that many people see the world as much meaner than it really is.*

Gerbner noted that violence is an easy fill for weak spots in a television story line. Also, in television, violence is an effective cliff-hanger before a commercial break.

While Gerbner's statistics are unsettling, there are critics who say his numbers make the situation seem worse than it really is. The Gerbner index scores acts of violence without considering their context. That means that when Bugs Bunny is bopped on the head, it counts the same as Rambo doing the same thing to a vile villain in a skull-crushing, blood-spurting scene. A poke in the eye on *The Three Stooges* also scores as a violent act.

Despite his critics, Gerbner provided a baseline for measuring changes in the quantity of television violence. Virtually every scholar cites him in the ongoing struggle to figure out whether media violence is something that should worry us all.

WHAT DO YOU THINK?

▶ Why do scholars need to measure incidence of media violence?

▶ Kung fu blood and guts or Bugs Bunny being bopped on the head—how do you classify the media depiction of violence?

▶ What do you make of Gerbner's observation that violence travels well?

inclined to gratuitous violence feel that their options for stirring the audience have become scarcer. The critics respond that this is a chicken-or-egg question and that the media are in no position to use the desensitization theory to excuse including more and more violence in their products if they themselves contributed to the desensitization. And so the argument goes on about who is to blame.

Desensitization is apparent in news also. In 2004 the New York *Times*, traditionally cautious about gore, showed a photo of victims' corpses hanging from a bridge in Fallujah, Iraq. Only a few years earlier there had been an almost universal ban on showing the bodies of crime, accident and war victims in newspapers and on television newscasts. Photos of U.S. troops torturing Iraqi prisoners, integral in telling a horrible but important story, pushed back the earlier limits. No mainstream media showed the videotaped beheading of U.S. businessman Nick Berg by terrorists in Iraq, but millions of people found the gruesome sequence online. This desensitizing did not come suddenly with the Iraq War and its aftermath, but the war has clearly established new ground rules.

It is undeniable that violence has had a growing presence in the mass media, which makes even more poignant the fact that we know far less about media violence than we need to. What do we know? Various theories explain some phenomena, but the theories themselves do not dovetail. The desensitizing theory, for example, explains audience acceptance of more violence, but it hardly explains research findings that people who watch a lot of television actually have heightened anxiety about their personal safety. People fretting about their own safety are hardly desensitized.

LEARNING CHECK ◄ ·····································

▸ **Does media-depicted violence desensitize us individually to be more tolerant of real-life violence?**

▸ **Is society more tolerant of real-life violence because of exposure to media depictions?**

VIOLENCE STUDIES

The mass media, especially television and movies that deal in fiction, depict a lot of violence. Studies have found as many as six violent acts per hour on prime-time network television. In and of itself, that may seem a lot, but a study at the University of California, Los Angeles, operating on the premise that the issue should not be how much violence is depicted but the context in which it occurs, came to a less startling conclusion: Slapstick comedic violence shouldn't be lumped with graphic homicide in counting depictions of violence. Nor should a violent storm.

● **Violence Assessment Monitoring Project**
Conducted contextual nonviolence studies and found less serious media depictions than earlier thought

The UCLA research, called the **Violence Assessment Monitoring Project,** concluded in its first year that distressing human violence was much less prevalent than earlier studies had counted. Of 121 prime-time episodes, only 10 had frequent violence and only eight had occasional violence. This was after comedic violence and nonhuman violence, such as hurricanes, were screened out. The next year, 1996, found violence in only five prime-time shows—half the number of the year before. Also, most of the shows didn't survive the season. In 1998 the number was down to two series.

● **William McQuire**
Found most media violence research flawed

The UCLA study added sophistication to counting acts of media-depicted violence but still didn't assess whether the violence affected people. In 1986 scholar **William McQuire** reviewed the literature on mediated violence and found that hardly any of the studies' evidence was statistically reliable. The exception was controlled laboratory studies, for which the statistics were more meaningful but didn't indicate much causality.

LEARNING CHECK ◄ ·····································

▸ **What difficulty do researchers have in measuring violent media content?**

Chapter Wrap-Up

Effects Theories (Page 402)

■ Early mass communication scholars assumed that media messages had powerful and direct impacts on people. At an extreme, the magic bullet theory said the media could immediately affect behavior. Further scholarship found that the magic bullet theory was simplistic and vastly overstated the effects of mass communication. This does not mean that the media are without effect but that the dynamics of the effects generally are gradual over time.

Lifestyle Effects (Page 405)

■ In most of the world, mass media are integrated into people's lives from the cradle. In fact, media have a large role in initiating children into society by instilling cultural values. It is worth asking whether the media's role in childhood development is good, bad or neutral. The answer is not obvious. It can said, however, that media reflect existing cultural values. This reflection, because values are in continuing flux, means that media content includes a rich mix of values. The mix includes traditional values as well as challenges to tradition.

Attitude Effects (Page 407)

■ Mass messages bring information and opinions to large numbers of people, in effect setting an agenda and conferring status on issues. What is missed by the media generally doesn't get on the public radar. But what are the effects of media content on attitudes and opinions? Scholars know a lot about the effect of stereotypes, which, when repeated, can have a compounding effect. Also, there is a copycat factor, at least for superficial issues like fashion and style. Which celebrity haircut will be the rage tomorrow? On more significant issues, shifts in attitudes and opinions generally are gradual.

Cultural Effects (Page 411)

■ Cultural values of dominant societies, as depicted in mass media content, have had unmistakable effects on developing societies. The extent of this so-called cultural imperialism can be debated, as can whether the effects are good, bad or nil. The export of dominant cultural values has been mitigated by the rise of indigenous media in developing countries, but there remains a lot of transcultural influence, some with content that imitates content from other countries and also the direct importation of content.

Behavioral Effects (Page 416)

■ Advertising research has found ways to tap into consumer psyches, sometimes with tactics so subtle as to be unrecognized for what they are. Precise control on hidden persuasion, however, is impossible. The larger the audience, the more exponentially the degree of influence decreases. Even so, a mythology exists about the effect of hidden persuasion. The power of subliminal communication has never been demonstrated conclusively to be a trigger of behavior. This is not to say, however, that media content has no effect on behavior. Media depictions of unacceptable behavior, especially when widely publicized, can have a dampening effect on such behavior. Also, media campaigns that explicitly encourage certain behaviors, as in Ad Council public-service announcements, can have an impact, albeit one that is difficult to measure.

Media-Depicted Violence (Page 417)

■ Media-depicted violence has been around forever. Read any Shakespeare lately? Despite anecdotal stories and testimony that "the media made me do it," scholars have come up empty in confirming the claim that media-depicted violence causes mentally healthy people to commit real-life violence. In fact, there is a line of reasoning dating to Aristotle that says witnessing violence sways people away from committing violence. There are, however, people, including the mentally deranged, who are susceptible to what's called aggressive stimulation. Research goes both ways on whether children are moved to violence by seeing it. The classic study on the issue says *some* children *may be* affected *some* of the time in *some* circumstances. That hardly is a firm conclusion of a predictable causal effect.

REVIEW QUESTIONS

1. Why has the magic bullet theory of mass communication effects lost support? What has replaced the magic bullet theory?

2. How is the role of mass messages in childhood development changing?

3. What are examples of the influence of mass communication on attitudes and opinions?

4. How has advertising perpetuated myths about the effects of mass communication?

5. What continues to fuel magic bullet theory beliefs about immediate, powerful effects of mass messages, including subliminal messages?

6. Identify and discuss different ideas about the effects of media-depicted violence.

CONCEPTS

cathartic effect (Page 418)

catalytic theory (Page 419)

cultural imperialism (Page 413)

powerful effects theory (Page 402)

TERMS

Bobo doll studies (Page 419)

magic bullet model (Page 403)

narcoticizing dysfunction (Page 404)

two-step flow (Page 403)

socialization (Page 405)

PEOPLE

George Gerbner (Page 420)

Elisabeth Noelle-Neumann (Page 404)

Wilbur Schramm (Page 420)

Orson Welles (Page 402)

Jim Vicary (Page 417)

MEDIA SOURCES

● Elizabeth M. Peers. *Media Effects and Society.* Erlbaum, 2001. Peers, a communication scholar, offers an advanced overview of studies on media effects, including their effect on public opinion and voting.

● Lisa Blackman and Valerie Walkerdine. *Mass Hysteria: Critical Psychology and Media Studies.* Palgrave, 2001. Blackman and Walkerdine draw on numerous psychology theories to examine the relationship between psychology and the mass media.

● Michael Pickering. *Stereotyping: The Politics of Representation.* Palgrave, 2001. As a social science researcher, Pickering sees limitations to stereotyping as a construct.

MASS-MEDIA EFFECTS: A Thematic Chapter Summary

In this chapter you have deepened your media literacy by revisiting several themes. Here are thematic highlights from the chapter:

Media Effects

Scholars know that mass messages don't have a sudden, bullet-like impact that affects behavior, but the idea of immediate, powerful media effects persists in our cultural mythology. A lot of the fears about the effects of media-depicted violence, for example, are drawn from the magic bullet theory. Scholars have come to the conclusion that the effects of mass messages are gradual, building up over time—a cumulative effect, not a bullet effect. **(Pages 402–405)**

Seeing is Doing? Personal experience tells us that media axe murders don't turn us into axe murderers.

Media and Democracy

On the Stump. No matter how good the campaign speech, most voters look to respected acquaintances for guidance in voting.

Pioneering studies by sociologist Paul Lazarsfeld in the 1940s discovered that most voters don't make their decisions based on campaign speeches, news accounts or advertisements. Lazarsfeld found that the greatest influence comes from opinion leaders with whom voters are regular contact, like a respected neighbor, a teacher, a wizened uncle. He concluded that media messages are their most effective when they reach these opinion leaders, who then, often not recognizing their influence, shape how people around them vote. **(Pages 403–404)**

Media and Culture

Media messages hardly are products of immaculate conception. They flow from their culture. Indeed, they are products of their culture. To find an audience, messages need to resonate fundamental values of the culture. Mass-media products thus perpetuate existing values, although there can also be challenges to tradition in mass messages. But messages never can be so out of line that they won't find an audience. This process is called cultural transmission. **(Pages 412–413)**

Stereotypes. Mass communication can strengthen stereotypes, as with loose characterizations of American Indians. Mass communication can also help dismantle stereotypes.

Media Globalization

Media content can be pivotal when cultures collide. Scholar Herbert Schiller called it cultural imperialism when media content from economically, politically and militarily dominant parts of the world, such as the United States, find audiences in less developed regions. Dominant values begin displacing native values, which can be lost forever. There is strong evidence of cultural imperialism at superficial levels—styles, fads, idioms. Contrarians note, however, that Schiller may have overstated his case. Not all displaced values are worth preserving, at least from a Western perspective. These include slavery, subjugation of women, and suppression of free expression. **(Pages 413–416)**

Cultural Imperialism. *Herbert Schiller cautioned that media-exported Western culture could wipe out indigenous values elsewhere.*

Media Economics

Advertising has found success in associating products with celebrities and other people with bigger-than-life reputations and followings. Golfer Tiger Woods is worth millions for helping sell Buicks, geriatric actor James Garner for reverse mortgages, Paris Hilton for her product du jour. The role model phenomenon, although hardly recent, especially worries traditionalists when cultural icons engage in errant behavior. Like it or not, 50 Cent has a following that translates into retail sales of a clothing line. **(Pages 408–409)**

Testimonials. *Celebrities and other cultural icons help motivate people toward buying products.*

17

Global Mass Media

The Hellfire Pictures

When journalist Hayatullah Khan heard that an important Al Qaeda commander had been killed in the tribal-controlled Waziristan region of Pakistan, he rushed to the scene. Khan took photos of the shambles of the house, where, the government said, the Al Qaeda leader had been making a bomb when it blew up. Khan's photos showed something else—fragments of a U.S. Hellfire missile. Khan's story, with photos, reported that the missile had been fired from a U.S. spy drone—a sensational report that contradicted both U.S. and Pakistani official insistence that the U.S. anti-terrorism resources were honoring Pakistan's sovereignty and staying within the borders of neighboring Afghanistan.

Officials at the U.S. Central Intelligence Agency, which operates drones, were displeased with Khan's reporting. So was the Pakistani government. Within days of Khan's revelations, Khan vanished. Six months later his body was found dumped in northern Waziristan, handcuffed and shot in the back.

Khan's family blamed the Pakistani government. The government blamed intrigue—somebody out to malign the government.

Whatever the truth, Khan's death is testimony to the danger facing war correspondents, especially in tribal no-man's territories. Over two years, five reporters who ventured into Waziristan were killed. Now almost all reporting from the area is second-hand, with reporters using telephones to call into the region from the relative safety of Peshawar and faraway cities.

LEARNING AHEAD

- Mass media reflect a nation's political system.
- War can force compromises in media freedom.
- Market forces are transforming some Arab media.
- Terrorists have adapted digital media as a propaganda tool.
- Media are central in a Cold War-style battle for reforms in Iran.
- China has the broadest censorship apparatus in history.
- Variations exist among national media systems, even in democracies.

Hellfire Evidence. *Missile fragments photographed by Hayatullah Khan suggest that the U.S. Central Intelligence Agency was responsible for a remote-control bombing in a remote Pakistani region that killed an Al Qaeda leader. It was contrary to official policy for U.S. military to be venturing into Pakistan.*

In this chapter you will discover how the mass media fit into the global geopolitical environment. The media are players not only in crisis moments, like war, but also in evolving globalization.

Mass Media and Nation-States

STUDY PREVIEW

The world's nations and media systems fall into competing, philosophically irreconcilable systems. Authoritarianism places confidence in political and sometimes theocratic leadership for governance. In contrast, libertarianism emphasizes the ability of human beings to reason their own way to right conclusions and therefore believes humans are capable of their own governance. Democracy and a free mass media are in the libertarian tradition.

GLOBAL COMMUNICATION

After the 2005 terrorist subway and bus bombings in London, the British news media flooded the streets and airwaves with stories about the suspects. Understandably, coverage was emotional. When the first arrests were made, the front page of the tabloid *Sun* blared: "Got the Bastards." Then the media went silent. British law forbids news coverage once a criminal charge has been filed. The rationale is to not prejudice potential jurors. It's a silly law by standards in the United States, where jury contamination is avoided through jury selection procedures, jury sequestering and relocation of trials. But the British system had accomplished the same purpose too—until now.

Hungry for news about the terrorism investigation and the people arrested, Britons needed to look no further than the Internet. The Internet's most-used coding structure is called the World Wide Web for a reason. And just down the street, newsstands stocked foreign newspapers and magazines full of ongoing revelations about the suspects. Legally, the imported publications, as well as Internet coverage, could be banned under the 1981 Contempt of Court Act. But how? The logistics would be overwhelming.

Throughout the world, not only in Britain, the power that governments once wielded over mass communication has eroded. The challenges for governments, especially in countries with repressive regimes, is how to impede unwanted outside messages from getting in. On a global scale, the struggle is between two intellectual

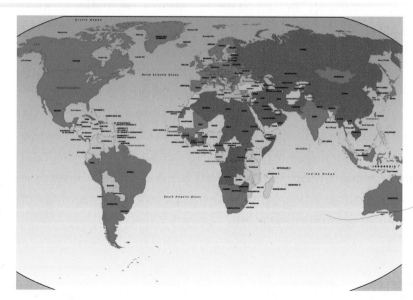

Color-Coding Freedom.
Freedom House, which tracks the freedom of the new media worldwide, reports relatively few countries where news and information flow freely within and across their borders. Green shows countries that Freedom House regards as free, yellow as partly free, and purple as not free. The number of free countries has grown over 20 years from 31 percent to 40 percent.

traditions—long-dominant **authoritarianism** and historically more recent freedom-favoring **libertarianism.**

LEARNING CHECK ◄ ••••••••••••••••••••••••••••••••••••••

▶ **What are the two philosophical traditions that define different media systems around the globe?**

AUTHORITARIANISM

Throughout mass-media history, authoritarian political systems have been the most common. The powerful monarchies were authoritarian. So were Nazi Germany and Franco Spain in the 1900s. The Soviets had their own twist on authoritarianism. Today, dictatorships and theocracies continue the tradition. A premise of authoritarian systems is that the government is infallible, which places its policies beyond questioning. The media's role in an authoritarian society is subservience to government.

■ **Henry VIII.** When Johannes Gutenberg invented movable type in the 1400s, authorities were enthusiastic. Early printers produced Bibles and religious tracts, which was consistent with the intertwined institutions of government and church. Within two generations, however, presses also were occasionally producing materials that bordered on sedition and treason. Authorities clamped down. What happened in England was typical. In 1529 King **Henry VIII** outlawed imported publications. So it was decreed that every printer must be licensed. Printers caught publishing anything objectionable to the Crown lost their licenses. In effect, they were put out of business. Remaining in the government's good graces brought favors. A license was a guaranteed local monopoly and a lock on government and church printing jobs.

In addressing a crisis of the time, Henry VIII became the model for authoritarian control of mass media.

■ **Censorship.** Authoritarian regimes have found numerous ways, both blatant and subtle, to control mass media. Censorship is one. The most thorough censoring requires that manuscripts be read by government agents before being printed or aired. To work, **prepublication censorship** requires a government agent in every newsroom and everywhere else that mass-media messages are produced. Such thorough censorship is hardly practicable, although governments sometimes establish censorship bureaucracies during wartime to protect sensitive military information and to ban information that runs counter to their propaganda. Most authoritarian regimes have opted instead for post-publication action against dissidents. The effect of the execution of a media person who strayed

Authoritarian Execution.
Authoritarian governments prevent mass-media criticism of their policies with numerous methods, including execution. In authoritarian England, the Crown made spectacles of executions. Here, a crowd gathered in 1619 to witness the execution of John de Barneveld, which had a chilling effect on other people who might have challenged the Crown.

Divine Right. *King James I, who fancied himself a scholar, wrote a treatise in 1598 that claimed monarchies were legitimate because of a pipeline to God. His theory, called the divine right of kings, is a classic defense for authoritarian political and media systems.*

beyond what's acceptable can be chilling to like-minded people. Consider the 1663 case of John Twyn in authoritarian England. This was the sentence imposed on Twyn, a printer: "You shall be hanged by the neck, and being alive, shall be cut down and your privy members shall be cut off, your entrails shall be taken from your body, and you living, the same to be burnt before your eyes."

■ **Bribery.** Another method of authoritarian control, bribery, can be either overt or disguised. Germany's "Iron Chancellor," Otto von Bismarck, maintained an immense fund for bribing editors in his 20-year reign beginning in the 1870s. Bismarck had picked up a lesson from 300 years earlier, when authoritarian England's licensing system rewarded supportive printers with lucrative government contracts. For decades the government of Mexico had a variation on bribery by controlling the supply of newsprint. Out-of-favor newspapers and magazines went to the bottom of the distribution list for paper. Bribery remains institutionalized today in impoverished regions, where journalists, earning subsistence salaries, accept gratuities on the side for putting certain stories in the paper and on the air.

■ **Authoritarian Effectiveness.** Authoritarian controls can have short-term effectiveness, but truth is hard to suppress for very long. In Franco's Spain, which was allied with Germany in World War II, the news media were mum for years about Nazi atrocities against Jews. Despite the media blackout, the Spanish people were aware of the Holocaust. People do not receive all their information through the mass media. Especially if people have come to distrust the accuracy or thoroughness of an authoritarian medium, they pay special attention to alternative sources. They talk to travelers. They read contraband publications. They listen secretly to transborder newscasts. They tap into the Internet. In recent years China has created the largest censorship apparatus in history to maintain ideological control, complete with electronic and Internet monitoring and intercepts, but the system leaks. It's an open question whether the Chinese will come to recognize the futility of prepublication censorship, as have earlier authoritarian-minded regimes.

■ **Global Authoritarianism.** Authoritarianism dies hard. The organization Freedom House, which monitors press freedom worldwide, lists 45 nations that deny a broad range of freedoms. The eight worst-rated countries include Cuba and North Korea, both Marxist-Leninist regimes. Turkmenistan and Uzbekistan in Central Asia are ruled by dictators with roots in the Soviet period. Arab countries Libya and Syria are under secular dictatorships. Sudan is under leadership that has elements of both radical Islamism and military juntas. Burma has a tightly controlled military dictatorship. Tibet, although not a country but under Chinese jurisdiction, rates among the bottom-most territories. So does the former Soviet republic of Chechnya, where an indigenous Islamic population is engaged in a brutal guerrilla war for independence from Russia.

LEARNING CHECK ◄ ···

▶ Give examples of authoritarian censorship and bribery.

▶ Why do authoritarian governments generally favor post-publication review to prepublication censorship?

AUTHORITARIAN PREMISES

Authoritarian media systems make sense to anyone who accepts the premise that the government, whether embodied by a monarch or a dictator, is right in all that it says and does. Such a premise is anathema to most Americans, but merely 400 years ago it was mainstream Western thought. **King James VII** of Scotland, who later became James I of England, made an eloquent argument for the **divine right of kings** in 1598. He claimed that legitimate monarchs were anointed by an Almighty and thereby were better able to express righteousness and truth than anyone else. By definition, therefore, anybody who differed with the monarch was embracing falsity and probably heresy.

● **King James VII**
Articulated the divine right of kings theory

● **divine right of kings**
Proper decisions follow the monarch's will, which is linked to an Almighty

As a novelist, Orhan Pamuk does what novelists do best—cast pressing problematic issues in such a powerful light that their resolution is hastened. In memoir-style best sellers Pamuk has explored controversial views of the culture of his native Turkey, particularly tensions between East and West, secularism and Islamism, and past and present. Although Pamuk's works have been lauded for their literary merit, his critics would rather some things be left unsaid. Some Turkish newspapers have editorialized that Pamuk should be "silenced for good." In 2005 he went on trial, charged with the crime of "insulting Turkish identity."

Pamuk personifies the difficulty of many tradition-bound countries in emerging from authoritarianism. Turkey, as an example, is torn between strong nationalism that dates to the Ottoman empire and the need to join the European Union to grow its economy. A condition for European Union membership is embracing fully the Western value of free expression. The European Court of Human Rights has been unequivocal about the right "to criticize public institutions in very strong terms." Although Turkey revised its laws on free expression in 2004, parts of old laws remain intact, including the provision against "insulting Turkish identity." At the time of Pamuk's trial, 65 free expression cases were before the courts in Turkey.

The Pamuk case grew out of an interview in a Swiss newspaper in which he discussed the deaths of 1 million Armenians and 30,000 Kurds in the late

Insulted the State. *Turkish author Orhan Pamuk found himself the victim of nationalist extremism for a critical assessment of Ottoman history. Although prosecuted for defiling Turkish national honor, Pamuk survived the trial. There were death threats. A provincial governor ordered his books burned.*

Ottoman period, which Western historians call the first genocide of the 20th century but which Turkey officially calls "internecine fighting." Pamuk also said that Turkish security forces shared responsibility for an estimated 30,000 Kurd deaths during separatist fighting

in the 1980s and 1990s. Pamuk did not use the hot-button word *genocide*, but he must have realized he was venturing into dangerous territory. About the mass killings, he said: "Nobody but me dares to talk about it."

For fierce Turkish nationalists, this was too much. A provincial governor ordered Pamuk's books burned, including several that contributed to his winning the German Peace Prize for literature. Despite the attacks and threats, Pamuk was defiant. Awaiting trial, he honed in on the Turkish dilemma: "What am I to make of a country that insists that the Turks, unlike their Western neighbors, are a compassionate people, incapable of genocide, while nationalist political groups are pelting me with death threats?"

In 2005 Pamuk's trial was adjourned on technical grounds. But under pressure from ultranationalists, the government continued to prosecute other writers, including journalists and scholars.

WHAT DO YOU THINK?

▶ Will European economic pressure on Turkey be effective over the long term in softening a nationalist streak that condones censorship?

The authoritarian line of reasoning justifies suppression of ideas and information on numerous grounds:

- Truth is a monopoly of the regime. Commoners can come to know truth only through the ruler, who in King James' thinking had an exclusive pipeline to an Almighty. Advocates of authoritarianism hold little confidence in individuals.
- Challenges to government are based on falsity. It could not be otherwise, considering the premise that government is infallible.

- Without strong government, the stability necessary for society to function may be disrupted. Because challenges to government tend to undermine stability and because challenges are presumed to be false to begin with, they must be suppressed.

To the authoritarian mind, media people who support the government are purveying truth and should be rewarded. The unfaithful, those who criticize, are spreading falsity and should be banished. It all makes sense if King James was right about his divine right theory. It's no wonder that John Twyn was sentenced to die so gruesomely.

An inherent contradiction in authoritarianism is the premise that the ruler is uniquely equipped to know truth. Experience over the centuries makes it clear that monarchs and dictators come in many stripes. Regimes have been known to change their definitions of truth in midstream, as in Henry VIII's change of heart on Roman Catholicism. A fair question to pose to authoritarianism advocates is whether Henry was right when he was a Catholic or later, when he was an Anglican.

LEARNING CHECK ◀ ┈┈┈┈┈┈┈┈┈┈┈┈┈┈┈┈┈┈┈┈┈┈┈┈┈┈┈┈┈┈┈

▶ **What is the notion of truth that is at the heart of authoritarianism?**

▶ **Was Henry VIII right when he was a Catholic or when he was an Anglican?**

LIBERTARIANISM

● **Enlightenment**
Period of rationalist thought; beginning foreshadowed by early libertarians

● **John Milton**
Early libertarian thinker

● **marketplace of ideas**
An unbridled forum for free inquiry and free expression

Libertarian thinkers, in contrast to authoritarians, have faith in the ability of individual human beings to come to know great truths by applying reason. This distinction is the fundamental difference between libertarian and authoritarian perspectives.

Physicists love telling young students the story of an English lad, Isaac Newton. Sitting in an orchard one late summer day, young Isaac was struck on the head by a falling apple. At that moment the law of gravity was instantly clear to him. It's a good story, although probably not true. Deriving the law of gravitation was a much more sophisticated matter for Newton, the leading 17th century physicist. But the orchard story lives on. It is a story also told to pupils in their first world history class to illustrate a period in intellectual history called the **Enlightenment.** In that version, young Newton not only discovered gravity at the very instant that he was bumped on the head, but he also realized that he could come to know great truths like the law of gravity by using his own mind. He did not need to rely on a priest or a monarch or anyone else claiming a special relationship with an Almighty. He could do it on his own. This revelation, say the history teachers, was a profound challenge to authoritarian premises and ushered in the era of rational thinking that sets the modern age apart. Individually and together, people are capable of learning the great truths, called natural law, unassisted by authorities. The insight was that human beings are rational beings. It was a realization that began quantum leaps in the sciences. The insight also contributed to the development of libertarianism, which held the intellectual roots of modern democracy.

Marketplace of Ideas. *A marital spat and a confrontation with the king led John Milton to write* Areopagitica *in 1644. The tract challenged royal authority on intellectual and moral grounds and paved the way for libertarianism. Milton made a case that everyone should be free to express ideas for the consideration of other people, no matter how traitorous, blasphemous, deleterious or just plain silly. It was a strong argument against restrictions on free expression.*

■ **Marketplace of Ideas.** An English writer, **John Milton,** was the pioneer libertarian. In his 1644 pamphlet *Areopagitica*, Milton made a case for free expression based on the idea that individual human beings are capable of discovering truth if given the opportunity. Milton argued for a free and open exchange of information and ideas—a **marketplace of ideas.** Just as people at a farmers' market can pinch and inspect a lot of vegetables until they find the best, so can people find the best ideas if they have a vast array from which to choose. Milton's marketplace is not a place but a concept. It exists whenever people exchange ideas, whether in conversation or letters or the printed word.

Milton was eloquent in his call for free expression. He saw no reason to fear any idea, no matter how subversive, because human beings inevitably will choose the best ideas and values. He put it this way: "Let Truth and Falsehood grapple: whoever knew Truth put to the worse in a free and open encounter." Milton reasoned that people would gain confidence in their ideas and values if they tested them continually against alternative views. It was an argument against censorship. People need to have the fullest possible choice in the marketplace if they are going to go home with the best product, whether vegetables or ideas. Also, bad ideas should be present in the marketplace because, no matter how objectionable, they might contain a grain of truth.

Milton and his libertarian successors acknowledged that people sometimes err in sorting out alternatives, but these mistakes are corrected as people continually reassess their values against competing values in the marketplace. Libertarians see this truth-seeking as a never-ending, lifelong human pursuit. Over time, people will shed flawed ideas for better ones. This is called the **self-righting process.**

- **self-righting process**
Although people make occasional errors in truth-seeking, they eventually discover and correct them

■ **First Amendment.** Libertarianism took strong root in Britain's North American colonies in the 1700s. Thomas Paine stirred people against British authoritarianism and incited them to revolution. The rhetoric of the Enlightenment was clear in the Declaration of Independence, which was drafted by libertarian philosopher Thomas Jefferson. His document declares that people have **natural rights** and are capable of deciding their own destiny. No king is needed. There is an emphasis on liberty and individual rights. Libertarianism spread rapidly as colonists rallied against Britain in the Revolutionary War.

- **natural rights**
Inherent human rights, including self-determination

Not everyone who favored independence was a firm libertarian. When it came time to write a constitution for the new republic, there was a struggle between libertarian and authoritarian principles. The libertarians had the greater influence, but sitting there prominently were Alexander Hamilton and a coterie of individuals who would have severely restricted the liberties of the common people. The constitution that resulted was a compromise. Throughout the Constitution, an implicit trust of the people vies with an implicit distrust. Even so, the government that emerged was the first to be influenced by libertarian principles, and "the great experiment in democracy," as it's been called, began.

- **First Amendment**
The free expression section of the U.S. Constitution

By the time the Constitution was ratified, it had been expanded to include the **First Amendment,** which bars government from interfering in the exchange of ideas. The First Amendment declares that "Congress shall make no law . . . abridging the freedom of speech, or of the press. . . ."

In practice there have been limits on both free speech and free expression since the beginning of the republic. Legal scholars debate where to draw the line when the First Amendment comes into conflict with other civil rights, such as the right to a fair trial. Even so, for 200 years the First Amendment has embodied the ideals of the Enlightenment. The United States clearly is in the libertarian tradition, as are the other Western-style democracies that followed.

■ **Global Libertarianism.** On its scale of *Free* and *Not Free*, the Freedom House organization, which tracks freedom globally, says that democracy and freedom are the dominant trends in Western and East-central Europe, in the Americas, and increasingly in the Asia-Pacific region. In the former Soviet Union, Freedom House says the picture remains mixed. In Africa, free societies and electoral democracies are a minority despite recent progress. The Middle East has experienced gains for freedom, although the region as a whole overwhelmingly consists of countries that Freedom House rates as *Partly Free* or *Not Free*.

LEARNING CHECK ◄

▶ **Explain how libertarianism is optimistic about human reason and how authoritarianism is pessimistic.**

▶ **How does the Enlightenment relate to libertarianism?**

▶ **How does the First Amendment embody the ideals of the Enlightenment?**

War as a Libertarian Test

STUDY PREVIEW

From the fog of war can come defining clarity on the irreconcilable clash between authoritarianism and libertarianism. The trials of combat, with national survival at issue, can put even the greatest democracies to a test of their libertarian ideals. Expedience can lead to contradictory policies—such as censorship and suppression of dissent.

COMBAT REPORTING

The ordeal of combat is perhaps the greatest test not only of personal courage but also of democratic nations' commitment to their ideals. In crisis situations, with national survival at issue, can a government allow unfettered news coverage? The struggle for an answer is rooted deeply in the American experience.

● **Edwin Stanton**
Union secretary of state who organized Civil War censorship of sensitive military news

■ **Civil War.** The Civil War was the first that had a large contingent of reporters accompanying the armies, about 500. After some fumbling with how to deal with the reporters, the secretary of war, **Edwin Stanton,** ordered that stories go to censors to delete sensitive military matters. In general, the system worked, from Stanton's perspective. Toward the end of the war General William Sherman marched all the way from Chattanooga, Tennessee, through hostile Georgia to the sea at Savannah, a nine-month campaign, without a hint in the press to tip off the Confederacy.

■ **World War II.** In World War II correspondents wore uniforms with the rank of captain and usually had a driver and a Jeep. The reporters generated lots of field coverage, but the reporting, reflecting the highly patriotic spirit of the times, as evident in the reporters wearing military uniforms, was hardly dispassionate and sometimes propagandist.

● **rice-roots reporting**
Uncensored field reporting from the Vietnam War

■ **Vietnam.** Reporters had great freedom in reporting the Vietnam War in the 1960s and 1970s. Almost at will, reporters could link up with South Vietnamese or U.S. units and go on patrols. The result, dubbed **rice-roots reporting,** included lots of negative stories on what was, in fact, an unsuccessful military campaign that was unpopular among many troops and a growing majority at home. For the first time the reporting was filmed for television, with gruesome footage being pumped by the networks into living rooms across the nation on the evening news, deepening opposition to the war.

Commanders didn't like negative reports, which some blamed for losing the public's support for the war. In the end, demoralized, the United States withdrew in defeat—the first war in its history the nation had lost.

■ **Grenada.** For the next wars, relatively quick incursions, the Pentagon had new rules. In 1983, when the United States took over the Caribbean nation of Grenada, a naval blockade kept reporters out. The war, secretly planned, surprised the news media. Scrambling to get on top of the story but barred from the action, enterprising reporters hired small boats to run the blockade but were intercepted.

Major newspapers, the networks and news agencies protested loudly at being excluded from covering the Grenada invasion. Acknowledging that the policy had ridden roughshod over the democratic principles on which the nation was founded, with an informed electorate essential for the system to work, the Pentagon agreed to sit down with news media leaders to devise new ground rules.

● **pool system**
Reporters chosen on a rotating basis to cover an event to which access is limited

The result was a **pool system,** in which a corps of reporters would be on call on a rotating basis to be shuttled to combat areas on short notice for the next quick war.

LEARNING CHECK ◄ ···

▶ Would news audiences have problems today with a policy to put journalists in military uniforms?

▶ What are the advantages and disadvantages of reporter pools?

media timeline

GLOBAL MASS MEDIA MILESTONES

1500s

Censorship
Henry VIII placed limits on imported publications (1529)

Licensing
British set up Stationers Company to license printers (1557)

Authoritarianism Justified
James I claimed kings held a divine right to rule (1598)

1600s

Areopagitica
John Milton argued for robust discourse in seeking truth (1644)

1700s

First Amendment
U.S. Constitution bars government control of press (1791)

1800s

Civil War
U.S. government limited war reporting (1862)

1900s

Global Shortwave
British Broadcasting Corporation created (1927)

Uniformed Journalists
U.S. government credentialed reporters (1942)

Airwave Propaganda
U.S. created Voice of America (1942)

Satellite Broadcasting
CNN launched a 24/7 news channel, later went global (1976)

Reporter Pools
Government allowed coverage of Panama invasion through reporter pools (1989)

Embeds
Reporters embedded with combat units (1993)

Al-Jazeera
Qatar sheik created Al-Jazeera news channel (1996)

2000s

Chinese Censorship
China installed filters on incoming Internet communication (2001)

Pan-Arab Media
Dubai launched media enterprise for multinational audiences (2003)

Iraq Infowar
Digital media used by Iraqi insurgents for propaganda (2003–)

King James saw divine anointment.

Milton would let Truth and Falsehood grapple

Voice of America as a Cold War tool

Al-Jazeera sought pan-Arab, global news audience

Liu Di under lifetime of Chinese government "permanent surveillance"

PIVOTAL EVENTS

- Printing presses throughout Europe (1500–)

- Age of Science, Age of Reason, Enlightenment

- Revolutionary War (1776–1781)

- Morse invented telegraph (1844)
- U.S. Civil War (1861–1864)

- World War II (1941–1945)
- Russian–Western rivalry triggered Cold War (1945)
- Vietnam War (1964–1973)
- Soviet empire imploded (1989)
- Persian Gulf War (1991)

- 9/11 terrorist attacks (2001)
- Iraq War (2003–)

437

For a story on U.S. soldiers on patrol in a ravaged Baghdad neighborhood, a three-person CBS television crew joined an infantry unit for the day. **Embeds,** the reporters were called. For most practical purposes, they were part of the unit, embedded. As their Hummer negotiated the streets, a yellow taxi alongside, packed with 300 to 500 pounds of explosives, was detonated remotely. Cameraman Paul Douglas and soundman James Brolan were wounded mortally. So were an Army captain and his Iraqi translator.

The wounded also included CBS correspondent Kimberly Dozier. Near death with shredded upper legs, severe burns and shrapnel in her head, Dozier was rushed to a combat hospital. Unconscious, having lost tremendous amounts of blood, Dozier's heart stopped twice. Technically she was dead. Both times surgeons brought her back and kept her alive.

Two dozen surgeries later back in the United States, Dozier was considering how to resume her work as a foreign correspondent. She had been in Baghdad three years, knowing every day the dangers. The work, she said, was essential: "The world is watching. The story needs to be told." At the same time, Dozier was hesitant to put her family through the trauma of her

● **embeds**
News reporters who are with military units on missions

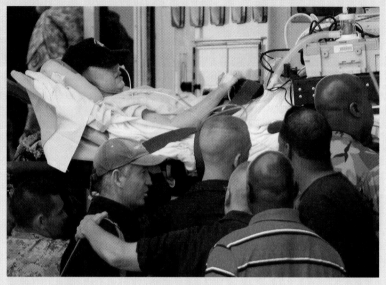

Medical Evacuation. *CBS reporter Kimberly Dozier survived a car bomb in which two crew members were killed, among 104 reporters who had died in the Iraq War by mid-2004. Also killed in the explosion were an Army captain and a translator.*

again being anyplace as dangerous as Iraq had become. By mid-2007 104 journalists had died covering the war.

She noted an irony about the embed duty for which she and Paul Douglas and James Brolan had volunteered the day they were attacked. They had chosen to go with soldiers assigned to a neighborhood thought to be relatively safe although a bomb had exploded there just the day before.

Another irony: The bomb that day was relatively small for the improvised

devices that insurgents had been perfecting since early in the Iraq War.

Although a veteran war reporter, Dozier said the experience that fateful day was a revelation: "You think how many lives, day after day after day, are being torn apart, how many sacrifices are being made. I thought I understood that, but I didn't really understand it until I lived through it."

WHAT DO YOU THINK?

▶ What if reporters were all afraid to volunteer for Iraq assignments?

EMBEDDED REPORTERS

The Iraq War, beginning in 2003, was covered by journalists like no other. The U.S. government, after flip-flopping on rules for war correspondents for 50 years, seemed to recognize the futility of trying to manipulate information in the digital age. Months before the invasion, the Pentagon chief for media relations, Victoria Clarke, invited news organizations to send reporters to special combat mini-courses to get up to speed—and also into physical shape—to go to war with combat units. Commanders were told to let the cameras roll whenever the journalists wanted.

The embed system has been fine-tuned as the war has ground on. Even so, the system has problems. A military unit with an embedded reporter needs to assign additional soldiers to address security. If a reporter is wounded, resources have to be diverted from the mission to evacuate the reporter. This became a growing issue in the Iraq War. By mid-2007, more than 100 reporters had been mortally wounded.

Pay-to-Publish

When the U.S. Defense Department realized it couldn't control news and information getting to Iraqis during the war in Iraq, it turned to private companies, including the Lincoln Group, a Washington-based public relations firm.

To Willem Marx, it looked like his dream of being a foreign correspondent was coming true. After his final semester at Oxford, he was offered an internship with Lincoln. Marx was ready for some real-world experience before starting journalism school in the fall.

In a tell-all piece in *Harper's* magazine, Marx described his job as choosing which stories submitted by U.S. military writers would be translated and published in Iraqi newspapers. He knew the stories were "far from exemplars of objective journalism." But, he said, he was told to think of them "not so much as news but as messages Iraqis needed to hear." Propaganda? That's the issue. Certainly, the stories being planted in Iraqi newspapers were not from the detached, neutral journalistic perspective that is the American democratic ideal.

During one two-month period the Lincoln Group proposed a $19 million multimedia blitz. Marx found an Iraqi company that would produce a half-minute television spot for $10,000. Iraq's national station said it could air the spot during its most expensive time for $2,000. The Lincoln Group was charging the military $1 million for the spot. Marx found himself driving through Baghdad with $3 million in cash in the trunk of the car. For his summer internship, Marx was paid $1,000 a month.

The Los Angeles *Times* broke the story about Lincoln's contract with the Pentagon to pay Iraqi news media to anonymously publish stories written by U.S. military personnel. Soon after, the Pentagon launched an investigation, which ultimately found that indeed the government could legally spread propaganda in foreign nations.

The Lincoln Group defended its work as an attempt to level the playing field in Iraqi media. Said one Lincoln adviser: "The opposition is very clever and basically gets a free run in the media over there." Other Pentagon defenders argued that different ethical standards are needed in a combat zone.

There is no evidence that the stories planted in Iraqi media were untrue. The controversy is whether the stories, for the sake of honesty and transparency, should have been attributed to the U.S. military.

Government manipulation of media content bothers John Schulz, dean of communication at Boston University. Schulz sees the issue going to the core of an American ideal. "In the very process of attempting to either lead by example or actually instill a democracy, which is the main mission in Iraq as we understand it now, we're subverting democracy at the very core by subverting the legitimate process of journalism," Schulz said. "There needs to be an agonizing reappraisal of what they mean about trusting the news media and whether soldiers and plants and public relations firms can function in the place of effective news media. I don't think so."

Old Tech Message. Despite a costly U.S. information campaign that vilified Iraq leader Saddam Hussein, the people of Fallujah renamed one of their streets the Street of the Martyr Saddam Hussein. Slickly produced media messages for television, no matter the budget or talent that goes into them, failed to offset insurgents' YouTube-type calls for resistance. George Bush was there, old-media style, and not getting through. Everybody, it seems, has a video cell phone.

DEEPENING YOUR MEDIA LITERACY

EXPLORE THE ISSUE

List the reasons the U.S. military would pay to have its own stories published in the Iraqi press. Then list ways that democracy and an effective media interact.

DIG DEEPER

Do you see any intersections between your two lists? Where do ethics fit into them?

WHAT DO YOU THINK?

Is a trust in the media necessary for a successful democracy? Is it OK to follow different media ethics in a new, unstable democracy? Was it worth the price the U.S. paid to get its stories in the Iraqi press?

Bureau chiefs for U.S. news organizations in Baghdad left it to individual reporters to decide whether to embed with a combat unit.

LEARNING CHECK ◄ ....

▶ Have embedded reporters given you a clearer feel for what's happening in the Iraq War?

▶ Does embedding as a policy resolve the vexing issue of how an independent news media can cover combat without jeopardizing military tactics?

▶ As a reporter in a Baghdad news bureau, would you volunteer for embed missions? Explain.

Arab Media Systems

STUDY PREVIEW

Media in Islamic regions do not fit a single mold. They operate in diverse political systems, some driven by theologies that themselves are inconsistent. Others are pragmatically oriented to create pan-Arabic mass audiences. Among the most successful is Al-Jazeera.

DIVERSE MEDIA STRUCTURES

Media systems of the nations comprising Islam-dominated regions are as diverse as the nations themselves. These nations span from northern Africa to southeast Asia. Many resemble classic authoritarian systems, some being among the planet's last theocracies with clerics dominating public policy. Variations, however, are significant. Islamic dogma ranges widely among sects vying for dominance. The civil war into which Iraq fell during the U.S. occupation, for example, was a clash of different traditions and strains of Islam going back centuries. In contrast, in the sheikdom of Dubai, whose governance resembles a monarchy, economic growth has trumped divisive issues with overt pan-Arabic attempts to accommodate diverse traditions.

Media systems in some Arabic areas reflect values from periods of overbearing European dominance, mixed with resurgent indigenous traditions and values. Some of this Western influence continued long after this dominance had ended. In the 1990s, for example, the British Broadcasting Corporation, with a history of international broadcasting in the region, spent two years setting up an Arab-language service. Obstacles led BBC to abandon the project in 1996. But, seeing a vacuum, the government of the tiny Gulf state of Qatar, already committed to creating itself as a regional media center, created a 24/7 television news service, modeled on U.S.-based CNN. Sheikh **Hammad bin Khalifa** put up the money. Thus **Al-Jazeera** was born, which today has been ranked the world's fifth-best-known brand.

● **Hammad bin Khalifa**
Founder of Al-Jazeera television news network

● **Al-Jazeera**
Qatar-based satellite news channel for Arab audiences; now global

LEARNING CHECK ◄ ....

▶ Describe the diversity in political systems and their media components in Arabic and Islamic regions.

AL-JAZEERA

Al-Jazeera picked up its journalistic tradition largely through Brits who had been with the abandoned BBC project. For the Middle East, the approach was fresh—live coverage of breaking news told dispassionately and as thoroughly as possible, no holds barred. Viewers glommed to the channel. Call-in shows were uncensored. Arabs suddenly had an avenue to unload on their governments, many of them despotic and unevenly responsive to public needs.

Al-Jazeera was applauded in the West as a voice for democracy and reform. But things changed after Arab terrorists killed thousands of people in New York City and Washington in 2001. As the Bush administration moved toward war in Iraq, the Arab perspective inherent in Al-Jazeera included independent reporting that sometimes was at odds with U.S. portrayals. Commentary was from all sides, including

Control Room. *The Al-Jazeera control room in Qatar is staffed by a mix of former British Broadcasting Corporation employees and Arabian journalists. Al-Jazeera's reporting during the U.S.-led war on Iraq displeased President Bush, who, according to British press reports, suggested to British Prime Minister Tony Blair in 2004 that the network's headquarters be bombed.*

insurgents whom the U.S. government wanted to deny a voice. According to news reports, in a 2004 meeting with the British prime minister, President Bush stepped out of the U.S. libertarian tradition in an unguarded moment and suggested bombing Al-Jazeera's headquarters in Qatar.

Meanwhile, Al-Jazeera's reporting continued in the BBC tradition, seeking multiple perspectives to get at the facts and truth. The reporting carried a high price to intolerant factions that claimed their own monopolies on truth. Twice Al-Jazeera bureaus were bombed, including a 2001 U.S. aerial attack on the Al-Jazeera bureau in Baghdad. Several Arab governments banned Al-Jazeera, although with little effect. The audience, already 50 million in 2000, has continued to grow.

So has Al-Jazeera's influence. In 2003 the network entered a news-sharing agreement with BBC. CNN added Al-Jazeera to its sources of video feeds. Al-Jazeera launched an English-language network in 2006 to extend its global reach. The English-language anchors have familiar faces, some formerly with CNN, Sky News and BBC.

LEARNING CHECK ◄ ··

▶ **What are challenges facing Al-Jazeera and its competitors in reaching Arab audiences?**

▶ **When agents of master terrorist Osama Bin Laden supplied video of his anti-Western political messages to Al-Jazeera, the network aired them as news. Was this the right thing to do?**

▶ **The White House said the Bin Laden tapes might carry embedded instructions to terror cells and asked U.S. television networks not to air the tapes. How would you as a network executive respond to the White House request?**

TRANSNATIONAL ARABIC COMPETITION

● **satcaster**
A television station that transmits to an orbiting satellite, which beams signals back down directly to individual receivers

The Arabic television field is becoming increasingly crowded. Saudi **satcaster** MBC has set up an all-news channel. Dubai TV's One TV has added an English-language entertainment network. Lebanon has become a powerhouse of pan-Arab television programming, including reality shows and talent contests. BBC, meanwhile, has decided to try an Arab-language news network again. The global reach of Arab media has extended to Latin America, where Telsur has gone into multinational satellite newscasts.

In Arab countries, the proliferation of satellite channels is expected to peak at some point soon. The survivors will be operations with deep, deep pockets. The business development manager at MBC in Saudi Arabia, Michel Constandi, estimates the combined operating budgets of the region's free satellite channels at $3 billion a year. The estimated ad market is only $30 million.

The significance of these multinational Arab media services is that, to attract large enough audiences to survive financially, they need to address audiences that subscribe to variations in Islamic readings of the Koran holy book, as well as divergent traditions, many of which have evolved confusingly and become intertwined with religious values.

LEARNING CHECK ◄ ···

▶ **How can media companies seeking pan-Arab audiences be successful in such a fractured part of the world?**

DUBAI MEDIA INCORPORATED

As a nation, Dubai might seem a mere speck of sand on the Persian Gulf—674,000 people, only 265,700 in its main city. From under the sand, though, has come oil that has brought spectacular wealth to the tiny emirate. But what will happen when the wells run dry? Resources extractable from the earth inevitably run out.

The government has set a deliberate course to create a post-oil financial infrastructure. The plan includes lavish hotels to transform Dubai into a tourism magnet. Beaches line the Gulf for miles, easily only a day's flight from major population centers in Europe, south Asia and, of course, the rest of the Arab world.

And so much sunshine. Could Dubai also become the Arabian Hollywood? It was California sunshine, after all, that drew the infant U.S. filmmaking industry from the East Coast to Hollywood early in the 1900s. The more sunshine, the more days for outdoor shooting. With moviemaking could come a host of related media industries—particularly television.

The brainstorming that began with a tourist-oriented Dubailand complex mushroomed. In 2003 the government converted its Ministry of Information into **Dubai Media Incorporated** to run the nation's television system. DMI is a quasi-government agency but is set up to operate like a private company. Ninety-seven billion dollars has gone into construction. More than 1,000 television and film companies have taken up residence, availing themselves of the sunshine and also the government's tax-free incentives.

Dubai Media Incorporated, with audience goals far beyond the emirate's borders, operates four television channels. These include an Arab-language general entertainment channel. The channel became the second-most-watched pan-Arabian satellite station, second only to the older Saudi-owned, London-based MBC. The Dubai Sports Channel, the only 24-hour Arab sports channel, has exclusive rights to the World Cup of horse racing. Arab soccer also is exclusive. An English-language service carries mostly movies and imported programs. In addition, a local channel aims at audiences within the United Arab Emirates, of which Dubai is part.

In the culturally and religiously fractured Arab region, Dubai TV and its competitors are on a tightrope in choosing content. Hussein Ali Lootah, chief executive, sees Dubai TV's greatest achievement in introducing Gulf-oriented programming that has not alienated Arabs on the Mediterranean. Creativity is within the bounds of local sensitivities, he says. For news, Dubai TV avoids the hard-hitting journalism of Al-Jazeera by having a deliberately friendly, informal approach. On magazine and talk shows there is more analysis, less polemics.

On the English-language One TV, programs and movies are chosen because they are "relevant and sensitive to our culture," says manager Naila Al-awadhi. Shows are subtitled and promoted in Arabic.

Dubai TV claims 50 percent market penetration, which means a reach of 100 million Arabs across the region. Dubai's pre-2004 predecessor earned less than $4 million. The 2006 gross reached $40 million. DMI claims English-language One TV can reach 70 million Arab households.

LEARNING CHECK ◄ ···

▶ **How is the emirate of Dubai seeking to become a global entertainment industry player?**

▶ **What obstacles does the Dubai enterprise face?**

● **Dubai Media Incorporated**
Quasi-government agency building Dubai to be a Mideast entertainment production center

Media and Terrorism

STUDY PREVIEW

Mass media are a new battleground in civilization's great struggles. Saudi Arabians have tackled terrorism with pan-Arab television drama. But old-style media may have maxed out their effectiveness. In Iraq, despite the high production quality and big spending, U.S. messages have failed to offset the insurgents' YouTube-style video calls for violent resistance.

SAUDI ANTI-TERRORISM

What a difference a major terrorism attack can make. Until November 2003, some members of the royal family that controls Saudi Arabia were channeling their oil wealth into Al Qaeda terrorism and to militant Islam imams who saw their holy book, the Koran, as justifying terrorism. Then came a 2003 terrorist bombing in Saudi Arabia itself. Eighteen people, all Arabs, were killed. It was a pivotal moment. Soon came a wave of mini-series and dramas, some produced in Saudi Arabia, challenging the notion that Islam somehow justifies terrorism. These programs play on Arab channels throughout the Middle East. Some, like *The Beautiful Virgins,* lead the ratings with an anti-terrorism theme woven into a trans-Arab story line with characters of Egyptian, Jordanian, Lebanese, Moroccan, Palestinian, and Syrian descent.

Beautiful Virgins, written by a former Al Qaeda member, is narrated by a Syrian girl who was burned in the 2003 attack. Amid all kinds of problems, including marital infidelity, drug addiction and wife beating, the core issue is the loving versus the dark side of Islam as told through the conflict within a young Saudi man torn between militant and moderate readings of the Koran. Which way does he go to find the virgins whom the Koran, at least metaphorically, says await good Islamic men in paradise?

Militant imams deride *Beautiful Virgins* as sacrilege, which points out that Islamic Arabs are hardly of one mind. The show was panned on militant Web sites. Station executives have received death threats. Even so, the show has led viewership not only in Saudi Arabia but also in other Islamic countries. At the Saudi-owned Middle East Broadcasting Corporation, based in Dubai, production manager Abe al Masry has described *Beautiful Virgins* as an integral part of the new Arab battle against terrorism.

It wasn't always so. The producer of a 2001 show, *The Road to Kabul,* which portrayed the Afghan Taliban negatively, caved to death threats after eight installments. But that was before the 2003 attack in Saudi Arabia. Today *The Rocky Road* story line hints at hypocrisy and Afghan corruption. Another show, *What Will Be, Will Be,* portrays conservative village sheiks as bumbling bumpkins, not unlike the sheriff in *The Dukes of Hazzard,* albeit with political edginess.

LEARNING CHECK ◄ ···

▶ **Why has anti-terrorism become fashionable in Saudi Arabian media?**

MEDIA AS TERRORISM TOOL

Islamic radicals including Al Qaeda have adapted low-cost digital media to their needs. During the U.S. presence in Iraq, insurgents have learned to plan multicamera, high-resolution video shots of large-scale attacks on U.S. forces. The videos are quickly edited into hyped narratives and spliced with stock clips of snipers felling U.S. soldiers, all with backgrounds of religious music or martial chants. The videos are meant to inspire triumphal passions. The videos sell in Baghdad markets, fundraisers for the cause. More potently, they make the video cell phone rounds incredibly quickly. Within minutes after an attack, video is in virtually unlimited circulation on handheld devices.

The adroit use of technology—all it takes is a laptop—figures into internecine tensions. A ghoulish sectarian video of a Sunni militiaman sawing off the head of a Shiite prisoner with a five-inch knife stirred Sunni emotion. The Shiites, of course, have no monopoly on the new tools of the information and propaganda war. When secretly shot video of the hanging of Iraqi leader Saddam Hussein leaked onto the Internet, his neck cracked in the noose, close up, incensed Shiites rioted in Anbar province.

New media can give underdogs an identity against forces that are superior by traditional measures. In Fallujah, an insurgent stronghold northwest of Baghdad, the United States created a multimillion-dollar campaign with traditional public relations and propaganda tools to win over the people. The other side, however, carried the day. The people renamed a major thoroughfare the Street of the Martyr Saddam Hussein.

LEARNING CHECK ◄

▸ How have underground forces glommed onto inexpensive new media forms to mobilize many Iraqis to their cause?

▸ How can the United States deal with grassroots media tactics that use new digital media?

Battle for Iran

STUDY PREVIEW

Geopolitically strategic Iran has emerged in the crosshairs of the East-West confrontation that has been shaped by global terrorism. In Los Angeles, where many Iranian expatriates live, satellite television stations aim at homeland reforms. The U.S. State Department, meanwhile, has implemented soft diplomacy with its own media messages. In reaction, the Iran government is trying to block transborder communication.

TEHRANGELES

● **Tehrangeles**
Nickname for Los Angeles as home to more Iranians than any city other than Tehran

Outside of Iran itself, no city is home to more Iranians than Los Angeles. The nickname **Tehrangeles,** however, didn't catch on much until Zia Atabay realized he could lease time on an orbiting satellite to send television programs from Los Angeles to anybody with a dish receiver in Iran. Atabay's goal: To encourage political reform and democracy in an Islamic society that's divided between old ways and new. Thus in 2000 was born, in Los Angeles, the National Iranian Television network.

Atabay poured $6 million into NITV, hoping it would become financially self-sustaining through advertising. It didn't. In 2006 the operation went dark. By then, however, 20 other satellite stations, funded by Iranians in the United States, were beaming signals to Iran. Although most are talk shows, programming at surviving Tehrangeles operations is all over the map. Think Iranian MTV. Or Iranian ESPN.

How effective has Tehrangeles television been as an alternative to state-controlled television and radio in Iran, all heavily censored? Measures are hard to come by. No doubt, though, the Los Angeles stations have audiences, judging by talk-show call-ins from Iran. Too, although satellite television is illegal in Iran, about half the population, roughly 20 million people, have dishes. But is it effective? The 2005 election of conservative Islamic Mahmoud Ahmadinejad as president has been called a backlash against the often-virulent anti-regime polemics from Los Angeles. Some observers say, however, that the music clips and sports on other satellite stations may be doing more to encourage social and other fundamental reforms by broadening the cultural exposure of Iranian young people.

LEARNING CHECK ◄

▸ Is it wrong for Iranian ex-patriates to try to influence public policy in Iran with appeals directly to the Iranian people?

▸ Can such projects succeed?

Tehrangeles. *Half a world away in Los Angeles, Alireza Nourizadeh offers commentary aimed at Iranian viewers of Channel One's* Window on the Fatherland. *Nourizadeh, who favors regime change, takes calls from Iranians in the country and out.*

Voice of America. *From studios in Washington, D.C., Luna Shadzi anchors a Persian-language news program beamed into Iran. Voice of America broadcasters believe Iranians deserve an alternative to the propoganda from their government.*

● **Radio Farda**
U.S. government-funded Farsi-language service aimed at Iran

● **Voice of America**
U.S. government-funded broadcast service sent into nations with state-controlled media to articulate U.S. policies directly to the people

U.S.-SPONSORED MEDIA

For years the U.S. government has funded **Radio Farda,** a 24-hour service in the Farsi language. Farda transmits from facilities in the Czech Republic. There also is a **Voice of America** satellite television service that the State Department beams into Iran. Unlike the fiery commercial stations broadcast from Los Angeles, the State Department hopes to sway Iranians with "soft diplomacy." This includes news programs that, although from a U.S. perspective, are not propagandistic.

The U.S. State Department has decades-long experience in broadcasting directly to people in repressed areas. Radio Free Europe and Voice of America were created after World War II, first under the guise of being citizen-generated projects. The goal ostensibly was to present information on U.S. positions on issues that were being distorted or unreported in Eastern Europe and the Soviet Union. It was soft-sell propaganda, but also was exposing people behind the so-called Iron Curtain to insights into Western pop culture and music, as well as dangling lures of advanced Western countries before repressed, impoverished people.

Old-style Voice of America and similar U.S. projects, including Radio Martí and television aimed at Cuba, also carried an antagonistic message to regimes in target countries. The projects have since added digital components. Attempts by the government to connect directly with Iranians, for example, include a Farda Web site. The main Iranian target is young adults, who tend to be well educated and technically savvy and more inclined as a group to political reform.

LEARNING CHECK ◄ •

▶ **What do you know about the role of Voice of America in facilitating the collapse of the Soviet Union and ending the Cold War?**

▶ **What are the prospects for the U.S. State Department's Radio Farda?**

IRAN BLOCKAGES

Typical of authoritarian regimes, the Iranian government tries to block signals from sources it considers unfavorable. The militia-like Revolutionary Guard jams signals. The British Broadcasting Corporation's Farsi service is a frequent target. The state Administration for Culture and Islamic Guidance assumed control of blogs in 2006

Web Censorship

China and Iran are the most aggressive nations in blocking political content from other countries but they are not alone. The Open Net Initiative—a consortium of Harvard, Cambridge, Oxford and Toronto universities—says at least 25 nations restrict citizen access to certain Web sites, some for political reasons, some for cultural reasons, some for both. The consortium noted that the study was limited to 40 countries and the Palestinian territories, so this may be only a partial picture of the state of the Web internationally. Besides China and Iran, the study reported that Myanmar, Syria, Tunisia and Vietnam focus on political content. Oman, Saudi Arabia, Sudan, Tunisia, United Arab Emirates and Yemen try mostly to filter socially unacceptable sites featuring pornography, gambling and homosexual material.

with robot and human censors and blocking. In addition, the agency hired hundreds of agents to create blogs carrying the government's message.

Blogging has worked against the government in specific cases. In 2006 word came from a prison that dissident journalist Akbar Ganji, who had been locked up five years earlier, was engaging in a hunger strike and could die. After bloggers spread the word about Ganji's prison treatment, re-igniting public interest in his case, the government freed him.

LEARNING CHECK ◄

▶ Eastern European regimes jammed Voice of America and similar programs during the Cold War but with limited success. VOA changed frequencies often. Would you expect Iran to be more successful in its blockage attempts?

China Media

STUDY PREVIEW

The struggle between freedom and tyranny plays and replays itself out with the mass media offering case studies on broader issues. Among major nations, China has suppressed challenges to government authority with the most labor-intensive censorship initiative in history.

CHINESE POLICY

● **Liu Di**
Under the pseudonym Stainless Steel Mouse, she satirized the Chinese government until arrested and silenced

Chinese authorities were less than amused at the free-wheeling satire of someone on the Internet going by the name Stainless Steel Mouse. The Mouse was tapping out stinging quips about ideological hypocrisy among the country's communist leaders. When government agents tracked the commentaries to **Liu Di,** a psychology major at a Beijing university, they jailed her for a year without charges. Finally, figuring the publicity about the arrest would be enough to chill other freethinkers into silence, the authorities let Liu Di go—on condition she not return to her old ways.

The government's rationale has been articulated at the highest levels. In a speech, President Jiang Zemin put the necessity of absolute government control this way: "We must be vigilant against infiltration, subversive activities, and separatist activities of international and domestic hostile forces. Only by sticking to and perfecting China's socialist political system can we achieve the country's unification, national unity, social stability, and economic development. The Western mode of political systems must never be copied."

LEARNING CHECK ◄

▶ How does China justify its tight controls on media content?

Chinese Quandary. *A guard on solemn duty at the bird's nest at National Olympic Stadium in Beijing metaphorically poses the question of how China would accommodate 20,000 foreign journalists for the 2008 Olympics in Beijing and also maintain the so-called Firewall, whose censors monitor all incoming communications. Reporters need unfettered communication back and forth with their editors back home to cover the games, which China wants to be a national showcase.*

Liu Di. *Government agents arrested college student Liu Di for her Internet essays, some of which mocked the government. Agents jailed her in a cell with a convicted murderer. After a year she was released subject to "permanent surveillance." She was told never to speak to foreign journalists.*

● **Emergency Response Law**
Chinese limits on news reporting of disasters, ostensibly to ensure social stability

CHINESE NEWS CONTROL

The rise of a market economy in China has loosened the financial dependence of newspapers on the ruling Communist Party. Competing for readers in this emerging marketplace, the predictable and dull propagandist thrust of many newspapers has begun to dim. More reporting is appearing, for example, on disasters and other previously off-limits spot news.

In 2005, after 121 Guangdong miners died in a mine flood, *China Business Times* launched a journalistic examination that concluded that mine authorities had known of safety violations and had taken bribes to look the other way. With the revelation, there was no choice but for the government to prosecute. Eighteen men, including a high-ranking government official, were hauled into court. In the past, misdeeds within the power structure had been ignored or dealt with quietly. That is no longer so easily done, now that a journalistic dragon is stirring.

Most accidents, even disasters, still go unreported. Of the 3,300 mine accidents in China in 2005, few garnered much coverage. But some newspapers have started going after these kinds of stories. When a Jilin factory explosion dumped 100 tons of toxic chemicals into the Songhua River, the government naïvely assumed it could keep a lid on the situation. Wrong. Chinese newspapers told the story, albeit in bits and pieces. The government was embarrassed when downstream Russians learned the river was dangerous. It was an international incident that the government blamed on the newspapers.

The extent to which the Chinese go to keep negative information out of circulation was demonstrated in 2007 when a contaminated ingredient imported from China began killing pets in the United States. When international inspectors arrived at the facilities of origin, the equipment was nowhere to be found. It was like the place had never existed. The Chinese explained that they had completed their own inspection and corrected any problems. No plant, no story.

To rein in journalism, the influential State Council has proposed an **Emergency Response Law** to "manage news" about emergencies. Censorship? The proposal's language is iffy. Permission would be required for reporting that "causes serious consequences." What does that mean? The State Council says "normal" reporting would be OK under its law, whatever that means.

The government's justification for the restrictions on coverage is to encourage stability. News about government corruption, as in the Guangdong mine flood, or government incompetence, as in disaster relief, does not inspire public confidence

Never Happened. A major industrial fire in China wasn't what authorities regarded as something that should be reported. A careful reading of Jilan newspapers, however, revealed bits and pieces that something catastrophic had occurred. When pollution from tons of toxic chemicals released in the explosions and fires reached the Russian border downstream, the fire became an international issue.

in the government. The nation's leadership is aware of an estimated 87,000 demonstrations in 2005 alone, many directed against public policies and government action—and inaction.

The Emergency Response Law would cover 812,500 news outlets. Some newspapers, feeling a new sense of journalistic self-empowerment, have taken strident positions against the proposed law. Editors have scoffed in print at the law's provision for local governments to be the sole source of disaster and accident information and to report such information in "a timely manner." The problem, the editors argue, is government cover-ups. And who defines "timely"? Who decides how much information is released? And which is, and which isn't?

LEARNING CHECK ◄

▸ **How would China's proposed Emergency Response Law affect reporting about disasters?**

▸ **If the United States had such a law, how would government sluggishness have been reported in the 2005 Hurricane Katrina disaster on the U.S. Gulf Coast?**

▸ **Do you accept the Chinese government's argument that restrictions on journalists are needed to prevent inaccuracies in reporting that could work against social and political stability?**

CHINESE FIREWALL

The Chinese government has expended major resources to limit Internet communication, particularly from abroad. To exclude unwanted messages, the Chinese government has undertaken numerous initiatives. One of them has been likened to a 21st century version of the Great Wall of China, a 1,500-mile fortress barrier built in ancient times along the Mongolian frontier to keep invaders out.

● **firewall**
A block on unauthorized access to a computer system while permitting outward communication

The Chinese didn't invent their **firewall.** It came from the U.S. network design company Cisco, which devised filters in the early 1990s for corporate clients to filter employee access to the Internet. The goal of these firewalls was productivity, to keep employees who are equipped with desktop computers from whiling away company minutes, hours even, on sites featuring entertainment and diversions. When Cisco went courting the Chinese as customers, the filters seemed perfect for China to block unwanted material from outside the country. Cisco filters soon were installed at the gateways for Internet messages into China. Here's how it works: The filters subtly "lose" messages from banned sites abroad. If a Chinese user seeks access to a verboten foreign site, an error message or a message saying "site not found" appears on the screen. Whether it's censorship or a technical glitch, the user never knows.

Chinese Web surfers who crave uncensored news have friends at a handful of U.S. companies that penetrate the Chinese government's firewall that's designed to block outside information. Bill Xia, a Chinese expatriate in the United States, operates one such company, Dynamic Internet Technology. Xia sets up Web sites with pass-through links to Voice of America and other outside sites that the Chinese government bans.

It works this way:

- The sponsor of a censored site, such as Voice of America, Human Rights in China, or Radio Free Asia, hires DIT to create a proxy site at a new Internet address.
- DIT sends mass e-mails to Chinese Web surfers with the address of the new site.
- Chinese Web users can then download software that hides their visits to the DIT site.

- When Chinese Web police identify the proxy sites and shut them down, often within 24 hours, never more than 72, DIT creates a new proxy site at a new address. And the process begins again.

It's cat-and-mouse and also a hassle, but DIT, always a step ahead of the censors, claims as many as 160,000 users. A few other companies, including UltraReach, provide similar proxy services.

Xia sees traffic spikes after the occurrence of major events on which the Chinese government has placed a lid. This happened when authorities tried in 2003 to conceal news of an epidemic of the virulently infectious SARS virus. It happened again in 2005 when police shot protesters in a village in south China.

Traffic also increased in 2006 when Google yielded to Chinese pressure to cooperate with the government's

censorship in order to be allowed to build its business in China. Microsoft and Yahoo earlier had made the same business decision.

DIT and other proxy companies reflect a zealous aversion to censorship. In some cases they reflect insurgent politics. DIT's Bill Xia, for example, is a member of the revolutionary Falun Gong movement, which Chinese leaders particularly fear. Concerned that his family back in China might be persecuted, Xia declines to be photographed or even to identify his home region or divulge his birthday. He won't even talk about DIT's location except to say that it's somewhere in North Carolina.

WHAT DO YOU THINK?

▶ Who will win the cat-and-mouse game between Chinese web censorship and companies like DIT? Could it go on forever?

There is dark humor among critics of the Chinese firewall. Noting the role of Cisco, they say: "The modern Great Wall of China was built with American bricks."

LEARNING CHECK ◀ ·······················

▶ How does the Chinese firewall work?

INTERNAL CHINESE CONTROLS

To control communication within the country, the Chinese Ministry of Public Security bans Internet service providers from carrying anything that might jeopardize national security, social stability—or even to spread false news, superstition or obscenity. As a condition of doing business in China, the U.S. company Yahoo agreed to the terms in 2002. So have Microsoft and other service providers. The system is called the **Golden Shield.** The shield complements the work of the firewall against unwanted foreign messages by controlling communication inside the country.

Even tighter control is expected through a huge intranet that the Chinese government is building within the country—the **Next Carrying Network.** CN2, as it's called for short, was designed from scratch—unencumbered by the older technical standards that have been cobbled together for the system that serves the rest of the planet. CN2's technical advantages include exceptional capacity and speed. Also, because CN2 uses its own technical standards that are not easily compatible with the global Internet, the system fits neatly with the government's policy to limit contact with the outside. Communications from abroad can be received on

● **Golden Shield**
Chinese system to control Internal Internet communication within the country

● **Next Carrying Network (CN2)**
Fast Chinese Internet protocols built on new technical standards; incompatible with other protocols

CN2 only after code translations that stall delivery and, not unimportantly, make them subject to more scrutiny.

LEARNING CHECK ◄ ••

▶ **How will China's CN2 strengthen the Golden Shield?**

▶ **How could CN2 work against Chinese integration into the global community? Could this work against China's commercial goals?**

CHINESE CENSORSHIP APPARATUS

● **prior censorship**
Government review of content before dissemination

Because **prior censorship,** reviewing messages before they reach an audience, is hugely labor-intensive, seldom in human history has it been practiced on a large scale. Past authoritarian regimes have relied almost wholly on post-publication sanctions with severe penalties against wayward printers and broadcasters to keep others in line. The Chinese, however, are engaging in prepublication censorship on an unprecedented scale.

Chinese censorship is partly automated. Internet postings are machine-scanned for words and terms like *human rights, Taiwan independence* and *Falun Gong* (a forbidden religious movement) and dropped from further routing. The system also catches other terms that signal forbidden subjects, like *oral sex* and *pornography*.

No one outside the government has numbers on the extent of human involvement in censorship, but there appears to be significant human monitoring at work. Western organizations, including Reporters Without Borders, occasionally test the Chinese system by posting controversial messages, some with terms that machines can easily spot, some with trickier language. Postings with easy-to-catch terms like *Falun Gong* never make it. Postings with harder-to-spot language but nonetheless objectionable content last a bit longer, although seldom more than an hour, which suggests a review by human eyes.

Who are these censors? How many are there? The consensus among experts outside the country is that China, whose Internet users number 100 million-plus, must be a massive censorship bureaucracy. A rare peek into the system appeared in a 2005 interview in *Nanfang Weekend* with a censor in Siquan, Ma Zhichun, whose background is in journalism. Ma discusses his job as an *Internet coordinator* in the municipal External Propaganda Office, where, without identifying himself online as a government agent, he guides discussions in the government's favor. Ma is part of elaborate mechanisms to keep online dialogue on the right track, particularly in chatrooms, but like thousands of other propaganda officers throughout the country, Ma is in a position to spot banned postings and report them.

LEARNING CHECK ◄ ••

▶ **If you were a Chinese censor, what terms would you use to intercept Internet content that should be checked?**

OVERT CHINESE CONTROLS

Although a lot of Chinese government control of Internet postings is invisible, some is overt. Because users are required to use a government-issued personal identification number to log on, citizens know they're subject to being monitored. Operators of blog sites, which number 4 million, need to register with the government. Cybercafés, which have been woven into the lifestyles of many Chinese, must be licensed. At cybercafés, cameras look over users' shoulders for what's on-screen. Police spend a lot of time in cafés looking over shoulders too.

The government's seriousness about regulating the Internet was unmistakable when thousands of illegal cafés were shut down in a series of sweeps in the early 2000s.

Arrests are publicized, which has a chilling effect. One especially notable case involved Wang Youcai, who, during President Clinton's historic 1998 visit to China, proposed an opposition political party in the U.S. tradition. Wang filed papers to register the China Democratic Party. Within a day, government knocked on his door, interrogated him for three hours, and hauled him away. He was sent to prison for 11 years and ordered into political abstinence for an additional three years for "fomenting opposition against the government."

The later case of the imprisonment of Liu Di, the Stainless Steel Mouse, for satirizing the government was a similarly chilling warning to those who want to engage in full and open dialogue.

LEARNING CHECK ◄ ·

▶ **Chinese punishments for bloggers who engage in frowned-upon content has a chilling effect. What is that chilling effect?**

▶ **As a traveler in China, would you be comfortable in a cybercafé engaging in the kinds of everyday Internet communication that you do at home?**

CHINESE BROADCASTING

Although political issues are the major focus of Chinese censorship, the government discourages what it sees as a creeping intrusion of Western values and sexuality. In a clampdown on racy radio gab and, lo and behold, orange-tinted hair on television, the State Administration for Radio, Film and Television issued an edict: Enough. To television hosts, the order was no vulgarity. That includes "overall appearance." Specifically forbidden: "multicolor dyed hair" and "overly revealing clothing." There also are new bans on things sexual. Violence, murder and horrors are out until 11 p.m. So too are "fights, spitting, littering and base language."

The restrictions, which are periodically issued as media stray, are consistent with the communist notion that government and media are inseparably linked in moving the society and culture to a better future. As the Chinese put it, the media are the *houshe*, the throat and tongue, of the ruling Communist Party.

Chinese nationalism takes unexpected turns. Broadcasters, for example, periodically are instructed to use only Mandarin. Foreign words, including Westernisms like *OK* and *yadda-yadda*, are not allowed. Not allowed either are dialects from separatist Taiwan. Also, a strict cap was put on imported soap operas and martial arts programs for television. Imports can't constitute more than 25 percent of the total of such programs.

Even in Hong Kong, the British colony that was returned to China in 1997 and that was to be governed by different rules that honored its tradition of free expression, Beijing-approved governors were appointed to comport with official policies. Political cartoonists also have been reined in.

Is government pressure effective? In Fujian province, the hosts of the program *Entertainment Overturning the Skies* gave up their blond dye jobs after one crackdown.

Yogurt Girl. *A touch of democracy swept China when people were asked to vote for their favorite talent in an Idol-style television show sponsored by the Mongolian Cow Sour Yogurt brand. Authorities didn't much like the idea. Whether societal reforms will be inspired by the show seems dubious, although Mongolian Cow Sour Yogurt Supergirl winners have catapulted their acts into entertainment careers.*

Some television programs imported from Taiwan, the United States and elsewhere suddenly and quietly disappear. Hong Kong radio is tamer. But clampdowns come and go. Kenny Bloom of the Beijing-based AsiaVision production house told a *Wall Street Journal* interviewer: "Commentators will follow the rules for a couple months, and then their clothes will get tighter and their hair will get wilder."

Even so, legal scholars Jack Goldsmith of Harvard and Tim Wu of Columbia, who have studied government controls on media content globally, say controls do not have to be absolute to be effective. Goldsmith and Wu offer copyright law as an example. Infringements of copyright in, say, illegal music downloads, are inevitable, but the threat of civil or criminal sanctions keeps violations at a rate that copyright owners are willing to live with. Such, they note, is the same with the censorious Chinese government. Nobody is so unrealistic to claim that all dissidence can be suppressed. The goal, rather, is to keep dissidence from breaking beyond an easily manageable level.

LEARNING CHECK ◄ ∙∙

▶ Why are Chinese media discouraged from using Westernisms in scripts, like *yadda-yadda* and *OK?*

EFFECTIVENESS OF CHINESE CONTROLS

An *Idol*-like mania swept China when an upstart television station in remote Hunan province put its show *Supergirl* on satellite. Despite admonitions against lyrics in English and gyrating hips, contestants pushed the envelope of government acceptability in front of huge audiences. That viewers could vote their preferences by mobile phones raised a specter of nascent democracy in a country where people can't vote for their leadership. Most analysts, however, have concluded that the phenomenon was an anomaly in the tightly controlled society. Even so, winners, who are called Mongolian Cow Sour Yogurt Supergirls, because of the dairy that sponsored the show, have gone on to singing and modeling careers.

LEARNING CHECK ◄ ∙∙

▶ Could *American Idol*-like television shows that encourage viewers to vote be a preamble to democracy in China?

Distinctive Media Systems

STUDY PREVIEW

Nations organize their media systems differently. Even largely similar systems like those in Britain and the United States have distinctive methods for funding. Some countries like India have unique features. Some countries have unique developmental needs.

BRITAIN

Almost everybody has heard of the BBC, Britain's venerable public-service radio and television system. Parliament created the British Broadcasting Corporation in 1927 as a government-funded entity that, despite government support, would have as much programming autonomy as possible. The idea was to avoid private ownership and to give the enterprise the prestige of being associated with the Crown. The government appoints a 12-member board of governors to run the BBC. Although the government has the authority to remove members of the board, it never has. The BBC has developed largely independently of the politics of the moment, which has given it a credibility and stature that are recognized worldwide.

The Beeb, as the BBC is affectionately known, is financed through an annual licensing fee, about $230, on television receivers.

The BBC is known for its global news coverage. It has 250 full-time correspondents, compared to CNN's 113. The Beeb's reputation for first-rate dramatic and entertainment programs is known among English-speaking people everywhere. The 1960s brought such enduring comedies as David Frost's *That Was the Week That Was* and later *Monty Python's Flying Circus*. Sir Kenneth Clark's *Civilisation* debuted in 1969. Then came dramatic classics like *The Six Wives of Henry VIII, War and Peace* and *I, Claudius*.

The great issue today is whether the BBC should leave the government fold. Advocates of privatization argue that the BBC could exploit its powerful brand name better if it were privatized. The privatization advocates also say that the BBC's government ties are keeping it from aggressively pursuing partnerships that could make it a global competitor with companies like Time Warner and Rupert Murdoch's News Corporation. But continuing to do business as always, they say, will leave the Beeb in everybody else's dust.

LEARNING CHECK ◄ ·······················

▸ **What sets the BBC apart from other international broadcast organizations?**

▸ **Is the BBC a government mouthpiece? Explain.**

INDIA

The world's largest democracy, India, has a highly developed movie industry that took root by providing affordable entertainment to mass audiences when the country was largely impoverished. The industry, called **Bollywood,** a contrivance of its historic roots in Bombay and the U.S. movie capital Hollywood, is adapting as India moves rapidly out of its Third World past. Today India is becoming a model for new media applications, like wi-fi, as the country brings itself into modern times.

● **Bollywood**
Nickname for India's movie industry

■ **Bollywood.** At 85 cents a seat, people jam Indian movie houses in such numbers that some exhibitors schedule five showings a day starting at 9 a.m. Better seats sell out days in advance in some cities. There is no question that movies are the country's strongest mass medium. Even though per capita income is only $1,360 a year, Indians find enough rupees to support an industry that cranks out as many as 1,200 movies a year, twice as many as U.S. moviemakers. Most are B-grade formula melodramas and action stories. Screen credits often include a director of fights. Despite their flaws, Indian movies are so popular that it is not unusual for a movie house in a Hindi-speaking area to be packed for a film in another Indian language that nobody in the audience understands. Movies are produced in 16 Indian languages.

Bollywood. The Indian movie industry, centered in Bombay and sometimes called Bollywood, pumps out an incredible 1,200 movies a year, Although India has some internationally recognized movie-makers, most Bollywood productions are formulaic action movies that critics derisively label "curry westerns."

The movie mania centers on stars. Incredible as it may seem, M. G. Ramachandran, who played folk warriors, and M. R. Radha, who played villains, got into a real-life gun duel one day. Both survived their wounds, but Ramachandran exploited the incident to bid for public office. He campaigned with posters that showed him bound in head bandages and was elected chief minister of his state. While in office, Ramachandran continued to make B-grade movies, always as the hero.

Billboards, fan clubs and scurrilous magazines fuel the obsession with stars. Scholars Erik Barnouw and Subrahmanyam Krishna, in their book *Indian Film*, characterize the portrayals of stars as "mythological demigods who live on a highly physical and erotic plane, indulging in amours." In some magazines, compromising photos are a specialty.

■ **Wi-Fi.** India has taken a lead in linking remote villages with the rest of the world through wireless technology. Villagers and farmers who once had to walk several miles to pay their power bills now go to a "knowledge center" as it's called—several rooms equipped with desktop computers, connected by **wi-fi** to the Internet—and pay online. Such "knowledge centers" are being installed in 600,000 villages in a government-enterpreneurial program launched in 2005. Eventually, all 237,000 villages in India large enough to have a governing unit will be equipped.

● **wi-fi**
Wireless fidelity technology, which offers limited-range downloading

The Indian experience is a model for extending mass-media links into isolated, poverty-ridden areas in Africa and eastern Europe. Farmers can learn market corn prices to decide when it's best to sell. Faraway doctors can diagnose illnesses through digital electrocardiography. In India a company named n-Logue has designed wi-fi kiosks for rural villages at $1,200 a unit, complete with a computer, software, a digital camera, paper and a backup power supply. Kiosks can have ATM banking too.

A remaining obstacle is the diversity in languages in many underdeveloped parts of the world. Google doesn't translate universally.

LEARNING CHECK ◄ ···

▶ **How do you explain the powerful influence of the Indian movie industry?**

▶ **Is wi-fi the way to bring remote parts of India into the country's mainstream economic expansion? How so?**

COLOMBIA

High drama is popular on Colombian radio stations, but it is hardly theatrical. In Colombia thousands of people, both wealthy and ordinary, are kidnapped captives. Families go on the air to express their love and support in the hope that their kidnapped kin are listening. It makes for powerful radio. Tragically, it's real.

Drug lords and petty criminals alike have found kidnapping to be lucrative in a country where anarchy is practically an everyday reality. The mass media are

After Jineth Bedoya Lima wrote about executions during a Bogota prison riot, she got word that a paramilitary leader inside the prison wanted to give her his side. "Come alone," she was told. Like all Colombian journalists, Bedoya, 25 at the time, was aware of the dangers of reporting news, especially on subjects sensitive to warring factions. Her editor and a photographer went with her.

As they waited outside the prison, the photographer left to buy sodas, then the editor followed him. When they came back, Bedoya was gone. Guards at the prison gate said they had seen nothing.

Many hours later, a taxi driver found Bedoya at a roadside garbage dump. She said that two men had grabbed her and forced a drugged cloth over her face. She regained consciousness in a nearby house, where her captors taped her mouth, blindfolded her and bound her hands and feet. They then drove her three hours to another city. They said they were going to kill her, as well as several other journalists they named. Then they beat and raped her and threw her out at the dump.

Her story, typical of violence against media people in Colombia, was disseminated widely by the Committee to Protect Journalists. It's a cautionary tale. Bedoya, who believed that she was still being trailed months later, was assigned two government bodyguards. Even so, she feels at risk. Why does she still do it? Frank Smyth of CPJ, writing in *Quill* magazine, quoted her: "I love my work, and I want to keep doing it. The worst thing that could happen has already happened."

In Pursuit of a Story. *Lima was kidnapped and raped while pursuing a story.*

WHAT DO YOU THINK?

▶ Consider a world where journalists refuse to take risks. How would society be different?

hardly immune. In the 1990s, according to the U.S.-based Committee to Protect Journalists, 31 journalists were killed because of their work. Sixteen others have died in incidents that may or may not have been related to their work. In a typical year, six to 10 journalists are kidnapped in a country whose population is less than that of the U.S. Pacific Coast states.

A political satirist, Jamie Garzón, was shot to death in 1999 after a television show. *El Espectador*, a leading newspaper, has armed guards at every entrance and around the perimeter, as do most media operations. Many reporters are assigned bodyguards, usually two, both armed. Two *El Espectador* reporters have fled the country under threat. The editor of another daily, *El Tiempo*, fled in 2000 after supporting a peace movement.

Beset with corruption fueled by the powerful cocaine industry, the government has no handle on assaults against the media. Although hypersensitive to negative coverage, the drug industry is not the only threat to the Colombian media. The Committee to Protect Journalists, Human Rights Watch, Amnesty International and other watchdogs blame renegade paramilitary units and guerrillas, some of whom are ideologically inspired. Also, the Colombian military itself and some government agencies have been implicated.

LEARNING CHECK ◀ •••

▶ What steps can be taken in a country like Colombia to create an environment in which newspeople can perform their highest service?

Chapter Wrap-Up

Mass Media and Nation-States (Page 430)

■ The world's nations and media systems can be measured on a scale of media freedom. At one extreme are nations in a libertarian tradition, which accords high levels of autonomy and independence to the mass media. Libertarianism emphasizes the ability of human beings to reason their own way to right conclusions and therefore believes humans are capable of their own governance. Democracy and a free mass media are in the libertarian tradition. At the other extreme are authoritarian nations with top-down leadership in control, sometimes overtly and onerously, sometimes less so. Libertarianism and authoritarianism are philosophically irreconcilable systems, a fact that explains many divisions in the world.

War as a Libertarian Test (Page 436)

■ For all of its attractions for Americans, whose traditions are libertarian, the concept has had a rough history. U.S. leadership hasn't always been responsive to the idea of grassroots governance nor to the ideal of a free press as embodied in the nation's Constitution. In times of war, even little wars like Grenada, leadership consistently has declared that national survival trumps free expression and a free press. The trials of combat put even the greatest democracies to the test of libertarian ideals. Contradictory policies result, including censorship and suppression of dissent.

Arab Media Systems (Page 440)

■ Although most nations in Islam-dominated regions are authoritarian, they also are diverse. Some are theocracies for all practical purposes, even when internal Islamic sects are hardly of one mind. Some of these countries, however, have moved beyond religion and pragmatically sought to be part of the modern world. Examples include the Qatar-based Al-Jazeera news network that seeks pan-Arabic, even global mass audiences. Media production centers, notably in Lebanon and Dubai but also elsewhere, are cultivating transborder and transcultural Arab and Islamic audiences.

Media and Terrorism (Page 443)

■ Terrorism has emerged as a major weapon in the global culture wars, aimed both at Western institutions from Islamic-dominated regions and at battling Islamic factions. The techniques of terrorism, low cost and mostly with easily mastered technology, have become a major propaganda tool in stirring odd mixes of religious pride and intolerance and also mindless hatred. Partisans find video cell phones a powerful tool for recruiting support. Insurgents in Iraq use YouTube-style videos to easily outflank sophisticated U.S. appeals for popular support.

Battle for Iran (Page 444)

■ Strategically located Iran, bristly in international relations, has become the target of outside media bombardment for reform. The U.S. State Department has fine-tuned its lessons from the Cold War and regeared its Voice of America to influence internal affairs in Iran. Meanwhile, in Los Angeles, home to thousands of Iranian expatriates, entrepreneurs have financed satellite television stations to encourage change. The satcast services are a transforming entry in global communication. In response, the government of Iran is employing traditional methods from the Cold War to block out transborder communication.

China Media (Page 446)

■ China's emergence as a global economic power hinges in part on its tightly controlling mass media. Government policy is to let nothing interfere with the stability necessary for the nation's economic engine to remain in high gear. The government has created the largest prepublication censorship apparatus in human history, called the Chinese Firewall, to monitor and censor incoming communication. Within the country, both entertainment and news media are kept in check—although signs of loosening appear from time to time.

Distinctive Media Systems (Page 452)

■ Nations organize their media systems differently. Even largely similar systems like those in Britain and the United States have distinctive methods for funding. Some countries like India have unique features. Some countries have unique developmental needs. In a nation like Colombia, where drug lords and gangs exercise heavy influence on media content through threats of violence, including kidnapping and murders, media have a unique set of obstudes.

REVIEW QUESTIONS

1. List countries that fit the definition of libertarian. List also those that fit the defintion of authoritarian. Justify your choices.

2. How well have various wartime efforts to accommodate free news reporting worked throughout U.S. history?

3. What generalizations can be made about government and media systems in Islam-dominated regions? How do these generalizations miss many realities?

4. Are insurgents destined to forever have an advantage through low-cost new technology in information and propaganda wars?

5. What are the echoes of the Cold War in the battle over information and ideas in Iran? What are the differences?

6. How effective have China's efforts at controlling mass media been? What do you see as the future of these efforts?

CONCEPTS	TERMS	PEOPLE
authoritarianism (Page 431)	Al-Jazeera (Page 440)	Henry VIII (Page 431)
divine right of kings (Page 432)	embeds (Page 438)	Liu Di (Page 446)
libertarianism (Page 431)	Enlightenment (Page 434)	Hammad bin Khalifa (Page 440)
marketplace of ideas (Page 434)	Emergency Response Law (Page 447)	John Milton (Page 434)
self-righting process (Page 435)	pool system (Page 436)	

MEDIA SOURCES

Scholarly journals that carry articles on foreign media systems and issues include the *International Communication Bulletin*.

● Thomas L. Friedman. *The World Is Flat: A Brief History of the 21st Century.* Farrar, Straus and Giroux, 2005. Friedman, a journalist, seeks an overview of how media resulting from new technology are transforming global economics.

● Michael S. Sweeney. *Secrets of Victory: The Office of Censorship and the American Press and Radio in World War II.* University of North Carolina Press, 2001. Sweeney, a scholar, examines the U.S. government's World War II censorship program and attempts to explain its success. Sweeney, once a reporter himself, draws on archival sources.

● Daya Kishan Thussu, editor. *Electronic Empires: Global Media and Local Resistance.* Arnold, 1999. Sixteen essays evaluate media globalization, especially television, from a diverse range of perspectives, including cultural imperialism and audience liberation.

In this chapter you have deepened your media literacy by revisiting several themes. Here are thematic highlights from the chapter:

Media Technology

Media technology that's accessible on a small budget is changing global mass communication. With $6 million, a fraction of what it would cost to build a traditional television station, Iranian expatriate Zia Atabay built a satellite station in Los Angeles to encourage political reform in his homeland. Now 20 such stations in the United States are beaming messages to Iran. Low-cost media technology is leapfrogging traditional media thinking. The government of Iran, for example, is trying old-style broadcast blocking and Internet intercepts with limited success. Elsewhere, financially accessible technology, especially cell phone videos, have given terrorists an advantage in propaganda wars against major powers, like the United States. **(Pages 443–446)**

Who's Watching? *The U.S. message to Iraqis, omniscient in a big-budget media campaign, hasn't carried the day. Meanwhile, insurgents are splicing motivational music with anti-American combat scenes and getting their message out on ubiquitous video cell phones.*

Media Economics

Advertising revenue goes to the media that amass audiences that advertisers covet. This financial incentive has become a factor in burgeoning broadcast services in Islamic-dominated regions. The 24-hour Arab television news service Al-Jazeera, for example, was designed to attract a pan-Arab audience that never existed before. Other Middle East enterprises have the same goal, some aiming for global audiences. **(Pages 440–442)**

Media and Democracy

The democratic ideal of government enacting the will of the people requires an informed populace. The ideal is from the philosophical school of libertarianism, which holds that people can reach good conclusions through the open exchange of ideas. This principle was articulated by the English poet and novelist John Milton in 1644. Libertarianism became the philosophical basis for the form of democracy pioneered by the United States when it was a new country in the late 1700s. **(Pages 434–435)**

Al-Jazeera. *The pan-Arab news channel has become the world's fifth most-recognized brand.*

Media Effects

Although media effects are difficult to measure, governments, including that of the United States, have invested heavily in directly reaching people in other countries to encourage political reforms if not outright revolt. The United States became heavily involved in transborder broadcasting during World War II with Voice of America. VOA and similar services continued into the Cold War with programming aimed at Russia and Eastern Europe. Today variants are targeting people in Cuba, Arab nations and wherever it suits U.S. national policy. Governments of target nations hardly see these projects as benign. Attempts are made to block incoming programs. **(Page 445)**

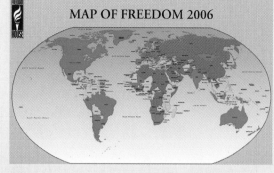

MAP OF FREEDOM 2006

Measuring Freedom. *The greening of the planet by Freedom House, which tracks global press freedom, has been gradual but steady for 20 years. Russia wobbles. Most of Asia and Africa have consistently been in the authoritarian tradition.*

Chinese Democracy. *Cell phone voting for the Mongolian Cow Sour Yogurt Supergirl may be as close as China has come to democracy. Could a taste of majority rule be a prelude?*

Elitism and Populism

Authoritarian government systems are elitist. A monarch or a coterie of governing elite are presumed to hold answers that common folks can't recognize without guidance. This monopoly on knowing what's best includes social policies, cultural affairs and other matters, including media content. In contrast, libertarianism has confidence in individual human beings. Given enough time to sort through even the most complex issues, according to libertarians, people individually and collectively will reach correct conclusions. To work well, libertarianism requires that mass media be an uncensored forum for people to gather information and exchange ideas. **(Pages 431–435)**

Rival Theorists. *What a conversation King James and John Milton would have had. The scholarly British king defended monarchal systems as divine and thus beyond criticism. Two generations later, Milton made the case for libertarianism in* Areopagitica.

Mass Media and Governance

Populist Appeals

Arnold Schwarzenegger had made up his mind. In advance of an appearance on the *Tonight Show*, he had told host Jay Leno, his friend, that he wouldn't run for governor of California. On the edge of the set before going on, Schwarzenegger stood chatting with his adviser, George Gorton, who held a news release ready to be issued. It began: "I am not running for governor." Then and there, as Gorton tells it, Schwarzenegger changed his mind: "Let's go do it."

The rest, after that August 2003 announcement, became history that raised anew questions about populism and the role of the mass media in the process of representative government. Schwarzenegger was in the tradition of populist candidates, who, as newcomers to politics, rally sectors of the society against existing institutions. "Hasta la vista, baby," Schwarzenegger taunted incumbent Governor Gray Davis, using a famous line from one of his movies. He vowed to clean house at the Sacramento Capitol. To attract support, he drew on public dissatisfaction with record state government deficits, college tuition hikes and higher auto registration fees.

Was Schwarzenegger qualified? His popularity came not from political experience. He had none. When he was a young man, Schwarzenegger was a photogenic, world-class bodybuilder. He later made a fortune in movies, the most successful being high-energy action flicks that were short on dialogue except for pithy deadpan phrases like "Hasta la vista, baby." Critics said that the media made Schwarzenegger—or, perhaps more accurately, Schwarzenegger used the media to create a persona.

LEARNING AHEAD

- The U.S. news media are a watchdog of government on the people's behalf.
- The mass media are major shapers of the public's agenda of issues.
- Government has many tools for manipulating media coverage.
- Watchdog performance is uneven, with voids in some government coverage.

Arnold Schwarzenegger. *Celebrity bids for public office can be disastrous—they can also be successes. Body-builder movie star Arnold Schwarzenegger, after a slow start, has won improving marks during his tenure as California's governor.*

Is populism a good thing? Critics note that populist appeals often are simplistic and don't work. Despite downsides, populist candidates can draw new voters to the polls, increasing political participation in the spirit of fuller democracy. Schwarzenegger, for example, proclaimed himself the "people's candidate." The core question, however, is whether people are participating knowledgeably and intelligently or responding to simplistic and panacean policy proposals that aren't well thought out. Populism carries a risk of uninformed though popular-at-the-time policy changes that end up doing more harm than good.

The mass media, of course, are key in helping people sort through issues as they participate in the political process. How hard do news reporters push candidates to defend their proposals? How responsible, forthcoming and honest are candidates in their advertising, photo-ops and other media manipulation? These are questions you will be exploring in this chapter on the mass media and governance.

Media Role in Governance

STUDY PREVIEW

The news media are sometimes called the fourth estate or the fourth branch of government. These terms identify the independent role of the media in reporting on the government. The media are a kind of watchdog on behalf of the citizens.

FOURTH ESTATE

Medieval English and French societies were highly structured into classes of people called *estates*. The first estate was the clergy. The second was the nobility. The third was the common people. After Gutenberg, the mass-produced written word began emerging as a player in the power structure, but it couldn't be pigeonholed as part of one or another of the three estates. In time the press came to be called the **fourth estate.** Where the term came from isn't clear, but **Edmund Burke,** a member of the British Parliament, used it in the mid-1700s. Pointing to the reporters' gallery, Burke said, "There sat a Fourth Estate more important by far than them all." The term is applied to all journalistic activity today. The news media report on the other estates, ideally with roots in none and a commitment only to truth.

The fourth-estate concept underwent an adaptation when the United States was created. The Constitution of the new republic, drafted in 1787, set up a balanced form of government with three branches: the legislative, the executive and the judicial. The republic's founders implied a role for the press in the new governance structure when they declared in the Constitution's First Amendment that the government should not interfere with the press. The press, however, was not part of the structure. This led to the press informally being called the **fourth branch** of government. Its job is to monitor the other branches as an external check on behalf of the people. This is the **watchdog role** of the press. As one wag put it, the founders saw the role of the press as keeping tabs on the rascals in power to keep them honest.

LEARNING CHECK ◄

▶ What is meant when the news media are called watchdogs?

▶ What did Edmund Burke mean by his term the *fourth estate*?

● fourth estate
The press as a player in medieval power structures, in addition to the clerical, noble and common estates

● Edmund Burke
British member of Parliament who is sometimes credited with coining the term *fourth estate*

● fourth branch
The press as an informally structured check on the legislative, executive and judicial branches of government

● watchdog role
Concept of the press as a skeptical and critical monitor of government

Governance Failure?
Journalistic Failure?

Bumper to bumper, commuters inched their way through a construction zone on a major federal highway across the Mississippi River in Minneapolis. Without warning the central eight-lane span collapsed. The 60-foot free fall was over in four seconds. Within another 10 seconds, other spans of the 1,900-foot bridge went down too. Miraculously, dozens of motorists survived, albeit many with injuries. Others were battered or crushed to death or drowned.

What had gone wrong? Within hours, journalists had access to reports that showed the bridge, part of the nation's government-built and maintained interstate highway system had received bad inspection marks for years. Neither federal nor state authorities responded with any type of repairs. Clearly there had been a failure of government.

News reporters were quick to divulge that the Minnesota highways department had been starved of funds for years. Money instead had been committed recently to build a lavish stadium for professional baseball. The dichotomy was ghoulish: Romanesque priorities of circuses and games over public safety.

Negligence? Lawsuits followed the Minneapolis tragedy.

The public policy question, however, is broader than the individual tragedies. How could the government have so distorted its priorities for always-limited financial resources—and done so for years? Public policy is in fact the operational vehicle through which society decides which decisions to make. It's like your checking account. There is never enough money to buy everything you want. You have to make choices. Government at many levels had made many, many wrong decisions.

The news media, true to their watchdog function, identified the failures. But too late. Journalists reacted to government's negligence only after the tragedy. The watchdog was sleeping. It was a government failure but a journalistic failure as well.

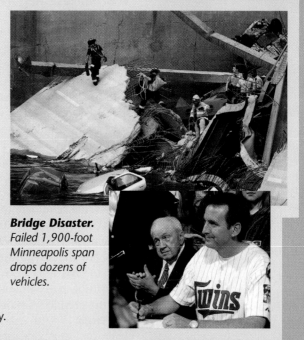

Bridge Disaster. *Failed 1,900-foot Minneapolis span drops dozens of vehicles.*

Safety vs. Circuses. *Minnesota Governor Tim Pawlenty had some explaining to do. Instead of backing highway infrastructure funding, he had to support the financing of a new Twins baseball stadium.*

DEEPENING YOUR MEDIA LITERACY

EXPLORE THE ISSUE

How complete is the coverage of state government in your news media? Check your daily newspaper for a day when your state legislature was last in session. Count the stories from the Capitol. Also count the words. Check the source of the stories—a staff reporter, a news agency, another newspaper. This will be a rough indicator of the resources your newspaper puts into covering state public policy decisions.

DIG DEEPER

For the same day 10 years earlier, count the Capitol stories and do a word count. Also note the sources of the stories—a staff reporter, a news agency, another newspaper.

WHAT DO YOU THINK?

From your two snapshots of state public policy coverage, what appears to have happened to public policy coverage in your state? Did you find any attention given to state or federal highway repair budgets in your snapshots?

Edmund Burke. *The British political philosopher Edmund Burke concocted the term* fourth estate *for the press. Pointing to reporters in the gallery, he told fellow members of Parliament: "There sat a Fourth Estate more important by far than them all." Burke was adding to the three recognized estates— the nobility, the clergy and the common people.*

● **equal time rule**
Government requirement for stations to offer competing political candidates the same time period and the same rate for advertising

● **fairness doctrine**
Former government requirement that stations air all sides of public issues

● **Don Burden**
Radio station owner who lost licenses because he favored some political candidates over others

● **Tornillo opinion**
The U.S. Supreme Court upheld First Amendment protection for the print media even if they are imbalanced and unfair

GOVERNMENT–MEDIA RELATIONS

Although the First Amendment says that the government shouldn't place restrictions on the press, the reality is that exceptions have evolved.

■ **Broadcast Regulation.** In the early days of commercial radio, stations drowned one another out. Unable to work out mutually agreeable transmission rules to help the new medium realize its potential, station owners went to the government for help. Congress obliged by creating the Federal Radio Commission in 1927. The commission's job was to limit the number of stations and their transmitting power to avoid signal overlaps. This the commission did by requiring stations to have a government-issued license that specified technical limitations. Because more stations were broadcasting than could be licensed, the commission issued and denied licenses on the basis of each applicant's potential to operate in the public interest. Over time this criterion led to numerous requirements for broadcasters, in radio and later television, to cover public issues.

Because of the limited number of available channels, Congress tried to ensure an evenhandedness in political content through the **equal time rule.** If a station allows one candidate to advertise, it must allow competing candidates to advertise under the same conditions, including time of day and rates. The equal time requirement is in the law that established the Federal Radio Commission and also the 1934 law that established its successor, the Federal Communications Commission. The rule has since been expanded to require stations to carry a response from the opposition party immediately after broadcasts that can be construed as political, like the president's state of the union address.

From 1949 to 1987 the Federal Communications Commission also required stations to air all sides of public issues. The requirement, called the **fairness doctrine,** was abandoned in the belief that a growing number of stations, made possible by improved technology, meant the public could find plenty of diverse views. Also, the FCC figured the public's disdain for unfairness would undermine the ability of lopsided stations to keep an audience. The commission, in effect, acknowledged that the marketplace could be an effective force for fairness—without further need for a government requirement.

Abandonment of the fairness doctrine was part of the general movement to ease government regulation on business. This shift has eased the First Amendment difficulties inherent in the federal regulation of broadcasting. Even so, the FCC remains firmly against imbalanced political broadcasting. In 1975, for example, the commission refused to renew the licenses of stations owned by **Don Burden** after learning that he was using them on behalf of political friends. At KISN in Vancouver, Washington, Burden had instructed the news staff to run only favorable stories on one U.S. Senate candidate and only negative stories on the other. At WIFE in Indianapolis he ordered "frequent, favorable mention" of one U.S. senator. The FCC declared it would not put up with "attempts to use broadcast facilities to subvert the political process." Although the Burden case is a quarter century old, the FCC has sent no signals that it has modified its position on blatant slanting.

■ **Print Regulation.** The U.S. Supreme Court gave legitimacy to government regulation of broadcasting, despite the First Amendment issue, in its 1975 **Tornillo opinion.** Pat Tornillo, a candidate for the Florida legislature, sued the Miami *Herald* for refusing to print his response to an editorial urging voters to vote for the other candidate. The issue was whether the FCC's fairness doctrine could apply to the print media—and the Supreme Court said no. As the Court sees it, the First Amendment applies more directly to print than to broadcast media.

This does not mean, however, that the First Amendment always protects print media from government interference. The Union Army shut down dissident newspapers in Chicago and Ohio during the Civil War. Those incidents were never

A political activist at the age of 9, Donna Brazile went on to become the first African-American woman to lead a major presidential campaign. The talented field operative and grassroots organizer grew up in poverty in a small town near New Orleans and began her political activism campaigning for a city council candidate who promised a playground in her neighborhood. The third of nine children, she was encouraged to follow her dreams by her grandmother.

On the road to being named Al Gore's campaign manager, Brazile worked on presidential campaigns for Democratic candidates Carter and Mondale in 1976 and 1980, the Reverend Jesse Jackson's first historic bid for the presidency in 1984, Mondale–Ferraro in 1984, Dick Gephardt in 1988, Dukakis–Bentsen in 1988, and Clinton–Gore in 1992 and 1996. It was Gore's 2000 loss to George W. Bush that was the most heartbreaking. Many political observers praised Brazile for her strategic planning and her get-out-the-vote effort, which resulted in Gore winning the popular vote, even though he lost in the electoral college.

Since then Brazile has served as a fellow at Harvard's Institute of Politics, where she has taught students how a multimillion-dollar presidential campaign is structured, managed and organized. The Gore campaign lost,

she says, "because we failed to educate voters, failed to remove structural barriers, failed to have every ballot counted."

In her autobiography, *Cooking with Grease: Stirring the Pots in American Politics,* Brazile named each chapter for a favorite dish, to reflect her lifelong habit of stirring the pot for social change. Now she wants to focus on the themes that have resonated through her life: voter participation, voter education, trying to make the system better and letting people vote without harassment, and she is the founder and managing director of Brazile and Associates, a political consulting and grassroots advocacy firm based in the District of Columbia.

Brazile, in her late 40s, is a contributor and political commentator on CNN's *Inside Politics,* MSNBC's *Hardball* and Fox's *Hannity and Colmes.* She is chair of the Democratic National Committee's Voting Rights Institute, which was established in 2001 to help protect and promote the rights of all Americans to participate in the political process. She told the Detroit *Free Press,* "I talk to the hip-hop generation 24/7, every day of my life. I want to be part of what they see as their vision of this country."

Political Strategist. *Although she failed in masterminding Al Gore's presidential campaign in 2000, Donna Brazile has emerged as a respected voice of reason, albeit from a partisan perspective.*

WHAT DO YOU THINK?

▶ What qualifies Brazile as a frequent talk-show guest on campaign politics?

▶ Is Brazile's partisan perspective an asset or liability when she offers campaign analysis?

challenged in the courts, but the U.S. Supreme Court has consistently said it could envision circumstances in which government censorship would be justified. Even so, the Court has laid so many prerequisites for government interference that censorship seems an extremely remote possibility.

■ **Internet Regulation.** The Internet and all its permutations, including chatrooms and Web sites, are almost entirely unregulated in terms of political content. The massive quantities of material, its constant flux and the fact that the Internet is an international network make government regulation virtually impossible. Even Congress' attempts to ban Internet indecency in 1996 and again in 1999 fell apart under judicial review. The only inhibition on Internet political content is through civil suits between individuals on issues like libel and invasion of privacy, not through government restriction.

LEARNING CHECK ◄

▸ **What controls does government exert over political news coverage in the United States?**

▸ **How do these controls comport with the First Amendment?**

Media Effects on Governance

STUDY PREVIEW

Media coverage shapes what we think about as well as how we think about it. This means the media are a powerful linkage between the government and how people view their government. A negative aspect is the trend of the media to pander to transitory public interest in less substantive subjects, like scandals, gaffes and negative events.

AGENDA-SETTING

● **Maxwell McCombs, Don Shaw**
Scholars whose agenda-setting ideas further displaced powerful effect theory

● **agenda-setting**
The process through which issues bubble up into public attention through mass-media selection of what to cover

A lot of people think the news media are powerful, affecting the course of events in godlike ways. It's true that the media are powerful, but scholars, going back to sociologist Paul Lazarsfeld in the 1940s and even Robert Park in the 1920s, have concluded that it's not in a direct tell-them-how-to-vote-and-they-will kind of way. Media scholars **Maxwell McCombs** and **Don Shaw** cast media effects succinctly when they said the media don't tell people *what to think* but rather *what to think about*. This has come to be called **agenda-setting.**

■ **Civil Rights.** The civil rights of American blacks were horribly ignored for the century following the Civil War. Then came news coverage of a growing reform movement in the 1960s. That coverage, of marches and demonstrations by Martin Luther King Jr. and others, including film footage of the way police treated peaceful black demonstrators, got the larger public thinking about racial injustice. In 1964 Congress passed the Civil Rights Act, which explicitly forbade discrimination in hotels and eateries, government aid and employment practices. Without media coverage, the public agenda would not have included civil rights at a high enough level to have precipitated change as early as 1964.

■ **Watergate.** Had the Washington *Post* not doggedly followed up on a break-in at the Democratic Party's national headquarters in 1972, the public would never have learned that people around the Republican president, Richard Nixon, were behind it. The *Post* set the national agenda.

■ **White House Sex Scandals.** Nobody would have spent much time pondering whether President Bill Clinton engaged in sexual indiscretions if David Brock, writing in the *American Spectator* in 1993, had not reported allegations by Paula Jones. Nor would the issue have reached a feverish level of public attention without Matt Drudge's 1997 report in his online Drudge Report about Monica Lewinsky.

By and large, news coverage does not call for people to take positions, but on the basis of what they learn from coverage, people do take positions. It's a catalytic effect. The coverage doesn't cause change directly but serves rather as a catalyst.

LEARNING CHECK ◄

▸ **How is news coverage catalytic in public decision making?**

▸ **What is media agenda-setting?**

A Failure of Government.
CNN deployed hundreds of staff to the Gulf Coast when Hurricane Katrina struck, documenting not only the disaster but the failure of the federal government to respond adequately. The coverage, including anchor Soledad O'Brien on the scene, kept the failure on the public agenda and forced President Bush to adjust his initially rosy claims about the federal response. The influence of the news media, particularly television, to propel issues powerfully into public consciousness has been dubbed the CNN effect.

● **CNN Effect**
The ability of television, through emotion-raising video, to elevate distant issues on the domestic public agenda

● **framing**
Selecting aspects of a perceived reality for emphasis in a mass-media message, thereby shaping how the audience sees the reality

CNN EFFECT

Television is especially potent as an agenda-setter. For years nobody outside Ethiopia cared much about the devastating famine. Not even after four articles in the New York *Times* was there much response. The Washington *Post* ran three articles, and the Associated Press distributed 228 stories—still hardly any response. The next year, however, disturbing videos aired by BBC captured public attention and triggered a massive relief effort. In recent years many scholars looking at the agenda-setting effect of television vis-à-vis other media have focused on CNN, whose extensive coverage lends itself to study. As a result, the power of television to put faraway issues in the minds of domestic audiences has been labeled the **CNN Effect.**

LEARNING CHECK ◄ ···

▸ **What examples of the CNN Effect have you seen in your campus news media? In other local news media?**

FRAMING

Related to agenda-setting and the CNN Effect is a process called **framing,** in which media coverage shapes how people see issues. Because the Pentagon has allowed news reporters to accompany combat units in the Iraq War, there has been concern that the war coverage might be decontextualized. Critics foresaw coverage focusing on tactical encounters of the combat units, missing larger, strategic stories. In other words, highly dramatic and photogenic stories from combat units might frame the telling of the war story in terms of the minutiae of the conflict. Too, Pentagon war planners were aware that reporters living with combat units would, not unnaturally, see the story from the soldiers' perspective. The Pentagon, in fact, had carefully studied the 1982 war between Britain and Argentina, in which embedded British journalists were entirely reliant on the military not only for access to the battle zone but even for such basics as food. The resulting camaraderie gave a not-unnatural favorable twist to coverage. As it turned out, scholars who analyzed the coverage concluded that the framing from combat zones is largely, though not wholly, as the Pentagon had intended. The tone is favorable to the military and individual combat units. However, the reports from embedded reporters are packaged in larger-perspective accounts that also include material from war protesters, mostly in Europe, and the fractured diplomatic front.

In the 2004 presidential campaign, advertising in support of President Bush hammered at inconsistencies in the Senate voting record of Democratic challenger John Kerry. The goal was to frame Kerry in the public mind as wavering and unreliable. The Bush campaign also emphasized consistency on national defense. Kerry, on the other hand, worked at framing Bush as single-minded, if not simple-minded, on military issues and as easily misled, even duped, by ideologues among his advisers.

Partisan framing is the easiest to spot. But news, though usually cast in a dispassionate tone, is also subject to framing. Framing cannot be avoided. Not everything about an event or issue can be compacted into a 30-second television story item or even a 3,000-word magazine article. Reporters must choose what to include and what not to. Whatever a reporter's choices, the result is a framing of how the audience will see the reality.

LEARNING CHECK ◄ ....

▶ Why is it impossible for the news media to be complete and comprehensive?

MEDIA OBSESSIONS

Although critics argue that the media are politically biased, studies don't support this. Reporters perceive themselves as middle-of-the-road politically, and by and large they work to suppress personal biases. Even so, reporters gravitate toward certain kinds of stories to the neglect of others, and this flavors coverage.

■ **Presidential Coverage.** News reporters and editors have long recognized that people like stories about people, so any time an issue can be personified, so much the better. In Washington coverage, this has meant focusing on the president as a vehicle for treating issues. A study of the *CBS Evening News* found that 60 percent of the opening stories featured the president. Even in nonelection years the media have a near-myopic fix on the White House. This displaces coverage of other important government institutions, like Congress, the courts, and state and local government.

■ **Conflict.** Journalists learn two things about conflict early in their careers. First, their audiences like conflict. Second, conflict often illustrates the great issues by which society is defining and redefining its values. Take, for example, capital punishment, abortion or the draft. People get excited about these issues because of the fundamental values involved.

Part of journalists' predilection for conflict is that conflict involves change— whether to do something differently. All news involves change, and conflict almost always is a signal to the kind of change that's most worth reporting. Conflict is generally a useful indicator of newsworthiness.

■ **Scandals.** Journalists know too that their audiences like scandal stories—a fact that trivializes political coverage. Talking about the coverage of Bill Clinton early in his presidency, political scientists Morris Fiorina and Paul Peterson said: "The public was bombarded with stories about Whitewater, Vince Foster's suicide, $200 haircuts, parties with Sharon Stone, the White House travel office, Hillary Clinton's investments, and numerous other matters that readers will not remember. The reason you do not remember is that, however important these matters were to the individuals involved, they were not important for the overall operation of government. Hence, they have been forgotten."

No matter how transitory their news value, scandal and gaffe stories build audiences, which explains their increased coverage. Robert Lichter and Daniel Amundson, analysts who monitor Washington news coverage, found policy stories outnumbered scandal stories 13:1 in 1972 but only 3:1 in 1992. During that same period, news media have become more savvy at catering to audience interests and less interested in covering issues of significance. This also has led to more negative news being covered. Lichter and Amundson found that negative stories from Congress outnumbered positive stories 3:1 in 1972 but 9:1 in 1992.

● **horse race**
An election campaign treated by reporters like a game—who's ahead, who's falling back, who's coming up the rail

■ **Horse Races.** In reporting political campaigns, the news media obsess over reporting the polls. Critics say this treating of campaigns as **horse races** results in substantive issues being underplayed. Even when issues are the focus, as when a

Helen Thomas grew up in Detroit, one of nine children of Syrian immigrants. Her father couldn't read or write English. Helen and her brothers and sisters read the newspapers to him. By high school she had decided to be a journalist. After graduating from her hometown Wayne University, she headed to Washington. That was in 1942, and prospects for women in the male-dominated capital press corps were not as bleak as usual because World War II was sucking almost every able-bodied male, including journalists, into the military. Helen Thomas landed a job as a copy girl with the Washington *Daily News* for $17.50 a week. Somehow she survived the pink slips that most women journalists received when men began returning to their old jobs from the war.

In 1961 Helen Thomas switched to the White House. Within a few years she found herself the senior reporter, which meant, by tradition, that she and the Associated Press reporter alternated asking the first question of the president at news conferences. Also as senior reporter, it fell to her to close news conferences after an agreed-upon 30 minutes by saying, "Thank you, Mr. President."

During her tenure Helen Thomas consistently improved the status of women in journalism and the respect they deserve. She joined the Women's National Press Club, which had been formed in 1908 because the National Press Club refused to admit women even to cover newsworthy speeches. Thomas became president of the women's club in 1960 and kept pressure on its male counterpart to admit women. Finally, in 1971, the National Press Club admitted women.

Things have changed dramatically since then in Washington journalism. Thomas herself was elected president of the National Press Club in 1975, and she broke gender barriers at the Overseas Press Club, the White House Correspondents Association and the Gridiron Club.

It was the 2006 Gridiron Club dinner that gave Thomas a segue into her most memorable news conference question with President George W. Bush.

Dean of White House Correspondents. *At age 85, Helen Thomas is as quick as ever with questions that go the core. She has covered news conferences of every president back to Franklin Roosevelt.*

THOMAS: After that brilliant performance at the Gridiron [dinner], I am . . . (*fellow reporters and Bush break into laughter*). You're going to be sorry. (*more laughter*)

BUSH: Well, then, let me take it back. (*more laughter*)

THOMAS: I'd like to ask you, Mr. President, your decision to invade Iraq has caused the deaths of thousands of Americans and Iraqis, wounds of Americans and Iraqis for a lifetime. Every reason given, publicly at least, has turned out not to be true. My question is, why did you really want to go to war? From the moment you stepped into the White House, from your Cabinet—your Cabinet officers, intelligence people, and so forth—what was your real reason? You have said it wasn't oil—quest for oil, it hasn't been Israel, or anything else. What was it?

It was the first time, three years after the U.S.-led invasion of Iraq, that a reporter had capsulized growing frustration at the war in a direct question to President Bush. In a few words, without showing disrespect for the office of the presidency, Thomas had framed a truth-seeking question in a way that was impossible for even the well-rehearsed president to sidestep gracefully. It was a tough question put honestly, directly and poignantly.

It also was the kind of question that Thomas, in her 2006 book *Watchdogs of Democracy?*, argued is too seldom asked anymore. The Washington press corps has gone soft, she argues. She said media owners, beholden to government for broadcast licenses, had incubated a get-along mentality. Tightened news budgets meant short-staffing that precluded lots of labor-intensive journalistic digging. She also blamed government for a growing aggressive tendency to wield its bully pulpit to discredit news reports and reporters who venture from the party line.

WHAT DO YOU THINK?

▶ A seating chart that aides gave President Bush for a late 2007 news conference had Thomas marked as someone not to call on. Why would that be?

▶ Is Thomas correct in criticizing the White House news corps as having become wimpy?

469

candidate announces a major policy position, reporters connect the issue to its potential impact in the polls.

■ **Brevity.** People who design media packages, such as a newspaper or newscast, have devised presentation formats that favor shorter stories. This trend has been driven in part by broadcasting's severe time constraints. Network anchors have complained for years that they have to condense the world's news into 23 minutes on their evening newscasts. The result: short, often superficial treatments. The short-story format shifted to many newspapers and magazines, beginning with the launch of *USA Today* in 1982. *USA Today* obtained extremely high story counts, covering a great many events by running short stories—many only a half-dozen sentences. The effect on political coverage has been profound.

The **sound bites** in campaign stories, the actual voice of a candidate in a broadcast news story, dropped from 47 seconds in 1968 to 10 seconds in 1988 and have remained short. Issues that require lengthy explorations, say critics, get passed up. Candidates, eager for airtime, have learned to offer quippy, catchy, clever capsules that are likely to be picked up rather than articulate thoughtful, persuasive statements. The same dynamic is apparent in *USA Today*-style brevity.

Some people defend brevity, saying it's the only way to reach people whose increasingly busy lives don't leave them much time to track politics and government. In one generalization, brevity's defenders note that the short attention span of the MTV generation can't handle much more than 10-second sound bites. Sanford Ungar, the communication dean at American University, applauds the news media for devising writing and reporting styles that boil down complex issues so that they can be readily understood by great masses of people. Says Ungar: "If *USA Today* encourages people not to think deeply, or not to go into more detail about what's happening, then it will be a disservice. But if *USA Today* teaches people how to be concise and get the main points across sometimes, they're doing nothing worse than what television is doing, and doing it at least as well."

While many news organizations have moved to briefer and trendier government and political coverage, it's unfair to paint too broad a stroke. The New York *Times*, the Washington *Post* and the Los Angeles *Times* do not scrimp on coverage, and even *USA Today* has begun to carry more lengthy articles on government and politics. The television networks, which have been rapped the most for sound-bite coverage, also offer in-depth treatments outside of newscasts—such as the Sunday-morning programs.

Candidates have also discovered alternatives to their words and views being condensed and packaged. Not uncommon are candidate appearances on Oprah Winfrey's, Jay Leno's and David Letterman's shows and even on *Saturday Night Live*.

LEARNING CHECK ◄ ···

▶ **What is the problem with political news that fits predictable models?**

▶ **How are people short-changed by sound bites and other media tools that are used for brevity?**

Government Manipulation of Media

STUDY PREVIEW

Many political leaders are preoccupied with media coverage because they know the power it can have. Over the years they have developed mechanisms to influence coverage to their advantage.

INFLUENCING COVERAGE

Many political leaders stay up nights figuring out ways to influence media coverage. James Fallows, in his book *Breaking the News,* quoted a Clinton White House official: "When I was there, absolutely nothing was more important than figuring

Presidents and the Media. Franklin Roosevelt was not popular with most newspaper and magazine publishers. Editorials opposed his election in 1932, and whatever sparse support there was for his ideas to end the Great Depression was fading. Two months after taking office, Roosevelt decided to try radio to communicate directly to the people, bypassing the traditional reporting and editing process that didn't always work in his favor. In his first national radio address, Roosevelt explained the steps he had taken to meet the nation's financial emergency. It worked. The president came across well on radio, and people were fascinated to hear their leader live and direct. Roosevelt's "fireside chats" became a fixture of his administration, which despite editorial negativism, would continue for 13 years—longer than any in U.S. history. John Kennedy used television as Roosevelt had used radio, and every political leader since, for better or worse, has recognized the value of the mass media as a vehicle for governance.

out what the news was going to be. . . . There is no such thing as a substantive discussion that is not shaped or dominated by how it is going to play in the press."

The game of trying to outsmart the news media is nothing new. Theodore Roosevelt, at the turn of the 20th century, chose Sundays to issue many announcements. Roosevelt recognized that editors producing Monday newspapers usually had a dearth of news because weekends, with government and business shut down, didn't generate much worth telling. Roosevelt's Sunday announcements, therefore, received more prominent play in Monday editions. With typical bullishness, Roosevelt claimed that he had "discovered Mondays." Compared to how sophisticated government leaders have become at manipulating press coverage today, Roosevelt was a piker.

LEARNING CHECK ◄

▶ **How do political leaders use the calendar and news flow to their advantage?**

TRIAL BALLOONS AND LEAKS

● **trial balloon**
A deliberate leak of a potential policy, usually from a diversionary source, to test public response

To check weather conditions, meteorologists send up balloons. To get an advance peek at public reaction, political leaders float **trial balloons.** When Richard Nixon was considering shutting down radio and television stations at night to conserve electricity during the 1973 energy crisis, the idea was floated to the press by a subordinate. The reaction was so swift and so negative that the idea was shelved. Had there not been a negative reaction or if reaction had been positive, then the president himself would have unveiled the plan as his own.

● **leak**
A deliberate disclosure of confidential or classified information by someone who wants to advance the public interest, embarrass a bureaucratic rival or supervisor, or disclose incompetence or skullduggery

Trial balloons are not the only way in which the media can be used. Partisans and dissidents use **leaks** to bring attention to their opponents and people they don't much like. In leaking, someone passes information to reporters on condition that he or she not be identified as the source. While reporters are leery of many leakers, some information is so significant and from such reliable sources that it's hard to pass up.

It's essential that reporters understand how their sources intend information to be used. It is also important for sources to have some control over what they tell reporters. Even so, reporter-source relationships lend themselves to abuse by manipulative government officials. Worse, the structures of these relationships allow officials to throttle what's told to the people. As political scientists Karen O'Connor and Larry Sabato said: "Every public official knows that journalists are pledged to protect the confidentiality of sources, and therefore the rules can be used to an official's

own benefit—but, say, giving reporters derogatory information to print about a source without having to be identified with the source." This manipulation is a regrettable, though unavoidable, part of the news-gathering process.

LEARNING CHECK ◄ •••

▶ **How do reporter relationships with sources affect news positively? And negatively?**

▶ **Should reporter–source relationships be transparent to news audiences? How?**

STONEWALLING

When Richard Nixon was under fire for ordering a cover-up of the Watergate break-in, he went months without a news conference. His aides plotted his movements to avoid even informal, shouted questions from reporters. He hunkered down in the White House in a classic example of **stonewalling.** Experts in the branch of public relations called political communications generally advise against stonewalling because people infer guilt or something to hide. Nonetheless, it is one way to deal with difficult media questions.

A variation on stonewalling is the **news blackout.** When U.S. troops invaded Grenada, the Pentagon barred the press. Reporters who hired runabout boats to get to the island were intercepted by a U.S. naval blockade. While heavy-handed, such limitations on media coverage do, for a limited time, give the government the opportunity to report what's happening from its self-serving perspective.

Recollection Lapses. The chief of the U.S. Justice Department later in the Bush administration, Attorney General Alberto Gonzales, frustrated congressional critics with repeated claims that he couldn't remember details about controversial decisions that raised constitutional issues. Gonzales didn't grant news media interviews. Critics challenged his credibility. After months of stonewalling he resigned.

LEARNING CHECK ◄ •••

▶ **Do "no comment" answers from political leaders serve democracy well?**

▶ **How about ducking questions or giving evasive answers?**

OVERWHELMING INFORMATION

● **stonewalling**
To refuse to answer questions, sometimes refusing even to meet with reporters

● **news blackout**
When a person or institution decides to issue no statements despite public interest and also declines news media questions

During the Persian Gulf buildup in 1990 and the war itself, the Pentagon tried a new approach in media relations. Pete Williams, the Pentagon's chief spokesperson, provided so much information, including video, sound bites and data, that reporters were overwhelmed. The result was that reporters spent so much time sorting through Pentagon-provided material, all of it worthy, that they didn't have time to compose difficult questions or pursue fresh story angles of their own. As a result, war coverage was almost entirely favorable to George H. W. Bush's administration.

LEARNING CHECK ◄ •••

▶ **How can newspeople deal with information overloads that work against sorting out significant news from lesser stuff?**

Political Campaigns

STUDY PREVIEW

Elections are a key point in democratic governance, which explains the scrutiny that news media coverage receives. Also, the partisanship inherent in a campaign helps ensure that media missteps are identified quickly. Some criticism of media is of news, other of advertisements that media are paid to carry.

CAMPAIGN COVERAGE

Critics fault the news media for falling short in covering political campaigns. These are frequent criticisms:

- **Issues.** Reporters need to push for details on positions and ask tough questions on major issues, not accept generalities. They need to bounce one candidate's position off other candidates, creating a forum of intelligent discussion from which voters can make informed choices.
- **Agenda.** Reporters need to assume some role in setting a campaign agenda. When reporters allow candidates to control the agenda of coverage, reporters become mere conduits for self-serving news releases and images from candidates. **Pseudo-events** with candidates, like visits to photogenic flag factories, lack substance. So do staged **photo-ops.** Reporters need to guard against letting such easy-to-cover events squeeze out substantive coverage.
- **Interpretation.** Campaigns are drawn out and complicated, and reporters need to keep trying to pull together what's happened for the audience. Day-to-day spot news isn't enough. There also need to be explanation, interpretation and analysis to help voters see the big picture.
- **Inside coverage.** Reporters need to cover the machinery of the campaigns—who's running things and how. This is especially important with the growing role of campaign consultants. Who are these people? What history do they bring to a campaign? What agenda?
- **Polling.** Poll results are easy to report but tricky and inconsistent because of variations in methodology and even questions. News operations should report on competing polls, not just their own. In tracking polls, asking the same questions over time for consistency is essential.
- **Depth.** With candidates going directly to voters in debates and talk-show appearances and on blogs, reporters need to offer something more than what voters can see and hear for themselves. Analysis and depth add a fresh dimension that is not redundant to what the audience already knows.
- **Instant feedback.** Television newsrooms have supplemented their coverage and commentary with instant e-mail feedback from viewers. Select messages are flashed on-screen within minutes. In some programs a reporter is assigned to analyze incoming messages and identify trends. While all this makes for

● pseudo-event
A staged event to attract media attention, usually lacking substance

● photo-op
Short for "photo opportunity." A staged event, usually photogenic, to attract media attention

The People's Questions. Pressing the flesh, historically a political campaign necessity, went virtual in 2008 with the CNN–YouTube debates during the primaries. Voters uploaded videos questions, some with clever animations and mini-skits. From thousands of submissions, CNN culled questions that were put to candidates. YouTube questions came mostly from young people, who have absorbed the video-upload site into their lifestyles.

"good television," the comments are statistically dubious as indicators of overall public opinion. Too much can be read into them.

LEARNING CHECK ◄ ·······································

▶ **Rank the list of common criticisms of campaign news coverage. How do you justify your ranking?**

ATTACK ADS

● **negative ads**
Political campaign advertising, usually on television, in which a candidate criticizes the opponent rather than emphasizing his or her own platform

The 2004 presidential campaign spawned **negative ads** in unprecedented quantity. With little regard for facts or truth, Republicans loosely connected to the Bush campaign, under the banner of Swift Boat Veterans for Truth, ripped at the war-hero record of Democratic candidate John Kerry. Then there was the entry in a campaign advertising contest that likened George W. Bush to Hitler, which an anti-Bush group, moveon.org, let sit on its Web site for days.

Negativism is not new in politics. An 1884 ditty that makes reference to Grover Cleveland's illegitimate child is still a favorite among folk singers. Negativism took center stage in 1952 when the Republican slogan "Communism, Corruption, Korea" slammed outgoing President Truman's Korea policy. Two hunkered-down soldiers, portrayed by actors, were lamenting a shortage of weapons. Then one soldier was killed, and the other charged courageously into enemy fire. The **attack ad** demonstrated the potency of political advertising in the new medium of television.

● **attack ads**
A subspecies of negative ads, especially savage in criticizing an opponent, many playing loosely with context and facts

● **527 status**
Used by groups unaffiliated with candidates or parties to collect and spend unlimited funds

■ **527 Financing.** The 2004 wave of attack ads were mostly from shadowy groups not directly affiliated with candidates or parties. These groups operated under what was called **527 status** in the federal campaign law. Unlike the parties and candidates, the 527s were allowed to collect unlimited money independently. The 527s had raised an incredible $240 million within a month of election day. Although there was widespread disgust at the nastiest 527 ads, experts who tracked polls concluded they had significant influence. When Congress reconvened in 2005, there were cries for reforms to curb the influence of the 527 organizations. Nothing happened.

■ **Making Light.** Amid the 2004 campaign negativity, Senator Russ Feingold of Wisconsin took a different tack—humor. Just as commercial advertising relies largely on evoking chuckles, Feingold did the same and won re-election. Whether easygoing self-deprecation and deft fun-poking are antidotes that will displace attack ads, or at least reduce their role, may be determined by whether 2008 candidates and their advisers have a good sense of humor and also decency and good taste.

LEARNING CHECK ◄ ·······································

▶ **Negative political advertising is easy to criticize, but what can be done about it?**

Chapter Wrap-Up

Media Role in Governance (Page 462)

■ The U.S. democratic system relies on the mass media as an outside check to keep government accountable to the people. The concept has many labels, including the press as a fourth branch of government. The similar label *fourth estate* comes from feudal European times. A more modern variation characterizes the press as a watchdog on government. The concept has given rise to the informally put goal of "keeping them honest." The First Amendment gives an autonomous role to the press, although government regulation exists, particularly of broadcasting, as an anomaly.

Media Effects on Governance (Page 466)

■ For lack of time and space to report all that might be reported, the media are selective in their coverage. What makes the news ends up on the public's agenda. The rest misses radar screens. This reality has been described in numerous variations, including agenda-setting, the CNN Effect and framing. What it all means is that we are dependent on the intelligence and goodwill of newspeople to use good judgment in their news choices. News people can be faulted for their focus on easily told aspects of stories, for superficiality, and for missing stories worth telling. Competition among news sources helps correct the worst shortcomings.

Government Manipulation of Media (Page 470)

■ Political leaders quickly learn techniques to influence if not manipulate news coverage in their favor. Floating ideas, sometimes with plausible deniability as to their source, is one method for peeking at how the media and the public might respond on an issue. It's called the trial balloon. Leaks of explosive information to the press, sometimes intended to damage reputations, are another method of bending the news media for ulterior motives.

Political Campaigns (Page 472)

■ The same factors that lead to formulaic and superficial government news coverage extend also to political campaigns. Issues take a backseat to the latest poll numbers, reducing campaigns to a kind of horse race caricature. Polls are important, but no less is citizens' thorough attention to candidates' character and positions. Besides news coverage, the mass media carry advertisements paid for by candidates and their supporters and, also, sometimes attack ads from opponents who can get really nasty and are not always accurate or honest. Dealing with the worst negative advertising is an unresolved issue. Everybody talks about it, but not much is being done.

REVIEW QUESTIONS

1. By what authority are news media the people's watchdog for government accountability?

2. How do mass media influence public policy?

3. What are major government tools for manipulating news coverage?

4. Why is news coverage of political issues often formulaic and superficial?

CONCEPTS

agenda-setting (Page 466)

fourth estate (Page 462)

fairness doctrine (Page 464)

Tornillo opinion (Page 464)

CNN Effect (Page 467)

TERMS

equal time rule (Page 464)

attack ads (Page 474)

stonewalling (Page 472)

527 status (Page 474)

watchdog role (Page 462)

PEOPLE

Edmund Burke (Page 462)

Maxwell McCombs, Don Shaw (Page 466)

MEDIA SOURCES

● Helen Thomas. *Watchdogs of Democracy? The Waning Washington Press Corps and How It Has Failed the Public.* Scribner/Lisa Dew, 2006. Thomas, a veteran White House reporter, blames adversarial news media on an unholy alliance of big government and big business to control the news, sometimes subtly, sometimes not.

● David D. Perlmutter. "Political Blogs: The New Iowa?" *Chronicle of Higher Education* (May 26, 2006), Pages B6–B8. Perlmutter, a political scientist, examines the potential of blogs in presidential campaigns. He has as many questions as answers about this new medium in candidates' quivers.

● Craig Crawford. *Attack the Messenger: How Politicians Turn You Against the Messenger.* Littlefield, 2005. Crawford, a *Congressional Quarterly* columnist, examines White House policies in the Bush administrations to undermine the mainstream news media.

MASS MEDIA AND GOVERNANCE:

In this chapter you have deepened your media literacy by revisiting several themes. Here are thematic highlights from the chapter:

Media Technology

Since the earliest days of the republic, political candidates and leaders have used leading media technology to seek public support. Newspapers were the medium of choice back then. Newspapers were joined by radio in the 1930s, when President Franklin Roosevelt combined the novelty of the emerging medium and a public yearning for leadership to solve the Great Depression. As a political tool, radio came of age during Roosevelt's four terms. In 1960, Senator John Kennedy exuded confidence, some said charisma, on television. He won the presidency. A former Vermont governor, Howard Dean, relied on the Internet to raise funds for his 2004 presidential bid and to spread his message. Dean washed out in later primaries. Nonetheless he wrote the how-to-book for other candidates on the potential of the latest mass medium and of blogging. **(Pages 470–474)**

Photogenic Candidates. *The role of television and other visual media in politics is undeniable. Could the portly William Howard Taft, who won the presidency in pretelevision 1912, be elected president today? Taft carried 321 pounds. In 1960 John Kennedy's calm command of issues won over voters in a televised debate as his opponent, Richard Nixon, sweated in obvious discomfort in the studio lights. Kennedy won.*

Elitism and Populism

British political philosopher Edmund Burke put a name to the role of the news media in the political life of a democratic society. Burke called the press a *fourth estate*, every much as powerful as the nobility, the clergy and the common people as institutions that influence the course of events. The founders of the United States saw the press as a conduit for information and ideas, back and forth between the people and the elected leadership. In the United States the press came to be called a *fourth branch* of government, in addition to the executive, legislative and judicial branches, but functioning outside the structure of the constituted branches. **(Page 462)**

Media and Democracy

Edmund Burke. *His contributions to modern political thought came in essays and speeches, mostly in the 1770s and later. Burke, who served in Parliament, saw the role of political parties as an important link between competing branches of government and as vehicles for continuity. He saw the press as a powerful vehicle in the political process. He called the press a* fourth estate *and declared it as powerful as the traditional institutions of society—the nobility, the clergy and commoners.*

Mass media have essential roles in democracy, including that of watchdog. Theoretically immune to government control under the U.S. Constitution, the media are like an outside auditor to assure the people of government accountability. The media accountability system, however, lacks the precision of audits in the sense of bookkeeping and works unevenly. Working against the accountability system is that political leaders have mastered tools for influencing news coverage to their advantage. Also, the media sometimes falter in their watchdog function. **(Pages 463–466 and 470–472)**

A Thematic Chapter Summary

Media Future

With the first $1 billion presidential campaign looming for 2008, most of it for television advertising, campaign spending reform is a bigger issue than ever. The costs have forced candidates into a financial dependency on big donors, many with self-serving public policy agendas. Existing limits on campaign spending donations are so big that deep-pocket donors could drive truckloads of cash through. Major advertising, for example, is funded by shadowy partisan organizations that support some candidates but have no direct ties to the candidates. Proposals also grew top give candidates free time for advertising on television, which is the most-used medium. **(Pages 472–474)**

Media and Culture

Lifestyle changes wrought by mass media technology don't settle easily with everyone. In political life, candidates and leaders with squeaky voices and shrill pitches don't come across effectively. The CNN-YouTube presidential debates in 2007 attempted to employ the immense new popularity of video sharing on the Internet, a sudden staple in the U.S. youth culture, in the public policy dialogue in the presidential campaigns. One candidate, Mitt Romney, at first declined to participate in the debates. He said he preferred questions from professional journalists and characterized YouTube questions as "disrespectful." **(Page 470–473)**

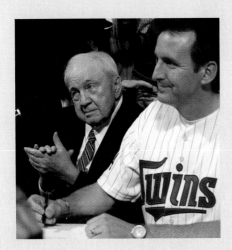

Fourth Estate. *The rationale for news being independent of government control worked, albeit too late, when a commuter-clogged bridge collapsed in Minneapolis because of unmended structural shortcomings. To the chagrin of Minnesota Governor Tim Pawlenty, news reports divulged the governor's support of state spending to build a new Twins baseball stadium even as the state's highway infrastructure was falling apart. The dichotomy was driven home by photos of Pawlenty grinning at Twins fans three months earlier while signing the stadium legislation. Within a week of the bridge collapse, however, Pawlenty announced that he had changed his position against a gasoline tax increase to generate new revenue for highway repairs.*

Not MyTube. *Presidential hopeful Mitt Romney turned down an initial invitation to the CNN-YouTube debates. He didn't want to encourage "disrespectful" questions. Whether Romney's refusal hurt his standing with young voters, many for whom YouTube is a favorite site, wasn't clear. One wag encouraged Romney to loosen up: "Maybe Mrs. Romney should put less starch in his boxers." In the end, Romney relented and participated in the debate.*

19

Mass-Media Law

Shaking Up Hollywood

By the age of 12 Jon Lech Johansen had written his first computer program. That made him a wunderkid of sorts. But nobody foresaw that he would, while still a teenager, devise programs that would shake the billion-dollar Hollywood movie industry to its core. His genius, also, would make him a folk hero to millions of movie-lovers worldwide.

Jon-Lech, as he came to be lionized in his native Norway, began his trek to notoriety unwittingly. He loved movies. By 15 he owned 360 DVDs. Some he bought at jacked-up Norwegian prices because Hollywood's geographical coding prevented European computers from playing U.S.-issued versions. Other DVDs he bought from U.S. sources, and with coding he invented, he played them on his computer in Oslo. It all was perfectly legal in Norway. He recalls reveling at his accomplishment when he first ripped copies of *The Matrix* and *The Fifth Element*.

"Why shouldn't others share my enjoyment?" he asked himself. A week later he posted his coding on the Internet.

Hollywood went ballistic, recognizing that Jon-Lech's coding could be used to bypass the encrypting that prevented their DVD movies from being easily swapped through file-sharing. The revenue loss could be devastating. The Motion Picture Association of America pushed Norwegian authorities to act. Police raided the Johansen home, confiscated Jon-Lech's computer, and put him through seven hours of interrogation. Confident he had done nothing wrong, Jon-Lech even gave police the password to his computer.

Waiting for the Judge. Jon Lech Johansen waits for his case to begin in a Norway court. The U.S. movie industry had gone after DVD Jon, as he came to be called, for publishing code that enabled others to copy disks. He was acquitted.

Johansen thus became the vortex of a continuing struggle between the rights of megamedia conglomerates that own creative material and the rights of individuals to do what they want with products they buy—in this case copying DVDs, and also music, to play on any number of their own devices.

For the trial, Hollywood executives flew to Oslo to argue that Johansen had unleashed software that facilitated movie piracy and could put the movie industry in ruins. Johansen responded that he had committed no wrongdoing, let alone piracy, and that he had a fundamental human right of free expression to share his coding however he wanted. In effect, he said: "Go after the pirates, not me." Jon-Lech fancied himself a consumer advocate, allowing people to use their DVD purchases as they wanted—on computers at home, on laptops on the road, on handheld devices anywhere else. The court agreed. In fact, when the prosecution appealed, the court again agreed.

In the run-up to the trial, Jon-Lech supporters worldwide distributed t-shirts and neckties printed with his software. In the May Day parade in Oslo, backers carried a banner "Free DVD-Jon." The issue inspired a haiku. Meanwhile, more than 1 million copies of his anti-DVD encryption software had been downloaded from Johansen's site.

For better or worse, depending on your perspective, Norway later revised its laws to forbid software that could be used to undermine copyright protections, as the United States had done earlier at the behest of giant media companies. But the issue lives on, as you will discover in this chapter on mass-media law. The chapter includes the most pressing media law dilemma in the early 21st century—the protection of intellectual property.

Intellectual Property

....

STUDY PREVIEW

Products produced by mass-media companies go by the legal name of intellectual property. Copyright law protects ownership rights to intellectual property. Other rights, including consumer rights and free expression rights, have arisen to challenge the long-held supremacy of copyright. Mass-media companies are worried.

COPYRIGHT

● **copyright**
Protects the ownership rights of creative works, including books, articles, lyrics

Copyright has been around since the beginning of the Republic. The founders wrote copyright law into the Constitution. When Congress first convened in 1790, the second law to be passed was for copyright. The whole idea was to encourage creativity. With creative work classified as property, creative people have a legal right to derive income from their works by charging for their use. An author, for

The Price of Free Music

Imagine opening an urgent e-mail from the Recording Industry Association of America accusing you of illegally downloading hundreds of songs onto your computer. Indeed, you have used a file-sharing program you found on the Internet to build your music collection. By doing this, the e-mail charges, you have violated federal copyright law. The law, you're reminded, grants rights to an artist, publisher or distributor for exclusive publication, production, sale or distribution of artistic work. The message from the RIAA is threatening: Settle now for several thousand dollars or we'll see you in federal court.

A hoax? Not for several hundred college students who have received these "prelitigation" e-mails. Most students settle, despite feeling that they were unfairly singled out. After all, it's estimated that more than half of all college students illegally download copyrighted music and movies. As one 20-year-old student who recently received the RIAA e-mail explained: "I knew it was illegal, but no one got in trouble for it."

But now people are getting in trouble. In addition to the lawsuits against individual music downloaders, the recording industry and other copyright owners have sued and won against several Web sites that either have file-sharing technology or encourage file-sharing with instructions on how to do it.

Yet, copyright violations continue to cost the artistic community billions of dollars. And with less money to reward artistic endeavors, some are concerned that artists will not be able to support themselves and that the companies that distribute the art will be less willing to invest because of diminishing returns. There are also those who argue that copyright violators hurt honest people because the artistic community has to increase prices to offset losses to copyright infringers.

With new technology constantly allowing for the possibility of copyright violations, the future is far from certain for both the artist and his or her downloading audience.

IF YOU CAN'T SEE THAT ILLEGAL DOWNLOADING IS STEALING THEN KEEP READING

1
2
3
4
5
6
7

If you download music illegally, you are stealing music.

Every month, thousands of students face university disciplinary action or lawsuits and fines that cost thousands of dollars.

Legal downloading doesn't cost much. The choice is yours. Pay a little now or a lot more later.

RIAA

Developed by university students for the RIAA.

Piracy Not Nice.
The recording industry, crippled by revenue losses from music file-swapping, has gone after downloaders, mostly college students, for copyright infringement. Legal settlements can run into thousands of dollars.

DEEPENING YOUR MEDIA LITERACY

EXPLORE THE ISSUE

Think of Web sites that allow people to download music or movies legally.

DIG DEEPER

Do you think that the lawsuits brought by the recording industry will solve the problem of illegal downloading? Are there alternatives? Would legislation help? How about education programs starting in grade school?

WHAT DO YOU THINK?

Individuals who download music may not be the only ones being sued. Media giant Viacom has sued YouTube because its users can illegally upload Viacom movies. The Viacom suit raises questions about the Digital Millennium Copyright Act, which Congress created to shield Internet service providers from the responsibility for copyrighted material posted by subscribers. Is it just a matter of time before individual YouTube users are also sued for sharing copyrighted media without permission?

example, can charge a book publisher a fee for publishing the book. Actually, it's a little more complicated, but that's the idea. The goal was to guarantee a financial incentive for creative people to keep creating. Why? The rationale was that a society is richer for literature and music and other creative works. Inventions, which are covered by patents, are a separate area of **intellectual property** law.

■ **Permissions.** Copyright law allows creators to control their creation. They can sell it, lease it, give it away, or just sit on it. The law is the vehicle through which creative people earn a livelihood just as someone in the trades, like a carpenter earning money from carpentry, or a landlord earning money by renting out real estate. Creators of intellectual property grant **permissions** for the use of their work, usually for a fee. Freelance photographers charge magazines that want to use their photographs. Composers charge music publishers that want to issue their music.

■ **Assignments.** As a practical matter, most photographers, composers, authors and other creators of intellectual property don't have the expertise or means to exploit the commercial potential of their work. Simon & Schuster, for example, can better market a hot murder mystery than the best whodunit author. Imagine Jay-Z without Def Jam. Or a Mark Burnett eco-adventure show without CBS. Although there are notable Lone Rangers, the resources of major media companies make it attractive for the creators of intellectual property to sell or assign their rights to a media company. In exchange for the **assignment** of their rights, the originating creator usually receives a flat fee or a percentage of the eventual revenue.

Also, media companies hire creative people whose work, as part of their employment, belongs automatically to the company.

For media companies these rights are a treasure trove. It's their product. It's what they have to sell. No surprise, media companies vigilantly guard their intellectual property against theft, or **piracy,** as they call it. Hollywood studios have dozens of attorneys who monitor for **infringements** of their copyrights. So do music companies. Magazines and newspapers are increasingly active in identifying infringements. Not uncommonly, media companies go to court against anyone who expropriates their property without permission and without paying a fee.

LEARNING CHECK ◄ ┄┄┄┄┄┄┄┄┄┄┄┄┄┄┄┄┄┄┄┄┄┄┄┄┄┄┄┄┄┄┄┄

▸ **Who are the various parties that can own a copyright?**

▸ **What recourse do copyright owners have against infringements?**

CONSUMER RIGHTS

Predictably, mass-media companies overreact when a threat to their tried-and-true business models presents itself. This has been no more true than in frenzied, almost Luddite attempts by media companies to apply copyright law to shield their old and comfortable ways of doing business. Time and again, media companies, wedded to the past, have failed to think outside the box and exploit new technologies. In fact, not since the glory days of RCA, which prided itself on research and development under David Sarnoff, have established companies been on the technological cutting edge.

Recent history has shown media companies merely making tepid applications of technology for modest advantages in efficiency. Then, wham, they find their existence on the verge of being upended by innovators who are seeing new basic infrastructures and saying to hell with old business models. Consider the movie industry in the Betamax case, the recorded music industry in the Napster and Grokster cases, and the book industry in the Google case.

■ **Betamax.** With copyright a core of their whole corporate structure, media companies went into a flailing frenzy in 1975 after Sony, the Japanese electronic hardware manufacturer, introduced its **Betamax** device, an advanced tape recorder for recording movies and other programs off television and also off other tapes. Hollywood sued, arguing that Sony was enabling people to infringe on

● **intellectual property**
Creative works

● **permissions**
Grant of rights for a second party to use copyright-protected work

● **assignment**
Transfer of ownership interest in a piece of intellectual property

● **piracy**
Theft of copyright-protected material

● **infringement**
A violation of copyright

● **Betamax**
An early home video recording-playback device that became the namesake for the U.S. Supreme Court decision that time-shifting was a fair use exemption under copyright law

copyrights by recording movies and swapping them, even selling them. As Hollywood told it, the future of the movie industry as an American icon was in jeopardy unless the intellectual rights of movie studios were protected. Ironically, Sony also owned the former Columbia studio and was itself a major producer of movies, but that didn't deter the earnestness of the rest of the industry's protest and legal action.

In court Sony responded that although its Betamax device could be misused, as can any invention, the idea was to allow people to record material for their own replay at a later, more convenient time. It was a moment in U.S. history when two powerful forces, the Consumer Movement, dating to the 1960s, and the Copyright Community, comprising the media companies, were in a dramatic confrontation. In a landmark decision, the U.S. Supreme Court bought Sony's argument for **time-shifting**—that recording for personal replay later was a legitimate activity and not protected by copyright.

Betamax devices now are history, eclipsed by VCRs and now DVD players. The lesson, though, is that Hollywood panicked—yet another demonstration of entrenched media companies lacking the imagination to adapt to new technology and restructure themselves fundamentally. Confronted with the hard reality of the U.S. Supreme Court decision, the movie studios realized that their old and comfortable ways of doing business were no longer viable. Thus began a Hollywood self-reinvention of the movie distribution infrastructure. Today 85 percent of Hollywood's revenue comes from rentals of the sort that Betamax made possible. Consumers have prevailed. By embracing the home video recording technology, Hollywood has emerged stronger than ever with an additional revenue base.

■ **Grokster.** A quarter century later the music recording industry, entrenched in its traditional ways of doing business, was in a frenzy with music-swapping software sales eroding profits dramatically. First with Napster, then other peer-to-peer music-sharing services, people were bypassing the retail CD bins. Napster was the first to hit the dust, in a 2001 federal court case. Then came the case against **Grokster,** another peer-to-peer service. Picking up a lesson from the Betamax defense, Grokster acknowledged that its software was neutral as to the rights and wrongs of copyright law. Yes, said Grokster, there could be misuses but the recording industry's legal target should be the misusers—not Grokster.

In deciding the case in 2005, the Supreme Court noted that Grokster had explicitly promoted the copyright-infringement potential of its software. It was right there in the company's own advertising. The self-incriminating ads, the Court said,

● **time-shifting**
Recording of television programs and movies for later viewing

● **Grokster**
Involved in U.S. Supreme Court case that said promoting the illegal copying of intellectual property is an infringement on copyright

Download Protest. *Among young people, emotions run high about music. A widely held view is that access to music should be free. When the U.S. Supreme Court was hearing the Grokster case over software intended to facilitate music downloads without the permission of copyright holders, protesters displayed their disdain for the record industry's initiative to shut down file-sharing.*

made the case substantively different from Betamax's. Grokster was out of business. Although the Betamax and Grokster decisions went different ways, the lesson from the cases is that infringement-enabling devices are all right as long as infringement isn't encouraged.

In any event, the music recording industry was shaken by Napster and look-alike systems like Grokster. The end result, after the legal battles, was that the industry came out of its decades-old buffered ways, which had been shielded by copyright law, and embraced the new technology. Even by the time of the Grokster decision, the Germany-owned global media giant Bertelsmann had bought the remnants of Napster to find ways to market its music online. Also, Apple's online music store, iTunes, introduced in 2002, was an instant success. Other online music sales outlets cropped up, sponsored by record makers, to capitalize on new technology—not to fight it or go into denial.

■ **Google.** The book industry, also entrenched in old ways, missed the potential of digital technology. Except for back-shop production efficiencies, which were invisible to readers, and marketing Web sites and minor forays with e-books, publishers had to be dragged kicking and screaming into the 21st century, like the movie and recording industries before them. Google was the reason.

Fueled with untold revenues from its massively successful search engine in the early 2000s, Google expanded rapidly into new ventures. In 2005 Google executives talked five major libraries into allowing it to digitize their entire collections, 15 million books in the English language. The goal, then, was to create a single on-line index system, the **Google Print Library Project,** with worldwide free access.

Publishers first bristled, then sued. The claim was that their intellectual property interests would be jeopardized through free online access to copyright-protected works not yet in the public domain.

The outcome of the suit against Googlization of entire books, unresolved at the time this edition went to press, may create new parameters on the protections afforded by copyright law. Whatever the outcome, the case further illustrates that mass media companies are less in control of the technology that is reshaping the world than are companies and individuals who specialize in the research and creative thinking that brings about technical revolution.

LEARNING CHECK ◄

▸ **How have the Consumer Rights movement and the Copyright Community collided?**

▸ **What lessons about copyright can be derived from the Betamax decision?**

▸ **What lessons about copyright can be derived from the Grokster decision?**

▸ **What are the copyright issues in the Google library project?**

● **Google Print Library Project**
Digitizes 15 million English-language books for online index access; by Google

Free Expression

STUDY PREVIEW

A core American value is that the government cannot impede free expression, which, of course, extends to the mass media. Although the U.S. Constitution bars government censorship, the courts have allowed exceptions. These exceptions include utterances that could undermine national security in wartime. In general the Supreme Court has expanded the prohibition on censorship over the years, all in the libertarian spirit articulated by John Milton in the 1600s.

● **John Milton**
Devised marketplace of ideas concept

● **marketplace of ideas**
People are capable of identifying good ideas among many as long as they have access to them all

IDEAS OF JOHN MILTON

Intellectually, the founders of the United States in the late 1780s were smitten with the ideas of **John Milton** from almost 150 years earlier. Milton had advanced the **marketplace of ideas** concept. In his essay *Areopagitica* in 1644, Milton saw free expression as the vehicle for putting a vast range of ideas into circulation.

His marketplace of ideas was akin to any marketplace, where people pick and choose the best—the more vendors, theoretically the better the chance of finding the very best items. Milton saw censorship as the enemy because censorship excludes potentially valuable ideas from consideration.

Milton, who also was a novelist, still is quoted for his eloquent summation of his concept. Paraphrased slightly: "Let truth and falsehood grapple, whoever knew truth put to the worse in a free and open encounter." Milton was confident that individual human beings could sort the wheat from the chaff.

The founders of the Republic were mostly **libertarians** like Milton, heady in a positive view of individuals and their power of reason. Censorship, at least theoretically, was anathema to letting individuals use their minds to chart their own best courses and also for society to find its way toward attaining common goals. In its purest form, libertarianism means uninhibited freedom of inquiry and expression.

LEARNING CHECK ◄ ···

▶ **How has John Milton's marketplace of ideas concept heavily influenced the role of the mass media in contemporary society?**

DISTRUST OF GOVERNMENT

In colonial times, before the formation of the United States, a critical mass of libertarians ascended into leadership roles as ill feeling grew against British authority. These people were still in critical leadership roles when the Revolutionary War ended. These included many luminaries of the time—Thomas Jefferson, Benjamin Franklin, James Madison, John Adams. Their rhetoric excoriated the top-down authoritarian British governance system.

In drafting the Constitution for the new republic, the founders, mindful of their experience as part of the British empire, were firm in their distrust of governmental authority. Also, true Miltonians, they exalted the ability of people individually and collectively to figure out their way to the best courses of action through free inquiry and free expression in an unregulated marketplace of ideas. The Constitution they put together prohibits government from interfering in free expression. The prohibition is in the Constitution's **First Amendment:** "Congress shall make no law . . . abridging the freedom of speech or of the press." The amendment, a mere 45 words, also prohibits government from interfering in religion. Also, it guarantees people the right to complain about the government and demand that wrongs be righted. Most relevant for media people are the free speech and free press clauses, which can be summed up as the **free expression provision.**

Implicit in the First Amendment is a role for the mass media as a watchdog guarding against government misdeeds and policies. In this respect, the media, in news as well as in other content areas, are an informal **fourth branch of government**—in addition to the executive, judicial and legislative branches. The media have a role in governance to, in effect, ensure that the government is accountable to the people.

LEARNING CHECK ◄ ···

▶ **Describe the roots of the First Amendment in libertarian principles.**

FIRST AMENDMENT REDISCOVERED

As ironic as it seems, merely six years after the Constitution and the First Amendment were ratified, Congress passed laws to limit free expression. People were jailed and fined for criticizing government leaders and policies. These laws, the **Alien and Sedition acts** of 1798, ostensibly were for national security at a time of paranoia about a French invasion. One of the great mysteries in U.S. history is how Congress, which included many of the same people who had created the Constitution, could so contradict the Milton spirit.

● **libertarian**
A person who believes human beings must be free, or *at liberty*, to pursue their individual fulfillment

● **First Amendment**
Prohibits government interference in free expression, religion and individual and public protests against government policies

● **free expression provision**
First Amendment ban against government abridgment of freedom of speech and freedom of the press

● **fourth branch of government**
The mass media

● **Alien and Sedition acts**
1798 laws with penalties for free expression

The fact, however, is that nobody paid much attention to the First Amendment for a century. It was a nice idea but complicated. Nobody wanted to tackle tough questions like, as in the case of the 1798 laws, whether there needed to be exceptions to free expression in times of war or a threat.

Many states, meanwhile, had laws that explicitly limited freedom of expression. The constitutionality of these laws, too, went unchallenged.

Not until 1919 did the U.S. Supreme Court decide a case on First Amendment grounds. Two Socialists, husband and wife **Charles Schenck** and **Elizabeth Baer,** had been arrested by federal agents for distributing an anti-war pamphlet. They sued, contending that the government had violated their free expression rights as guaranteed by the First Amendment. The Supreme Court turned down their appeal, saying that censorship is reasonable in war, but the justices acknowledged in the case, usually called *Schenck* v. *U.S.,* that freedom from government restraint is a civil right of every citizen.

Numerous other censorship cases also flowed from World War I. In 1925 the Court overruled a New York state law under which anti-war agitator **Benjamin Gitlow** had been arrested. Gitlow lost his case, but importantly, the Court said that state censorship laws in general were unconstitutional.

LEARNING CHECK ◄ ··

▸ **Explain the anomalies of the 1798 Alien and Sedition Acts.**

▸ **Explain the Supreme Court's 130 years of First Amendment silence.**

PRIOR RESTRAINT

On a roll with the First Amendment, the Supreme Court in 1931 barred the government in most situations from silencing someone before an utterance. The ruling, in **Near v. Minnesota,** banned **prior restraint.** A Minneapolis scandal sheet had been padlocked by the sheriff under a state law that forbade "malicious, scandalous and defamatory" publications. John Milton would have shuddered at the law, as did the U.S. Supreme Court. In a landmark decision against government acts to preempt free expression before it occurs, the Court ruled that any government unit at any level is in violation of the First Amendment if it suppresses a publication because of what might be said in the next issue.

Since *Near* the Supreme Court has moved to make it more difficult for the government to interfere with freedom of expression. In an important case, from the perspective of free expression advocates, the Court overturned the conviction of a white racist, **Clarence Brandenburg,** who had been jailed after a Ku Klux Klan rally in the woods outside Cincinnati. Brandenburg had said hateful and threatening things, but the Court, in a landmark decision in 1969, significantly expanded First Amendment protection for free expression. Even the advocacy of lawless actions is protected, according to the Brandenburg decision, as long as it's unlikely that lawlessness is imminent and probable. This is called the **Incitement Standard.** The distinction is that advocacy is protected up to the moment that lawlessness is incited. According to the Incitement Standard, authorities can justify silencing someone only if:

- The statement advocates a lawless action.
- The statement aims at producing lawless action.
- Such lawless action is imminent.
- Such lawless action is likely to occur.

Unless an utterance meets all four tests, it cannot be suppressed by the government.

LEARNING CHECK ◄ ··

▸ **How can restrictions on free expression be justified in view of the absolutist language of the First Amendment?**

▸ **What was the significance of *Near* v. *Minnesota*?**

● Charles Schenck, Elizabeth Baer
Principal plaintiffs in 1919 U.S. Supreme Court opinion decided on First Amendment grounds

● Benjamin Gitlow
Principal in 1924 U.S. Supreme Court decision that barred state censorship laws

● *Near* v. *Minnesota*
U.S. Supreme Court case that barred government interference with free expression in advance

● prior restraint
Prohibiting expression in advance

● Clarence Brandenburg
Ku Klux Klan leader whose conviction was overturned because his speech was far-fetched

● Incitement Standard
A four-part test to determine whether an advocacy speech is constitutionally protected

Jay Near and Howard Guilford, who started a scandal sheet in Minneapolis in 1927, did not have far to look for stories on corruption. Prohibition was in effect, and Minneapolis, because of geography, was a key U.S. distribution point for bootleg Canadian whisky going south to Chicago, St. Louis and other cities. Police and many officials were knee-deep in the illicit whisky trade and bribery.

Hearing about the kind of newspaper that Near and Guilford had in mind, the crooked police chief, aware of his own vulnerability, told his men to yank every copy off the newsstands as soon as they appeared. The *Saturday Press* thus became the first U.S. newspaper banned even before a single issue had been published. Even so, Near and Guilford put out weekly issues, each exposing scandals.

Two months after the first issue of the *Saturday Press*, Floyd Olson, the prosecutor, was fed up. He went to court and obtained an order to ban Near and Guilford from producing any more issues. Olson based his case on a 1925 Minnesota gag law that declared that "a malicious, scandalous and defamatory newspaper" could be banned as a public nuisance.

Despite their crusading for good causes, Near and Guilford's brand of journalism was hard to like. Both were bigots who peppered their writing with references to "niggers," "yids," "bohunks" and "spades." Could they get

● **Jay Near**
His appeal resulted in a strong ruling against government prior restraint on expression

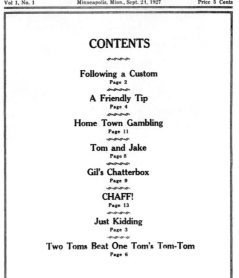

The Saturday Press

Vol 1, No. 1   Minneapolis, Minn., Sept. 24, 1927   Price 5 Cents

CONTENTS

Following a Custom
Page 2

A Friendly Tip
Page 4

Home Town Gambling
Page 11

Tom and Jake
Page 8

Gil's Chatterbox
Page 9

CHAFF!
Page 13

Just Kidding
Page 3

Two Toms Beat One Tom's Tom-Tom
Page 6

1927 Scandal Sheet. *Page one of Jay Near and Howard Guilford's inaugural issue looked bland enough, but inside were stories that infuriated officials. The officials eventually declared the* Saturday Press *a public nuisance and shut it down to head off further incriminating coverage of local corruption. In the landmark court case that resulted,* Near v. Minnesota, *the U.S. Supreme Court ruled that such prior restraint is unconstitutional.*

away with saying such things in print?

The U.S. Supreme Court said "yes" in a landmark decision known as *Near v. Minnesota*. The court said that no government at any level has the right to suppress a publication because of what it might say in its next issue. Except in highly exceptional circumstances, such as life-or-dealth issues in wartime, legal action against a publication can come only after something has been published—not before.

WHAT DO YOU THINK?

▶ Does the argument make sense that the First Amendment protects obnoxious and objectionable media content?

▶ Should the First Amendment be scrapped? Amended?

ALLOWABLE ABRIDGMENTS

In its wisdom the U.S. Supreme Court has avoided creating a rigid list of permissible abridgments to freedom of expression. No matter how thoughtfully drafted, a rigid list could never anticipate every situation. Nonetheless, the Supreme Court has discussed circumstances in which censorship is sometimes warranted.

■ **National Security.** The federal government jailed dozens of anti-war activists during World War I. Many appealed, prompting the U.S. Supreme Court to consider whether the First Amendment's prohibition against government limitations should be waived in wartime. A federal prosecutor had gone after Charles Schenck of Philadelphia, general secretary of the Socialist Party, and his wife, Elizabeth Baer,

Martyred Political Prisoner.
Eugene Debs, a Socialist Party leader, had run four times for the presidency, in 1900, 1904, 1908 and 1912. He ran a fifth time, in 1920—this time from prison. Here, party officials pose with Debs at the prison after notifying him that he had been nominated. He had been sent to jail for making an anti-war speech, a conviction that was upheld by the U.S. Supreme Court because of special national security considerations in time of war. Debs's 1920 campaign photograph showed him in prison garb with bars in the background—the martyred political prisoner. He won almost 1 million votes. A year later, President Warren Harding pardoned Debs, who by then was aged and ailing.

for handing out leaflets aimed at recently drafted men. The pamphlets made several points:

- The draft violated the 13th Amendment, which prohibits slavery.
- The draft was unfair because clergy and conscientious objectors, like Quakers, were exempted.
- The war was being fought for the profit of cold-blooded capitalists, who, the leaflets claimed, controlled the country.
- Draftees should join the Socialists and work to repeal the draft law.

As the government prosecutor saw it, the leaflets encouraged insubordination and disloyalty in the military, even mutiny. The Supreme Court agreed that the government can take exceptional prerogatives when the nation is at war. Schenck and Baer lost.

Since *Schenck* in 1919 the Court has repeated its point that national security is a special circumstance in which government restrictions can be justified. Even so, the Court's thinking has evolved in specifics, and many scholars believe that Schenck and Baer today would have prevailed. Support for this assessment of the Court's revised thinking came in an important 1972 case, during the Vietnam War, when the Court overruled the government for threatening the New York *Times* for a series of articles drawn from classified defense documents. In the so-called **Pentagon Papers** case, the Court said that the people's right to know about government defense policy was more important than the government's claim that the *Times* was jeopardizing national security.

■ Public Endangerment. In the Schenck case, the eloquent Justice **Oliver Wendell Holmes** wrote these words: "The most stringent protection of free speech would not protect a man in falsely shouting 'Fire' in a crowded theater and causing panic." His point was that the First Amendment's ban on government abridgment of freedom of expression cannot be applied literally. Holmes was saying that reasonable people agree that there must be exceptions. Since then, lesser courts have carved out allowable abridgments. Some have been endorsed by the Supreme Court. On other cases the Court has been silent, letting lower-level court decisions stand.

In a 1942 New Hampshire case, the police were upheld in jailing **Walter Chaplinsky,** who had taken to the streets to deride religions other than his own

● **Pentagon Papers**
Case in which the government attempted prior restraint against the New York *Times*

● **Oliver Wendell Holmes**
Justice who wrote that shouting "Fire!" in a crowded theater would be justification for abridgment of freedom of speech rights

● **Walter Chaplinsky**
Namesake for the case in which the Fighting Words Doctrine was defined

Clarence Brandenburg worked by day as a television repairman in a suburb of Cincinnati. By night he was an Ohio Ku Klux Klan leader. One day, in the mid-1960s, he called a reporter for a Cincinnati television station and invited a television crew to a rally.

About a dozen hooded figures, some with firearms, burned a large wooden cross. There were no spectators—just the Klansmen and the news crew. The only record of what Brandenburg said is the news film. Although the sound on the film is not always clear, it seemed that Brandenburg's speech rambled and was loaded with non sequiturs and imprecise, sometimes nonsensical expressions and words. Derogatory things were said about blacks and Jews. Brandenburg urged sending "niggers" back to Africa and Jews to Israel. Here are some passages transcribed from the news film:

"This is an organizers' meeting. We have had quite a few members here today which are—we have hundreds, hundreds of members throughout the State of Ohio. I can quote from a newspaper clipping from the Columbus, Ohio, *Dispatch*, five weeks ago Sunday morning. The Klan has more members in the State of Ohio than does any other organization.

"We're not a revengent organization, but if our President, our Congress, our Supreme Court, continues to suppress the white, Caucasian race, it's possible that there might have to be some revengeance taken.

"We are marching on Congress July the Fourth, 400,000 strong. From there we are dividing into groups, one to march on St. Augustine, Florida, the other group to march into Mississippi. Thank you."

Authorities who saw the television news coverage decided to act. Soon

Court Voids Law on Urging Violence

Special to The New York Times

WASHINGTON, June 9 — Ohio's criminal syndicalism law, a prototype of the kind of antiradical statutes that were passed by a score of states during the post-World War I "red scare," was declared unconstitutional today by the Supreme Court.

The Court ruled in an unsigned opinion that the law violated the free speech guarantee of the First Amendment.

The statute makes it unlawful "by word of mouth or writing [to] advocate or teach the duty, necessity or propriety of crime, sabotage, violence or unlawful methods of terrorism as a means of accomplishing industrial or political reform," for the first time to convict a Cincinnati Ku Klux Klan leader, Clarence Brandenburg.

were said to be plotting insurrection. Officials of those states told the Justices that the black militants' capacity to attempt insurrection was great enough to justify the use of these laws.

Allen Brown of Cincinnati argued for Brandenburg. Leonard Kirschner, assistant prosecuting attorney of Cincinnati, argued for the city.

Associated Press
Clarence Brandenburg, the Ohio Klan leader whose conviction was reversed.

Klan-Talk Protected. *The U.S. Supreme Court says the First Amendment protects obnoxious utterances, even those advocating violence unless the violence is imminent. The issue was forced by Clarence Brandenburg's racist fomenting at a Ku Klux Klan rally.*

Brandenburg was indicted for violating a 1919 Ohio law that barred violence directed at the government. This law made it a crime to advocate "violent means to effect political and economic change that endangers the security of the state." Brandenburg was convicted. In 1969, however, the U.S. Supreme Court found 9-0 in his favor. The court said the First Amendment protects advocating ideas, including the overthrow of the government. This protection, however, stops short of unlawful acts. The court was making an important distinction between advocacy of ideas and advocacy of unlawful action. In other words, you may teach and advocate an overthrow but you can't do it. Nor can you prod someone else into doing it.

In short, the state needs to prove a real danger exists. In Brandenburg's case, such was impossible. Although

his muddled expressions may have seemed to advocate violence against leaders of the national government, his prosecutors could not seriously argue that Brandenburg was a real threat to the Republic. Whatever violence Brandenburg advocated was hardly imminent. The woods in southwest Ohio were a long way from the Potomac, and there was no way the prosecutors could demonstrate that violence was likely.

WHAT DO YOU THINK?

▶ Few people today would value Clarence Brandenburg's ideas or even want him as a neighbor, but how about banning the views he expressed?

▶ Should criticism of government be allowed? How about criticism that calls for an overthrow of the government?

● **Fighting Words Doctrine**
The idea that censorship can be justified against inciting provocation to violence

as "rackets." Somebody called the police. Chaplinsky then turned his venom on the marshal who showed up, calling him, in a lapse of piety, "a God-damned racketeer" and "a damned fascist." From these circumstances emerged the **Fighting Words Doctrine.** The Court said someone might be justified taking a poke at you for using "fighting words," with perhaps a riot resulting. Preventing a riot was a justification for halting someone's freedom of expression. Again, whether courts today would uphold Chaplinsky being silenced is debated among legal scholars. Nonetheless, the Fighting Words Doctrine from *Chaplinsky* remains as testimony to the Court's willingness to consider public safety as a value that sometimes should outweigh freedom of expression as a value.

The courts also accept time, place and manner limits by the government on expression, using the **TPM Standard.** Cities can, for example, ban news racks from busy sidewalks where they impede pedestrian traffic and impair safety, as long as the restriction is content-neutral—an important caveat. A newspaper that editorializes against the mayor cannot be restricted while one that supports the mayor is not.

● **TPM Standard**
Government may control the time, place and manner of expression as long as limits are content-neutral

LEARNING CHECK ◄

▶ What are the allowable exceptions to the First Amendment prohibition on government interference with free expression? What is the basis for these exceptions?

▶ What is the Fighting Words Doctrine?

▶ Can you give an example of the TPM standard allowing government to ban a publication's distribution?

Broadening Protection

STUDY PREVIEW

The U.S. Supreme Court's initial First Amendment decisions involved political speech. The justices had no problem applying protections against government interference to political discourse, which is essential in democracy. It became apparent, however, that a fence cannot easily be erected between political and nonpolitical discourse. Gradually, First Amendment protections have been broadened.

POLITICAL EXPRESSION

The strides of the U.S. Supreme Court in the 20th century for free expression first were limited to political expression. The justices saw free exchanges of political ideas as necessary for a functioning democracy. Entertainment and advertising initially were afforded no First Amendment protection. They were considered less important to democracy than political expression. New cases, however, made it difficult to draw the line between and political and nonpolitical expression.

■ **Literature.** A 1930 tariff law was used as an import restriction to intercept James Joyce's *Ulysses* at the docks because of four-letter words and explicit sexual references. The importer, **Random House,** went to court, and the judge ruled that the government was out of line. The judge, **John Woolsey,** acknowledged "unusual frankness" in *Ulysses* but said he could not "detect anywhere the leer of the sensualist." The judge, who was not without humor, made a strong case for freedom in literary expression: "The words which are criticized as dirty are old Saxon words known to almost all men, and, I venture, to many women, and are such words as would be naturally and habitually used, I believe, by the types of folks whose life, physical and mental, Joyce is seeking to describe. In respect to the recurrent emergence of the theme of sex in the minds of the characters, it must always be remembered that his locale was Celtic and his season Spring."

● **Random House**
Fought against censorship of James Joyce's *Ulysses*

● **John Woolsey**
Judge who barred import law censorship of *Ulysses*

Woolsey was upheld on appeal, and *Ulysses*, still critically acclaimed as a pioneer in stream-of-consciousness writing, remains in print today.

Postal restrictions were used against a 1928 English novel, *Lady Chatterley's Lover*, by D. H. Lawrence. The book was sold in the United States in expurgated editions for years, but in 1959 **Grove Press** issued the complete version. Postal officials denied mailing privileges. Grove sued and won.

● **Grove Press**
Fought against censorship of D. H. Lawrence's *Lady Chatterley's Lover*

In some respects the Grove case was *Ulysses* all over again. Grove argued that Lawrence, a major author, had produced a work of literary merit. Grove said the explicit, rugged love scenes between Lady Chatterley and Mellors the gamekeeper were essential in establishing their violent yet loving relationship, the heart of the story. The distinction between the *Ulysses* and *Lady Chatterley* cases was that one ruling was against the customs service and the other against the postmaster general.

■ **Entertainment.** Courts had once claimed movie censorship as involving something unworthy of constitutional protection. But movies can be political. Witness the movies of Michael Moore. The Supreme Court in 1952 widened First Amendment protection to movies in striking down a local ban on a controversial movie, *The Miracle,* in which a simple woman explained that her pregnancy was by St. Joseph. Some Christians saw the movie as blasphemy. The Court found, however, that government could not impede the exploration of ideas under the Constitution's guarantee that expression should be free of government control.

■ **Advertising.** Advertising, called **commercial speech** in legal circles, also was not easily separated from political speech, as the Supreme Court discovered in a libel case out of Alabama. The case originated in an advertisement carried by the New York *Times* to raise money for the civil rights cause. The ad's sponsors included negative statements about Montgomery, Alabama, police. Was this commercial speech, being an ad? Or was it political speech, being on a public policy issue? In the landmark *New York Times* v. *Sullivan* case in 1964, the Court found the ad to be political speech and began opening the door for First Amendment protection of advertising—although the process of full protection for advertising remains a work in progress.

■ **Silent Statements.** The broadening of First Amendment protections eventually was extended to unspoken statements, sometimes called **symbolic speech.** In a breakthrough 1969 decision, the Supreme Court found in favor of three junior high school children in Des Moines, Iowa, who showed up in school with black armbands to protest the Vietnam War silently. They were suspended, but the U.S. Supreme Court decided that wearing armbands was constitutionally protected, especially considering that there had been no disruption at the school.

■ **Emotive Speech.** Polite society has never been particularly tolerant of vulgarities, but what if the vulgarity is clearly political? The issue was framed in the Vietnam war-protest era when a young man showed up at the Los Angeles courthouse wearing a jacket whose back carried a message: "Fuck the Draft." Paul Robert Cohen was sent to jail for 30 days. The Supreme Court overturned the conviction. Justice John Harlan wrote that linguistic expression needs to allow for "inexpressible emotions,"

sometimes called **emotive speech.** As one wag put it: Cohen wouldn't have been arrested if his jacket had said, "The Heck with Conscription" or "I Really Don't Like the Draft Very Much." Instead Cohen chose more charged language, the F-word. His jacket conveyed the depths of his feelings about the draft. Justice Harlan said: "One man's vulgarity is another's lyric. Words are often chosen as much for their emotive as their cognitive force."

■ **Flag Burning.** In another controversial application of toleration for offensive expression, the Supreme Court has recognized the burning of a U.S. flag as an expression that is protected from government interference. Although revisited many times in the courts, the main Supreme Court decision goes back almost a quarter of a century. At the 1984 Republican national convention in Dallas, **Joey Johnson** marched with a hundred or so other protesters to City Hall. There he doused a U.S. flag with kerosene and lit it. Johnson's supporters chanted: "America, the red, white and blue, we spit on you." The flag burning was a powerful gesture, a political gesture, against President Ronald Reagan, whom the Republicans were renominating. Johnson was arrested and convicted under a Texas law, similar to laws in many states, that forbade defacing the flag.

The U.S. Supreme Court found that the arrest was wrong. Said Justice William Brennan: "If there is a bedrock principle underlying the First Amendment, it is that the government may not prohibit the expression of an idea simply because society finds the idea itself offensive or disagreeable."

Joey Johnson. *Flag-burning protester whose conviction was overturned on First Amendment grounds.*

■ **Hate Speech.** Emotions run high on First Amendment issues when national security is at stake or when expression is obnoxious or even vile. The Supreme Court, however, takes the position that a society that is free and democratic cannot have a government that silences somebody just because that person's views don't comport with mainstream values. In effect, the Court says that people need to tolerate a level of discomfort in a society whose core principles value freedom of expression.

This point, made in the Brandenburg case, has come up in Court decisions against **hate speech** laws that grew out of the political correctness movement of the 1990s. Especially notable was *R.A.V.* v. *St. Paul*. Several punks had burned a cross, KKK style, on the lawn of a black family in St. Paul, Minnesota. They were caught and convicted under a municipal ordinance against "hate speech." One of them, identified only as R.A.V. in court documents, appealed to the U.S. Supreme Court on First Amendment grounds. The Court found that the ordinance was aimed at the content of the expression, going far beyond allowable time, place or manner restrictions. The decision was a slap at the political correctness movement's attempts to discourage language that can be taken offensively.

LEARNING CHECK ◄

▶ What kinds of expressions beyond political speech have been gaining First Amendment protection?

▶ Would you regard black armbands as political speech? What are the arguments on both sides?

▶ Does the U.S. Supreme Court see four-letter vulgarities as protected by the First Amendment? How about flag burning? How about hate speech?

BROADCAST REGULATION

Early commercial radio was a horrendous free-for-all. Government licensing was a joke. Stations went on the air at any frequency with as much wattage as they wanted. As the number of stations grew, they drowned each other out. To end the cacophony and create a national radio system, Congress established the Federal Radio Commission in 1927 to facilitate the orderly development of the new radio

John Brinkley and his bride arrived in Milford, Kansas, population 200, in 1917 and rented the old drug store for $8 a month. Mrs. Brinkley sold patent medicines out front, while Brinkley talked to patients in a back room. One day an elderly gentleman called on "Dr. Brinkley" to do something about his failing manhood. As the story goes, the conversation turned to Brinkley's experience with goats in the medical office of the Swift meat-packing company, a job he had held for barely three weeks. Said Brinkley, "You wouldn't have any trouble if you had a pair of those buck glands in you." The operation was performed in the back room, and word spread. Soon the goat gland surgeon was charging $750 for the service, then $1,000, then $1,500. In 1918 Brinkley, whose only credentials were two mail-order medical degrees, opened the Brinkley Hospital. Five years later he set up a radio station, KFKB, to spread the word about his cures.

Six nights a week, Brinkley extolled the virtues of his hospital over the air. "Don't let your doctor two-dollar you to death," he said. "Come to Dr. Brinkley." If a trip to Milford was not possible, listeners were encouraged to send for Brinkley compounds. Soon the mail-order demand was so great that Brinkley reported he was buying goats from Arkansas by the boxcar. "Dr. Brinkley" became a household word. *Radio Digest* awarded Brinkley's KFKB its Golden Microphone Award as the most popular radio station in the country. The station had received 356,827 votes in the magazine's write-in poll. Brinkley was a 1930 write-in candidate for governor. Harry Woodring won with 217,171 votes to Brinkley's 183,278, but Brinkley would have won had it not been for misspellings that disqualified thousands of write-in ballots.

Also in 1930 the KFKB broadcast license came up for renewal by the Federal Radio Commission, which had been set up to regulate broadcasting.

● **John Brinkley**
Radio quack who challenged
government regulation of radio

Goat Gland Surgeon.
Eager for publicity, John Brinkley obliges a photographer by placing a healing hand on a supposedly insane patient he is about to cure. Broad-casting such claims from his Kansas radio station, Brinkley developed a wide market for his potions. Because of his quackery, he lost the station in a significant First Amendment case.

The American Medical Association wanted the license revoked. The medical profession had been outraged by Brinkley but had not found a way to derail his thriving quackery. In fact, Brinkley played to the hearts of thousands of Middle America's listeners when he attacked the AMA as "the meat-cutter's union." At the license hearing, Brinkley argued that the First Amendment guaranteed him freedom to speak his views on medicine, goat glands and anything else he wanted. He noted that Congress had specifically forbidden the FRC to censor. It would be a censorious affront to the First Amendment, he said, to take away KFKB's license for what the station put on the air. Despite Brinkley's arguments, the FRC denied renewal.

Brinkley challenged the denial in federal court, and the case became a landmark on the relationship between the First Amendment and U.S. broadcasting. The appeals court sided with the FRC, declaring that broadcast licenses should be awarded for serving "the public interest, convenience and necessity." It was appropriate, said the court, for the commission to review a

station's programming to decide on renewal. Brinkley appealed to the U.S. Supreme Court, which declined to hear the case. The goat gland surgeon was off the air, but not for long. In 1932 Dr. Brinkley, proving himself unsinkable, bought a powerful station in Villa Acuna, Mexico, just across the Rio Grande from Del Rio, Texas, to continue peddling his potions. By telephone linkup from his home in Milford, Brinkley continued to reach much of the United States until 1942, when the Mexican government nationalized foreign-owned property.

WHAT DO YOU THINK?

▶ How do you explain the skirting of First Amendment issues in early court decisions about federal regulation of broadcasting?

▶ Do you see a problem in a government agency establishing the requirements for a license to broadcast?

▶ Can you defend the broadcast licensing standard of "public interest, convenience and necessity"?

493

industry. A no-nonsense licensing system was put in place with licenses going to stations that could best demonstrate they would operate in "the public interest, convenience and necessity."

Wait a minute? Government licensing based on performance sure smacks of government regulation. What about the First Amendment?

To sidestep the First Amendment issue, Congress embraced the concept that the airwaves, which carried radio signals, were a public asset and therefore, somewhat like a public park, were subject to government regulation for the public good. The **public airwaves** concept was useful for justifying regulation of the 1927 chaos on the airwaves, but it also was problematic. Some stations that lost licenses made First Amendment objections, but the courts declined to address the inherent constitutional contradictions. The radio industry overall was pleased with the new federal regulatory structure. The system, today under the Federal Communications Commission, later was expanded to television.

Over time many early restrictions have been relaxed. No longer, for example, are stations expected to air public affairs programs as a condition for license renewal. Although the FCC talks tough about on-air indecency, old bans have become loosened with the times.

● **public airwaves**
Concept that broadcast should be subject to government regulation because the electromagnetic spectrum is a public asset

LEARNING CHECK ◄ ·····································

▶ How has government regulation of broadcasting been justified when regulation of print media is clearly unconstitutional?

Defamation

STUDY PREVIEW

When the mass media carry disparaging descriptions and comments, they risk being sued for libel. The media have a strong defense if the libel was accurate. If not, there can be big trouble. Libel is a serious matter. Not only are reputations at stake when defamation occurs, but also losing a suit can be so costly that it can put a publication or broadcast organization out of business.

LIBEL AS A CONCEPT

If someone punched you in the face for no good reason, knocking out several teeth, breaking your nose and causing permanent disfigurement, most courts would rule that your attacker should pay your medical bills. If your disfigurement or psychological upset causes you to lose your job, to be ridiculed or shunned by friends and family or perhaps to retreat from social interaction, the court would probably order your attacker to pay additional amounts. Like fists, words can cause damage. If someone writes false, damaging things about you, you can sue for **libel.** Freedom of speech and the press is not a license to say absolutely anything about anybody.

● **libel**
A written defamation

If a libeling statement is false, the utterer may be liable for millions of dollars in damages. The largest jury award to date, in 1997 against the *Wall Street Journal*, was almost twice the earnings that year of the *Journal's* parent company, Dow Jones Inc. The award was reduced substantially on appeal, but the fact remains that awards have grown dramatically in recent years and can hurt a media company seriously.

LEARNING CHECK ◄ ·····································

▶ What is the rationale for libel law?

RECKLESS DISREGARD

Elected officials have a hard time winning libel suits today. Noting that democracy is best served by robust, unbridled discussion of public issues and that public officials are inseparable from public policy, the U.S. Supreme Court has ruled that public

MASS-MEDIA LAW MILESTONES		PIVOTAL EVENTS

1700s

Intellectual Property
Congress passed first copyright law (1790)

Free Expression
States ratified First Amendment to U.S. Constitution (1791)

- Revolutionary War (1776–1781)
- Alien and Sedition Acts (1798)

1800s

Censorship
Wartime newspapers closed (1864–1865)

- Civil War (1861–1865)

Opposition newspapers padlocked on Lincoln's watch

1900s

Cherry Sisters
Iowa Supreme Court ruled that performers must accept criticism of performances (1901)

Prior Restraint
Justice Oliver Wendell Holmes coined "Fire!" in a crowded theater example for prior restraint (1919)

Book Ban
Court overruled import restriction against *Ulysses* (1930)

Landmark Case
U.S. Supreme Court banned prior restraint in *Near* v. *Minnesota* (1931)

Sullivan Case
U.S. Supreme Court ruled that public figures can sue for libel only if media were reckless (1964)

Obscenity
U.S. Supreme Court ruled that local community standards determine obscenity (1968)

National Security
U.S. Supreme Court banned prior restraint in Pentagon Papers case (1971)

Celebrated and ridiculed vaudeville troupe

Jay Near won against prior restraint.

- World War I (1914–1918)
- Right to vote extended to women (1920)
- Great Depression (1930s)
- World War II (1941–1945)
- Civil Rights movement (1960)
- Humans reached moon (1969)
- Vietnam War (1964–1973)
- Nixon resigns presidency (1974)

2000s

Download Piracy
Recording industry won case against Grokster and other Internet file-swap enablers (2005)

Napster-like file-swaps outlawed

- 9/11 terrorist attacks (2001)
- Iraq War (2003–)
- Hurricane Katrina (2005)

figures can win libel suits only in extreme circumstances. The Court has also said that people who thrust themselves into the limelight forfeit some of the protection available to other citizens.

The key Court decision in developing current U.S. libel standards originated in an advertisement carried by the New York *Times* in 1960. A civil rights coalition, the Committee to Defend Martin Luther King and the Struggle for Freedom in the South, escalated its antisegregationist cause by placing a full-page advertisement in the *Times*. The advertisement accused public officials in the South of violence and illegal tactics against the civil rights struggle. Although the advertisement was by and large truthful, it was marred by minor factual errors. Police Commissioner L. B. Sullivan of Montgomery, Alabama, filed a libel action saying that the errors damaged him, and he won $500,000 in an Alabama trial. On appeal to the U.S. Supreme Court, the case, **New York *Times* v. *Sullivan*,** became a landmark in libel law. The Supreme Court said that the importance of "free debate" in a democratic society generally was more important than factual errors that might upset and damage public officials. To win a libel suit, the Court said, public officials needed to prove that damaging statements were uttered or printed with the knowledge that they were false. The question in the *Sullivan* case became whether the *Times* was guilty of "**reckless disregard** of the truth." The Supreme Court said it was not, and the newspaper won.

Questions lingered after the *Sullivan* decision about exactly who was and who was not a public official. Lower courts struggled for a definition, and the Supreme Court eventually changed the term to *public figure*. In later years, as the Court refined its view on issues raised in the *Sullivan* case through several decisions, it remained consistent in giving the mass media a lot of room for error, even damaging error, in discussing government officials, political candidates and publicity hounds.

- **Government officials**. All elected government officials and appointed officials with high-level policy responsibilities are public figures as far as their performance in office is concerned. A member of a state governor's cabinet fits this category. A cafeteria worker in the state capitol does not.
- **Political candidates**. Anyone seeking public office is subject to intense public review, during which the courts are willing to excuse false statements as part of robust, wide-open discussion.
- **Publicity hounds**. Court decisions have gone both ways, but generally people who seek publicity or intentionally draw attention to themselves must prove "reckless disregard of the truth" if they sue for libel.

How far can the media go in making disparaging comments? It was all right, said a Vermont court, when the Barre *Times Argus* ran an editorial that said a political candidate was "a horse's ass, a jerk, an idiot and a paranoid." The court said open discussion on public issues excused even such insulting, abusive and unpleasant verbiage. Courts have generally been more tolerant of excessive language in opinion pieces, such as the Barre editorial, than in fact-based articles.

LEARNING CHECK ◄ •

▶ How did *New York Times* v. *Sullivan* significantly change libel law?

▶ How many people can you name who fall into a gray area between public figure and private figure? Discuss their ambiguous status.

COMMENT AND CRITICISM

People flocked to see the **Cherry Sisters'** act. Effie, Addie, Jessie, Lizzie and Ella toured the country with a song and dance act that drew big crowds. They were just awful. They could neither sing nor dance, but people turned out because the sisters were so funny. Sad to say, the Cherry Sisters took themselves seriously. In 1901, desperate for respect, the sisters decided to sue the next newspaper reviewer who gave them a bad notice. That reviewer, it turned out, was Billy Hamilton, who included a lot of equine metaphors in his piece for the Des Moines *Leader*: "Effie is

---

● *New York Times* v. *Sullivan*
Libel case that largely barred public figures from the right to sue for libel

● reckless disregard
Supreme Court language for a situation in which public figures may sue for libel

● Cherry Sisters
Complainants in a case that barred performers from suing critics

Fair Comment and Criticism.
*Upset with what an Iowa re-
viewer had written about their
show, the Cherry Sisters sued.
The important 1901 court decision that resulted said that
journalists, critics and anybody
else can say whatever they
want about a public performance. The rationale was that
someone who puts on a performance for public acceptance
has to take a risk also of public
rejection.*

● **fair comment and criticism**
Doctrine that permits criticism of
performers, performances

an old jade of 50 summers, Jessie a frisky filly of 40, and Addie, the flower of the family, a capering monstrosity of 35. Their long skinny arms, equipped with talons at the extremities, swung mechanically, and anon waved frantically at the suffering audience. The mouths of their rancid features opened like caverns, and sounds like the wailings of damned souls issued therefrom. They pranced around the stage with a motion that suggested a cross between the *danse du ventre* and the fox trot—strange creatures with painted faces and hideous mien. Effie is spavined, Addie is stringhalt, and Jessie, the only one who showed her stockings, has legs with calves as classic in their outlines as the curves of a broom handle."

The outcome of the suit was another setback for the Cherrys. They lost in a case that established that actors or others who perform for the public must be willing to accept both positive and negative comments about their performance. This right of **fair comment and criticism,** however, does not make it open season on performers in aspects of their lives that do not relate to public performance. The *National Enquirer,* for example, could not defend itself when entertainer Carol Burnett sued for a story that described her as obnoxiously drunk at a restaurant. Not only was the description false (Carol Burnett abstains from alcohol), but Burnett was in no public or performing role at the restaurant. This distinction between an individual's public and private lives also has been recognized in cases involving public officials and candidates.

LEARNING CHECK ◄ •

▶ How did *New York Times* v. *Sullivan* enable news reporters to do their work better?

▶ Disparaging comments about an individual in the mass media are acceptable for some situations but not others. Consider a major celebrity. What's off-limits? What's not?

TRESPASS, FRAUD AND LIBEL

An emerging legal tactic against the news media for disparaging coverage is not libel but trespass and other laws. In 1998 the Utah Restaurant Association sued television station KTVX for a report on roaches in restaurant kitchens and unsanitary food handling and storage. Wesley Sine, attorney for the restaurants, did not sue for libel.

Sine argued instead that it was illegal for news reporters to go into a private area, like a kitchen, without permission.

Such end runs around libel law worry media people. The defenses that usually work in libel cases are hard to apply if the media are sued over disparaging reports on grounds other than libel. This was a factor in a case involving the Food Lion supermarket chain that resulted in a $5.5 million jury verdict against ABC television. Food Lion was riled over a 1992 report on rats and spoilage in store backrooms as well as unfair labor practices. In its suit, Food Lion never challenged ABC's accuracy. Rather, Food Lion said, among other things, that ABC had committed fraud by sending undercover reporters to get on the Food Lion payroll to investigate the backrooms. On appeal, the damages against ABC were reduced almost to zero—a moral victory for ABC, but it took seven years and lots of expensive lawyers.

LEARNING CHECK ◄

▶ **What alternatives to libel law are litigants using against defamatory reporting that is accurate and true?**

Indecency

STUDY PREVIEW

Despite the First Amendment's guarantee of freedom of expression, the U.S. government has tried numerous ways during the past 100 years to regulate obscenity and pornography.

PORNOGRAPHY VERSUS OBSCENITY

● **pornography**
Sexually explicit depictions that are protected from government bans

Through U.S. history, governments have attempted censorship of various sorts at various levels of jurisdiction. But since the *Ulysses* and *Lady Chatterley* cases, much has occurred to discourage censorship.

The U.S. Supreme Court has ruled that **pornography,** material aimed at sexual arousal, cannot be stopped. Import and postal restrictions, however, still can be employed against obscene materials, which the Court has defined as going beyond pornography. Obscenity restrictions apply, said the Court, if the answer is yes to *all* of the following questions:

- Would a typical person applying local standards see the material as appealing mainly for its sexually arousing effect?
- Is the material devoid of serious literary, artistic, political or scientific value?
- Is sexual activity depicted offensively, in a way that violates state law that explicitly defines offensiveness?

LEARNING CHECK ◄

▶ How are pornography and obscenity different?

PROTECTING CHILDREN

● **indecency**
Term used by the Federal Communications Commission to encompass a range of words and depictions improper on public airwaves

Although the Supreme Court has found that the First Amendment protects access to pornography, the Court has stated on numerous occasions that children must be protected from sexually explicit material. It's a difficult double standard, as demonstrated by 1996 and 1999 federal forays into systematically regulating media content that were ill-conceived communications decency laws. Without hearings or formal debate, Congress created the laws to keep smut away from children who use the Internet. Although hardly anyone defends giving kids access to indecent material, the laws had two flaws: the difficulty of defining **indecency** and the impossibility of denying questionable material to children without restricting freedom of access for adults.

Before a Philadelphia federal appeals court that reviewed the 1996 Communications Decency Act, witnesses from the Justice Department testified that the law went ridiculously far. The law, they said, required them to prosecute for certain AIDS information, museum exhibits, prize-winning plays and even the *Vanity Fair* magazine cover of actress Demi Moore nude and pregnant.

■ **Access.** When it reviewed the 1996 Communications Decency Act in 1999, the U.S. Supreme Court noted that the Internet is the most democratic of the media, enabling almost anyone to become a town crier or pamphleteer. Enforcing the law would necessarily inhibit freedom of expression of the sort that has roots in the Revolution that resulted in the creation of the Republic and the First Amendment, the court said. The 7-2 decision purged the law from the books.

How, then, are government bans of indecency on radio and television justified but not on the Internet? Justice John Stevens, who wrote the majority Supreme Court opinion, said the Internet is hardly an "invasive broadcasting." The odds of people encountering pornography on the Internet are slim unless they're seeking it, he said. Underpinning the Court's rejection of the **Communications Decency Act** was the fact that the Internet lends itself to free-for-all discussions and exchanges with everybody participating who wants to, whereas other media are dominated by carefully crafted messages aimed at people whose opportunity to participate in dialogue with the message producers is so indirect as to be virtually nil.

Even while politicians and moralists rant at indecency, people seem largely unperturbed by the issue. The V-chip, required by a 1996 law to be built into every television set, allows parents to block violence, sexual explicitness and vulgarity automatically. Although the V-chip was widely praised when it became a requirement, hardly anybody uses it.

In 2006, when Congress was in a new dither over objectionable content, movie industry lobbyist Jack Valenti came out of retirement to lead a $300 million campaign to promote the V-chip. Valenti made the point that stiff fines being levied against broadcasters for indecency are unnecessary because people already have the tool they need to block it, if they want.

LEARNING CHECK ◄··
▶ **What is the difficulty of enforcing indecency restrictions for children but not adults?**

PATRIOT ACT

Immediately after the 9/11 terrorist attacks on New York and Washington, in 2001, the Bush administration quickly drafted multiprong legislation to give authorities more power to track terrorists. Despite criticism among civil libertarians that some provisions would allow federal agents to ignore constitutionally guaranteed citizen rights, Congress reasoned that it was better to be safe than sorry and went along, passing the **Patriot Act** by an overwhelming majority.

The book industry mobilized against a provision that allowed federal agents to go into bookstores, unannounced and without close judicial oversight, and confiscate customer records to see who had bought books that might be used to aid or promote terrorism. The provision also allowed agents to go into libraries to see who had been reading what. To book publishers, authors, librarians and indeed all civil liberty advocates, the implications were alarming. They launched a massive lobbying effort to rescind parts of the law that could chill citizen inquiry and expression. Their point was that the law's effect would be to discourage people from reading works on a secret or even nongovernment list of seditious literature.

Four years later, as fear about massive, imminent terrorism eased, Congress pushed to delete Section 215 from the Patriot Act. Earlier attempts in U.S. history to place federal limits on what citizens read had failed too—though through the courts, not the executive or legislative branch of government.

The Patriot Act was rigorously defended in its entirety by President Bush, including Section 215, which especially concerned the book industry, librarians and

● **Communications Decency Act**
Failed 1996 and 1999 laws to keep indecent content off the Internet

● **Patriot Act**
2001 law that gave federal agents new authority to pre-empt terrorism

civil libertarians. Bush argued that the provision had not been used much. But, he said, it needed to be in the government's anti-terrorism arsenal. The law remained in force.

LEARNING CHECK ◄┄┄┄┄┄┄┄┄┄┄
▶ **What is Section 215 of the Patriot Act?**
▶ **Why do the book industry, librarians and civil libertarians object to Section 215?**

Chapter Wrap-Up

Intellectual Property (Page 480)

■ Copyright law protects mass communicators and other creative people from having their creative work used without their permission. It's an issue of property rights. Also, copyright law encourages creativity in society with a profit incentive for creative people. They can charge for the use of their work. The financial structure of mass-media industries has been built around the copyright concept. Time and again technology has challenged media control over copyrighted content, most recently with downloaded music and video.

Free Expression (Page 484)

■ The First Amendment to the U.S. Constitution guarantees freedom to citizens and the mass media from government limitations on what they say. The guarantee has solid roots in democratic theory. Even so, the U.S. Supreme Court has allowed exceptions. These mostly common-sense exceptions include utterances that could undermine national security in wartime. In general, however, the Supreme Court has expanded the prohibition on censorship over the years, all in the libertarian spirit articulated by John Milton in the 1600s.

Broadening Protection (Page 490)

■ The U.S. Supreme Court addressed First Amendment issues for the first time after World War I and had little problem in declaring that government limitations were unacceptable for political discourse, albeit with specific exceptions. It turned out, however, that political speech has lots of crossover with literature, entertainment and advertising. Over time, the Supreme Court has broadened First Amendment protection into these additional areas of expression—although less exuberantly than for political issues. An odd exception has been broadcasting, for which the Court has never squarely addressed the contradictions of federal regulation.

Defamation (Page 494)

■ Someone who is defamed can sue for libel. This generally is not a constitutional free expression issue but a civil issue. If the defamation was false and caused someone to suffer public hatred, contempt or ridicule, civil damages can be awarded by the courts. Judgment can be severe, sometimes approaching $100 million. The courts have found some defamations excusable. The landmark *New York Times* v. *Sullivan* decision of 1964 makes it difficult for public figures to recover damages unless there has been reckless disregard for truth. Also, performers cannot sue for criticism of their performances, no matter how harsh.

Indecency (Page 498)

■ Indecency revolts many people, but the U.S. Supreme Court in struggling with the issue has said, in effect, that indecency like beauty is in the eye of the beholder. The Court says the media are guaranteed freedom to create pornography and citizens are guaranteed freedom of access. However, sexually explicit material that goes too far—obscenity, the Court has called it—cannot be tolerated. But the Court has never devised a clear distinction between pornography, which is protected, and obscenity, which it says is not. In both categories, however, the Court has endorsed laws to punish purveyors of sexually explicit material to children.

REVIEW QUESTIONS

1. What is the rationale underlying copyright law?

2. Why is the First Amendment important to mass media in the United States?

3. What was the direction of court interpretation of the First Amendment in the 1900s?

4. Who can sue for libel?

5. How are obscenity and pornography different?

CONCEPTS	**TERMS**	**PEOPLE**
copyright (Page 480)	fair comment and criticism (Page 497)	Cherry Sisters (Page 496)
libel (Page 494)	First Amendment (Page 485)	Clarence Brandenburg (Page 486)
indecency (Page 498)	Incitement Standard (Page 486)	John Milton (Page 484)
marketplace of ideas (Page 484)	pornography (Page 498)	Jay Near (Page 487)
	prior restraint (Page 486)	Charles Schenck, Elizabeth Baer (Page 486)

MEDIA SOURCES

● Robert J. Wagman. *The First Amendment Book*. Paros, 1991. This lively history of the First Amendment is a solid primer on the subject.

● Clark R. Mollenhoff. "25 Years of *Times* v. *Sullivan*," *Quill* (March 1989), pages 27–31. A veteran investigative reporter argues that journalists have abused the landmark *Sullivan* decision and have been irresponsibly hard on public figures.

● Fred W. Friendly. *Minnesota Rag: The Dramatic Story of the Landmark Supreme Court Case That Gave New Meaning to the First Amendment*. Random House, 1981. A colorful account of the *Near* v. *Minnesota* prior restraint case.

In this chapter you have deepened your media literacy by revisiting several themes. Here are thematic highlights from the chapter:

Media Technology

New technologies keep creating new mass-media legal issues. The first home video recording equipment in the 1970s, Betamax, raised questions of whether people have a legal right to duplicate copyright-protected movies. Despite Hollywood's objections, the answer of the U.S. Supreme Court was yes. For more than a century, photography has created poignant privacy questions that nobody ever thought about before. The problem with copyright law is that lawmakers are no better than the rest of us at seeing what future technology will bring. Copyright law has been revisited over and over in the history of the Republic, most recently because of Internet-related issues like unauthorized downloading that have shaken media industries. **(Pages 480–484)**

Free Stuff. Feelings run strong on the recording and movie industries call for court protection against downloading and file-swapping that threatens their franchises.

John Lech Johansen. He became Hollywood's Norwegian nightmare with software that cracked regional coding for movies

Media Economics

At the core of mass-media infrastructure is copyright law, which gives exclusive rights to creative people to profit from their creations. The Internet has broken the control of media companies on distribution of their creations. Anybody with a few pieces of low-cost, easy-to-use computer equipment can distribute media content for free downloading by anyone on the planet. Most threatened have been the recording and movie industries, which have scrambled in the courts for protection of assets under copyright law. Both industries have cast the issue as economic survival. **(Pages 479–484)**

Media and Democracy

The democratic ideal of self-governance through grassroots political participation requires that people have full access to information. The ideal also requires that people have the freedom to sort through and hash out the facts to arrive at the best possible public policy. The First Amendment to the U.S. Constitution guarantees these freedoms of inquiry and expression to all citizens and to the mass media. The guarantee, however, is limited only to a ban on government interference in inquiry and expression. Citizens who feel wronged can seek compensation from other citizens and corporate entities, including media companies. Also, the courts have carved out some areas, including national security, in which the government can restrict access to and sharing of information. **(Pages 484–490)**

Prior Restraint. The sheriff was wrong to padlock the Minnesota paper.

Media and Culture

The polarizing Culture Wars that have divided American society in recent years are not new except in their shrill intensity. Sexual explicitness is a hot-button cultural issue that goes way back. The U.S. Supreme Court has barred government interference with adult access to sexually explicit material. The Court has said that the access is a right under the free expression guarantee of the First Amendment, but the Court also has created limits. Some of these limits are clear, like protecting children. Some are vague, like the distinction between pornography, which is acceptable, and obscenity, which is not. In short, though, the mass media have had growing latitude in dealing with sexuality through the First Amendment. (Pages 498–500)

Public Figures. *They must take criticism as well as praise.*

Elitism and Populism

Elected and appointed governing elites have been largely stripped of the ability to sue their critics. In a landmark 1964 decision, *New York Times* v. *Sullivan,* the U.S. Supreme Court ruled that a democracy requires full and robust citizen discourse on public policy issues. The Court said that defamations that occur in this discourse are excusable, except for egregious and intentional untruths. The *Sullivan* decision gave new leeway for criticism of political leadership to the people and also to the media. The decision also opened up the range of negative comments on a broad range of other public figures. (Pages 490–498)

Media Tomorrow

Our understanding of the First Amendment is evolving. It's been clear since the U.S. Supreme Court began examining the First Amendment after World War I that discussion of political issues must be protected for democracy to function. But numerous practices, also endorsed by the courts, leave many contradictions unresolved. For example, the government in 1927 gave itself the authority to decide who could broadcast and who couldn't. Criteria for a broadcast license still include on-air performance expectations, a kind of government content control that the Court would never countenance for print media. Also not addressed squarely by the courts so far are a wide range of government restrictions on advertising. (Pages 484–494)

Lingering Issue. *Can government restrict on-air quacks?*

20

Ethics

Does Illegal Equal Immoral?

Jim DeFede, a hard-hitting Miami *Herald* investigative reporter, was home late in the afternoon when his phone rang. It was an old friend, former city and county Commissioner Arthur Teele Jr. Teele was distraught that another newspaper had outed him for trysts with a transvestite prostitute. "What did I do to piss off this town?" Teele asked. The transvestite allegation had followed 26 charges of fraud and money laundering. Teele said he was being smeared by prosecutors. He was afraid the transvestite story would hurt him with "the ministers and the church."

Worried about his friend's anguish, DeFede turned on his telephone recorder to record Teele's pain. He also asked if Teele wanted to go public about the prosecutors using the media to smear him. Teele said no, but the discussion meandered back and forth to a potentially explosive story for which Teele said he had documents. A couple hours later Teele called and said he was leaving the documents for DeFede. Then he hung up, put a pistol to his head, and shot himself dead.

DeFede briefed his editor, Judy Miller, who told him to write a Page One story. In the meantime, higher executives at the *Herald* realized that DeFede had violated a state law that forbade taping a telephone conversation without permission. Over Miller's objections, publisher Jesus Diaz Jr. and corporate attorney Robert Beatty and two other corporate executives decided to fire DeFede—even though the *Herald* had once fought the Florida law, even though anyone who calls a reporter implicitly is consenting to being quoted, even though tape recording is just a more detailed form of

LEARNING AHEAD

■ Mass-media ethics codes cannot anticipate all moral questions.

■ Mass-media people draw on numerous moral principles, some inconsistent with each other.

■ Some mass-media people prefer process-based ethics systems, while some prefer outcome-based systems.

■ Potter's Box is a useful tool to sort through ethics issues.

■ Some mass-media people confuse ethics, law, prudence and accepted practices.

■ Dubious mass-media practices confound efforts to establish universal standards.

Jim DeFede. *Reflexively, Miami* Herald *columnist Jim DeFede did what seemed right when a suicidal friend called. He taped the call. But in Florida taping a call without permission is against the law. But does being illegal make an act necessarily wrong? Such are the issues that make ethics essential to understand.*

note taking—and even though, in this case, *Herald* executives decided to draw on DeFede's notes from the taped conversation to be used in a Page One story on the suicide.

If indeed DeFede had acted unethically, then how about the fact that the *Herald* drew on his information from the phone call? And how's this for a twist to make the issue murkier? The state's attorney cleared DeFede of violating the anti-recording statute. Also, only 12 states, including Florida, have such a law. If what DeFede did was unethical in Florida, is it less so in the 38 states that don't have such restrictions?

Clearly, the law and ethics don't coincide lockstep, which is a major issue in media ethics. In this chapter you will learn tools that have been developed through the centuries to sort through complexities posed by dilemmas of right and wrong, when choosing a course has downsides as well as upsides.

The Difficulty of Ethics

STUDY PREVIEW

Mass-media organizations have put together codes of ethics that prescribe how practitioners should go about their work. Although useful in many ways, these codes neither sort through the bedeviling problems that result from conflicting prescriptions nor help much when the only open options are negative.

PRESCRIPTIVE ETHICS CODES

● **code of ethics**
Statement that defines acceptable, unacceptable behavior

● **Canons of Journalism of the American Society of Newspaper Editors**
First media code, 1923

● **prescriptive ethics**
Follow the rules and your decision will be the correct one

The mass media abound with **codes of ethics.** The earliest was adopted in 1923, the **Canons of Journalism of the American Society of Newspaper Editors.** Advertising, broadcast and public relations practitioners also have codes. Many newcomers to the mass media make an erroneous assumption that the answers to all the moral choices in their work exist in the prescriptions of these codes, a stance known as **prescriptive ethics.** While the codes can be helpful, ethics is not so easy.

The difficulty of ethics becomes clear when a mass communicator is confronted with a conflict between moral responsibilities to different concepts. Consider:

■ **Respect for Privacy.** The code of the Society of Professional Journalists prescribes that reporters will show respect for the dignity, privacy, rights and well-being of people "at all times." The SPJ prescription sounds excellent, but moral priorties such as dignity and privacy sometimes seem less important than other priorities. The public interest, for example, overrode privacy in 1988 when the Miami *Herald* staked out presidential candidate Gary Hart overnight when he had a woman friend in his Washington townhouse.

■ **Commitment to Timeliness.** The code of the Radio–Television News Directors Association prescribes that reporters be "timely and accurate." In practice, however, the virtue of accuracy is jeopardized when reporters rush to the air with stories. It takes time to confirm details and be accurate—and that delays stories and works against timeliness.

■ **Being Fair.** The code of the Public Relations Society of America prescribes dealing fairly with both clients and the general public. However, a persuasive message prepared on behalf of a client is not always the same message that would be prepared on behalf of the general public. Persuasive communication is not necessarily dishonest, but how information is marshaled to create the message depends on whom the PR person is serving.

LEARNING CHECK ◄···

▶ **How can codes of ethics help media people make the right decisions? Do codes always work? Why or why not?**

▶ **Is it always a virtue to respect privacy? Why or why not?**

CONFLICT OF DUTIES

Media ethics codes are well-intended, usually helpful guides, but they are simplistic when it comes to knotty moral questions. These inherent problems become obvious if you consider how the various duties of mass communicators can conflict. Media ethicist Clifford Christians and others have examined, for example, conflicts in duties to audience, to employer, to society, to the profession and to self.

■ **Duty to Self.** Self-preservation is a basic human instinct, but is a photojournalist shirking a duty to subscribers by avoiding a dangerous combat zone?

Self-aggrandizement can be an issue too. Many college newspaper editors are invited, all expenses paid, to Hollywood movie premieres. The duty-to-self principle favors going: The trip would be fun. In addition, it is a good story opportunity, and as a free favor, it would not cost the newspaper anything. However, what of an editor's responsibility to readers? Readers have a right to expect writers to provide honest accounts that are not colored by favoritism. Can a reporter write fairly after being wined and dined and flown across the continent by movie producers who want a gung-ho story? Even if reporters rise above being affected and are true to conscience, there are the duty-to-employer and the duty-to-profession principles to consider. The newspaper and the profession itself can be tarnished by audience suspicions, whether or not they are unfounded, that a reporter has been bought off.

■ **Duty to Audience.** Television programs that reenact violence are popular with audiences, but do they do a disservice because they frighten many viewers into inferring that the streets are more dangerous than they really are?

Tom Wicker of the New York *Times* tells a story about his early days as a reporter in Aberdeen, North Carolina. He was covering a divorce case involving one spouse chasing the other with an ax. Nobody was hurt physically, and everyone who heard the story in the courtroom, except the divorcing couple, had a good laugh. "It was human comedy at its most ribald, and the courtroom rocked with laughter," Wicker recalled years later. In writing his story, Wicker captured the darkly comedic details so skillfully that his editor put the story on Page 1. Wicker was proud of the piece until the next day when the woman in the case visited him. Worn-out, haggard, hurt and angry, she asked, "Mr. Wicker, why did you think you had a right to make fun of me in your paper?"

The lesson stayed with Wicker for the rest of his career. He had unthinkingly hurt a fellow human being for no better reason than to evoke a chuckle, or perhaps a belly laugh, from his readers. For Wicker, the duty-to-audience principle would never again transcend his moral duty to the dignity of the subjects of his stories. Similar ethics questions involve whether to cite AIDS as a contributor to death in an obituary, to identify victims in rape stories and to name juveniles charged with crimes.

■ **Duty to Employer.** Does loyalty to an employer transcend the ideal of pursuing and telling the truth when a news reporter discovers dubious business deals involving the parent corporation? This is a growing issue as the mass media become consolidated into fewer gigantic companies owned by conglomerates.

In a classic case, the executive producer of the NBC *Today* show, Marty Ryan, ordered a reference to General Electric deleted from an affiliate-provided news story

Unusual among U.S. newspapers, the Shelton, Washington, *Journal* prints the names of rape victims and even gets into X-rated details in covering trials. The publisher, Charlie Gay, knows the policy runs against the grain of contemporary news practices. It's also, he says, "good basic journalism."

Most newsrooms shield the names of rape victims, recognizing a notion, flawed though it is, that victims invite the crime. This stigma sets rape apart from other crimes, or at least so goes one line of thinking. Thus, naming should be at the victim's discretion, not a journalist's. To that, Charlie Gay says balderdash. Silence and secrecy only perpetuate stigmas, he says. As he sees it, only with the bright light of exposure can wrong-headed stigmas be cleansed away.

Gay says the journalist's duty is to tell news fully and fairly. "If we did follow a policy of no victims' names, we'd be horribly unfair to the other party, the person who's picked up for the crime and who is innocent until proved guilty," he says. It's unfair reporting to be "stacking everything against the accused."

In a speech to the Shelton Rotary Club, Gay said: "The *Journal* is reporting a crime and a trial. We're not trying to protect one party or make judgments about one party." The ideal to Gay is full, fair, detailed stories that inform without prejudicing.

The *Journal's* victim-naming policy has rankled many readers. Letters flood the opinion page with every rape case. The newspaper has been picketed. Critics have tried organizing an advertiser boycott and called on readers to cancel subscriptions.

At one point the state legislature responded. After lengthy debate about whether naming names should be outlawed, the legislature decided to bar reporters from naming child victims. The law was later ruled unconstitutional. It violated the First Amendment because government was abridging freedom of the press. The flap, however, demonstrated the intensity of feelings on the subject.

Police, prosecutors and social workers generally want names withheld, saying that some victims won't come forward for fear of publicity. Gay is blunt about that argument: The job of the press is to report the news, not to make the job of government easier. He says it is the job of government agents, including police and social workers, to persuade victims to press charges.

Although decidedly with a minority view, Gay has some support for including names and gripping detail in reporting sex crimes. Psychologist Robert Seidenberg, for example, believes that rape victims may be encouraged to report the crime by reading the accounts of victims with whom they can relate because details make compelling reading that helps them sort through their own situation more clearly.

For a thorough discussion of the issue, including the interview with Charlie Gay from which this Media People box was drawn, see Richard J. Riski and Elinor Kelley Grusin's research article "Newspaper's Naming Policy

Rape Names. *Editor Charlie Gay sees a journalistic duty to include victim names in rape stories.*

Continues Amid Controversy," in the Fall 2003 issue of the *Newspaper Research Journal*.

WHAT DO YOU THINK?

▶ What do you think of the rationale for publishing the names of accusers in criminal cases, including rape?

▶ Will the policy of the Shelton *Journal* contribute to eliminating an undeserved stereotypical stigma that some rape victims feel?

▶ Should the First Amendment protect news organizations that choose to publish the names of crime victims?

---

on untested and sometimes defective bolts in jet engines manufactured by GE. The owner of NBC is GE.

■ **Duty to the Profession.** At what point does an ethically motivated advertising agency person blow the whistle on misleading claims by other advertising people?

■ **Duty to Society.** Does duty to society ever transcend duty to self? To the audience? To the employer? To colleagues? Does ideology affect a media worker's sense of duty to society? Consider how Joseph Stalin, Adolf Hitler and Franklin Roosevelt would be covered by highly motivated communist, fascist and libertarian journalists.

Are there occasions when the duty-to-society and duty-to-audience principles are incompatible? Nobody enjoys seeing the horrors of war, for example, but journalists may feel that their duty to society demands that they go after the most grisly photographs of combat to show how horrible war is and, thereby, in a small way, contribute to public pressure toward a cessation of hostilities and eventual peace.

LEARNING CHECK ◄···

▶ **If you were a college newspaper editor and were offered an all-expenses-paid trip to a Hollywood movie premiere, would you accept? In explaining your decision, keep in mind that avoiding controversy may be an attractive response but would be a weak ethical choice.**

Media Ethics

··

STUDY PREVIEW

Media ethics is complicated by the different performance standards that mass-media operations establish for themselves. This is further complicated by the range of expectations in the mass audience. One size does not fit ail.

MEDIA COMMITMENT

A single ethics standard is impossible to apply to the mass media. Nobody holds a supermarket tabloid like *News of the World*, which specializes in celebrities being visited by aliens, to the same standard as the New York *Times*. Why the difference? Media ethics, in part, is a function of what a media operation promises to deliver to its audience and what the audience expects. The *News of the World* commitment is fun and games in a tongue-in-cheek news context. The New York *Times* considers itself a "newspaper of record." There is a big difference.

CNN touts accuracy in its promotional tagline: "News You Can Trust." Explicitly, the network promises to deliver truthful accounts of the day's events. CNN establishes its own standards. A lapse, like a misleading story, especially if intentional or the result of sloppiness, represents a broken promise and an ethics problem.

A media organization's commitments may be implicit. Disney, for example, has cultivated an image of wholesome products with which the whole family can be comfortable. It's a commitment: Nothing bordering on smut here.

AUDIENCE EXPECTATION

The audience brings a range of ethics expectations to media relations, which further thwarts any attempt at one-size-fits-all media ethics. From a book publisher's fantasy science-fiction imprint, readers have far different expectations than they do from *NBC News*, which, except for plainly labeled opinion, is expected to deliver unmitigated nonfiction.

A range in the type of messages purveyed by the mass media also bespeaks a variety of ethics expectations. Rarely is falsity excusable, but even the courts allow puffery in advertising. The news releases that public relations people produce are expected, by their nature, to be from a client's perspective, which doesn't always coincide with the perspective expected of a news reporter.

Media messages in the fiction story tradition don't unsettle anyone if they sensationalize to emphasize a point. Sensationalistic exaggeration in a serious biography, however, is unforgivable.

ETHICS AS AN INTELLECTUAL PROCESS

A set of rules, easily memorized and mindlessly employed, would be too easy. It doesn't work that way. Ethics, rather, needs to be an intellectual process of sorting through media commitments, audience expectations and broad principles. But even on broad principles there is more.

LEARNING CHECK ◄ ·······································
▶ **Why do ethics expectations differ among media organizations?**

Moral Principles

STUDY PREVIEW

Concern about doing the right thing is part of human nature, and leading thinkers have developed a great number of enduring moral principles over the centuries. The mass media, like other institutions and also like individuals, draw on these principles, but this does not always make moral decisions easy. The principles are not entirely consistent, especially in sorting through dilemmas.

Aristotle. *Shown in the fashions of the 15th-century artist who painted this portrait, the Greek thinker Aristotle told his students almost 2,400 years ago that right courses of action avoid extremes. His recommendation: moderation.*

● **Aristotle**
Advocate of the Golden Mean

● **Golden Mean**
Moderation is the best course

● **"Do unto others"**
Judeo-Christian principle for ethical behavior

● **Immanuel Kant**
Advocated the categorical imperative

● **categorical imperative**
A principle that can be applied in any and all circumstances with moral certitude

THE GOLDEN MEAN

The Greek philosopher **Aristotle,** writing almost 2,400 years ago, devised the **Golden Mean** as a basis for moral decision making. The Golden Mean sounds simple and straightforward: Avoid extremes and seek moderation. Modern journalistic balance and fairness are founded on this principle.

The Golden Mean's dictate, however, is not as simple as it sounds. As with all moral principles, application of the Golden Mean can present difficulties. Consider the federal law that requires over-the-air broadcasters to give equal opportunity to candidates for public office. If one candidate buys 30 seconds at 7 p.m. for $120, a station is obligated to allow other candidates for the same office to buy 30 seconds at the same time for the same rate. On the surface this application of the Golden Mean, embodied in federal law, might seem to be reasonable, fair and morally right, but the issue is far more complex. The equality requirement, for example, gives an advantage to candidates who hold simplistic positions that can be expressed compactly. Good and able candidates whose positions require more time to explain are disadvantaged, and society is damaged when inferior candidates win public office.

"DO UNTO OTHERS"

The Judeo-Christian principle of "**Do unto others** as you would have them do unto you" appeals to most Americans. Not even the do-unto-others prescription is without problems, however. Consider the photojournalist who sees virtue in serving a mass audience with a truthful account of the human condition. This might manifest itself in portrayals of great emotions, like grief. But would the photojournalist appreciate being photographed herself in a grieving moment after learning that her own infant son had died in an accident? If not, her pursuit of truth through photography for a mass audience would be contrary to the "do-unto-others" dictum.

CATEGORICAL IMPERATIVES

About 200 years ago, German philosopher **Immanuel Kant** wrote that moral decisions should flow from thoroughly considered principles. As he put it, "Act on the maxim that you would want to become universal law." He called his maxim the categorical imperative. A **categorical imperative,** well thought out, is a principle that the individual who devised it would be willing to apply in all moral questions of a similar sort. In a way, Kant recast the Judeo-Christian "do unto others" admonition but more intellectually and less intuitively.

Kant's categorical imperative does not dictate specifically what actions are morally right or wrong. Moral choices, says Kant, go deeper than the context of the immediate issue. He encourages a philosophical approach to moral questions, with people using

media timeline

	ETHICS MILESTONES		PIVOTAL EVENTS

Early eras

Aristotle
The Golden Mean (400 B.C.)

Jesus Christ
"Do unto others as you would have them do unto you" (20)

- Greek defeat of Persians at Marathon (490 B.C.)
- Athenian democracy (430 B.C.–)
- Roman domination of Mediterranean (250–300 B.C.)

1700s

Immanuel Kant
Categorical imperatives (1785)

- Johannes Gutenberg's movable metal type (1440s)
- Martin Luther launched Reformation (1517)
- Age of Science, Age of Reason began (1600s–)
- Isaac Newton's natural laws (1687)
- Industrial Revolution (1760s–)
- Revolutionary War (1776–1781)

Kant, less intuitive on ethics, more intellectual

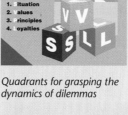

Quadrants for grasping the dynamics of dilemmas

1800s

John Stuart Mill
Utilitarianism (1865)

Wayland Ayer
First advertising agency (1869)

Yellow Press
Sensationalism grew as factor in news (1890s)

- Morse invented telegraph (1844)
- Darwin's seminal work on human evolution (1859)
- U.S. Civil War (1861–1864)
- Railroad link of Atlantic and Pacific coasts (1869)

1900s

John Dewey
Pragmatism (1903)

World War I
U.S. government stirred war enthusiasm with comprehensive promotion (1917)

News Ethics
Upton Sinclair exposed newsroom abuses in *The Brass Check* (1919)

Ethics Code
American Society of Newspaper Editors adopted first media ethics code (1923)

Social Responsibility
Hutchins Commission urged media to be socially responsible (1947)

Ethics as Process
Ralph Potter devised quadrants as a model to deal with dilemmas (1965)

John Rawls
The veil of ignorance (1971)

Hutchins, a paradigm shift to social responsibility

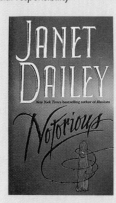

Copycat romance novel a plagiarist embarrassment

- Right to vote extended to women (1920)
- Radio emerged as mass medium (1920s)
- Great Depression (1930s)
- World War II (1941–1945)
- Television emerged as mass medium (1950s)
- Humans reached moon (1969)
- Netscape browser ignited the Internet as a mass medium (1997)

2000s

Interest
Plagiarism swelled with growing access to digitized media (2000s)

- 9/11 terrorist attacks (2001)
- Iraq War (2003–)
- Hurricane Katrina (2005)

John Dewey. *He saw decisions as ethical if the ascertainable outcomes were good.*

● **John Stuart Mill**
Advocated utilitarianism

● **principle of utility**
Best course bestows the most good for the most people

● **John Dewey**
Advocate of pragmatism

● **pragmatic ethics**
Judge acts by their results

● **John Rawls**
Advocated egalitarianism

● **veil of ignorance**
Making decisions with a blind eye to extraneous factors that could affect the decision

● **egalitarianism**
Treat everyone the same

John Rawls. *He favored putting a blind eye to all issues except rightness and wrongness. The* veil of ignorance, *he called it.*

their intellect to identify principles that they, as individuals, would find acceptable if applied universally.

Kant does not encourage the kind of standardized approach to ethics represented by professional codes. His emphasis, rather, is on hard thinking. The point has been put this way by scholar Patricia Smith, writing in the *Journal of Mass Media Ethics*: "A philosophical approach to ethics embodies a commitment to consistency, clarity, the principled evaluation of arguments and unrelenting persistence to get to the bottom of things."

UTILITARIAN ETHICS

In the mid-1800s British thinker **John Stuart Mill** declared that morally right decisions are those that result in "happiness for the greatest number." Mill called his idea the **principle of utility.** It sounds good to many of us because it parallels the democratic principle of majority rule, with its emphasis on the greatest good for the greatest number of people.

By and large, journalists embrace Mill's utilitarianism today, as evinced in notions like the *people's right to know,* a concept originally meant to support journalistic pursuit of information about government, putting the public's interests ahead of government's interests, but which has come to be almost reflexively invoked to defend pursuing very personal information about individuals, no matter what the human toll.

PRAGMATIC ETHICS

John Dewey, an American thinker who wrote in the late 1800s and early 1900s, argued that the virtue of moral decisions had to be judged by their results. Dewey's **pragmatic ethics,** like other ethics systems, has problems. One is that people do not have crystal balls to tell them for sure whether their moral actions will have good consequences.

EGALITARIAN ETHICS

In the 20th century, philosopher **John Rawls** introduced the **veil of ignorance** as an element in ethics decisions. Choosing a right course of action, said Rawls, requires blindness to social position or other discriminating factors. This is known as **egalitarianism.** An ethical decision requires that all people be given an equal hearing and the same fair consideration.

To Rawls, a brutal slaying in an upscale suburb deserves the same journalistic attention as a similarly brutal slaying in a poor urban neighborhood. All other things being equal, a $20,000 bank burglary is no more newsworthy than a $20,000 embezzlement.

SOCIAL RESPONSIBILITY ETHICS

The **Hutchins Commission,** a learned group led by intellectual **Robert Hutchins** that studied the U.S.

Immanuel Kant. *This 18th-century philosopher urged people to find principles that they would be comfortable having applied in all situations. He called these universal principles categorical imperatives.*

John Stuart Mill. *Americans tend to like Mill's utilitarianism, which favors actions that result in the greatest good for the greatest number of people. This approach to ethics dovetails well with democratic theory and majority rule.*

Robert Hutchins. *His commission elevated social responsibility as a factor in ethics decisions in mass communication.*

● **Hutchins Commission**
Advocated social responsibility as
goal and result of media activities

● **Robert Hutchins**
Called for the new media to emphasize its social responsibility, not only
its freedom

● **social responsibility**
Making decisions that serve society
responsibly

mass media in the 1940s, recommended that journalists and other media people make decisions that serve the society responsibly. For all its virtues the **social responsibility** system, like all ethics systems, has difficulties. For one thing decision-makers can only imperfectly foresee the effects of their decisions. It is not possible to predict with 100 percent confidence whether every decision will turn out to be socially responsible. Also, well-meaning people may differ honestly about how society is most responsibly served.

LEARNING CHECK ◄ ···

▶ **Can you identify the ethics principle or system most associated with Aristotle? Immanuel Kant? John Stuart Mill? John Dewey? Robert Hutchins? John Rawls?**

Process Versus Outcome

STUDY PREVIEW

The various approaches to ethics fall into two broad categories: deontological ethics and teleological ethics. Deontologists say people need to follow good rules. Teleologists judge morality not by the rules but by the consequences of decisions.

DEONTOLOGICAL ETHICS

● **deontological ethics**
Good actions flow from good
processes

The Greek word *deon*, which means "duty," is at the heart of **deontological ethics,** which holds that people act morally when they follow good rules. Deontologists feel that people are duty bound to identify these rules.

Deontologists include people who believe that Scripture holds all the answers for right living. Their equivalent among media practitioners are those who rely entirely on codes of ethics drafted by organizations they trust. Following rules is a prescriptive form of ethics. At first consideration, ethics might seem as easy as following the rules, but not all questions are clear-cut. In complicated situations, the rules sometimes contradict each other. Some cases are dilemmas with no right option—only a choice among less-than-desirable options.

Deontological ethics becomes complicated, and also more intellectually interesting, when individuals, unsatisfied with other people's rules, try to work out their own universally applicable moral principles.

Here are some major deontological approaches:

● **theory of divine command**
Proper decisions follow God's will

● **theory of divine right of kings**
Monarchs derive authority from
God, not from their subjects

● **theory of secular command**
Holds that authorities legitimately
hold supreme authority although not
necessarily with a divine authority

● **libertarian theory**
Given good information and time,
people ultimately make right
decisions

● **teleology**
Good decisions are those with good
consequences

- **Theory of divine command.** This theory holds that proper moral decisions come from obeying the commands of God, with blind trust that the consequences will be good.
- **Theory of divine right of kings.** This theory sees virtue in allegiance to a divinely anointed monarch.
- **Theory of secular command.** This theory is a nonreligious variation that stresses allegiance to a dictator or other political leader from whom the people take cues when making moral decisions.
- **Libertarian theory.** This theory stresses a laissez-faire approach to ethics: Give free rein to the human ability to think through problems, and people almost always will make morally right decisions.
- **Categorical imperative theory.** This theory holds that virtue results when people identify and apply universal principles.

TELEOLOGICAL ETHICS

Unlike deontological ethics, which is concerned with the right actions, teleological ethics is concerned with the consequences of actions. The word **teleology** comes from the Greek word *teleos*, which means "result" or "consequence."

Teleologists see flaws in the formal, legalistic duty to rules of deontologists, noting that great harm sometimes flows from blind allegiance to rules.

Here are some major teleological approaches:

- **Pragmatic theory.** This theory encourages people to look at human experience to determine the probable consequences of an action and then decide its desirability.
- **Utilitarian theory.** This theory favors ethics actions that benefit more people than they damage—the greatest good for the greatest number.
- **Social responsibility theory.** This theory judges actions by the good effect they have on society.

SITUATIONAL ETHICS

Firm deontologists see two primary flaws in teleological ethics:

- Imperfect foresight.
- Lack of guiding principles.

● **situational ethics**
Make ethics decisions on the basis of situation at hand

Despite these flaws, many media practitioners apply teleological approaches, sometimes labeled **situational ethics,** to arrive at moral decisions. They gather as much information as they can about a situation and then decide, not on the basis of principle but on the facts of the situation. Critics of situational ethics worry about decisions governed by situations. Much better, they argue, would be decisions flowing from principles of enduring value. With situational ethics the same person might do one thing one day and on another day go another direction in a similar situation.

Consider a case at the *Rocky Mountain News* in Denver. Editors learned that the president of a major suburban newspaper chain had killed his parents and sister in another state when he was 18. After seven years in a mental hospital the man completed college, moved to Colorado, lived a model life and became a successful newspaper executive. The *Rocky Mountain News* decided not to make a story of it. Said a *News* official, "The only reason for dredging up [his] past would be to titillate morbid curiosity or to shoot down, maliciously, a successful citizen."

However, when another newspaper revealed the man's past, the *Rocky Mountain News* reversed itself and published a lengthy piece of its own. Why? The newspaper that broke the story had suggested that *News* editors knew about the man's past and had decided to protect him as a fellow member of the journalistic fraternity. *News* editors denied that their motivation was to protect the man. To prove it, they reconsidered their decision and published a story on him. The *News* explained its change of mind by saying that the situation had changed. *News* editors, concerned that their newspaper's credibility had been challenged, thought that printing a story would set that straight. Of less concern, suddenly, was that the story would titillate morbid curiosity or contribute to the destruction of a successful citizen. It was a classic case of situational ethics.

Flip-flops on moral issues, such as what happened at the *Rocky Mountain News*, bother critics of situational ethics. The critics say that decisions should be based on deeply rooted moral principles—not immediate, transient facts or changing peripheral contexts.

LEARNING CHECK ◀ •

▶ As someone who reads newspapers and watches newscasts, do you favor deontological or teleological ethics? Which system do you think most journalists favor? Why?

▶ What is the attraction of situational ethics for sorting out dilemmas? And what is the problem?

Potter's Box

STUDY PREVIEW

Moral problems in the mass media can be so complex that it may seem there is no solution. While ideal answers without any negative results may be impossible, a process exists for identifying a course of action that integrates an individual's personal values with moral principles and then tests conclusions against loyalties.

FOUR QUADRANTS

● **Ralph Potter**
Ethicist who devised Potter's Box

● **Potter's Box**
Tool for sorting through the pros and cons of ethics questions

A Harvard Divinity School professor, **Ralph Potter,** devised a four-quadrant model for sorting through ethics problems. The quadrants of the square-like model, called **Potter's Box,** each pose a category of questions. Working through these categories helps to clarify the issues and leads to a morally justifiable position. These are the quadrants of Potter's Box:

■ **Situation.** In Quadrant 1 the facts of the issue are decided. Consider a newsroom in which a series of articles on rape is being developed and the question arises of whether to identify rape victims by name. Here is how the situation could be defined: The newspaper has access to a young mother who has been abducted and raped and who is willing to describe the assault in graphic detail and to discuss her experience as a witness at the assailant's trial. Also, the woman is willing to be identified in the story.

■ **Values.** Moving to Quadrant 2 of Potter's Box, editors and reporters identify the values that underlie all the available choices. This process involves listing the positive and negative values that flow from conscience. One editor might argue that full, frank discussion on social issues is necessary to deal with them. Another might say that identifying the rape victim by name might discourage others from even reporting such a crime. Other positions: Publishing the name is in poor taste. The newspaper has an obligation to protect the victim from her own possibly bad decision to allow her name to be used. The purpose of the rape series can be accomplished without using the name. Readers have a right to all the relevant information that the newspaper

Ralph Potter

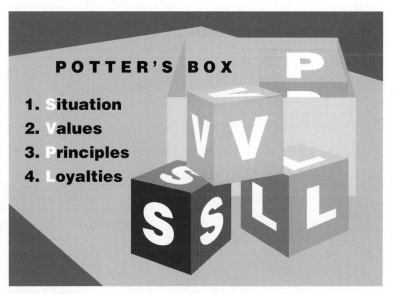

Clarifying Process. *Potter's Box offers four categories of questions to help develop morally justifiable positions. Ralph Potter, the divinity professor who devised the categories, said to start by establishing the facts of the situation. Then identify the values that underpin the options, recognizing that some values may be incompatible with others. Then consider the moral principles that support each of the values. Finally, sort through loyalties to all the affected interests. Potter's Box is not a panacea, but it provides a framework for working through ethics issues in a thorough way.*

can gather. An editor who is torn between such contrary thoughts is making progress toward a decision by at least identifying all the values that can be posited.

■ **Principles.** In Potter's Quadrant 3, decision makers search for moral principles that uphold the values they identified in Quadrant 2. John Stuart Mill's principle of utility, which favors the majority over individuals, would support using the victim's name because it could add poignancy to the story, enhancing the chances of improved public sensitivity, and perhaps even lead to improved public policy, all of which, Mill would say, outweigh the harm that might come to an individual. On the other hand, people who have used Immanuel Kant's ideas to develop inviolable operating principles—categorical imperatives—look to their rule book: We never publish information that might offend readers. One value of Potter's Quadrant 3 is that it gives people confidence in the values that emerged in their debates over Quadrant 2.

■ **Loyalties.** In Quadrant 4 the decision maker folds in an additional layer of complexity that must be sorted through: loyalties. The challenge is to establish a hierarchy of loyalties. Is the first loyalty to a code of ethics, and if so, which code? To readers, and if so, which ones? To society? To the employer? To self? Out of duty to self, some reporters and editors might want to make the rape series as potent as possible, with as much detail as possible, to win awards and bring honor to themselves and perhaps a raise or promotion or bigger job with another newspaper. Others might be motivated by their duty to their employer: The more detail in the story, the more newspapers it will sell. For others their duty to society may be paramount: The newspaper has a social obligation to present issues in as powerful a way as possible to spur reforms in general attitudes and perhaps public policy.

Potter's Box does not provide answers. Rather, it offers a process through which the key elements in ethics questions can be sorted out.

Also, Potter's Box focuses on moral aspects of a problem, leaving it to the decision-maker to examine practical considerations separately, such as whether prudence supports making the morally best decision. Moral decisions should not be made in a vacuum. For example, would it be wise to go ahead with the rape victim's name if 90 percent of the newspaper's subscribers would become so offended that they would quit buying the paper and, as a result, the paper would go out of business?

Other practical questions can involve the law. If the morally best decision is to publish the name but the law forbids it, should the newspaper proceed anyway? Does journalistic virtue transcend the law? Is it worth it to publish the name to create a First Amendment issue? Are there legal implications, like going to jail or piling up legal defense costs?

Is it worth it to go against generally accepted practices and publish the victim's name? Deciding on a course of action that runs contrary to tradition, perhaps even contrary to some ethics codes, could mean being ostracized by other media people, whose decisions might have gone another way. Doing right can be lonely.

LEARNING CHECK ◄

▶ **You are a news reporter. A candidate for mayor tells you that the incumbent mayor is in cahoots with organized crime. It's a bombshell story! Use Potter's Box to decide whether to rush to your microphone with the story.**

Ethics and Related Issues

STUDY PREVIEW

Right and wrong are issues in both ethics and law, but ethics and law are different. Obedience to law, or even to professional codes of ethics, will not always lead to moral action. There are also times when practical issues can enter moral decisions.

Tennis champion Arthur Ashe was glad but then leery to hear his old high school chum Doug Smith on the phone. Smith, tennis reporter for *USA Today*, wanted to see him for an interview. It was not unusual for reporters to call on Ashe. He was the first world-class black American male tennis player, and after his athletic prime he had campaigned vigorously against apartheid. But by 1992 he worried with every interview that the question of whether he had AIDS would surface.

Ashe, in fact, did have AIDS. He had contracted the virus apparently in 1983 during surgery. Five years later, when doctors found the infection, Ashe began therapy for the debilitating and fatal disease. He decided against going public with the fact that he had the disease, and his family and friends went along with what Ashe called "a silent and generous conspiracy to assist me in maintaining my privacy."

When Doug Smith showed up for the interview, he asked the dreaded question: "Do you have AIDS?" Although Ashe realized that some reporter someday would ask the question, it nonetheless caught him off guard. "Could be," he quipped. Then he recognized how much more revealing his words were than he intended. The secret was out.

The next afternoon, before Smith's article could appear, Ashe called a news conference to announce that he suffered from AIDS. Although he was gentle on *USA Today,* Ashe criticized the mass media for intruding into the private lives of people. In the news conference, carried live by CNN, Ashe said, "I am sorry that I have been forced to make this revelation at this time. After all, I am not running for some office of public trust, nor do I have stockholders to account to. It is only that I fall in the dubious umbrella of, quote, public figure, end of quote."

Private Issue? *Tennis hero Arthur Ashe objected that news media inquiries about his AIDS violated his privacy.*

Ironically, *USA Today* had decided against going with the story, but Ashe's news conference nonetheless epitomized one of the great media ethics questions of our time: Who prevails when the mass media are at the intersection of the public's interest in knowing certain information and an individual's interest in preserving personal privacy? Like all vexatious ethics questions, people on both sides feel strongly and mount powerful arguments for their positions. Journalists themselves are hardly of one mind.

Among those supporting *USA Today's* initiative was Gerry Callahan of the Boston *Herald*. Callahan said that the violation of Ashe's privacy was committed by whoever in his circle of friends tipped the newspaper anonymously. The newspaper, he said, merely was performing its function of checking out tips.

Not everyone saw it that way. *USA Today* received almost 1,100 calls, with 60 people canceling their subscriptions. Among journalists, there were negative reactions too: Mona Charen, a syndicated columnist, wrote that the fact that Ashe was a great athlete who had established a milestone for blacks was "no reason to treat his personal struggle as a peep show."

WHAT DO YOU THINK?

▶ Would ethics questions in an AIDS case be less poignant today, almost 20 years after Arthur Ashe died?

▶ To what extent do celebrities forfeit their privacy?

▶ Should editors decide whether to pursue a story because public outrage is a risk?

517

DIFFERENTIATING ETHICS AND LAW

Ethics is an individual matter that relates closely to conscience. Because conscience is unique to each individual, no two people have exactly the same moral framework. There are, however, issues about which there is consensus. No right-minded person condones murder, for example. When there is a universal feeling, ethics becomes codified in law, but laws do not address all moral questions. It is the issues of right and wrong that do not have a consensus that make ethics difficult. Was it morally right for *USA Today* to initiate coverage of tennis superstar Arthur Ashe's AIDS?

Ethics and law are related but separate. The law will allow a mass-media practitioner to do many things that the practitioner would refuse to do. Since the 1964 *New York Times* v. *Sullivan* case, the U.S. Supreme Court has allowed the news media to cause tremendous damage to public officials, even with false information. However, rare is the journalist who would intentionally push the *Sullivan* latitudes to their limits to pillory a public official.

The ethics decisions of an individual mass-media practitioner usually are more limiting than the law. There are times, though, when a journalist may choose to break the law on the grounds of ethics. Applying John Stuart Mill's principle of "the greatest good," a radio reporter might choose to break the speed limit to reach a chemical plant where an accident is threatening to send a deadly cloud toward where her listeners live. Breaking a speed limit might seem petty as an example, but it demonstrates that obeying the law and obeying one's conscience do not always coincide.

LEARNING CHECK ◄ ··

▸ **Can breaking the law ever be justified?**

ACCEPTED PRACTICES

Just as there is no reliable correlation between law and ethics, neither is there one between accepted media practices and ethics. What is acceptable at one advertising agency to make a product look good in photographs might be unacceptable at another. Even universally **accepted practices** should not go unexamined, for unless accepted practices are examined and reconsidered on a continuing basis, media practitioners can come to rely more on habit than on principles in their work.

● **accepted practices**
What media do as a matter of routine, sometimes without considering ethics implications

PRUDENCE AND ETHICS

● **prudence**
Applying wisdom, not principles, to an ethics situation

Prudence is the application of wisdom in a practical situation. It can be a leveling factor in moral questions. Consider the case of Irvin Lieberman, who had built his *Main Line Chronicle* and several other weeklies in the Philadelphia suburbs into aggressive, journalistically excellent newspapers. After being hit with nine libel suits, all costly to defend, Lieberman softenend the thrust of his newspapers. "I decided not to do any investigative work," he said. "It was a matter of either feeding my family or spending my whole life in court." Out of prudence, Lieberman decided to abandon his commitment to hard-hitting, effective journalism.

Courageous pursuit of morally lofty ends can, as a practical matter, be foolish. Whether Irvin Lieberman was exhibiting a moral weakness by bending to the chilling factor of libel suits, which are costly to fight, or being prudent is an issue that could be debated forever. The point, however, is that prudence cannot be ignored as a factor in moral decisions.

When Government Defines Ethics

Dead bodies make gruesome footage. People avert their eyes or avoid them altogether. After Hurricane Katrina decimated the U.S. Gulf Coast, killing more than 1,000 people and displacing a million, the Federal Emergency Management Agency (FEMA) issued a "zero access" order for news photography of the dead. Why? On the front line of the disaster, agency people lectured video-shooters on ethics:

• The dead deserve a dignity that photographs would violate.
• Decent people don't want to see loathsome images.
• Why intrude on the sanctity of the victims?

FEMA's attempt to block photographers wasn't anything new. In recent years, government agencies have increasingly tried to cloak restrictions on news coverage in the language of ethics. The fact, though, is that ethics are hardly so simple.

CNN, thwarted in their Katrina coverage, rushed to court to overturn the FEMA ban. The court agreed. The ban was nullified. Newsrooms, not government, were left with the ethics choices in how to tell the story of one of the worst disasters in U.S. history.

So who was right—FEMA or CNN? The Katrina case illustrates the difficulty of media ethics and why quick answers are hopelessly simplistic.

By definition, ethics issues are dilemmatic. Even after agonizing review, right-minded people can arrive at conflicting conclusions. CNN's premise was that thorough reporting necessitated access to all aspects of the unfolding Katrina disaster. Without the facts, people would be less well equipped to assess the seriousness of the situation. And why should coverage of a domestic disaster be softer than that of disasters abroad? Horrific images from the Indian Ocean tsunami disaster less than a year earlier were still fresh in people's minds. FEMA critics noted, too, that the agency had a stake in minimizing coverage of its own failure to respond quickly and adequately. The more intense the coverage, the worse the agency would appear.

Whose Ethics? While government disaster-relief executives were proclaiming their handling of Hurricane Katrina a success, even with President Bush joining the upbeat choir, the government was trying to keep news reporters from reporting the grisly realities.

DEEPENING YOUR MEDIA LITERACY

EXPLORE THE ISSUE

Consider the amateur images of U.S. soldiers torturing prisoners at the Abu Ghraib prison, which surfaced on the Internet in April 2004. The government released its files only after the Internet postings had stirred public outrage.

DIG DEEPER

Check archived newspapers or magazines in your library or reliable Web sources for the debate over Abu Ghraib issues.

WHAT DO YOU THINK?

Was the government policy ethical in serving the public's interest? Or was the government protecting itself from criticism, or even from losing support for broad policies? In deciding what belongs in public discourse, would you trust a mainstream newsroom or a government agency that has the ability not only to control access to lots of information but also to suppress the release of information?

Unsettled, Unsettling Questions

STUDY PREVIEW

When mass-media people discuss ethics, they talk about right and wrong behavior, but creating policies on ethics issues is not easy. Many standard media practices press the line between right and wrong, which muddies clear-cut standards that are universally applicable and recognized. There is further muddiness because many ethics codes confuse unethical behavior with behavior that may appear unethical but is not necessarily so.

PLAGIARISM

● **plagiarism**
Using someone else's work without permission or credit

Janet Dailey

Copycat Romance.
Widespread Internet access is facilitating plagiarism, much of it among people who don't know better. But it remains a taboo in media work. Janet Dailey's Notorious *was withdrawn and shredded by publisher HarperCollins after rival romance writer Nora Roberts spotted passages that Dailey had lifted.*

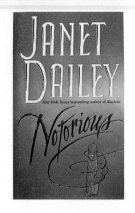

Perhaps the most fiercely loyal media fans are those who read romance novels and swear by a favorite author. In an Internet chatroom in 1997, romance writer Janet Dailey found herself boxed into an admission that she had plagiarized from rival writer Nora Roberts. There is no scorn like that of creative people for those who steal their work, and Roberts was "very, very upset." HarperCollins recalled *Notorious*, Dailey's book that contained the plagiarism, and Roberts' fans, many of them longtime Dailey detractors, began a hunt for other purloined passages.

What is **plagiarism?** Generally, it's considered passing off someone else's creative work as your own, without permission. It's still plagiarism even if the original is changed a tad, as was Dailey's loose paraphrasing.

The fact that Dailey's 93 books over 20 years had sold an average of more than 2 million each made the scandal all the juicier. In the end Roberts proposed a financial settlement, and the proceeds went to promote literacy.

Everyone agrees that plagiarism, a form of thievery, is unethical, but the issue is not simple. The fact is that in many media, people draw heavily on other people's ideas and work. Think about sitcom story lines that mimic each other or the bandwagon of movies that follow an unexpected hit with an oddball theme that suddenly becomes mainstream. Journalists, most of whom consider themselves especially pristine compared to their media brethren, have standard practices that encourage a lot of "borrowing."

Among factors that make journalists uncomfortable when pressed hard on plagiary questions are:

- Institutionalized exchanging of stories.
- The role of public relations in generating news stories.
- Monitoring the competition.
- Subliminal memory and innocent recall.

This all is further complicated by a cut-and-paste mentality that has been facilitated by digitized messages on the Internet. A whole new generation is missing a level of sensitivity to traditionally recognized rights of people who create or own intellectual property to control its reuse.

■ **Swapping Stories.** Some creative work, like scholarship, requires that information and ideas be attributed to their sources. Journalists are not so strict, as shown by story swapping through the Associated Press. The AP picks up stories from its members and distributes them to other members, generally without any reference to the source. Some publications and broadcasters do not even acknowledge AP as the intermediary.

Conditioned by 150 years of the AP's being a journalistic model and under pressure to gather information quickly, many journalists have a high tolerance for "borrowing." When the Chicago *Tribune* was apologizing for a story cribbed from the Jerusalem *Post*, for example, one of the writer's colleagues defended the story: "Everybody rewrites the Jerusalem *Post*. That's how foreign correspondents work."

Incredible as it seems, journalistic tolerance for plagiarism once even allowed radio stations to pilfer the local newspaper for newscasts. Sometimes you could hear the announcer turning the pages. A sad joke that acknowledged this practice was that some stations bought their news at 50 cents a copy, which was cheaper than hiring reporters to cover the community. So pervasive was the journalistic tolerance for "borrowing" that few newspapers protested even mildly when their stories were pirated.

MISREPRESENTATION

Janet Cooke's meteoric rise at the Washington *Post* unraveled quickly the day after she received a Pulitzer Prize. Her editors had been so impressed with her story "Jimmy's World," about a child who was addicted to heroin, that they had nominated it for a Pulitzer Prize. The gripping tale began: "Jimmy is 8 years old and a third-generation heroin addict, a precocious little boy with sandy hair, velvety brown eyes and needle marks freckling the baby-smooth skin of his thin brown arms." Janet Cooke claimed that she had won the confidence of Jimmy's mother and her live-in male friend, a drug dealer, to do the story. Cooke said she had promised not to reveal their identities as a condition for her access to Jimmy.

The story, which played on the front page, so shocked Washington that people demanded that Jimmy be taken away from his mother and placed in a foster home. The *Post* declined to help authorities, citing Cooke's promise of confidentiality to her sources. The mayor ordered the police to find Jimmy with or without the newspaper's help, and millions of dollars in police resources went into a door-to-door search. After 17 days the police gave up knocking on doors for tips on Jimmy. Some doubts emerged at the *Post* about the story, but the newspaper stood behind its reporter.

Janet Cooke, 25 when she was hired by the *Post*, had extraordinary credentials. Her résumé showed a baccalaureate degree, magna cum laude, from Vassar; study at the Sorbonne in Paris; a master's degree from the University of Toledo; abilities in several languages; and two years of journalistic experience with the Toledo *Blade*. Said Ben Bradlee, editor of the *Post*: "She had it all. She was bright. She was well spoken. She was pretty. She wrote well." She was also black, which made her especially attractive to the *Post*, which was working to bring the percentage of black staff reporters nearer to the percentage of blacks in the newspaper's circulation area.

Six months after "Jimmy's World" was published, the Pulitzer committee announced its decision and issued a biographical sheet on Janet Cooke. The Associated Press, trying to flesh out the biographical information, spotted discrepancies right away. Janet Cooke, it turned out, had attended Vassar for one year but had not graduated with the honors she claimed. The University of Toledo had no record of awarding her a master's. Suddenly, doubts that had surfaced in the days immediately after "Jimmy's World" was published took on a new intensity. The editors sat Cooke down and grilled her on the claims on which she was hired. No, she admitted, she was not multilingual. The Sorbonne claim was fuzzy. More important, they pressed her on whether there was really a Jimmy. The interrogation continued into the night, and finally Janet Cooke confessed all: There were no confidential sources, and there was no Jimmy. She had fabricated the story. She resigned, and the *Post*, terribly embarrassed, returned the Pulitzer.

In cases of outright fabrication, as in "Jimmy's World," it is easy to identify the lapses in ethics. When Janet Cooke emerged briefly from seclusion to explain herself, she said that she had been responding to pressures in the *Post* newsroom to produce flashy, sensational copy. Most people found the explanation unsatisfying, considering the pattern of deception that went back to her falsified résumé.

There are **misrepresentations,** however, that are not as clearly unacceptable. Much debated are the following:

■ **Staging News.** To attract favorable attention to their clients, public relations people organize media events, a practice known as **staging news.** These are designed to be irresistible to journalists. Rallies and demonstrations on topical issues, for example, find their way onto front pages, magazine covers and evening newscasts because their photogenic qualities give them an edge over less visual although sometimes more significant events. The ethics question is less important for publicists, who generally are up front about what they are doing. The ethics question is more serious for journalists, who claim that their job is to present an accurate, balanced account of a day's events but who regularly overplay staged events that are designed by publicists to be photogenic and easy to cover.

■ Re-Creations. Some television **reality programs** feature **reenactments** that are not always labeled as such. Philip Weiss, writing in *Columbia Journalism Review*, offered this litany: shadows on the wall of a woman taking a hammer to her husband, a faceless actor grabbing a tin of kerosene to blow up his son, a corpse in a wheelbarrow with a hand dangling, a detective opening the trunk of a car and reeling from the smell of a decomposing body. Although mixing re-creations with strictly news footage rankles many critics, others argue that it helps people understand the situation. The same question arises with docudramas, which mix actual events and dramatic re-creations.

■ Selective Editing. The editing process, by its nature, requires journalists to make decisions on what is most worth emphasizing and what is least worth even including. In this sense, all editing is selective, but the term **selective editing** refers to making decisions with the goal of distorting. Selective editing can occur in drama too, when writers, editors and other media people take literary license too far and intentionally misrepresent.

■ Fictional Methods. In the late 1960s many experiments in media portrayals of people and issues came to be called the **new journalism.** The term was hard to define because it included so many approaches. Among the most controversial were applications of fiction-writing methods to topical issues, an approach widely accepted in book publishing but suddenly controversial when it appeared in the news media. Character development became more important than before, including presumed insights into the thinking of people being covered. The view of the writer became an essential element in much of this reporting. The defense for these approaches was that traditional, facts-only reporting could not approach complex truths that merited journalistic explorations. The profound ethics questions that these approaches posed were usually mitigated by clear statements about what the writer was attempting. Nonetheless, it was a controversial approach to the issues of the day. There was no defense when the fictional approach was complete fabrication passing itself off as reality, as in "Jimmy's World."

LEARNING CHECK ◄ •••••••••••••••••••••••••••••••••••••

▸ **How have mass-media practices muddied plagiarism as an issue?**

▸ **If plagiarism is so bad, why do more and more people do it? Are there any ethics principles or systems that would condone plagiarism?**

GIFTS, JUNKETS AND MEALS

In his 1919 book ***The Brass Check,*** a pioneer examination of newsroom ethics, **Upton Sinclair** told how newspeople took bribes to put stories in the paper. Today all media ethics codes condemn gifts and certainly bribes. Even so, there are still people who curry favor with the mass media through gifts, such as a college sports publicist who gives a fifth of whisky at Christmas to a sportswriter as a gesture of goodwill. Favors can take many forms: media-appreciation lunches; free trips abroad, known as **junkets,** especially for travel writers; season passes to cover the opera; discounts at certain stores.

Despite the consistent exhortation of the ethics codes against gifts, favors, free travel and special treatment and privileges, there is nothing inherently wrong

- **reality programs**
Broadcast shows with a nonfiction basis

- **reenactments**
Re-creating real events

- **selective editing**
Misrepresentation through omission and juxtaposition

- **new journalism**
Mixing fiction techniques with nonfiction

- *The Brass Check*
1919 book that exposed newsroom corruption

- **Upton Sinclair**
Author of *The Brass Check*

- **junket**
Trip with expenses paid by someone who may expect favors in return

in taking them if they do not influence coverage and if the journalist's benefactor understands that. The problem with favors is more a practical one than one of ethics. Taking a favor may or may not be bad, but it *looks* bad. Many ethics codes do not make this important distinction. One that does is the code of the Associated Press Managing Editors, which states: "Journalists must avoid impropriety and *the appearance of impropriety* as well as any conflict of interest or *the appearance of conflict.* They should neither accept anything nor pursue any activity that might compromise or *seem to compromise* their integrity" [italics added]. The APME admonitions at least recognize the distinction between the inherent wrongness of impropriety, which is an ethics question, and the perception that something may be wrong, which is a perception that is unwise to encourage but is not necessarily unethical.

● **freebies**
Gift for which the giver may expect favors in return

While ethics codes are uniform in prohibiting **freebies,** as gifts and favors are called, many news organizations accept free movie, drama, concert and other tickets, as well as recordings, books and other materials for review. The justifications are usually that their budgets allow them to review only materials that arrive free and that their audiences would be denied reviews if the materials had to be purchased. A counterargument is that a news organization that cannot afford to do business right should not be in business. Many news organizations insist on buying tickets for their reporters to beauty pageants, sports events and other things to which there is an admission fee. A frequent exception occurs when a press box or special media facility is available. With recordings, books and free samples, some media organizations return them or pass them on to charity to avoid any appearance that they have been bought off.

When junkets are proposed, some organizations send reporters only if they can pay the fare and other expenses. The Louisville *Courier-Journal* is firm: "Even on chartered trips, such as accompanying a sports team, or hitchhiking on a State Police plane, we insist on being billed for our pro-rata share of the expense." An exception is made by some news organizations for trips that they could not possibly arrange on their own, such as covering a two-week naval exercise aboard a ship.

Some media organizations address the issue of impropriety by acknowledging favors. Many quiz shows say that "promotional consideration" has been provided to companies that give them travel, lodging and prizes. Just as forthright are publications that state that reviews are made possible through season passes or free samples. Acknowledging favors does not remove the questions, but at least it is up front.

LEARNING CHECK ◄ •

▶ **As a news editor, how would you handle a proposal from the National Guard to ferry a reporter in a Guard aircraft to hometown unit training exercises? "Just have the reporter bring a pad, pencil and camera," says the Guard public relations officer. "We'll provide lodging, field meals, flak jackets and everything else—even a souvenir t-shirt and Guard baseball cap."**

Chapter Wrap-Up

The Difficulty of Ethics (Page 506)

- Media people have no shortage of ethics codes. Every professional organization has one. This multitude of ethics codes makes it easy for people to infer that ethical behavior is a simple matter of learning and obeying the rules. But they are missing the complexity of moral issues. No matter how well intentioned the ethics codes, they have limited usefulness. Merely to follow prescribed rules with unique, sometimes nuanced subtleties make for a particular dilemma. No prescriptive code, cast in broad terms as they must be, can replace a good mind and the application of broad, universal principles.

Media Ethics (Page 509)

■ Mass communicators try to do good in an often-confusing combination of obligations. One fundamental obligation, for example, is to serve the audience. But who decides what serves the audience best? The editors of the New York *Times* and the *National Enquirer* could debate endlessly on that. Imagine the conflict of advertising-supported media when the interests of advertisers and listeners don't coincide. That's been the crux of ethics debates on sugary, fat-laden snacks marketed to kids.

Moral Principles (Page 510)

■ Philosophers have struggled over the centuries to devise overarching principles to sort through moral dilemmas. In the 1700s Immanuel Kant proposed *categorical imperatives*—broad principles that everyone would see as acceptable for dealing with any and all situations. The Kant idea is not prescriptive as much as it is a call for thorough consideration, clarity of thinking, and consistency.

Process Versus Outcome (Page 513)

■ Nothing better demonstrates the complexity of ethics than the conflict between deontologists and teleologists. Deontologists emphasize creating good rules. As deontologists see it, applying good rules results in good behavior. Whoa, say the teleologists. They can cite all kinds of well-intentioned rules that backfired in particular situations. Teleologists argue that behavior can be judged better by the results. A third school of ethicists approach each moral dilemma from scratch. The idea is to consider the facts of a situation without any larger or philosophical framework. Critics of situational ethics note, however, that no two human minds work alike. Without agreed-upon principles, people end up with very different ideas of how to handle a dilemma. Not everyone can be right.

Potter's Box (Page 515)

■ By definition, a moral dilemma has no perfect solution. That's what makes a dilemma a dilemma. A useful process for working through problems, called Potter's Box, is to start with the facts and apply values and principles—and then to sort through loyalties that affect everyone involved. Potter's Box emphasizes not rules but an intellectual process in finding answers.

Ethics and Related Issues (Page 516)

■ Ethics and law often are confused. The confusion is no better illustrated than by someone claiming to have been ethical for following a law. Ethics is not so simple. Think about the long history of whistleblowers who have violated national security laws and been lauded as heroes for exposing wrongheaded government policies. Sometimes ethics is confused with standard and accepted practices in a profession. The fact, however, is that accepted practices need continuing reconsideration as to their efficacy. Mimicking old ways of doing things may or may not be practicing good behavior.

Unsettled, Unsettling Questions (Page 520)

■ Many standard media practices border on the shady. None is more problematic than plagiarism. Everybody condemns plagiarism as thievery and dishonesty, but a tremendous amount of "borrowing" occurs in creating media content. The rash of movies picking up on a blockbuster theme is one example. It's similar with misrepresentation, which is easy to condemn. But what about John Howard Griffin, a white man who dyed his skin black and traversed the South in the 1950s to see racial injustices, which helped trigger the civil rights movement? Griffin misrepresented himself. Was it the right thing to do? Or was it wrong?

REVIEW QUESTIONS

1. Why can't ethics codes anticipate all moral questions? And does this limit the value of codes for mass-media people?

2. List and explain moral principles that mass-media people can use to sort through ethics questions.

3. How can mass media people come to different conclusions depending on whether they use process-based or outcome-based ethics?

4. How is Potter's Box a useful tool to sort through ethics issues?

5. Is ethics the same as law? As prudence? As accepted practice?

6. Discuss dubious mass-media practices that are inconsistent with many moral principles.

CONCEPTS

deontological ethics (Page 513)

teleology (Page 513)

veil of ignorance (Page 512)

theory of divine command (Page 513)

libertarian theory (Page 513)

TERMS

categorical imperative (Page 510)

pragmatic ethics (Page 512)

situational ethics (Page 514)

junket (Page 522)

freebies (Page 523)

PEOPLE

Aristotle (Page 510)

Immanuel Kant (Page 510)

John Stuart Mill (Page 512)

Robert Hutchins (Page 513)

Ralph Potter (Page 515)

MEDIA SOURCES

- Thomas Bivins. *Mixed Media: Moral Distinctions in Advertising, Public Relations and Journalism*. Erlbaum, 2004. Professor Bivins stresses identifying the impact of ethics decisions in choosing courses of action.

- Clifford G. Christians, Kim B. Rotzoll and Mark Fackler. *Media Ethics,* sixth edition. Longman, 2002. These scholars are especially good at describing Kant's categorical imperative and other philosophical systems on which media ethics can be based.

- Ralph B. Potter. "The Structure of American Christian Responses to the Nuclear Dilemma, 1958–1963." Potter describes what came to be known as Potter's Box, in his Harvard University doctoral dissertation in 1965.

- Richard L. Riski and Elinor K. Grusin, "Newspaper's Naming Policy Continues Amid Controversy," *Newspaper Reseach Journal* (Fall 2003), pages 64–76.

ETHICS: A Thematic Chapter Summary

In this chapter you have deepened your media literacy by revisiting several themes. Here are thematic highlights from the chapter:

Media Technology

Changing technology through the history of the mass media has posed ethics challenges that never could have been anticipated earlier. A growing contemporary issue is a lack of sensitivity among a new generation whose practices include wholesale cutting of Internet material and pasting it into their own work without credit. Plagiarism has always been a difficult issue for the mass media, especially with the vagaries imposed by deadlines and the continuing repackaging of material. For better or worse, media people have agreed upon all kinds of conditions and rules for swapping information. Even these accepted practices cause purists in some academic fields to shudder—"Egads! No footnotes?" The issue is becoming more critical with broadening acceptance of the rampant copying that's facilitated by digitization. Old ways of doing things need to be reconsidered. (Page 520–521)

Media Economics

Advertising-dependent media have an obligation to advertisers as their financial supporters. But media also have obligations to other interests and values, including to their readers, to their owners and, let's not forget, to the truth. Weighing these obligations can expose all kinds of moral dilemmas. Consider a magazine that is financially dependent on ads for dubious Viagra substitutes. To turn away the ads could mean the magazine goes belly-up. What kind of service is that to readers who would benefit from the magazine's articles? (Pages 507–510)

Media and Democracy

For democracy to work as it should, people need accurate, timely and useful information. Ethical media conduct includes providing full reports, but are there no limits? During the 2000 presidential campaign, when an intrepid reporter in Maine unearthed a nearly 30-year-old drunken-driving conviction against George Bush, the Bush campaign people were irate and used words like *irrelevant, unfair* and *smear*. Others saw evidence of Bush not owning up to his past. They argued that he had wanted to conceal his record, which they saw as a character flaw that voters should know about. (Page 519)

Elitism and Populism

Digitization has given almost everyone a mass-media megaphone. Look around you. Who doesn't have the capability to set up a MySpace or Facebook page or become a blogger? This democratization of the mass media has triggered a need to reassess the rules by which traditional media have operated. Ethical conduct, for example,

Social Responsibility. *In 1947 a blue-ribbon task force of intellectuals headed by Robert Hutchins placed a premium on the media acting in socially responsible ways. The Hutchins ideas came to be embraced by the media, albeit with notable exceptions. But the media are no longer the easily identified companies that had the equipment and means to reach huge audiences. New technology has enabled just about anyone to enter the media marketplace, many who never heard of the Hutchins Commission and are completely oblivious to the Hutchins legacy.*

had been conditioned over the centuries and decades by conventions of copyright and widely accepted bounds on defamation, privacy and decency adopted by media organizations and the trained professionals who crafted media messages. These conventions were fortified by a broad range of institutions, including journalism schools and other career-oriented educational programs. Today, nobody needs a degree to blog or go on Facebook. **(Pages 506–523)**

Media Tomorrow

Professional media associations will continue to tweak their ethics codes, especially to address issues that could never have been anticipated because of changes wrought by technology and evolving values in society. These codes will place pressure on media people who operate at the fringes of appropriate behavior, but, lacking the force of law, will wield influence mostly through moral persuasion. On complex issues with conflicting duties, the codes will continue to have limited roles in finding answers. Only through hard thinking can moral dilemmas be addressed and even then not to universal satisfaction. **(Pages 506–523)**

Arthur Ashe. *The tennis Olympian had sought to stay private about his HIV infection from tainted blood. But suspecting that the news media wouldn't honor the privacy he wanted, Ashe went public. It was a personality distressing disclosure at the intersection of conflicting virtues in media ethics codes. By definition, ethics issues are dilemmatic and not easy, sometimes painful. Universally satisfying prescriptive answers are elusive.*

Index

PHOTO CREDITS

Images/Paul Sakuma; 138B (134B, 495B): Napster logo and marks reprinted with the permission of Napster, LLC; 139: © Kim Kulish/CORBIS; 140L: © Hulton Archive/Getty Images; 140R: © AP Images/Mark Lennihan; 143 (148C): © Kevin Winter/Getty Images; 144: © Ethan Miller/ACMA/Getty Images; 145: © Reuters/CORBIS; 150 (viiiT): © Kino International/Courtesy Everett Collection; 151: Courtesy Everett Collection; 153: © Buena Vista/Courtesy Everett Collection; 154 (180B): © Focus Films/Everett Collection; 155 (286B): © Jeff Riedel/Contour by Getty Images; 157L: © Gregg Segal Photography; 157R (162B, 180T): © WARNER BROS/DC COMICS/THE KOBAL COLLECTION; 160 (181T): © Lions Gate/Courtesy Everett Collection; 161L (162TC): © AP Images; 161R: © Hulton Archive/Getty Images; 163L: Courtesy Everett Collection; 163R (162T): © Photofest; 166: © AP Images; 167 (162BC, 181B): © AP Images; 169: © DreamWorks/Courtesy Everett Collection; 170 (180C): © Jeff Fusco/Getty Images; 171 (51B): © The Granger Collection, New York; 173: © K.C. Alfred/SDU-T/ ZUMA Press; 175L: © EPOCH/THE KOBAL COLLECTION; 175R: © UNITED ARTISTS/THE KOBAL COLLECTION; 182 (viiiB, 204B): © AP Images/Bruce L. Flashnick; 187 (185C, 205M): © AP Images; 189 (204T): © AP Images/CBS Inc.; 191 (51C, 205TL): © Spencer Platt/Getty Images; 192L (205TR): © Bettmann/CORBIS; 192R (185T, 205TC): © Bettmann/CORBIS; 198: Courtesy "Fresh Air with Terry Gross," produced in Philadelphia by WHYY. Photo by Miles Kennedy; 199: © AP Images/Gregory Bull; 200 (185B, 205B): Courtesy XM Satellite Radio; 206 (ixT, 221C, 230T): Copyright Broadcasting & Cable Magazine, Photo Illustration by Forest Evashevski; 208: © DANIEL ACKER/Bloomberg News/Landov; 210 (230C): © Jonathan Nourok/PhotoEdit; 213: © & ™ Fox/Photofest; 214: © HBO/Courtesy Everett Collection; 215: © The Cable Center; 219L: Courtesy LG Electronics MobileComm; 219R (231C): Copyright 2008, Tribune Media Services. Reprinted with permission; 220L: Cliff Lipson/© CBS/Courtesy Everett Collection; 220R (230B): John Filo/CBS, copyright 2005 CBS Broadcasting, Inc. All Rights Reserved; 221B (231B, 458TR): © Justin Sullivan/Getty Images; 224T: © Alex Wong/Getty Images for Meet the Press; 224B (231T): © AP Images/Jim Cole; 226: © NBC Universal, Inc.; 232 (ixB, 256T): © 2005 Shawn G. Henry; 239 (241T, 256TR): © AP Images; 240: © Bettmann/COR-BIS; 243 (241BC, 256TL): © Justin Sullivan/Getty Images; 245T (256C): © 2004-2005 Geoffrey R. Hutchison, licensed under a Creative Commons License; 245B (256B): © AP Images/Paul Sakuma; 247: Courtesy Wonkette.com; 248: Courtesy Glenn Reynolds, photo by Christian Lange; 249 (241B): © Copyright 2007 Strategic Forecasting Inc. All rights reserved; 252: © Kevin Morris; 253: © ERIC FEFERBERG/AFP/Getty Images; 258 (xT): © M. Kaia Sand, Courtesy Jules and Maxwell Boykoff; 261 (269T) and 264T (269TC, 287C): Copyright © North Wind Picture Archives. All rights reserved; 264B (286T, 322T): © Bettmann/CORBIS; 265 (269C): © Mathew Brady/Henry Guttmann/Getty Images; 266TL (102T), 266T (269BC) and 266BL: © Culver Pictures, Inc.; 266BR (267): © Bettmann/CORBIS; 272: © Matt Dellinger/The New Yorker; 273T (269B, 287T): © SuperStock; 273B: © AP Images; 278: © Paul Chinn/San Francisco Chronicle/CORBIS; 283 (126B): © The Granger Collection, New York; 286C: © AP Images/Brian Kersey; 288 (290, xB): Courtesy Rocket Racing League; 292 (314B): © General Motors Corp. Used with permission of GM Media Archives; 297L (294T): © The Granger Collection, New York; 295L (314T): © AP Images; 295R: Courtesy Colorado Historical Society; 297R: © AP Images; 300 (294B, 314C): © AP Images/Gerald Herbert; 301: Courtesy Dawn Bridges; 302: © AP Images/Reed Saxon; 305L (294C): © Kevin Horan; 305R: © Abe Frajndlich; 306 (315B): Used with permission from McDonald's Corporation; 307: © NICHOLAS KAMM/AFP/Getty Images; 311: © Bettmann/COR-BIS; 316 (xi): © Fred R. Conrad/The New York Times; 319 (342B, 426C): © AP Images/Charles Dharapak; 324: © www.adbusters.org; 325: © AP Images/Pat Sullivan; 326: © ABC Photo: Gail Adler/Photofest; 329: DaimlerChrysler/Screenshot from Tony Hawk's Pro Skater 2, Courtesy Activision Publishing, Inc. © 2000 Activision Publishing, Inc. All Rights Reserved; 330L: SCHWEPPES is a registered trademark of Dr Pepper/Seven Up, Inc. © 2007 Dr Pepper/Seven Up, Inc.; 330R (322TC): Courtesy Ogilvy & Mather; 331L: © RoadsideAmerica.com, Kirby, Smith & Wilkins; 331R: © LUKE FRAZZA/AFP/Getty Images; 332 (322B): © AP Images/Brian Kersey; 334 (343): Courtesy Miralus Healthcare; 335: Courtesy Ogilvy & Mather, London and Ford of Europe; 336 (315TL): Courtesy Bamboo, Inc.; 337 (322BC): © Richard Pasley; 338 (342T): © CBS/Landov; 344 (xiiT): © FRANCIS SPECK-ER/Landov; 347 (370B): © Robert Voets/CBS/Courtesy Everett Collection; 348: © Lester Cohen/WireImage (Awards) via Newscom; 350: © Kevin Mazure/WireImage/Getty Images; 351: Ben Kaller © TNT/Courtesy Everett Collection; 353: © Michael Ochs Archives/Getty Images; 354 (371B): © AP Images/Dima Gavrysh; 355: © AP Images/Jeff Christensen; 359: © Ted Streshinsky/CORBIS; 360: © Andreas Rentz/Getty Images; © AP Images/Gretchen Ertl; 366 (371T): © EZIO PETERSEN/UPI/Landov; 370T: © Paul Spinelli/Getty Images; 372 (xiiB): © BRENDAN MCDERMID/REUTERS/Landov; 376T (380BC): Courtesy The Gallup Organization; 376B (380T, 399T): © AP Images; 379: Courtesy Andrew Kohut, Director of Pew Research Center for People & the Press; 385L and 385R (380TC, 380BL, 398TR, 398B): Courtesy Nielsen Media Research; 387 (398TL): © AP Images/The Free Press, Mankato/John Cross; 389 (380BR, 399B): © Dennis Kitchen/Getty Images; 390T: © NEW LINE/THE KOBAL COLLEC-TION/DITTIGER, JAMES; 390B: © Ryan Miller/Getty Images; 400 (xiiiT, 406C): © Culver Pictures, Inc.; 404 (406B): © Patrick Seeger/dpa/Landov; 409 (427B): A BAND APART/MIRAMAX/THE KOBAL COLLECTION; 411T (426B): © AP Images/Tony Dejak; 411B: © Lincoln Journal Star Library; 413 (427T): © SIO Archives, UCSD; 414T: Provided by Virgin Comics, LLC. © 2006 DEVI, All rights reserved; 414B: © TIM OCKENDEN/PA Photos/Landov; 415: © J. Emilio Flores/Getty Images; 420: © Bettmann/CORBIS; 423L (22B, 50C, 426T): © Lions Gate/Courtesy Everett Collection; 423R: © Kyle Cassidy, ASC; 428 (xiiiB): © Hayat Khan/epa/CORBIS; 430 (459T): Freedom House; 431: Copyright © North Wind Picture Archives. All rights reserved; 432 (437T, 459BL): © Bettmann/CORBIS; 433: © AP Images/Michel Euler; 437C: Courtesy Voice of America; 438: © Win McNamee/Getty Images; 439 (458TL): © AP Images/Kamran Jebreili; 441 (437BC, 458B): © RABIH MOGHRABI/AFP/Getty Images; 445L: Courtesy Voice of America; 445R: Courtesy Channel 1 and Alireza Nourizadeh; 447T: © RUSSELL BOYCE/REUTERS/Landov; 447B (437B): © AFP/Getty Images; 448: © AP Images/Chi Haifeng/Xinhua; 451 (459C): © China Photos/Getty Images; 453: Courtesy Video Sound, Inc., NJ; 454: © AP Images/Anupam Nath; 455: © Reuters/CORBIS; 460 (xivT): © ROBERT GALBRAITH/ REUTERS/Landov; 463T: © RICHARD TSONG-TAATARII/MCT/Landov; 463B (477L): © AP Images/Ann Heisenfelt; 464 (476B): © Stock Montage/Hulton Archive/Getty Images; 465: © PAUL J. RICHARDS/ AFP/Getty Images; 467: © CNN. All rights reserved; 469: © EDUARDO SVERDLIN/UPI/Landov; 471L (22T): © Bettmann/CORBIS; 471R (476T): © Bettmann/CORBIS; 472: © AP Images/Dennis Cook; 473L (477R): © BRIAN SNYDER/REUTERS/Landov; 473R: © CHRISTOPHE MORIN/Maxpp/Landov; 478 (xivB, 502C): © Len Irish; 481: This advertisement, created by students enrolled in RIAA-EdVenture Partners classes, was provided courtesy of the Recording Industry Association of America (RIAA); 483 (502T): © Dennis Brack/Bloomberg News/Landov; 487L (502B): From the collection of the Minnesota Historical Society; 487R (495BC): © Star Tribune. All rights reserved; 488: © Underwood & Underwood/CORBIS; 489: Copyright © The New York Times Company. Reprinted with permission; 492: © David Leeson/Image Works/Time Life Pictures/Getty Images; 493 (503B): © Bettmann/CORBIS; 495T: Courtesy Library of Congress; 497 (495TC, 503T): © State Historical Society of Iowa, Iowa City; 504 (xv): © AP Images/Wilfredo Lee; 508: Courtesy Charles Gay; 510 (406T): © Erich Lessing/Art Resource, NY; 512TR (511T): Copyright © North Wind Picture Archives. All rights reserved; 512BR (511C, 526): © Fritz Goro/Time Life Pictures/Getty Images; 512TL: © Bettmann/CORBIS; 512C: Copyright © North Wind Picture Archives. All rights reserved; 512BL: Courtesy Harvard News Office; 515: Courtesy Office of Communications Arts at Harvard Divinity School; 517 (527): © AP Images; 519: © AP Images/Eric Gay; 520T: © Ed Lallo/Time Life Pictures/Getty Images; 520B (511B): © David M. Grossman.

STUDY GUIDE

CHAPTER 1 Mass Media Literacy

MEDIA LITERACY ACTIVITY
BROADCAST OR NARROWCAST:
WHAT'S THE DIFFERENCE?

The ultimate goal of narrowcasting is to market a product to consumers individually. It's a daunting goal. If only the precision were available to identify consumers by the likelihood of their purchasing a given product, then manufacturers, distributors and retailers would save millions of their marketing dollars by super-targeting advertisements. The challenge was recognized by Philadelphia department store magnate John Wanamaker in the late 1880s. At the time, newspapers were the hot vehicle for advertising. Wanamaker said he knew he was wasting half of his ad budget reaching people who would never shop at his stores. "But," he added, "I don't know which half."

Today, advertisers have found ways to reduce wasted advertising dollars. In broadcasting, for example, advertisers can split the traditional mass *broadcast* markets of national networks and local stations into multiple, and often more lucrative, *narrowcast* markets. Sure, the result is a smaller audience, but it's an audience with a far higher quotient of interested consumers.

The differences between broadcasting and narrowcasting start with an assessment of the target audience for an advertisement. A *broadcast* message—*broad*, get it?—does not target a specific audience because it can communicate to people fitting diverse demographics at the same time. Everyone can access a message, whether it's pertinent to them individually or not. A narrowcast message, often packaged with narrowly focused entertainment messages, is aimed at a select audience. These are people who, when the narrowcasting strategy works well, are interested in whatever is being pitched.

Narrowcasting can be done on a large scale, as in an ad campaign that targets several different demographics. For example, the TV commercial with the Mac guy and the PC guy targets an older audience by showing that Mac is simpler to use. At the same time it targets a young tech-savvy audience by showing that Mac is more stable than PC. Narrowcasting can also be on a small scale, as in a church newsletter.

Narrowcasting aims to disseminate a message that is ultra-relevant to an audience's interests or needs, like an online newsletter for green builders.

Narrowcasting can be understood in terms of specialized content development. Public television, for example, is narrowcasting because the programming isn't designed to reach the general mass audience. Specialized television programming for children or other age groups, ethnic or religious groups on the PBS network, for example, is hardly what the major networks have traditionally broadcast in their quest for the largest possible audience. It must be noted,

though, that the big commercial networks recently have bowed to pressure from advertisers and have started narrowcasting by programming shows that appeal to similar audiences such as young children or ethnic groups back-to-back.

A political candidate may use both broadcasting and narrowcasting to get a campaign message out. The candidate may create a website, which is a broadcast, but on the website try to segment the audience by offering narrowcast options, such as an email newsletter, premium content, password-only pages, members-only networks, RSS-only articles, user-generated news, or social media mullets. Another political candidate may decide that a blog is the best way to reach a broadcast audience. Podcasts might be added to the candidate's blog, which can be considered both broadcast and narrowcast. Theoretically, podcasts are limited to those who subscribe to them, but anyone who comes across them on the Web can download them, so in a way they are also broadcast.

- If you were a candidate for the city council, would you advertise through narrowcasting or broadcasting? Why?
- If you were running for the U.S. Senate, would narrowcasting or broadcasting be a better vehicle for your advertising? Why?
- If a candidate creates a Facebook page, is the message narrowcasting or broadcasting?
- If a candidate is interviewed on a local, low-power radio station, is that narrowcasting or broadcasting?
- What are these media—broadcast or narrowcast?
  Cable television
  Satellite radio
  AARP the magazine
  Rolling Stone magazine
  The New York *Times*
  The Aurora *Sentinel* in a Denver suburb
  MySpace
  A video on YouTube

PRACTICE QUIZ

1. The simultaneous exposure to messages brought to you by different media is called _____.
2. _____ is the technology-assisted process of delivering messages to large, often faraway audiences.
3. The vehicles that convey messages to a mass audience are called _____.
4. _____ is communication between two people, or at most a small group of people, usually face-to-face.
5. Fragmenting the audience into smaller and smaller, more specialized segments is a process called _____.

6. It is important to note that most media outlets are for-profit endeavors. They depend on a(n) _____ to continue their operations.
7. _____ is an important revenue stream for many mass media outlets, including television, radio, and newspapers.
8. The non-advertising part of your newspaper is called _____.
9. The process of creating larger and larger media corporations through corporate mergers and acquisitions creates _____.
10. Mass media used to have a(n) _____ effect on society. But today, with more specialized content attracting more segmented audiences, that effect is becoming less apparent.
11. Democratic societies such as the United States encourage the free and open exchange of ideas; that exchange is made possible by the mass media. John Milton, an English philosopher who studied the process of persuasion, originally put this concept, called the_____, forth in his essay titled *Areopagitca*.
12. _____ is possessing the knowledge to be competent in assessing messages carried by mass media. It is essential in this age of mass communication so citizens can exercise their rights and enjoy their day-to-day lives.

PRACTICE TEST

1.1 Multiple Choice Questions

1. Media literacy is
   a. the process of understanding messages delivered by the mass media.
   b. possessing the knowledge to be competent in assessing messages carried by the mass media.
   c. understanding the dynamics that shape media content.
   d. all of the above.
2. Media effects refers to
   a. how messages delivered by mass media create effects in our lives.
   b. what messages we pay attention to in the media.
   c. special effects, such as effects in movies, created by the media.
   d. both a and b.
3. Mass communication is
   a. sending a message to a great number of people using communication technology.
   b. communicating with a heterogeneous mass audience.
   c. generally lacking in immediate feedback, although feedback may still be possible.
   d. all of the above.

4. Feedback is important in interpersonal and small group communication because
   a. it communicates the receiver's response to the message.
   b. it allows the communicator to change or clarify the message.
   c. it demonstrates expertise on a subject.
   d. both a and b
5. Television became a societal unifier
   a. because huge audiences converged on networks, all promulgating the same cultural fare.
   b. because news coverage of major events is similar on various channels.
   c. because sets were manufactured in the United States.
   d. both a and b

1.2 True/False Questions

___ 1. The media, in covering controversy, can become divisive to society.
___ 2. Narrowcasting, as opposed to broadcasting, is the mass media seeking niche audiences.
___ 3. Advertising generates most of the revenue for newspapers, magazines, radio and television.
___ 4. A media chain is a group of media companies owned by a large corporation. An example would be Gannett, a media conglomerate that owns many newspapers, some television stations, and other media enterprises.
___ 5. Mass media operate through a process called mass communication which amplifies messages, sending them to massive audiences.
___ 6. John Milton's concept of the marketplace of ideas refers to how people can use their power of reasoning to know truths through the free exchange of ideas. It is the basis of our concept that the mass media are the primary vehicle for persuasive discourse.
___ 7. There is an interdependence between the mass media and media consumers. People need the media to gain information, be entertained, and to live their daily lives. Media outlets need audiences to survive financially.
___ 8. Some types of mass media can invade our lives on a subconscious level.
___ 9. Media literacy requires the audience to distinguish between the message and the messenger. For example, media messengers are not advocating the use of recreational or illegal drugs because they write about them.
___ 10. Submass audiences—or niche audiences—are segments of an audience made up of people with very specialized interests. These audiences were created when the media focused on narrower audience segments in a process called massification.

1.3 Completion Questions

1. _____ is a significant driver of media behavior. It gravitates to media products that deliver audiences of the most likely customers.
2. _____ is a term that means broadcasting directly to consumers through the use of satellite technology.
3. _____ is an Australian media mogul who inherited a chain of newspapers and then expanded his media empire into other countries, including the United States, where he purchased 20th Century Fox with the intent of starting a fourth television network. His media corporation operates under the name News Corp. and has become a worldwide corporation to create and deliver media content.
4. Every teenage girl wanting to wear fashion made popular by her favorite musical artist is an example of the _____ effect of the media.
5. Media _____ was accelerated in the 1980s with the technology that gave cable television the ability to deliver dozens of channels.

1.4 Essay Questions

1. Compare and contrast the concepts of the theories of media unification and division in society. What caused the media to move from unification to division?
2. Discuss the statement: Television's product is not really programming. It is the audience it delivers for its advertisers.
3. What caused the movement toward media chains and conglomerates?
4. If we spend two-thirds of our waking hours with the media, either consciously or unconsciously, then we need to cultivate our media literacy. How can we do that?

CHAPTER 2 Media Technology

MEDIA LITERACY ACTIVITY
KNOW YOUR GATEKEEPER

All media, no matter what technology it uses, has gatekeepers. Whenever you read, hear or see a media message, you should be aware of who your gatekeeper is.

Why should you care? Because the gatekeeper chooses the message. No news organization, no matter how large, can run all the news. Gatekeepers decide what news is worthwhile, what stories can be done effectively and efficiently, and what news will affect a substantial portion of their readers, viewers, or listeners.

You don't have time to read, listen to, or view every news report from every news organization. How can you decide which gatekeeper has your best interests in mind?

Here are a few criteria to consider, as suggested by Steven Petranik, 24/7 news editor for the Honolulu *Advertiser*, a Gannett newspaper, during a visit with University of Hawaii students:

1. Does your gatekeeper have a mission statement or a code of ethics? Journalistic codes of ethics seek to ensure fairness and accuracy in news reporting. If your gatekeeper has a code, does he follow it?
2. Does your gatekeeper include diverse opinions, including opinions critical of the publication?
3. Does your gatekeeper run corrections?
4. Does your gatekeeper quote a variety of sources? Does the gatekeeper challenge your beliefs and sometimes take you out of your comfort zone? (Why bother with a gatekeeper who tells you what you already know or simply reinforces your opinions?)

And here's one more: Does your gatekeeper disclose conflicts of interest? Not only is transparency in how a gatekeeper makes decisions important, so is your gatekeeper's integrity.

"When you read, watch or listen to news, know your gatekeepers," warns Petranik.

Check out the websites npr.org and foxnews.com. As you look at the sites side-by-side to analyze their differences, forget that they are considered polar opposites politically. Look for quantifiable differences. Write a 300-word comparison of how their gatekeepers function.

Here are a few things to look for to get you started:
1. Can you find a mission statement or code of ethics? You might check the "About" link for this.
2. Look at the opinion pages side by side. Do they carry diverse opinions? Are any of the opinions critical of past stories? Do they have any opinions from common people in their audience, or is it all by pundits or experts in their fields? What else do you see that makes them different? Use actual numbers and headlines or short summaries of the opinion pieces.
3. Do they run corrections?

Write about these and any other comparisons you make as you analyze these two sites.

PRACTICE QUIZ

1. _____ is necessary for mass communication, which makes mass communication unique within forms of human communication.
2. _____ was invented by Johannes Gutenberg in the mid 1440s in Germany.
3. Media technology incorporates several different technologies. Name the four technologies as discussed in the text.
4. Illustrations were done with engravings until Frederick Ives invented the process of using a(n) _____, the reproduction of an image using various tones of gray or color produced by variously sized dots of ink.
5. The process of photography is rooted in the technology of _____. Photography made it possible to illustrate the written word, bringing new possibilities to newspapers and magazines.
6. Taking photography one step further, movies allowed audiences to see moving images. The _____ is the phenomenon that fast-changing still photos create the illusion of movement. It makes use of the fact that the human eye retains an image for a fraction of a second and if those images are changed rapidly, the eye is tricked into perceiving continuous motion.
7. Electricity and the mastery of electromagnetic waves brought new delivery systems for mass messages. Electronic media include _____, _____, _____, and _____.
8. Satellite and fiber optic technology increased the _____ and _____ of delivering mass messages.
9. The _____ is the medium through which a message is sent.
10. All receivers of messages _____ those messages. This process may impede communication.
11. _____ are media people who decide which messages merit inclusion and which messages do not.
12. Anything that interferes with the communication process before the message reaches its intended receivers is called _____.

PRACTICE TEST

2.1 Multiple Choice Questions

1. Noise is
   a. anything that impedes communication before it reaches its intended receivers.
   b. sloppy wording by the communicator
   c. anything within the environment that interferes with the communication.
   d. all of the above.

2. Receivers of messages filter the message in many ways, including through
   a. informational filters such as the receiver's knowledge of the subject.
   b. psychological filters including the receiver's state of mind and background.
   c. physical filters, such as the receiver's state of awareness.
   d. all of the above.
3. Harold Lasswell proposed a narrative communication model to explain how people process certain messages. His model poses questions, including
   a. whether the receiver is knowledgeable.
   b. who says what.
   c. what channel carries the message.
   d. b and c.
4. Arthur C. Clarke devised the concept of placing satellites in orbit so that the satellite's orbit matches perfectly the earth's orbit. This is called
   a. corrected orbit.
   b. balanced orbit.
   c. geosynchronous orbit.
   d. simple orbit.
5. Television was invented by Philo Farnsworth when he theorized that
   a. light could be converted to electrons.
   b. light could be transmitted very quickly as a beam.
   c. a beam of light could be spread back and forth across a surface to create an image.
   d. all of the above.

2.2 True/False

___ 1. A landline is a conventional telecommunication connection using cable laid across land, typically buried or strung on poles.
___ 2. Mathew Brady brought the horrors of war home when he recorded the awful injuries and death of World War I.
___ 3. Persistence of vision refers to the phenomenon that fast-changing still pictures can create the illusion of movement because the human eye retains an image for a fraction of a second.
___ 4. The phonograph was invented in 1877 by Thomas Edison.
___ 5. The telegraph was invented by Samuel Morse in 1844.
___ 6. Heinrich Hertz demonstrated the existence of radio waves in 1887.
___ 7. Johannes Gutenberg invented moveable metal type in the mid-1440s, which made the printing press an agent for mass communication.

___ 8. The newest media technology, the Internet, is built on chemical technology.
___ 9. A quartertone is an image created by the use of various tones of gray or color produced by variously sized dots of ink. It made it possible to mass produce images in books, newspapers, and magazines.
___10. Both photography and movie technology draw on chemical technology.
___11. The Internet is a high-capacity global telegraph network that links computers.
___12. Digital technology is technology through which media messages are coded into 1s and 0s for delivery transmission and then decoded into their original appearance.

2.3 Completion Questions

1. Through the development of digital technology, there has been a melding of print, electronic and photographic media into digitized form. This melding is called _____.
2. A(n) _____ is a silicon chip that is used in digitization.
3. The _____ model notes that communication starts with a message or idea at the center and then ripples outward to the receiving audience.
4. _____ are non-media people who influence messages. An example would be a censoring organization that regulates which books are published.
5. The telegraph, which originates a message at one point and then transmits it to another point, with the sender controlling the message, is an example of _____ communication.

2.4 Essay Questions

1. Discuss how the Internet has made early mass communication models obsolete.
2. Discuss the obstacles for a message to reach a mass communication audience as noted in the concentric circle model of communication.

CHAPTER 3 Books

MEDIA LITERACY ACTIVITY
THE NEW BOOK

How innovative is the new technology of books? We have e-books, i-books, print-on-demand books, networked books, and now waterproof laptops that would allow us to read a book in the bathtub. But is any of this really new? Or are these innovations just "paper book mimes"?

E-books, or electronic books, are now available at many libraries and bookstores and online. They are displayed on a reader, a hand-held device that shows pages similar to those in the physical book. Instant books, or i-books, are available on Espresso Book Machines (EBMs) which print library-quality paperbacks from a digital file in minutes. Print-on-demand (POD) companies proliferate on the Web, and make it possible for anyone to upload a book and have it printed in hardback or paperback in days. EBMs are also POD devices. You can also read a book online on your computer that is networked to the World Wide Web.

Critics say that all this technology is great, but basically all it does is mimic the current book form. We can now bring books as we currently know them to more people faster. But so far, no one has come up with something that is a radical change from today's physical book—at least not something that gives the same satisfaction and interaction with the reader's mind.

Among all the recent innovations, only audio books take a different form from printed books, but hearing a book being read to you does not engage your mind in the same way as reading it yourself. Explains Scott Condon, of the Everett, Washington, Public Library, in a paper presented to the 2007 Washington Library Association Conference: "Books are composed of printed words; they demand literacy; they are accessed and decoded through the sense of vision; the reading of books is self-paced; and they are evoked in the highly individualized circuitry of each reader's mind, heart and imagination. Audio books are non-literal; the language component reaches us through the sense of hearing; the pace is not controlled by the user; and the text is interpreted by the performer(s)."

Publishers may be reluctant to push for a new technology, but it seems that increased screen reading has not been linked to print decline. The Association of American Publishers, the national trade association of the U.S. book publishing industry, estimates that U.S. publishers had net sales of $25 billion in 2007—a 3.2 percent increase from 2006 with a compound growth rate of 2.5 percent per year since 2002.

Many large publishers have bought e-book readers for their staffs to help eliminate the massive piles of paper a book uses as it passes through various departments on its way to publication. Having a book in digital form also eases the process of making changes as it's edited by various people. Could the book of the future be interactive with not just editors, but also the reader, in ways we can only imagine now?

What is the future of the physical book? Will it continue in its present form, either digitally or physically? Will it co-exist with some other way of exchanging knowledge? Will it become interconnected with the reader in some way no one has thought of yet? Will it cease to exist altogether?

- List the problems the traditional book faces in the digital age.
- List some possible remedies for those problems.
- Write a 300-word blog about what your lists tell you, and answer these questions: Is a new form of the book on the horizon? Will it be a natural extension of the history of the book? If not, why not?

U.S. Book Publishing Industry

	2007	Increase from 2006	Compound growth rate from 2002
Total Net Sales	$25 billion	3.2%	2.5%
Audio Books	$218 million	19.8%	8.8%
e-books	$67 million	23.6%	55.7%

Information from the Association of American Publishers

PRACTICE QUIZ

1. Books are the _____ vehicle used by new generations for education in society's values and to learn the lessons of the past.
2. Choosing not to read, even though able to do so, is called _____.
3. A book unavailable because slow sales do not warrant the cost of reprinting and warehousing the books is said to be _____.
4. Modern technology has made it possible to print and bind fewer books, even a single copy at a time. This process is called _____.
5. Portable electronic devices for on-screen reading of books downloaded from the Web are called _____.
6. _____ invented moveable metal type which made mass production of the written word possible.
7. Harriet Beecher Stowe's book _____ is said to have propelled the antislavery movement to the fore and helped cause the Civil War.
8. University-sponsored publishers, called _____, focus on publishing scholarly work.
9. Not all books are best sellers. Some, called _____ titles, are books for which publishing houses expect modest sales, and, as a result, are promoted only modestly by the publisher.
10. General interest titles, including fiction and non-fiction, are called _____.
11. Jimmy Wales founded a massive online encyclopedia, written and edited by users, called _____.

PRACTICE TEST

3.1 Multiple Choice Questions

1. Wikipedia, the online encyclopedia, is written by_____.
   a. its users
   b. a competent staff
   c. Jimmy Wales
   d. a professional newspaper editor
2. *The Spy*, a novel written by James Fenimore Cooper, brought Americans_____.
   a. entertainment
   b. a sense of an identifiable American culture
   c. a better way to print books
   d. a and b
3. _____ founded the online book retailer Amazon.com. It was the first major use of the Internet for commerce.
   a. Jeff Bezos
   b. Jimmy Wales
   c. Charles Darwin
   d. Johannes Gutenberg
4. One of the first blockbuster books, _____, sold 200,000 copies in just three weeks. That book told of the horrors of slave life in the South and became pivotal in propelling the antislavery movement and the Civil War.
   a. *Uncle Tom's Cabin*
   b. *Silent Spring*
   c. The Bible
   d. *Unsafe at Any Speed*
5. *Origin of the Species* was written by _____. The book argued that all species evolved from common ancestors through a process he called natural selection.
   a. Charles Darwin
   b. William Holmes McGuffey
   c. Thomas Paine
   d. John Howard Griffin

3.2 True/False Questions

___ 1. Rachel Carson wrote a famous book which jump started the environmental movement.
___ 2. *Black Like Me*, written by Harriet Beecher Stowe, offered insights into the injustice and travesties African Americans suffer. It helped set the stage for a renewed civil rights movement and major reforms that became law.
___ 3. El-hi is the name for books that are used in elementary schools and high schools.
___ 4. Trade books are those books that are traded, not purchased.

___ 5. Not all books are best sellers. Some, called mid-list, are only expected to generate modest sales and are only modestly promoted by publishers.
___ 6. With new printing technology, it is possible to print only a few copies, or even a single copy, of a book. This is called print on demand.
___ 7. Johannes Gutenberg invented electronic printing technology.
___ 8. E-books are portable electronic devices for on-screen reading of books that have been downloaded from the Web.
___ 9. The Google Print Library is a massive project to put all the books in every language in a searchable database.
___10. Refusing to read, even though you have the capability to read, is called being aliterate.

3.3 Completion Questions

1. A publisher associated with a university that focuses mainly on scholastic titles is called a(n) _____.
2. Once a book is no longer popular, publishers stop printing copies of it. Such a book is said to be _____.
3. The modern consumer movement got a major boost when _____ wrote *Unsafe at Any Speed* about the Chevrolet Covair.
4. Wikipedia, created by _____, is a massive online encyclopedia that is written by its users.
5. Books fall into two broad categories: _____ and textbooks.

3.4 Essay Questions

1. Discuss how books have transformed human existence and helped cultures define themselves.
2. Discuss how book publishing has been affected by the trend toward mergers and acquisitions that has resulted in fewer and fewer publishing houses.
3. Discuss how the Internet has changed book publishing.

CHAPTER 4 Newspapers

MEDIA LITERACY ACTIVITY
WILL NEWSPAPERS SURVIVE?

As newspapers continue to lose readers to the Web, they're desperately trying to figure out how to compete in this new world. Some of them are more successful than others. NYTimes.com was introduced in 1996. By 2008 it claimed 13 million unique users, and it had more than 30 blogs and 12 daily and weekly podcasts. It also generated 100 plus original video segments a month.

The *Wall Street Journal,* which caters to a select audience, found success with its fee-based website. In 2007 it had a paid subscriber base of nearly 1 million customers. Now under the ownership of Rupert Murdoch's News Corp., the *Journal* is considering the idea of eventually converting WSJ.com to a free site.

Unbundling has been the problem for newspapers moving online, writes Nicholas Carr on a blog forum on the future of newspapers at Britannica's (yes, the encyclopedia people) website. Carr is a member of Britannica's Editorial Board of Advisors and author of *The Big Switch: Rewiring the World, from Edison to Google.*

He says the traditional print newspaper is "an array of content—local stories, national and international reports, news analyses, editorials and opinion columns, photographs, sports scores, stock tables, TV listings, cartoons, and a variety of classified and display advertising—all bundled together into a single product. People subscribe to the bundle, or buy it at a newsstand, and advertisers pay to catch readers' eyes as they thumb through the pages. The publisher's goal is to make the entire package as attractive as possible to a broad set of readers and advertisers. The newspaper as a whole is what matters, and as a product it's worth more than the sum of its parts."

That all changed when newspapers went online. "The bundle falls apart," Carr asserts. Readers go directly to a particular story that interests them. Often they don't even see the "front page" of the newspaper. "They may not even be aware of which newspaper's site they've arrived at."

The result of this unbundling is that each story becomes a separate product and it must stand on its own economic merits, Carr says. That means the big question for newspapers is how to continue to be able to afford to create quality content in the online world. So far, no one has found the answer to that question.

Look up Britannica's blog forum, *Are Newspapers Doomed? (Do We Care?): Newspapers & the Net* Forum. Read Nicholas Carr and three others, including at least two of these four: Clay Shirky, Charles Madigan, Colette Bancroft, and Jay Rosen.

Write your own blog about this subject. Start with a summary of what each of these authors has to say about the future of newspapers, and be sure to include the future for journalists and writers, and your opinions about how the Web will change print newspapers. Based on the ideas of the bloggers you chose to read, describe the ones you think are most on target, which are viable and why. Do you agree that unbundling is the problem for newspapers as they migrate to the Web?

Then write your own thoughts about the future of newspapers and the Web. What will they look like? How will they make money to pay reporters? Will they have traditional reporters? How will they attract readers? Who will be their readers? Will readers in the future want to read long, investigative pieces, or will newspapers only write short, entertaining stories about easy subjects? Will newspapers continue to publish print editions? Will print newspapers survive?

What's Wrong with Newspapers in the Internet Age?

Here are some of the criticisms young people have of print newspapers:

- They don't want bulky newspapers cluttering their homes.
- They don't want to get their hands dirty from newsprint.
- They want to customize their reading experience and are used to picking their reading from lists of headlines on the screen instead of flipping through numerous print pages to find what they want.

What would you add to this list? What is sacrificed in the process of people moving to the Web for their news?

PRACTICE QUIZ

1. In 1908, _____ founded the *Christian Science Monitor*, a Boston-based national newspaper, which seeks to address major issues and problems around the world.
2. The _____ were published by the New York *Times* and led to a U.S. Supreme Court decision that discouraged censorship. It has been said the publication of these papers helped to end the Presidency of Richard M. Nixon.
3. Newspapers come in two sizes, _____ and broadsheet. The size does not denote quality of content, merely the size of the pages.
4. The term for posting newspaper stories on the Web after they have been published in a print edition is called _____.
5. Some newspapers are geographically close to each other and owned by the same publisher. This is called a(n) _____.

6. In the past newspapers were owned by publishers who were local. But with the trend towards media mergers and acquisitions, many newspapers are now run under _____, where the top chain executives do not live in the communities the newspaper covers.

7. A(n) _____ is an advertising newspaper, distributed for free, that does not contain any news, only advertising.

8. The *Wall Street Journal*, *Christian Science Monitor*, and *USA* Today are three nationally recognized _____ newspapers.

9. *USA Today* was created by _____. This newspaper is well known for its visually interesting design and multitude of varied stories.

10. The *Wall Street Journal* had some humble beginnings, first as a collection of notes sent to clients, then as a newsletter, and, finally, as a newspaper. Originally it was based on financial information. The paper was founded by _____ and _____.

PRACTICE TEST

4.1 Completion Questions

1. _____ was a newspaper publisher who determined that he could multiply profits by owning more than one newspaper. He put together a chain of papers in the late 1880s.
   a. William Randolph Hearst
   b. Benjamin Day
   c. Charles Dow
   d. Edward Jones

2. _____ co-founded the *Wall Street Journal* in 1882.
   a. Charles Dow
   b. Barney Kilgore
   c. Allen Neuharth
   d. Mary Baker Eddy

3. _____ expanded the definition of the *Wall Street Journal*'s news coverage to everything that somehow relates to earning a living.
   a. Edward Jones
   b. Barney Kilgore
   c. William Marcy Tweed
   d. George Jones

4. Though *Christian* appears in its name, the *Christian Science Monitor* is not a preachy, religious newspaper. The newspaper tries to emphasize _____ news and allows only one plainly labeled religious article per issue.
   a. positive
   b. national
   c. local
   d. sensationalistic

5. Arthur Sulzberger, publisher of the New York *Times*, says he is a _____, noting the company is not so much in the newspaper business as in the news business. The content generated by the organization is more relevant than the medium that delivers it.
   a. newsman
   b. platform agnostic
   c. Pulitzer prize winner
   d. television personality

4.2 True/False Questions

___ 1. The *North Star* was an abolitionist newspaper founded by Frederick Douglas in 1847.

___ 2. Mary Baker Eddy founded the *Christian Science Monitor* on the principle that there should be a newspaper that ought to be an alternative to the rampant sensationalism found in most papers of her day.

___ 3. Charles Dow and Edward Jones founded the *Wall Street Journal* in 1889, mostly to report financial news.

___ 4. Circulation in the daily and weekly newspapers in the United States is growing.

___ 5. Newspapers can offer a wider variety of content and stories, and they can cover issues in greater depth than the electronic media.

___ 6. Because a newspaper is published in tabloid format, it means the paper is prone to sensationalism.

___ 7. Granite is a national newspaper chain with 90-plus daily newspapers.

___ 8. When a newspaper's headquarters are located in some other city than where the paper is circulated, that is called absentee ownership.

___ 9. Newspapers have often been involved in the "watchdog" function of the media and have exposed various fraudulent activities as well as government scandal. The Tweed Scandal was exposed by the New York *Times* reporter George Jones when the paper published the story of how William Marcy Tweed, a city council member, built a fortune through fraudulent streetcar franchises, sales of nonexistent buildings, and double billing.

___10. The trend has been to large corporate chains owning groups of newspapers, often in a close geographic area, is called a newspaper cluster.

4.3 Completion Questions

1. The _____ were published by the New York *Times* and led to a U.S. Supreme Court ruling that discourages censorship.
2. _____ is the term for newspaper content that has been posted on the Web after it was published in the newspaper.
3. A(n) _____ is a publication in newspaper format but that contains only advertising, not editorial copy.
4. Allen Neuharth founded _____, a national newspaper with visual interest due to its advanced use of photos, color and graphics.
5. Roving reporters using communications technology, including cell phones, laptop computers, and video cameras are called _____.

4.4 Essay Questions

1. Younger citizens are not reading newspapers like their parents and grandparents did. What has caused this?
2. Weekly newspapers provide news of local events better than the large dailies. Why can they provide the best delivery of local news?

CHAPTER 5 Magazines

MEDIA LITERACY ACTIVITY
WEB MAGAZINES: IS BEING ONLINE ENOUGH?

Independent magazines are not part of an established media organization. Many of them are started online with minimal staff and investment. Starting a print magazine not only involves higher costs, especially for printing and distribution, but it's a risky investment these days because advertisers have been shifting their dollars to the Internet.

One reason to start an independent magazine is to get noticed by the big boys. But many independent magazines are published just for the love of it.

Grist, the non-profit online magazine that publishes environmental news and opinion, was launched in 1999. The magazine, known for its in-depth coverage and its tongue-in-cheek humor, has won numerous awards and has been called *The Daily Show* for the environment. David Roberts, a *Grist* staff writer, says bringing humor to the headlines has become the magazine's signature. *Grist's* taglines are "Gloom and doom with a sense of humor" and "A beacon in the smog."

Seven, sevenglobal.org, addresses key issues from the seven continents. It launched as an online magazine in November 2005 and boasts that it "provides young and emerging writing talent with a platform on which to address the real issues that affect the planet we live on." *Seven* wants to bring global issues to a global readership. Marc Cameron developed the project with former fellow student Michelle Akande, and it won the Business Concept competition run by the London Centre for Arts and Cultural Enterprise in 2005. But really the inspiration for *Seven* came from an internship Cameron did with a New York magazine that left him thinking the magazine industry was "pretty soulless" and too focused on celebrities.

When MySpace considered publishing its own magazine, the social networking site decided instead to collaborate with a magazine on a reader/website audience-produced print product. MySpace chose *Marmalade,* a London underground magazine with a cult following among creative types. The deal was a first step towards leveraging the popular social networking website to multiple platforms. But as John Plunkett, a blogger for the *Guardian,* asks, "The idea…was to give print space to up-and-coming talent. Which begs the question—why would up-and-coming talent want to appear in print when they have got the whole of the Web instead?"

Nevertheless, *Marmalade* and MySpace have found some success with their collaboration. Apparently up-and-coming talent on MySpace wants to be picked for the print pages, and the partnership with MySpace provides lots of free content for *Marmalade.* It also was a smart marketing ploy by *Marmalade,* one that resulted in it being one of the first print publications to be featured on MySpace's homepage.

Kirsty Robinson, co-founder and managing editor of *Marmalade,* says the magazine treats MySpace contributors the way it treats regular contributors. In another savvy marketing move, the magazine hired a MySpace editor to "help facilitate the community conversation" and to verify that *Marmalade's* MySpace "friends" are the creative types to whom the magazine is targeted. These steps have created a sense of exclusivity for those who make the jump from the Web to print.

- Visit three or four Web magazines. What do they have in common? How are they different? Are they elitist or populist? Do they contribute to the national identity? Do they do original reporting? How are they financed?
- Write a proposal for an independent magazine start-up. Include the magazine's name, proposed audience, potential advertisers, proposed format (online, print, or both), and why. How big will your staff be? What kinds of stories will you publish? What needs will your magazine fulfill?

PRACTICE QUIZ

1. Magazines survived the assault of television by reinventing themselves and pursuing a narrower segment of the mass audience. This is called _____.
2. _____ is advertising jargon for cost per thousand, or the cost of running the ad per thousand people who are exposed to its message.
3. Magazines became very popular in the 1800s with their _____, lengthy treatments of subjects that go beyond spot news.
4. Investigative reporting has a long history in magazines. In 1902 _____ exposed the Standard Oil monopoly in *McClure's* magazine.
5. Stories in magazines that were investigative in nature were called _____. These stories were forerunners of modern investigative journalism.
6. Cross media ownership is created when a single entity owns a combination of media outlets, such as newspapers, radio stations and television stations. This cross ownership is encouraged by _____, the concept that such a combination creates more than the sum of the parts.
7. The _____ is a scale used for determining reader satisfaction. It provides a quantitative measure of qualitative information that transcends circulation numbers, number of ad pages or even ad revenue.
8. Hugh Hefner shook the magazine industry's foundation when he published _____, a magazine that carries nudity as well as articles and stories on various topics.

9. _____, along with Yale classmate Briton Hadden, founded *Time* and later *Life* magazine. *Time* created a new genre of magazines, the news magazine, to provide more in depth analysis of news.

10. Margaret Bourke-White traveled the world to bring her photo images to the pages of *Life* magazine. She was one of the first _____.

PRACTICE TEST

5.1 Multiple Choice Questions

1. _____ was the pioneer editor of *National Geographic* magazine.
   a. Gilbert Grosvenor
   b. Upton Sinclair
   c. Theodore Roosevelt
   d. Ida Tarbell

2. Magazines survived the assault of television by reinventing themselves and appealing to a narrower, more focused audience. This process is called _____.
   a. competition
   b. sponsored magazines
   c. demassification
   d. fragmenting

3. In 1902 _____ exposed the Standard Oil Company's business practices in an investigative journalism piece in *McClure's* magazine.
   a. Sara Josepha Hale
   b. Ida Tarbell
   c. Gilbert Grosvenor
   d. Harold Ross

4. _____ are those magazines sold on the newsracks, as found in grocery and book stores.
   a. Trade magazines
   b. Professional journals
   c. Consumer magazines
   d. Paperback books

5. Some magazines, such as _____, are reserved for circulation only to an organization's members.
   a. *Reader's Digest*
   b. *AARP The Magazine*
   c. *McClure's*
   d. *Time*

5.2 True/False Questions

___ 1. Briton Hadley and Henry Luce introduced the newsmagazine genre with the publication of *Time* magazine.

___ 2. *American Magazine*, published by Andrew Bradford, was the first magazine printed in the colonies. It was followed a few weeks later by Benjamin Franklin's *General Magazine*.

___ 3. In-store magazines, with content and ads to appeal to shoppers in a particular store, began in the early 2000s when Bella Price created *All You* for Wal-Mart shoppers.

___ 4. Long-term journalism means short treatments of news subjects covered over a longer period of time.

___ 5. Sometimes the combination of things creates something that is more than the sum of its parts. This is called synergy and was found to happen when existing media companies merged.

___ 6. In-depth personality profiles began in newspapers. They were pioneered in the 1920s by Harold Ross of the *New Yorker* newspaper.

___ 7. Hugh Hefner started *Playboy* magazine in 1953. It is a magazine that mixes artful nude photos with articles and interviews.

___ 8. CPM is the term for cost per million—the cost of exposing your message to one million people.

___ 9. High brow slicks is the term used for magazines whose content appeals to the very intelligent or well educated. Examples are the *New Yorker* and *Atlantic*.

___ 10. The first women's magazine, with content appealing to women, was founded by Sara Josepha Hale. It was called *Ladies' Magazine*, later to become Godey's *Lady's Book*.

5.3 Completion Questions

1. _____ is the term applied in the early 1900s to investigative reporting. The term was coined by President Theodore Roosevelt

2. The _____, or _____, is a scale for measuring reader satisfaction with a publication. It is used to ascertain positive and negative responses by readers.

3. A _____ is a magazine used to keep members of a profession or trade informed as to the latest news in that profession.

4. When Congress passed the _____, it recognized the role of magazines in creating national culture and literacy. The law allowed a discounted postal rate for magazines.

5. _____ was an early Time Warner initiative to place magazines online. It was started in the mid 1990s as a massive website.

5.4 Essay Questions

1. Magazines are said to have helped shape American culture. Explain how this happened, using specific examples from the text.

2. Ben Bagdikian, a well-known media critic, says media chains and cross media ownership harm diversity in content and public interests. Explain.

CHAPTER 6 Sound Recording

MEDIA LITERACY ACTIVITY
WHAT'S AN ARTIST TO DO?

Is the music business going down the drain? A lot of people say yes, it is, but musician and artist David Byrne, formerly of Talking Heads and winner of Grammy, Oscar and Golden Globe awards, believes that "this is actually a great time, full of options and possibilities."

Byrne foresees a future where mega pop artists will still need "that mighty push and marketing effort for a new release that only traditional record companies can provide." But for others, he sees the possibility that the traditional record company will be replaced by a small company that funnels income and invoices from the various entities and keeps the accounts in order.

What are these "various entities?" Traditionally, a record company provided lots of services to its artists, including funding recording sessions; manufacturing, distributing, and marketing the product; advancing money for expenses like touring; and handling the accounting.

Today, artists are discovering less expensive ways of doing these things on their own. The cost of recording has dropped significantly, as have the costs of manufacturing and distribution. Touring has become an income source for artists, not just a way to promote a new album.

It seems, then, that artists should be making more money than ever. So why are some of them so steamed about how little they make when they sell their work digitally, through services like iTunes? According to *DownhillBattle*, a record album of 12 songs sells on iTunes for $11.88. Apple sends the record company $7.80. The record company then distributes the artist's royalty, which often has been reduced by 20 to 50 percent because record companies treat downloads as "new media/technology." And, even though there is no packaging involved, many labels still deduct a 25 percent packaging fee from the artist's check. Bottom line: the label and Apple get 96 percent of the price paid for the album; the artist gets 4 percent. If the same album sells as a CD on Amazon.com for $14.98, the artist gets 31 cents per song, instead of the 0.045 cents on a digital download. *DownhillBattle* figures that would mean an 85 percent reduction in income for the artist to sell online.

What's an artist to do?

Contemporary jazz guitarist Chris Standring believes that artists who want to make money should write their own music. That's because there are two royalty sources available to artists. The first is "artist" royalties. This is what an artist receives from record sales. Usually an artist is offered anywhere from 10 to 20 royalty points. The second type, "mechanical" royalties, are paid to the songwriter and the publisher. The standard rate for 2007 was 9.1 cents per song. So for a song that sells 100,000 copies, the mechanical royalties (which are usually split evenly between the songwriter and the publisher) would equal $9,100, although that rate is often negotiated lower by a record company.

Byrne advises artists to hold on to their publishing rights if they can. That way they get paid if someone covers, samples or licenses their song for a movie or commercial. Byrne calls it an artist's pension plan. And he says artists also should try to hold on to the copyrights for their recordings. This can pay off if someone wants to use their work in some other medium in the future.

Artists' opinions vary on how they should derive income from online sales. Some think it's OK to give away their music in the hopes that it will spur CD sales. Others think that's not the way to go, and that everything that is downloaded should result in income for the artist. Ultimately, though, Byrne thinks the changes we're seeing in the recording industry will be good for the artists and for the audiences. Audiences will have more choice, and artists will have more control.

Stories abound about successful artists who are broke. Courtney Love wrote a scathing letter about the situation to her fellow artists in 2000 urging them to form a new organization that would "represent their interests in Washington and negotiate fair contract terms with record companies."

- Find out what is happening today: Are successful artists still going broke? Who has been successful financially? How did they do it? How are record companies treating royalties owed to artists from Internet sales? Is there an alternative contract model supported by most artists?

PRACTICE QUIZ

1. One of the newest online applications for the recording/music industry is the _____ music store created by Steve Jobs of Apple Computers.
2. _____ is under the table payment to radio disc jockeys to encourage them to play a certain piece of music to plug a product in the mass media.
3. _____ is sharing music, usually as individual tunes, over an Internet source.
4. The illegal duplication of music and movies for black market sale is called _____.
5. Upstart performers without dependence of a studio contract are called _____.
6. _____, chief executive at Time Warner, defended artist's free expression as an essential value in a free society.
7. The _____, a group led by wives of influential members of Congress, crusaded for labels on "objectionable" music.
8. Napster was invented by _____. It was the first online music swapping software.
9. Independently owned record making companies, not part of the Big Four, are called _____.
10. Every recording artist competes for _____, radio time devoted to a particular recording.

PRACTICE TEST

6.1 Multiple Choice Questions

1. _____ was a pioneer in podcasting technology.
   a. Steve Jobs
   b. Adam Curry
   c. Gerald Levin
   d. Shawn Fanning

2. In the past the recording industry maintained tight control over recording artists. The powerful _____ units "made" the performers, choosing their music, controlling their "look," and controlling their recording sessions.
   a. A&R or Artist and Repertoire
   b. garage bands
   c. Parents Music Center
   d. Time Warner

3. _____ is the process of making illegal duplicates of music and movies for black market sale.
   a. File swapping
   b. Downloading
   c. Pirate dubbing
   d. Napsterizing

4. A major scandal in the 1950s over how disc jockeys decided which music to play uncovered a system of _____, or paying radio personnel to play certain music, giving that music more airplay.
   a. graft
   b. corruption
   c. payola
   d. all of the above

5. _____ is a hybrid form of music, which became rock 'n' roll.
   a. Rockabilly
   b. Protest music
   c. Hill billy music
   d. Classical

6.2 True/False Questions

___ 1. Digitization allowed the development of compact discs.

___ 2. Streaming made downloading from the Web feasible.

___ 3. *Garbage bands* is the term applied to recording artists who do not rely on a recording contract with a major recording company.

___ 4. The wives of influential members of Congress formed the Parents Music Resource Center because they were concerned with objectionable music that was being produced.

___ 5. Steve Fanning is the driving force behind the Apple Computer revival, iPod and iTunes.

___ 6. The first Hollywood billionaire, David Geffen, became rich by building Geffen Records from scratch. He sold the company for three quarters of a billion dollars.

___ 7. Elvis Presley was called the "white boy who sang colored" and helped pave the way for racial integration.

___ 8. The so-called Big Four recording companies are Universal, Sony BMG, EMI and Warner. Only one is a U.S. company.

___ 9. Napster and other file-sharing technology that facilitates music swapping seriously eroded music sales and record industry viability until 2005 when the U.S. Supreme Court intervened.

___ 10. Recording artists were beholden to record companies under the old A&T unit system that gave control of the artist and his or her music to the recording company.

6.3 Completion Questions

1. A(n) _____ status is awarded to recording that sell 500,000 albums or 1 million singles.

2. _____ is the term to describe how winning a prestigious award can affect sales.

3. _____ is the Apple-owned online retail site for recorded music.

4. The _____ was founded by the wives of influential Congress members who were concerned about the messages music consumers, often young people, heard in their music.

5. _____, Time Warner chief executive, is famous for his statements defending recording artists' freedom of expression.

6.4 Essay Questions

1. Radio has been said to have an uneasy partnership with the recording industry. Each needs the other. Explain.

2. With the development of new recording technology, performers are no longer tied to the large recording companies. Does this allow more artistic freedom for the recording artists? How does it affect their messages?

CHAPTER 7 Motion Pictures

MEDIA LITERACY ACTIVITY
WITHOUT DISTRIBUTION A FILM GOES NOWHERE

Distribution can make or break a film. For the maker of a docu-ganda who hopes to change hearts and minds, a lack of distribution can also be heartbreaking.

Alex Gibney's *Taxi to the Dark Side* depicts the final days of Dilawar, a young Afghan man who was arrested in 2001 by the U.S. military and beaten and tortured to death. Dilawar had volunteered to drive the taxi for his small village and had never spent the night away from home until he was imprisoned. It was eventually revealed that the attackers themselves fingered him as a participant in a rocket attack on the Americans.

At first everything seemed to be going well for *Taxi to the Dark Side.* It could be seen in movie theaters across the country, it had been nominated for an Academy Award, and the Discovery Channel bought the television rights to the film. But just before Gibney's Oscar nomination, Discovery told him it had no intention of airing the film. The Discovery Channel is owned by John Malone, the conservative media mogul who owns Liberty Media. At the time, Malone was negotiating with Rupert Murdoch's News Corp. for control of Murdoch's DirecTV satellite television system and they were waiting for approval of the deal from the Bush administration's Federal Communications Commission.

After *Taxi* won the 2007 Academy Award for best documentary, HBO managed to buy the television rights to it and aired the film in September 2008. Discovery said it would debut the movie on its smaller Investigation Discovery channel in 2009. Pundit Amy Goodman points out that date put the debut "after the election, after its business with the Bush administration is wrapped up."

Body of War also found distribution difficult. The moving anti-war film set against the backdrop of the 2002 congressional debate about the Iraq War was conceived by 72-year-old Phil Donahue, who is often referred to as the "father of the modern daytime TV talk show." In 2004, his friend Ralph Nader took him to visit Tomas Young, a 25-year-old war veteran who was paralyzed from the chest down when he was shot during his first week serving in Iraq.

Donahue teamed with Ellen Spiro, a documentary filmmaker teaching filmmaking at the University of Texas in Austin. Despite their differing artistic visions—Donahue wanted hard-hitting clips of Congress, and Spiro wanted to let the film's poetry make the point—they eventually compromised to tell both sides of the story in a powerful way that neither could have done alone. Eddie Vedder of Pearl Jam wrote two original songs for the film. *Body of War* premiered at the Toronto International Film Festival to a standing ovation, and it was short-listed for a 2007 Oscar nomination, although it didn't make the final cut. Even with all the film's accolades, Donahue and Spiro had to fight for distribution. *Body of War* finally went into limited national distribution in spring 2008.

In contrast, consider another difficult documentary, *Darfur Now,* which opened in theaters in November 2007. According to director Theodore Braun, it was "surprisingly easy to sell." The reason may be that it targeted young audiences ages 16 to 25, the same group that was most active in protesting the situation in Darfur. Braun also believes the film's message of hope helped sell it to Participant Productions and Warner Independent Pictures. The film described the genocide, but it focused on upbeat activists around the world. MTV's mtvU wing partnered to promote campus screenings, and Jessica Biel, Brad Pitt, Magic Johnson and others taped 30-second public service announcements with ties to the film.

The war in Iraq spawned a number of anti-war films. Pick four of them and summarize the point of view and message of each one.

- Are they elitist or populist?
- Who is their audience?
- Which ones had you heard of before you started this assignment?
- Have they or will they succeed in putting their issues on the public agenda? Why or why not?
- What do you think the effect is of docu-gandas and anti-war films on democracy?

PRACTICE QUIZ

1. People carry their own experiences and realities with them when they attend a movie. It is the responsibility of the movie maker to encourage _____, which occurs when you suspend your doubts about the reality of a story and become caught up in it.
2. The _____ is the term for the mass production, distribution and exhibition process for movies. As part of that system, the star system made actors into celebrities in order to increase movie audiences.
3. A(n) _____ is a low-budget movie, usually without any artistic aspirations.
4. _____ is the term for movies that are filmed, edited, distributed and exhibited digitally. Mark Cuban is an early advocate of this process.
5. _____ was an early movie director known for his innovations in his film *Birth of a Nation*.
6. Today's special effects, through the use of _____, use three-dimensional graphics to create scenes that were impossible in early films. *The Matrix* is an example of a film that used this system.
7. _____ was the first documentary filmmaker.
8. Walt Disney was a pioneer in animated films. His _____ eventually became the beloved Mickey Mouse.

9. _____ occurs when one company controls multiple stages of production of movies. It makes it difficult for smaller production houses to compete and limits audience access to multiple messages.

10. _____ is what movie houses do: they show movies.

PRACTICE TEST

7.1 Multiple Choice Questions

1. The _____ was a system by which Hollywood studios made actors into celebrities to increase movie audiences.
   a. star system
   b. studio system
   c. block booking
   d. vertical integration

2. A _____ is a video examination of a historical or current event or a natural or social phenomenon.
   a. docu-ganda
   b. documentary
   c. fiction movie
   d. B movie

3. _____ describes the function movie houses fulfill.
   a. Exhibition
   b. Multiplex
   c. Display
   d. D-cinema

4. _____ is the name for the area in Los Angeles that was the early center for movie making. Today, as more and more movies are made in different locations, it is more a synonym for the movie business.
   a. San Francisco
   b. Seattle
   c. Hollywood
   d. San Diego

5. People need to experience _____ when they watch a movie to surrender doubts about the reality of the story and become caught up in it.
   a. suspension of disbelief
   b. imagination
   c. movie clarity
   d. belief

7.2 True/False Questions

___ 1. A B movie is a low-budget movie, usually produced with little artistic aspiration.

___ 2. A blockbuster is a movie that is a great commercial success. The term is also used to describe a very successful book.

___ 3. Today's movie houses often show many movies at the same time, giving moviegoers a chance to choose which movie they would like to see. These movie houses are called group houses.

___ 4. *The Jazz Singer* with Al Jolson was the first movie to use new Warner Brothers technology that allowed moviegoers to hear sounds along with the visual.

___ 5. Movies were originally played in black and white. That all changed when the *White Pirate* became the first feature movie to be shown in color.

___ 6. Today, we enjoy movies with visual effects considered impossible not very long ago. Early special effects appear almost amateurish compared with the computer-generated imagery (CGI) used in movies and television today.

___ 7. Mark Cuban, owner of the Landmark chain, is leading the move toward digital exhibition, or d-cinema, which includes adding more luxurious surroundings to make moviegoing more memorable.

___ 8. D.W. Dubois was an early movie director known for innovations in his film *Birth of a Nation*. He successfully explored the storytelling capabilities of movies.

___ 9. Walt Disney was a pioneer in the creation of animated films. His *Bambi* was the first full-length animated film.

___10. Robert Flaherty was the first documentary filmmaker. Documentaries examine historical or current events and natural or social phenomena.

7.3 Completion Questions

1. The _____ was a U.S. government requirement from 1949 to 1987 that broadcast presentations must include both sides of any competing public issues.

2. The _____ is the term used to describe the mass production, distribution and exhibition process for movies. Adolph Zukor, the innovative creator of Paramount as a major movie studio, exemplifies the system.

3. When a single company controls or owns various stages in the production and distribution process, it is called _____. This makes it difficult for smaller movie producers to compete.

4. A movie that tells a story, much like a stage play, is called a(n) _____.

5. A rental agreement through which a movie house has to accept a batch of movies in order to get the one they really want to show is called _____.

7.4 Essay Questions

1. It has been said that movie audiences who see the movie in a movie house have a different experience than those who see it at home on their television screens. Explain.

2. Movies generate revenue through more than just selling tickets to moviegoers. Discuss the other ways movies can generate revenue.

CHAPTER 8 Radio

MEDIA LITERACY ACTIVITY
RADIO'S REIGN OF TERROR

When three journalists went on trial for war crimes committed during the Rwandan genocide in 1994, they were the first journalists to be accused of crimes against humanity since Julius Streicher, the Nazi editor who was executed after his trial at Nuremberg in 1946.

Two of the men, Ferdinand Nahimana and Jean-Bosco Barayagwiza, founded a "nominally private" radio station in Rwanda in 1992 called Radio Television Libre des Mille Collines. The third man, Hassan Ngeze, edited an extremist newspaper, and his anti-Tutsi writing was often broadcast on RTLM. In the months leading up to and during the 1994 Rwandan genocide against the Tutsi, RTLM became a popular spot on the radio dial.

At Nahimana and Barayagwiza's trial it was revealed that RTLM sought to create the impression that the Tutsis were planning an attack that would topple the government and, by some reports, enslave Hutus. One of the findings of the trial was that "government officials easily manipulated information about the Tutsi-dominated Rwandan Patriotic Front and security issues as a pretext to incite violence against Tutsi civilians." RTLM attempted to create the impression that Hutus had no choice but to slaughter Tutsis to save themselves from the inevitable conflict. The hate radio broadcasts also sought to demonize and dehumanize Tutsis to create the impression that killing them wasn't the same as killing other human beings, and to make it every Hutu's responsibility to participate in the slaughter. As gangs took to the streets with nail-studded clubs and sharpened sticks, the radio broadcasts grew increasingly chilling, court records show. One RTLM announcer advised: "Look at a person's height and his physical appearance. Just look at his small nose and then break it."

RTLM learned to disguise its propaganda from the rest of the world. It generally broadcast in two languages, French and Kinyarwanda. The broadcasts in Kinyarwanda were more virulent than those in French, and there were virtually no translations available of the Kinyarwanda broadcasts.

How did this happen? "Even the poorest African families haunt their neighbors' houses to catch snatches of government newscasts. The first thing Africans buy when they get a job is a radio...in rural parts of Rwanda, radio is king," reported Dina Temple-Raston, an award-winning journalist now working for NPR, in the *Columbia Journalism Review.* She quoted a Rwandan journalist who said, "In Rwanda, the radio has become like the voice of God, telling people what to do."

The United Nations did not intervene during the massacres, but afterward it set up an international court in Tanzania. Eight years after the genocide, in 2002, the United Nations tribunal convicted the three men of genocide for media reports that fostered the killing of about 800,000 Rwandans, mostly of the Tutsi minority. In sentencing them, the presiding judge said, "Without a firearm, machete or any physical weapon,

you caused the deaths of thousands of innocent civilians." The three-judge panel said the radio station openly called for the extermination of the Tutsi, luring victims to killing grounds and broadcasting the names of people to be singled out. Nahimana and Ngeze were sentenced to life in prison. Barayagwiza was sentenced to only 27 years because, according to the judges, his rights had been violated early in the case. The prosecutors contended that about seven out of 10 Rwandan Tutsis were killed in the 101 days of genocide.

- Find out how many radio stations exist in your listening area and who owns them, including satellite, low-power, public radio, computer, corporate, and commercial terrestrial radio.
- Define hate radio.
  - Do any of the stations in your listening area broadcast hate radio?
  - How do shock jocks fit into this picture?
  - Where in the world is hate radio most prevalent? Where is it most effective? Why?
- Do you think today's radio innovations might have made a difference in Rwanda?

PRACTICE QUIZ

1. Because radio uses _____ that are owned by the public to transmit its messages, the federal government says broadcast should be subject to regulation.
2. Government regulation was lessened in the 1980s through _____, where the old limits were relaxed, including limits on how many stations a single business entity could own.
3. The _____ established the Federal Radio Commission, which was designed to prevent radio chain ownership.
4. _____ is a delivery system in which radio programming originates at one source and is then broadcast to a satellite for delivery to individual end users.
5. _____ reinvented radio using narrow formats to appeal to very specific audiences.
6. The term for radio that is transmitted over land-based towers is _____.
7. A(n) _____ station is a station that is locally licensed and has an affiliation with a network to carry the network's programming along with its local programming.
8. Because the government recognized _____, an insufficiency of radio frequencies, in the 1920s, they felt some kind of regulation was necessary.
9. The Corporation for Public Broadcasting was established by the _____.
10. A(n) _____ is an announcer whose style includes vulgarities and taboos.

PRACTICE TEST

8.1 Multiple Choice Questions

1. The Federal Radio Commission, which regulates radio, was established by the _____.
   a. 1927 Radio Act
   b. Constitution
   c. 1st Amendment
   d. Fairness Doctrine
2. _____ is the radio listener survey company that determines what programming is popular and the demographics of the listeners.
   a. FCC
   b. Arbitron
3. _____ reinvented radio with narrow formats to appeal to more specific audiences in the 1950s.
   a. Gordon McClendon
   b. Edward R. Murrow
   c. Don Imus
   d. Rush Limbaugh
4. The _____ awards radio licenses to applicants that are expected to broadcast in the public interest, convenience and necessity.
   a. Radio Licensing Board
   b. state governments
   c. Federal Radio Commission
   d. Deregulation Authority
5. _____ is the term used to identify traditional radio audio transmission from land-based towers, as opposed to transmission via satellite.
   a. Old fashioned
   b. National Public Radio
   c. Terrestrial radio
   d. Corporate radio

8.2 True/False Questions

___ 1. An announcer whose style includes vulgarities and taboos is said to be a shock jock.
___ 2. Deregulation is the trend that began in the 1980s increase government regulation of business.
___ 3. The marketplace concept says that people will choose the radio stations they want and will not choose something with which they are not satisfied. In effect, people will "vote" with their radio dials.
___ 4. The concept that broadcasting should be subject to government regulation springs from the idea that it is transmitted over public airwaves. The government argues that the electromagnetic spectrum is a public asset.
___ 5. The trusteeship concept says that the government serves as a trustee for the public's interest in regulating broadcasting, as do the licensed station owners.

___ 6. Edward R. Monroe was a famous radio, and later television, broadcaster who is known for his coverage of World War II and his exposing Senator Joseph McCarty's hypocrisy and unfairly accusing famous people of being affiliated with the Communist Party.
___ 7. All-news radio is a niche format that delivers all news and news-related content and commentary.
___ 8. Joan Kroc, wife of the founder of McDonald's, was a passionate radio listener who bequeathed $200 million to National Public Radio when she died in 2003. National Public Radio is a network of noncommercial radio stations.
___ 9. Associate stations are fully licensed stations that carry network programming along with local programming.
___10. A playlist is a list of songs a radio station plays.

8.3 Completion Questions

1. _____ are reports, often live, on events as they are occurring.
2. The _____ established the Corporation for Public Broadcasting, a quasi-government agency that funnels funds into noncommercial radio and television broadcasting.
3. _____ is a delivery method of radio programming that emanates at a single source and is beamed to an orbiting satellite for transmission directly to individual end users. An example is Sirius.
4. A new industry-adopted standard, _____, allows old style analog and new style digital radio receivers to pick up either signal at the same spot on the radio dial. In essence, it allows multiple programming on the same channel.
5. Unlike analog radio, digital signals are encoded as 1s and 0s, which means multiple programs can be _____ on the same channel.

8.4 Essay Questions

1. Some claim that corporate radio provides listeners with a bland sameness of programming. Explain.
2. It is said Edward R. Murrow brought war into people's homes for the first time with his coverage of World War II. Explain.

MEDIA LITERACY ACTIVITY
BIG BROTHER: A 24/7 FLY ON THE WALL

One of the biggest hits of reality television has been *Big Brother.*

The concept of Big Brother first made an appearance in the 1949 George Orwell novel *1984,* where Big Brother is the all-seeing, all-knowing force behind a dictator who has everyone under constant surveillance. The television series confines 10 to 15 contestants to the House for three months. They are isolated from the outside world, and they are filmed 24/7 by hidden cameras. The highlights are edited together and make up the weekly TV show. Addicts can also log onto a website for further live coverage.

The contestants regularly nominate a number of their fellow housemates for eviction, and viewers are then given the opportunity to vote on those with the most nominations. When the "evictee" is announced, he is interviewed live by the show's host.

The show has been a commercial success around the world. It originated in Holland and then spread to other countries, including Germany, Spain and the United States. In most countries, it has remained true to its original fly-on-the-wall style, but in the U.S. *Big Brother* now has more emphasis on strategy, competition, and voting.

In addition to broadcast television, the show is available on the Internet with a continuous 24-hour feed from multiple cameras. In some countries, the webcast is supplemented by email updates and material that is available on mobile phones. In some countries there is a charge for access to the *Big Brother* websites. In addition, the House is shown live on satellite television, although some countries require a 10-to 15-minute delay to allow the removal of libelous or unacceptable content.

Although producer Peter Bazalgette says that television's *Big Brother* is "nothing but entertainment; it never pretended to be a genuine social experiment; it's just a game show with a prizewinner," critics deride the show's voyeuristic qualities. In pursuit of cash prizes and fame, the contestants give up their privacy. They have been likened to caged animals who are being watched to see how they behave and how their relationships develop.

At times, the contestants have been sexually involved with one another, sometimes going so far as engaging in intercourse in front of the cameras. The British and American shows edit out this material, but the Germans broadcast allows it to air. And, the salacious content is available on the Internet stream, leading some other countries to ask for an end to the popular show.

Big Brother may be an amalgam of the new directions of the reality television show, allowing reality and fiction to morph into each other. Are the contestants on *Big Brother* living in isolation or community? How about those of us watching them? Screenwriter-director Andrew Niccol said, "Television blurs boundaries between reality and fiction, and it unites, but in a way that also separates us. Watching is what we share, not proximity."

- Make a list of the elements of *Big Brother* that make it so successful.
- Compare *Big Brother* to the game show programs of 20 or 30 years ago.
- How do other types of successful programs, like news shows, comedies or dramas, compare with their historic counterparts?
- Do these changes reflect what is happening in society?
- How does the experience of watching *Big Brother* compare to your experience watching other kinds of shows, like a documentary or a soap opera?

PRACTICE QUIZ

1. _____ is the term for when the audience has control of when to view a program.
2. _____ is when a company is subsumed into the ownership of another company.
3. Originally the United States' broadcast infrastructure was called a(n) _____, meaning it had one tier of locally licensed stations, and another of national networks.
4. _____ was the FCC chair who said television was "a vast wasteland."
5. In 1975, _____, a young executive at Time Inc. devised a way to create a network exclusively for cable stations to augment what they were picking up from over-air stations. He used orbiting satellites to relay exclusive programming to local cable systems.
6. The _____ is a quasi-governmental agency that channels tax-generated funds into the U.S. noncommercial television and radio system.
7. New technology has made _____ possible, allowing viewers to tune in to programs at any time they choose, no matter where they are.
8. _____ is a television entrepreneur whose interests include DirecTV, Liberty Media, Discovery, QVC, and more.
9. _____ are companies, many subsidiaries of large media companies, that own several local cable television delivery units, usually in different, far-flung communities.
10. A(n) _____ is a mini-movie, generally only four minutes in length, on the Web that is sponsored by and sometimes includes the advertiser as part of the story line.

PRACTICE TEST

9.1 Multiple Choice Questions

1. When the audience has control of the time they view a television program, it is called _____.
   a. direct broadcast
   b. time shifting
   c. digital transmission
   d. upfront broadcasting

2. _____ built the first CATV system in Astoria, Oregon, in 1949.
   a. Ed Parsons
   b. Gerald Levin
   c. Stanley Hubbard
   d. Philo Farnsworth

3. _____ is noncommercial television with an emphasis on quality programming to meet the needs of the public.
   a. Webisodes
   b. Sponsored television
   c. Public television
   d. On-air delivery

4. When one company is subsumed into the ownership of another company it is called _____.
   a. an ownership meld.
   b. merging.
   c. a partnership.
   d. a transmission meld.

5. The _____ is a quasi-governmental agency that channels tax-generated funds into a U.S. noncommercial television and radio system.
   a. Corporation for Public Broadcasting
   b. Carnegie Commission on Educational Television
   c. Public Broadcasting Act
   d. Public Broadcasting Service

9.2 True/False Questions

___ 1. With new technology, people can carry television with them anywhere. This has created space shifts, or changes in where people watch television.

___ 2. Originally, infrastructure of television in the United States had a two-tier system, one of locally licensed stations, the other consisting of national networks.

___ 3. Stanley Hubbard was the FCC chair who coined the term "a vast wasteland" for television.

___ 4. John Malone built Liberty Mutual into a television programming powerhouse including Discovery, QVC, other cable channels, websites, and Starz movie pay-per-view. With DirecTV he controls a significant platform for delivering his programming.

___ 5. Time shifting devices allow people to watch programs at their convenience. Video-on-demand mechanisms allow viewers to tune in any time they choose.

___ 6. An advance contract system locks advertisers into buying network advertising time slots for specific shows many months in advance.

___ 7. A *multisystem operator* is the term for a company that owns several local cable television delivery units in different, usually far-flung communities.

___ 8. Sat Tom is the term for a satellite company that delivers television.

___ 9. The Federal Radio Act of 1927 was the original law for government regulation of broadcasting in the United States. It was revised in 1935 to include television.

___ 10. Edward R. Monroe was a pioneer radio broadcaster who made the switch to television broadcasting.

9.3 Completion Questions

1. _____ used orbiting satellites to relay exclusive programming to local cable television systems in 1975.

2. The _____, a handheld device made by Apple, allows users to listen to music and view video whenever and wherever they choose.

3. With upfronts, most advertising slots during a specific show are spoken for months in advance. But, if the show does not meet expectations, advertisers may be given _____, or additional spots, to compensate for a smaller than anticipated audience.

4. _____ are mini-movies, generally only four minutes in length, shown on the Web. They are usually sponsored by and often include the advertiser as part of the story line.

5. _____ was a pioneer of direct-to-viewer satellite television delivery. Called direct broadcast satellite, it is the transmission of television signals directly from orbiting satellites to viewers without a local station or cable system as intermediary.

9.4 Essay Questions

1. How have time shifting and space shifting changed television for the stations, advertisers and viewers?

2. In 1961 FCC chair Newton Minnow said television is "a vast wasteland." Explain his comment.

CHAPTER 10 Internet

MEDIA LITERACY ACTIVITY
NET NEUTRALITY: IT'S A QUESTION OF CONTROL

Should Internet users have the freedom to access the content, services, applications, and devices of their choice, or should their Internet Service Providers be the ones to determine access?

Although the Internet was supposed to democratize mass communication, evidence that providers were beginning to control access to the Internet for their customers surfaced as early as 2006 when North Carolina telco Madison River blocked Vonage VoIP traffic and was fined by the Federal Communications Commission. Next to surface were anti-union actions of the Canadian ISP Telus, which stopped on-site employees' access to a labor union website.

In 2007, Pearl Jam complained that a Lollapalooza concert in Chicago that was webcast on AT&T's Blue Room was censored. Lyrics that Eddie Vedder altered in the song "Daughter" to express his anti-President Bush feelings—"George Bush, leave this world alone; George Bush, find yourself another home—were bleeped out."

Both fans and the band were outraged. Pearl Jam called for action on its website saying, "AT&T's actions strike at the heart of the public's concerns over the power that corporations have when it comes to determining what the public sees and hears through communications media"—were bleeped out.

For its part, AT&T said the whole thing was a big mistake. Since the Blue Room has no age restrictions, AT&T hired a webcast partner to bleep out curse words. The partner, said AT&T, was overzealous. "The editing of the Pearl Jam performance…was completely contrary to our policy," the company said in a statement. "AT&T does not edit or censor performances."

In May 2008 the Max Planck Institute in Germany released the results of a study that showed that both Comcast and Cox Communications were blocking Web traffic over their networks. It found that the widespread blocking of BitTorrent peer-to-peer file transfers only happened in the U.S. and Singapore, and most of the hosts who were observed blocking belonged to a few large cable Internet Service Providers. In the United States most of those were Cox and Comcast networks. In Singapore, all the blocked hosts were connected using the StarHub network. The study found that all the hosts that were observed blocking were doing so in the upstream direction, and that the blockages happened throughout all hours of the day, not just during high-traffic times as Comcast had previously claimed. Of 788 Comcast subscribers who participated, 62 percent had their connections blocked. At Cox, 54 percent of the 151 subscribers were blocked.

Investigations by the Electronic Frontier Foundation and the Associated Press also found that Comcast monitored usage of file-sharing applications such as BitTorrent. When users tried to upload large files, Comcast sent messages blocking the communica-tion. The messages appeared to come from the user receiving the file.

In its filing with the FCC, Comcast defended its practices by saying that broadband network operators needed to be able to engage in reasonable network management to ensure that their customers could enjoy a positive broadband experience. "Network management is best left to the sound, good-faith judgment of the engineers and proprietors who run and own the networks and who are best able to remedy customer service issues promptly, rather than to regulation."

In response to these and other complaints, a new bill was introduced in Congress in 2008. Called the Internet Freedom Preservation Act, the bill sought to put the FCC's nondiscrimination principles into law, in language general enough to be open to regulatory discretion.

- Find out if Internet Service Providers always provide equal bandwidth for upstream and downstream traffic. If there is a difference, do you think it's because of censorship or their bottom line? When would it cross the line from an economic consideration to censorship?
- Find out what happened with the proposed Internet Freedom Preservation Act. Is net neutrality a real issue in the U.S. where our freedom of speech is guaranteed? Do you think laws are needed to guarantee net neutrality?
- Find out if net neutrality is an issue in other parts of the world. What about countries that don't have freedom of speech? Or countries with emerging world economies?

PRACTICE QUIZ

1. An informal general term used for Internet commercial sites, most of whose online addresses end in .com, is _____.
2. _____, a silicon chip used in digitization, functions as an on/off switch, converting information into 1s and 0s so they can be transmitted in rapid fire pulses and reconstructed at the other end of the transmission.
3. _____ devised the protocols, or codes, for the World Wide Web.
4. The technology that makes a message more compact by deleting nonessential underlying code is called _____.
5. _____ is the term used to describe the economic distinction between impoverished groups and societal groups with the means to maintain and improve their economic well being through computer access.
6. Two University of California researchers, _____ and _____, are credited with inventing the transmission protocols, TCP for short, that allow local networks to talk to each other.

7. The _____ is a system that allows global linking of information modules in user-determined sequences.
8. _____ is the coding that allows computers to talk with each other to read Web pages. With it people's computers can read Internet files.
9. The computer language that allows someone to click on a link and be transferred to another on-line address is called _____.
10. A(n) _____ is a website, usually personal in nature on a narrow topic. It can be a kind of Internet diary.

PRACTICE TEST

10.1 Multiple Choice Questions

1. A(n) _____ is where an institution or individual establishes its Web presence.
   a. Internet site
   b. streaming site
   c. ARPAnet
   d. Lexis site
2. The technology that makes a message more compact by deleting nonessential underlying code is called _____.
   a. data packets
   b. compression
   c. streaming
   d. dynamic routing
3. _____ devised the protocols, or codes, for the World Wide Web.
   a. Marc Andreesen
   b. Vint Cerf
   c. Glenn Reynolds
   d. Tim Berners-Lee
4. _____ is the technology that allows playback of a message to begin before all the components have arrived.
   a. Streaming
   b. Data packets
   c. Hypertext transfer protocol
   d. Hypertext markup language
5. _____ and _____ are co-authors of Transmission Control Protocol or TCP, sometimes called the Fathers of the Internet. TCP allows local networks to talk with each other.
   a. Vint Cerf
   b. Bob Kahn
   c. Marc Andreesen
   d. a and b
   e. b and c

10.2 True/False Questions

___ 1. The digital divide is the economic distinction between impoverished groups and groups with the means to maintain and improve their economic well being through computer access.
___ 2. Wireless fidelity technology know as wi-fi, allows Internet access anywhere through radio waves.

___ 3. A fiber optic cable is made of copper strands capable of carrying data at the speed of light.
___ 4. The Telecommunications Act of 2008 repealed many limits on services that telephone and cable companies could offer.
___ 5. The diffusion of innovation is the process through which news, ideas, values and information spread.
___ 6. The melding of print, electronic and photographic media into digitized form is called technological convergence.
___ 7. Search Inside is Amazon.com's search engine that can find a term or phrase in every book whose copyright owners have agreed to have it scanned into Amazon's database. It demonstrates possibilities for the library of the future.
___ 8. An informal, general term for Internet commercial sites, most of whose online addresses end with the suffix .com, is dot com.
___ 9. An entry point for further Internet access is called a door.
___ 10. Bandwidth is the space available in a medium, such as cable television or the electromagnetic spectrum, to carry messages. It limits the number of messages a medium can carry at a given time.

10.3 Completion Questions

1. A(n) _____ is a website, generally personal in nature, on a narrow subject, such as politics. The term is short for Web log.
2. Digitization would not be possible without _____, silicon chips that act as on/off switches, changing data into 1s and 0s and then transmitting them as rapid fire pulses and reconstructing them at the other end.
3. _____, a system for nonsequential reading, allows people to interrupt themselves while reading material in a linear manner and transport themselves in a nonlinear way to other related materials. In other words, it allows you to move to another website through a system of links.
4. The technology that makes every wireless device a vehicle for furthering a message along to its destination, rather than having it move along a structured network, is called _____. The ad hoc network created for each single message to reach its destination is called mesh networking.
5. _____ is the term for a Web protocol that allows users to choose a level of privacy. In essence, this technology automatically bypasses websites that do not meet a certain level of privacy.

10.4 Essay Questions

1. It is said that Internet users need to exercise caution with the information they may find on the Web. Explain. How would you check the quality of information you find on the Web?
2. Netscape was the first browser that make the Web easily accessible to personal computer owners. Explain what Netscape does.

CHAPTER 11 News

MEDIA LITERACY ACTIVITY
THE DAILY SHOW: *UNBURDENED BY OBJECTIVITY, JOURNALISTIC INTEGRITY OR EVEN ACCURACY*

"Balance" in media stories has been blamed for a slow awakening to the climate change issue.

The U.S. media presented the issue as an equal argument between scientists who said global warming was occurring and those who said it wasn't. Actually, a very small number of scientists refuted the body of evidence supporting global warming, but coverage of the issue didn't reflect that. In their zeal to be "fair" and "balanced" America's mainstream media gave each side equal weight. Was the resulting news about this issue authentic? Was it accurate?

Martin Kaplan, associate dean of the University of Southern California's Annenberg School for Communication, says the modern perception of balance has overtaken the concepts of accuracy, truth and objectivity. Today's journalists portray issues as controversy between two opposite sides, "and the journalist is fearful of saying that one side has it right, and the other side does not." He explains that today's media audiences have to figure out where the truth lies for themselves after reading a story that says "Some say black is black, and some say black is white." "So whether it's climate change or evolution or the impact on war policy of various proposals, it's all being framed 'on the one hand, on the other hand,' as though the two sides had equal claims on accuracy."

What's a reader or viewer to do? Many seek out alternatives in the Internet blogosphere or on television with Comedy Central's *The Daily Show* with Jon Stewart. Much like NBC's Tim Russert, who put newsmakers' quotes on screen and asked them about what they said, Stewart also shows us how newsmakers contradict themselves, but Stewart goes even further in the hypocrisy-exposing business—and, since his news is faux, he gets the laughs. Stewart took over *The Daily Show* in 1999, and with his sharp, intelligent, humorous parodies of the news of the day, he's built the show into a major media player. Surveys show that more than 20 percent of young Americans look to satirical programs like *The Daily Show* as their primary news source.

Stewart and his fake correspondents "know how to crystallize an issue on all sides, see the silliness everywhere," says Hub Brown, chair of the communications department at Syracuse University's S.I. Newhouse School of Public Communications. Bill Moyers describes Stewart's show as "a compendium of news, interviews and features, held up to a fractured mirror to reveal a greater truth." Stewart himself explains "We just are so inundated with mixed messages from the media and from politicians that we're just trying to sort it out for ourselves."

USC's Kaplan says Stewart isn't afraid to make fun of the journalistic concept of balance or to have "a bull***t meter and to call people spinners or liars when they deserve it. I think as a consequence some viewers find that helpful and refreshing and hilarious."

- Listen to or read two different mainstream media reports of an event or issue. Then watch *The Daily Show* to see how it "reported" the same event or issue. (You could also do this by visiting the organizations' websites.)
  - Did *The Daily Show* report all sides of the issue? Was it objective? Fair?
  - What, exactly, was the difference between Stewart's report and the original, mainstream reports, other than that one is funnier than the other?
  - Do you think the mainstream media reports or *The Daily Show's* report of this event or issue was more informative?
  - No one is suggesting that "serious" journalists should stop gathering the news to give us factual information, but is there a case to be made that more journalists should try to emulate Jon Stewart's honesty? What would be the consequences if "serious" journalists adopted Stewart's style of reporting?

PRACTICE QUIZ

1. _____ was a newspaper publisher who defied authorities by criticizing the governor of the colony of New York.
2. The organization of a newspaper newsroom and its staff is credited to an early editor of the Penny Press, _____.
3. _____ and _____ proved the power of the press with their investigative reporting of the Watergate break-in.
4. _____ is the fanciful term for a serious type of reporting: investigative reporting.
5. _____ allow journalists to protect the identification of their sources who wish to remain confidential.
6. The term _____ refers to the news media's role in monitoring the performance of government and other institutions of society.
7. The _____ is the space left over in a newspaper or news broadcast after the paid advertising has been placed.
8. Seeing things on the basis of your own personal experiences or values is called _____.
9. Those members of the media whose job it is to decide which stories will reach the media consumers are _____.
10. The _____ discouraged criticism of the government in the colonies. These acts affected newspapers and their publishers and the stories they could publish.

PRACTICE TEST

11.1 Multiple Choice Questions

1. Enterprise reporting that reveals new, often startling information that official sources would often rather not have revealed is called _____.
   a. investigative journalism
   b. blogging
   c. independent reporting
   d. beat reporting

2. _____ defied authorities in New York and founded a newspaper that was in competition with the Crown-sponsored newspaper. This paper antagonized the governor and the publisher was ultimately arrested, though later he was freed.
   a. Arthur Schlesinger
   b. Benjamin Harris
   c. John Peter Zenger
   d. James Gordon Bennett

3. The _____ is the person in a media organization who decides whether or not to use a story and whether to shorten or change it en route to a mass audience.
   a. gatekeeper
   b. writer
   c. editor
   d. graphic artist

4. _____ is information media consumers can use. It is often said to be a report on change.
   a. News
   b. Yellow journalism
   c. Filtered information
   d. Shock journalism

5. The _____, generally considered to have occurred during late 1800s, was a period of journalism marked by sensationalism where stories were not always reported with attention to truth and honesty.
   a. Yellow Period
   b. Victorian Period
   c. Great Depression
   d. World War I

11.2 True/False Questions

____ 1. Joseph Pulitzer was a newspaper publisher who emphasized human interest stories and later sensationalized stories when he found his papers in competition with those of another famous newspaper owner, William Randolph Hearst.

____ 2. Carl Bernstein and Bob Woodward were reporters for the New York *Times* when they broke the Watergate story, which linked President Richard M. Nixon to a crime, ultimately resulting in the President's resignation.

____ 3. The Alien and Sedition Acts discouraged criticism of the U.S. government by the media of the time.

____ 4. The concept in journalism that news should be gathered and reported without bias is called objectivity.

____ 5. News that is geared to satisfying the audience's information wants, not needs, is said to be soft news. It includes self-help, lifestyle tips, and human interest stories.

____ 6. A leading Penny Press newspaper editor, James Gordon Bennett, was the first to organize methodical news coverage with a newsroom and reporting staff.

____ 7. The New York *Sun* published by Herbert Gans changed the newspaper industry. At a penny a copy it was affordable to everyone and its content focused on items of interest to the common people and was written in a style they could understand.

____ 8. *Publick Occurrences* was the first colonial newspaper.

____ 9. Horace Greeley started placing content that expresses opinions on an editorial page.

____ 10. The inverted pyramid form of organizing a news story places the most important information first. It was developed because war correspondents often transmitted their stories over telegraph lines and there were no assurances they would not suffer a disconnection.

11.3 Completion Questions

1. _____ was a muckraker journalist famous for her series on monopolistic corruption at Standard Oil Company.

2. News reporting that continues 24/7 is called _____.

3. News is a competitive profession, with media outlets competing with each other to get the "scoop" first. Media scholar Leon Sigal calls this competitive nature between news outlets the _____.

4. The space left for news in a newspaper after all the paid ads have been inserted or the time left in a newscast after the commercials is called the _____.

5. Since the founding of this country, the media has been expected to fulfill a _____: to monitor the performance of government and other societal institutions, keeping them honest and responsive to the public.

11.4 Essay Questions

1. A number of variables affect the news. Discuss what might affect whether or not a story is used.

2. During the Colonial period of U.S. history many concepts that still guide news outlets today were set into place. Discuss.

CHAPTER 12 Public Relations

MEDIA LITERACY ACTIVITY
FAKE STUDENT TOUTS ANTI-COUNTERFEITING MESSAGE

Students in a public relations class at Hunter College in New York thought they'd come up with a winning campaign.

Their class was one of several across the country that was funded through a grant from a member company of the International AntiCounterfeiting Coalition (IACC). IACC members include companies like Apple, Levi Strauss & Co., Louis Vuitton, and Rolex. The anti-counterfeiting organization recruited the colleges to its *Get Real* campaign, which was launched to dissuade consumers from buying knock-offs. Students play the role of an agency pitching an anti-counterfeiting campaign to the "client." The *Get Real* campaign is itself run by a public relations firm, Paul Werth Associates, based in Columbus, Ohio.

Schools that have participated include Ohio State University, the University of Miami, and California State University in Sacramento. A number of campaigns created by classes at these schools got the hoped-for results, and students said they thought the experience was educational and a helpful look into the real world of public relations. At California State, the class got a grant from Cisco Systems and came up with a campaign, *Fear the Fraud,* with a website, T-shirt and wristband giveaways and testimony before the Sacramento City Council. Fearthefraud.com got more than 48,000 hits its first week, and more than 700 visitors signed an online pledge to eschew counterfeit goods.

But at Hunter College something went wrong.

The school received a grant of $10,000 from Coach, a company know for high-end fashion accessories, for the class. Hunter asked an assistant professor in the film and media studies department to teach the class. He said he wasn't qualified, but he was pressed into the job anyway.

The students in his class pitched four different campaigns to representatives of Coach. The Coach people chose a combination of two of the pitches, one which featured a fictional student and another with the tagline, *Break the Chain.*

The students hung posters around campus that read, "MISSING — $500 reward!" for the return of a lost Coach bag. On the posters was the picture of the woman who lost the bag, Heidi Cee. Tear-off tabs listed her phone number, blog, MySpace page, and Facebook profile. Visitors to the blog, which drew more than 15,000 hits, learned the bag was a gift from an ex-boyfriend serving in Iraq. Days later, she blogged that the bag had been returned, but the next day she told the world that the bag was a fake and she had been scammed for the reward. She was outraged. She told her readers that she had researched counterfeit goods and found that they're linked to criminal activity and child labor. She posted a YouTube video about counterfeiting. She also organized an anti-counterfeiting event on campus that offered free food and T-shirts.

The problem with all this was that Cee was a fake. Cee's 32nd and last blog entry included a press release, which was also linked to the social networking sites, telling readers: "Here is the catch—I am totally not real!"

Critics say this acknowledgement was too little, too late, and investigations into what happened were launched. Critics said the Hunter campaign violated parts of the Public Relations Society of America's code of ethics, namely truthfulness and transparency. It was, they said, a classic example of how buzz-seeking stunts can backfire.

Public relations professionals acknowledge how difficult it can be to design ethical online campaigns. Even the pros have crossed the line. There was the fan blog for PlayStation that was outed when it was found that it was registered to Zipatoni, an agency working for the game maker. Sony had to apologize. In 2006, the couple blogging as Wal-Marting Across America was outed when it was discovered that their trip and blog were organized by Wal-Mart's public relations firm, Edelman. In an attempt to appease outraged Wal-Mart customers, Richard Edelman wrote on his own blog, "I want to acknowledge our error in failing to be transparent about the identity of the two bloggers from the outset."

- Find out more about the Wal-Mart and Playstation fiascos. Write about how they compare to the Hunter College affair.
  - At what point did the three campaigns cross the ethical line?
  - What could each campaign have done differently to prevent the backfire?
  - Why do think consumers react with anger when they find out about campaigns like these?

PRACTICE QUIZ

1. _____ is a dialogue-based approach to negotiating relationships.
2. Paul Garrett devised the notion of _____, or mutually beneficial public relations.
3. A comprehensive program that links public relations and advertising is called _____.
4. _____ is a management tool to establish beneficial relationships.
5. _____ is the application of Darwin's survival of the fittest theory.
6. _____ is attacking critics openly.
7. A(n) _____ is a public relations message that takes an editorial position and appears in paid space or time. It is a term contrived from the words advertisement and editorial.
8. _____ is the process of trying to influence public policy, usually legislation or regulations. It is a form of public relations.
9. Dealing with the press and other media is called _____ in public relations.
10. _____ was an early public relations practitioner whose practice and scholarship helped define the field.

11. _____ was another public relations pioneer who laid out the fundamentals in the practice of public relations.

PRACTICE TEST

12.1 Multiple Choice Questions

1. _____ was a pioneer in the field of public relations. He laid out the fundamentals of the field.
   a. Ivy Lee
   b. William Henry Vanderbilt
   c. Paul Garrett
   d. Jack Abramson
2. _____ was an early public relations practitioner whose practice and scholarship helped define the field.
   a. William Henry Vanderbilt
   b. Edward Bernays
   c. Paul Garrett
   d. Peter Diamantis
3. Good public relations should be mutually beneficial. This is called enlightened self-interest and was postulated by _____.
   a. Paul Garrett
   b. Charles Darwin
   c. Ivy Lee
   d. Leslie Unger
4. An _____ is a public relations message that takes an editorial position and appears in paid advertising space or time.
   a. advertisement
   b. information boycott
   c. advertorial
   d. adversarial
5. During World War I, _____ demonstrated that public relations could work on a mammoth scale.
   a. George Creel
   b. P.T. Barnum
   c. John D. Rockefeller, Jr.
   d. Elmer Davis

12.2 True/False Questions

___ 1. Puffery is inflated claims or hyperbolic boasts, often used in early advertising.
___ 2. A social media news release is a newspaper-based news release with links to other related material.
___ 3. Dialogic theory is a dialogue-based approach to negotiating relationships—a kinder, gentler practice of public relations.

___ 4. The Public Relations Society of America is a major professional association. It works to regulate the practice of public relations through its volunteer membership.
___ 5. Charles Darwin devised the survival-of-the-fittest theory that, when extended to society, became social Darwinism.
___ 6. Companies that provide public relations services are called public relations agencies.
___ 7. Political communications refers to advising candidates and groups on public policy issues, often tied to elections.
___ 8. Crisis management is the term used to describe the policy of developing programs in advance of an emergency.
___ 9. Proactive media relations is taking the initiative to release information before requested. This full disclosure tends to head off false rumors.
___10. Whitewatering is the term used for covering up a wrongdoing, usually some kind of abuse or embarrassment, without correcting it.

12.3 Completion Questions

1. _____ is the management tool to establish beneficial relationships between a person, organization, corporation, or government entity and the publics that affect it.
2. _____ is a comprehensive program that links public relations and advertising.
3. When public relations attacks critics openly it is _____.
4. _____ is the process of trying to influence public policy, usually legislation or regulations.
5. _____ is the component of public relations that deals with press and other media.

12.4 Essay Questions

1. In the past public relations and advertising were kept apart from each other. Today, however, often under integrated marketing communication, the two fields are combined. Public relations practitioners may find themselves running both the public relations and advertising functions of their organization. Discuss why you think this happened and why it has been a successful concept.
2. The origins of modern public relations are in the turbulent times of the late 1800s and early 1900s when U.S. businesses were developing. Many big companies found themselves in disfavor for ignoring the public good to make a profit. Discuss how public relations helped big business and the public cultivate a better relationship.

CHAPTER 13 Advertising

MEDIA LITERACY ACTIVITY
THE SEX(IST) SALES PITCH

Americans don't think twice about seeing naked bodies in commercials and print ads. Everyone knows that "sex sells." We see partially clad bodies selling everything from beer and cars to shampoo, and some of these ads are blatantly sexist. In other parts of the world, ads that are considered sexist are banned. Norway and Denmark prohibit sexist ads, and at the same time they prize their freedom of speech. They don't see any conflict between the two.

In early 2008, Sweden considered a similar ban on sexist advertising. A special report calling for the ban defined sexist advertising as any message distributed "with a commercial aim that can be construed as offensive to women or men."

"Sexist advertising affects the shaping of people's identities and is counter-productive to society's goal of achieving gender equality," said the report. The Swedish government rejected the report, saying a ban on sexist advertising would compromise the country's freedom of speech.

"I don't want to infringe on fundamental human freedoms and rights for a legislation the efficacy of which I question. This is not the way to win the fight for gender equity," said Swedish Gender Equity Minister Nyamko Sabuni. The country's Equality Minister, Malin Engstedt, said the Swedish government was confident that efforts made by the country's advertisers themselves—including the introduction of an ombudsman similar to Denmark's to oversee advertisements—would be more effective. "They are more than capable of finding other ways of advertising their products," she said.

Sweden's neighbors Norway and Denmark have strict limits on the use of sexist content for commercial gain. In Norway, ads can contain sexual images, but they must be relevant. "Naked people are wonderful, of course, but they have to be relevant to the product. You could have a naked person advertising shower gel or a cream, but not a woman in a bikini draped across a car," explains Sol Olving, head of Norway's Kreativt Forum, an association of the country's top advertising agencies. "Basically, if something is offensive or it makes the viewer feel uncomfortable when they look at it, it shouldn't be done." Norway has outlawed sexist advertising in 2003. The ban is part of a broader law that places limits on how ads handle religion, sexuality, race, and gender. A company that refuses to remove or alter an ad after a complaint has been upheld faces a fine of 500,000 Norwegian kroner (62,500 euros). Olving says there have been no complaints about the law from advertisers, and they have found less obvious ways to sell their products.

Similar guidelines have been in effect in Denmark since 1993. Ombudsman Henrik Oe says that he receives about 10 complaints a year about sexist advertising, and that companies usually remove the offending images quickly. He says advertisers are becoming increasingly creative, using humor instead of sex to stretch the boundaries and to appeal to consumers.

In countries with no bans on sexism in advertising, critics claim that sexism has become "normalized," and that means that media consumers don't question or challenge the sexism.

Deline Beukes, executive director of the Advertising Authority of South Africa, says, "Whether or not an advertisement is sexist depends on a society's value systems and where the advert is placed."

- Several ads have created a stir in other countries because of their sexism. Find one of them through an Internet search.
  - Do you think the ad's effectiveness would be compromised without the sex appeal?
  - Would such an ad be considered normal in the United States? Would it appear normal in Botswana? How about in Denmark?
  - Do sexist ads appeal to the lowest common denominator among consumers?
  - Do sexist ads contribute to the common course of informed decision-making that is the basis of democracy? If not, is freedom of speech really compromised by a ban on sexist ads?

PRACTICE QUIZ

1. _____, devised by Rosser Reeves, is an advertising concept that emphasizes a single feature of a product or service.
2. _____, developed by Jack Trout, targets ads for a specific consumer group.
3. Advertisements, often subtle, that are placed in unexpected places are called _____.
4. _____ refers to the potential circulation of periodicals that are seen by more than one person.
5. The first ad agency was founded by _____.
6. Ad agencies are paid for their services in a number of ways. With a _____, the agency earns expenses and an agreed-upon markup for the client, plus bonuses for exceeding minimal expectations.
7. The term _____ describes how the cost effectiveness of different media is calculated.
8. The Internet has opened new opportunities for advertisers. Some online ad resources include _____, an on-screen hot spot to move to another online advertisement.
9. _____ is enhancing a product image with a celebrity endorsement or the use of an already established brand name.
10. People are exposed to so many ads each day that it is a challenge for the advertiser to actually have their message seen or heard. This overabundance of ads is called _____.

PRACTICE TEST

13.1 Multiple Choice

1. The first advertising agency was founded by _____.
   a. Wayland Ayer
   b. Benjamin Day
   c. William Caxton
   d. John Campbell

2. _____ championed the concept of brand imaging when he said, "give your product a first class ticket through life."
   a. Sam Walton
   b. David Ogilvy
   c. Jack Trout
   d. Dave Balter

3. Benjamin Day's newspaper, the _____, was the first penny newspaper that brought advertising to a new level within its pages.
   a. Washington *Post*
   b. Chicago *Tribune*
   c. Boston *Globe*
   d. New York *Sun*

4. _____ was a British printer who is credited with printing the first advertisement to promote one of his books.
   a. William Caxton
   b. John Campbell
   c. Benjamin Day
   d. Wayland Ayer

5. Contemporary advertising uses a concept called unique selling proposition, emphasizing a single feature, which was developed by _____.
   a. Rosser Reeves
   b. Jack Trout
   c. Harry McMahan
   d. John Clio

13.2 True/False Questions

___ 1. The Clio Award is presented for excellence in advertising creativity.

___ 2. Stealth ads are an illegal form of advertising.

___ 3. Product placement is adding a brand name product into a television or movie script. Advertisers pay for this placement.

___ 4. Enhancing a product image with a celebrity or already established brand name, regardless of the intrinsic connection between the product and the image is called branding.

___ 5. Messages geared to the largest possible audience are written to the highest common denominator.

___ 6. Pass along circulation is an estimate of all the possible people who may see a message in a periodical.

___ 7. How long a periodical remains in use is called publication life.

___ 8. The circulation claims of periodicals are verified by the Bureau of Circulation.

___ 9. Ad agencies create media plans when they decide where to place ads to reach their target audience.

___10. CPM or cost per thousand is a tool to determine the cost effectiveness of different media.

13.3 Completion Questions

1. People are assaulted by so many ads each day that the ads lose their impact. This phenomenon is called _____.

2. A(n) _____ is a sponsored online game, usually for an established brand at its own site.

3. An advertising agency with a(n) _____ earns an agreed upon percentage of what the client spends for time and space when purchasing ads, usually 15 percent.

4. Jack Trout devised the concept of _____, targeting ads to specific consumer groups, not to the lowest common denominator.

5. A _____ or _____ refers to an intense repetition of ads: placing a series of ads instead of only one.

13.4 Essay Questions

1. A brand's image is important and companies take great care to prevent their brands from being tarnished. What does a brand contribute to a corporation's image?

2. Explain unique selling proposition in advertising.

CHAPTER 14 Entertainment

MEDIA LITERACY ACTIVITY
THE NEW ENTERTAINMENT: CAGE FIGHTING?

Is it a human cockfight or a human game of chess? A new sport, called cage fighting or extreme fighting, has stirred up its share of controversy in the United States and abroad. Called an "entertainment sport," it's a battle between two amateur fighters who face off in a ring in a no-holds-barred combat of fists and feet.

The first incarnations of the sport in the early 1990s were incredibly violent and gladiatorial, and Republican Senator John McCain coined the term "human cockfighting" when he worked to get the unregulated sport banned.

After several deaths and much opposition, the sport reorganized in 2000 with stringent rules and regulations under the corporate banner of Ultimate Fighting Championship. McCain said the sport had "grown up" and dropped his opposition. Bans were lifted and licenses granted, and it's become a billion-dollar industry.

"It is the fastest growing sport in the world," said Jonny Burrows of CageWars Productions. "It is a see-saw spectacle, a human chess match. You're thinking four or five moves ahead….Thugs and brawlers do not last in this sport, you need to be clever to do it, and the guys at the top are very intelligent." Scottish Mixed Martial Arts contender Anthony Thompson, 24, whose nickname is Cougar, said almost everyone he has fought or trained with is highly educated. The MMA allows combatants to use an array of fighting styles such as kickboxing and martial arts. Cougar is a philosophy student at the University of Glasgow. "The guys who run my gym both have sports science degrees, and one of the other guys is an astrophysicist… Another guy is an engineer who builds submarines." He said the sport is very technical, "so the more intelligent you are, the better you get at it." When the first MMA bout was staged in 2007 it was condemned as violent and barbaric and protesters wanted to see further bouts banned. But in spite of the criticism, the sport continues to attract huge audiences.

Critics point to the loud music and strobe lighting that are used to get the crowds excited, and they worry how people spend that energy when they leave the fight. They also worry over the fights' billing as family entertainment.

The pay-per-view Ultimate Fighting Championship television show is now available on Spike TV. Called *The Ultimate Fighter*, it's a cross between a reality show and a sports event. Thirty-two contestants enter a tournament held at the UFC complex in Las Vegas. They are whittled down to 16 middleweights who are evenly split into teams which are coached by professional fighters. Single-elimination bouts, each a show with titles like "No Poseurs," "The Heebie-Jeebies," and "Piece of Meat," determine the two finalists who tangle in the live season-ender.

The show has created an explosion of amateur, copy-cat organizations holding their own cage combats, some of them are fly-by-night promoters. The competitions have caused problems in many small towns where they are held in bars or community centers with few, if any, rules or regulations. Several states have now banned ultimate fighting or cage combat events, and others are considering bans.

- Is *The Ultimate Fighter* television show authentic or mediated?
- Find out who advertises on *The Ultimate Fighter*. Who is their target audience?
- How has the media shaped this sport?
- Susan Sontag said that pop art "broadens the common experience of a society." Does cage fighting fit the definition of pop art? Does it broaden the common experience?

PRACTICE QUIZ

1. _____ says that pop art has some inherent value.
2. Broad thematic categories of media content are called _____.
3. A live, on-site performance is a(n) _____.
4. A message that has to be adjusted to be effective when carried by the mass media is a(n) _____.
5. _____ music is a folk genre derived from the rural Appalachian, Southern white experience.
6. The radio station that pioneered sports broadcasting in the 1920s was _____ in Pittsburgh.
7. Sexually explicit media depictions that the government can ban are termed _____.
8. A(n) _____ is a filmmaker recognized for significant and original treatments.
9. The _____ view says that the media should not pander to the tastes of low culture audiences, but should gear its content to high culture audiences.
10. _____ is a pejorative word for anything that is trendy, trashy, low art.

PRACTICE TEST

14.1 Multiple Choice Questions

1. _____ is the ABC television executive who established the network as <u>the</u> place to watch sports with the Wide World of Sports in 1961.
   a. Roone Arledge
   b. Henry Luce
   c. George Carlin
   d. James Gordon Bennett

2. Social commentator _____ said all pop art is kitsch, a pejorative word for trashy, trendy or low art.
   a. George Carlin
   b. Susan Sontag
   c. Dwight Macdonald
   d. Sam Phillips
3. _____ is art that tries to succeed in the marketplace. It is art that appeals to common people and tends to be trendy and have short-lived popularity.
   a. Popular art
   b. Middlebrow
   c. Highbrow
   d. Lowbrow
4. _____ is the term used to describe a filmmaker recognized for significant and original treatments. Andre Bazin, a French film critic, coined the term.
   a. Artistic director
   b. Editor
   c. Creative director
   d. Auteur
5. When a performance has been modified or adjusted for delivery to an audience by mass media it is called _____.
   a. mediated performance
   b. authentic performance
   c. amateur performance
   d. scripted performance

14.2 True/False Questions

___ 1. Broad thematic categories of media content are called genres.
___ 2. The lyrics of black music dwell on depressing events.
___ 3. Rap is music with intense bass, rhyming riffs, and often defiant, antiestablishment lyrics.
___ 4. James Gordon Bennett was the New York newspaper publisher who first assigned reporters to sports events on a regular basis.
___ 5. Sometimes businesses, even media outlets, sell a product at a loss to attract customers. This item is called a loss product. Networks sports programming is often broadcast at a loss.
___ 6. Media theorists describe levels of media content sophistication that coincide with audience tastes. These levels are said to be highbrow (high art such as ballet or fine art paintings), middlebrow (with artistic merit but not highbrow sophistication, such as *Star Trek*), and lowbrow (popular art, such as *Superman* or *Rambo*).

___ 7. A distinctive form of black music that became popular in the 1930s was called rhythm and blues.
___ 8. Hillbilly music is a folk genre of music from the historic, Southern black experience.
___ 9. Sexually explicit media depictions that the government can ban are called pornography.
___10. Susan Sontag is called the High Priestess of Pop Art because she sees cultural and social value in pop art.

14.3 Completion Questions

1. The _____ movement says that pop art has inherent value.
2. The _____ turned moviemaking into a kind of factory process in the 1920s.
3. The _____ view argues that the mass media does society a disservice by pandering to low tastes. It says the media should use programming designed to expose the audience to high art in the hopes of elevating the audience.
4. The _____ view says mass media should seek the largest possible audiences and direct its content to appeal to the largest number of people through low art that appeals to almost everyone.
5. _____ was a Memphis music producer and disc jockey who promoted early rock music.

14.4 Essay Questions

1. Discuss how music has contributed to the perpetuation of culture, from black music to rock 'n' roll and on to rap and hip hop.
2. Elitists say pop art has little value. Populists say pop art has inherent value. The pop art revisionism movement supports the value of popular art. Discuss the value of popular art.

CHAPTER 15 Media Research

MEDIA LITERACY ACTIVITY
SURFING FROM YOUR CELL PHONE

If you use a cell phone to surf the Web, chances are that you use Opera as your browser. Opera Software says its Opera Mini is the world's most popular software for connecting a cell phone to the World Wide Web.

Opera started out as a research project in Norway's largest telecom company, Telenor, in 1994. By 2005, the company's browser software was in use at the Massachusetts Institute of Technology, Harvard University, and Oxford University. The schools could customize the browser's design by adding the school colors and mascot to buttons, backgrounds, and borders of the user interface. They could insert news or other announcements for students, an important feature on today's security-conscious campuses.

By 2008, Opera claimed its Opera Mini browser software was more widely used than Apple's Safari for the iPhone or proprietary software on Nokia phones and BlackBerry devices from Research in Motion. Opera's main business strategy is to provide a browser that operates across devices, platforms and operating systems, and that can deliver a faster, more stable and flexible Internet experience than its competitors.

In 2008, Opera using aggregated data to study the Internet habits of more than 44 million Opera Mini users worldwide and reported that there were major differences in how people used the mobile Web. They found that people who use their cell phones to surf the Web tended toward social networking sites like MySpace and Facebook ahead of news, maps or weather. Worldwide, about 40 percent of mobile web traffic headed to social networks and 25 percent to content portals or search engines. In the United States, South Africa and Indonesia, 60 percent of mobile web traffic clicks led to social networks.

In Russia, Ukraine and Indonesia, where an inexpensive cell phone may be the only form of Web access for many people, Opera had its highest market shares. In its biggest market, Russia, Opera attracted between 20 and 25 percent of mobile users.

The allure of the Opera Mini browser is that it compresses full websites for mobile use so users can check out the same kind of content on their phones that they would from a desktop computer. The company reported that about 77 percent of all mobile web traffic in 2008 was for "full web surfing."

"It really is one Web, with people using whichever device they choose to connect on the Internet," said chief executive Jon von Tetzchner.

- Look up the research that was done by Opera in 2008 on cell phones and Internet habits.
  - What are the patterns the research revealed about use in different countries?
  - Which country's users flocked to entertainment and sports sites?
  - Which chose search engines first?
  - Who checked email the most?
  - Which country's users shopped most?
  - Which of these countries are democracies?
  - Which have stable economies?
  - How do you think research like this might be used?

PRACTICE QUIZ

1. The _____ is the term for when television viewers leave during commercials to go to the bathroom or get a snack.
2. _____ are used to monitor pulse and skin responses in people who volunteer to view programming to determine their reaction to it.
3. A _____ is a prototype television show that is given an on-air trial.
4. _____ introduced probability sampling, or the selection of survey populations which every member of the population has the same chance of being selected to answer the survey questions.
5. In order for a survey's results to provide a 95 percent confidence level and a less-than 5 percent margin of error, _____ people should be included in the selected sample.
6. _____ is a demographic tool used to identify marketing targets by common characteristics.
7. Breaking down a population by its lifestyle characteristics is called _____.
8. _____ founded the survey firm that still bears his name today. It is involved in determining the ratings, or measurement of audience size, for broadcast media.
9. The Audit Bureau of Circulations checks the _____ of a periodical.
10. With the development of new technology, the A.C. Nielsen Company has a plan to integrate audience measurement on a wide range of video platforms. This is called _____.

PRACTICE TEST

15.1 Multiple Choice Questions

1. _____ conducted the first polls on broadcast audience size.
   a. Archibald Crossley
   b. George Gallup
   c. A.C. Nielsen
   d. Susan Sontag
2. _____ founded the Institute of American Public Opinion and introduced probability sampling.
   a. Susan Whiting
   b. George Gallup
   c. Rupert Murdoch
   d. Andy Kohut

3. _____ means every person in the group has an equal opportunity to be sampled.
   a. Quota sampling
   b. Straw sampling
   c. Demographic sampling
   d. Probability sampling
4. _____ is the director of the widely cited Pew public policy polling organization. He says polls should be independent, distributed for free, and unconnected to commercial endeavors.
   a. Andy Kohut
   b. George Gallup
   c. Jonathan Robbin
   d. A.C. Nielsen
5. The _____ is the organization that checks newspaper and magazine circulation data.
   a. Audit Bureau of Circulations
   b. Nielsen Ratings
   c. Arbitron
   d. U.S. Department of Publications

15.2 True/False Questions

___ 1. Psychographics divides the population into groups determined by their lifestyles.
___ 2. The VALS system identifies broad categories of people based on their geographic locations.
___ 3. Cohort analysis is the demographic tool used to identify marketing targets by common characteristics.
___ 4. Jonathan Robbin was a computer whiz who devised the PRIZM geodemography system to identify population characteristics by their zip codes.
___ 5. The process of drawing conclusions from statistical data, or a segment of the whole, is called extrapolation.
___ 6. No survey can be 100 percent certain it is correct. The percentage that a survey may be off the mark is called the percent of wrong answers.
___ 7. The kind of sampling through which the population sampled coincides with the makeup of the entire population is called quota sampling.

___ 8. Ratings are the measurement of a broadcast audience size. They are important for advertisers in choosing where to place their ads; they are important to broadcasters in setting prices for ad time.
___ 9. Circulation refers to the number of readers of a publication.
___10. Anytime Anywhere Media Measurement or A2/M2 is the system devised by Arbitron to integrate audience measurements for a wide range of video platforms.

15.3 Completion Questions

1. It is difficult at best to measure Internet audience size and usage, but _____ is a service that uses a two track system to determine how many people view websites.
2. _____ founded the major broadcast survey firm that still bears his name today.
3. _____ are survey techniques that may be conducted face-to-face, by mail or by phone.
4. Periods when broadcast ratings are being conducted are called _____.
5. Consulting companies are hired by television stations to measure audience reaction to programming. Besides surveys, these companies use _____ to monitor pulse and skin responses to stimuli provided by the programs and ads viewed.

15.4 Essay Questions

1. A lot of time, effort and money goes into producing media content, so media producers use many different methods to measure probable success before actually printing or broadcasting the messages. Name some of these scientific methods.
2. No matter how hard a survey organization tries, it cannot be sure it is 100 percent correct in its results. Discuss how the organization can minimize its margin of error.

CHAPTER 16 Mass-Media Effects

MEDIA LITERACY ACTIVITY
VIRAL MESSAGES: DO THEY PERPETUATE CULTURE?

An accepted outcome of E.M. Rogers' diffusion of innovation theory is that the most effective media messages are based in traditional values. Therefore, media messages help instill traditional values in new generations. In 1995, when Rogers made his case, text messaging was in its infancy and social networking had yet to be conceived. Can today's youth learn traditional values from today's media messages?

Consider these examples of new media messages that have enjoyed phenomenal success.

At first Tieko Kawakami was just a former bar hostess and bookstore clerk, an obscure singer who started writing an Internet diary from her home in Japan. Her blog is about how we are always doing our best at living.

American blogs tend toward news, politics and technology. In Japan, and elsewhere in the world, blogs are more personal. Kawakami's poetic, street-wise writing caught on. In 2008, the 31-year-old won the Akutagawa Award, Japan's most prestigious honor for a new writer.

"At first, the blog was the only place I had for my writing," said Kawakami. "You know how many people are accessing it, and so you know right away when you've written something that's drawing interest." When she started blogging in 2003 she had a handful of readers. In 2008 she was averaging about 10,000 a day. "She writes in a frenzied, urgent prose that gurgles with furor," says Yuri Kageyama of the Associated Press. He says she exploits the dialect of Osaka, the city where she grew up, which is emerging as the language of Japan's modern-day standup comics and vernacular slang. Her award-winning novella, *The Breast and the Egg*, explores the ideas of divorce and solitary womanhood, themes that are relatively new to Japanese literature.

Other bloggers who found success in the publishing world include Julie Powell, author of *Julie and Julia: 365 Days, 524 Recipes, 1 Tiny Apartment Kitchen*, which chronicles her attempts at famous chef Julia Child's recipes. Colby Buzzell, a U.S. soldier in Iraq, wrote *My War: Killing Time in Iraq*.

Think of the YouTube videos that soar into instant fame:

- "Stop the Clash of Civilizations," a serious video by the global organization avaaz.org.
- "Battle at Kruger," which shows a baby water buffalo surviving an attack by lions and a crocodile in the African prairie.
- "Don't tase me, bro!", a clip of a University of Florida student pleading with police as they removed him from a John Kerry forum.
- "I Got a Crush on Obama" by the Obama Girl.

Tay Zonday morphed from an unknown musician to an Internet superstar who got booked on national television after his song. "Chocolate Rain," an amateur clip of his baritone crooning that he posted on YouTube, went viral in 2007.

Such instant phenoms owe their fame to viral buzz, word-of-mouth—or, more precisely, word-of-keyboard—marketing that spreads as fast as a virus. Research has shown that people are more inclined to believe word-of-mouth advertising or referrals than more formal forms of promotion. This is true for corporations marketing a message as much as it is for individuals writing about their lives. Do the media messages that go viral resonate with traditional values? Do these new media messages help instill a culture's values?

- Find a media message—an ad, a television show, a book, a blog or a piece of art—that reflects your fundamental values.
  - How was this achieved?
  - Have traditional marketers learned to use new media to deliver the same messages to new audiences?
  - What effects might this message have on people younger than you? How about on people older than you?

PRACTICE QUIZ

1. The _____ says people release their violent inclinations by seeing media depictions of violence.
2. The theory that says the media have powerful and immediate effects on audiences is the _____.
3. W.P. Davison devised the _____, which says that people overestimate the impact of media messages on other people.
4. _____ notes that media attention enhances attention given to issues, people and subjects.
5. Learning to fit into society is called _____.
6. _____, a communication scholar, says that the media have reduced generational and gender barriers.
7. Choosing to wear clothes like those worn by your television idol is a form of _____.
8. Communication of cultural values to future generations is called _____.
9. One culture's dominance over another is called _____.
10. _____ speculated that democracy is endangered by media violence.

PRACTICE TEST

16.1 Multiple Choice Questions

1. Yale psychologist _____ studied World War II propaganda and developed a model of mass communication: who says what, in which channel, to whom and with what effect.
   a. Walter Lippmann
   b. Harold Lasswell
   c. W.P. Davison
   d. Paul Lazarsfeld
2. W.P. Davison devised the _____, which says people overestimate the effects of media messages on other people.
   a. third person effect theory
   b. minimalist effects theory
   c. two-step flow theory
   d. powerful effects theory
3. The _____ dates back to Greek philosopher Aristotle and argues that people who watch violence actually release their violent inclinations by seeing them portrayed.
   a. aggressive stimulation theory
   b. desensitizing theory
   c. cathartic effect theory
   d. scapegoating
4. _____ says that media violence is among the indicators that someone will commit real life violence.
   a. Catalytic theory
   b. Aggressive stimulation theory
   c. Cathartic effect theory
   d. Magic bullet theory
5. _____ found that watching violence in the media stimulates aggressive actions in children.
   a. Seymour Feshbach
   b. Aristotle
   c. Albert Bandura
   d. Walter Lippmann
6. _____ refers to the dominance of one culture over another.
   a. Cultural imperialism
   b. Revisionism
   c. Contemporary transmission
   d. Diffusion of culture

16.2 True/False Questions

___ 1. The communication of cultural values to earlier generations is called historical transmission.
___ 2. Subception is receiving subconscious messages that trigger behavior.
___ 3. Sub-hearing messages are messages that cannot be consciously perceived.
___ 4. The theory that people learn behavior by seeing it in real life, and in depictions of real life, is called observational learning.
___ 5. Seymour Feshbach conducted studies that found evidence to support the cathartic effect theory that says people release their violent inclinations through seeing them portrayed.
___ 6. The Voodoo dolls study says that children seem to be more violent after they view violence in movies.
___ 7. Opinion leaders, or people who influence family and friends, are important to the two-step flow theory of media effects.
___ 8. Walter Lippmann and Don Shaw said the media tell people what to think about, not what to think.
___ 9. George Gerbner, a leading researcher in the effects of screen violence, speculated that democracy is endangered by media violence.
___ 10. The Violence Assessment Monitoring Project at the University of Illinois conducted contextual nonviolence studies and found effects from media depictions of violent acts to be less serious than earlier thought.
___ 11. The minimalist effects theory says that media effects are mostly indirect.

16.3 Completion Questions

1. _____ are people who are respected by others and to whom others look for information and opinions.
2. The theory that people are inspired to violent acts through watching media violence is called _____.
3. _____ is the Austrian neurologist who theorized that the human mind is unconsciously susceptible to suggestion.
4. _____ pioneered motivational research that explores how subconscious appeals can be used in advertising.
5. The process through which news, ideas, values and information is spread is called the _____.
6. The communication of cultural values to different cultures is called _____.

16.4 Essay Questions

1. Early mass communication scholars thought the media worked like a bullet or hypodermic needle, injecting people with ideas and opinions. Since then we have found it is not that easy to explain the effects of media on audiences. Discuss how the media affects people.
2. Some media scholars think media violence encourages violent behavior in media consumers. Discuss how media violence affects audiences.

CHAPTER 17 Global Mass Media

MEDIA LITERACY ACTIVITY
A LONGER LEASH

The media in China are entirely state-controlled, but after a devastating earthquake in 2008, the media put itself on a longer leash.

Some of the state's control had been slipping during the economic reforms of the 1990s. As China's media became more commercialized, although still timid by Western standards, racier content and more aggressive headlines emerged as organizations competed for audiences and advertising.

In 1976 Maureen Fan of the Washington *Post* reported the death toll of 240,000 from an earthquake that razed Tangshan was treated as a state secret for years. In 2008, when a 7.8 earthquake hit southwestern China on May 12, China's media began reporting the tragedy immediately and nearly nonstop with television footage, Internet coverage, and newspaper coverage. Editorials called for building industry and other reforms. They didn't wait for state approval. When an editor ordered continued coverage of the earthquake in spite of the latest edict ordering domestic news media not to send any more journalists to Sichuan, he said, "If everyone pays no attention to this, then it won't really be a ban."

The coverage mobilized the Chinese and the world to donate blood, money and labor. This is not what usually happens after a catastrophe in China. Explains Tom Doctoroff of the *Huffington Post* who has lived on the mainland for more than a decade, middle-class Chinese are typically "ruthlessly competitive and money-hungry." He says the bottom-up empathy for earthquake victims was heightened by two "new" influences. Unlike propaganda mouthpieces, the Internet told real tales of agony and triumph by real people. The coverage inspired millions of new generation netizens to give to a far-away cause. Second, Doctoroff says, the flow of information from the government was, relatively speaking, factual and fast. "Prime Minister Wen Jiabao's immediate, ubiquitously broadcast trek through quake wreckage convinced the nation that the disaster was *tian zai,* an act of heaven, not *ren huo* caused by official malfeasance or inefficiency, and, therefore, a 'worthy' national rallying cry."

For the Chinese it was incredible to see CCTV anchor Zhao Pu struggle to compose himself as he reported the earthquake. Chinese anchors on the state-controlled television are expected to be staid and rigid, and this was something new. Zhao was widely praised for showing emotion, but his openness made the Chinese government anxious that they were no longer shaping the story and overall agenda. The coverage encouraged citizens to raise questions about sincerity of the rescue effort and about why scores of schools and other buildings collapsed.

"The transparency of information can unite everybody to fight against the big tragedy," said Min Dahong, a journalism professor at the Chinese Academy of Social Sciences. "This is a good opportunity to establish a system that will encourage the press to report in a timely and open manner."

However, Doctoroff called it a blend of "managed transparency." The media were allowed to report a climbing death toll every day, which by the end of May had reached nearly 70,000, but that news was always accompanied by propagandistic tales of inspiring heroism.

Nonetheless Doctoroff sees changes afoot. Facilitated by modern technology and a less defensive government, "China may emerge stronger, more confident, less prickly."

- Find out how the Chinese government dealt with the media during the Tiananmen Square protests of 1989 and during the riots in Tibet in 2008, just months before the earthquake. Also look at how it dealt with the international media during the Olympics, which were held in 2008, just a few months after the earthquake.
  - What factors contributed to any change in how the Chinese government dealt with media inside and outside China?
  - Do you think any changes will last?

PRACTICE QUIZ

1. King James VII said proper decisions follow the monarch's will, which he linked to the Almighty. This is called _____.
2. _____ is the system that says given time and access to good information, people will ultimately make the right decisions. This is the basis for democratic form of governance.
3. A _____ is a television station that transmits to an orbiting satellite, which beams signals back down directly to individual receivers.
4. _____ is the Qatar-based Arab satellite news channel founded by Hammad bin Khalifa.
5. The Chinese government keeps tight control of the media. The government's _____ limits news reporting of disasters, ostensibly to ensure social stability.
6. Reporters who are assigned a specific military unit to cover during a war are called _____.
7. _____, an early libertarian thinker, argued for a free and open exchange of ideas, called the marketplace of ideas, based on the concept that people are capable of discovering the truth if given a chance.
8. _____ is the U.S. government-funded Farsi language service aimed at Iran. It is part of a long-standing effort by the U.S. government to broadcast directly to people in repressed areas.
9. _____ is the nickname for the movie industry in India.
10. Although people occasionally make errors in truth seeking, they eventually discover them and correct them. This is said to be _____.

PRACTICE TEST

17.1 Multiple Choice Questions

1. Throughout mass media history, _____ political systems have been most common. This top-down governance, as in dictatorships and monarchies, gives government major control over the mass media.
   a. authoritarian
   b. democratic
   c. republican
   d. strict

2. _____ argued for a free and open exchange of ideas, a marketplace of ideas, in which everyone should be free to express their ideas for consideration by others.
   a. Henry VII
   b. John Milton
   c. King James VII
   d. Orhan Pamuk

3. _____ is wireless technology that allows limited range downloading, without hooking up to a wire system.
   a. Wi-fi
   b. Next Carrying Network
   c. Fireconnect
   d. Golden Shield

4. Reporters who are assigned to a specific military unit are said to be _____.
   a. volunteers
   b. assignments
   c. embeds
   d. investigative reporters

5. The Chinese State Council proposed a(n) _____ to limit news reporting of disasters, ostensibly to ensure social stability.
   a. boycott
   b. emergency response law
   c. shield law
   d. protection law

17.2 True/False Questions

___ 1. Henry VII was the British monarch who began cracking down on print materials in 1529.

___ 2. Libertarianism says that given time and access to good information, people will ultimately make the right decisions. It is the basis of democratic governance.

___ 3. Under an authoritarian system, authorities usually see material only after it is disseminated.

___ 4. Bollywood is the nickname for India's movie system.

___ 5. Prior censorship is the government's review of content before dissemination.

___ 6. Censorship is always an issue during times of war. John Milton was the Union Secretary of State who organized Civil War censorship of sensitive military issues.

___ 7. Hammad bin Khalifa founded Al-Jazeera, a Qatar-based satellite news channel geared toward Arab audiences. Al-Jazeera also operates a global news channel.

___ 8. A sat-station is a television station that transmits to an orbiting satellite, which beams signals back down directly to individual receivers.

___ 9. Liu Di was a Chinese college student who, under the pseudonym Stainless Steel Mouse, satirized the government. She was jailed, but eventually released on the condition that she never speak to journalists.

___10. The divine right of kings, as articulated by King James VII, says kings are gods.

17.3 Completion Questions

1. Although people make occasional errors in truth-seeking, they eventually discover the errors and correct them. This is called _____.

2. Inherent human rights, including the right to self-determination, are called _____.

3. The _____, in which reporters are chosen on a rotating basis to cover an event to which access is limited, was devised during the invasion of Grenada.

4. The period in history of rationalist thought that foreshadowed the beginning of early libertarianism is called _____.

5. The _____ includes the free expression segment of the U.S. Constitution. It bars the government from interfering with the free exchange of ideas.

17.4 Essay Questions

1. Covering events during wartime is a special challenge for the media. Discuss some concerns about war coverage.

2. The media in China is an example of a media system that is suppressed by the Communist government. Discuss some of the challenges of being a journalist in China.

CHAPTER 18 Mass Media and Governance

MEDIA LITERACY ACTIVITY
CASUALTIES OF GLOBAL WARMING

Most scientists agree that global warming makes super-strong hurricanes more likely because it creates hot oceans, which are just what hurricanes need to get started. It follows that as global temperatures rise, hurricanes are becoming more powerful. That was the conclusion Kerry Emanuel, a professor at the Massachusetts Institute of Technology who has studied hurricanes for 20 years, came to in a paper in the scientific journal *Nature*, published several weeks before Hurricane Katrina struck New Orleans in 2005. As he put it, by adding more greenhouse gases to the earth's atmosphere, humans are "loading the climatic dice in favor of more powerful hurricanes in the future."

"But most Americans heard nothing about Hurricane Katrina's association with global warming," said Mark Hertsgaard in a 2006 article in *Vanity Fair*. Instead, media coverage reflected the views of the Bush administration—specifically, the National Oceanic and Atmospheric Administration, which declared that the devastating hurricane was the result of natural factors. An outcry from NOAA's scientists led the agency to backtrack from that statement in February 2006, but by then it had already been set in place as conventional wisdom. "Post-Katrina New Orleans may eventually be remembered as the first major U.S. casualty of global warming, yet most Americans still don't know what hit us," Hertsgaard wrote.

Public discussion about climate change in the U.S. is years behind the conversation in Europe. The way the global warming story was handled in the U.S. media in the 1990s and early 2000s is a classic example of agenda-setting. Much criticism has been leveled about the media's insistence to include balancing viewpoints from a very small number of dissenting scientists, many of whom were on the payroll of big corporations that didn't want to make any changes to help stop or slow the warming process. But beyond the way individual stories were handled, critics charge that the U.S. media also failed to keep the issue in front of the American public.

In 2006, Charles Alexander, a former environmental editor at *Time*, complained that while coverage had improved, media executives continued to regard climate change as just another environment issue, rather than the overriding challenge of the 21st century. "Americans are hearing more about reducing greenhouse emissions from BP (British Petroleum) ads than from news stories in *Time*, the New York *Times*, or any other U.S. media outlet. This will go down as the greatest act of mass denial in history."

The internal watchdog for the National Aeronautics and Space Administration (NASA), the agency responsible for the U.S. space program and for aerospace research and scientific discovery, charged that its own press office "marginalized or mischaracterized" studies on global warming between 2004 and 2006. In a report released in June 2008, NASA's inspector general office called it "inappropriate political in-terference" by political appointees in the press office. The report found that National Public Radio's allegations that it was denied access to top global warming scientist James Hansen were true. It also found that NASA headquarters press officials canceled a press conference on a mission monitoring ozone pollution and global warming because it was too close to the 2004 presidential election. In dozens of instances, the report found that NASA's public affairs office had edited or downgraded press releases having to do with global warming or denied the press access to scientists. NASA's head of public affairs said the report was old news and claimed the problem was fixed, but the Union of Concerned Scientists is still fighting for legislation and regulatory action that will keep scientists independent of government.

- Pick a current global warming story and read about it in several different sources.
  - Do the stories help set the public agenda on the global warming issue?
  - Do they add to the public discussion?
  - Do they include trivial "balancing" viewpoints from scientists?
  - Do you think the problems cited here have been fixed?
  - Who is more to blame for the way global warming was covered in the United States—the press or the Bush administration?

PRACTICE QUIZ

1. The press has been called _____, a term whose origin is not exactly clear, but may have emerged in the mid-1700s as a addition to the social structure of the time, which consisted of three estates—the clergy, the nobility, and the common people. Many credit its origin to Edmund Burke.
2. The _____ says that broadcasting stations must offer competing political candidates the same amounts of time and the same rates for advertising.
3. Scholars _____ proposed a theory on media effects that says what mass media decides to cover tells people what subjects to think about, not what to think about those subjects.
4. The _____ is the term for the ability of television, through emotion-raising video, to elevate distant issues on the domestic public agenda.
5. Political ads, usually on television, in which a candidate criticizes the opponent rather than emphasizing his or her own policies, are called _____.
6. The process of the media telling people what issues they should pay attention to is called _____.
7. _____ is the term for selecting aspects of a perceived reality for emphasis in a mass media message, thereby shaping how the audience sees the reality.
8. The actual voice of someone in the news, sand-

wiched into a correspondent's report, is called a
_____.

9. A deliberate disclosure of confidential or classified information by someone who wants to advance the public interest, embarrass a bureaucratic rival or supervisor, or disclose incompetence or skull-duggery is called a _____. Sometimes, a deliberate disclosure of a potential policy, usually from a diversionary source, is used to test the public's response. This is called a trial balloon.

10. Often an election campaign is treated like a game by the media, with reporters calling who's ahead, who's trailing and who's coming up on the rail. Critics say treating campaigns like _____ results in substantive issues being underplayed when they should garner more attention.

PRACTICE TEST

18.1 Multiple Choice Questions

1. The press has been called _____, a term whose origin is not exactly clear, but many think it started in the mid-1700s as an addition to the existing social structure of the time, which consisted of the clergy, nobility, and common estates. Many credit its origin to Edmund Burke.
   a. the fourth estate
   b. watch dog
   c. fourth branch of government
   d. the press power

2. The _____ says that stations must offer competing political candidates the same amounts of time and the same rates for advertising.
   a. fairness doctrine
   b. framing law
   c. equal time rule
   d. media rule

3. Scholar _____ proposed a theory on media effects that says what mass media decide to cover tells people what subjects to think about, not what to think about those subjects.
   a. Maxwell McCombs
   b. Don Shaw
   c. Don Burden

4. The _____ is the ability of television, through emotion-raising video, to elevate distant issues on the domestic public agenda.
   a. CNN effect
   b. Framing effect
   c. Agenda setting
   d. Sound bite effect

5. Political ads, usually on television, in which a candidate criticizes the opponent rather than emphasizing his or her own policies, are called
   _____.
   a. positive ads
   b. moderate ads
   c. negative ads
   d. stonewalling ads

18.2 True/False Questions

___ 1. Attack ads, a subspecies of negative ads that are especially savage in criticizing an opponent, often playing loosely with context and facts.

___ 2. There are many laws that regulate campaign financing. Groups unaffilialed with candidates or political parties who can collect unlimited amounts of money independently have a 527 status.

___ 3. A pseudo-event is an event staged to look like a social event.

___ 4. A photo-op, short for photo opportunity, is a staged event that offers good visuals for photos to attract media attention.

___ 5. When a person refuses to answer questions, or even meet with reporters, they are said to be stonewalling.

___ 6. When a person or organization decides not to issue a statement, make a comment or to answer questions from the news media despite public interest, they are engaging in a news boycott.

___ 7. Calling the media the fourth branch refers to its role as a watchdog to the official three branches of government.

___ 8. The fairness doctrine refers to a former government rule which stated that whenever the media covered an issue with two sides they were required to present both sides of the issue.

___ 9. In the Burden opinion, the U.S. Supreme Court upheld the First Amendment protection of the print media, regardless of balance or fairness in coverage.

___ 10. Donna Brazile was a radio station owner who lost licenses because she favored some political candidates over others.

18.3 Completion Questions

1. The media telling people what issues they should pay attention to is called _____.

2. Selecting aspects of a perceived reality for emphasis in a mass media message, thereby shaping how the audience sees the reality, is called
   _____.

3. A _____ is the actual voice of someone in the news inserted into a correspondent's report.

4. A deliberate disclosure of confidential or classified information is called a _____.

5. Critics say treating political campaigns like _____ results in substantive issues being underplayed when they should garner more attention.

18.4 Essay Questions

1. Political leaders are well aware of the importance of media coverage and have developed mechanisms to influence coverage. Discuss some of these mechanisms.

2. Critics fault the media for falling short in its coverage of political campaigns. Discuss some of the challenges faced by the media in campaign coverage.

CHAPTER 19 Mass-Media Law

MEDIA LITERACY ACTIVITY
INDIANA JONES AND THE COMMUNIST PARTY

Banning films is not a new phenomenon. Movies have been banned for one reason or another around the world almost since the industry began, but two recent attempts targeted actors, not just the films themselves.

When the new Indiana Jones movie hit the big screen in 2008, the Communist Party central committee in St. Petersburg saw red. They said the film promoted crude, anti-Soviet propaganda. In *Indiana Jones and the Kingdom of the Crystal Skull,* Harrison Ford, who plays the swashbuckling Indiana Jones, is pitted against a sinister KGB agent, played by Cate Blanchett, in the hunt for a skull endowed with mystical powers. The film is set against the backdrop of the Cold War in 1957.

Sure that their teenagers, unaware of what happened in 1957, would see the film and think that their country made trouble for the United States and almost started a nuclear war, St. Petersburg's Communist Party's ideology committee called the film "an insult to the Soviet and Russian people, who remember the difficult Fifties when our country was concluding its reconstruction after the Great War, but did not send merciless terrorists to the USA." The committee also pointed out that Russians had loved Harrison Ford in previous serious roles, but it concluded in an open letter, "You have no future in Russia any more. Speaking plainly, it is better for you not to come here. You will be beaten and despised."

The party leaders urged Russian moviegoers to boycott the film and called Ford and Blanchett "capitalist puppets." On the party's website Ford and Blanchett were referred to as "second-rate actors serving as the running dogs of the CIA. We need to deprive these people of the right to enter the country."

Despite the party's protests, the film was released on 808 screens in Russia, a record for a Hollywood film.

After the devastating May 2008 earthquake in China, actress Sharon Stone said, "I'm not happy about the way the Chinese are treating the Tibetans because I don't think anyone should be unkind to anyone else. And then this earthquake happened, and then I thought, is that karma? When you're not nice that the bad things happen to you?" In response, the founder of one of China's biggest cinema chains said his company would not show her films in his theaters. He called her comments "inappropriate," and said that actors should not bring personal politics to comments about a natural disaster that left 5 million Chinese homeless.

A Chinese website devoted solely to disparaging Stone's comments sprang up as her words created a swell of anger on the Internet. Stone has at least four movies due to be released between 2008 and 2010.

Although these recent attempts targeted actors, many films have been banned through the years for various reasons, including *The Da Vinci Code, Saving Private Ryan, Day of the Dead* and *Bruce Almighty.*

- Find eight more movies that have been banned. Include at least two movies that have been banned in the United States. List offending qualities of the films you chose and of those mentioned above.
- Categorize the reasons for the bannings into religious, political, moral, or other reasons.
  - How many of the reasons other countries use for banning films would stand up today in the United States?
  - Looking at your categorizations, what conclusions can you draw?
  - What do you think are viable reasons for a country to ban a film?

PRACTICE QUIZ

1. The _____ were a musical group who did not appreciate negative reviews. They sued and lost, ultimately causing the fair comment and criticism law to be formulated.
2. _____ protects the ownership rights of creative works such as books, articles and lyrics.
3. _____ is the term used to define creative works.
4. The _____ prohibits government interference with free expression, religion and individual and public protests against government policies.
5. _____ is defined as sexually explicit depictions that are protected from government bans.
6. Prohibiting expression before it is disseminated is called _____.
7. The _____ is a law passed in 2001 that gives federal agents new authority when investigating possible acts of terrorism.
8. Several laws have been written to try control indecent content on the Internet. The U.S. Supreme Court rejected the _____, both in 1996 and 1999, noting the Internet is not an invasive broadcasting medium.
9. _____ is an offensive expression, especially one directed at racial, ethnic and sexual minorities.
10. In law, advertising is called _____.

PRACTICE TEST

19.1 Multiple Choice Questions

1. The _____ were a musical group who did not appreciate negative reviews. They sued and lost, ultimately causing the fair comment and criticism law to be formulated.
   a. Cherry Sisters
   b. Groksters
   c. Charles Schenck Trio
   d. The Cherrettes

2. _____ protects the ownership rights of creative works such as books, articles, and lyrics.
   a. Trademark
   b. Patent
   c. Copyright
   d. Free expression rights

3. _____ is the term used to define creative works.
   a. Creativity
   b. Intellectual property
   c. Property of the mind
   d. Mindworks

4. The _____ prohibits government interference with free expression, religion, and individual and public protests against government policies.
   a. First Amendment
   b. Sixth Amendment
   c. Second Amendment
   d. Fourth Amendment

5. _____ is defined as sexually explicit depictions that are protected from government bans.
   a. Obscenity
   b. Pornography
   c. X-rated film
   d. Indecent movie

19.2 True/False Questions

___ 1. Slander is written defamation.
___ 2. Indecency is the term used by the Federal Communications Commission to refer to a range of words and depictions considered improper on public airwaves.
___ 3. John Milton devised a concept called the marketplace of ideas that says people are capable of identifying good ideas among many as long as they have access to them all.
___ 4. The Indictment Standard is a four-part test to determine whether an advocacy speech is constitutionally protected.
___ 5. Prior restraint is prohibiting expression in advance.
___ 6. Jay Near was a publisher who was involved in a legal case that resulted in a strong ruling against government prior restraint on expression.

___ 7. If someone wants to use copyrighted work, they need to get permission.
___ 8. Theft of copyrighted work is called stealing.
___ 9. Clarence Brandenburg was a Ku Klux Klan leader who was arrested because he said hateful and threatening things. His conviction was later overturned because his speech was far-fetched and not an imminent threat.
___ 10. Charles Schenck and Elizabeth Baer were arrested for distributing anti-war pamphlets about the Vietnam War. Their case was decided on First Amendment grounds. During their appeal the U.S. Supreme Court decided that censorship was reasonable in times of war, but acknowledged freedom from government restraint of expression is a right of every citizen.

19.3 Completion Questions

1. The _____ is a law passed in 2001 that gives federal agents new authority when investigating possible acts of terrorism.
2. Several laws have been written to try to control indecent content on the Internet. The U.S. Supreme Court rejected the _____, both in 1996 and 1999, noting the Internet is not an invasive broadcasting medium.
3. _____ is an offensive expression, especially one directed at racial, ethnic and sexual minorities.
4. Advertising is called _____.
5. First Amendment rights were eventually extended to non-verbal expressions that are still expressive. This is called _____.

19.4 Essay Questions

1. Freedom of expression is protected under the First Amendment, but that does not mean you can say anything about anyone without repercussions. Discuss some of the limits on freedom of expression.
2. As communications technology has developed, we find we need to consider the control or freedom of many types of expression that could not have been imagined by the signers of the First Amendment. Discuss.

CHAPTER 20 Ethics

MEDIA LITERACY ACTIVITY
STUDENTS IN THE NATIONAL SPOTLIGHT

There is a lot to be learned by making a national uproar.

Student newspapers on college campuses often test the limits of free speech and university administrations. In the process, they go further than reporting the news—they make the news.

At Colorado schools, there is long tradition of creating national uproars.

In the early 1960s, Carl Mitcham, a student at the University of Colorado, wrote guest editorials about political issues for the official student newspaper. In one, he called Arizona Senator Barry Goldwater, the Republican presidential candidate, "a fool, a mountebank, a murderer, no better than a common criminal." Goldwater was notified of the column, and the university president apologized, but that wasn't enough for the politician, who demanded further action. The university president refused, saying he would not "silence" the students. Mitcham did, however, lose his scholarship and had to drop out of school for a year. His editor was fired for publishing the piece. Half the newspaper staff walked out in response. Mitcham is now a professor of ethics and philosophy at the Colorado School of Mines.

A few years later, Bob Ewegen wrote an editorial, also for the same student newspaper, that got him in trouble. The owner of one of the student bookshops was arrested for selling "obscene" lapel buttons. One of which was a two-word attack on censorship that used the F-word. Ewegen wrote an editorial with a tongue-in-cheek headline that said "(expletive) the Constitution." When being disciplined for the incident, Ewegen explained that it, obviously, was not the newspaper's attitude toward the Constitution, but he had to apologize to a board that oversaw student publications for being wrong in a matter of taste. Ewegen is now deputy editorial page editor for the Denver *Post.*

As a student journalist, David McSwane contributed to a report on a Denver television station that won a Peabody Award. A high school senior, he posed as a dropout with a drug problem to find out how far recruiters would go to try to sign him up. He was advised to get a fake diploma online and given advice on how to beat a drug test. In 2007, as student editor of the Colorado State University newspaper, he wrote a four-word headline to an editorial: "Taser This ... F— Bush." the editorial was written in response to the tasering of a vocal student at the University of Florida who questioned U.S. Senator John Kerry after a speech. It was printed in banner-headline type. Condemnation was swift and predictable.

"We as an Editorial Board made a statement," he wrote in response to the criticism. "We stand by that statement, and I intend to defend our right to do so. We feel this statement, albeit unpopular, was necessary in communicating our opinion that it's time college students challenge the current political climate and speak out." The Board of Student Communications admonished McSwane for violating the student newspaper's code of ethics, which bars profane or vulgar words in opinion writing. Advertisers threatened to pull their advertising from the newspaper, a potential loss of $50,000 in revenue. School officials decided the newspaper staff would have to take an across-the-board 10-percent pay cut to make up for the losses.

A year later, McSwane was named one of the top 100 student journalists in the country by UWire, which describes itself as "a community-driven service devoted to the needs of student journalists." The organization solicited nominations from student journalists and advisers across the country, with emphasis given to candidates' "potential to shape the media industry in the years ahead."

- Look up the ethics codes used by a couple of college newspapers. Imagine that you are McSwane's adviser on the student newspaper at one of those colleges. Write a memo to your dean explaining the ethical decision-making process the editor and his staff engaged in before publishing the four-word headline on the editorial and how the students reached their decision to publish. Tell your dean if the students should be allowed to continue publishing, and why or why not.

PRACTICE QUIZ

1. A statement that defines acceptable and unacceptable behavior for a person or organization is called a _____.
2. Aristotle, a Greek philosopher, said moderation is the best course. That came to be called _____.
3. The _____ principle for ethical behavior is "Do unto others as you would have them do unto you."
4. Immanuel Kant, a German philosopher, introduced the _____, a principle that can be applied in any and all circumstances with moral certitude.
5. The _____ says morally right decisions are those that result in happiness for the most people.
6. _____ says that good actions flow from good processes.
7. _____ says that you should make ethical decisions based on the situation at hand.
8. The _____ gives a tool for sorting the pros and cons of ethics questions.
9. Stealing the work of another and claiming it as your own is _____.
10. _____ are gifts given to media from which the giver may expect favors in return.

PRACTICE TEST

20.1 Multiple Choice Questions

1. Aristotle, a Greek philosopher, devised a basis for moral decision-making called _____.
   a. the Judeo-Christian principle
   b. categorical imperative
   c. the Golden Mean
   d. theory of divine command

2. _____, a German philosopher, wrote that moral decisions should flow from thoroughly considered principles and can be applied in any circumstances with moral certitude.
   a. Immanuel Kant
   b. John Stuart Mill
   c. John Milton
   d. Wayland Ayer

3. _____ says everyone should be treated the same, with blindness to their social position or other factors.
   a. Deontological ethics
   b. Teleology
   c. Egalitarianism
   d. Utilitarianism

4. _____ advocated a system of utilitarian ethics that says the best decisions are those that result in the happiness of the greatest number of people.
   a. John Stuart Mill
   b. John Dewey
   c. Immanuel Kant
   d. John Rawls

5. _____ says that good actions flow from good processes, or people act morally when they follow good rules.
   a. Deontological ethics
   b. Theory of Devine Command
   c. Theory of Pragmatic ethics
   d. Libertarian theory

20.2 True/False Questions

___ 1. Libertarian theory says people will make good decisions given information and time.

___ 2. Telegraphy says good decisions are those with good consequences.

___ 3. Most ethics codes are uniform in prohibiting freebies, or gifts for which the giver may expect favors in return. Junkets, trips or tickets to an event, are other forms of freebies that are prohibited.

___ 4. A code of ethics is a statement that defines legal behavior.

___ 5. Making decisions with a blind eye to extraneous factors that could affect the decision is called the veil of ignorance.

___ 6. The theory of divine command says that proper decisions follow God's will, with blind trust that the consequences will then be good.

___ 7. Making decisions without considering whether or not they serve society is social responsibility.

___ 8. Pragmatic ethics says we should judge an act by its results.

___ 9. Situational ethics says decisions should be based on the situation at hand.

___10. Ralph Potter, an ethicist and divinity professor, created Potter's Box, a tool for sorting through the pros and cons of an ethical question.

20.4 Completion Questions

1. The _____ was a group that studied U.S. mass media and advocated social responsibility as a goal and result of media activities.

2. Using someone else's work without permission is called _____.

3. _____ is creating an event to attract news media attention and coverage.

4. Misrepresentation by omission and juxtaposition is called _____.

5. Mixing fiction technique with nonfiction is called _____.

20.4 Essay Questions

1. The media often face a conflict of duties—a reporter, for instance, may be faced with an ethical dilemma and find it impossible to be ethical to all involved. Name some people and organizations to which a reporter has a responsibility.

2. Explain the Potter's Box method of examining an ethical dilemma.